A Thru-Hiking Trilogy

Three Trails ~ Three Adventures

Three-Book Box Set Containing:

The Journey In Between
The Last Englishman
Balancing on Blue

Keith Foskett

A Thru-Hiking Trilogy

By Keith Foskett
www.keithfoskett.com

Produced by Createspace.com
(ISBN: 978-1539004462)

Edited by Alex Roddie
www.alexroddie.com/pinnacle-editorial

Copyright © 2016 Keith Foskett. All rights reserved.

The Journey In Between (ISBN: 978-1480176393)

The Last Englishman (ISBN: 978-1480169111)

Balancing on Blue (ISBN: 978-1480176416)

Illustrations in *Balancing on Blue* by Derek Smith

The right of Keith Foskett to be identified as the author of this work has been asserted by him in accordance with the Copyright, Designs and Patents Act of 1988

This book is sold subject to the conditions that it shall not, by way of trade or otherwise, be lent, resold, hired out, or otherwise circulated without the authors prior consent in any form of binding or cover other than that in which it is produced and without a similar condition including this condition being imposed on the subsequent purchaser

Contents

The Journey In Between   1

The Last Englishman   219

Balancing on Blue   511

The Journey In Between

A 1000-mile walk on El Camino de Santiago

With love:

To Mum, who never doubted any of my crazy adventures and always shared in my excitement.

To Dad, for passing on the Foskett walking gene.

To Bam Bam and Nan, I know you are both always with me.

Introduction

Clarification

The bar commanded a worthy view over the rooftops of Heraklion as a subtle, orange evening light softened the concrete world outside. Looking back now I know that's where it all started.

Monis Agkarathou Street is home to the hostel whose name has left me now, although I know I could return and find it tomorrow should I wish. A few travellers littered the room as the owner, Yanis, stifled a yawn and turned pages of a local paper with one hand, whilst twiddling his fingers around the beer pump with the other. Despite the lack of people in there, they were all drinking well, probably due to the eight flights of steps just to get up there; anyone would need a drink after that.

Bob was a Kiwi whom I'd met briefly the previous evening, and he beckoned me over to sit with him.

"Any idea what you're going to do?" he asked.

I shrugged my shoulders, raised my eyebrows and took a few gulps of Mythos.

"I want to walk, Bob. Not just for a few days, for weeks," I replied.

"Where?"

"I don't know. Somewhere warm with no rain, somewhere with history, culture and great food. Oh, and Latin women, you know? Dark hair and olive skin?"

He nodded and grinned.

"Yeah, I know what you mean. I was talking to someone on the south coast a few days ago who had walked somewhere in Spain for a few weeks last year. He absolutely loved it, he's going back to do it again. It's an old pilgrimage route, like really old, centuries old. Christ, what was the name of it?"

He screwed his face up and buried it in his hands. I waited expectantly, feeling as though someone had the answer to my life for the next few weeks at least, and was going to let me down at the last minute.

"Bloody hell mate, I can't remember. No! Wait! The Camino, Santiago... Yeah, the Camino de Santiago."

A chance meeting with a stranger. I wasn't looking for answers – indeed I didn't really have any questions – but that conversation with Bob inadvertently steered me down one turn of a crossroads and took my life in a whole new direction. I didn't realise it at the time but now it's obvious.

Yes, that's definitely where the journey started.

* * *

I have fond memories from my early teens of family holidays driving to Wales or Dartmoor in a sky-blue Triumph Herald, with my sister or, when she got bored of such things, a best mate. I was more into skateboards, girls and Abba at the time, but Dad would cunningly con us into walking somewhere a couple of hours away because there was a great ice cream place halfway or Mum would promise to give the new skateboard thing some serious consideration. So, most of the time I found myself walking and running about with my mate over hillocks, through streams, getting filthy and having a great time, oblivious to the fact that we were only, really, walking.

At around fourteen I discovered tents, not so much because it meant spending a night in the woods but because it meant a night away from home, a grown-up thing to do. I was, however, getting hooked on real walking, as opposed to an occasional ramble with the folks. When Dad suggested a friend and I try the South Downs Way, which at around 160 kilometres isn't too easy a prospect, I jumped at the chance for my first real adventure. It was close to home, so I had an escape clause with a bus or train back, some of the landscape and route were familiar, and the weather forecast promised great things.

I roped in Andrew Boyd after dismissing some poor

objections, such as missing his favourite TV programme and being away from his girlfriend for that length of time (even though I knew she was seeing someone else). I thought his lack of actual interest in walking, which was the main problem, might be rekindled by the great outdoors. Besides, all my other mates were not interested, on holiday or listening to Spandau Ballet.

Dad dropped us off around South Harting one evening. Our tent was so flimsy it would have fallen down in a mild breeze. The sleeping bags took up most of our packs, leaving just about enough room in mine for Mum's saucepan, a Camping Gaz stove, several cans of baked beans, numerous Mars bars, a couple of T-shirts and a rain jacket. As long as it didn't rain or get windy, we'd be fine.

Four days in, on Kithurst Hill above Storrington, it did both. We had pitched on open ground right on top of the Downs and the expedition was going well up to that point. I noticed some alarmingly black clouds and a slight breeze just before I zipped up the tent, but had full faith in our little shelter. I woke up about an hour later with Andrew screaming and a rain-lashed canvas slapping me in the face. Every few seconds lightning lit up the scene and all I could see was my mate wrapped around the support pole down one end of the tent, with petrified eyes, looking like a cat up a lamp post with a dog underneath.

"Hold your tent pole!" he screamed. "Hang on or the whole tent's gonna go!"

Thunder crashed all around us for two hours as we battled to keep the tent upright, terrified that one of the poles would be hit by lightning. It felt as if we were in the very centre of the storm itself. Every so often, when the lightning illuminated our world, I expected to look down the other side of the tent and see a pile of charcoal briquettes instead of Andrew. Then the water started to trickle in. After thirty minutes we were paddling around in a pool, very cold, scared shitless and with arms hurting so much from holding the poles we couldn't actually feel them.

By the time the storm had finished with us it was daylight. We struggled out of the tent, sopping wet, tired and thankful to be alive. Catching the train back home, both of us fell silent as we gave camping out some serious reconsideration.

I completed the South Downs Way the following summer

with another mate. It never even threatened to rain on us once and I remember thinking that the elements owed me one.

In my twenties, cycling took over as my main activity. I travelled to various countries and indulged in the occasional hike here and there, just to remind the leg muscles that I might call on them again. I made regular trips to Wales, the Lake District and Scotland. I dabbled in mountaineering but became frustrated at the mechanics of it. The need to wear harnesses, use ropes, tie knots, and other distractions frustrated me. It took away the simplicity of putting one foot in front of the other, so, whenever I went up a mountain, which I loved, I chose the route that could simply be walked.

The uncomplicated act of walking is one of the appeals. I have never been one to require an in-depth understanding of something to appreciate it. If it works, then I have no questions – the simpler the better. Walking is the most natural and oldest form of travel. It is designed to get us from one point to another with the minimum of fuss and at a pace that allows us to notice things that we would normally miss. If it weren't so normal, so natural, then I'd consider it a revelation.

We live in a world where we seem to want to make everything quicker in order to free up more time, which in turn we fill up with other stuff. When it all gets too meaningless for me, I feel the need to escape and walk. To be part of the outdoors, with all your belongings strapped to your back, to be able to camp wherever takes your fancy, and to have no decisions to make other than where and when to sleep and eat clarifies, simplifies and puts the world in perspective.

Late one summer, I decided my world was in sore need of a little clarification…

Chapter One

Getting to the Start Line

People lose it at airports. Excitement gets the better of them, frustration makes them pick arguments with people they have never met and say things they wouldn't normally say. People cry, laugh, become emotional and you can observe it all from a suitable vantage point. Emotion spotting is the new trainspotting. Order yourself an espresso, grab a seat and take it all in.

I sugared my coffee and considered adding more, but I was on a health phase. The sort of health phase where you try, but never really do anything of any importance. Like having one less sugar, but then having another coffee. Or changing your brand of cigarettes and fooling yourself into thinking the new ones are better for you.

I took a sip and let the sweet nectar sit on my tongue whilst glancing around the Lyon airport terminal. A young woman was trying to settle two children who were throwing a tantrum. Her expression was one of near boiling point and complete frustration. The children were stamping their feet up and down and raising hell outside the Duty Free. I observed their faces, a mixture of mischievous contentment when they thought they had got away with something and then exasperation when they discovered they hadn't. A man bearing a striking resemblance to Jack Nicholson was trying to cut his croissant in half but appeared to be having trouble because he was still wearing sunglasses. A young couple were kissing and groping with a sense of urgency but also tenderness as his hand brushed away a stray curl of hair from her cheek. I was trying to decide if they were soon to be parted or had just been reunited.

People from all walks of life milled around – business types clasping laptops under their arms, budget travellers leaning precariously forward, almost dragging hands on the floor like Neanderthals to counteract the load of a rucksack. Passengers running to catch flights, couples gesticulating over who forgot the tickets. Drivers and chauffeurs were waiting at arrivals holding up cards with clients' names on them. I could tell the companies that were efficient and well organised, as the names had been printed neatly, with the company logo just underneath. Even the drivers were well turned out, with name badges and pressed clothing, their shoes reflecting the airport lighting. Then there were the cab drivers. Fags dangling from their mouths, hair greased back, stubble casting a grey shadow, and shirts unbuttoned as far as they dared. They had pulled bits of cardboard out of the bin and scribbled something indistinguishable on it. I had always harboured a strange desire to be one of those drivers just so I could hold up a board with someone's name on it. As the client saw me and walked over with a smile of recognition, I would promptly turn it over so they could see the back which read 'Only joking'.

I had arrived from London that morning with my possessions stuffed into a bright yellow backpack, sweating the spirit of adventure, and slightly the worse for wear after a very dubious ham and salad roll courtesy of the airline. My stomach sounded like a cement mixer churning thick porridge. As I clutched my stomach with one hand and puffed out my cheeks, I must have looked like a walking advert for indigestion tablets.

I was in the middle of an eight-year period of 'sporadic travelling'. This entailed working, usually as a temp, doing whatever was available from filing to emptying dustbins. I would scrimp and save for a few months, and when I had collected an amount of money that was nowhere near enough for the next trip, I would head off again. A few months later I would return to England and start the whole process over again. It was unpredictable but that was the attraction. I had spent most of the summer working at a yoga retreat in Greece. Having finished earlier than expected and still with a relatively moderate bank balance, I realised I still had some of the summer left to plan a trip. So I found myself back at my parents' house, holed up in my old eight-foot-square bedroom. It was the middle of August and I wondered what I was going to do for the rest of the season. I didn't really need to work, which was a blessing because that's a serious waste of good weather. I had thought about flying to America to do a long-distance hike, but it was too late in the season. Options on the other side of the equator such as Australia and Latin America were impractical because of flight costs.

The conversation with Bob in Heraklion had stayed with me when I returned from Greece, and I arrived back home eager for research. As I gleaned what information I could on my computer screen, it began to emerge as the perfect walk which ticked all the right boxes. It was the right distance I was looking for, about 1,600 kilometres. This translated to about three months' hiking. With luck the weather would hold right up to October and November. The flight was inexpensive, and the Spanish make damn fine red wine. Not to mention those Latin women.

Over the next couple of days I sat by the PC surrounded by empty cups with black treacle on the bottom where coffee had once been. Crumbs dotted used plates, and pieces of A4 littered the room with scribbles and notes. I left the room only to bond with my cat and explain why I was leaving him again after having only just returned.

Eventually, succumbing to tired eyes and an aching spine, I leaned back in the chair with my hands clasped behind my back and smiled. I had no maps, just a guidebook from the local shop with what seemed like reasonable directions. Anyway, it had a really nice picture of a bridge on the cover. The walk was on.

The ancient path I had chosen to walk came under many guises. As well as the Camino de Santiago, it was also referred to as El Camino, the Way of St James, the Way of St Jacques or the Pilgrims Way. To confuse the issue further, pilgrims, as walkers on the route are fondly known, could choose from numerous starting points. In fact, a true pilgrimage by definition starts at one's home. From the south coast of England to the north-west coast of Spain would have been a great walk, but I had limited time before the first snows fell over the Spanish mountains. Most pilgrims start their trek from Saint Jean Pied de Port in France. This small town nestles at the foot of the tail end of the Pyrenees, about a day's walk from the Spanish border and about 750 kilometres from the finish at Santiago de Compostela in north-west Spain. Saint Jean is easy to get to, has many facilities, and thousands of potential pilgrims start there each year. Novices choose this as their starting point because they feel there is safety in numbers.

Other starting points include Paris, Vézelay, Arles and Le Puy in France, or Seville in Spain. But don't let that fool you. Walkers can start from wherever they choose. There is no rulebook of the Camino saying you must begin at any one particular point. Indeed, to qualify for the coveted Certificate of Completion at the end of the walk in Santiago cathedral, you need actually walk only a minimum of 100 kilometres, a little more if you choose to cycle or ride a horse.

I had, literally, as much time as I wanted. However, walking in cold weather has never been my idea of fun. So, I had blessed myself with three months to complete my mission and this pretty much determined my starting point for me. Le Puy en Velay, the guidebook assured me, was two and a half months' walking to Santiago de Compostela. This would get me to my destination before winter gripped northern Spain, and give me a couple of weeks to boot as a buffer zone. I was sorted.

El Camino is old, very old. If it were a person, they would have had their bus pass for twenty years. If it were a movie, you would be watching through a lens and winding a handle at the side. The first documented journey along the route was made somewhere around AD 1145 by a certain Amery Picaud, a French cleric, and pilgrims had already been walking the route for many years before that – well over a thousand years to date in fact.

A religious pilgrimage is the primary reason for doing the walk. I'm not religious, but a brief acquaintance with the story of the walk is enough to whet anyone's appetite.

The legend began after the death of Christ. One of his disciples, St James, travelled to Spain to spread the gospel, with little success. He returned to Jerusalem, where Herod obviously took a dislike to him and had him beheaded some time around AD 44, making him a martyr. Disciples took his body and brought him back to Spain, where they buried him in a tomb on an empty hillside.

For the next several centuries, no one held any knowledge of the burial site, until a hermit named Pelagius received a vision of the location of the grave, guided by a star. The remains were exhumed and identified as those of the saint. A church was built on the site, and grew to become the present-day Santiago de Compostela, although the grand cathedral now towering there was built much later.

As news spread of the find, the location began to fulfil all the criteria of a potential pilgrim site. It was difficult to reach, over rough terrain, requiring the crossing of rivers and mountains. The trail was riddled with such dangers as bandits and wolves. The prevalence of disease in the area, coupled with the fact that Spain was at war with the Moors, compounded the difficulties and meant a true pilgrim would have to endure suffering to reach their goal. Regardless of what the history books tell you, my understanding of a pilgrimage is a very long, difficult journey where there's a reasonable chance you'll get killed.

Towns and villages began to grow along the route. Accommodation, food establishments, hospitals and all manner of amenities appeared to service the pilgrims, and the route became more famous as each year passed. It follows, therefore, that the Camino is rich in history, culture, sights, energy and an unusually high number of churches. When pilgrims first started walking to Santiago, it was said that the churches were their map and guide. The route stretches east to west. They could tell which way was west by the sun and other simple navigation aids, so their method was to look in a westerly direction for a church spire. A church spire would mean a village or town, and they would be pretty sure that was the direction they had to head.

Pilgrims in the past walked in simple sandals, one long item of clothing like a cloak, and perhaps a hat as shade from the fierce sun bearing down on them. A staff would help their balance and provide friendship, aiding their climbs up as they leaned on it and supporting them on the steep descents. Perhaps tied to this would be a small bag containing food or water. Provisions were procured on the trail by buying, trading or begging. And of course dangling around their neck would be a scallop shell, the emblem of the Camino to this day.

Supposedly, when the boat carrying St James originally

landed on the Spanish coast, a man was riding on horseback along the beach. The horse was startled by the boat and plunged into the sea, and both rider and horse eventually emerged covered in the shells. Even to this day, many of the beaches in the area of Galicia are strewn with scallop shells, particularly the curved white sands at Finisterre. And it is a sure way to spot a pilgrim from a day tripper when you see the shell stitched on to their pack or swaying from their staff or neck. Although Santiago is the true finishing post, many then walk the extra five or so days to Finisterre on the Atlantic coast and I had promised myself to do the same.

So, why walk 1,600 kilometres? Or even 100? Why do some pilgrims come from as far away as Canada and Australia? Why strap your life on your back to walk for three months? There are several reasons.

The obvious first choice is religion. It is the same principle for Christians, Catholics, Jews, Hindus, and all faiths to make a pilgrimage to a place of great importance in their faith. After all, St James was a disciple of Christ. The Camino ranks as high in importance as Jerusalem and Rome. Individuals make their way to the cathedral at Santiago to kiss the statue of St James, and feel safe in the knowledge that they have 'suffered' to make the trip.

Spirituality also plays a big role. Various books have been written on the Camino, fuelling this aspect. Many pilgrims make the challenge in the hope of maybe receiving enlightenment or enjoying some spiritual experience. It is true the Camino is full of natural energy lines, known as ley lines, following its course from east to west. These lines date back thousands of years and, although we know they exist, we have not been able to explain their importance or even how they work. When in proximity to one, especially for extended periods, people have noticed an increased 'awareness' of their surroundings and a feeling of being happier, closer to feeling 'complete'. It is true that some experience events of the kind they were hoping for and I think it is fair to say everybody emerges as a changed person. I didn't experience anything of cosmic proportions, although I encountered many nights with two, three or maybe four vivid dreams, one of which was a premonition of events happening the following day. Most people I met looked happy and content; you could argue that anybody would if they had a couple of months to partake in something they love. This is true, but it was certainly more than satisfaction. I was certainly aware of an energy, an energy that made me feel free, with little to worry about, and had a regular trick of putting a smile on my face.

In the Middle Ages people were sent to walk the Camino as a punishment for a crime and a chance to repent when they arrived in Santiago. Some pilgrims journeyed as a way of gaining merit and improving their standing in society, earning respect. Some even completed the walk for others. The wealthy of the day would pay lesser mortals to complete the pilgrimage for them. I hoped that method was still being used, as my funds were a little limited.

Me? As I said, I'm not religious. I would admit that I was hoping to receive some sort of spiritual encounter, maybe an insight into the meaning of life. I certainly wasn't undertaking it as a punishment (although at times it seemed like one). I wasn't even after any merit, and I never did find someone to pay me. I just simply fancied a long walk.

* * *

I ambled over to the Airport Tourist Information Office, places I have never held in great esteem. I concede they are mines of information and extremely useful. However, first, they label me as a tourist, which I hate. Even though most of the clientele, myself included, are indeed of this breed, to me it's a dirty word. It reeks of someone looking lost and confused, with a Kodak dangling around their midriff, white socks and sandals, scratching insect bites and with the unnatural glow of a lychee fruit. Even though I suppose I was a tourist, I cower from seeing or even hearing the 'T' word.

Secondly, you take your chances with the character found on the other side of the counter. The ones that appear the most intelligent are usually the most ignorant. Light travels faster than sound – this is why some people appear bright until they actually speak. They are either extremely helpful, with a genuine smile, or they would rather be somewhere else. Unfortunately, as usual,

I got stuck with the latter. I was secretly wishing her companion would become available first, as she seemed a little more natural and perhaps helpful, but there wasn't a lot separating the two of them.

I dispensed with trying a little French as that would have only confused the issue.

"Hi, can you please tell me how I get to Le Puy?" I enquired. I had pronounced Le Puy the way I thought it should be, as 'Le Poo'. This simple, innocent error cost me valuable minutes.

"Le Poo?" she replied, looking very confused.

I thought eye contact would improve the situation, so I removed my sunglasses.

"Yes, Le Poo. I need to get to Le Poo. Can you tell me the best way to get there please?"

"Ah, you mean Le Pwee!" Her smile and expression let slip that she found my ignorance a little amusing.

"OK," I said, "Le Pwee. How do I get there?"

"The quickest way is the bus to Lyon train station, and then the train via St Etienne. You can get a ticket for the bus just behind you at the desk. There should be one every fifteen minutes. Enjoy your time in France."

The securing of the bus ticket was, thankfully, trouble-free. As I stepped outside the air terminal, the mid-afternoon August sun rushed over my face like the breeze on opening the window of an air-conditioned car in midsummer Miami. I looked up and squinted as numerous postcard-perfect clouds streamed overhead. Lyon was visible a few miles to my left as the occasional church spire broke through the skyline. Cars stopped, people alighted. It made me feel that I was somehow on the verge of escaping all the commotion of modern life, as though my journey was starting and my pace was slowing down. Like driving for an hour on a motorway, then turning off down a country lane. For the first time since deciding two weeks before that I was going to walk El Camino, I felt a little uneasy about the task. My knees wobbled a bit, I sighed and bowed my head. Not out of sadness, you understand. I was looking forward to the whole experience with relish. The little pause for thought was just to try and comprehend actually walking 1,600 kilometres. I could board another plane and fly to Santiago and back all in

The Journey in Between

that same afternoon. It was possible to visit the Avis desk, sort out a nice little sports coupé and spend a couple of weeks doing the trip in air-conditioned luxury. But no, it was the actual walk that was the challenge. That was the reason I was here, and if it hadn't been the Camino, it would have been somewhere else.

The coach stopped at the kerbside and hissed as the brakes were released. I dodged through passengers retrieving luggage, threw my pack into the hold and then waited patiently as the amorous couple from the airport tried to negotiate the steps on to the bus without letting go of each other. They took their places; he had the aisle seat while she sat next to the window. As he became more affectionate, kissing her harder and clutching her waist, he pushed her up against the window. Like a cartoon character that hits a wall high up, and then slowly starts to slide down to earth, she began to slide up. I saw a guy walking past outside the coach grin as he observed two squashed buttocks stuck to the pane.

We sped along the motorway for thirty minutes, making occasional stops. Nothing outside looked like a railway station but I kept asking the driver just in case.

"Station?" I asked, raising my eyebrows.

"No," and he would make some sort of gesture to his watch suggesting more time.

When we did arrive he turned around and smiled, revealing an alarmingly big gap in his teeth, and gave the thumbs up. I disembarked and had to quickly bang on his door as he began to pull away again so I could get my bag back.

The station was huge; it seemed bigger than the airport. It was all I could do to keep my eyes ahead of me as I entered this massive hall: I just wanted to look up as though I had just entered a church. People were milling about everywhere, spilling out of little cafés, tapping their toes with folded arms as they waited in line for a sandwich and shuffling forward inch by inch to a roped-off area that was the horror of the ticket line. Think of banks on a Saturday morning, multiply by twenty, and you have some inkling of the picture. The roped area wound back and forth like a concertina. It reminded me of Philadelphia airport a few years previously. The queue for passport control was so long, they had kindly built a room for the sole purpose of dealing with the influx of visitors. There was enough rope winding back and forth in that place to kit out the rigging on a small ship. At Lyon they had also thoughtfully installed the system with the little black, electronic sign that flashes up a number in red and a directional arrow when a desk becomes available. The Post Office back home loves those toys. When I get to the end of the line, there always seem to be two counters with staff behind them doing absolutely nothing. They just look into space, and when they see me looking at them with an 'Any chance you can push your button?' look on my face, they bury themselves in a pile of TV licenses. At least fifty people appeared to be contemplating suicide as they stared into space waiting for a counter. The line was painfully long, and I wasn't looking forward to communicating my needs in French. There was a small tourist office with a cute French girl sitting behind it. It was a real dilemma, a long queue or the 'T' counter. I went for the counter and it proved the right choice. Not only did she speak word-perfect English and give me the platform number, time of departure and arrival, but she also smiled and offered to supply me with the ticket.

"Result!" I thought as I walked past the other queue with a smirk on my gob. I was starting to like France.

The train carriage was like a blast from the seventies, and actually, it probably was. Brown plastic fabric covered the seats, trying to imitate leather. The lino on the floor had been reduced to a strip of wood in the middle where it had played witness to thousands, probably millions of commuters, and looked so worn in places that I feared I may actually fall through to the line whizzing by underneath. To my surprise, people were smoking. Not that this bothered me – it was just a pleasant change to be given the choice of a smoking compartment when nowadays signs adorn most establishments telling you that you can't. Unlike the English rail system, this one actually worked. The train left when it was supposed to. It wasn't exactly Concorde, but it was moving.

I arrived at St Etienne to change trains, a place name somehow evoking romantic ideals. There were a couple of hours before my connection so I did a short scout of the area outside the station. I sat down in the park and wondered where the

The Journey in Between

population had vanished to. The place was deserted. A few people walked their dogs, but that was it. The shops were shut, traffic was non-existent, even the birds were on a tea break. Drizzle started to fall so I sat under an oak tree and played with my dictaphone. A shop door rattled across the road as the owner unlocked it. Small bells tinkled as she jammed it open and placed advertising clapboards in the street, which reflected perfectly in the puddles. I wandered over, paid for a couple of EEC regulation-shaped bananas and walked back to the tree. I wasn't hungry, just needed something to break up the monotony of a damp, lifeless afternoon in the big town. An overcast blur streamed past overhead. Trees swayed in the wind, and a fine spray smoked across the park. The black path was broken up with mirrors of water as I made my way back to the train station for my connection to Le Puy, reminding myself that someday I would return to St Etienne to see if anyone actually lived there.

The remaining section of the journey was uneventful save for brief glimpses through the trees of a landscape dipping and curving, a result of volcanic activity thousands of years before. Valleys, gorges, rivers and hills littered the area and the greenery seemed more intense and vivid. Le Puy straddled this unusual scenery as it rippled up and down. Rocky peaks dominated the town, rising up like stalagmites, some topped with statues or buildings. They were long, tall, slender, and dwarfed everything else. One was topped with the Chapel of Saint Michel d'Aiguilhe, and another with a statue of Notre-Dame de France. It was like surveying a giant sand-coloured cardiograph.

I neglected to bring a guidebook to France, apart from my one on the Camino, reasoning that I needed to save weight. So, standing outside the entrance to Le Puy station, I wondered where I would sleep. Under normal circumstances, I would have checked the guide, decided whether hostel or campsite would do the trick for the night and make my way there. Without the guide, I had to find out for myself. A wave of jealousy washed over me as I watched loved ones being collected, kids being ushered to waiting cars and more couples kissing and groping each other. It's one of the few aspects of travel that doesn't appeal, finding a place to spend the night. First it's a case of deciding which offering would be most suitable based on criteria such as location, distance, price, and whether they let females in the male dorms. Then it's a case of finding them.

A sign on a building opposite promising 'Cheap Hotel' tempted me. However, budget mode kicked in and I began studying the town map decorated with cigarette burns, which had melted the plastic covering, rendering 'Campsite Bouthezard' as something indistinguishable. Nevertheless, I calculated a quick stroll of about forty minutes and I would be checking in. Sure enough, I found the place beautifully nestled among poplar trees, resting up between two rivers. Three euros secured me a shady spot underneath one of the trees, among a smattering of other tents and caravans.

I had expected more walkers, as Le Puy is one of the main start points for the Camino. There was a handful scattered around, but not many. The rest of the campers were a random mix of nationalities, with random modes of transport. German cycle tourists had cordoned off one section of the best grass and set about making it their own. A precise washing line doubled as a boundary fence, as the male positioned each piece of laundry with fanatical attention to prevailing wind direction and the sun's position. His girlfriend was sorting equipment on the ground with such precision that I thought any minute she would inform him that they were missing a rubber band. An Austrian couple were near to me, and seemed to be in more of a holiday mode. Far from being organised, they were just slouching in two deck chairs and sinking Kronenbourgs like they were going out of fashion. The obligatory English couple plus two kids were doing the 'family holiday' thing. Mum was peeling the spuds while Dad was trying to figure out why the barbecue was too hot. As he lifted up and peered with upturned nose at the hard, black slab that was once a hamburger, I think he had pretty much decided that they were dining out tomorrow.

French campsites have always amazed me. The French love and place great value on their camping expeditions and traditions. The grass is always plentiful, soft and springy. There is always a toilet and wash block, and while they do vary in cleanliness, they are generally well presented and have everything a town camper should require. I had last camped in France as a teenager on a cycle trip, and remember being

The Journey in Between

grateful for the camping facilities then. After all, in those days, £18 a week wages from working in a supermarket didn't get a traveller very far. We English could learn a few lessons from our French counterparts about communal campgrounds. Back home, I would by this stage have no doubt endured a delayed train journey, and found myself in a field in the middle of nowhere that was pretending to be a campsite, full of cow shit, boasting as many amenities as, well, your average field.

After washing off the rigours of a day's international travel in the shower, I spent the evening just lying on the grass by my tent taking it all in. I cooked some pasta and then lay on my back, drinking fresh coffee, courtesy of my new camping percolator, watching my cigarette smoke curl up and out of sight. I thought about the little planning that had got me here, my complete lack of training and my limited financial supplies. Odds were a little stacked in the Camino's favour but I had one ally, and a powerful one at that: determination to succeed.

I gazed up at the leaves on the poplars, which appeared to sigh as they lifted up gracefully, then relax as the passing breeze caught them unawares, like that last, deep breath we take before falling asleep. The sun had slid under the horizon for another day, leaving only a blazing memory of golden hues streaking above me. A rainbow was arching gracefully over the Chapel of Saint Michel D'Aiguilhe, teetering on a fulcrum at the hill's apex, providing a colourful and stark contrast to a deep black, merciless cloud mass bubbling behind. The whole vision was still curing, still maturing, and improving by the second. I took it as a portent that the Camino was sure to be beautiful, but there would be difficulties under the façade. I zipped up my sleeping bag, listened to a few raindrops explode on the canvas inches from my head and dozed off with that secure feeling of being safe and warm whilst the elements stirred around me.

The Camino was always going to be an unknown and invisible journey in that I did not know what would be around the next corner. I had few expectations of what it would hold. Most of them were to be surpassed. All of them were met with conviction. I did not know whom I would meet, what I would see, smell, hear or taste. It would be a pathway hiding its secrets and surprises, a journey along the line of fate. It had a beginning and it had an end, but those were the only aspects of its character that were certain. Everything else was ensconced between these points waiting to be experienced. The unpredictability was dangerously exciting.

Tomorrow I would start walking sixteen hundred kilometres to Santiago de Compostela.

Chapter Two

Breaking Myself in

I awoke the next morning with an enthusiasm eager for release. The little rain during the night had dispersed, to be replaced with perfect walking weather, as if it knew my journey was beginning. Pure white clouds eagerly socialised with a gentle breeze, resisting the urge to move. The sun was already gliding along its east–west journey, creating shafts of light which cast shadows on the grass like moving apparitions. A squirrel played up and down a nearby oak tree, flocks of birds swooped and rose almost as though they were riding waves. Ducks flapped in desperation, trying to take off, while silver water droplets tumbled off their ochre feathers.

I felt wide awake but my eyes were having difficulty opening, as they often do at the start of the day. I entered the campsite bar searching for a caffeine fix. It was empty except for a woman resting on her side of the counter reading a newspaper. I offered a feeble "Good morning." She paused on the football results and looked up just in time to catch me peering down at her cleavage. Smiling, she adjusted her left breast, took one look at the narrow slits where my eyeballs had once resided and started fiddling with the dials on the coffee machine. It hissed, spluttered and eventually she handed me a very strong espresso accompanied by a stale croissant.

My memories of previous visits to France were all returning to me as I walked through Le Puy. Battered old Citroëns with hay bales stuffed in the back belched out black clouds as they bumped down uneven streets. Old men sat outside rustic cafés, sipping their coffees and brandies, a Gitane stuck to their bottom lip wafting up smoke the same colour as their ageing hair. They conversed with their mates while throwing elaborate gestures with arms and hands to emphasise certain points, all interspersed with eruptions of laughter. I stopped to savour the tormenting aroma of fresh baked bread from one of the numerous bakeries. Shop shutters clattered noisily as they were pulled up. A couple were engaged in an animated, heated exchange: in most countries this would draw disapproving looks, but in France it was part of everyday life. Everyone seemed relaxed and in no hurry. Assistants in shops laughed with customers; even the estate agents seemed genuinely busy.

Before I could truly get going, I had to obtain a pilgrim's passport, or *créanciale*, for the Camino from the Cathedral. The *créanciale* is a piece of card about the size of a passport, except it is folded like a concertina and when opened out stretches from hand to shoulder. Your basic details are included (name, address, etc.) and the rest of the card consists of about eighty printed, matchbox-sized squares. Each one of these sections is designed to be stamped at certain establishments along the route with their own particular design. The gîtes (in France these are cheap, hostel-like accommodations) and their cousins the refuges in Spain were the main source for these stamps, along with some restaurants, bars, museums and even shops. The primary purpose of all this is to provide proof to the Cathedral authorities in Santiago de Compostela that the owner has actually completed the route he or she claims to have walked and is thereby eligible for the coveted certificate of completion. The *créanciale* is not just a good idea; more a necessity. It also rewards you with cheaper accommodation than your average tourist, and discounted meals at establishments displaying the *pilgrims' menu*. All the walkers I met had one – you just don't walk El Camino without it.

Classic architecture stared back at me, proud, intense, almost arrogantly boasting its heritage. Streets and alleys split off randomly and aimlessly around me, as if I were standing in a hole in a broken pane of glass, the shatter lines radiating out. Attractive women meandered leisurely around me, finding solitude in shop windows displaying the new autumn fashions.

The Journey in Between

There were a few pilgrims peering into their guidebooks and squinting anxiously at street names. Locals were picking at breakfast on wrought iron tables, which spilled on to polished cobbles. Tourists were strolling around, hands clasped behind their backs, bending over to get a closer look in souvenir shop windows. I felt somehow different, even famous. I wasn't one of those people on holiday for two weeks. I was on a different mission. I felt like crying out, "Look at me! I'm going to walk from here to the Atlantic coast," but I doubted anyone would have listened.

I made my way to the Romanesque cathedral of Notre Dame, where my research had assured me I could obtain the *créanciale*. The steep streets and steps up to the cathedral had me seriously questioning my sanity before I had even set foot on the actual Camino. My lungs were exploding from three weeks of inactivity. I felt like I was wading through knee-deep snow hauling an oil tank behind me. By the time I reached the top of the steps leading to the cathedral, I was a wheezing wreck.

The huge wooden doors were slightly ajar. I entered to feel a rush of damp, moist air surround me. A gloomy corridor wove around the main seating area. Polished wood panels adorned the walls, giving way to a bleak stone floor; I could almost feel the coldness of it rising through my boots. I found a small souvenir room at the rear of the cathedral, where, judging by a small number of pilgrims, the elusive *créanciale* was there for the taking, but it didn't prove that easy. I approached a very rotund nun sitting behind a desk. I have nothing against people with a larger frame, but it was hard not to stare. Her chin hung down in several layers like molten lava; her attire was at stretching point. I half expected her buttons to ping off, or the stitches to fray and snap any second. If she were wearing high heels, she would have struck oil.

We had a serious language barrier, as usual. I always assumed that I could get by in France by letting roll with a sentence containing predominantly English words, with the odd French noun thrown in, and mask the whole mess up with a crap accent. Well, it seemed to work last time I was here.

"Excoos eem mwoir madame, I em lookeen fur le creanceearlee por Le Camino." I realised as soon as I said it that my theory stood about as much chance of success as a fart in a hurricane. I knew the reply before it even came.

"Pardon?" she replied with a smile that suggested customer service was not her main priority. I managed to communicate what I was after by pointing to a small pile of *créanciales* on the desk in front of her.

"Ah, oui, oui!" she said, a wave of enlightenment rising up over her face. "Moment." She pointed to some chairs positioned around the room. I spent the next hour alternately sitting down and wandering around the room looking at the exhibits. Every once in a while she would look in my direction, nod her head and smile. All the time, she dished out passports like they were cakes going cold. With a mixture of impatience, and perhaps thinking she had misunderstood me, I made my way to the desk again. A young chap bearing a striking resemblance to Adrian Mole ambushed me in mid-stride.

"Sir, I eem sowee for le wait, my friend speaks no English. Perhaps I can elp you." He peered at me through small, round glasses. His hair was slicked back with oil so all the comb marks were visible like furrows in a field, and it was so shiny I could see the stained-glass windows reflected in it. He stood nervously playing with a hanky and occasionally jerking his right arm.

"Yeah, hi. I am walking the Camino, and from what I understand, I can obtain a *créanciale* here to assist me, a pilgrim's passport," I explained, doing a double take when I saw the diminishing pile on the desktop.

"Oui, sir, we do provide *la créanciale*. Please, first I must ask a few questions."

Now, I am a laid-back sort of guy. It takes a lot to rattle me. I was, however, reaching a point. I had been waiting for nigh on two hours. In that time walkers had come and gone after receiving their passport. I was tired, in desperate need of a smoke and so hungry that everything I looked at was starting to resemble sweet pastries.

Luckily, Mr English speaker processed my request relatively smoothly, after I provided some basic information. I also had to promise that I was not looking to acquire the passport by means of deception, or to use it for any purpose other than that for which it was intended. I paid a small fee, and also purchased a small pendant depicting the church for my neck chain.

By the time I got outside, I was drawing on my cigarette as though I was trying to suck a pea through a straw. I took a couple of photos, had an argument with the straps on my rucksack, and stumbled off towards town, and the start of the Camino.

"This is it," I said to myself. "This is the start of all my lack of planning." The start of twelve weeks of walking. Twelve weeks! I still couldn't wrap my head around the prospect of travelling by no means other than putting one hiking boot in front of the other for that period of time. Sixteen hundred kilometres! That's like walking from my parents' house to my sister's, and back, three times!

It was August the 18th. I walked back down the cathedral steps, along Rue des Tables, left at the Choristes fountain and on to Rue Raphaël. When I emerged into the Place du Plot, considered the traditional starting point for the Le Puy pilgrim, the weekend market had already been plying its trade since the early morning. Wooden tables filled the square and buckled under the weight of local produce. Mushrooms lay jostling for space among blood-red tomatoes and white papery garlic. Onions tied in strips were dangling from rain covers like plaits of ginger hair. Golden yellow apples appeared ripe and juicy and nestled among green pears and rich black plums. Vegetables had been groomed to perfection, displaying virtually every hue of the rainbow. Colour engulfed me; it was like a paint-box riot. I felt obliged to buy something, even though I didn't need anything. Then I remembered an umbrella. I had waterproofs and a cover for my rucksack, but it took ten minutes of delving into its furthest caverns to retrieve them and put them on. By which time, invariably, it had stopped raining. An umbrella, I figured, would be worth it for those short showers.

Perhaps, subconsciously, I was thinking of Nicholas Crane, walker and author, who traversed from Spain to Turkey a few years back entirely on foot. 'Que Chova' was the name he had christened his friend to shelter him from the rain and to fend off a few dogs. I felt like I wanted to be part of the experience he had written about, the careful search for the perfect companion, the perfect umbrella. In the end, all it amounted to was picking the lightest and cheapest version. I squeezed in the shop, hitting people with my rucksack and sending postcard stands spinning. I wasn't in the mood for shopping. That was one of the horrors of society I had come out here to escape. I pondered the thought of christening it with some well-thought-out, profound name. Several options came to mind, like old friends, relatives and pets, all of whom had meant something special to me at some point in my life, and who would perhaps bless this umbrella to look after me in the coming storms. Something meaningful, something different and something unexpected. After deliberating this for thirty minutes I eventually settled on 'Brolly'.

Boulevard St Louis merged into Rue des Capucins, and then rose steeply. The buzz of the market faded to just a colourful memory. Le Puy en Velay was shrinking each time I turned around. It all merged into one brown and grey mass; the only redeeming features were the church spires breaking the blot. Soon I was encapsulated in a kind of meditative walk. My feet were on autopilot, and I was just lost in my own thoughts. The steep hill out of the city eventually flattened out and merged into the French countryside. I stopped, slid my rucksack on to the grass on the Camino's edge, retrieved my peanuts and lay with my back in the grass looking up at the sky as thousands of pilgrims before me had done, perhaps in this very spot.

The sun was hot, burning my exposed flesh. I had expected hot days, but I was still thankful. Sun to me is sometimes the very essence of a good walk. To take advantage of a beautiful day and to walk while the sun disperses its heat. I felt as though I was the luckiest person on the planet, with little money, but everything I needed to live on was squashed, in no particular order, in my rucksack. I did not have to suffer an intrusive alarm clock for three months, and my life consisted of a stony track weaving in and out of classic countryside. Things were exactly how I liked them, uncomplicated. After my initial fears about the distance I had to walk faded, I came to realise it wasn't going to be so much of a walk but more of an experience. You can admire the peak of the mountain, but it's the journey up that holds the real pleasures.

As I heaved my rucksack on to my back and the fabric

moulded into the ridges and curves of my spine, I realised something that I had missed during my walking meditation. My rucksack was seriously heavy. I had packed with care, two pairs of socks and liners, two pairs of underwear, two T-shirts, a pair of light hiking trousers, shorts, waterproofs and the usual camping equipment one would expect to take. So why, when I had placed it down on the scales at check in, had I been horrified to see sixteen kilos displayed? Some pilgrims I had seen in Le Puy had rucksacks so small that I would have struggled to squeeze in a food allowance.

I do pack carefully; I *had* packed carefully. I was thorough and had omitted some items that I normally would have taken. However, I need certain 'comfort' items that always come with me; I think we all do. Some people make do with a cup of instant coffee in the morning. I wouldn't go near the stuff and for years scoured the hiking shops for a small, lightweight piece of equipment that brews proper, fresh coffee. I ended up securing an insulated mug with a built-in plunger while travelling in Canada a few years before. I probably didn't 'need' the umbrella, but had grabbed it, again for comfort. I would rather have an extra half-kilo and know I could sleep at a beautiful spot, and pull out my stove for a hot coffee. The thing is, if you want to have a light load, you do have to be careful about packing. Every single item has to be looked at for its merits. I've seen people pay ten pounds each for a titanium spoon, fork, and knife. Fine, they have saved weight. If they put a modicum of thought into it, however, they should have realised that only a spoon is needed to cook and eat with, and they would have a cutting edge on their penknife. I have seen people pack hairdryers, three pairs of shoes, four pairs of trousers, six pairs of underwear and even a CD radio cassette player, and then complain that the load is too much for them. I end up somewhere in between. I buy lightweight gear, and then ruin it all by taking too much of it.

It's worth noting that many people on the Camino, in fact most, stop at some point to post equipment back home because they need to lose some weight. In the end, I decided to carry as little food as possible and buy provisions few and often. The heaviest items a walker carries are usually food and water. I would become fitter as the walk progressed anyway, and if I was still struggling later on, then I would post some equipment back home to Nerve Centre HQ, better known as Mum.

I passed my first *balise*. These markers direct pilgrims on the correct route, like a wooden footpath or bridleway sign back home. I think someone did a lot of walking with a brush and paint pot, marking any suitable medium vaguely found in the right place. Rocks, fences, trees, houses, walls all got the treatment. These soon-to-be-familiar logos were to become my friends over the next few weeks, until I reached the border with Spain, where they changed into the Spanish version. They consisted of a horizontal white rectangle on top and a red pointer underneath. The white rectangle remained the same always, a red rectangle running parallel underneath signifying that the pilgrim should carry straight on. The other two variations, where the red segment would point left or right, were self-explanatory. The last option consisted of the white rectangle on a diagonal, with the red crossing it on the opposite diagonal – your basic cross on its side. This proved to be invaluable, as it advised that the pilgrim had taken a wrong turn and should reverse back to where he or she had seen the last sign. I started to say "Thank you" every time I saw one showing I was going the right way. And when I needed one, I would ask, and the Camino would oblige. One seemed to appear at exactly the time I was most in need of it. I carried on this method throughout the entire Camino. I don't know why I started to be grateful but it worked. Except for a few times when the trail was confusing and seemed to give no clear direction, my thanks and requests were always answered.

I walked gently and deliberately that first day. I wanted to break my body in slowly, but more importantly I wanted to establish a rhythm. I needed the Camino to be a memorable experience, not a physically demanding mission defined by schedules and plans. It was more of a stroll than a walk. I spent time studying and surveying what was around me. The track itself varied from well-worn stone ruts, with grass lining the middle, to shingle on the newer stretches. Occasional small bridges hopped over busy brooks, grasses caught in the soft current like long, flowing locks of emerald hair. Fields of corn the colour of sand stooped over in the breeze. Irregular-shaped meadows were patched with clumps of oak trees, like spots on a Dalmatian.

I turned around to check my progress and caught sight of another pilgrim on the trail, about a kilometre behind me. I wasn't in any hurry, so he soon caught me up. He was walking as if he had just robbed the bank in Le Puy and the police were in hot pursuit. I wondered what his hurry was, and why he wasn't taking his time and savouring the experience. When he got to a few feet behind me, I turned around, smiled and said "Bonjour". He said nothing. No eye contact, no facial expression, no body language. I repeated the greeting in case he hadn't heard me, but still he didn't respond. He just walked on with his head down, without a word. I began to wonder what his problem was and even became paranoid, for some reason, that the church had forgotten to impart some vital piece of information that we pilgrims were not supposed to speak. What if I had to walk all the way and as a penance to God I was not allowed to utter a word while I walked? I was very relieved when, shortly afterwards, I passed a pilgrim sunbathing. He smiled and said "Bonjour."

I had decided to camp out the first night. I would just pick a nice spot and set up camp away from any prying eyes. However, after about five hours and fifteen kilometres' walking, I passed the small hamlet of Montbonnet. It was quiet, unobtrusive and just seemed to exist, not bothering anyone. There were a couple of farms, dogs were running around in the yards on chains, chickens pecked at whatever small morsel they could find. There was the odd hum of a tractor in a nearby field, harvesting the fruits of the summer's labours. The only disturbance to the tranquillity was the occasional 2CV zooming past on the small country road.

I always have good intentions to camp out, and when I do, I don't regret it. Sometimes, however, my brain accelerates towards logical mode and demands I seek a little comfort. But I do love getting back to nature. I enjoy finding the perfect spot to pitch camp. Maybe by some water, a nice flat area for the tent, some firewood close to hand. On clear nights I rarely pitch the tent, preferring to sleep out. There are few experiences as simple as lying on your back picking out the constellations, snuggling down in a sleeping bag, and feeling a chilled waft of night air brush you cheeks.

A voice in my head offered: "Fozzie, why camp out in a miserable field when there is a gîte a hundred metres down the road? Why get into your sleeping bag when you're filthy, when they are sure to have a piping-hot shower? Why make do with your provisions when they will probably have food to buy and a cooker to rustle something up on?"

I relented, swerved a sharp right along the road, and then turned right again into the small farmyard. Perhaps I had subconsciously asked for shelter, and if I did, how would I know this was the right place? I got my validation immediately. Two border collies came bounding out, tails on overdrive, tongues slapping with a look of devotion in their eyes. "This will do nicely," I thought.

I knocked on an old oak door studded with lead rivets. An attractive woman in her early thirties answered with a genuine smile and an expectant look on her face, as though she thought I should speak first.

"Er, bonjour, mademoiselle. Avez-vous une... place to sleep?" I offered. She giggled sheepishly and put her hand to her mouth.

"Excuse me," she replied, "I do not wish to be rude, but that's the worst French I have heard in a long time!"

"Well, that is good news. Yesterday it was really crap, so I'm glad things are improving."

Wavy, blonde hair tumbled down the sides of her face like dangling party streamers. Her only make-up was a subtle pink lipstick, which highlighted her tanned skin. She was perspiring in the heat and moisture droplets winked back at me from the nape of her neck as they caught sunlight. Flour marks smudged a blue apron and her hands. She left a little on her nose as she brushed off a fly and blew a lock of hair from her eye.

In the space of five minutes she had given me the guided tour. There was indeed a good kitchen with a few groceries to buy. Hot showers were on tap, so to speak, and the rooms were dormitory-style. I opted to camp in the grounds as a compromise and save some funds. She offered breakfast of bread and jam plus juice and coffee, which I accepted, and I watched her slink back to her house.

After showering and watching what little fatigue I had swirl its way down the plughole, I rustled up some soup and rice, and blagged two boiled eggs and some bread off a couple of French cyclists. The French are generous like that, always ready to dish out some provisions if you show them what little you have with a resigned look. I went outside and played with the dogs for a while, and chilled out with a coffee and a smoke. It was about seven pm and the sun was still up, and still warm. I remember thinking it would be quite a change two months down the road. The sun would have already set, it would be chilly, probably raining, maybe even snowing in Spain. But for now I was content, very content. Fifteen kilometres in a day was hardly breaking any records, but I hadn't intended to. I needed a casual, gentle first day of breaking myself in. My back and shoulders felt fine and, most importantly, my feet showed no signs of any blisters. Sure, I was tired, had been hungry and needed a long night's rest.

Satisfied with both my pace and my fitness, I dwelt once more on what was in store; and it brought a huge smile to my face.

By the time I had finished daydreaming, the sun had set. I ran for my tent as a few fat droplets of rain began to land around me. I hurriedly zipped up the shelter and looked up to see clouds the colour of soot racing up as though someone were drawing the blinds over the sky. They were billowing over me with frightening ferocity, transforming a star-splattered arena into a shade darker than night itself. There was a storm building.

Chapter Three

Pushing Too Hard

The elements had indeed stirred overnight; a vicious thunderstorm kept me awake for over an hour. I opened the zip of the tent and lay there taking in the spectacle. Electricity lit up the French countryside every few seconds like a million fireworks, illuminating the surrounding hills and providing a split-second glimpse of the dark sky overhead. Each thunderous clap made me cower as if expecting a lightning strike to pinpoint my safe little haven. Raindrops smacked on the grass, transforming the area into a waterlogged dance floor. The ground appeared to move and become alive as the drops collided and exploded in a myriad of small splashes. It was an awesome, energetic display of Mother Nature at her cinematic best.

I awoke at sunrise and clambered outside. France had received a spring-clean – everything was wet and glinted in the sunlight, smelling fresh and moist. I went into the farmhouse breakfast room, which the family had long since left for another day's toil in the fields. The lady of the house welcomed me again, and invited me to eat as much as I could. There was fresh coffee, orange juice, limitless crusty baguette and homemade jams, the classic continental breakfast. A woman joined me. Shoulder-length grey hair curled around the sides of her face, disguising the outline and giving her a soft appearance. She was probably in her sixties, and wore glasses with frames so big that she might have been able to see what was behind her. She looked in good shape and I got the impression she was a walker. Eating carefully and attentively, she seemed to savour each portion as if it were her last meal. I had not noticed her last night, perhaps preoccupied with my thoughts.

She spoke a little English, and we chatted about the Camino, for she too was on her second day after starting from Le Puy en Velay. The conversation followed what was soon to become a familiar pattern every time I chatted to pilgrims. Where we had started, where we were going, where we were from, and the reasons for succumbing to El Camino's lure in the first place. She left before me; I was in no hurry. I was to meet this woman several times over the next few weeks. I never did ask her for her name and I don't know why. Usually when I am introduced to someone, I forget their name straight away, and end up asking them again. It didn't seem to matter with this woman, who showed an equal lack of curiosity about my name. I spotted her walking past the window shortly afterwards, smoking a cigarette, so I decided to call her the smoking woman.

I settled up with the owner, the grand sum of about two euros, and she bade me farewell as I strode off. It was always refreshing to meet the proprietors of hotels, guesthouses and the like on the Camino – they seemed genuinely happy. Imagine having twenty or more walkers hanging around your house every night in peak season, and still be able to appear totally relaxed, provide a warm and genuine smile, and be helpful, and then do exactly the same thing the following day. I'd go nuts if I had to do that all the time.

I left and crossed over the road and back into the countryside, through fields bordered by haphazard old stone walls about waist height. They yielded to the Camino, which wove left and right and then entered a pine forest. I spotted a pilgrim through the trees in a small clearing, relaxing after his breakfast and soaking up the warmth. I love pine forests: they remind me of magical, secret places, and bring back memories of books such as *The Hobbit* and children's fairy tales with a touch of wizardry and the mystical. Unicorns prancing among the pine needles, medieval cavalry charging by and perhaps a glimpse of Merlin. I wanted to camp there and spend the night experiencing the atmosphere, but smiled when I realised this would be just the first of many, many chances along the way.

I dipped sharply down among deep green woods. The decline was severe and because of the rain it was also slippery. Coupled with the weight of my rucksack, this made me feel as though I was taking my first, tentative move on skis. If I leaned too far forward, my body toppled forward; too far back, and it felt as though any second my feet would be snapped away, flung up in the air, and I'd land on my arse, like a cartoon character slipping on a banana skin.

Reaching the pit of the mini gorge, I skipped over puddles and a brook, and climbed again for a few minutes. A dog saw me and started barking wildly, straining at a chain. The entire garden of the house was fenced in, and I wondered why people take on beautiful animals and then keep them imprisoned.

The stones and mud yielded to tarmac. I crested the hill and arrived in the village of Saint Privat D'Allier, a beautiful place sitting on the edge of the gorge, and apparently threatening to topple over any second down to the river below.

I put down my rucksack, indulged in a sugar fix with a soda and a bar of chocolate and sat on a bench to watch life go by. It was the beginning of the week, but it felt more like a Sunday. Everyone proceeded without any hurry, a practice they have mastered well in Europe. People were walking dogs, buying their bread for the day and chatting to their friends in the shop, or just strolling around without a care in the world, as if they were all on holiday. I was so drawn in to the whole ambience that I just hung out on the bench for an hour or so.

* * *

I was determined to walk every step of the Camino, every single metre of the sixteen hundred kilometres. I did not want to accept any lifts, take a bus or catch a train. I knew that on arrival in Santiago de Compostela, pilgrims presented themselves to the cathedral authorities to obtain their certificate of completion. I was aware that they asked a few questions, which they were obliged to do, to weed out walkers who tried to obtain the certificate by means of deception.

Playing a scenario in my head, I imagined myself sitting in the square outside the cathedral, and being approached by a sinister-looking character.

"Fozzie?" he asks, clamping a clipboard firmly in one hand, a pen poised in the other. He is wearing a badge displaying the words 'Fake-Pilgrim Spotter', and he peers at me over half-framed spectacles. His head is bald save for some long wisps of white hair dangling from each side, and he is wearing a long, brown cloak with sandals just peeking out at the bottom.

"Yep, that's me."

"I understand you are requesting the coveted certificate of completion from the authorities here at Santiago."

"Er, yep. That's correct."

"I am sure you won't mind just answering a few questions. We have to be careful in these situations. People have been passing themselves off as pilgrims, in order to get a certificate. First, where did you start from?"

"Le Puy un Velay in France," I would say, feeling a little nervous, albeit proud.

"Le Puy? That is a fine walk; you have done well, pilgrim. When did you start?"

"Erm, August the 17th."

"Ah, I see you have progressed well. Le Puy to Santiago is a long walk – I see that you wanted to make the most of your time on the Camino. Congratulations."

"Thank you." At this point my fingernails are firmly rooted in my mouth, and taking a hammering.

"Now, let me see," he says, scanning down the paper on his clipboard and sliding his spectacles up his nose. "Ah, yes. Can you tell me if a pilgrim should turn left or right out of the campsite in Le Puy en Velay in order to start the Camino?"

"Well... he would turn... lef... No! Sorry, right."

"Excellent, excellent," he says. I smile, thinking maybe this isn't so bad after all. But then he continues the inquisition.

"Very well, imagine the Camino descending out of Conques. Please enlighten me as to the name of the river you cross before the sharp incline."

I shift nervously, looking down at my feet. "The river? Conques? The river, the river, the river... there isn't one! Hah! Trick question!"

"Actually, it's not. It's called the River Dordou."

"Oh... shit. I knew that. Really, I did. Have I failed, then?"

"No," he says, with the same malicious chuckle that my

maths teacher would have been proud of. "We would not expect 100%. That would be unfair."

"Oh, great, 'cause it was just a lapse of concentration. I knew there was a river, really."

"One incorrect answer is available to you. Let us see how you acquit yourself with my other questions. You are sitting by the river in Espalion. A fine bridge, quite possibly my favourite. Please tell me what you see on the other side."

"Huh! Now that *is* a trick question! I need to know what side I am sitting on before I can tell you that!"

"Yes, excellent, well spotted. Let us say, the north side, looking south."

"O... K... I would see the park on the other side, poplar trees running right to left along the path. There are a few men playing boules and some laughing children nearby. There is a football pitch with a grandstand, and if I look through the seating, I can just make out the café." I sit back, smirking.

"Good ... very good. Now, one more question, answered correctly, and I can leave you in peace, Mr Foskett."

"Please call me 'Fozzie'. Would you like a cigarette?"

"No, I do not smoke. Cast your mind back along your route. Follow from the beginning to the end, and observe. Tell me how many churches you visited."

"Oooh... five?" I offer, a bit hesitantly now.

"Five? FIVE? Is that all? I cannot be expected to authorise a certificate to a pilgrim who has visited only five churches on the entire route! That is ludicrous!" And the man, becoming more and more the villainous accuser with every passing moment, roars with laughter.

"Wh... wha... what do you mean? There's nothing in the transcripts that dictates I must visit a certain number of religious establishments. Excuse me, but that's nonsense."

"I beg your pardon?" He stares at me.

"If you're going to fail me on that question, then I demand to see your manager... now!"

He opens his mouth to reply but is cut off before he can do so by another, kinder-looking man, who towers imposingly over both of us.

"Manuel! There is no need to question this poor man any

The Journey in Between

further. Please leave – I will see you in my office shortly. Go!" Manuel cowers like a trapped dog under the glare of his master.

"Mr Foske... sorry, 'Fozzie'. Please accept my sincerest apologies for the behaviour of my colleague. He takes his job a little too seriously at times."

My daydreaming was interrupted when I caught sight of the smoking woman sitting by the side of the trail.

"Cigarette break, huh?" I smiled.

"Oui. It is one of a few weaknesses," she replied, squinting as she looked up at me.

"Nothing wrong with a few weaknesses. I'm guilty of a few myself, smoking included."

We exchanged a few pleasantries and I continued, through tunnels created by stumpy oak trees curving over me and the familiar stone walls cluttering either side. I reached the small hamlet of Rosiers, having walked a total of around eighteen kilometres that day. The soles of my feet felt strange. It was a feeling I had experienced when hiking before. It felt like blisters, but I knew it was just soreness. My shoulders were also aching from the constant rubbing of the rucksack straps. I should have stopped, checked out the situation and stayed there for the night. Foolishly, however, I decided to carry on to the large town of Saugues, where I told myself I could check out my aches and pains, and spend the night in a cheap, communal gîte. I was also low on food, so I would be able to stock up in the town.

This turned out to be a huge mistake. I had walked too far, too soon. My body was still being run in. I should have been building my distances up slowly and resting often. By the time I reached Saugues I was in agony. I was barely hobbling and my shoulders felt as though someone was rolling their knuckles up and down on them. I must have looked like a runner who had just crossed the finishing line in a marathon and collapsed into someone's arms.

I winced my way to the first gîte, which was full. Then to the second, also full. I stocked up on food and limped down to the last communal gîte by the River Sauge. As I leaned over to one side to take off my rucksack, something gave in my right shoulder. I yelled with pain, much to the bemusement of the guy sitting at reception.

My shoulder felt as though someone had driven a skewer straight through it. I couldn't move for about five minutes, and was stuck there, standing but leaning over to one side, bent forward, scared even to breathe, my face contorted with the excruciating pain.

This is it, I thought. My attempt on the Camino was over, after just three days.

After a while I eased my body upright, which seemed to take forever. The pain, still intense, seemed to abate slightly. I booked in for two nights, somehow tentatively hoisted my rucksack on again, then struggled for another five minutes to the communal room where I would spend the night with three other pilgrims.

My shoulder, I was to discover, was just one of two problems. I had deliberately delayed looking at the soles of my feet, for fear of what lurked there. I knew it was bad because it felt bad. Whatever the problem was, it was minor compared to my shoulder. My feet seemed like a mere distraction.

My morale, which up until now had been good, dipped to a low and it was an effort to snap myself out of a bad mood and try to convince myself that the day's events were just a hiccup.

I knew deep down blisters were causing the pain, I just couldn't fathom why. My boots were well worn. They had been broken in over the course of a year's worth of weekend hikes, and I had worn them while working in Greece for four months that year. I had good socks, and wore thin liners underneath. I washed my feet religiously every night, and gave them a good massage to ease away the aches. It couldn't be blisters.

I sat on the edge of my bunk and eased off my boots, then slowly peeled off my socks as one would carefully peel a plaster off an open wound.

"Bollocks," I muttered to myself as the full picture was revealed on one foot. It was worse than I had imagined. On the sole, a line of skin running parallel to my toes, stretching from my big toe to the third toe, had pushed up into a ridge, like a chain of mountains rising out of the plains. There were also blisters on my little toe and on the sole of my heel. My other foot was pretty much the same.

I was out of action, at least for tomorrow, and decided to take

The Journey in Between

a rest day to see if things would improve.

I remembered reading somewhere once that when we get injured, our reaction to the problem and how we deal with it can determine how it heals. For example, if we take the view that the injury is disastrous or, conversely, if we consider that it is not as bad as it looks, then the body 'listens', takes heed and acts accordingly. Having a positive state of mind can affect our body's capability to make itself better. Whether it worked or not, I always tried to follow this thinking.

I tried to concentrate on imagining that both the blisters and the shoulder were minor problems, and pushed my fears to one side. It seemed to work. To my astonishment, after a short time, my shoulder felt as though there had never been a problem to start with. The blisters were obviously still there, but after I had punctured them, squeezed out the liquid and patched them up, they also seemed much better. My good spirits slowly returned.

In any case, while planning the walk, I had decided to incorporate a rest day once a week, so the timing couldn't have been better. Filling my mind with positive thoughts, I roamed around Saugues. It entailed hobbling a little because the blisters still hurt, but at least I could walk. There was no way that I was going to give up now, whatever hardships. Short of breaking a leg, I fully intended to be admiring the Cathedral at Santiago de Compostela in a few weeks.

Too many times in the past I had set out on a direction, be it a job, a challenge or some other test, and failed. I always wanted to succeed but for some reason I would turn back halfway down the road. I was determined the Camino would not end up as another one of the failures that seemed to be speckling my life. Maybe I was subconsciously learning the valuable lesson that if I put my mind to something, then I could do it. I knew from the start that the main problem would be state of mind. I was physically fit, my stamina was fine, and I knew my body was well capable of the task. I just had to persuade my mind not to throw negatives in the way.

Over the next few days, my blisters continued to cause pain in both feet. The difficult part was getting going first thing in the morning, and after every rest stop. Once I was moving, the pain subsided, and I actually forgot at times I was suffering. As soon as I stopped, however, even for five minutes, it took ten minutes of hobbling and wincing before the pain abated and I could settle into a normal stride once more. I was wondering how long this would go on. Unlike this walk, my previous treks had lasted only a week or so and I had rarely suffered from blisters, and at most only for four or five days. This was therefore unfamiliar territory.

The smoking woman was also in town and she had made friends with a French couple, with whom I also became acquainted. One of them, Reginald, was a retired teacher. The first thing I noticed about him was that he sort of bounced when he walked. His knees seemed to be incredibly flexible, and when he placed one leg on the ground, his whole body lowered much more than you would expect, and then seemed to ricochet slowly back up to repeat the process. Like a bungee jumper, falling quickly at first, slowing to a stop as the elastic broke the fall and then slowly rising again. It sounds very ungraceful, but believe me, if walking was a work of art, this guy was the Mona Lisa. His whole demeanour suggested a well 'worn-in' hiker. His rucksack and equipment were soiled, but not exactly dirty. He had brought along tried and trusted friends, stuff that he knew worked, and the occasional piece of dependable new gear. He had every gadget in his bag, perhaps a little battered and grimy from years of service but in full working order.

His features were also somewhat the worse for wear, but still working perfectly, with oil in all the right places. He constantly had a pipe balanced in his mouth, his teeth stained from the smoke. A couple of days' stubble shadowed his face.

"Your rucksack appears large," he said, peering out through 1960s spectacles and replacing his pipe in his mouth between sentences.

"Yeah. It's around sixteen kilos, but I like to be self-sufficient," I explained, trying to sound convinced myself. "It's nice to be able to stop where I want to in the woods, and just set up camp. Unfortunately, I have a weight penalty for the privilege, but I'll get used to it. I can always post some stuff back home if it gets too much."

"I too like to be self-sufficient. I carry a sail from a small boat. I use it as a tarp when I camp out. It works perfectly, and weighs one tenth of a tent," he proclaimed, as if it were commonplace.

I left Reginald in no doubt that he would bounce all the way to Santiago.

The weather had improved. The first week or so had seen the odd rainy day. Now it was hot. It was a treat to walk in the shade, and I relished entering woods as they cut out the sun and provided a musky coolness. It was bliss to take off my rucksack and turn into the breeze so my moist T-shirt could slap my back and make me shiver. Sweat ran down my arms and on to my trekking poles. It mixed with sunblock and wove a route over my eyebrows, sometimes dripping into my eyes and making them sting. Instinctively wiping them, I made matters worse by leaving a fresh deposit of cream from the backs of my hands.

Because the Camino runs to the west, it was a comfort never to actually have to face and squint into the sun until the evening. Its heat would singe the back of my neck in the morning, and my left arm would receive the attack during the heat of the afternoon, but by the time it was trying to overtake me on the left side I had usually hung up my boots for the day.

I began to know exactly which way I was heading just from my position in relation to the sun. If the rays smacked me straight in the face when I was looking forward to lunchtime, then I knew the Camino had swerved to the south. If I was closing in on the day's end, and the left side of my body was stroked by the sun's warmth, I knew I was walking north. And if I set off for the day's walk in the morning and found myself squinting into direct sunlight, I knew I had not had enough coffee, was still half asleep, and had begun walking the wrong way. This happened on more than one occasion.

The actual surface of the Camino varied greatly. Parts were sandy, others gravel. Some areas wove across fields of deep green, which was always welcome as it was kinder on the muscles. Sometimes sunken boulders and slabs broke the surface and I'd amuse myself by hopping from one to the next. Certain stretches of the Camino seemed to exude a richer past. I could tell that it was the original way just by the look and feel of it, the way it wove and the buildings and landmarks it brushed against. Over the centuries, the Camino has been redirected in places, mainly because of land ownership. These new stretches are sometimes just gravelled over. Other parts I could see had been renewed through a swath of recently cut trees. The original Camino just had a feeling about it. It's difficult to put into words; I just knew. This section was littered with large cobblestones, about the size of a telephone directory. Thousands of feet had worn away the tops into smooth slabs, the edges rounded and sleek. Grass sprouted and eased through where it could, and a classic stone wall on one or both sides usually accompanied the path.

I soon learned to enjoy the tarmac stretches. At the beginning, I just relished the chance to walk on old tracks, and be rid of the bitumen. However, it had its advantages. First, it was smooth, with no obstacles. Rougher stretches threatened sprained ligaments if I didn't keep both eyes on careful foot placement. When I reached a road, I was able to look around me all the time without fear of tripping and falling on my face.

Second, roads usually meant that a town or village was approaching. Occasionally, I would be ambling down a leafy dirt lane, and be surprised to emerge into a hamlet without warning. That wasn't the norm. My guidebook would usually indicate when I was coming near to civilisation, and that was almost a relief when I was hungry and a road would appear, winding down to a bakery or small shop.

On some occasions when I reached a road, there would be no sign, and my guidebook would be sketchy as to the correct direction. I only had to look at the verge on the roadside, and I could see a clear line, a slightly lighter shade of silver green, where the blades had been flattened by passing pilgrims. And sure enough, when the way left the road again, the grass would return to its upright position.

I reached the highest point of the French section when I came into Chapelle Saint Roch, at an altitude just short of 1,300 metres. There was nothing here except a small shelter for bad weather. I had mistakenly thought it might offer some facilities such as beds or a stove, which it didn't, so I carried on seeking a gîte. Further on I detoured down the D987, which the guidebook assured me would take me to three guesthouses. The first of the three had a bad vibe. I meandered around the rear of the old house, to come face to face with a rather stern-looking madame.

"Hi, is it possible to camp here?" I enquired sheepishly. She thought about my request for a few seconds, running her tired eyes up and down me.

"Er, oui," she replied eventually and unconvincingly. I waited for her to maybe add directions or to point out some spot in the yard where I could be remotely near some facilities. Nothing, she just stood there.

"Merci," I retorted. "Where?"

She led me over to a fence commanding a view back up the hill I had just come down, and pointed to a spot about twenty metres into a field. I made my way back around the house, into the field and began pitching my tent. After a few minutes, I heard her shouting something and flapping her arms around so wildly that I thought it was some sort of warning, as if the local bull had spotted me. She then began to point further up the hill and made motions with her arms as though she were pushing a car.

"Great," I thought to myself, "as if moving another fifty metres up the hill is going to make that much difference." So I picked up my gear, plodded over to the area she had indicated and continued. After another few minutes, a pilgrim who had already booked in came over to me in the field.

"I think she wants you to move to the next field. There is some sort of problem if you pitch tent here," he said.

"Thanks. Do you know exactly where she means?" I said, scratching my head and laughing.

"Yes, I think she means up there," he said. "Come, I will show."

I followed him back up the hill, clutching all my equipment beneath folded arms, and tripping over dangling guy ropes trailing on the ground. He showed me a small area next to a run-down garage. The ground was bare and dusty, full of cow pats, and I would have had to negotiate a barbed-wire fence every time I needed to get out. The whole place looked as if it might be advertised in the local land for sale column of the paper as 'To clear'.

"Look, thanks, but don't worry," I said, feeling a little stupid that he had taken the trouble to show me the spot, and now I was going to reject it. "I think I'll walk on into the village and look for something else."

I mooched further into La Roche de Lago, and after a while I stumbled across the gîte logo swinging from one nail, and clinging to a dark green picket fence. It looked perfect. I was tired, hungry, needed a shower and my blisters were complaining. I made a deal with myself that if I couldn't stay here then La Roche de Lago just wasn't meant to be and I'd go camp in the woods.

As I unlatched the gate, I caught sight of the robust and challenging figure of a madame watching me curiously from the kitchen window, like a guard dog itching to pounce. She opened the front door and came down the path using the same arm-flapping routine.

"Monsieur, le gîte est complet," she cried dramatically, as if she were auditioning for a part in a movie. My heart sank. All I wanted was hot water tumbling over my sore limbs. I went for the 'This is my last resort, or I will die here' routine.

"But madame, I have une tente," I implored. I pointed to the green bag squeezed between tie cords on the back of my pack. I gave her a classic puppy-eyed look with upturned palms and slouched a little to swing things in my favour. To my astonishment, the woman had understood my word-perfect French. She beckoned me to follow, somehow squeezing her large frame between the house and a wall running up one side. My tent plot was secured amongst rampant chickens, basking in the last of the sun's warmth. Madame and I communicated somehow and it was arranged that she would cook a meal for me if I came to the house in two hours. Success!

After a reviving torrent of hot water in the shower and some relaxing, I made my way back to the front of the house and knocked on the door. She beckoned me to take a seat at a huge wooden table dominating a traditional, rustic farmhouse kitchen. I didn't know what to expect. In the end she just busied herself around an old cast-iron stove, tinkering with this pot and that, checking the oven and clanking about.

First she served me an entrée of vegetable soup, then salad, rice with a steak, and a mountain of cheese and fruit to finish, all accompanied with limitless crusty baguette, red wine and water.

It was all in perfectly sized portions, as if she knew my stomach storage capabilities and I finished the whole lot, feeling extremely satisfied.

She gave me a steaming cup and I sat on a rickety old bench outside sipping sweet coffee. The evening dimmed gradually, encroaching on the last orange glow of the sun on the hills opposite. The crickets started their chorus, the stars were intensifying, and the ambience was becoming more and more serene.

"Good idea to come here," I thought as I laid my head on my folded-up fleece and snuggled up inside my sleeping bag. The chickens gradually stopped scratching about and the light on the tent changed from the orange of a sinking sun to the silver of a rising moon.

Chapter Four

The Bag Rustlers

Saint Alban sur Limagnole appeared below me, its terracotta rooftops forming a patchwork of patterns which crowned the town like a chequerboard, as the bells of the church of Saint Alban cried out the midday call. I followed the route carefully, occasionally looking up to familiarise myself with the town's layout. After what seemed an endless descent from the hills, I emerged from an alley on to the quiet main street. Smack in front of me was a pharmacy, which no pilgrim could fail to notice. The owner would appear to have been the ultimate marketing ace, as the whole front window proudly boasted a display of a leading brand of blister patches, known as 'second skin'. He must have been making a fortune.

He also had perfect timing, or, rather I did, for as I turned left on to the Grand Rue, having stocked up on supplies, my left leg buckled as I felt another blister squelch. I meandered down the street, wincing, past a couple of small cafés. "Fozzie! FOZZIE!" It was Hans and Louise, a Dutch couple I had met in Saugues.

"You want a coffee? You look like shit!" Hans had a knack of quickly getting to the point.

"You must have read my mind, that would be fantastic," I replied.

I slouched down rudely between them and let the sun wash all over me. We discussed my blisters and the fact that they appeared to be getting worse.

"Where are you staying?" I asked.

"There's a campsite about three kilometres out of town," said

Louise, and then tempted me further, "with a bar and a swimming pool."

That was all I needed to hear. I had to sort out my feet once and for all, and if that took several days, so be it; I didn't have any deadlines. I followed them out of town on the road and they left me to check in as they strolled off to their pitch. I checked in for two nights and erected my tent between three trees, on a spot commanding a great view over the whole site. As I wouldn't be doing much moving about for the next few days, I figured I might as well entertain myself with a good view of everyone else's business.

After trying and failing to hitch a ride, I walked all the way back to town to stock up on supplies for my convalescence from the local shop. The store chain was called Casino, very apt when you take into account that it's a gamble whether they actually have anything you want.

That evening 'Operation Blister' began. It was a delicate procedure, requiring a deft touch. There was actually a far better method of dealing with blisters, but unfortunately I would not learn this for another week or so. The secret was to keep everything clean and sterile. First, I prepared my faithful Swiss army knife, holding it in the flame of my lighter to sterilise the scissors. Then, while I propped myself up in a very poor half-lotus position, I snipped each blister in the middle and let the liquid ooze out on to a tissue. Carefully cutting four lines radiating out from the centre to the edge and snipping off these four bits of skin, this left just the tender, pink skin underneath. At one point, losing concentration, I inadvertently plunged the tip of the scissors into this exposed area. I tried desperately to stifle a cry, but it got the better of me. I grasped my foot and rocked back and forth, cradling it like a baby, wincing with eyes shut tight.

Once the pain had subsided, and realising that my sterile wipes had run out, I looked around. There was an old French couple staying in a tiny caravan next to me. First I tried to get the woman's attention by waving, looking helpless, and calling out. No luck. So I hopped over to her, pointed to the hole in my little toe and, from memory, muttered something like 'sterilisation'. Amazingly, she opened a cupboard door and produced a bottle of sterile cleaning fluid for wounds. That's one of the great bonuses of campsites, you can blag just about anything.

Teeth gritted and one eye closed, I gave blister number one a generous squirt. It was like squeezing lemon juice on an open wound, excruciating. This time I managed to stifle any obscenities until the pain stopped. Instead of applying a blister patch, I used a plain strip of gauze. This enabled me to keep dirt off the area, but still let air get to the wound, as my priority was to dry the wounds out.

At night I removed the gauze and let the blisters breathe fully. Each day I cleaned and changed the dressing, just as the nurse tells you to do, on each of the six blisters. And each day I would stay next to the tent, moving only to pee or shower, or sit by the stream. Whenever I ventured out, I had to balance and walk on my heels, much to the amusement of the camp residents, who would nudge each other and nod my way with stifled giggles.

A friend had emailed me with an interesting method of dealing with blisters that he had been taught in the South African army. These unfortunate recruits would have to fill a syringe with methylated spirits, pierce the wound and squeeze the liquid in, forcing the ooze out. The meths apparently dried out the skin, made it tougher and it was of course sterile. I did consider this method, but, knowing my luck, I'd be smoking at the time and end up with third-degree burns everywhere.

Saint Alban sur Limagnole eventually became my home for four nights. It got boring at times: there's not much a guy can do when he can't really move. It got to the stage where I was actually looking forward to having a shower because it killed a few minutes. I did eat well, though. Now I had been gifted with plenty of time, I made the most of it. One night I produced sausages, fried onions, mashed potatoes and peas with gravy. Not bad with one camp stove.

I went to bed early and got up late. Other interests that kept me occupied during the long days were reading chocolate wrappers, feeding my new friend, a baby chick I named Rachel, guessing what my neighbours were cooking from the smell, staring into space and convincing myself that I wasn't going senile.

On my last day I decided to go into town for a lunch treat. Luckily, as I waited by the entrance to the campsite, I got a lift. I chose the same place where I had drunk coffee with Hans and Louise and found the locals tucking into some reasonably edible-looking offerings, so I sat down and ordered a cold beer. After amusing myself for a bit trying to translate a discarded French newspaper and look like a local, I called to the waitress, who resembled someone from the eighties Gothic era.

"Bonjour, mademoiselle," I smirked, "s'il vous plaît le menu?"

"Oui, monsieur," she replied, bounding back inside.

I waited, and I waited some more. Every time I tried to attract her attention, she would be looking the other way. Eventually she arrived. No menu, but she did place a plate in front of me containing a slice of pizza and a very attractive parsley garnish. By the time I could react, she had bounded back off again. So I ate it anyway, and very tasty it was too. I thought it no use trying to explain the misunderstanding when she arrived back at my table to take my empty plate, and just went for dessert.

"Une crème brûlée," I said.

The waitress pointed obligingly to a woman at the next table eating a crème brûlée and asked me in broken English to confirm if that was what I meant. I replied it was.

She then nipped off again and after a few minutes returned, leaving a plate in front of me containing a portion of French beans, pasta twirls and a steak. I ate that too and, although I eventually did get my crème brûlée, I had to stifle a laugh when a pilgrim appeared and asked for 'le menu'. I was just leaving when he received a mixed salad. I learnt a few days later that my misunderstanding came about because the menu in French is 'Carte'; 'le menu' will just get you the set course.

After the fourth night I decided my feet had improved sufficiently, and I was desperate to get back into the swing of the Camino. All the regular faces I had become accustomed to seeing would be a few days ahead of me now, so I would be making new friends. For a brief second, while I walked the bridge over the stream out of the campsite, I was sorry to be leaving. I needed new scenery, different trees, a river that made new sounds and unfamiliar birds. Rachel chirped and looked very sorry to see me go.

The countryside was calling in the end of summer. Hay was piled up into cone shapes in the field, and the air full of the sweet smell of the harvest. Tractors bumped along ungracefully, and dusk advanced just that little bit earlier each day.

I had been trying, unsuccessfully, to locate a camping gas cartridge, as my existing canister was nearly empty after my unscheduled rest. The village of Aumont Aubrac promised great things, but didn't deliver. There were numerous shops selling everything the average hiker didn't need and nothing that they did. If you required meat, the butcher would oblige. Those in need of a trim would be spoilt for choice by the four hair salons. I could even purchase a hunting knife that would have made Rambo jealous.

In the end I decided it was an omen that I wasn't meant to find the cartridge. As I left town I decided to camp in the forest, and make a fire to cook on. I found a great spot on the edge of the trees in a small field. It had a good supply of firewood, was blocked from prying eyes on the Camino, and faced east to capture the first of the sun in the morning. Before long, the crickets were in chorus and my fire crackled and sprayed out an orange glow, matching the setting sun behind. The pines were silhouetted, and my only reminder of the modern world was the gentle hum of traffic on the road a way off.

I lay on my back while soup bubbled on the fire, and looked up at the void of black spread out above me, splattered with the constellations. I picked out the Big Dipper and the North Star, directing travellers as it had done for thousands of years. Orion was visible, guarding the sky. The tips of the pines swayed from side to side, almost choreographed, and creaked from time to time. It was great to have new scenery at last.

* * *

One of the great experiences of the Camino is the history. It just sort of smacks you in the face. Because many of the villages, towns, hamlets and even cities sprang up to cater for the ever-increasing numbers of pilgrims, you encounter cultural aspects at every turn. The buildings in this area of France use huge, rectangular blocks of stone for the walls. The bottoms of the roof tiles are curved as a decorative touch. Farms are common; indeed, many of the so-called hamlets are in fact just a couple of farm buildings. Cow dung is cemented to the road and farm animals still pull carts and plough fields. Wherever you go, you hear wildly barking dogs. Timber beams protrude from walls, awnings lean out perilously, and everything looks as if it might collapse at any moment, although it has clearly been like that for centuries.

Iron crosses on top of large stone foundations reminded me I was on the right track. Some were constructed from wood, others had been elaborately forged from iron, the strips curled and wound by some expert blacksmith of years gone by. Some were barely waist-height, some towered over me, demanding attention by their very stature. Virtually every settlement was blessed with a church, a necessity for the pilgrims who travelled the Camino when religion was the law. Some were small and simple chapels, usually growing in grandeur with the size of the town. In places I could look at my surroundings and imagine I was in the Middle Ages. Few, if any modern distractions intruded; even the planes overheard seemed silent.

I had stopped at a café called Chez Régine in the small hamlet of Les Quatre Chemins. I ordered a Coke and a croque monsieur because that was all I could understand. I sat outside and looked around. No one was hurrying. An old tune wafted out from a radio, sharing the breeze with fragrances from the kitchen. Plastic Coca-Cola tables, faded from red to pink from the sun, broke up the small area at the front. I wrestled with the sunshade for a while and kicked my heels in the dust while over the road geese cackled and chickens pecked. Apart from the occasional clang of a saucepan from the kitchen, all was quiet.

That café marked the start of the Aubrac plateau. After diving in and out of forests and woods since the start, the route suddenly emerged into an area devoid of trees. The scenery reminded me of Dartmoor in south-west England: no trees, tracks meandering in no particular direction pinned in by waist-high granite walls, tall grasses bent over in the breeze. The ground was a rich chocolate brown, and occasionally I would have to skip over and around boggy areas. I remembered when I was about ten years old, on one of our regular family holidays in Dartmoor, the feeling of the peat giving under my feet, the stiff breeze stealing the sweat off my forehead, and the rolling hills rising like the folds of a big blanket dumped on the floor.

There were still occasional clumps of trees, and as I walked through one, a sign led me to a spring with an old iron table and a couple of chairs. I shivered and gritted my teeth as I ducked my head under the cold water. It tasted somehow sweet and I must have taken a litre without coming up for air. As I was resting on one of the chairs, a French couple joined me. The woman spoke good English and we chatted as her companion gave my trekking poles a test run.

I had not used trekking poles before coming out to the Camino, but they had proved to be a godsend. At first I felt self conscious, worried I might look like a skier, but I soon felt lost without them. On the few occasions I forgot them after resting somewhere, I needed to walk only a few paces before I knew something was missing. On the flat terrain they were really just a means of rhythm. My arms would have something to do as well as my legs, and it felt good. I became accustomed to the click, click, click as the carbide tips hit the ground and I nicknamed them 'Click' and 'Clack'. On the descents they provided stability and balance. Some sections of the Camino are very steep and riddled with stones and boulders, sometimes wet and slippery from the rain. Add to this the weight of your pack, and you come to realise how treacherous some areas are. One slip could have meant the end of the walk for me, and Click and Clack held me up.

The real bonus was going uphill. Imagine how much easier it is if there is a handrail to hold on to when you are climbing stairs. Click and Clack were my handrails: I could really lean into them and almost pull the rest of my body after. Sometimes, just to remind myself what a blessing they were, I used to stop using them suddenly, pulling them abruptly off the ground and parallel with the road, like a downhill skier. Immediately my pace would slow down, and I had to make more effort. I don't think I would consider hiking anywhere without them again.

The French guy seemed impressed as well, to judge from his approving nods.

The Journey in Between

"Why are you walking the Camino, Fozzie?" his companion Floret asked me.

"I'm not too sure," I replied. "Several reasons I think. Spare time for an adventure, for a nice, long walk, spiritual energy and maybe just because it's here."

"It is interesting that you say spiritual energy," she said. "How would you describe the energy you feel here?"

"I just feel great to be alive. Doesn't everything seem more colourful out here? Don't you notice the birds and the insects more? I can't explain something like that, I just know."

She smiled. "Yes, I know exactly what you mean. I feel it too, everybody feels it, and some notice it more than others."

I asked her why she was walking the Camino.

"I lost my husband some thirteen years ago. It was a hard time for me, and I realised then that I should have done something like this. A space as vast as this gives you opportunity to think about what has happened, and where you are going; it provides you with somewhere for your grief. And this is why I am walking with my friend: he lost his wife three months ago. I remembered how I felt, and suggested he walk here as I should have done. I came for him, really, but I am loving it."

I turned to her friend. He spoke no English so had not understood our conversation, but I could tell from the look in his watery eyes that he didn't need a translation. I felt mine well up a little as well, and we smiled and nodded at each other to recognise understanding.

"I'm sorry," I said. He nodded that he understood.

"He is much better," she interjected. "The walk is doing him good. We have been walking for only two weeks, but already I notice the change. But what do you mean 'Because it's here'?"

I laughed. "I guess it's an English expression. Mountaineers say it about why they climb mountains. It means we do something simply because we can, maybe to prove to ourselves we are capable of it."

"I understand," she said. "I wish I could walk all the way too."

"What's stopping you?"

"Oh, you know. The house, bills, leaving my town, family."

I tried my best to encourage her. "Everyone is capable of

travelling. What we think are obstacles are just inconveniences that can be overcome. First, you can let the house. The tenants are then responsible for the bills. Your friends will be there when you get back, and no doubt extremely proud of you. I have seen lots of the world, and I will see more. I never wanted to get to the stage of being old and having regrets about not seeing anything that this planet has to offer. The number-one issue for you, and anybody in your position, is having the courage to get up and make the decision. The rest is easy. I have been where you are, so I know how you feel. Sometimes, our problems are just up here," I said, tapping my head.

She smiled in agreement. "I know you are right. It is getting past the comfort zone of your normal life, and doing something out of your usual routine. It's a little scary."

"Well, I hope you have a great time, and I hope you both come back next year and finish the whole thing."

* * *

As I entered the town of Nasbinals, I decided a comfy night in a gîte was suitable reward for cranking out 29.5 kilometres that day, the most so far. There was a street market careering all over the road, just packing up for the day. I bought a slab of salami and some cheese to supplement my dwindling food stocks.

The gîtes were generally of a good standard, and this one was no exception. I found a spare bed in the upstairs dormitory and headed off for the shower. I had just soaped up when I was interrupted by a rapping on the door and someone calling.

"Hey, man!"

I turned off the shower, and keeping my eyes shut because of the shampoo, called back, "Hello? Yeah? What's up?"

"Man, stop using the shower, it's running all down the stairs!"

"OK, hang on a sec." I turned the shower back on, knowing it would cause a commotion when they heard it outside, but I had a head full of shampoo and a body covered in soap that needed to come off. Sure enough, there was a rapping on the door. "Hey man, turn off the shower!"

I carried on, the whole rinse procedure taking little more than thirty seconds.

"Hey! There's water coming out! Turn off the shower! Can you hear me?"

"Yeah, I can hear you," I said, tearing open the door and coming face to face with a French Canadian guy. Feeling a little tired and probably short tempered, I replied, "What the fuck did you expect me to do? I had a head and face full of shampoo. I had to rinse it off, I couldn't see a thing, MAN!"

"Look, I'm sorry, I thought you couldn't hear me," he said, backing off a little.

"No worries." I shook his hand, smiled to disperse any friction, and helped him and a couple of others mop up the mess.

His name was Gerard. He was in his mid-forties with a little grey hair poking through above his ears. He had a penchant for saying "Man" like some time-warped hippie from the sixties, made all the more amusing by his French accent. His casual gear was hiker-branded material; he liked the best – and liked to advertise it. He was walking all the way from Le Puy to Santiago with his wife Chantelle and four friends. Other French Canadians had tagged on and the group had swelled to about ten.

After the little contretemps of our first meeting, Gerard and his entourage were a regular sight on the Camino and I used to look forward to seeing them, which happened at least every couple of days. Often I'd come across them sitting in the grass munching on their supplies, and Gerard would always greet me with, "Fozzie, hey, man, how's it going?"

The following morning I was rudely awoken at 5:15am. The plastic bag rustlers were out in force. A lot of pilgrims set out on their walk as early as possible, any time between 5:00 and 7:00am, so that they could finish the day's walking by midday, avoiding the higher temperatures and having the afternoon to recuperate. It makes perfect sense, I know, but logic does not apply when walkers stuffing their belongings into supermarket carrier bags wake you up every day. They seemed the perfect solution to keeping gear dry and sorted. In fact, I used them myself. But that irritating daily rustling noise was starting to grate on my and others' nerves, and was greeted by moans and angry faces and the wrapping of pillows over heads by those still in bed.

At first, people were genuinely concerned about waking other pilgrims. However, no matter how hard they tried, it was impossible to move those bags quietly. Eventually the rustlers, acting on the principle that everybody was awake already, just did their packing more loudly, ramming clothes into bags, ramming the bags into backpacks and so on, until the anti-bag-rustling lobbyists were almost ready for armed revolt. Why the hell, I wondered, didn't the early starters pack their shit the previous evening?

Although the bag packers usually woke me early, I would eventually drop off again. I have never really been an early riser. I resented having to get up at some unearthly hour to go to work, and the phrase, "So, we'll make an early start then!" far from rousing me enthusiastically, generally did the opposite. I get up when my body feels ready, and if I find I am struggling to wake up or get out of bed, then I assume that it is plainly too early to be attempting it.

Five o'clock in the morning for me is no-man's-land, a twilight zone, an area I don't mess with. I usually got up around eight, slapped some water on my face, breakfasted on whatever I found in my food supplies, drank three cups of strong coffee, smoked a few roll-ups, threw my stuff in my pack and headed off around nine thirty. So, I would be walking in the sun, so what? I would rather be walking in sun than darkness for the first hour. It would be hot. So what? Rather hot than a bit of a chill. So, I would finish around three or four in the afternoon. So what? That left ample time to wind down, eat and maybe go and do some sightseeing. And, to all potential pilgrims who read this, it would provide ample time to pack my kit before I went to bed!

Chapter Five

Finding My Pace

Some days I would remove my watch, a simple act, with interesting results. I would have to rely on my body to tell me when I needed things and take more notice of how I was feeling. Out on the Camino, I had no real need for the time. My watch had a compass, an altimeter and a barometer, which I used on occasion and came in handy, but mostly they were just toys.

During the early days of my walk, I would take a break for a cigarette after an hour, stop around one o'clock for lunch and set a goal to finish the day's walk around four. Without my timepiece it was different altogether. I went for a couple of hours without even realising I needed a cigarette.

One day, I decided I would stop for lunch when I was hungry, and when eventually I did stop to eat and check my watch, I discovered it was three o'clock. The pleasure of that surprise soon waned when I felt the familiar pressure of blisters again. It had been ten days since my improvised hospitalisation at the campsite at Saint Alban sur Limagnole, and despite the odd twinge, my feet were holding up well. I had walked only seventeen kilometres that day, but couldn't go any further. I had asked the universe for a solution several times: this was the day it was to arrive.

The town of Saint Chély d'Aubrac was very cute, but I was too angry and full of self-pity to notice. As I was sitting on a stone wall with a Coke and a cigarette, I heard someone say my name.

"Hi, Fozzie."

It was Walter. I had chatted to him briefly a few days earlier.

He was walking with his wife, Barbara, and a friend called Oulie.

"You OK? You look a little down," he observed.

"Yeah, I guess so. I've got bloody blister problems again, can't seem to get rid of the things."

"Tell you what, Fozzie. I have to go into town to get some supplies. We are staying at the gîte here. I'll be back here in thirty minutes and I will take a look at your feet for you. I am a doctor of medicine."

"Fantastic!" I said, smiling broadly. "That's really good of you."

When he came back, he bade me follow him to the garden at the rear of the gîte. Barbara and Oulie were reclining on iron chairs, chatting and sipping on lemonades under low trees. If there had been a few ample-bosomed females in long, white lace dresses daintily carrying parasols, the scene could have passed for something out of *Pride and Prejudice*.

I lay back on a sun lounger and slipped off my socks and boots. Wincing, I pulled off each of the six or so blister patches on each foot, and waited for the worst.

"Fozzie, this is no problem at all."

I was a little taken aback by his initial prognosis.

"Are you sure?"

"Certainly. I thought your blisters may have been hurting because they were infected."

He was checking each one with the precision of a watchmaker.

"I am pleased to tell you that these are the cleanest-looking blisters I have ever seen, even cleaner than mine."

I felt a strange little flush of pride.

"So why do they hurt so much, why do I keep getting them, and why won't they go away? I even rested for a few days a week or so ago to let them heal."

Walter's answer came as a big surprise.

"That was probably the worst thing you could have done. The best advice I can give you, and I tell you this from experience of my walks, is to keep walking. Grin and bear it. If you stop to rest them, then the skin will just soften, which is the main problem in the first place. The trick with blisters is to keep plodding on. The more you walk, the more your skin toughens up and adapts to the task that is being asked of it. The human body is a wonderful thing, it can deal with lots of things, and sometimes it just needs a little time. Sometimes you just have to trust it."

His advice was starting to make sense.

"Each evening," he continued, "pierce them with a sterile needle and squeeze out the juice. You might want to give them a squirt of antiseptic liquid to be sure. Just make sure they are clean, and repeat the process the next evening. I guarantee you that your feet will take care of the rest. After a while the skin will become hard in the problem areas, and you can leave them be."

"Thanks, Walter, I feel better already." The way he explained things was wonderfully reassuring.

"What are you doing tonight?" he asked.

"Dunno. Why?"

"Come to dinner with us. There is a nice little restaurant in the main street, our treat."

"Look, I appreciate the offer, but I couldn't..."

He brushed my objections aside.

"We'd like your company, and it looks like you could do with some cheering up."

It was a good evening: the first real meal at a decent restaurant I had encountered on the Camino. We communicated in French, German, English and Greek. The wine flowed; the food was great. No cooking, no clearing up. We exchanged email addresses as we parted and I wobbled, a little worse for wear from the wine, back to the gîte, where I tripped up the steps and woke a few people up, including three French Canadians in my room. However, they were inveterate bag rustlers, so I drifted off to sleep, content with a little revenge.

The following morning I was raring to go. Although the blisters were still painful, I was confident about Walter's advice. It was a beautiful morning. As I made my way down a hill out of town, the early morning mist was still clearing. I passed over a small bridge spanning the River Boralde and up past the cemetery dominating the hill. The Camino entered a silver birch wood set halfway up a long slope. It was eerily quiet. The sun's rays spliced through the damp air from my left, like a torch shining through the smoke from a fire. The ground was soft and I felt good, really good.

According to the guidebook, this was gorge country; no huge ravines, but rocky outcrops littered the area. Trees clung to cliff edges, their exposed roots grasping helplessly to the edge like giant hands. The clear waters of streams meandered around millions of polished stones, gently shelving into the water like a series of small beaches. Sunlight lit up leaves as the branches swayed, and cast constantly moving shadows. The beautiful smell of damp, peaty earth reached me from time to time.

I started to climb. I hadn't really encountered much in the way of steep inclines up to this stage. This one wasn't very long, perhaps a kilometre or so, but when I reached the top I was dripping with sweat. There was a farm, boasting a fridge, which looked completely out of place by the side of the trail. It was stocked full of sugary goodies – cans of Coke and other fizzy mixtures, chocolate, mini cakes. A sign on it asked pilgrims to take what they needed and leave the money in the basket. There was even a register to sign. I picked out a few treats and wandered off, munching. This, I thought, must be the only known fridge in the Western world equipped with a visitors' book.

At lunchtime I wandered into a small grocery store in Saint Côme d'Olt. My salami was perspiring alarmingly, and the cheese was sprouting furry stuff. It was one of those classic places that specialised in nothing, but had pretty much everything, including the elusive camping gas cartridge, just visible over the side of a box tucked into a corner. My existing one had lasted longer than I had expected, even though for the last few days it had been running off fumes.

As I shuffled through the aisles, something else took me by surprise.

"Well, fancy seeing you here," I said to myself. "I never expected to see you in the middle of France."

But there she was, a tin of Heinz Baked Beans, her head covered in a layer of dust, nestling among inferior friends. I took her to the till, feeling her coldness in my hand, paid and tucked her safely in my pack.

That afternoon I crossed the River Lot, where the locals

frolicked in the water to escape the burning temperature. The river on my right kept me company for a couple of hours. To my left, huge automatic sprayers sent curving jets of water over the tall, thirsty parallel lines of maize that loomed over me. Before long, the Pilgrims' Bridge over the river came into view as I reached the striking town of Espalion. Medieval buildings with beams emaciated from years of weather abuse leaned perilously over the river. The park was alive with the clinks of boules, children yelled, fisherman cast nets into the shallow waters and lovers strolled. The place just beckoned me to rest there the night. There was a gîte, somewhere, but it looked so tranquil by the river that I decided I would sleep rough.

I crossed over the bridge, turned right and wove through narrow streets until the river appeared again. A small area of water by the bank was calm and devoid of any current, hemmed in by some strategically placed stones, perhaps as a swimming area. I took it as a hint that I needed a bath and stripped down to my underwear. Then, realising that most of the locals must have seen a naked bottom at some time, removed them as well. The relief was enormous as the water momentarily chilled me and washed away the day's sweat and filth. It felt fantastic. As I surfaced, I caught sight of a couple of old ladies chuckling at me from the other bank.

What would have been the reaction in other countries, I wondered? In England, I might have received a few disapproving glances, some finger pointing and some stifled chuckles. The Italian police (my personal favourites) would have eventually moved me on politely, but not before stopping for a chat, bringing me an espresso and offering me a smoke. In India, I probably would have had several hundred locals for company also washing and doing laundry. In America, I probably would have been arrested, first for indecent exposure and then for loitering, with 'probable intention to dive dangerously' thrown in for good measure. Here, the inhabitants of the town just walked their dogs at dusk, smiling an acknowledgment my way, giving me the odd wave. With the river tumbling a few feet away and some good fresh air, I enjoyed the best sleep I'd had in days.

In the morning, I wanted to check my emails, but discovered

that Espalion was devoid of any public internet facilities. Internet cafés, I was told by the woman at the tourist information desk, can be found only in the larger towns and cities like Paris.

"Jeez," I muttered, checking my guidebook on the way out. "There are 5,000 people living here, how large do you want it?" But I could sympathise with their wish to hang on to their culture and I would rather have a town full of character with no internet café than the reverse.

* * *

Some people go as far as to refer to hiking as meditation. Others simply like it as relaxation, some as exercise. To me it provides all of the above. I got lost in my own thoughts many times on the Camino, and often when I stopped for a rest I had forgotten the past few kilometres.

Walking does this to me. I get into my own mind: where I am going, where I have been, the next step of my life, plans, ideas, goals, etc. It gives me the chance to sort out my life. Dreaming like this on the Camino, I would miss direction signs and have to retrace my steps to find the way. Other times I would forget when I saw the last marker, and have no idea when the next one would appear.

Sometimes, exercising my mind became more conscious. When it was a bleak and boring stretch of walking, for example, I played games to pass the time. A song might pop into my head for no particular reason, and I would end up singing it for the rest of the day. Back at home, that song of the day was usually the first song I heard on the radio in the morning; it would worm its way into my subconscious as I struggled to emerge from under the duvet. Out here, I had no source to feed me tunes, except the odd radio.

There were the obvious favourites that I had accumulated over the years. And there were also those dreadful songs that you might hear on a pub jukebox – offerings from Abba, early stuff from Madonna, maybe even the Bee Gees. On exceptionally bad days, my desperate subconscious really comes up with some crap. Trouble is, as hard as I try, once embedded, that song of the day is nigh on impossible to root out. There was little I could do when I realised I was humming along to Showaddywaddy or doing a rendering of *This Ole House* by Shakin' Stephens. Today, however, I plummeted to new depths, involuntarily humming the theme tune to Cagney and Lacey.

* * *

Autumn was approaching. I could sense it, even without the obvious visual reminders. The air smelled different, night trespassed a little earlier each day, bringing the occasional chilly spell. Leaves started to change from summer greens to browns, yellows, golds and rubies, and each day there would be a few more fluttering about on the ground. The sun seemed to take a little longer to heat the air and on some mornings a mist hung low, obscuring the countryside like a translucent window. I love the summer; I dislike the winter. Autumn is that pleasant interim period where I am sad that the hot days have passed, but am not yet quite dreading the cold ones. If summer were a fresh chocolate éclair with cream oozing from the sides, and winter was a cream cracker, then autumn might be a jam doughnut. It was pleasant security.

I reached Golinhac late evening after climbing for what felt like hours, although in fact I had probably covered only about ten kilometres. I pitched my tent in the grounds of the gîte. There I met a Dutch guy called Gare, who was finishing his two weeks on the Camino the following day and who plied me with offerings that he no longer needed: blister patches, antiseptic cream, needles, medi-tape. The true godsend, though, was some herbal cream, designed for aching feet. Gare demanded that I try it there and then. I tell you no lies when I describe this stuff as foot orgasm in a tube. It was awesome. The harder I rubbed, the better it felt, if you'll pardon the pun.

I had decided to head for Conques and take a day's rest. I had heard much about this historic medieval town, a national monument. There I could recuperate in classic surroundings, with some good food, a hot shower – and, I hoped, the chance to see the World Cup soccer qualifier between England and Germany. Boy, would I be pissed off if I missed that one.

Conques lived up to its reputation and then some. It was

touristy, but as it was the end of August, the numbers were dwindling. I had deliberately left only fifteen kilometres or so to walk in the morning, so I could arrive relatively early, have a leisurely afternoon, and make the most of my rest stop the following day.

The village clung to the side of a small, tree-choked valley, blocking the view of the river. Conques seemed to have become caught in a time warp, resisting change. Not only were the streets cobbled, probably with the original stones, but there was even straw here and there, spilt off the back of a cart.

Little stone channels in the middle of streets ferried water away after a passing storm I had just missed. The uneven stone surface still glistened with the moisture. Moss stuck in the cracks glowed a radiant green. Medieval buildings unscathed through the centuries displayed dark timber beams, ancient stone and brickwork. Stairs disappeared up and down. Alleys wound back and forth. The whole place was a maze, a labyrinth of pristine comeliness. Hand-painted signs in black and gold dangled over shop doors. Small, cosy, smoky cafés plied for trade. Children giggled shyly, as though the serenity of the locality affected them too. It was almost as if Conques had survived from the eighth century, through countless battles, because the enemy couldn't bear to destroy it.

The town was blessed with two relatively economical places to stay. Gare had advised me to take advantage of the lodgings at the Abbey of St Foy, rather than at the gîte. I passed the gîte on the outskirts and took a look out of curiosity. It was clean enough, but there were no facilities to cook or even eat. The beds were so close together that if you were to turn over in the middle of the night, you would probably end up on top of the person next to you. So I carried on down into the village centre to seek out lodgings in the Abbey.

It took a while backtracking down streets and passages to locate it. I couldn't exactly miss the Abbey, which loomed out of the centre, attempting to grasp the clouds. As usual, when all else failed, there was security in following the other pilgrims. They were either heading out on the Camino or looking for somewhere to stay. I walked down past the tourist office, down some steps to an inner courtyard with a well in the centre, where laughing kids were trying to fish money out of the water. Passing under a stone archway, I saw the path lead up to a door, which swung open, revealing a glimpse of an inner yard through yet another archway. A map displayed the route of the Camino, and as I went for a closer look, a voice floated over from an office on the left. I turned and saw a woman looking at me, confirming she was talking to me.

"I'm sorry," I said to the middle-aged lady behind the desk. "I don't speak French. Do you speak English?"

The woman smiled and pointed to a seat in front of her. She called to someone in French, and after a while a man appeared, who took her place behind an old wooden desk, smiled and adjusted his glasses.

Before he or I could speak, we were interrupted.

"Please, I really want to. Please?"

I glanced over my shoulder to see an American woman, perhaps in her early twenties. She looked despondent.

"No," the man replied. "I told you, first you must finish the Camino. I'm sorry, that is the way we and all of the gîtes operate. There are no exceptions. Now please, I have to help this gentleman." He motioned to me, and she puffed her shoulders and stormed out.

"She stayed here for a week," the man explained, turning to me, "fell in love with the Abbey, and with Conques, and wanted to volunteer to work here."

"Is that a problem?"

"No, not really. We get many requests each week, people wanting to work here. We have a rule. People who want to volunteer here, well, we need to know they are serious, and not just out for a summer of free lodging, even if they are working. They need to know what it is like to have finished the Camino. They need to be able to answer pilgrims' questions. How far it is to there, what the terrain is like, where to stay. But most importantly, to prove to us that they are willing to complete a goal to contribute to what we do here."

"I see." I nodded.

"If she is serious about helping here, she will be back. We already have applications from pilgrims who have finished the Camino to work here next year. All the positions are taken, and we have more applications waiting. Anyway, I presume you want to stay here?"

"Yes, for two nights please. I am taking a day's rest tomorrow."

"This is not a problem. We have plenty of space. Do you want any meals? We have breakfast and evening meal."

"Er, no thanks. I'll be fine."

He looked genuinely concerned.

"I don't want to force you into eating here," he said, "but Conques is expensive, very expensive. It is teeming with tourists, and the restaurants know it. We have great staff and they really do a fantastic meal in the evening, several courses. Breakfast is all you can eat, coffee, orange juice, muesli, toast. The…"

"OK, OK. You persuaded me. How much is it?"

"Eleven euros. That is your bed and meals for one night. So, twenty-two euros for the two nights."

It was about twenty-two pounds. I would struggle to find even bed and breakfast for one night at that amount back home. He led me up a stone spiral staircase to the dormitory, giving me a mini guided tour as we went. It was a beautiful place. The stone had softened over the years to a series of curved edges and pastel shades. Windows and arches offered glimpses of the village and valley; closed doors made me wonder what was on the other side.

"By the way, I want to see a soccer game on Saturday night. Do any of the bars here have satellite TV, or do you know of a place where I might be able to see it?"

"I don't think you will have much luck," he said. "There is no satellite reception here because the dishes go against planning laws. There are a few bars that do have TVs, but they will probably show the French game. It may be worth asking."

The whole place was scrupulously clean. Old and basic, but spotless. Even the tiles in the washroom gleamed, with not even a streak mark. My dormitory room held about fourteen bunk beds. Large windows were open and a cool breeze wove through, rustling papers, playing with clothing hung on beds and cooling me off. My window looked down on a small garden on the edge of the village. All I could really see were plants and trees and the valley tumbling away. I could have been in a cottage, alone in the middle of nowhere.

There must have been fifty pilgrims eating that night. It reminded me of the school canteen: long tables with people facing each other, rubbing their hands in anticipation. Before the food was served, the man who checked me in gave a small speech welcoming us all. Then we all joined in with a communal song, the lyrics of which had been written on a board.

It was called *Ultreya,* and although in French, I could tell it was a hymn of faith of some kind. That song stuck with me for the rest of the Camino, becoming my 'song of the day' several times, and I often heard others humming and reciting the words as they walked. The words were written in visitors' books everywhere, it was sung around meal tables and I even saw Ultreya written as graffiti on walls by the side of the road or in the dust on the trail. I didn't need to know the translation. If there was one word that meant El Camino, it was Ultreya. We walkers only needed to see the word somewhere, and we would grin and relive our experiences of the past few weeks. It was not until some five years later that a friend told me that Ultreya was a Spanish word derived from Latin, meaning *Onward!* It was in common use by pilgrims to greet and encourage one another along the way.

That evening I did a tour of the bars to find out if any planned to show the England game the following evening. I'm not a hardcore soccer fan but for me the world stops when England plays, especially if our opponents are Germany. And I'm not alone: passions fly, tempers fray, emotions burn and pride matters. Short of falling off a cliff, I was determined to watch it.

The responses were not good. Wherever I went, I was told they would be showing the French game, not the England game because of the lack of satellite dishes. Dejected, I realised I would have to leave Conques and seek out some hotel where I was assured coverage.

Leaving Conques was hard, but I made an early start for once and followed the Camino down to the valley floor, where it crossed over the River Dordou. As I turned around, a breath of mist was creating eddies over and around the Chapelle Saint Roch perched above me. The outline was silhouetted by the early morning sun. It was beautiful, eerie, and an awesome farewell.

I had reached the first day of September, the day I had always regarded as the end of the summer and the start of autumn, at least back home. There was a definite chill in the air and I hoped I could make it to Santiago before winter really took a grip. I also passed the 200-kilometre mark on leaving Conques, which, I calculated, meant I had done two-fifteenths of the total distance of the walk. I had been going for sixteen days. That put me bang on course for three months to complete the trip. I felt a little surge of excitement. Perhaps I would actually do this thing! I had two cigarettes on my break to celebrate.

I arrived in Decazeville early afternoon, a disappointingly ugly town with all the trimmings of the twentieth century. Most places were shut until around three, so I treated myself to a burger and fries and a chocolate éclair, all washed down with a Coke. Good staple, healthy nourishment...

At the tourist office, a middle-aged woman peered up at me from behind the counter. Thick, bifocal glasses made her look like a cartoon character about to realise that a train is about to run them over.

"Bonjour," I said. "Parlez-vous Anglais?" My French lessons at school had never covered the possibility of asking for a hotel room for the night with cable facilities capable of showing an England international game.

"Yes, I speak English. How can I help?" she responded. Things were definitely looking up.

"Erm, well, it's a bit of a strange request, really. I need a room tonight, but I need to watch a football game that will only be on cable or satellite. Somewhere cheap, as long as it has this facility."

"OK. I don't think it will be a problem. There are two or three places that come to mind." She leafed through a booklet and circled two options. "These two are around twenty to twenty-five euros. They both have cable. Would you like me to call one of them to confirm, and make a reservation for you?"

"That would be great, thank you."

A few minutes later I was bounding along with a serious spring in my step humming 'Football's Coming Home'. What

The Journey in Between

made the game that much more important was that if we didn't win, England had very little chance of qualifying for the World Cup.

The Hotel Foulquier was set back from Avenue Victor Hugo and from the outside looked like an American motel. The interior was like a throwback from the eighties. The colour scheme was pink and black. Flowery curtains clashed with striped wallpaper, all bottomed off with a grey carpet. At least it was clean, and at least it had a TV. I made a pre-game sweep of the channels. Eurosport was available, as well as a French sports channel which would certainly be showing the French game, but might offer highlights of the main match. These were two promising options. I restrained myself from becoming too excited, but did manage a subdued yelp.

The art of watching football is that you get up only once during a match to stretch your legs, at half-time. This means all necessary requirements must be to hand. There is a syndrome known as 'absent scoring'. Most fans will confirm that the moment you get up from the game to have a pee or make a coffee, someone will score. This is why it is imperative to visit the toilet, make your drink, kiss your girlfriend and apologise for the ensuing abuse of expletives, and do whatever else needs to be done, before you sit down. I had prepared well. A meal from the hamburger joint lay beside me. Several cans of Guinness nestled within easy reach of my right hand. Popcorn was at the ready. I had even rolled several cigarettes beforehand so I would not have to avert my eyes. It was perfect.

The TV flickered to life. Sure enough, the French game was the main offering. I turned to Eurosport, shut my eyes, then slowly squinted through the cracks in my eyelids hoping to see little men running around a green pitch. No such luck. What were they showing? Clay pigeon shooting! Bloody clay pigeon shooting! I was furious.

I suffered two hours of clay pigeon shooting on one channel and the French national team on the other, hoping in vain they would tempt me with some highlights. I eventually managed to grab a report from CNN around midnight. At least we won, 5:0. I was ecstatic. It took me a week to get over it.

* * *

Pilgrims don't only walk the Camino, although that is easily the most popular method. I saw many riding bicycles and a few on horseback. Bernard, whom I met one day, had different ideas. Plodding alongside him was a donkey, which carried all his gear, so Bernard was able to afford a few luxuries. All he carried was a day pack containing a few sandwiches.

"Donkeys do have drawbacks as well as benefits," he told me. "For starters, they walk slower. I cannot walk ahead because he would get lost. So I have to walk at his pace. It's frustrating at times but I have got used to it. After all, I am not in any hurry. Secondly, he needs food. And by food I mean prime hay. He can nibble on grass during the day for his snacks, but he needs his hay fix in the evening. If he doesn't get his hay, he doesn't go anywhere. Thirdly, he knows his distance. When we hit twenty kilometres at the end of the day, his built-in mileage gauge kicks in, and he just stops. I can't budge him; he's there for the night. So I am limited, but we have a pattern now. After all, he is doing me a favour. It's only right I should indulge his little whims."

For some reason the approach to Figeac was lacking in water supplies. Usually I would pass a couple of water sources each day, which was all I needed. By lunchtime I had run out. As I walked past a house attached to a large barn, an old chap was cutting his whiskers, holding a small hand mirror.

"Bonjour, monsieur," I called, asking in my limited French whether he had any water and pointing to my empty water bag. This was a mistake. If my French hadn't confused him, then the water container with a tube dangling around my knees certainly had. He came down and, holding the bag gingerly, with two fingers, peered in and smelt it as if it were some sort of enema equipment.

I tried to explain, making glugging noises with my throat, and imitating turning a tap with my hand and holding the bag under it. I was just about to crawl along the ground holding up a pleading hand like a soul lost in the desert when he smiled and led me up the stairs to his modest two-roomed flat. He filled the bag for me, and gave me two glasses of first-rate French plonk as a bonus. I remember thinking as I left him that I should practice this method more often. Not only was this a genuine opportunity to obtain water and to get to know some French people, but I might even get the odd titbit of food thrown in. I spent the rest of the day practising my French, pulling hungry and thirsty facial expressions, and generally trying to look weary for my next attempt.

If I had known more about plants, I could probably have survived the whole Camino living off the land. There were blackberry bushes everywhere. Hedgerows groaned and stooped over and walls disappeared as the season's fruits, sprouting from all locations, tumbled and draped over them. Mint plants poked their heads through grass at the side of the path. In fact, I could smell them before I saw them. I was reminded of my grandmother, who used to throw a handful of leaves into the pot of boiling new potatoes. In autumn, chestnuts turned the path into a shimmer of mahogany. The fields were full of sweetcorn, tender and bursting with freshness. I could have dined on mushrooms and in Spain there were even cumin plants, releasing an inviting waft of curry into the air, which puzzled me until I finally figured out where it was coming from. Rosemary bushes, huge and deep green in colour, had me scrambling over walls to retrieve a small stock. I would 'steal' a few potatoes from the edge of crop fields, and boil or roast them with mint or the rosemary. Apples were regular friends; plums glistened in the light like precious stones. Indeed, the whole Camino was one mammoth outdoor fruit and vegetable market.

Chapter Six

From a Good Plan to a Bad Plan

Kurt Cobain and Nirvana had been rolling around in my head for a couple of days. I rarely remember the titles of songs; I just know the ones I like. 'Nothing on top but a bucket and mop, and an illustrated book about birds,' Kurt warbled. I just hummed the rest because I couldn't remember most of the lyrics either.

I was on the approach to Le Causse, a limestone plateau with scrubby vegetation and scruffy, stunted trees. I stopped at Gréalou. My food stocks had dwindled pathetically to a cereal bar and a spoonful of rice. The épicerie promised in my guidebook was long gone, and the only option was the café. My budget winced, but the craving in my stomach was overriding the logic in my head. A pilgrim walked out.

"Hello," he said. He was French but somehow knew I was English. His name was Gérard.

"Hi," I replied.

"If you're looking for something to eat, I wish you good luck. The madame has been left on her own. Her assistant has gone off somewhere, so she is doing everything by herself. Cooking, drinks, being a waitress, and she is trying to have her lunch as well. She's a bit stressed."

"Thanks, I'll watch my back," I said, smiling.

The place was empty except for a group of four pilgrims and another couple flirting in the corner. "How hard can it be to run this place with six customers?" I wondered as I approached the bar. After waiting a while, I 'accidentally' dropped my loose change on the counter to attract some attention. There was movement and the owner appeared through a doorway. She approached in a menacing manner with a hard stare, sort of like a boxer eyeing up the opposition. She stopped by me, wiped some stray lunch from her chin, put both hands on the bar and looked at me, saying nothing.

"Bonjour," I offered. For some reason I derive great pleasure from toying with people who are already annoyed. It's like playing with a lighter and fireworks at the same time. I smiled and let a silence hover for a few seconds to get some sort of reaction.

"Oui!" she spat.

Wiping the spit out of one eye, and giving her another annoying smile, I scanned the bar.

"Une Coke. And... er... avez-vous a menu, please?"

"No menu," she stammered and then volleyed off a few, rapid sentences of which I understood nothing.

"She said she only has a meat sandwich, a kind of salami. I had one myself, it wasn't good, but it's edible if you're hungry." One of the pilgrims, who I later learned was called Bernard, had come up to the bar to help; he must have known I would have problems with my limited French.

"Thanks," I replied. The look on his face suggested he was enjoying watching her suffer too. I ordered the sandwich and a packet of crisps.

As she opened the fridge, most of the contents crashed over the floor. She released a hurl of abuse so frightening that half the customers cowered under their tables.

I escaped outside with Bernard, and his wife joined us. He offered me the rest of his wine as they were heading off.

"Thanks for all that," I said.

"No problem," he replied. "See you on the trail."

The salami in the sandwich resembled old leather, but it tasted OK. The Coke was barely cold, and the crisps were stale. I was too hungry to care. I berated myself for letting my food supplies dwindle. There is nothing worse than having nothing to eat and nowhere to buy anything. I remembered a cycling trip through Europe a few years earlier. It was Saturday, and the shops all closed on Sundays, so I had procured all the necessities to last me the weekend. On the Saturday evening I settled down at my campsite to cook up a stew with the fresh vegetables in my bag. It was then I realised my stove was out of fuel.

Le Causse was, indeed, a strange area of France. The plants and trees seemed stunted somehow, as though they were trying to grow but a higher force wouldn't oblige. The trees were mainly oak, but barely managed a height of ten feet. A type of gorse bush grew everywhere, tugging on my clothing as I brushed past. Chalky rocks protruded from reddish soil. My guidebook had given me the impression that the trees on Le Causse were sparse, as on the Aubrac plateau. On the contrary, however, most of the landscape was taken up by these diminutive trees. It was eerie, even scary at times.

Part of my mission on this walk was to hone any spiritual skills I had, to become more in tune with my feelings, to take more notice of events and their meanings. I wanted to be able to experience what was going on around me. I did succeed; after all, I was blessed with plenty of time to practise. I walked into a wood and immediately felt ill at ease. It was dark, the sunlight struggled to make any inroads and it smelled damp and musty, not a pleasant dampness, more a stench of rot. The trees were stunted, twisted, misshapen. Plants were pathetic shades of green, flowers limp and with incomplete petals. There was no breeze, nothing moved and it was silent. I felt as though not one but many people were watching me, like in those cartoons when someone is walking through the dark and little white eyes appear behind them.

I began to walk faster. I felt as though I were being chased, as though if I looked around something would be running after me. Eventually the trees thinned and I reached a small road. I crossed and entered another similar wood, but I felt totally secure there. Everything looked the same, but there were noises, a breeze would ruffle my hair once in a while, it felt safe. So what had happened? To this day I wonder. I just knew something bad had happened in that place. It was as though a hundred souls had been lost in there.

In the early days of the Camino, the route was riddled with bandits. They would pick on pilgrims, and they knew the most productive areas to lie in wait. Woods and forests were ideal. They could hide a few feet from the path and be totally hidden from view. Many pilgrims were robbed of what little possessions they carried. Many were murdered. Had that wood been such a place? Was it still harbouring the energy of what had happened there? I have experienced similar emotions in certain situations in the past. However, it never felt as strong and certain as it had done that day in that place. I was sincerely glad to get out.

I carried on churning out the kilometres. By this stage I was so attuned to my walking speeds and distances that I knew exactly, almost to the minute, when I would arrive somewhere. My natural speed, I calculated, was about four and a half kilometres an hour. I could push up to as much as seven kilometres an hour but I hardly ever needed to. I wasn't in a hurry, and there were very few occasions when I had to be in a certain place at a certain time. It also damn near killed me every time I kept this pace up. However, it was interesting to experiment.

By now I was even confident enough to question the guidebook. The author, quite rightly, had based her calculations on an average speed. So, when I read about a detour of 'seven hundred and fifty metres, or about eleven minutes', I would say to myself, "Actually, that's only about ten minutes". When other pilgrims said they were aiming for a town to rest overnight, and they would be there at five o'clock, I knew I would probably be relaxing on my bunk when they arrived, as my pace was just a little faster than theirs. Not something to be particularly proud of, just the way I'm made.

Cajarc appeared below me as I crested a hill. As I carefully made my way down the remaining thirty minutes or so, it became clear how beautiful not only the town was, but also its setting. It was completely encircled by chalk cliffs, like the sides of a volcano crater. If this place had ever come under attack in the past, it must have been easy pickings. Any opposing army would simply have set up their trebuchets on the surrounding hills and flattened the place.

The campsite was ideal. Neat little trimmed hedges bordered each plot; it was like having your own garden. Most of the tourists had retreated back home in time to get their children to school for the new term. I had stocked up at the shop with lots of goodies to refresh my aching limbs and now badly needed a carbohydrate fix.

A French guy had set up camp in the next plot. After he had tinkered with his motorbike and finished an hour-long conversation on his mobile, he came over.

Christoph, who spoke good English, was a motorbike mechanic on a two-week biking holiday. He had a friendly demeanour, and we sat and talked for a while as potatoes bubbled on my stove.

"You want a beer?" I asked after I had eaten.

"Sure, we can go into town," he said, looking excited and rubbing his hands in anticipation.

Cajarc was spookily quiet. I realised that most of the locals were tucked up in the bars that dotted the centre. We chose a suitable spot and sat down outside. Although it was the beginning of September and well into the evening, the nights were still warm. Christoph sipped on a vivid yellow drink that I had not seen before.

"It is called Suze," he explained. "It is brewed from the roots of a plant that grows in this region. You may have seen them, the flowers are yellow and it is quite common, about so high." His hand indicated his waist.

"Yeah, I have seen them. How does it taste?" He let me have a sip. It was very sweet, with a taste so unusual I was unable even to describe it, but it was damn good.

We chewed the fat for a couple of hours, talking of the Camino, motorbikes, the weather and McDonald's. I am not a huge fan of the great burger chain, but I do succumb to the odd Filet-O-Fish. Since my arrival in France they had been few and far between.

"They are here," Christoph began to explain, "but we put them where they belong, a good couple of kilometres out of town."

"Because you want to keep your villages as they are, your heritage intact?"

"Yes, exactly. We do not want to become part of this Westernisation process, where all the local businesses are forced to close because a large garden centre or supermarket has opened up. We do not want huge shopping malls dominating our culture, destroying our villages and towns. In the large cities like

Paris maybe, but not in places like this."

"It's a good attitude," I said. "I feel the same way about England. We are slowly destroying our small village businesses and shops by letting the large chain stores take over. It saddens me too."

"Here in France," he agreed, "we value what we have. Look at this square here. We still have the butchers and the bakers. You can buy your vegetables fresh every day from the greengrocer who is trading with the local farmer. The cake shop continues to bake as it has done for years. It is how people like it; they are comfortable with it. If the council receives an application from McDonald's or some DIY chain to build in the centre, it is often rejected or, at best, given permission to build out of town, but they know that is not the ideal spot, so sometimes they give up. We don't need change. We just want France to retain some sort of individuality. We still keep the same opening hours, nine to twelve and two to seven, or thereabouts," he went on, warming to the theme more and more. "People here don't want to be able to go and buy an electric chainsaw at ten in the evening. We don't need a twenty-four-hour pharmacy. If we need a new carpet, we call Pierre, the carpet guy. Maurice services our vehicles and Claude deals with the plumbing. It works. Why do people feel they need to change it?"

We staggered out of the bar around midnight. I lost count of how many times we both tripped over something, laughed out loud at something not really that funny and generally behaved extremely immaturely, as only two drunks know how.

I woke in the morning fully clothed with both legs inside the tent and the rest of my body outside, resting on the grass. To my surprise, I had no hangover, which I put down to the Suze and made a mental note that it was acceptable to drink too much of the stuff.

* * *

I am a glass-half-full sort of guy but I'm also a realist. I know the law of averages dictates that it is highly unlikely that anyone can walk 1,600 kilometres without at some point falling over, or at least coming close. That morning, walking out of Cajarc, I proved myself right.

It was innocent enough. I was merrily walking down a narrow track pinned in by bushes at head height when they suddenly cleared on my left to reveal a low stone wall. On the other side a family had obviously spent the fruits of their labours on their dream cottage, renovated to perfection. Beside the swimming pool lay an extremely attractive, bikini-clad woman, soaking up the sun. Her legs were endless, her tanned skin glistened with droplets of perspiration, and she... well, you get the picture. After three weeks of meeting backpacking women clad in hiking boots and ridiculous sunhats, you can imagine how I felt. My pace naturally slowed a little. Actually it slowed a lot. In fact, if I'd been going any slower, I would have stopped. She looked up. I looked at her. I smiled, she smiled. We held each other's gaze, still smiling.

It was like that scenario you see in the movies sometimes. Man and woman lock eyes, man walks into lamp post. There were no lamp posts here, but there was one hell of a huge boulder. As my right foot smashed into it, I felt myself going over, the weight of the pack pushing me forward. My arms flung and flapped around, scrabbling fruitlessly for anything to grab. It was all happening in slow motion. God only knew how it must have looked from her angle. One minute there was a torso bobbing up and down behind her wall, the next moment it had disappeared.

Somehow, I didn't hit the deck but ran on all fours trying to retrieve my balance, and eventually I did. I popped up behind the wall a few metres further on, to see her hand over her mouth and her breasts bobbing in sync with her giggling. I bowed, she applauded, and I walked off to save further loss of face.

I was getting fitter, feeling less tired as each day passed and climbing hills like a man possessed. I felt good, really good. Muscles were starting to bulge in my legs where I didn't even know there were muscles. Even my upper body was firming up from using the trekking poles. My breathing was less laboured. I had always considered myself relatively fit. I cycled, on occasion I went to the gym, I jogged, and I swam. But the Camino was giving my body newfound energy. My daily distances were slowly creeping up too. At this stage I was averaging around twenty-two kilometres a day, although I knew I was capable of doing around thirty.

One day I was slumped on a bench under an oak tree in the little hamlet of Bach, pencil in one hand and notebook in the other, totalling up the distance for the day. I had two surprises. First, I had finally managed to break the elusive thirty-kilometre barrier. To me it was like completing a marathon. I had come close before – twenty-seven, twenty-nine. Better still, I had reached the milestone without much fatigue.

Secondly, as I wrote my journal that night, it hit me that, after walking for nineteen days, I had covered over three hundred kilometres, one fifth of the total distance of the Camino. At first I was elated with the realisation that I was actually capable of doing this thing. Then my excitement waned as I took in what a small dent it actually was. Twenty per cent; it was nothing really. The pros and cons twisted round in my head. I was proud of my achievement to date, but battering their way through these positive feelings were the memories of those tough days, all those monotonous stretches that I thought would never end and the knowledge that I had a whole lot more to get through. I couldn't figure out why these negative thoughts insisted on pushing their way forward. I concluded that I was just making the challenge tougher than it was, to prove to myself that, for once in my life, I was capable of reaching a goal. I was determined not to be beaten into submission this time, not to take the easy option. I was becoming stronger, learning to take the route that might be more difficult but that offered bigger rewards.

I woke to a serene morning. As I crawled out of the tent, a veil of mist undulated over the field as though an artist had just painted it, his brush merely glancing the canvas. Dew shone in the grass, each blade bent over with the weight of a moisture droplet. The toll of the church bell in Bach seemed hushed as though it was embarrassed to break the silence, and horse hooves clattered a way off. I arched my back and stretched, trying to find some sunlight through the trees to warm myself. While my pan lid rattled over the boiling water, I rummaged around in my food bag and tore off pieces from a stale baguette. I cleared up, hoisted my pack and wandered away, my mind occupied with thoughts of nothing more than another day's stroll.

I had been wondering why, during the past couple of weeks, a lot of the gîtes were booked before I even got there. Even when I was one of the first to arrive the owners usually shrugged their shoulders with a resigned look. Several times I had been forced to walk out of town and camp; not that this was a problem but a shower and a restaurant always lifted the spirits at day's end. A French pilgrim I met enlightened me.

"I have my mobile with me. I stay at gîtes every night but I call and book three nights in advance," he said.

I had deliberately left my mobile at home, horrified by the thought of it ringing, beeping and disturbing the ambience of the Camino. I had come to walk precisely to escape such modern distractions. It seemed wrong to me that those of us who didn't carry a mobile were being deprived of a bed for the night by those who did. Where was the camaraderie in that? I looked forward to arriving in Spain, where the refugios, as the lodgings are known, do not accept bookings. It was at it should be, first come first served. I am not saying that everyone should leave their mobile behind. To a lone pilgrim, this little device may provide a lifeline in an emergency. In the meantime, I was content with camping out for five or so nights a week, and taking my chances at the gîtes when I got there.

Other walkers had GPS units. If you are lost in the middle of the Sahara or in an uncharted jungle, then they are a necessity. What would we need them on the Camino for? You're never more than a day's walk from anywhere, and there's a nice little track in front of you, with markings on it to tell you where to go. It made no sense to me. One American I met was the proud owner of one of these units. According to the guidebook, one stretch of the Camino was four kilometres long.

"Actually, Fozzie," he said with pride, "I consulted my GPS because I thought it seemed longer. And it was. The actual distance was six kilometres! Imagine that!"

"Imagine that, indeed," I replied, trying to look interested before wandering off to the nearest bar.

* * *

The Journey in Between

I had been walking over ground resembling moorland for an hour or so. As I crested the brow of a hill, the large settlement of Cahors appeared below me. It was tucked up in a huge loop created by the River Lot, which I had been following on and off over the past few days. The famous Pont Valentré was just visible spanning the water on the outskirts. It was an impressive sight. The whole panorama was laid out like a huge map on a cartographer's desk. I could even plot my way through town and out again from my perch.

I descended a steep road, crossed the Pont Louis-Philippe, walked up Gambetta, and before long I had paid for two nights' lodgings at the hostel on Frédéric Suisse Street. I immediately warmed to Cahors. It was friendly and clean, and the locals looked as though they were genuinely happy to live there. It was alive and bustling, but never overwhelming. In the busy cafés circling Place Aristide Briand, tobacco smoke and freshly brewed coffee smells caught the breeze, as did peals of genuine laughter.

I recognised a guy sitting outside the hostel tending his feet. We hadn't met but I had seen his face a few times. His name was, appropriately, France.

"Blister problems?" I enquired.

"Yes, nothing until now, and then this," he replied, pointing to the offending bulges on the small toes on each foot. "I took my boots to a cobbler to see if he could adjust them. He did, but it has made no difference." He stuck a pin in one of them, making me cringe as the liquid oozed out and dripped on to the ground. 'Blistering', as I now referred to it, was a regular sight on the Camino. Because everyone assumed that everyone else was in the same boat, most pilgrims would tend to them, regardless of where they were, or in whose company.

I passed on Walter's advice, happy that my blisters had been replaced by hard skin, so hard that I could actually tap it.

Blisters aside, I was now encountering a new problem. Although I'd never suffered from insomnia before, my sleeping patterns now were a chaotic tangle. Since day one of the Camino I had been experiencing the most vivid dreams, on occasions two or three a night, waking after one and falling asleep again until the next woke me. I presumed it was something to do with the Camino's energy and the ley lines. I began to write the dreams down, but could never make any sense of them.

My lack of sleep was starting to bother me. I would go to bed around ten or eleven, much earlier if I was camping. By two in the morning I had probably managed one hour of shallow slumber, tossing and turning and becoming more frustrated with each minute. I usually slept OK in the tent, in the fresh air, but not at the gîtes. It was starting to annoy me.

By three in the morning at the hostel in Cahors, I had given up. I got up and wandered down to the TV room, where I found a French teenager drawing on a joint and clearly stoned. I sipped a coffee (probably not the best solution to insomnia) and smoked. He turned around and constantly tried to converse with me in French, waving the TV remote around and looking at me through bloodshot and distant eyes as he brushed ash off his arm. I decided after five minutes that lying awake in my room was the more attractive option and told him in English that he looked like a Jack Russell, that he should get a haircut and that the French can't play football for shit. He nodded his head in approval, smiled and waved goodbye.

The following day, miserable for lack of sleep, I deliberately stayed out of everyone's way and concentrated on cheering myself up with some alcohol and food. I found a little café down a side street and sat down to three courses with wine at lunch, then sat by the Pont Valentré for what seemed like all afternoon. It is a beautiful piece of architecture stretched across the River Lot and its fortifications must have been a formidable sight for approaching enemies. The shimmering water, the grass on my back and the breeze tickling my legs improved my mood considerably.

On the way back to the hostel I stopped at a phone box and called Trish, a friend in Greece. I had spent most of the few months before the Camino on Crete and made some great friends. Trish and I shared a hunger for adventure that needed constant feeding, so we would head off around the island on our mopeds just to explore. We found all the best tavernas, the most beautiful walks and the most deserted beaches.

She sounded confused but excited. We had talked in depth

about starting our own vegetarian restaurant on Crete. For the time being, she was finishing her time at a yoga retreat, and we were both looking for a reason to return to Crete the following year. She had spoken to a taverna owner who was planning to go to America at the end of the season, and needed someone to take over the following year. It sounded perfect. Trish would be given free rein to experiment with the menu and make her mark on the place.

"Go for it, Trish!" I said enthusiastically. "If that's what you want, and it means you are where you want to be next year, then do it."

"Fozzie, I know. I'm just a bit lost. There's so much to sort out if I do it. My head's all screwed up. You need to be here. All the money stuff and the legal angle. I'm all wobbly just thinking about it all."

I spent the rest of the evening wandering around in a daze, wondering if I should have asked the question that I wanted to ask. I phoned her the following morning.

"Fozzie, what are you doing calling me in the morning? You usually call in the evening. You were lucky to get me."

"Trish, are you asking if you want me to do this thing with you?"

"Yes."

"Well," I said, "the answer is yes, but I can't make any promises to get out there before the end of the season. My priority is to finish this walk first, you know that, and that will take until the beginning of November, sooner if I can increase my distances. Then I could get out there for the last two weeks of the season, see everyone, and we can talk to this guy and sort it out. How's that?"

"I think it would work, Fozzie."

I replaced the receiver. The full impact of what I had done suddenly hit me, and I didn't like what I felt. I had inadvertently given myself a schedule. From being in the position of having no timetable to keep to, walking as far as I wanted to each day, resting when I damn well wanted to, I now had to complete by a set date, the middle of October. All these freedoms lay in tatters on the ground by the phone box. I cursed. I was feeling excited at the prospect of returning to the island I had fallen in love with, but frustrated in equal measure. I cursed again.

According to my original plan, to finish by early November, I would have needed to walk an average of twenty-seven kilometres each day, six days a week. It was a loose plan, based solely on the weather. If the Spanish winter was late or mild, then I had the option of extending the trip. If, however, I were to finish by the 10th of October or thereabouts, I would have to walk thirty-five kilometres each walking day. It wasn't exactly out of the question, but it was difficult. It meant eight or nine hours of walking each day. Throwing in an hour for lunch and a couple of breaks, I would need to start no later than eight in the morning. This meant only one thing: I would be up with the bag rustlers.

Up to this point I had finished each day tired but not exhausted and, once revived, ready to do the same the following day. To increase my distance by ten kilometres meant I would be a physical wreck each evening. Although I hadn't made a promise as such, I felt I had an obligation to fulfil. I began blaming myself for getting into the position to start with, of ruining the Camino I had been blessed with. Nevertheless, I decided to give it my best shot. I would aim for thirty-seven kilometres each day, two more than I needed: that way, perhaps, I could do a little less one day a week, say twenty-five.

As I left Cahors, a place I resolved to revisit someday, and crossed the Pont Valentré one last time, I encountered the steepest section of the entire Camino. It was only about three metres long, but it was pretty much vertical. There was another option, a footpath that curved around and finished at the same spot, but this looked more fun. If there had been no metal grab rails embedded into the rock, it would not have been possible. I hauled myself up, my pack doing its utmost to haul me back down again. It was fun. It may have only been a minute's worth of mountaineering, but it got the blood squirting around my body.

I came up behind a guy loudly singing Ultreya, as if he didn't care who heard him. Pierre, who came from the north-east of France, was in his sixties and had grey hair that was ruffled and untidy from the breeze and sweat. He was the first real pilgrim I had met who completely took his time and relaxed on the

Camino. He ambled along, humming and singing and looking all around him, often stopping to take a closer look at a plant or the view.

When he heard Click and Clack on the tarmac, he turned round and said hello. We introduced ourselves.

"Are you walking all the way to Santiago?" he asked.

"Yes, all the way."

"You walk very quickly," he said with a smile.

"Long story, which I won't get into. Unfortunately I have given myself a time limit."

We talked only briefly. I kept making false starts before he would say something and I felt obliged to pause and answer. I must have looked stupid and awkward. I felt a little angry with him, guiltily, for having the freedom that I had surrendered.

The schedule I had set was still fresh in my mind and for most of the day I concentrated on nothing but plugging out the kilometres, head down, trying to keep my speed up to six kilometres an hour, checking my watch at lunch breaks and making sure I didn't overrun. If I had only thirty minutes for lunch, I could relax a little.

By the time I hit Montcuq in the early evening, I was a wreck physically and mentally from straining to be at a certain point at a certain time. The soles of my feet were on fire. I literally had to lift them off the ground with my hands and rest them on top of my pack. The only time they didn't ache was when I removed my boots and socks and exposed them to the air. My right calf hurt, and threatened to get worse. I had two fresh blisters on my ankles. I hadn't taken the least notice of what was around me because I'd been focusing on a point two metres in front of me all day, watching my step.

I was destroying myself, and my Camino.

Chapter Seven

The Trail Telegraph

It always amazed me how and where I bumped into familiar faces on the Camino. I saw some people almost every day, other people once a week, maybe once a month. Sometimes I would overtake the people I had come to know, at other times they would overtake me, all of us oblivious to the fact we had passed each other. I might see them resting in a field, looking at a church or drinking at a bar. I knew then I was ahead of them – not that it was a race, everyone just developed a need to know where all their friends were at a given point. Sometimes we would lose each other.

"Fozzie, have you seen Pierre?" someone would ask.

"Yeah, two days behind," I would reliably inform them.

"What about France?"

"Last time I saw him was Cahors; he was taking a day's rest. I left a day before him, so he's about a day behind."

I guess we all developed a mental map of the Camino. Mine took a bird's-eye view, covering perhaps a week's walk in length. Dotted along it would be other pilgrims, marked by little flags marked with their names sticking out of their packs. It was easy to find out where a particular person was, or how they were doing. As I passed someone, or they me, I would update my mental map.

Then there was the trail telegraph. As most of us didn't have mobiles, messages and information were passed from person to person until they arrived at the intended recipient. You would imagine such a haphazard method would prove unreliable but in fact it was surprisingly successful, perhaps because it was a pleasantly different way of communicating. On any given day hundreds of messages would be moving along the Camino at various stages, waiting to be delivered to the right pilgrim, whether it was 'Tell Gerard that I've got his spoon, he left it at the gîte', or 'If anyone sees Chantelle, can she meet me at the church in Lauzerte lunchtime tomorrow?' You could pretty much arrange an evening meal for ten at a certain town on a certain day if you sent out the messages a week before and gave them plenty of time to reach your friends.

In an age where we all seem to be relying on technology, it was wonderful to rely on such a basic method of communication.

* * *

I encountered my first day of rain. I had been camping and it must have started in the early hours. For the first time, I had to walk in waterproofs, which I hate: even with today's breathable materials, you end up being cocooned in your own microclimate. Waterproofs keep the rain out, but if your body is working a little hard, you get damp from the sweat anyway, so why bother protecting yourself from a little moisture?

If you bear in mind that, apparently, we lose a litre of water just when we sleep, you can imagine how much we lose in a summer rainstorm with sixteen kilos plugged on your back, walking up a hill, wrapped up in protective gear. When the rain eventually stopped, I would peel off the layers at the first opportunity. My T-shirt would be wringing wet and stuck to my back and my shorts would have damp blotches over them as if I had failed to make it to the gents on time. Others on the trail would be doing the same, frantically whipping off their outer clothes as vapour rose off them like morning dew escaping from a wall when the sun hit it.

My pack also needed protection. At the first sign of rain, my usual course of action was to go under the nearest tree to see if it would only last a few minutes. If this were not the case, then I would commence 'Operation Keep Dry'. First, I had to drop my pack and find the waterproofs. As it rained quite rarely on my walk, these items were classed as 'not used often', and therefore at the bottom under everything else. Hence, everything else would have to come out – and inevitably also got wet. Trousers would go on first. They had zips around the ankles so that I could, in theory, put them on without removing your boots, only some idiot designer had obviously not taken into account the actual size of hiking boots, so they would have to come off as well. The jacket thankfully was pretty straightforward. After that I had to fix on the 'one-size' rucksack cover. I am always wary of anything described as one size. No matter how I adjusted it, how far I pulled it over the top or stretched it over the bottom, there was always some part not covered.

And I am not exaggerating when I say that seven times out of ten, by the time I had gone through this rigmarole, it had stopped raining anyway. I need not explain 'Operation Remove Waterproofs', let alone 'Operation Throw a Huge Tantrum'. By this stage I had no umbrella: brolly had snagged on a tree somewhere after Cahors.

I seemed to be the only one who used this method on the few occasions that it did rain. The humble poncho is making a comeback and all because of its wonderful simplicity. I watched with a mixture of admiration and intense jealousy when other pilgrims hit a rainstorm. They would stop, retrieve their poncho from a side pocket, stick their head through the hole, and let the whole thing just fall over them, and their pack. The poncho didn't need to be particularly breathable because all the air circulated underneath it. It was a miracle of design, and got me wondering how they ever went out of favour in the first place.

* * *

Sunflowers grew everywhere in this part of France and I often walked through fields blazing with their yellow faces. I reached Lauzerte, an historic fortified village dating back to 1214. It commanded a lofty perch on top of a hill, giving uninterrupted views for miles all around. It was my birthday and birthdays mean indulgences, in this case food. The obvious choice was the village centre. The cobbles looked as if they had just been varnished after a passing shower. Pigeons cooed and flapped around, sending the local cats into frenzied bouts of frustration. I wiped off a seat at the café that seemed to be drawing a larger crowd than most. My policy of eating at establishments that were busy had served me well, up until this point at least.

After a good fifteen minutes of deliberately avoiding eye contact with me, the young waitress eventually came over. A greasy slick of hair flapped against her face and she wore a permanent frown. Pencil poised over her order ticket, she stood, bored and resolutely unhelpful, squinting through ultra-thick glasses.

"Can I use your glasses as an ashtray?!" I asked. I knew she didn't speak English, as one of the other guests had given up on that venture.

She looked puzzled.

"I said, if I ordered breakfast now, would that be enough notice for you to get it to me in the morning?"

I'm not that rude really. It's just that she was treating the whole café like a waste of her time. She was ignoring everyone, taking a decade to bring out orders, and kept tutting all the time, as if everything was an imposition.

The table with the English tourists had heard me. At first they looked at me in astonishment, then they just started to giggle. I winked at them.

Smiling now, I ordered a Coke and a croque monsieur. She scribbled down the request and sauntered back to the haven of the kitchen, returning briefly to place my Coke on the table.

I waited for forty minutes. Eventually I went into the bar and gave her the money for the Coke.

"Monsieur, le croque monsieur?" she said, surprised.

"Well, where the hell is it?" I stammered. "I ordered the bloody thing forty minutes ago. It's your basic cheese on toast with some frilly extras. You know? Cheese on to toast, under grill and there you go. What are you doing? Milking the damn cow?"

If it weren't for the fact that when it arrived five minutes later it was the best-tasting croque monsieur I had eaten on the entire Camino, I would have gone off to one of the other establishments. I can't remember the name of the place, but, for all future pilgrims entering the market place in Lauzerte, it's the one on the far right-hand side in the corner, with the red chairs. Try the one with the nice yellow chairs on your left instead.

I stumbled into Moissac that evening in the dark after walking thirty-eight kilometres, literally incapable of going any further. I still had to find somewhere to sleep and something to eat. What a birthday! I happened on a café serving up such delicacies as hot dogs, chips and burgers. There were illuminated photos of the options above the serving area. I realised my hunger was borderline dangerous and ordered two huge baguettes each stuffed with three hamburgers. The cook raised one eyebrow slightly, smiled and muttered something about pilgrims as he slapped six hamburgers on the grill. I collapsed into one of the chairs outside and devoured the food like a wolf with a chicken.

"How far is the campsite?" I asked the waitress.

She replied that she thought it was closed for the season. I had forgotten that some French campsites shut at the beginning of September; it was time to sleep rough again and it needed to be close.

On a trip with a friend a few years previously, we had slept rough most nights. It was obviously cheap, which was a major concern at that time, and we became experts at finding pretty comfortable places to spend the night. The knack was to have your amenities on hand. We referred to potential locations as 'hotels' and graded them according to the facilities nearby, which were, in order of importance: shelter, lighting, toilets, water, seating, privacy and ground comfort. Shelter essentially meant anywhere where we would remain dry if it rained, such as a bus stop or even some trees. Lighting could come from a street light or a window. If there were public toilets, we didn't have to rely on restaurants. Water was a tricky one. It could always be obtained from somewhere such as a bar or by calling at someone's house but far better was a tap or water fountain. We could use our sleeping mats as seating, but preferred a bench or seating area. Ground comfort ideally meant soft grass as opposed to concrete. A poor 'hotel' would offer one or two of these amenities; if we found three or four we were usually quite chuffed, fives were a rarity and sixes and sevens happened once in a blue moon.

The place I had found in Moissac rated about four and a half, the half coming from the fact that there was light, but not very strong. There was a bench to sit on and toilets a short stroll away, so I could have a wash and get water to brew coffee in the morning. Top marks went to privacy: my actual sleeping location was a hollow hedge, and people, such as the occasional dog walker, could be a metre from me and have no idea I was there. Unfortunately there was no shelter, but thankfully it didn't rain that night. This just goes to show that the best hotels don't necessarily come with roofs and a bathroom.

Moissac was a large town, but somehow still retained that sleepy feel about it. I walked up Rue de la République and came into the main square flanked by the abbey of St Pierre. I studied the portal, with the apocalypse depicted in the stone, and marvelled at the time it must have taken to carve it.

It had been at least two weeks since I had seen her, but now I spotted the smoking woman limping towards me and looking a bit sorry for herself.

"Hey," I said and gave her a peck on the cheek. "You look a bit sad. What's the matter?"

"Big problem with my leg. I see doctor and he tell me not good. Must go easy and rest. So, I go to St-Jean-Pied-de-Port by a train, and walk from there. Then I still can do Camino but walk slowly." Dejectedly, she looked down, like a naughty child waiting to be punished.

St-Jean-Pied-de-Port was just before the border with Spain, and about halfway to Santiago. It was, give or take, seven hundred and fifty kilometres from Le Puy en Velay and the same distance again to Santiago.

"I'm really sorry," I said. Even though I still didn't know her name, and had not really met or talked to her many times, I liked her immensely. As she was the first pilgrim I had met, not only did she occupy a special place in my affections but she glowed with courage. She was perhaps in her late sixties, and less capable than most of us, yet she had struggled to be here and she had made it with determination and grit. I wished I had half her determination and hoped that when I reached that age I would still be capable of walking such distances.

"I wish you luck," I said. "I'm sure Spain is as beautiful as France, if not more so. And it sounds like a good plan you have.

Just take the rest of the walk at a slow pace, don't rush it, and make sure you rest. Muscles heal with rest. By the way, what is your name?"

"Ann, my name is Ann. Yours?"

"Fozzie."

"It is nice to know your name at last. I used to call you the smoking man. Good luck Fozzie."

She turned and walked off before I could reply.

That's one of the things about the Camino people don't really take into account. It's great to be determined, to set your eyes on the goal of Santiago. But anything may happen. We can trip or fall, be injured, become ill. That would be the end of the walk, at least until the next attempt. There is a memorial in Spain just past the village of Salceda. A bronze sculpture of two bronze boots set into a wall reminds pilgrims of Guillermo Watt, aged 69, who died there in 1993. He was one day short of Santiago. That is why, when people said to me, "Fozzie, you will make it," I always used to reply, "I will accept I have made it when I know I am there."

France also appeared in the square. He was always glad to see me, and I him. He sat down and we talked for a while over a coffee. I went over to the church portal to take a photo and when I returned he had gone. I went to pay but the waitress explained that France had already met the bill. I looked down the street to see him gleefully waving and running away, smiling back at me. I knew I'd see him again to thank him, and he knew it too.

* * *

As I have explained, pilgrims on the Camino carry a card called a *créanciale*, which we can have stamped at various establishments, as proof for the cathedral authorities in Santiago that we have been to the places we say we have. The *créanciale* is also a unique souvenir, but mine was looking decidedly empty.

I was under the impression that I could obtain the stamps only at gîtes and churches. I stayed in a gîte maybe once a week, and as I am not a religious person, my 'churches visited' collection was skimpy, to say the least. When Pierre unfolded his card and showed me his impressive collection of stamps, about four times more numerous than mine, I thought it was time to do something about it. He explained I could also obtain stamps at tourist information offices, and even at some restaurants and bars.

From that point on, I went all out on a mission to fill up my *créanciale*. It was like being a kid again and trying to get my entire football album filled up with stickers as fast as possible.

A welcome sight greeted me as I left Moissac. The terrain ahead, which I calculated was a couple of days' walk, was flat. Oh, joy of joys! No hills, no inclines. The builders of the canal had spotted this also, and for most of the day the Camino clung to the bank. Although it was pretty much dead straight, it was a beautiful walk. The water was still like polished steel, broken only by the wake of an occasional boat or a fish jumping for a fly. Trees stood to attention on both sides like symmetrical soldiers guarding the entire length. Sunlight filtered through chinks in the foliage and there was a pleasant smell of damp earth. It was peaceful, and a distinct and pleasant change to experience such uniformity after such irregularity.

I had noticed my calf muscle was becoming more painful, but I had resolved to increase my daily distance travelled. Inevitably, whenever I started walking again after a rest stop, I was hobbling for fifteen minutes before the muscle loosened up and the pain abated. Logically I knew I should rest it for at least two days, preferably three or four, but if I did that, I would lose valuable time. Again I cursed myself for putting a restriction on my adventure.

"I'll tell you a short story about my experience, Fozzie," said Fabian at the gîte at Saint Antoine. Fabian was a Frenchman on a mission to complete the Camino in super-quick time. He ate super-quick as well, shovelling spoonfuls of ravioli into his mouth and storytelling at the same time. It was dangerous to sit opposite him.

"I pulled a ligament too. Like you, I ignored it because I had a schedule to keep. I must keep going, I thought. Eventually it became so painful that my friends had to issue threats to get me to rest. I rested for two days and continued. It wasn't long enough. After a few days more, the problem had returned tenfold. The consequence was that I had to hole up in Conques for a whole week. Rest it now, Fozzie. You will lose more time if you don't."

"OK, I hear what you are saying," I said, wiping a piece of ravioli from my forehead. "I know it makes sense. I'm going to give it two days and see what happens. If no improvement then I will rest. Where are you heading to tomorrow?"

"I will make Condom tomorrow evening," he replied.

"Condom!" I exclaimed, looking at him as if he were deranged. "That's sixty-three kilometres! Are you crazy?"

"I am doing about sixty kilometres every day," he explained. "It is long, I know, but I too have a schedule. I have to return to Paris to study, and this is the distance I need to walk each day to complete. I would rather do this than not walk at all. Besides, I walk with no pack."

"So where is all your stuff?"

"There is a courier service. You pay them ten euros and they take your bag on for you, pretty much to anywhere."

I was puzzled. "Don't you think that is like, well, cheating? Don't you feel a little guilty?"

"At first yes, but I have little choice. I cannot walk these distances in a day with my pack."

He slept in the reception area, so as to make an early start around six o'clock without waking others. Unfortunately the other pilgrims staying at the gîte did not have Fabian's consideration. The noise of rustling plastic the following morning sounded as though someone had thrown a hyperactive octopus into a skip full of carrier bags. As the last culprit left, a Canadian pilgrim had obviously reached the end of his tether and literally manhandled him back into the room, pointed to the light switch, then to the fluorescent light blinking on the ceiling.

"I've listened to your noise for the last half an hour. Please have some respect for others next time you wake early in the morning. We would appreciate it. And make sure you turn the fucking light off when you leave!"

There was a definite chill in the air at eight in the morning. In fact, it was cold. As I left St Antoine I was tempted to put on trousers and a fleece, but I knew after half an hour I would be too hot. Sure enough, as the day progressed I was comfortable. The air was crisp, with an autumnal chill that lasted just that bit longer each morning before the sun burnt it away.

I had decided to meet Fabian's policy halfway. I would walk for a day, and if there was no improvement in the calf that evening, I would rest for two days. I imagined Fabian shaking his head and wagging his finger at me.

For the last two weeks a white butterfly had been keeping me company, appearing every day for a few minutes. It seemed as if he was egging me on, giving me the enthusiasm to go that extra mile. I used to wonder where he was every day if I hadn't seen him, but sure enough, at some point, I would catch a flash of white out of the corner of my eye, look over and there he would be. Sometimes he would dance around my head, at others fly alongside and rest occasionally on plants. I pretended it was the same butterfly every day; whether it was or not, I looked forward to seeing him and felt reassured by his presence.

My calf was showing no signs of improvement and Fabian's warning was ringing around my head for most of the day. I decided caution was the best option. The town of Lectoure seemed perfect for a two-day, three-night recuperation stop. It had everything I would need: a couple of supermarkets to buy food I could cook for myself, and the gîte even had an oven! There was a collection of bars, cafés and restaurants and, remarkably, the post office had internet access.

Everyone seemed to rally around. When my buddies found out I was resting for two days because of my calf, all manner of remedies appeared. They plied me with pills, lotions, oils and every piece of advice available. I thanked them all but told them I would rather work on the problem myself, hoping my mental strength was enough to sort it out. That and a bottle of a very fine rosé each night to aid the healing process.

To pass the time, I checked my email, ate, drank and took more photos than was necessary. In between times, I wandered around aimlessly, hoping that something would catch my attention. I do not like wishing days away, but I was going a little crazy having to stay put, however attractive Lectoure was. My body had become used to churning out twenty-five kilometres every day and didn't seem to know what to do with all the stored-up energy. I was surprised by how much I missed the walking.

I escaped the town's confines, as planned, on the third day. My calf had improved, which made the decision easy, although boredom had played a big part. I managed an early start and before long my waterproofs were on. They didn't come off for the day, as it rained on and off and was cold too. Autumn was starting to take a grip.

Pulling off the way at Chapelle Sainte Germaine to search for water, I spotted a little old lady feeding chickens in her yard. She must have been in her nineties, and spoke no English at all. My usual routine with my water bag produced puzzled looks. I found a tap (which was not working) and held the bag under it. That seemed to do the trick. Why she didn't give me water from her house I don't know. Instead, she led me up her drive and pointed to the top of the hill. As we were walking, she passed wind three times extremely loudly and never batted an eyelid. Her apparent total ignorance of what had happened had me creased up with silent laughter, and I had to get away quickly in case she thought I was being rude.

It was a great day and I felt extremely content just to walk. Putting aside the issue of distance, I went back to how I had been walking at the start, a month before, taking my time, looking around me, noticing every scene and sight. My calf was giving me no pain at all. There was a noticeable decline in the number of pilgrims, no doubt because of the approach of winter. Or maybe they were all taking a rest day as well.

When I actually managed to obtain some water at a house a little further on, I carried on walking for a short distance with the full water bag in my hand, intending to place it in the rucksack when I stopped for a rest. Then it struck me – my pack was so much lighter. My water bladder held two litres, which weighed about two kilos. The lightness of my pack was remarkable. I started to ponder on the weight issue more as the day rolled on. I figured that I could send my tent and cooking equipment back home. My tent was just less than two kilos. As great as it was to camp out, did I really need it? The refugios in Spain were plentiful and cheap. In fact, many of them operated on donation only. Therefore I would have a roof over my head most of the time. Even if I did want to spend a night in the woods, the weather in the early part of Spain was still predictably warm, with little rain, so I would not need shelter anyway.

As for the cooking equipment, I was only really using it for brewing tea and coffee and it could be dispensed with without too much loss of comfort. I could cook in some of the refugios with cooking facilities, and if there weren't any, I would simply have a cheap meal at a bar or eat something cold. Four kilos was the total weight I would be able to save. That was twenty five per cent of my pack. I decided to ditch the gear when I got near to the Spanish border.

I passed through Condom, which, although beautiful, did not appeal as a place to spend the night. By the time I reached the three or so houses known as Le Carbon, dusk was falling. I was intending to make a detour of about one kilometre to the fortified town of Larressingle, but then spotted that one of the houses was empty, and being renovated. The front door creaked open to reveal rooms full of nothing but dust. I'm not keen on sleeping in dark, empty houses on my own, so opted instead for the open garage at the side, which gave me a 'hotel' score of around three.

What was also particularly pleasing was that I had broken the elusive forty-kilometre barrier. I also realised that I had completed a third of the Camino. I slept with a smile on my face.

The following day I passed a couple sitting on the grass, eating their lunch, in front of a church that was catching the full light of the midday sun. By the look on the guy's face I knew he was going to try and stop me to make conversation. I just wasn't in the mood for talking, so I avoided eye contact except for the customary nod in their direction.

"You walking the Camino?" he called.

"Yeah," I replied, not slowing my pace.

"Where you heading to?"

"Santiago."

"When you plan on getting there?" He was firing questions like a machine gun.

"Another four weeks," I replied, and waited for him to disagree.

"Four weeks! That's not possible! It's too far," he stuttered, disbelief all over his face.

I just smiled and carried on.

***

The vast majority of other pilgrims are a decent bunch. What astounded me was the lack of respect some walkers had for others, and the countryside, when it came to defecating. I used public facilities whenever I could, but hey, we all get stuck sometimes. In these situations, I would walk off the Camino, a good twenty metres into the woods or fields. I did not carry a trowel, but usually picked a soft piece of ground that I could at least kick a hole into, or I used a stick. Business done, I would burn my toilet paper, and cover the whole lot over.

It was a shame some other pilgrims didn't share my practices. I regularly walked past piles of foul-smelling shit on the sides of the Camino, some even in the middle, surrounded by soiled toilet paper. I failed to comprehend how people could have such a flagrant disregard for others, the countryside and the Camino. The path to me represented a way full of natural energy, where millions of pilgrims had passed; and more importantly, millions more would pass. It was sacred. How could someone desecrate it in this way? How much extra effort, when they have already walked five hundred kilometres, was it to go twenty extra metres into the bushes?

Pierre told me of an unpleasant experience when he had once gone into the woods to take a pee. On finishing, he picked up his pack, only to realise he had put it down in a pile of someone else's excrement. Worse, he had grabbed the bag where a prime nugget had been squelched against the fabric, and succeeded in soiling his hand in the stuff. All he could do was wipe his hand on the grass and get the worst off his bag until he reached somewhere where he could wash it.

It wasn't just human waste that was causing a problem. Litter was another. What possessed people to throw their refuse on the ground? Did they not have pockets? Had they not yet comprehended the idea of holding on to their litter until they reached a bin? Discarded food wrappers, socks, shorts, even boots and shoes were scattered along the path. Now, I don't have an exceptional memory, but I'm pretty sure I would realise that I had no boots or shoes on and must have left them behind.

***

I posted the tent and cooking gear at the mail office in Aire sur l'Adour. It felt as though someone had been hanging on to my shirt up until now, weighing me down, and had just let go. I had a new lease of life. I also got into the habit of filling my water bladder only half full in the morning, which made all the difference. If I were to do a similar hike in the future, I would pick and pack my equipment much more judiciously.

The landscape had changed from rolling hills and trees to characterless agricultural monotony. On the flat fields, large crops of maize loomed over me on all sides. There were few hedges or trees, and the pattern was symmetrical, straight lines at right angles. I got lost, had to retrace my steps for a kilometre or two, checked the book, but found it did not conform to what I was seeing before me. In the end it was guesswork. I became frustrated and grouchy, my mood worsening with the sun beating down on me. For most of the day I just walked in the vague direction I thought was right. How I made it to Arzacq Arraziguet I don't know.

To cheer myself up, I booked into the gîte, where the warden took me up a flight of steps to one of the dormitories. She wasn't sure if there was a spare bed or not. A woman and two guys were chatting on the stairs outside.

"Is there a spare bed in here?" the warden asked.

The three looked at each other, waiting for someone to say something. I got the impression they were a single group walking together and didn't want anybody intruding on their space.

"There may be," one of the guys suggested.

"Screw this," I was thinking to myself. "I can do without this at eight in the evening."

"Do you snore?" the woman asked, smiling.

"Yeah, I do," I said. "But only when I sleep on my back. And I fart a lot as well, especially when I have eaten beans, which I may have tonight. How about you?"

There was some giggling and banter and one of the guys assured me that she not only snored but also talked in her sleep.

"Are you American?" I asked her.

"Sure am," she said warily. "Why?"

"Sorry, I didn't mean to sound condescending," I said. "I'm just surprised, that's all. You're the only American I have met on the whole Camino." I held out my hand. "My name is Fozzie."

"Fozzie? What sort of a name is that?" she giggled again.

"Long story," I said. "I prefer it to Keith, my real name."

"Yeah, it's kinda cute. I'm Jeannie."

"Pleasure." I shook her hand. "So, can I stay in here or not?"

"As long as you don't snore or fart."

As it transpired, no one slept at all. Every time one of us even breathed, the springs on the beds reverberated around the whole room. For once, spending most of the night awake was almost worth it for the entertainment Jeannie provided with her sleep talking.

Chapter Eight

In the Company of Jeannie

I had made the decision at the beginning of the trip not to walk with a companion for any length of time. A day? Fine, no problem. I just didn't want company for an extended period. I enjoyed conversation but didn't want to be in a situation where I felt I had to make it all the time, and I liked being in a position where the only plans I needed to make concerned me. So, it was after much deliberation that I asked Jeannie the following morning if she wanted to walk with me that day. She appeared tired of the bickering and backstabbing in the rest of the group, and I thought the experience would do me good. I knew she would probably not be walking as far as I did each day, but I was approaching the stage where I was tired and fed up with cranking out thirty-five-kilometre days. Perhaps, deep down, I knew it would give me the opportunity to take the Camino at a more relaxed pace. I was starting to think that I would rather slow down to my original pace and be late to Greece than continue rushing the walk. I was tired of missing out on the sights.

She agreed. We talked pretty much non-stop for the morning. It was good to talk and walk, to have someone alongside who walked differently to the way I did, and had different methods of dealing with the Camino. For one, she insisted on stopping at every church: not just for a look at the outside, to check out the inside as well. I usually peered inside each one, murmured something like, 'Yeah, very nice,' and sat outside smoking while she carried on.

It's not that I dislike churches, but to me, if you have seen one, you have seen them all. I'm not religious either, so I had no need to go in to each one and feel at one with God. It's like museums: they bore the crap out of me as well. They seem to have an atmosphere of the old school, of rules and regulations. You feel out of place if you raise your voice, and most of the displays are static. I know you couldn't really expect to walk into the Natural History Museum and expect Tyrannosaurus Rex to be getting on down with the Jackson Five but at least some movement would be good. Everything is in cabinets, behind screens, ropes or barriers. That said, I respect people who are interested in museums or indeed churches. So Jeannie's insistence on making a foray into every church worked out pretty well: I would have stopped for a smoke at some point anyway, so we were killing two birds with one stone.

I tried to educate her on the wonders and pleasures of smoking a decent roll-up. She had taken to the bad habit of smoking Gitanes, a French brand of fierce cigarettes without filters. She had been using them because she was ignorant about European brands.

"I only smoke it because it's the nearest I can get to a joint. I don't really even like the stuff," she told me.

"Well, at least smoke a decent brand," I suggested and offered her some of mine. Enlightenment slowly rose up her face when she lit and inhaled. After that my tobacco depleted rapidly.

"You don't have any, do you?" she asked.

"Have any what?"

"Weed."

"No, I don't really like it. Have smoked it in the past, but don't really get a good vibe from it."

"Well, you obviously haven't had any good stuff."

"Well, let me know when you have got some good stuff," I said, "and I'm sure I'll be up for a smoke."

Jeannie was in her mid-forties. Ridiculously long red hair, worn in a plait the thickness of a substantial piece of rope, fell down the middle of her back. She had a habit of pursing her lips as she spoke, and smiled most of the time. I liked her sense of humour. It was crude, to the point and didn't pull any punches. She told it as it was.

She had come from Florida with one of her friends, Valerie, whom I had met the previous evening, and had also started in Le Puy, intending to walk all the way to Santiago. She had left her daughter and boyfriend to look after her house, taken care of what needed to be taken care of, and accepted Valerie's invitation to join her. Things were not going as planned between them. They walked apart most of the time and didn't communicate much. There seemed to be some sort of personality clash.

"What do you do back home?" I asked.

"I'm a painter, an artist. Just starting to make a living out of it. I paint the female torso."

"Just the torso?" I asked.

"Yeah. No arms or legs, and usually with lingerie. It's classed as modern art, and I'm doing well out of it. I've had a few successful exhibitions. I've sold some examples. What do you do?"

"Well, at the moment, nothing. I've done a lot of stuff and never really had a career because I've travelled a lot. My CV is a disaster. Three months here, then travelled. Managed a year here and... travelled. So I go home and usually do temporary jobs. I guess what I like doing, and want to do, is to cook."

The villages were becoming distinctly more Mediterranean in style, with whitewashed walls supporting terracotta roofs that shone against deep blue skies. There were vines winding over porches and frameworks, and the earth was scorched.

I was taking a few photos of the view, when my eyes were drawn up to the top of the camera frame.

"Jeannie! Jeannie!" I cried.

"What's up?"

"Take a look in the viewfinder," I instructed, pointing to the camera.

"Why? What is it?"

"Just look! It's the bloody Pyrenees!" I pointed to the horizon. Just beyond those mountains, I knew, was Spain. It was maybe three days' walk to St-Jean-Pied-de-Port, that busy little town burrowed into the mountains' base, teeming with eager pilgrims ready to get going. It was a marker, a big, bold proof that I had nearly completed half the walk. It couldn't have been more dramatic, unless someone had stuck a sign on top of one of the peaks proclaiming 'Halfway on the Camino, Spain this way'.

* * *

No matter how hard I tried, I couldn't get rid of my dilemma about Greece. I felt I should be pushing out the kilometres, but I was enjoying walking with Jeannie. She walked slower than I did, but that was the attraction. Some days I would say to her that I really needed to do forty kilometres. She would just shrug her shoulders, say "OK," and keep with me for the morning, and then I would lose track of her. That made me sad because I enjoyed her company, and would much rather have stayed with her than keep plugging on. Some days I walked a long distance, kept up a fast pace and left her behind, then waited for her to catch me up by the evening.

I stopped at a picnic table by a river; Jeannie was behind so I ate and rested. I forget where I had purchased it, but I had an absolute cracker of a tomato. It was blood red, juicy and sweet, and together with tuna and a lump of crusty baguette it was a match made in France.

Food was a very important part of the Camino for me. The thought of lunch and dinner provided energy to push me along. I would set myself a goal of lunch in a certain spot or town, and could taste the flavours long before I got there. It provided more than just energy. It was a goal, direction and reward. If I was staying in a place with a bakery, then I would be there at the door in the morning, smelling the flavours wafting out: baguette straight out of the oven, cheese puffs, croissants and doughnuts. I would usually buy a croissant and a pain au chocolat. Couple these with a strong coffee and a cigarette, and I was ready to take on anything.

Lunch would consist of a baguette, stuffed with whatever I had available, maybe cheese with tomato or canned tuna nestling in with some cucumber. Possibly a bag of crisps, some biscuits and an apple or banana would round things off. Then I would find a suitable spot, perhaps some soft grass or propped up at the base of a large tree, and have a short siesta. Well, it would have been rude not to – do as the locals do!

Dinner was the best meal of the day. Sometimes I would treat myself to a meal at a bar or restaurant if I couldn't be bothered to cook. Plenty of establishments would offer cheap meals if pilgrims produced their *créanciale*. The food was of variable standard, but in general pretty good. One thing you realise pretty quickly is that, after a long day's walk, even the worst food tastes great.

When I did cook for myself on the camp stove, I made the effort to produce something I knew well. Sometimes I would crave potatoes, sometimes rice or pasta. It is remarkable what can be produced on one stove. In fact, I sometimes wonder why we have four burners on our conventional cookers at all. It was all a case of balancing two pans and keeping food warm while I cooked something else. At first I thought it would be limiting cooking with one pot and one burner but after a short space of time you become remarkably adept at knocking out decent food quickly.

Having a camp fire was even better as I didn't have to conserve fuel and could have endless hot water. I could cook stuff in the fire, such as jacket potatoes in tin foil. Or I would slice a banana lengthwise, push chunks of dark chocolate in the slit, wrap it in tin foil and place it in the ashes for fifteen minutes. When the foil was peeled off, the chocolate would have melted into the banana flesh, creating a sweet, gooey mush to spoon out. One time I pigged out on roast potatoes with onion, a rare slab of steak, peas and ice cream. OK, so I wasn't carrying a portable camping freezer, and the ice cream was a little runny, but it was still a damn fine meal.

* * *

It was a Thursday morning and I was on a final push to St-Jean-Pied-de-Port. I wanted to get there on Friday evening, and have the Saturday off to relax. That meant walking seventy-five kilometres in two days. I had done a similar distance in that time before, but I was tired of doing it. Jeannie had not kept up that morning, but was aware of my intentions, so we had agreed to meet up later.

It was a strange day. It seemed quieter than usual. I saw no pilgrims the whole time. The weather was cloudy but very hot. Somehow the walk seemed to be in another country, maybe some sort of partial wilderness; it just didn't seem like the Camino I had grown used to. I followed tracks aimlessly, not caring if I was on the designated route or which direction I was taking, and I failed to take note of the *balises*. The only security I had was the sun's position either ahead of me or to the left.

Needless to say, I got lost. My list of gîtes promised me one in Sorhapuru. I was struggling to even find the village, let alone the gîte. In the end, I just took a road that felt right, and after a short walk arrived in a hamlet that was about as likely to host a gîte as it did an internet bar. What I read in the guidebook seemed to bear no relation to what I saw around me. It looked as if it ought to have been in Austria or Bavaria. The residents were wearing strange clothing I had not seen before and they even seemed to be speaking in a different language. I began to imagine that I had entered some kind of time warp. I asked directions from a farmer and his wife. Although we spoke only our native tongues, the man was clearly insisting there was no gîte there, but advised me there was one at Larribar, another two kilometres further on.

How I managed to walk that extra distance I don't know. I stumbled in to Larribar, to find that there was no gîte and nothing but a few houses and a church. I had no extra strength left, not even enough to walk a little further to find a place to camp. I started to look around for possible 'hotels'. I cursed when the door of a shed was locked, but then came to the church, where some women were cleaning the stone floor inside. They looked up and smiled.

My feet were on fire, my legs throbbing, I could feel the blood pulsing around the arteries. I sat down on the church steps and ate the only food I had, a cold can of ratatouille with stale bread. A dog kept creeping closer and closer until she finally let me pet her, bribing her with a piece of bread. The women went off into the night, chatting and chuckling. A car parked and the occupants went into the house opposite, the children grinning shyly at me, the parents waving. The bells chimed softly, almost as if trying not to break the ambience. I laid out my sleeping bag in the shelter of the church porch and stretched out. It took two hours for my feet and legs to finally relax, and I fell asleep. The following day I realised I had walked fifty-two kilometres.

The church bells woke me at seven. I sat up, rubbing my eyes and getting my bearings. It was cold and damp. A thick, deep, eerie mist covered the valley. Nothing moved, and the sun was just poking over the hills, its rays splicing the moisture swirling around me. I yawned and stretched, my ribs cracking. I dressed quickly and then strode off, the only things on my mind being a large coffee and a pain au chocolat. Both were a long way off.

I crossed a bridge above the River Bidouze. The water was clear and fresh and the bottom littered with red and yellow stones. I dropped down to the bank, cupped the water with my hands and splashed it onto my face. Above the damp track, water droplets clung to orange leaves and eventually plummeted down to join small trickles weaving their path around tree roots and stones. The Chapelle de Soyarza was visible at the summit of the next hill, a 210m climb away. Solitary and isolated, it seemed to mock me. As I ascended, the mist covering the valley resembled a cloak of white silk haphazardly left in a pile on the floor, undulating against the knolls and hills. Birds dived and soared on thermals like boats on choppy water, disappearing into the translucent dankness. A dog howled somewhere in a village, and soon a chorus erupted as others joined in.

The summit was quiet. I looked at my watch: it was eight o'clock. Still nothing stirred; I was on my own. Pilgrims were no doubt walking, but they would have slept in gîtes and be far behind me. There was a map carved on a granite plinth depicting the panorama in front of me. The Virgin Mary watched me from the chapel behind, her crisp, white stone contrasting against the dark oak beams around her. A small room next door for visitors would have made a perfect place to rest the previous evening if I had had the strength to make it. I wrote a message to Jeannie in the visitors' book: '21st September. 08:00 am. On the final push to St Jean, will make it today, see you there.'

I was ravenous, not having eaten anything remotely nutritious for twenty-four hours. After ten kilometres I saw Ostbat Asme on a distant hill, but it seemed to take forever to get there. I entered the town as pilgrims in the past had always done, snaking my way along a path riddled with trickles of water, mud and livestock excrement. The lower part of town was where, traditionally, the poorer pilgrims would rest and take shelter. The upper town had higher-grade establishments and was reserved for those with money. In appearance at least, nothing much had changed. I reached a small square, where there was an épicerie also selling fresh baked delicacies. I stocked up on food and sat outside with a coffee and croissant, as cats played with my bootlaces and cows meandered down the street more often than cars.

Now that I had eaten, St-Jean-Pied-de-Port was within striking distance. The terrain started to roll in preparation for the Pyrenees beyond, as if someone had ruffled the landscape like a rug. The mountains, thrusting up from the depths of the earth, loomed a little closer each time I dared look at them. St-Jean-Pied-de-Port played 'catch me if you can' for most of the day. Every time I came to a cluster of houses I thought I was on its outskirts, but I was merely passing through hamlets on the approach to it.

When I did eventually arrive, the change was startling. I passed under the Porte St Jacques and came into a town bursting with Camino energy. There were pilgrims all over the Rue de la Citadelle, spilling out of cafés, talking on corners, walking in their multi-coloured clothes, like a moving border of spring flowers; veterans and novices, those hardened by walking and those who had yet to discover both the trials and the splendours of the Camino. I lapped the whole scene up with relish, beaming contentedly.

I had made it half way.

One of the start points of the Camino, St-Jean-Pied–de-Port, or St-Jean as it's affectionately known, is an attractive town and a wonderful place to rest. Somehow it had managed not to generate that tacky atmosphere that hangs about many tourist towns. Apart from the odd postcard stand outside a shop, there was a noticeable lack of cheap establishments offering out-of-fashion hats, T-shirts and fluffy toys.

The Citadelle overlooked the town, but from most angles was obscured by trees. Traditionally, pilgrims entered the town, as I had done, by the Porte St Jacques, just down the slope supporting the fortifications. The path followed the Rue de la Citadelle, a steep, cobbled street leading down to the lower town. Bridges crossed the River Nive where many a photographer had snapped the reflections of houses rising out of its waters.

I was tired and didn't know where the refuge was so asked directions from a local who obviously misunderstood me and I ended up in a small, cheap hotel. Not wanting to walk back to town I sat on the single bed to test out the comfort factor. It collapsed inward, momentarily trapping me like a sandwich filling with my knees in my mouth. I chose the bottom bed of the bunk instead and was just preparing to inspect the bathroom when an extremely attractive young woman glided in effortlessly.

"You are walking Camino, yes?" she said in English. I always found it amazing how people knew I was English just by my looks. Perhaps it was the Union Jack boxer shorts that gave it away.

"Yes I am." She made motions to sit on the single bed.

"Er, that's not a great bed," I warned. "There's no support."

She tested it by pressing with one hand and screwed up her face in disapproval. Looking at the only other option of the top bunk and seeing my gear on the bottom one, I thought my luck was in when she announced:

"It's OK, I sleep on top of you."

Jeannie found me in the morning aimlessly walking around, taking it all in.

"Hey! When did you get in?" she called from over the road.

"Yesterday, as planned. You?"

"Last night. I got a ride into town!"

Jeannie had discovered the delights of hitchhiking. Using transport of any kind was generally frowned upon by the pilgrim masses, probably rightly; if you did, you could hardly say you had walked the Camino. We had discussed the pros and cons one day. I was determined to complete the whole distance without stepping on a train or bus, accepting a lift or indeed asking for one. Jeannie had a different outlook. She said that if she was tired or stuck somewhere with nowhere to sleep, then she would stick her thumb out. It made no impression on her conscience. I used to back her up when she came in for criticism from others. I guess, when all is said and done, Jeannie still walked a distance most people cannot even begin to comprehend.

"Where're you hanging out?" She crossed over the road to meet me, skipping like a ten-year-old.

"I'm at this gîte a little way out. It's not bad, actually, but I wish I had taken something closer to town. What about you?"

"There's this fantastic place by the Porte St Jacques. There's a lot of people there, and this old woman runs around the kitchen, grabs everyone's food and cooks it for them, whether they want her to or not! It's awesome, you should come take a look, in fact come up at seven, bring some food and wine. We'll eat and get pissed. Oh, and Fozzie," she called after me, "believe it or not, there's an Irish couple there. They're starting to walk tomorrow."

This doesn't exactly sound like world-shattering news. However, at this point, after seven hundred and fifty kilometres, or thereabouts, I had met no English walkers whatsoever and no Irish, Welsh or Scottish. As far as I knew, I was the only guy from Great Britain on the entire Camino. Not that it bothered me, but it would have been nice to catch up with a fellow countryman, check out what was happening back home, take the piss out the French, and so on.

I called Trisha in Greece to get the latest news on the taverna. I didn't know whether to feel sad or happy when she told me it was all off. The owner had apparently changed his mind. I moped around town for a while, walking aimlessly up and down streets, trying to come to grips with it all. Then I realised my Camino would be back to how it was at the start. Once again, I had no schedule; and anyway, something else would materialise in Greece, I was sure. Gradually my good mood was restored.

The gîte Jeannie was staying in was a cracker. It was right on the Rue de la Citadelle. Traditionally built, it fell away on a severe slope, so that you could walk in the entrance at ground level, go down three flights of steps and emerge at street level again. I hardly recognised anyone.

"Fozzie, meet Roberta and Sean," Jeannie announced.

"Hi, I'm Fozzie. How far you planning on going?"

"To Santiago, we hope," Sean said. Roberta just lay on her bunk looking at us. It was all she could do to raise her hand to shake mine when I offered it. I just knew, at that moment, that she wouldn't make it. I doubt whether she even had the inclination to get out of bed. Sean looked more determined and enthusiastic, but they both looked underequipped. Their packs were tiny, and Sean's was more of a duffel bag, made from leather. If it rained, his gear would get soaked.

I squeezed myself in to the basement kitchen with Jeannie. There were about twelve of us in there, including a couple of faces I recognised. They had all brought down their own food to cook but the old woman cordoned off the stove and cooked it all, letting no one else come near. Some found this amusing, as I did, but others scowled. As it turned out, not only was she a damn fine cook, but she knew what everyone had been intending to prepare, and produced it for them. The German guys looked astounded when she plonked a pot of spaghetti bolognese in front of them. Somehow, in all the confusion, Jeannie managed to sneak in and whip up a salad. I don't know how she managed to get past the security, but, knowing Jeannie, she gave as good as she got.

It was one of those meals where everyone shared, where food kept coming from nowhere, and the wine flowed freely. Occasionally, a few of us would open the back door and go outside for a cigarette. The street lamps of St Jean winked back at us from below. People would leave, others would arrive. We ate whatever was going, drank whatever was offered. We laughed, talked, joked, told stories and enjoyed the atmosphere. I remember most of the Camino, but certain situations shine more brightly in my memory. That evening was one of them.

The trek out of St Jean to the Spanish hamlet of Roncesvalles is infamous, at least among pilgrims. A few had already walked it, and were back to do it again. Some had heard of it, a few had read up on the road that winds up to around 1,350m above sea level, but everyone was talking about it. It's by no means a huge elevation, but except for the route up to El Cebreiro in Spain, it is the toughest section of the entire Camino and is to the Camino what Everest is to the Himalayas. Named the Route Napoléon, after the conqueror himself had led his army over it, it takes the traveller over the border into Spain, and for those who start at Le Puy en Velay, as I had, it meant the start not only of the Spanish section but also of the second half of the walk. I was looking forward to it immensely.

The weather, however, was threatening. Most of my stay in St Jean had been interrupted by huge downpours, and although on the big day it wasn't raining, the sky over the pass and surrounding area was black enough to make me cower every time I looked skywards. Jeannie had started earlier than I did, but we had agreed to meet 'somewhere' on the way to Roncesvalles, the first place to stay in Spain.

As I trudged upwards, kicking at the damp leaves, St Jean melted into green, lush fields. The sun had broken through and the road blazed and glistened, making me squint. Ahead, coloured ponchos curled ever up, looking like twinkling Christmas lights. My mental jukebox settled on 'Viva España' as song of the day.

Fourteen years previously, I had driven down from England with a Spanish friend to the north coast of Spain and discovered this wonderful country. Those distant memories needed rekindling. France was beautiful, no question about that, but I was eager to experience a different country, and my appetite for new sights, new traditions and new spectacles was ravenous. I had imagined dusty landscapes and blistered earth. Sitting at bars nursing a Spanish beer and being plied with various tapas. Tomatoes and pimientos drying on rooftops. Smiling Latin woman with black hair. Olive trees and old, rustic villages.

I walked without stopping to the half-way point of the pass, the Vierge d'Orisson. A small statue of the Virgin Mary stood by the side of the road and it was there that I looked over and saw Jeannie, who waved. She had taken the opportunity to rest with Sean, Roberta, a Korean girl called Yoko and a Spanish guy called Antonio. We were joined by a French Canadian woman called Pascal. We sat on the damp grass taking in the view and munching on snacks. Hills and peaks rollercoastered before us. The high of the previous evening still lingered, and everyone seemed happy and relaxed. The steady procession of walkers crept past us towards the summit, where the way toppled down again.

The Journey in Between

At half past two in the afternoon, we rounded a corner and saw the border crossing. I don't know what I was expecting really. In the Europe of my younger days, border crossings were places that were stringently policed and held in wary respect. Unable to shake off that image, I imagined a Spanish border guard who sported a huge, black moustache and had a cigarette dangling on his lower lip. His feet would be propped up on a chair, his arms folded over a bulbous stomach, snoring with the odd grunt as he shifted his position, just like in the movies. The reality was quite different: just a cattle grid and gate. I admit to having been a little disappointed. I half wanted to be asked to step to one side while they went through my bag and looked at me suspiciously. I wanted that overweight security guard to scan the pages of my passport and ask me ridiculous questions, questions so irrelevant and useless that they could be asked only at those forbidding border crossings of the eighties. I demanded hassle. I wanted those memories rekindled.

While waiting for the others to come, I took photos of Pascal, then Antonio, Sean and Roberta, with Yoko and Jeannie bringing up the rear. We told silly frontier jokes. Someone ran over the cattle grid and back several times, shouting, "Should I stay or should I go?" and we all rolled about giggling.

We continued up to the summit. As we separated out again, finding our own pace, we entered the clouds that had been threatening all day and I donned my waterproofs. Through the clouds that occasionally broke up at the top, I glimpsed the rooftops of the monastery at Roncesvalles, set among trees below me. We all walked down together, the drizzle clearing as we came out of the clouds once more. Steaming hoods and ponchos were removed, jackets peeled off.

Some local people were searching for fungi among the grasses on the slopes around us, occasionally bending over, pointing and gesticulating, beckoning others over for verification, and filling up their wooden baskets with edibles.

As we arrived alongside the monastery, a woman opened one of the countless windows and beckoned us down a shortcut to the rear. This was to be our first refugio. More common in Spain than the gîtes were in France, they were a whole new experience and proved to be good and bad, some so comfortable that they were like hotels, others just grubby, dilapidated buildings. Some wardens were helpful and friendly, others would have done an admirable job in charge of a prison.

The monastery was certainly an impressive baptism. It was Augustinian, founded in the early twelfth century and was huge; even the hospital building, which housed pilgrims, was a maze of rooms and corridors. We didn't know where to bed down or whom to see. In the end we dumped our packs in an empty room with a few bunk beds scattered around and Jeannie found the office where we were required to sign in.

At the end of a long, cold stone office stood a desk, dwarfed by the size of the room, and seemingly an endless distance away from the door. A woman perched behind it and a gentleman stood by her shoulder with an air of authority. We produced our pilgrims' passports, which she duly stamped, and then logged our details in a huge, leather-bound book that appeared older than the monastery. When we had made our donation, the man instructed us to collect our bags and follow him. No one dared argue.

He led us down steps and through passageways to a smaller room, already crammed with damp pilgrims and I grabbed the first available bottom bunk. He spewed out a list of regulations in Spanish, and then broken English. There was no food available except in the small restaurant across the square. We must respect the values of the monastery; everyone must be in bed by 22:00 and leave by 08:00 in the morning.

I was still not sleeping well, but the later I stayed up, the more tired I became, and the more chance I had of beating my insomnia. I was not looking forward to the restless night that was bound to follow an early bedtime. As he left the room, some people stood up and saluted, some bowed. At first we looked at each other in silence, taking it all in. The shock dissipated after a few minutes when someone giggled, and soon we were all laughing and joking at being incarcerated.

Curfews and strict rules, we were to discover, were commonplace at the refugios. In some places we felt as if we were literally being locked up. In others the regime was a lot more relaxed. However, refugios were a godsend, whichever way you looked at them, regardless of our complaints. Providing the rudimentary basics for the pilgrim, they were perfect: a roof over your head, occasionally somewhere to cook, sometimes a hot meal, showers, a haven to be with others and all in return for a mere donation. I would not have been without them for a second and I take my hat off to the people who give up their time to become volunteers there.

Some of us went over to the restaurant to eat. I propped up the bar for most of the evening with Christian, a cyclist. We downed San Miguels with gusto, savouring the new taste. Pilgrims mixed with local people. There was a permanent smoke haze, glasses clinked, espresso machines gurgled and spluttered, laughs burst out and the odd cheer erupted as the local football team scored on the TV. I was already being drawn in to the Spanish way, and I was loving every second of it.

Over the next few days, I spent a lot of time getting to know new faces and characters. Sean and Roberta were an interesting young couple and a constant source of amusement, annoyance and bewilderment. When I had first met them in the refuge in St-Jean-Pied-de-Port, Sean's face shone with an eager look that I have seen before in people who realise that some long-held dream has suddenly come to fruition. Disregarding the fact that he was due to return to Ireland to continue his studies, he often seemed to be straining at the leash. Roberta had apparently just come along for the ride, because her boyfriend was doing it, and most of the time she was the one pulling back on that leash. They were constantly bickering, even on day one, and it wasn't uncommon to round a corner and find Sean being beaten around the head by Roberta's walking stick, sometimes supplemented by a few punches.

Roberta was incredibly immature, and Sean, for some reason that escaped me, doted on her, which she milked mercilessly. He would run around doing her favours, bringing her food and drink, every time she waved her hand. What he saw in her I don't know. She was attractive, there was no denying, but she must have received a privileged upbringing, or perhaps being lazy was second nature, for she was used to getting what she wanted. Their relationship very nearly came to an abrupt end on day two, after a massive argument and several blows of the walking stick. By evening she had him doing her bidding like a servant.

I had no time for Roberta but I liked Sean. He had a free spirit, which I could imagine him nurturing over the coming years by travelling the world, seeking experiences and answers. He was extremely intelligent and amusing, and had a genuine desire to become a writer. He was the only person I met on the Camino, apart from me, who carried a dictaphone to make notes. One day, when we were alone, he told me he planned to write a book and wanted to ask me a favour.

"Really?" I said. "I want to write a book too. What's yours going to be about?"

"Well, it's going to follow the format of *The Canterbury Tales*. I want some short stories from walkers on the Camino. They don't have to be true. They can be experiences, dreams, hopes, anything. They don't even have to be about the Camino."

"Sounds like a great idea," I said. "So, I'm assuming the favour is you're gonna ask me to contribute. I'm very flattered."

"No, I wanted to bum a smoke." We both laughed. "Yeah. I would like you to give me one of the tales. All I need is for you to borrow my dictaphone one day, and just talk into it. Around fifteen minutes should be fine."

Yoko, the Korean girl, found her own pace and obviously preferred to walk on her own. I took a liking to Pascal; in fact, I had a bit of a crush on her. She was way too tall, her wavy hair was tied back in a bob, and she always seemed to look great despite, like the rest of us, oozing sweat and being flecked with dust for most of the day. When we joked about and flirted, she would giggle and screw her face up, her eyes reducing to narrow slits as she playfully hit me. I found her French Canadian accent romantic, and I admit to being a little disappointed when she eventually explained she had a boyfriend, and, worse still, he was coming out to walk with her.

Antonios was a battler. He was Spanish, short and built like a tank. He reminded me of a Rottweiler, someone you wouldn't want to get into a fight with. He was obviously struggling with the walk, but whenever I saw him or walked with him, he had such an air of determination I never once doubted that he would succeed. He was usually behind most of us, and he stopped often, but would emerge at the end of the day, sweating, panting and red in the face, but with a cheeky look reflecting pride in his achievement.

This eclectic collection of people formed itself loosely into a group. We would usually start the day together and then drift apart to walk alone or with a companion, taking rests with or without the others. No one asked if they could walk with us, and no one assumed we were even a group, but you knew each day that you could round a corner and either be confronted with an Irish guy being beaten up by his girlfriend, a sweaty Rottweiler, a Korean drifting along in her own world, a cute girl scrunching her features up or a mad American woman.

Pamplona was the largest settlement I had encountered so far on the Camino, and the experience of being thrust into a large metropolis caught me unawares. It is home to the tradition of the running of the bulls during the first two weeks of July, when hundreds of young Spanish men, with a few tourists, run for their lives through Pamplona's streets while being pursued by a herd of bulls. Unfortunately it was a spectacle I had missed.

I entered the suburbs with Jeannie. For an hour or so we made our way through the uninspiring outskirts interwoven with quieter, countrified lanes, between nondescript old and modern buildings, failing to discover any real sense of identity in this place, reputed for its beauty and culture. As we crossed the River Arga over the Puente de los Peregrinos, the tall, grey buildings gave way to the old town. The change was instantaneous. We gawped up at the inner set of ramparts towering above us, crossed over the drawbridge on Calle del Carmen, the wooden planks thudding and bouncing under our boots, and wound our way through to the true centre. I am not a fan of cities but I immediately fell in love with Pamplona, and if I had to live in one, this would be top of the list.

Grand stone buildings hemmed in wide, pedestrianised streets, full of people bustling about without any sense of urgency. Most were impeccably dressed, the women in autumn fashions, designer sunglasses and long, sepia-toned coats. Tapas bars abounded, along with a thousand pavement cafés serving good coffee. There were laundries (a rarity in France), several internet establishments and even a condom shop! For me, though, a country boy at heart, it was heaven.

Somehow we managed to find the refugio, which was situated on the first floor of a tall building. As we climbed what seemed like an endless flight of steps, I had the feeling I wasn't going to like it.

A squat, grim and severe-looking man sat behind a desk, flanked by an older woman peering over the top of half-framed glasses. Having booked us in, he told us we should be back at the refugio by 21:30, lights out was at 22:00 and we had to leave by 08:00. I was furious. I walked off before they got the full brunt of my frustration, and avoided the others, to give myself time to calm down.

"Fozzie, whoa! You look pissed! What's up?" Sean said.

I let it all out. I think he was sorry he asked.

"It's these fucking refugios. They're driving me insane!" I spat. "In bed by such and such a time, leave by this time, don't do this, don't do that! What is it with the bloody Spanish that makes them think pilgrims must suffer? Why do we have to learn to accept hardship, just to be 'true' pilgrims! It's all bullshit!"

He looked at me in silence.

"All I want to do," I continued, "is to be able to go out once in a while, just once, and have a few drinks with my friends, or have a leisurely meal with good conversation and not have to worry about getting back to a refugio by half past bloody nine. I feel like I'm seven years old!" I looked at Jeannie. "If you wanna share a hotel tomorrow night then I'll go halves with you. In fact, I'll bloody pay for it! How's that?"

She grinned, and said, "Sure," which is probably all she wanted to risk saying.

"I'm going to have a shower, put on some clean clothes, and then I'm going out to get pissed – you know, not drunk – really, really trolleyed. You're welcome to join me."

"Sure," she said with another grin.

Sean had retreated to the security of his bunk, as half of the dormitory looked at me as if I had lost it. I sheepishly averted my gaze and began sorting out some gear.

By the time I had showered and left Colditz I had calmed down a little. The streets were just starting to fill up with people looking for food, fluid and fun. We checked out a couple of places and decided on a tapas bar with some cheap, tasty-looking offerings. Two American guys whom Jeannie knew joined us at the table, and we all started laying into the whisky. My worries melted away amid a blurred fusion of scotch, animated conversation, laughter and good food. Pretty soon we were a raucous bunch of drunken idiots. Everyone was slurring, laughing uncontrollably, walking sideways to the bar and trying to focus on anything that was relatively stationary and offered a secure bearing. We wolfed down octopus, chips, tortilla, salads and various other delicious dishes before grudgingly heading back just before 22:00.

The others went to bed. I tried to sober up a little, and retreated to the kitchen where I hoped the warden wouldn't check for stragglers. At 21:55 (I know this because I looked at the clock on the wall), the warden opened the door, looked at me, held out his watch and tapped the face. "Doce minutes," he said. "Si," I muttered, returning to my book.

A few minutes later Jeannie and the two Americans came in. They couldn't sleep, they said, and we started to joke around, though trying to keep quiet. We could hardly have known what deep trouble we were in. The door flew open and there stood the squat warden, shaking with rage, legs apart, clearly trying his utmost to look threatening. One hand gripped a cordless phone as if he were trying to throttle it, while the other forced the door back. He made us all jump and his threatening behaviour could have been taken quite seriously had he not been wearing pink-striped pyjamas. I couldn't decide whether we were in a horror movie or a comedy.

"Usted vallase a dormir o si no llamare a la policia!" he screamed. We all looked at each other. No translation was needed: the phone in his hand and the words 'policia' and 'dormir' told us all we needed to know.

"He's going call the police?" I asked, gobsmacked.

"Actually," said one of the Americans, "I'm not sure of the exact translation, but basically he says that if we don't go to sleep, he will call the police." We were all desperately trying to stifle giggles, hands clasped over mouths, avoiding eye contact in case it set one of us off.

"What's he going do?" I said. "Arrest us for not sleeping?"

That was the spark for the flame. Jeannie drunkenly collapsed on the table, giggling so uncontrollably that she looked as though she was having involuntary spasms. The two Americans rocked back on their chairs in hysterics, holding their stomachs.

"Usted vallase a dormir o si no llamare a policia!" he screamed again, brandishing the phone like a dagger. Jeannie and the other two ran out laughing and went to bed. For some reason he seemed to forget about me, and by some miracle I stayed in there for another hour or so, reading. I deeply hoped he would come back in, as I would have loved to make him call the police, just for the hell of it. He never came back – nor did the police show up.

When I did eventually climb up to my bunk, the snoring in the room had reached epidemic proportions. I lay there for what seemed like an eternity, staring at the ceiling and following lines of cracks. I turned to my right so I could see one of the offenders, separated from me by an aisle. I crept out of bed and retrieved my trekking pole, then returned to my bunk, extended it to full length, gingerly maneuvered it to above the guy's leg and smacked him just above the knees. He gurgled a little, twitched his nose and swung his palm in front of his face as if swatting a fly. He stopped snoring for a few seconds, gurgled some more and fired up again. I must have hit him five or six times, with more frustration in each blow. Another pilgrim was observing and chuckling at my antics. I decided a new approach was called for. Again I steered the pole over towards him, but this time I positioned the end directly over his nose, made delicate contact and pushed down. He snorted, grumbled, turned over while muttering something about carrots and stopped snoring. Amazingly, at that precise moment, the pilgrim below stopped also. The guy who was watching mimed a round of applause and, shortly after, about forty-two pilgrims managed to get some shut-eye.

All we heard of the warden in the morning was the dormitory door being opened, the light clicking on and the door being closed again. It was 06:45.

Jeannie and I gingerly emerged on to the streets of a city still immersed in darkness. As I squinted around for an illuminated café, Jeannie grabbed my arm and pulled me in the opposite direction, pointing to the faint glow of a pastry and coffee shop. As we drank and munched, we laughed at the previous night's events.

It was time for a rest day and, having no schedule, I was free to explore this fantastic city and do all kinds of things I hadn't been able to do on this walk so far: sleep in a decent bed, with crisply laundered linen, experience the wonders of tapas bars, drink red wine, sample a good Spanish café au lait, eat sweet pastries, amble around and check out the shops, buy something I didn't need just for the sake of it, take some photos and generally indulge myself.

When the daylight became reasonable we headed off to what looked like a promising hotel that the tourist office had inked on a map for us. As we walked past a bar, our two American friends called to us and we joined them for more coffee and laughter. They were off to hike around the Picos de Europa, a range of mountains to the north, and we shook hands and wished them well. We also bumped into Monica, a Swiss pilgrim, who led us to the fantastic hotel she had found. Before long we had checked in and were making full use of our newfound freedom, strewing gear randomly around the room just for the hell of it. We watched some TV, and I dived into a hot bath. It was total luxury.

Smelling of hotel soap, we forayed out again into Pamplona. We pigged out on croissants and omelette wedged into a warm baguette. Sitting on chairs on the pavement, we sipped coffees, and I gave in to the temptation of reading a newspaper, looking up every now and then to watch the world walk past. It was nearly October but the sky was blue and I lapped up the heat, wearing just shorts and a shirt. Having finished breakfast and brunch, we moved rapidly into lunch, which included red wine and portions of the tastiest-looking offerings I had yet seen. Glass cabinets lined the bars, filled to breaking point. I didn't even have to speak Spanish. I would just catch the barman's eye, point to a dish and nod. Bowls of octopus salad squeezed up against small slices of bread decorated with all manner of toppings. Huge, dried hams hung from the ceiling. I had died and gone to food and drink heaven.

I even managed to grab a good night's sleep. A firm mattress, soft sheets, a gentle breeze, the hum of the street below and a few glasses of Rioja had me slumbering like a baby. I was out for eleven hours straight. The following morning we left late and in no hurry, satisfied but with a heavy heart at leaving Pamplona.

The landscape was quite different from the greens of France. The wind caught dust and sent it spiralling up from the trail in mini whirlwinds. We passed through small, quiet hamlets, their sand-coloured buildings looking as though they had been hewn from the very earth itself. But for a few tumbleweeds blowing around and a sleeping bandit hidden under a sombrero, we could have been in a Mexican movie scene.

The climb up the Monte del Perdon loomed ahead, dotted with a line of some forty white, glistening windmills. At the top, so the story goes, Satan accosted a pilgrim, who promised to show the thirsty man a hidden fountain, but only if he renounced god, the Virgin Mary and St James. The pilgrim refused. St James himself then appeared as a pilgrim and led the man to the fountain, much to the disgust of the devil.

The view from the summit was stunning, and I was to encounter similar views many times in Spain. From here we could see the way spread out before us, like a three-dimensional map, the Camino linking three villages: Uterga, Muruzabal and Obanos, like a piece of string.

It was then that I saw a pilgrim I had noticed earlier when she passed me having lunch. She was tall, with curves in all the right places, and seemed to glide along effortlessly. Her long, ebony hair hung down her back as though it was wet. She was, quite frankly, beautiful. As I looked up, I smiled. She had smiled back.

"Jeannie, I'll stop in Uterga for you!" I called through the wind.

"What are you doing?" she called back. I nodded towards the pilgrim who had just passed, winked and smiled. Jeannie understood and winked back, calling "Good luck," she cried.

It took me two kilometres to catch up with her. I figured her long legs were giving her an unfair advantage. As I finally pulled alongside her, she smiled again, almost as if she was expecting me.

"What is the problem with your leg?" I asked. She was

wincing with each step. She spoke little English, but somehow we managed to string a conversation together. It was an old injury that had sprung up again, and, as with many walkers, it centred on the knee. I got the impression it was something to do with a past skiing trip. To be honest, I wasn't too concerned: I was just glad to be talking to her. She told me her name was Tamar.

We talked for fifteen minutes or so until we arrived at Uterga. It was deathly quiet, an elderly couple sitting outside their house offering the only signs of life. The woman gave me a toothless grin. Her husband sat in a wheelchair next to her. Tamar told me that there was a refugio in the village somewhere, but it was not marked in any of the guidebooks. She decided to walk on to the next town, and as she strode off, I stood there, eyes wide, looking like a puppy that had mislaid its bone.

Jeannie arrived shortly after.

"Any luck?" she said, smiling and winking again.

"I'm working on it. Tamar was saying there's a refugio here somewhere, it's not in any of the books, some sort of a mysterious, local secret."

I was in one of those moods where I couldn't be bothered to apply even a modicum of effort to anything. Jeannie soon noticed and kindly offered to do some groundwork.

"Sorry," I offered, "Just want to sit down. Just feeling like a lazy bastard."

Jeannie went about the task with gusto and walked up to the old couple near us. After a few bits of murmured conversation, she called to me while triumphantly motioning towards a building. "It's in here!"

"What?" I questioned.

"This woman looks after it! We were sitting looking at it!"

It seemed a doctor had reserved one room in his building for pilgrims. It had one bunk bed and a shower room. I couldn't believe it.

"I wonder why she didn't say anything?" I said.

"Perhaps she just thought we were resting before carrying on," Jeannie said.

I came across similar scenarios a few times in Spain. The guidebook might say there was a shop in a particular village, but then in brackets note, "It is unmarked. Ask for it." These secret shops, bars and refugios were everywhere, but were kept quiet. I never did figure out why. Normally, if you are running a business, you want to advertise it. But I guess that if you live on the Camino and have a few thousand foreigners walking past every summer, asking stupid questions in strange languages, you might just want to keep what you have to yourself.

Chapter Nine

Roasting Peppers

The further I walked into Spain the more it affected me. Except for a package holiday to Salou one year, I had affectionate memories of this country. Now, though, I felt I was out there in the thick of it. I saw fields still being ploughed by man and horse. Onions were hung out to dry. People still roasted all their peppers, peeled the skin off, and preserved them for the winter. They ate what was grown in the back yard. Supermarkets hadn't really made their mark out in the countryside, where there was no real need for them. I saw old women making cheeses by hand, pleased to let me taste when I asked. Families would want to make conversation when I went over to them. They would give me a bunch of grapes that had literally just been pulled off the vine. They would offer me a slug from the bottle of wine they had, and tempt me with meat crackling over a lunchtime fire. All I had to do was cast envious eyes at picnickers' food and they would obligingly call me over.

On the approach to Ciraqui the rain I had been avoiding for so long caught me up. For three hours Jeannie and I walked along tracks transformed into torrents of water and mud. The elements pounded us relentlessly. Strangely, I was enjoying it. First, it was a new experience, one I had not encountered often on the Camino and, as much as I normally hated rain, I realised that I had sorely missed it. Second, the waterproofs were doing me proud. After I had cocooned myself in, the feeling that I was dry, and would remain that way despite the efforts of Mother Nature, gave me a feeling of security. Jeannie was faring a little worse.

She had no pack cover and tried unsuccessfully to strap a space blanket over the whole thing as it wriggled and writhed in the gusts.

We found shelter in a pedestrian tunnel under the road, and sat there reading messages on the walls left by pilgrims stretching back years. We kidded ourselves that we were drying off, and smoked a couple of cigarettes. We splashed on to Ciraqui, which offered nothing in the way of overnight shelter; even the church was locked.

Under dark clouds we trudged on for another seven kilometres, skirting around freshly ploughed fields, making slow headway as thick, red mud clung in huge lumps to the tread of our boots. It felt like autumn. Lorca loomed above us like a garrison perched on an impregnable hill, and I felt I was a medieval soldier planning the best line of attack. We pushed up to the top, through stone streets glinting in the evening sun. The air was ripe with the sweet smell of peppers and charcoal, and we passed people with sooty hands peeling off the pepper skins next to orange and red embers that glowed and faded with the fluctuating breezes.

Two men were working on a car.

"Ola!" I called. "Donde esta el refugio?"

Jeannie did her best to translate as the younger man explained that there was nowhere to stay in the town.

"Shit, Fozzie! I dunno if I can go any further! I'm finished!" She dropped her head and let her eyes roll up at me like a child who had been caught doing wrong.

"OK, I don't need the puppy-eyed routine," I said. "I owe you one for the other day anyway, so I will secure lodgings!"

Again the church was shut; in fact, everything seemed firmly fastened as if another storm was expected. The village had an air of abandonment and decay about it, as if the residents had moved on and let it rot. The occasional drip from a gutter would slap the top of my head and send a trickle down my neck that made me shiver. To my surprise, I noted that the guidebook mentioned 'Rooms'. I walked back to the mechanic.

"Habitaciones?" I said.

"Si." He pointed across the street about twenty metres to a little house. Jeannie and I looked at each other and then at him, with palms up and raised eyebrows.

"Why didn't he tell us that when we asked him?" I wondered.

She shrugged her shoulders and gave me a cheeky grin, as though she were the same kid who had just been given some sweets.

When I knocked at the door, a kind-looking woman appeared. She took one look at our sopping hair and red faces, held her hands up in pity and manhandled us both into the front room. It was like a little Swiss chalet inside, with wooden beams and walls of carved, dark wood. We took our damp gear to the loft, where she showed us lines to dry it on. We delicately stepped around huge piles of nuts being stored on the floor. The bedroom was like something out of Moulin Rouge: vibrant red and gold wall coverings reflected in glass-covered tables, and an elaborate chandelier reflecting the last of the sun's rays around the room.

After a bath, I wandered back out onto the streets, zipping my fleece tighter around my chin and trying without much success to stretch it over my ears, stomping my feet and watching my breath rise out of sight. The mechanics had given up for the day, the last sign that anyone actually still lived there. Nightfall shrouded my surroundings in blacks, greys and whites. Menacing clouds parted like theatre curtains to reveal a blazing moon, sending streaks of silver racing through the streets. The whole scene looked like the set for the opening sequence of a fifties horror movie.

"Buenas noches." A man startled me. He walked past me, washed his hands in the central fountain and emptied black-coloured water from a huge saucepan, then he refilled it.

"Pimientas?" I enquired, the only piece of Spanish I could muster. I assumed the dirty water was from the burnt skins of the peppers.

"Si," he replied. I pointed to my eyes and then to my mouth, suggesting I would like to see him work.

"Si," he said again, smiling, and gently took my arm. He led me to a garage door and pushed it open. An older man, perhaps eighty, and two kids of about fourteen looked up at me and smiled. They beckoned me to sit on the floor. For half an hour I watched as they carefully arranged their pickings from the summer and prepared them for preservation over the winter. In one corner was an oil drum cut in half, with a grid resting over it. Halves of the red peppers were sweating, spitting and blistering as they finally surrendered to the heat. One of the boys would occasionally fetch them and put them in the large pan of water the man had collected, and restock the cooker with a new batch. The other boy and the two men sat on old beer crates, pulling out the pepper halves and removing the skin in several peels, occasionally dipping the piece back in the water to rinse off the burnt flakes. The liquid took on a dark hue, with black pieces of skin floating on the surface like dirty oil. Lastly, the old man would take the now juicy, bright-red pieces of flesh and bottle them with a preservative of olive oil. Once in a while, they passed me a piece to taste. With the slightest suggestion of a bite, the piece would disintegrate and the flavour burst out. They ate pieces themselves, rolling their eyes upwards and grinning to display their enjoyment.

* * *

The following morning I felt the need to be alone. Jeannie, always understanding, walked with me for a short way and then let me go. I walked through Estella and bumped into Tamar stuffing food from a petrol station into her pack. I asked her how her knee was getting on, and she said it seemed to be making progress. We casually agreed that we might see each other in Los Arcos, my destination for the day.

The afternoon walk between Azqueta and Los Arcos was like being on another planet. For three hours I trod smooth, gravelled tracks. I did not need to concentrate on the surface, so let my eyes wander around at the surroundings. Every once in a while the scenery would change dramatically. In the morning I had walked through damp, green woods and lush grass; now, I was passing through a shallow valley, dry and desolate, with small hills curving up either side of me like a cupped hand. Occasionally a ruined stone building would come into view on the hills as the trees parted. I could see for miles, and still make out the worn surface of the Camino, beige against the ochre soil, coiling away to the distant hill. I wrote my name in the soil with my trekking pole, as I had been doing through most of Spain. Other pilgrims often said they liked to see a familiar name etched in the ground.

Los Arcos seemed like an eternity away. The scenery, bare for miles around, offered no clues until the last minute, when, cresting a hill, the town appeared just a kilometre away. It caught me completely by surprise, as I thought I had more walking to get there. Its premature arrival put a smile on my face. As I entered the town, I heard Pascal's familiar laugh from a shop doorway. I peered in and poked her in the back.

"Fozzie! Where you been?" she said, swinging round to see me.

"Walking... slowly. Did you find the refugio yet?"

"Oui, come, we show you."

It was a modern building on the outskirts and, like many, right on the Camino and hence teeming with pilgrims. It caught me unawares. I had experienced a thoughtful and serene day, I was relaxed and to suddenly be thrown into the hubbub put me on edge. I had to squeeze past people to sign in, squeeze up the stairs and squeeze through the dormitory. I wondered where they had all come from; the Camino had been quiet for a few days and now it seemed as though a coach load of new pilgrims had emptied out. My checking-in time was perfect, as they had just opened a new room, and as I was the last to check in it remained mine for the night, with a door to screen off the snorers.

I had agreed to cook a meal for Monica, who had kindly shared half the shopping bill in return. As I cooked, Tamar and some others seemed to be watching. I was hungry and needed to relax, the ideal environment for me to cook in, and soon the wine began to soothe me. I prepared kedgeree, a rice dish with fish, eggs, onion and curry powder. I tossed sliced potatoes in butter and rosemary, flecked with black pepper. A small salad completed the meal.

Meanwhile, Tamar, who, when I had first met her, had seemed a loner, quiet and reserved, was eating watermelon with parma ham and suggestively kept feeding me pieces. She seemed carefree, happy, as if some problem had been resolved, and could scarcely string a sentence together for giggling. Whenever our eyes met, we would hold each other's gaze for a few seconds, and then laugh. I had a funny feeling in the pit of my stomach, the sort where you are excited about something, enjoying the anticipation. I realised I was seriously smitten.

* * *

There were few things about the Camino that annoyed me – the wardens and rules in some of the refugios, inability to find a meal when everyone was having a siesta – mundane things that I had to learn to deal with. Snoring, on the other hand, was really starting to get to me. Having had ample opportunity to study the practice I decided an in-depth analysis was in order.

There was a definite pattern emerging, and amongst the dormitory carnage in the middle of a night – some snored like their lives depended on it – I began to figure out that there were, essentially, only four types of snorers.

The most common type is the *back snorer*, a person who snores whilst lying on their back. Some people believe, falsely, that this is the only position that people snore in.

Slightly less common is the *side snorer*, and obviously is someone who snores whilst sleeping on their side.

The *front snorer* is a difficult one to spot, often because their noise is muffled but they are not uncommon. Occasionally responsible for other innocent sleepers being accused of snoring.

Finally, and a rare breed, is the *all-position snorer*. Accomplished in the art of sleeping and snoring in any position and for extended periods, and is to be avoided at all costs if possible.

Unfortunately, there is little one can do to stop a snorer. The only remedy is earplugs, which were a common sight in the refugios. I never bothered getting any, and suffered as a result.

You can try the aggressive approach, which worked for me a couple of times. A carefully aimed, quick and precise swing of a pillow to somewhere around the head area may result in a temporary respite. To avoid being discovered, lean over, aim, swing, make contact and immediately feign sleep. Trekking poles are useful, as I have already explained, and more precise. One remarkable method, which I did not employ, but saw used on one occasion, was highly successful. After I had tried the pillow method unsuccessfully and several pilgrims had even thrown objects at the offender, two pilgrims got up, came over, politely shook the guy awake, turned on his torch, apologised for waking him and explained he was snoring, keeping the whole dormitory awake. They finished off by apologising again, and requesting he sleep on his stomach to reduce any possible risk. It worked – but because he was, luckily for us, only a back snorer.

Still worse were the rare occasions when several snorers were going at it in harmony, a category I didn't mention above known as *orchestral snoring*. One culprit snored as they exhaled while another filled in the quiet spaces with his own variation on the theme.

The last resort, if faced with snoring situations, is to pick up your mattress and bedding and get the hell out of it. Many a morning I would wake up in reception area or in the common room and then realise why. Of course nobody wants to up sticks in the middle of the night but it is pretty much the only wholly reliable method to beat the snorers.

* * *

I had lost contact with Jeannie. She had not arrived in Los Arcos the night before. It wasn't a big deal: we had not bound ourselves to being at any place at a certain time, nor were we walking companions. By this stage, we walked together often but never felt obliged to. I knew I would see her before the Camino ended.

I set off that day with Monica, who kindly asked if she could walk with me as opposed to presuming that it would be all right. We found a great café in Torres del Rio and tucked in to bacon and eggs, endless coffees and orange juice; not exactly authentic local cuisine but it hit the spot.

For the rest of the day I walked occasionally with Monica, sometimes with Tamar and also with an Australian girl called Fiona, although she preferred everyone to use her surname of Breeder. I was scared to ask her why!

I stopped in vineyards taking photos of local people. Often I would be invited to sit among the grapes with them and share their lunch of steak cooked over an open fire, washed down with wine. They were a joy to be with, for they were always laughing and joking around. The route dipped and dived into mini canyons ranging in depth. Cracks appeared on the soil crust like crazy paving and olive trees appeared, back from the trail, their silver leaves shyly peering over shrubs and small trees.

By this stage of the Camino I was completely at ease and at one with the walk. My rush to get to Greece had been cancelled so I had all the time in the world. I had blended in with a great group of perhaps thirty or so friends with whom I was sharing and enjoying the experience. No one in this informal group had a particular companion. Some days I would be alone, some days I would be with one pilgrim, other days I would walk with five others. Some evenings there may be a couple of familiar faces dotted around a refuge and other days I would go to a local bar for a beer and end up laughing and shouting with fifteen others who had made the same plan. By this time, walking had become a way of life for us. We were nonchalant about it, feeling that whatever was thrown at us we could take in our stride. We got up each morning and did what came naturally, walk. The strange part was that we never thought of the end – finishing was a thought we didn't entertain. Our life was here, now, doing what we loved. It was as though we had accepted that it was our destiny to be on the Camino for the rest of our lives.

It was now October. The sun was still out every day, and the temperature hovered around twenty degrees. A pollution cloud hung low in the skies over the city of Logrono as I made my way down the quiet track that would eventually merge into busy streets and roads. I stopped by an old lady at the side of the road and bought a scallop shell, the symbol of the Camino, which she tied on to my pack so I didn't need to take it off. I left a message in her book, scanning the pages to see who was ahead of me. Breeder had passed the day before, and I recognised the shooting star symbol that Val, Jeannie's friend, had left. I regularly saw it on the Camino as well. Although they had parted, she was still leaving her sign for Jeannie.

The refugio was not open until three thirty, so I had a cappuccino at a bar, whose owner kindly agreed to let me leave my bag there so I could go and explore the town freely. I found the tourist information office and subsequently the internet café, where Tamar's shining deep black hair caught my eye and I gave her head a playful tickle as I walked past. As I glanced back, her eyes peeked over the top of the monitor and I could tell she was smiling. It was all I could do to concentrate on fiddling with my keyboard. When she had finished, she walked over and said she would wait for me outside so we could go and get a drink somewhere. I completed the rest of my emails in around half a minute.

We sat under a covered walkway with people milling about and waiters trying to dart through the cross traffic. Her English was better than I had originally thought and with a little imagination we got by pretty well. She even read my palm, told me that the back pain I occasionally suffered was due to worrying about money too much, and told me to give up smoking. Whether there was any truth in what she said I didn't know, but it didn't seem to matter. I was surprised to learn that she was married, with a young daughter. I don't know why I was surprised – I just didn't picture her with a husband or a child – or perhaps it was truer to say I had hoped she didn't have a family. My spirits lifted a bit when she said she was getting divorced. She seemed to be plying me with all this information to test the water and see how I would respond. I don't know or much care how she interpreted my reaction. I had become infatuated with her. She walked back with me to the centre of town.

"Fozzie, do you want to walk with me?" she asked.

"I can't," I said. "I'd love to and I will – soon – but today I have walked all I planned to and now I need to rest. I hope you understand."

We hugged, and as she walked off out of Logrono, leaving me in the middle of the city, I wondered what it would be like to kiss her. I tried to figure out why I had refused her offer and rapidly came to the conclusion that I was a complete bloody idiot.

* * *

Some roads on the Camino entail taking your life into your own hands. The French appear to have taken this problem seriously. Most of the roads I walked on in France were quiet, country back roads with little or no traffic. Although the Spanish were aware of the problem and were taking measures, some sections were appalling.

I had just left Navarette and was forced to walk on the road. This, unfortunately, was not a pleasant little country side road, more a main artery route with lorries and trucks hurtling towards me at a hundred kilometres an hour or racing past me perhaps two metres away, creating a dust and grit-filled slipstream that made me turn my head away and stop in my tracks, eyes tightly shut and breathing paused. I walked on the hard shoulder, leaving it whenever possible for a thin slice of gravel running alongside, the beginnings of the local authorities diverting the way away from such roads. Occasionally a welcome stretch of white shingle sloped away from the road where the Camino ran parallel for a while, but it would always eventually slope up again to throw me back into the fray.

My guidebook was pretty accurate and the direction signs were always there, somewhere. But now I wanted a map so I could see if there were any alternatives to walking on the road. I abandoned the idea because I wanted to walk on the Camino regardless, and it had always followed these roads, from the time when they were just dirt tracks. I wanted to walk the same way pilgrims had always done, see what they had seen and experience the same adventure. I followed pretty much its every whim and wish. If it detoured through a wood for a kilometre, even though I knew where it reappeared, I would follow it slavishly, resigned to its demands, even taking the longer of two possible variants when they came up. I needed to make sure I had walked the entire length and not cheated. I had nightmares that I had missed out a section. I even went as far as making sure every morning that I started to walk from the very spot where I had finished the previous day.

Chapter Ten

New Faces

Two days out of Logrono, I caught up with Tamar and we walked together for the day. Arriving in Santo Domingo de la Calzada, we came to one of the town's two refugios and decided to take a look inside.

The dormitory area, housed in a sort of abandoned warehouse, was huge, with a ridiculously high ceiling, so that you had to shout to hold a conversation with someone on the other side. The beds were arranged all around the outside, leaving a huge rectangular space in the middle. A rare luxury in refuges, it had real single beds, not bunk beds. I liked it straight away: it was weird, different, but certainly inviting.

Monica had checked herself in to the finest hotel this side of Paris, a plan she had been talking about for days. All she could think about was stuff like wrapping herself up in three immense, fluffy towels after a steaming hot bath, watching a bit of TV, calling room service just for the hell of ordering a coffee and generally revelling in the opulence. She had invited me to a meal in the evening. I took my time wandering through the hotel searching for her room. Tourists were mingling around reception, where one was leaning over the reception desk complaining and demanding a refund. Bell boys were running around as taxis dropped off new clients and picked up those leaving.

"Yes, who is it?" she said as I rapped on the door.

"It's Fozzie."

She opened the door, indeed cocooned in big, fluffy towels.

"You look like you're enjoying yourself," I said.

She smiled and invited me in, disappearing off to the bathroom. I flicked aimlessly through the TV channels just because I could and settled on a 1950s Western dubbed in Spanish. It was either that or a 1930s documentary featuring a woman yodelling in the Alps. The choice was a little limited.

"What time is the meal?" I said to Monica when she came back and plopped on to the bed next to me.

"Eight thirty. Have you seen the restaurant?"

"No. I don't know where we are eating. Have you found somewhere?"

She laughed. "Fozzie, I am treating you to a meal here, at the hotel, as my guest!"

"Oh! Wow!" I exclaimed. "I thought you were taking me out on the town to a small bar or something. Look… you don't have to do that, really."

"It's my pleasure. I'll meet you in reception at, say, eight?"

"Yeah, fine. Listen… thanks!"

I went back to the refugio, had a shower, did the laundry and took a siesta. I explained to Tamar about the meal. Then it hit me. The restaurant opened at eight thirty: the refuge shut its doors at nine thirty.

"I don't believe it," I muttered to myself. "Shit!"

Foiled again! The chance of dining in a top-flight restaurant spoilt by a damn refuge restriction. There was no way I could do it, even if we rushed through the meal, but doing that would make a nonsense of the whole experience.

The warden would have none of it. I explained it would just mean staying open a little longer or leaving the back door ajar. Nothing doing. I was tired and didn't want extra hassle, so I plodded dejectedly back to the hotel and explained to Monica. She understood, and even said she could keep the offer 'in the bag' for another time. I ended up with Tamar in a quaint little bar munching on portions of tapas and sipping red wine. Afterwards we walked back through quiet streets to the refuge, where most of the pilgrims were already asleep and the lights were off. Returning from the bathroom, and as we talked some more, she sat on the edge of my bed, letting her hair fall down one side of her face as she ran a brush through it. I realised I had probably not even put that much thought into how to get around the curfew problem earlier. I could have crashed on Monica's floor, left a window open at the refuge – there were a number of options. I hadn't really tried because I just wanted to spend the time with Tamar instead. Eventually, without the need for words, she slipped in bed beside me.

She had to leave the Camino soon for a week to attend a wedding, so we spent two days walking together. I liked to walk in silence most of the time, fully content just taking in my surroundings. She couldn't seem to grasp this idea and was becoming frustrated at not being able to converse constantly. We walked apart for a few kilometres and by the time we reached the disappointing village of Belorado there was an atmosphere. As we ate a picnic lunch on the steps leading down from the church, she called a taxi.

"We won't end up together, Fozzie," she said.

I looked at her with a little surprise and then realised she was probably right.

"I know," I said. "It's frustrating sometimes. We go through these times when you are angry with me and I with you, but I still love being with you."

"Email where you are," she continued. "After the wedding, I will come back to the Camino and walk again. Please contact me some time and tell me where you are."

"I will."

The refugio was the worst I had stayed in. There was one shower for the whole place, which yielded a pathetic trickle of water dripping on to dirty, broken tiles. The mattress on the bunk bed sagged alarmingly and the whole dormitory reverberated with rusty springs twanging and pinging. The other room consisted of two benches and a table, possibly rescued from the skip outside. One camping gas stove had spluttered to death as two pilgrims tried to brew coffee. It was depressing.

I was in a bad mood anyway. The conversation with Tamar and her subsequent departure had made me irritable. A group of pilgrims I had briefly chatted to in recent days were occupying the other table. One of them, James, an English guy, the first I had met on the Camino, was suffering with blisters. He had started at St Jean and was experiencing the same problem I had after a couple of weeks of walking. At first I was sorry for him, but soon he started to annoy me with his constant whining, as if he were the only one suffering. When I returned to the room after going outside for a cigarette, he was lying on the table while two of his pals performed surgery on his ailments. He was milking it for all it was worth. I raised my eyes to the ceiling and one of his friends smiled in agreement.

I went over and introduced myself to a middle-aged man lying on his sleeping mat in the corner. Sleeping next to him was his dog, which opened one eye when I approached, gave a sigh and fell asleep again. A mountain bike was propped up against the wall with a trailer bolted behind it.

"Lovely dog. What's his name?" I asked.

"Boom," the man said. "After a book I read once called *Me and a dog named Boom*, or something like that anyway."

He spoke with a hint of Scottish accent. His hair was short and grey, he was well built and, to judge from his equipment, he might have cycled from Nepal. Everything was scuffed and dusty. An odd piece of tape held battered bags and straps. In fact, he looked as though he had spent his whole life travelling.

"Two German guys just left him at one of the refuges," he continued, scratching Boom's head as if to let him know he was the subject of conversation. "I couldn't leave him there, so brought him along. I can't figure out why they left him, he's such a great dog. I set off in the morning on the bike, and he just runs alongside me. Eats anything I give him, treats me like a best friend, he's great. I'm Ian, by the way."

"Sorry," I replied. "I have a bad habit of asking dogs' names and never asking the owners. I'm Fozzie."

He laughed. "At least you show a genuine interest," he said. "I can tell just from the attention you pay him that you love dogs. Do you have one?"

"No, although I've lost count of the number of times I have been down the rescue centre and nearly brought one back with me. But I travel too much. And there are all those quarantine restrictions. I have a cat, but a dog would probably end up residing at my parents' place for the summer and coming back with me for the winter – if I ever go home, that is. I hope to get one when I am settled in one place. Interesting method of travelling," I said, nodding towards his bike. "You Santiago bound?"

"Probably. I have to go to Germany to get married in a week or so, a lady I met at one of the refuges. She was a warden. I'll take it as it comes."

He declined my offer of a beer, saying he needed to make an early start and get some sleep. Outside, drizzle chased by a strong wind was streaming past the street light. A constant stream of lorries made the two-hundred-metre dash to the bar a death zone, and a wet one at that. I sat at the counter in El Pajero and ordered a beer. Munching on pistachios and smoking an endless stream of cigarettes, I tried to be interested in a Spanish soap on the TV. For the first time in several weeks I was properly depressed.

I awoke to rain pounding on the windows. I wiped a circle in the condensation on the glass and peered out. The sun had yet to come up, darkness covered everything and the occasional car sent up a cloud of spray. I could just make out the moon, trying desperately to peer through racing dark clouds. I dived back into my sleeping bag and waited, snoozing, until most of the other pilgrims had got up and filed out.

When I eventually got going after endless coffees and omelettes at El Pajero, the rain had given up, but grey clouds still streamed overhead, blocking out the blue, and the way was damp, the soil reduced to a sticky mix of clay and rotting leaves. I walked on fire tracks through forest for most of the day, dodging the puddles and kicking imaginary footballs to send up huge clods of earth that had stuck to my boots. I could see Ian's tracks: three lines representing his machine, and the odd set of paw prints to one side. 'He must have struggled through this shit,' I thought.

After twelve kilometres I came to San Juan de Ortega, a cluster of old buildings huddled in the drizzle. The church of San Nicolas de Bari stood proudly at the head of the small street. It was constructed in such a way that, on the spring and autumn equinoxes at five in the evening, the setting sun illuminated the capital depicting the Annunciation. I went inside to check it out, imagining the rays streaming in like something out of *Raiders of the Lost Ark*. Apart from the fact I had missed the equinox, it was still raining and there was no sun. I comforted myself with the fact that I could at least add one more church visit tick to my limited list. The fake-pilgrim spotter in Santiago would surely be impressed now.

I carried on along freshly tarred, jet-black roads that wound through ancient hamlets. At the end of a long stretch of tarmac that never seemed to end, I came to Atapuerca. After the miseries of the previous night, this small village seemed like some sort of peace offering. Its damp empty streets reminded me of Damascus in Syria, where I had spent some time a few years earlier. It was pleasant enough, but the true reward was the refugio. As I gripped the round iron latch, opened the door and stepped inside, faces peered back at me through the darkness. I made out about ten pilgrims huddled around a table and occupying themselves swatting a huge resident fly population. Blister-ridden James was reciting the wincing script again, and there was that same exasperated look on his friends' faces.

It was one of the best refuges I had stayed at. Recently restored, it reminded me of a Stone Age hut with a few mod cons. The ceiling was high, wooden beams spraying off in a haphazard fashion, with what looked like mud plaster clinging on for dear life in between them. The walls had been distressed with a thin terracotta wash. There were nooks and crannies in the dormitory to rest books, torches and anything else one might need in the middle of the night. A separate bathroom housed three showers with an endless supply of steaming water. The kitchen area and table where the others were recuperating sported a wood-burning stove. We wrote our diaries in relative silence, except for the odd moan from James, and set about lighting the stove.

Firewood was limited so three of us were sent out into the elements on fuel-securing missions. The rain was intermittent, but now it was windy and the temperature had plummeted. I began to wonder if I would make it over El Cebreiro, three hundred and fifty kilometres away before the first snows fell. We stripped an area six metres in circumference around the refugio of anything that looked vaguely combustible and retreated back inside. A German woman was struggling with a pile of ashes in the stove, which sent up the occasional pathetic puff of damp smoke, like a dragon coughing on its death bed. We would keep stuffing in toilet roll, one would hold the lighter, one would throw in the odd piece of kindling, whilst another two would blow and make comments such as "The wood's too damp," or "Open the air vent, it needs more air." This usually culminated in the orange glow behind the glass receding dangerously low as the vent was accidentally shut instead. I dreamt that night of walking through snow up to my waist, homing in on an orange glow that never got any nearer. I deliberately didn't analyse it in the morning: it seemed bad whichever way I looked at it.

The wind did its best to blow me off the road in the morning as I scampered from the refugio to a nearby bar for breakfast. At this stage of the Camino I was struggling to get going without at least three coffees, a Spanish omelette and several cigarettes. I had worked my way through enough eggs in the previous couple of weeks to be contemplating a cholesterol test. I asked for an espresso and watched as the waitress expertly operated the coffee machine. I love those things; ridiculously wide, dials and handles sprouting all over the front, warm cups stacked on top, steam rising up, leaving moisture on the chrome, with stainless steel nozzles pointing in all directions. Underneath there would be a wooden drawer, battered and worn at the top by the constant smack of the grounds holder. There's nothing like real coffee. The flip of the grinder depositing the ground beans into the holder, its compression compacting the powder, the sound of the holder being thrust and turned in the receptacle and the sight of that rich, deep brown treacle dripping out bring a smile to my face every time. I know then it is only a short wait before I get my hit.

I sat in the corner watching the weather report on the TV, which promised great things. The silence was shattered abruptly as the door burst open and a seemingly never-ending stream of pilgrims filed in, rubbing their hands. The bar was transformed from a silent haven to a bustling rabble of walkers gossiping and overjoyed at having found somewhere that was open. Damp waterproofs were pulled off, hats and gloves removed to reveal faces red and raw from the wind.

Among them was France, whom I hadn't seen since Lectoure,

six hundred kilometres back.

"France!" I shouted. "Bloody hell! How are you?! I thought you were way ahead of me."

"Fozzie! Hey, how are you? I thought you were way ahead of *me*!" His face lit up with surprise.

He came and sat with me, turning around, tapping everyone on the shoulder and saying, "Hey, *this* is Fozzie!"

One guy saw the confused look on my face.

"Oh! You're Fozzie!" he said.

"Er... yes."

"I've been seeing your name carved into the dirt since St Jean! It's great to finally meet you!"

France and I looked at each other and laughed hard.

"Have you seen Jeannie?" I asked.

"The American woman who stays on the public phones for an hour at a time?"

I laughed again. "Yeah, that's Jeannie."

"She's about two, maybe three days back."

We caught up on everything that had happened since Moissac: where everybody was, who was ahead, who was behind. He left shortly before me and said he would see me that night in Burgos.

As I ventured back outside, the wind had intensified. It was by far the coldest day on the Camino I had experienced. I began to worry that the Spanish hills in Galicia were going to be deeper in the grip of winter than I had thought. I had completed two thirds of the Camino but still had five hundred kilometres left to walk.

My poles dug into the chalky soil on the hill out of Atapuerca, walking past pilgrims as I found my pace and everyone spaced out to their own speed. I passed a young woman to my right.

"Ola!" she said.

"Hi," I nodded. I was walking faster than she was and carried on past, not in the mood for a day's company, but she merely increased her speed to stay with me. I relented, thinking some company might do me good after all.

Tania was Mexican, and hovered around twenty years old, maybe a little younger. She was a strong walker, and had been clocking up thirty to thirty-five kilometres a day since St Jean. We smoked and walked. She had shiny hair arranged in a braided fashion framing an attractive face. She smiled a lot and made eye contact often. Her English was excellent with just a hint of Spanish, and she had an infectious humour about her that was just what I needed. After ten minutes I decided I liked her.

We talked away the eighteen or so kilometres to Burgos, a city I was looking forward to as I had planned a rest day and a night in a hotel. We depleted such topics as spirituality, photography, travel and cooking.

France walked with us on and off for the day. As we went through small villages, each one promising the outskirts of the city but not delivering, we reached a motorway. I looked up in astonishment at the Camino sign, which pointed to the other side.

"We gotta cross this!" I exclaimed, laughing.

"No way," Tania replied, in a disbelieving tone.

"Well, that's where the sign is suggesting." We walked for a short way, thinking there was a tunnel underneath but were disappointed. I looked in my guidebook.

"Uh-oh," I said.

"What?" Tania was peering over my shoulder trying to read as well.

"Well, I'm quoting from the book. It says *cross motorway*." We looked at each other and then at the road. France joined us and we explained the situation. Streams of cars were whizzing past, interspersed with the occasional lorry and the odd motorbike for good measure. I was reminded of something my dad had said to me years earlier when I set off to walk the hundred or so miles that comprise the South Downs Way in West Sussex.

"Remember, when you get to a road, be careful. For one, you will probably be tired. For another, that pack on your back has a funny habit of making you think it's not actually there. The end result is a mad dash through a hole in the traffic and you suddenly realise you're making no headway and there are two cars bearing down on you."

The words repeated in my head. In the end, we ran like pilgrims possessed to a small strip of concrete in the middle, an island, a safe haven, where we could launch the next attack. As we caught our breath on the other side, France said that the law of averages would suggest that, with several thousand pilgrims walking here every year, a few probably ended up in Burgos accident and emergency.

The three of us made our way into Burgos, which presented the familiar pattern of uninspiring outskirts gradually giving way to the older buildings nearer the centre. It struck me as another pleasant city, with plenty of green spaces, wide walkways and original architecture. It bustled in a friendly way.

The refuge nestled in an expanse of grass a short walk from the Arco de Santa Maria, a fortified gateway taking the pedestrian into the old city. Bunk beds were crammed alarmingly into a couple of rooms, and the buildings themselves reminded me of the temporary huts I was schooled in, designed to last for five years but still going strong at thirty. There were plenty of pilgrims claiming their preference of bunk position, going to or returning from showers, or blistering. My assumption that any hot water had long gone was confirmed when I entered the shower area to hear cries of pain from the cubicles as the water was turned on. I decided something to eat would be a better idea; I could come back for a shower later.

A short distance from the refuge was a small restaurant advertising a pilgrims' menu, so Tania and I took a table and, as space was limited, invited some Australian guys to join us.

"Oh, you're Fozzie," said Steve, who sported a white trilby and lilac T-shirt printed with the slogan *In your dreams, sugar puff.*

"I am," I said, putting my arm around Tania just to confirm my sexual orientation.

"I thought so. I was walking with a woman called Monica and she said you were attractive. She also advised me not to eat with you."

"Not to eat with me?"

"Yes. She said you eat like a horse. She said you'll eat any tapas within your reach, regardless of whom they belong to."

"Thanks," I replied. "I had no idea my eating habits were held in such high regard. I'll have words when I see her. Well, anyway, I'm not mad on onion soup but you'd better guard your fries with your life."

The food, as in most establishments with pilgrims' menus, was good. Walkers filled the place and many, like us, stayed after we had eaten. Waiters whisked around with coffees, beers and spirits. Glasses were raised, conversation wafted around, people laughed and leant back in their chairs with their tired legs outstretched. I would occasionally catch a glimpse of someone I recognised and hold up a glass or nod my head in their direction. Somehow we managed to find our way back to the refuge and I sat down by Boom, who was sleeping outside, scratching his head for what must have been fifteen minutes. I slept well, dreaming of walking a route that took the rest of my life to finish, with a dog running alongside.

Chapter Eleven

Dreams of Home

I headed off in the morning to find a good hotel for a day's rest and to make up for a missed shower. Stopping at the post office, I picked up a parcel that a friend had sent out and sat down at a café to open it. Inside was a large tub of peanut butter, a delicacy in short supply in Spain. I asked the waiter for some fresh baguette and spent several minutes reacquainting myself with my favourite spread, even going so far as hiding it under the table when some American pilgrims sat a few tables away.

After trying two hotels, which were full because it was the last public holiday of the year, I eventually found a cracker a few minutes' walk from the centre. Damp laundry spread around the room, rucksack contents deposited everywhere, I dozed off into a premature siesta and dreamt that I was in my parents' back garden with a storm raging all around me. The base of a tree trunk was swinging violently as the wind tore at it. The wet soil was giving way as each gust pushed and pulled it further back and forth, tugging it from either side. Eventually it fell. I woke up shortly afterwards and called my mum, not because of the dream, just to catch up and report on my progress.

"How's the weather doing?" I asked.

"Oh, Keith, we had a storm last night. Really strong winds and heavy rain. It pushed over a tree in the back garden."

Perhaps the Camino was nurturing my spiritual side after all.

* * *

Pamplona was still sitting pretty at the number-one spot of Spanish cities, although Burgos produced a valiant and worthwhile attempt at nudging it into the number-two spot. It was pretty close but Pamplona held on by a whisker. A number of ornate bridges span the chasm of the River Arlanzon, whose waters gush and fall over stones, the banks are coated in rich, green grass and a few trees and bushes. Lovers walked along the banks, dogs charged and swerved, glad to be unleashed. People strolled down tree-fringed avenues. There was a hum of small engines as workers blew up great swirls of leaves into pyramid-shaped piles.

Tamar sounded reluctant to speak on the phone when I called her. She was due in Burgos that evening, and I said she should come to the hotel.

"OK, fine, do whatever," I said, and slammed down the receiver. I couldn't figure out her mood swings: one minute she was attentive and tender, the next she acted as though she had just met me.

I hung around with Tania. We cordoned off a table in one of the numerous cafés, and went back to our discussions, mainly on books again. I ordered food far too expensive for my budget, sipped wine and relaxed. It was that Sunday feeling. I swear someone could pick me up and dump me anywhere in the world, without telling me what day of the week it was, and sure enough, I would know instantly when Sunday arrived. My body would feel relaxed: all I would want to do was read and drink coffee and generally do all the things I didn't have time for in the week. I made the most of it.

That evening Tamar and I met at a bar, and while I sipped on Johnnie Walker Black swimming in ice, she told me she had been unable to talk earlier as her husband was in the room with her. Everything, it appeared, was back to sweetness and light as we returned to my hotel. She was due to meet a friend of hers called Espe who was to share her room and walk the rest of the Camino with her. She left my room late in the evening to meet her.

I left Burgos the following morning on my own, knowing that Tamar and Espe would catch me up. I waved and giggled as Ian sped past on his bike with Boom scampering alongside. Before long Burgos was behind and the welcoming Spanish countryside engulfed me once more. I felt calm again, the late autumn sun warming my back as I slowed my pace to take in my surroundings.

In Tardajos, I stopped at a bar where people were staring into their drinks as if someone had just died. The whole place had the atmosphere of a morgue. The saving grace was the TV showing the movie *Big,* and the scene where Tom Hanks is in the toyshop playing the keyboard with his feet. I was humming the tune for the rest of the day. Before leaving town, I loaded up my pack with bananas and oranges from a truck selling fruit and vegetables on the roadside.

The Camino was filtering out into vast, open spaces with little more than scrub and dust for company. I could see for miles. Hornillos del Camino appeared in the distance two hours before I actually arrived there. As I was unpacking in the refuge there was a tap on my shoulder and I turned around to see Pierre.

"Pierre! Holy crap!" I exclaimed. "Long time no see! Where you been?"

"Taking my time," he replied. "Lots to see, take more in when I walk slowly."

"I agree, I am getting to the stage now where Santiago is actually becoming a reality, and I feel myself slowing down each day."

It was true. I had about four hundred and fifty kilometres left. After the initial doubts, the long days where nothing was going right for me, Santiago de Compostela now seemed within reach. Everyone was in a similar mood. It was as though the end of the walk was starting to rear up, to creep a little closer each day, like a cat prowling through long grass, and we knew that there would be a massive moral crash when we had all finished. We would wake up at the refugio in Santiago, or Cape Finisterre for those who continued to the coast, to realise it had all finished. There would be no more walking to do. Decisions would have to be made about the next step. Back home? Stay in Spain to wind down? At times, when I imagined how my spirits would be at the end, I almost saw myself turning around to start to walk back to Le Puy again. I didn't want it to end.

To my surprise, the French Canadians were in the village as well. People I hadn't seen for weeks had somehow concentrated into this small, dusty place out in the middle of nowhere. I entered the only bar, where Gérard looked up from his packet of peanuts.

"Fozzie! Hey, man! What you doing!"

His familiar hippy tones resonated around the place. The others looked up and smiled. I hadn't seen them since Conques, which seemed an eternity ago. We all shook hands, pecked cheeks, patted each other on the back. Although I knew them, it felt as if we were at the stage where a kiss or a handshake wasn't quite cutting it. We would soon be on the rostrum where hugs were the norm. These people, friends, pilgrims whom I had known for a few weeks, would be going their separate ways and we sort of knew we had to make the most of the time we had left on the walk. I was back among friends, happy, and walked around for the rest of the day with a huge grin.

When the warden tapped me on the shoulder the following morning and pointed to his watch, which displayed a time of eight fifteen, I just glared at him. The refuges weren't bothering me any more. In fact, the whole rules and regulations crap was starting to amuse me. I would get up around eight o'clock, the time by which you should have already left, and pack at my own speed, ignoring any reproving looks. At this stage of the Camino, approaching mid-October, pilgrim numbers were dwindling. There were no queues of tired walkers waiting to get a bed for the night. We didn't have to leave early to provide bed space; there was plenty. Everyone was aware of this, so we took our time and generally bypassed the restrictions.

I walked with Espe and Tamar, who had arrived later the previous evening, for part of the morning, but then let them go ahead. I wanted to come to terms with this new part of Spain. I rested more often, content with just sitting at the side of the track, listening to only the birds, insects and the rustle of the grass as the wind whipped through it. Everything seemed intensified. Sounds were amplified, demanding that I stop and listen. I felt I could hear things that I would normally miss. My senses were becoming more acute and refined. I took an endless stream of photos to try and capture it all, but I knew the real experience could never be taken back with me, except in my memories.

* * *

A group of pilgrims had stopped at the only bar for twenty kilometres. Any visit from a health inspector and it would have been closed down long ago. On entering, I could smell the owner before he appeared from an adjoining room. He looked as if he hadn't washed in a month. Filth and grime streaked his white vest. Dirt lined his cracked fingernails and his hands looked as though he had just completed an oil change on a tractor, and then used the old lubricant to slick back his receding hair over a shiny bald patch. His establishment fared little better. Food scraps littered the bar. Flies buzzed around as though they were on vacation. Cured ham rested on an ancient slicing machine that was caked in dust and filth. A bread sack was propped up in the corner, the contents spilling onto the floor. As I ordered coffees for me, Tamar and Espe, he dipped three glass cups into a sink full of murky grey water, wiped them on his shirt, and placed them under a coffee machine, which spluttered into life as if it were overdue a service.

I retreated to the warmth outside. Tamar followed me out and we started arguing about something trivial that eventually had me donning my pack and storming off at such a speed that I knew she had little chance of catching up.

I stopped at Hospital San Anton, where an imposing archway stretched across the road. Pilgrims had left scribbled notes on pieces of paper, weighed down by small stones in niches on the wall – messages to friends yet to pass, poems and tales, or simply a few words to brighten up someone's day.

11th November. Jeannie, keep going, girl! Love, Fozzie, I wrote, and placed it near the front under a scrap of stone that had once been part of the stone arch.

I continued down a road as straight as a datum line, leading to Castrojeriz. Its castle, perched up high, dominated the town. Spotting a rosemary bush climbing the walls of a ruined house, I slid down an embankment and picked a twig to fasten to my shoulder strap. Its scent stayed with me for hours.

Tamar eventually appeared in the evening with Espe. I didn't know whether I wanted to see her or not, but she was affectionate, as if nothing had happened.

"I just don't understand her sometimes," I said to Espe.

"She is walking the Camino to sort out a lot of problems in her head," she replied, and then added:

"And, she said the very same thing today about you."

Chapter Twelve

Into Autumn

The sun was making an appearance a little later every day and leaving me a little earlier. It wasn't really light until eight thirty. There were fewer sunny days and the air carried a chill in the early morning. Most of the time it was overcast but, thankfully, rain was still rare. Laying claim to being the wettest area of Spain, Galicia was sure to give me a pounding this time of year. I thought the weather reports in England were unreliable; in Spain, when I caught reports on the TV, I saw those familiar black cloud symbols, but the forecast rain just never seemed to arrive.

The leaves were in classic autumn colours, like the tones of a Turkish rug: reds, yellows, dark and light browns all ducked and weaved in the breeze. The Camino was drenched in a new carpet of colour that comforted the feet. I kicked up leaves and watched them fall back again into the camouflage. Trees arched over in the wind like ballet dancers warming up and stretching to one side, the trunks groaning, the leaves whistling and whispering above me, caught in wind eddies, twirling, spiralling and plummeting. Soon those coats of trees would reveal the dark skeletons beneath.

It was the perfect time of year to walk. Although I loved the feeling of the sun burning into my back, autumn is designed to be hiked in. On some mornings, for the first few minutes my breath emerged as a cloud of mist and the cold snapped at any exposed skin. It was a weird sensation, feeling snug once I had warmed from the walking, when my face and hands still tingled.

The Journey in Between

The hills at the latter end of the Spanish section would be even colder. Snow was becoming a real threat and I hoped I could make it over the hills of El Cebreiro before their tops turned white. I must have been one of the last pilgrims to walk the Camino that year, even though there were still a few behind me. I played a cat-and-mouse game with the elements, having left my departure later than considered normal. The wet season was due now as well, but my luck was holding and rain was still rare.

After Ledigos, the Meseta started to undulate gently and the way started to weave. I walked through a couple of hamlets, unfortunately neither of them with bars, and trees and rivers began to appear. After what seemed like an eternity on the mundane Meseta, my morale started to lift.

In my haste to maintain a brisk pace to keep warm, I had completely missed the town centre at Sahagun and had to backtrack, walking under the Portada del Templo Abacial, an imposing stone arch spanning the road.

I was ravenous and also in the mood for blowing the financial budget for the day. I craved sugar, coffee, tapas and something cocooned in puff pastry. There were three bars in the centre, from which I chose a very upmarket-looking one, which by a minor miracle had something made from puff pastry in the window.

Inside, light bounced off endless glass and polished brass. Copious quantities of tapas attracted my attention, and an interesting choice of *She's a Model* by Kraftwerk piped though somewhere above my left ear. The place even boasted lights in the toilet that came on by movement sensors. The clientele seemed posh, all done up in their Sunday best (well, Monday best actually). Ladies sat with crossed legs and twiddled with model-perfect hair while throwing their heads back in mock laughter at bad jokes. With my grubby clothes and matted hair, I felt out of place but I didn't care; there was food to devour, and that always had my undivided attention.

Three kilometres out of Sahagun the Camino threw up a choice of routes, two of which ran through an area that I had been reading about for weeks. I had heard pilgrims discussing the area with fear in their voice. It is known as the Calzada de los Peregrinos, or *the carriageway of the pilgrim.*

One of the routes was considered drastically worse than the other, with little or nothing to look at. The other offered a slim chance of finding something to eat or drink if needed. Both routes were the same distance, thirty kilometres. I needn't have spent the time pondering as the bad option meant I had another thirty kilometres before the next refuge, and I had already walked eighteen that day. The days when I walked forty kilometres or more were long gone. So I picked way number two, called Camino Real Frances, and hoped it wasn't as bad as I had been led to believe.

After crunching along a gravel track for a while, I lay down in the grass to savour a spectacular storm assaulting the countryside. Clouds loomed up from the horizon, multiplying like bacteria. In the foreground, the church of Ermita de Perales looked like a lost child, alone and crying in the middle of nowhere.

The path dipped and crossed the River Coso, where a headstone sat in memory of a pilgrim who had died there in 1998. Many pilgrims have died over the years on the Camino, most of them as a result of a traffic involvement. However, there was a sad and quiet, almost mysterious air to this location and it made me wonder how the pilgrim had died in such a secluded spot.

The walls of the houses in the next town, Bercianos del Real Camino, were made mainly from a mixture of mud and water, like something out of an African village. It was silent save the rustling of leaves and debris flying past me at street corners as though they had been waiting in ambush. Following yellow direction arrows splashed on walls, I soon caught up with two Dutchwomen with whom I had become acquainted, called Helen and Ancha. They told me a friend of theirs had stayed at the refuge a couple of years previously and in the absence of beds had been forced to sleep on the floor. This didn't exactly do my perception of the place any favours. No beds suggested it was lacking in funds and this in turn meant all the other facilities would probably be sparse.

I need not have worried. The arrows led right up to the door and I stepped inside. It was like walking into a small castle. An impressive wooden door riddled with studs was ajar and led to a porch area with small pebbles set into the floor. It was dark, a little musty and very old, but it enveloped me with a feeling of welcome and friendship. I checked in.

"Leave when you want in the morning," the middle-aged woman said, smiling. "Breakfast and evening meal are included, and any donation is welcomed."

"Thanks," I replied. "Is there a bar in the village? I have a coffee craving."

"Please, have a seat in the dining room. I will make one for you. Is espresso OK?"

They couldn't have done more for us if they had tried. OK, so we had to sleep on the floor (albeit with the welcome addition of a mattress) and the facilities were basic, but the refugio at Bercianos del Real Camino squeezed in to my top ten favourites. It just goes to show that you should listen to rumours with a dose of scepticism: what travellers experienced in the past may no longer be the case now. The donation I gave was four times more than I would have normally given.

I awoke in the morning after everybody had left and ventured outside to retrieve my laundry, only to be met by an eerie fog that enveloped pretty much everything. I needed a map to find the clothesline. It was dead quiet; I wouldn't have known if someone was standing four paces away. For most of the morning I walked through countryside from a movie scene, perhaps *The Hound of the Baskervilles*. I could barely see ten metres in front of me and half expected to be savaged by a rabid hound any second. It was at this point I realised with horror that I had left my peanut butter at one of the refuges a couple of nights earlier, and very nearly shed a tear.

Stopping for an early lunch at Burgo Ranero, I pondered the approach to food and eating found in various countries. To me, England seems to charge excessive prices for food, profit taking precedence over everything else. I have no problem with this in theory: after all, making a profit is the fundamental basis of any business. However, in mainland Europe, in particular the Mediterranean, I get the impression that the attitude is different and most places are actually there simply to provide food; if they happen to make a profit, all the better. In Spain and some other countries you often see the inhabitants having a full-blown lunch in the middle of the week, because they can afford to do so. For them, food is a God-given right and most establishments genuinely seem to enjoy feeding the masses.

France appeared from the fog and joined me.

"In France and other Mediterranean countries," he said, when I explained what I had been thinking, "I notice the food is much more reasonable than in England and generally of a higher standard. I don't mean to say that English cuisine is bad, it is not, it just seems of a poorer standard than elsewhere and costs more."

Commercialism plays its part too. To take things a step further, we now have large companies that care about nothing else except squeezing the maximum amount of coinage from the public, while dishing up rubbish. They're not there to provide an experience of eating, just to swipe your credit card at the end of the meal. Their ingredients are delivered frozen twice weekly and thrown in the deep-fat fryer by a recycled juvenile delinquent. The chairs are designed to be comfortable for thirty minutes so you don't hang about and then the next lot gets herded in.

I do indulge in the occasional McDonald's and rumour has it I have been spotted in Pizza Hut, but I can honestly count on two hands the number of times I go to those establishments in a year.

We are what we eat: never a truer word spoken. The more we take a basic food and process it, the worse it becomes. Ingredients are altered genetically, and then sprayed with endless chemicals. Your average hamburger from a fast-food chain consists of bread with all the goodness removed, and meat derived from poor cuts and trimmings from cows injected with hormones and the like to produce as much beef as possible in the shortest amount of time. A slice of plastic cheese is thrown on top with a generous dollop of mayonnaise, plus a token lettuce leaf for the 'healthy' bit. I have walked through cities in Italy and seen babies and children munching on fresh asparagus tips, fruit and water.

Thinking about all this that day, I made a determined decision to eat more healthily and go vegetarian... in the New Year.

France had walked with me for a while but stopped in a

supermarket to restock. The fog had cleared and the temperature had risen enough to make me sweat. A rare sight on the Meseta now met my eyes: not a fork in the track, or even a path coming in from one side, but a crossroads. To add to the confusion, a car was stuck behind a tractor. It was gridlock in the middle of nowhere. I just had to laugh at the preposterousness of it all.

I entered Leon and followed signs to the Youth Hostel, purely because it seemed easier than locating the refuge. The building was huge and resembled a prison block. The thermostat registered thirty degrees, and on the rise. I bumped into Tamar in the corridor with her daughter. Apparently her husband had driven the little girl down to see her. They left shortly after and we both ventured into Leon for food and wine. Espe very kindly offered to swap her room for mine so Tamar and I could be alone for the night.

My opinion of Tamar plummeted in the morning when she suggested all three of us go to *Cortez del Inglese* for breakfast. For those of you unfamiliar with this Spanish establishment, think of British Home Stores or Debenhams. Not my first choice for a breakfast location but Tamar insisted. They virtually had to drag me into the place as I peered through tapas bars on the way, pleading with the diners: *For God's sake, HELP ME!*

They pulled me in the door and marched me through the underwear section, past the sports department, up some escalators and into an eating hall where instrumental cover versions of dire pop songs piped through. Needless to say, all I could do was to down an espresso and hope that Tamar and Espe finished their croissants quickly.

As soon as we were out, I went looking for the nearest tapas bar.

"But, Fozzie, you just had..." protested Tamar.

"Sorry, but I look forward to my coffee and eats in the morning before I start walking, and that place wasn't quite cutting the mustard."

"Cutting? Mustard?" She tilted her head to one side and narrowed her eyes with a puzzled look.

"It doesn't matter," I said. "I mean I wanted to eat in a tapas bar. I like the Spanish food. To 'cut the mustard' is an English expression for being good. I didn't like Cortez del Inglese, and wanted to come here for my breakfast. Understand?"

"Si... I mean yes. I understand." She sank back into her chair and gave me the odd glance as I munched on my tortilla. I sensed something big was on her mind. Espe had gone off to the toilet, but had been keeping her distance anyway.

"Fozzie?"

"Yes?"

"I lied to you. I told you I wanted fun and that I was not in love with you. I am in love with you."

I stopped chewing and stared at her, expecting more information, but knowing she had said her piece.

"Tamar, oh God, Tamar. I don't know what to say."

The whole place seemed to stop and wait for me.

"You're beautiful, really beautiful, and when we get along, we really get along. But most of the time we argue, and that's when we can understand what we're both saying. The way you look is more than I could ask for in a woman, but we clash Tamar, we clash big time."

"Clash?"

"Clash, yes," I continued. "Our personalities don't match, we find fault and upset each other, apologise and then do it again. It's a constant circle and I struggle with it. We can take each other's company in small amounts, but too much is, well, too much."

"So you don't want to know me any more?"

"No, not at all. I just don't think we are going anywhere from a love point of view. I still want to be a friend to you, but a relationship would be a disaster. I'm sorry, Tamar, it just wouldn't work."

"I know, I understand," she said, smiling. "We would kill each other."

She got up and kissed me on the cheek.

"See you on the trail."

* * *

Jato the Faith Healer, now there's a title. Forget Queen of this or Prince of that. I had heard numerous stories about this guy who runs a refuge on the Camino at Villafranca del Bierzo, most of them from Jeannie, who in turn was enlightened by pilgrims she knew from last year. Apparently Jato had the ability to heal using his hands, mind and nothing else. I guessed he couldn't be making much money out of it or he wouldn't be needing the refuge. But, as stories go, it was a good one and I was looking forward to staying with him and seeing what he was all about. My calf was still playing up a little, so at least I was a good test case.

Jato was three or four days away and I had set myself a target of thirty kilometres a day to get there – a bit more than I had been used to walking of late, but hardly breaking any records. I had decided to move to the Leon refuge from the hostel to spend my rest day.

The building was centuries old with a little sprinkling of character to match. It was one of the most cramped I had stayed in but it was nice to see loads of friendly faces. The French Canadians were there, John and Yetty from Canada, as laid back a pair of pilgrims as I had met, and numerous others including Pierre.

Most of them went to a nearby restaurant to eat in the evening but I declined. I wandered the streets for about an hour, just needing my own company, feeling the cobbles through my soles, letting my hands run along cold, damp stone, feeling the indentations, cavities, nicks and dents. Modern lighting recessed in the ground sent shafts of light up against the walls like searchlights, casting eerie shadows. A slight mist hung in the air and created rainbows of light around the street lamps. And then, suddenly, a side alley would throw me back into one of the main streets, to be engulfed by shoppers, like a leaf floating in a stream entering a powerful river.

As my head hit the pillow, the loudest snorer I encountered on the entire walk made his presence known. As always seemed to be the case, he was sleeping in the bunk beneath me. It was frankly unbelievable that the noise he made didn't wake him up.

The room was pretty well lit from outside so when I sat up and looked around the room several pairs of eyes looked back at me with pained and amazed expressions.

"You got to be fuckin' kidding me," said one guy a few bunks away, setting off giggles from around the room.

I had already slapped the guy around the head with my pillow several times, but he didn't even break breath. On other bunks, heads dived under pillows and feet kicked up and down in anguish, in the hope it might do the trick and stop him.

The solution was remarkable. The crazy thing about a snorer keeping everyone awake is the courtesy his victims accord him. Nobody wants to wake him up. They think it would be rude! I feel the same way myself sometimes. I mean, how crazy is that? One person keeping everyone awake and everybody just lives with it?

This time it was different. A redhead, three bunks away, faced me. She was constantly smiling, and I, naturally, smiled back a lot as well. As it transpired, she was smiling at the guy in the next bed from her, which was rather disappointing. After a while, during which they had been discussing what to do, they both got out of bed and made their way over to the culprit. The conversation that followed still makes me chuckle now.

The girl proceeded to shake him several times until he came around. In fact, at one point, if she had shaken any harder I think his head would have flown off. He awoke, looking a little dazed.

"Excuse me," the woman whispered ever so gently.

"Huh? What?" came the puzzled reply, as he rubbed his eyes. He then smiled broadly, presumably thinking his luck was in, as you might expect after being woken by a gorgeous-looking woman in the middle of the night.

"I'm sorry to wake you," she said, "but you're snoring really loudly and keeping everyone awake. Would you please mind turning over on to your side? There's less chance you may snore there. Thanks very much, I'm sure everyone appreciates it." She walked back to her bunk. I peered over the bunk and smiled at the guy, who looked up at me in amazement, raised his eyebrows and went back to sleep.

I awoke in the morning to the usual buzz of pilgrims packing and discussing the day's walk, some holding a mug of coffee, some with toothbrushes hanging out of their mouths, some bouncing about on one foot trying to get the other sock on.

"Hey, Fozzie, make sure you check you have everything this morning. OK?" Gérard said.

"Yeah," I managed, rubbing my eyes and homing in on the

coffee machine.

"Morning, Fozzie. Check you pack everything this morning, won't you? Make sure nothing is missing," John said.

"Yeah, will do," I replied, letting some hot, black caffeine slide down my throat.

"Hi Fozzie, good morning," Pierre said, stopping right in front of me and blocking my way.

"Pierre, sorry, I don't wish to be rude but I ain't good at conversation first thing in the morning."

He laughed.

"No problem. Make sure you double check your bag, huh?"

"Yeah, I will," I said, as he started to walk off. "Hey! What? Pierre! Come here a sec. You're the third person this morning who's told me to check my stuff. What the hell is going on, or am I imagining things?"

"Haven't you heard?"

"Heard what?"

Pierre took the chair by me, swung it round and rested his hands on the back rest the way they do in the Westerns. He looked concerned.

"Fozzie, I thought you would have heard. Several people reported items and belongings missing this morning as they packed."

"Right, I'm listening."

He continued. "Well, apparently, someone caught a guy going through their rucksack in the early hours, helping himself to anything he fancied. The victim called the warden and the guy handed over a sack full of booty. It was weird. All I heard when I got up was people saying they couldn't find stuff, where was this, where had they left that? The guy must have been through practically everyone's bags during the night. Do you not have anything missing?"

"Well, yeah, now you mention it, my karabiner has gone." This was a small clip that I used to hang my damp laundry on to my pack so it would dry during the day's walk.

"Well," Pierre said, "go and see the warden, tell him what's missing, and I bet he's got it in the booty bag."

The warden was sitting in the kitchen, and a few pilgrims were queuing up to see him. When I got to him I explained what the karabiner looked like, and to my amazement he pulled it from the bag. Next to him was the thief himself. As I looked at him, his dejected head raised and his eyes met mine. If ever I had seen someone looking sorry for himself, this guy got the Oscar. I actually felt pity for him; he looked genuinely remorseful. I thanked the warden and walked back to Pierre.

"He had the karabiner," I stammered. "I couldn't believe it, thought I'd lost it. I mean it's not valuable or anything, but I would have missed it."

"Apparently," Pierre explained, "when the guy caught him going through his stuff, he just held up his hands, admitted to everything, claimed he was a kleptomaniac, and said he deserved everything that was coming to him. The police are coming later, but for sure he'll lose his pilgrim's passport. His days on the Camino are finished."

Leaving Leon was depressing. The sky was thick with ripe clouds, blocking out any light whatsoever. The rain kept stopping and starting. I didn't really want it to rain, but wished it would – just so I would have confirmation of a decision. I observed the elements from a sheltered café on a street corner, watching Leon get to work. Traffic hooted, showers of road spray hung in the air. People dashed across the road bracing their umbrellas against gusts, or stood with their feet in puddles at the kerbside.

At nine I gingerly ventured out of the café and started trying to establish how to actually leave the city. The guidebook was no use; I may as well have been in another country. Camino signs were non-existent. I saw the occasional rucksack, so presumed there was a reasonable chance that I was on the right way, although we could all have been having the same problem.

I passed John and Yetty amongst a cacophony of car horns and traffic.

"Morning, John," I said. "Nice, peaceful and tranquil morning!"

"I don't get off on cities," he replied and smirked to show he still had a sense of humour.

Six kilometres out of Leon, I met Pierre and walked with him for the rest of the day. I had developed a great liking for this man, although on first meeting I hadn't taken to him, maybe because I was at full throttle trying to finish early for Greece and probably not the best company. Then this guy more or less forced me to stop and I felt resentful for it. It pissed me off that I had to struggle with distances and a schedule when he was the exact opposite and could hardly have taken the Camino at a more relaxed pace.

Pierre was sixty-three, tall and lanky, with a slick of silver hair that used to stand erect when a south-easterly caught it. The expression *they're so laid back that they're horizontal* sprung to mind although Pierre's walking was so laid back that he had passed the horizontal, done a couple of loops and finished back somewhere past horizontal at diagonal. When he walked, he often hummed or sang *Ultreya*, the song we had sung at the monastery in Conques.

We arrived at the ghost town that was Villar de Mazarife late afternoon. No one was about. It was way past siesta, and too damn cold and wet for one anyway. We found the refuge up a small side street and peered around the open front door after several knocks had failed to produce a reaction.

An estate agent might describe this house as 'in serious need of renovation'. Plaster flaked off walls, fading paint clung on wherever it could. It was the sort of place where budget was clearly the primary concern, and if something needed to last another year, it damn well better had. When the last building inspector had viewed it, I surmised, he left after five minutes to call for backup.

But I loved the way it oozed character. There was a courtyard at the rear, and a rickety wooden balcony framed three of the walls above where mattresses were spread out. People could sleep outside but the drizzle was working its way under the overhanging roof. I would have killed to have been there in the summer, sitting out in the garden with a late-night drink and chatting to other pilgrims, with the laughter echoing off the walls. The showers were outside but at least hot. Bed for the night was a bare mattress on a wooden floor, just the way I liked it. Wind whistled through cracks around doors and windows and brushed past my face.

"G'day, mate!"

I swung around to be met by a short, well-built woman of

about thirty-five. She was totally out of place, especially as the Australian accent just didn't fit. But it didn't matter: the place kept getting more quirky every minute.

Blancetta (pronounced Blanketar, not, as we kept being reminded, Blanchetar) was, well, funny. She had long, dark hair that made her look ten years younger than she was. Her Aztec excuse for a jumper looked as if it had been knitted from a dead yak; fishnet stockings bulged out around her legs and were met at the bottom by a pair of Dr Martens. Pierre took a dislike to her bubbly manner, and his temper began to fray, which made her bite back.

"So," I interjected, to break off another spitting match, "Blanchetar, what on earth are you doing out in the middle of remotest Spain, running a wreck of a refugio, but a unique wreck at that, with an Australian accent?"

"It's BLANCETTA, not Blanchetar. I'm originally from Spain anyway. My mother is Spanish, Basque to be precise, and she married an Ozzie. I moved to Australia when I was about five and grew up out there. The other kids used to take the piss because I had a Mediterranean complexion, so I grew up learning how to take care of myself. I completed the Camino a month ago and came straight back to this place because I want to buy it, renovate it and spend the rest of my life here."

She handed me an A4-size piece of thin card.

"Look, this is probably the first time you have seen one of these."

"Oh, my God!" I exclaimed. "Pierre, look at this, it's the certificate we get in Santiago."

We both studied it, poking it, almost to see if it were alive.

"They write your name in Latin usually," Blancetta explained. "But they couldn't find mine on the list so it stayed the same."

This had totally thrown me. I was holding what was in some weird way a glimpse of the finish line. It was recognition that the end was coming.

"Blanchetar, what, I mean why, sorry, how exactly do you get it once you've arrived?"

The fake-pilgrim spotter was creeping back into my thoughts. I half expected her to confirm my fears with tales of torture dungeons.

"It's BLANCETTA, not Blanchetar. Well, mate, you just kinda go to this room at the back of the cathedral where two very nice Spanish girls ask you a few questions, check your name in Latin, ask you to fill out a couple of forms and they hand it over. There's no big ceremony or anything."

"Questions? What sort of questions?" My eyes narrowed.

"Just name and address, that sort of thing. You know, tourist information to compile reports and all that."

"Oh... OK."

I fell asleep with a draught on my face, listening to the floorboards creaking, and wondering if the Camino could throw up any more surreal surprises.

Chapter Thirteen

Villafranca del Bierzo

After an eternity, the Meseta at last started to fade out after Leon. Bends and turns became more frequent, and hills appeared, along with a certain scenic randomness which everyone had missed. The occasional stream flirted with the Camino and trees grew along its side. After travelling a path that seemed almost obsessively straight, I felt I was in a new playground, the change gratefully accepted. For the first time, I walked with hat, gloves and a neck buff. On the hills a stinging wind whipped my face.

On Sunday 21st October I awoke to accusations that I had been snoring. The refuge in Astorga was a cramped affair. Bunk beds were not two, but three storeys high, balanced like uncertain skyscrapers and the narrow space between them lent a certain claustrophobic element to the dormitory. There were a lot of people jammed into a small space, hence there were several witnesses to back up the claim, which came from Chantelle, one of the French Canadians. At first I gave her my best look of horrified innocence, but after several pilgrims nodded in agreement, I backed down and apologised, admitting that I did occasionally snore when I slept on my back.

I have a proven and precise method of getting to sleep, which had obviously been disturbed, otherwise I wouldn't have ended up sleeping on my back. On retiring for the night, I lie on my back, tuck my feet under the end of the duvet, roll to the left and tuck in again, and then roll to the right and do the same. The pillow sits under my head and I pull the corners so they sit on top of my shoulders. I cross my left leg over my right, and place both my hands on my heart. I then tense every muscle in my body for about ten seconds and let go, which relaxes me. After about thirteen minutes I roll over to my right side, tuck in again, and place both hands just below my chin. This position suits me for about another twelve minutes, when I complete the falling asleep regime by rolling over to my left side to assume the same position. I'm usually asleep in this position after a further few minutes. Clearly, on the night of the snoring episode, I had not made positions two and three, and had been so tired that I fell asleep on my back.

I just couldn't understand why no one took my side when I explained all of this.

After a little frustration getting out of Astorga, the day blossomed into one of the best since Le Puy. As it was Sunday, there was little traffic, so even though I walked by the side of the main road for a few kilometres, there was a weird silence. The sun was warm and low, providing the chance to take some good photos of autumnal colours and long shadows. A collection of hot air balloons drifted above and around me, sending out the occasional roar from their burners. It reminded me of the fairground, for some reason, maybe eliciting some forgotten childhood memory. I walked in a T-shirt and shorts and let the sun keep me warm.

Everyone else sensed what a perfect day it was. No one was in a hurry, and they were all smiling, taking their time, apparently putting aside their worries about finishing the walk and what might come after. It was like one of those classic autumn Sundays in the park when people were out strolling, hands in pockets and holding their faces to the sun as if to soak up the last seasonal warmth before winter arrived.

I passed pilgrims on the grass just off the Camino sipping wine and having a picnic. People I knew would acknowledge me and smile or wave and not say a word, because words weren't needed. No one had to focus on the walking; their legs automatically carried them, leaving them free to look around and experience the day.

Hills were visible in the distance, the last major hurdle before Santiago. Heathers erupted in greens and purples everywhere. It reminded me of Scotland. After walking with Pierre again for a couple of hours, we pulled off the way, about half an hour short of Rabanal del Camino, to where Ancha and Helen were resting under a magnificent oak tree. The tree and the small clearing underneath lured us in, a place to rest and capture the last of the daylight hours. The two Dutchwomen had sensed it as well. Pierre said he had heard about a large oak tree before the village, which, it was claimed, beckoned people to it.

I climbed a short way up the trunk, like a little kid, and let my legs dangle either side of a stout branch, with my head resting on my hands. I focused my mind on the tree and soon familiar wisps of white energy started to dance around, emanating out and up. None of us spoke, simply absorbing the experience.

The refuge in Rabanal del Camino rounded off a splendid day. It nestled in the corner of a small square, flanked by a church. Everything was hewn from stone or carved from deep brown wood. Smoked wafted out of chimneys, reminding me the nights were colder now.

The beautiful refuge had been recently restored and was being run by two Englishwomen from the St James Society back home. They were motherly figures, old and grey, with kind features. Tea and cakes adorned the kitchen like a patisserie shop. The rooms, indeed the whole place was immaculate. They even had a spin dryer, which took me back a few years to my mother's kitchen, where she would sit on the dryer to prevent it from taking off after ignition, and then from bouncing down the hall and ending up in the garden. A deep orange fire roared in the common room, where pretty much everyone ended up reading or writing diaries, talking a little and savouring the perfect day they too had experienced.

The morning could not have produced a more dramatic change. By eight o'clock I was walking in what felt like a horror movie. Intermittent rain slapped haphazardly against me, streaming across the landscape, whipped into a frenzy by gusts of wind. The sun had not risen, but I doubt if it would have had any effect. The sky, barely discernible in the low light, looked menacing, to say the least. Soot-black clouds sped over me, barely seeming an arm's length away. The road snaked over the hills and shimmered from the night's rain. Huge, dead, black trees loomed over the road like terrifying giant hands.

It was the road to the Cruz de Ferro. At an altitude of 1,504m, this large iron cross is perched on top of a huge cairn of stones left by pilgrims over the years as a representation of their worries. The tradition goes that you start the walk with a stone from your home and deposit it at the cross so that you leave your worries behind. I had decided at the start to leave my neck pendant from the church at Le Puy here. It was lucky I had been unaware of the tradition when I left home.

Numerous other artefacts adorned the site: photos pinned to the cross, messages scrawled on scraps of paper, underpants, glasses, you name it. If some archaeologist happened on this site in ten thousand years' time, it would be the find of a lifetime.

A long procession of sodden pilgrims wiggled down to the tiny hamlet of Manjarin, famous for being the home of a Camino legend. It was tiny, a few stone houses limply scattered along the road, all of them abandoned years ago except for one. It had been made inhabitable by whatever material was available: plastic sheets, corrugated tin, wood. It looked like a salvage yard. I was drawn up its path by medieval-type music wafting out of a vintage stereo. Two or three pilgrims were reading an article in the window about the guy who lives there. I realised it was a man Jeannie had told me about a few weeks earlier.

The Knights of the Templar, guardians of the Camino, were entrusted centuries ago with ensuring the safe passage of pilgrims. The occupier of this run-down shack way up in the mountains was referred to as Thomas the Knight. He claimed he was a true Templar Knight and had left his middle-class existence to come to Manjarin, set up his home and provide shelter and food for the walkers.

I peered inside the mess that was the refuge, to be met with the sight of two puppies climbing over each other in squalor. It was disgusting, not to mention cruel. The decision not to stay there, despite Jeannie's recommendation, was pretty easy. All credit to the guy for setting up the place, but it wasn't for me.

From the village of El Acebo to Ponferrada the going was all downhill. The rain, trying to make up its mind since sunrise, finally relented and stopped mid-afternoon. I made my way down to the town through sodden vegetation. Everything shone in the sunlight and water droplets glinted as they fell to earth from glistening leaves. Grass seemed twice as green as usual and streams gushed over boulders and stones. I smelt incense and looked around, expecting to see someone burning a fragrance stick somewhere. Eventually I fathomed the source. Small brown seed pods in the small bushes that lined the path had burst open and were releasing this fantastic perfume. I later found out they were called Cistus bushes and the smell is indeed likened to incense.

I walked through the charming village of Molinaseca, dodging streams of water from overhangs and gutters. The narrow streets made dusk seem more severe, and slimy cobbles reflected the moon like a thousand cat's eyes. Black clouds whisked past, occasionally clearing to reveal a vividly blue night sky, tinged with a fading orange from a setting sun.

I had walked about one kilometre out of town and was about to turn back because I thought I must have missed the refuge, when a giggle from one of the French Canadians made me execute a sharp left to an old church. It had been completely refurbished with pilgrims in mind, and the warden proudly boasted that Shirley MacLaine had stayed there on her pilgrimage.

Downstairs had the feel of a Middle Eastern room. A log fire was crackling right in the centre and the walls were lined with cushioned benches close to the ground.

Hearing a constant squealing and whimpering from outside, I went to investigate. The warden's dog had given birth to a pup whose rear leg was deformed and useless. The bitch, unable to accept it, was picking it up with her teeth and literally flinging it against the wall. If it hadn't been for the noise, I might have let Mother Nature take her course, but my conscience took over and I brought the pup inside by the fire. I imagine it was probably the best night of her life. Practically everybody gave her a bit of love, not to mention numerous food scraps. She was running around, ears pricked up, and playfully nipping at people's legs. I didn't have the heart to send her back outside to be beaten up again, so she spent the night curled up on my bed, never stirring once.

In the morning fat clouds still threatened, their bellies

The Journey in Between

glowing orange from the sunrise. One particular cloud seemed to be winning the daily beauty contest, and when a rainbow joined the scene, I knew it was one of those once-in-a-lifetime photo opportunities. By the time I retrieved my trusty camera from the rucksack, however, the cloud had left and the rainbow had faded. I had to settle for taking a shot of the road winding down to Ponferrada.

I found the town disappointing. I tried to picture the place in summer, which didn't help. Modern concrete apartment blocks looked dirty from traffic pollution. Uninspiring architecture just inflamed the ugliness, and there was the constant smell of industry. To be fair, I should say that I entered the town on the west side, which was built more recently. Another branch of the Camino brings you through the prettier and culturally richer east side, which slopes down from the hill where the thirteenth-century castle built by the Knights Templar perches. This part of the town is well worth seeking out if you want a more pleasant entrance.

A huge slag heap on the way out of town seemed to be summing up a depressing day, but the afternoon couldn't have been more different. The town filtered out to countryside that seemed to be throwing an autumnal party. The sun kept appearing through huge breaks in the clouds, illuminating everything like a lightning strike. Distant hills and mountains flashed and changed as shadows and rays swept over them. The changing light was astonishing. Colours seemed more intense and vivid, even blinding. The vineyards mutated from one colour to another as their lines of perspective merged and ran on a rollercoaster up to the horizon. It was extraordinary, a visually magical afternoon.

Little did I know that when I came into the beautiful town of Villafranca del Bierzo I wouldn't be leaving for ten days. I had every intention of spending the night and leaving in the morning. By the time I did actually leave, nearly two weeks later, I could spell its name without checking the handbook, and give directions to the post office. I even knew what evenings the bar was showing the European football matches.

Jeannie told me to stay at one of the two refuges in town because Jato the faith healer ran it. It was shadowed by the church and immediately I could tell it was going to be special. Jato built the place with his bare hands, and it just sweated character. It had been constructed in stone and wood, made to look as old as the church, and it worked.

Upstairs in the dormitory, I shunned a bunk bed for a mattress on the floor in order to be blessed with some good sleep on the firm surface, even if I only had a modicum of headroom, as the roof slanted down steeply. Everywhere I went, it seemed, I either had to duck under a low beam or walk up little stairs. One dormitory had a sign pinned to the door saying *Over 40s only*. I peered in to check that didn't entitle them to any perks we didn't have. It was worrying that the woman I passed coming out nodded and smiled at me as if I were in that age bracket.

The dining area was the main focal point, where people gathered to eat, drink, write, read or sit by the stove. Food was included each night for a small fee, and I took full advantage after seeing the huge portions of Spanish dishes on offer.

On the first evening I got talking to Kylie, a Canadian guy, whose favourite phrase was 'Yeah, but I'd have some issues with that'. He was about twenty-two, but looked seventeen. He was short, with ruffled hair, a beard and looked a bit like Kevin from Coronation Street. I asked if he knew Jeannie and it turned out he had walked with her for a while.

"Me too," I said. "We were together for a couple of weeks coming over the border."

"Wait a minute, are you Foz?"

The accusation made me feel mildly famous.

"Yep, that's me."

"Jesus, I've heard about you from loads of people. Jeannie, Barry the Irish guy and someone else."

I was just about to say that I didn't class four as 'loads' when he continued.

"I've been seeing your name etched on the Camino for weeks!"

I laughed. It seemed my name in the mud was sticking in loads of people's minds – well, at least two to date.

Together with an American called Warren, they were helping Jato build an extension on to the existing property. Jato's own inimitable style of building meant it was kind of thrown together with whatever materials were available on a given day. I watched him often and he would stop every once in a while, scratch his stubble, cock his head for a closer look at something, then seem to decide that although it probably didn't meet building regulations, if indeed there were any, no one would ever need know.

When he was doing some groundwork, he had found what he thought was an old pilgrim bath. There had apparently always been a refuge on the site, and the bath was centuries old. It was made of stone and about six times the size of a normal bath. It would make a great attraction to the place, especially if it was in full working order. You could tell from the way he looked at it that he was trying to work out the plumbing plans.

The first morning, I awoke to the usual bustle and rustle of pilgrims preparing for the day's march. The sun didn't penetrate our room, as there were no windows, but I knew it must be roughly eight o'clock. I was tired, Villafranca seemed like a pleasant enough place, and I was due a rest day. Then I thought, 'Screw it! Why do I have to be DUE a rest day? Why can't I have a day off whenever I feel like it? Why do I have to be owed one?' So, that's exactly what I did.

I wandered bleary-eyed down to the common room. Warren and Kylie were having the last mouthfuls of breakfast before another day of mixing mortar and throwing bricks around under Jato's watchful eye. I did manage a brief bit of faith healing with the man himself, though. My toes occasionally suffer from loss of feeling. He removed my sock, placed my outstretched leg on his knee and began rubbing the area. His eyes closed and his features contorted as if trying to locate a fly buzzing around the room. He seemed to get fed up after a while, patted my foot and went off to do some building. I decided the village might be more interesting.

I walked down the steep streets to the central square, built in the architectural style I had become accustomed to, with a church commanding the scene, a smattering of bars and restaurants skirting the edge.

It was a good place to rest. Villafranca had all the usual amenities, plus a few interesting diversions as well. The first was the photographic shop. I had to go in to get film anyway, but ended up spending a good hour in there. The owner, who had walked the Camino, had displayed on the walls several of his excellent black-and-white prints of life on the trail.

At a café I treated myself to a good old greasy fry-up. Feeling full, I did manage to squeeze in dessert.

A hair trim was also in order. My hair was long, so all I needed was a shave on the back of my neck under the hairline to get rid of that fluffy stuff, and a sideburn tidy up. Trouble was, as my Spanish was non-existent, I was always terrified of going into the barbers in case they misunderstood me and cut the whole lot off. There were four women inside, one of whom, I deduced, must be the stylist and another, with blue hair, her current customer. The stylist sat me down on an ageing chair and after a lot of pointing, gesturing and saying "por favour" "no" and "si," I finally got the trim I wanted. This was the limit of our conversation until she had finished, when she asked "Pilgrim?"

"Si," I replied, reaching for my wallet.

"No, no. Pilgrim. OK?" Gesturing no money was required.

"OK, gracias. Muchas gracias."

I called Trish as her job in Greece was due to end soon, and I wanted to discover what her plans were.

"How are you?" I said.

"Erm, I'm a bit wobbly, really, Fozzie. Season's finished and I'm at that 'what to do next' stage." She sounded tired of making decisions and considering her options.

"Trish, listen," I said. "Why don't you come out and walk the last two weeks with me? I know the impression you got last time was that I wanted to walk this thing on my own, and I did, but the end is in sight now and it would be great to see you and have some company. It's apparently the best two weeks of the whole walk, at least in terms of scenery. I'm in no rush and I can hang somewhere while you get yourself sorted. Plus, you get to walk into Santiago de Compostela! What do you think?"

"I'd love to, Fozzie."

We discussed a rough itinerary and I said I'd call again in a few days. It would be great to walk with her, and enter the square at Santiago with a companion. I couldn't wait.

The problem now was how to kill those few days. I didn't want to carry on walking because Trish wanted to see the mountains and they started after Villafranca. It was pointless backtracking, so I decided to chill where I was. Then I had an idea. If Jato wanted someone else on the construction site, I could do that and at worst, get my food and board thrown in. He scratched his stubble briefly when I asked him and then he said yes.

On the first day I was helping myself to breakfast with Kylie and Warren in the common room, expecting to spend the day shaping some stone bricks, mixing a bit of cement and sitting on my arse when Jato wasn't looking. He came in, muttered a few words and beckoned us to follow him. Carrying spades and shovels, we walked in thick fog up the hill at the back of the refuge and stopped by a pile of dirt and rubble about two metres high. Kylie and Warren, both of whom spoke good Spanish, listened as Jato instructed them before he walked off back down the hill.

"What's the deal?" I asked.

"We sit down, have a smoke, and admire the scenery when the fog lifts. We talk for a bit more, then do a few minutes' work. Then we repeat again," Warren advised with a smirk on his face.

"What's going on with all this dirt?" I enquired.

"We prop this old bed frame up and then take shovels of dirt and throw them at the springs," said Kylie. "It sieves out all the crap and we're left with a nice, fine dirt to mix with water and use as a finish over the cement. It's so it looks as if the stones are held together in the old-fashioned way. Basically, we're going to be his sieve bitches."

And there it was. We spent most of the day talking, smoking, eating grapes, and every once in a while, we would all get up and go crazy throwing dirt at an old bed so that it looked as though we had done some work. At two thirty we took a break and walked back down the hill to lunch prepared by Jato's wife, a woman of few words. Of short stature, with a crop of dyed black hair not quite covering the grey roots, she spent most of the day preparing food and throwing abuse at Jato. But she was a damn fine cook. She would poke her little head out of the kitchen door, do a quick squint around the tables, then scuttle back in and out again with a top-up of whatever dish had been finished. Occasionally she would sit down, grab a few swigs of vino, eat a couple of mouthfuls, throw some smiles and make some conversation. Then she would go back to the kitchen.

I was sleeping well after the work and food but had developed an annoying habit of getting up in the night to pee. I always thought that was something I would experience in later life, but the problem had started, it seemed, earlier than expected. A woman I knew once told me how, regular as clockwork at three am, she would wake up and go to the toilet, then go back to bed again. This happened every night, whatever she had eaten or drunk before going to bed, and she had just come to accept it as a fact of life. Now I found the same thing happening to me, but rather than accept it, I took to going to the toilet every night before hitting the sack, in the hope that my head would remind my bladder that it wasn't time to wake up yet. No such luck. It is a major operation getting me out of bed at any time, let alone at three in the morning. For an hour or so I would fight the feeling, kidding myself that I could actually go another five hours without relenting, but eventually I let out a sigh and caved in. It was of paramount importance to do the job quickly, but it was always bloody freezing and I could never be bothered to get dressed for the sake of five minutes.

I would unzip the sleeping bag and sit up, usually forgetting there was a big rafter just above my head. Next I had to fumble and grope aimlessly around in the dark to find the stairs. I didn't want to turn on the lights because I was a considerate pilgrim and didn't want to wake anyone. Think of the ending to *The Silence of the Lambs*. Clarice Starling has found the killer's house but he has just done a runner and turned off all the lights. Switch to what the suspect is seeing through his night-vision goggles. Our heroine's arms are outstretched in front of her, waving helplessly from side to side. Her face is green except for these two big golf balls as eyes, staring blankly at nothing. She touches something and then jumps because she doesn't know what it is. Well, that was me. First I had to find the handrail so I knew where the stairs would start, then down three steps and turn right to find the other handrail for the second flight. Once I was at the bottom I turned on the outside lights so I could see better. At this point I was shivering and stood at the urinal shaking, impatiently waiting for my bladder to empty. I usually turned on the lights to get back in bed because I was in such a hurry to be warm again.

* * *

One day a local guy called Jose turned up and he helped with the building for the rest of my time there. He was in his mid-thirties, with a short, tight perm. His skin was Spanish olive and he wore the same pair of jeans and white T-shirt every day. His favourite word was undoubtedly 'tranquil'. Jose liked to take regular breaks and do little work, so he fitted right in immediately. Cigarette breaks, tea breaks, coffee breaks, sit-down breaks, eating breaks, laughing breaks, talking breaks, you name it. When in full flow, though, we would blitz the work. I remember one day, from eight to four, we must have worked for at least three hours!

I had, by now, been promoted to staff quarters. A door leading from the main dorm led to where Kylie, Warren, Jose and I had our own space to retreat to at night, away from the bag rustlers. In the late evening we enjoyed quality relaxation time. Warren would probably write his diary or draw stupid pictures. Kylie would be trying to decide whether to have a snooze or darn his socks. Jose would be smoking marijuana and I would probably be reading or dreaming about mountains. My new quarters afforded increased head space, although it was in the loft, so there was still some crouching involved. It had bags of character, a couple of dormer windows let in some light and we each had a mattress and some personal space. There was only one light bulb so at night we lit some candles. It was a far cry from luxury but we liked it.

The following day I was getting dressed on my bed when I looked over to see Kylie standing in the doorway with a grin on his face.

"Someone to see you," he smirked and stepped to one side.

In the split second that followed, 'someone' came sprinting towards me, arms outstretched, with a huge smile on her face. It was Jeannie. She hit me head on and the momentum carried us over and we landed in a heap on Warren's mattress, much to his surprise.

"You little fucker! Where the hell you been? You fucking went off and left me, you bastard!" she screamed. We just lay there in a heap, giggling uncontrollably until we hurt.

"I got your note," she cried. "Foz! Where the hell you been?!"

My mouth hurt so much from laughing I couldn't speak.

"Walking!" was all I could muster, and we both collapsed again.

Chapter Fourteen

A New Companion

Jeannie could sell anything to anyone. By the time evening had arrived, she had secured a job cleaning for a few days and Virginia, the manager, was her new best mate. It transpired she had never been much more than two days behind me. That was the thing with the Camino. You could meet someone and then not see them for four weeks and it would turn out they were always just a few kilometres behind you, when you thought they were days ahead. Walkers make friends and then lose them, not realising that they probably pass them a few times a week sitting in a bar or staying at a different refuge.

Pierre had also arrived, looking a little the worse for wear but with a glint in his eye confirming he would make it. Reginald, the only walker I had really known all the way from Le Puy, also arrived, sporting the same old pipe held together by the same sticky tape. He was as surprised to see me as I him.

"Fozzie!" he exclaimed, actually removing the pipe from his mouth which I took as a compliment. "Why, I thought you'd be finished for sure!"

"I thought the same about you, Reginald."

I entered the dining room the following morning to find Jato with his head buried in his hands and snapping at people when they asked him where the food was. Virginia had failed to arrive to cook the breakfast, but she eventually huffed and puffed her way through the door at nine, calmed everyone down and sorted out food. Jato perked up immediately and when we left for work he was laying healing hands on a very worried-looking Austrian lady.

He was leaving for Madrid at the weekend, so Virginia was left in charge. When we asked her what we were to do, she simply shrugged her shoulders and muttered something about looking busy. So we climbed up the hill one more time on the pretence of an attempt to work, and spent 95% of the day talking – a new record.

"Every man's revolution is a tap on the snooze button," Kylie said at one point. All three of us nodded sagely at this piece of nonsense and muttered a few 'Yeah man's.

The conversation covered such profound areas as fair-trade coffee, organic farms, revolution in Mexico, oh, and the benefits of online gaming. Kylie and I shared a passion for medieval warfare games – sad, at my age, I know. Warren was struggling to see the attraction.

"You can learn more from gaming than from history books," I explained. "The gaming is based, more or less, on actual war units, infantry, siege weapons and such. You learn where and when to use a particular unit, what to counter with, war planning, lines of attack, surprise hit and runs. It's cool."

"You sad, English boy."

Virginia took her new role to heart and gave us the afternoon shift off. This would have provided me with an afternoon siesta for once, had Warren not been engaged in throwing wet pieces of bog roll at me and refusing to turn down his radio because the volume button was broken.

To my surprise, I was getting tired of Villafranca. Jato was getting on my nerves and I could see myself getting stuck there like Kylie and Warren, like a fly in treacle. They were happy muddling along but I could see they had lost the spirit of the Camino. Maybe it was because of the fear of finishing, the dread of actually reaching the stage where you don't have to walk any more. Perhaps, I thought, that was why they were there, because they knew if they stayed at Jato's then the finish wasn't getting any closer. I could feel myself starting to stick as well. I had not heard from Trish and it was getting on for a week since I had arrived. The work was getting monotonous, I begged for new scenery, my legs were getting restless and I wanted to feel my pack on my back again.

The place did have its advantages, though. It was undeniably a beautiful village, I wasn't spending any money and it was the only place where Trish could get hold of me so I couldn't move anyway.

Occasional events broke up the boredom. Jeannie and Jose had been caught by the police for smoking marijuana amongst some bushes in the park. Naturally, this worried me when I found out. I mean, what was she doing with Jose in the bushes?

They had been spending a lot of time together and flirting around. A few of us had gone into town one evening for a meal and the two of them had wandered off for a walk. Villafranca park was a maze of short, cropped bushes about waist height, with the occasional bench. As night fell, they had sat down, laughing and joking around, and decided a little harmless substance smoking was called for, for which they obviously had to use a lighter. This proved a very inviting beacon for the local police patrol, who put two and two together and called six colleagues. Before Jeannie and Jose knew what had hit them, eight law enforcement officers jumped over the hedges from various angles, blinded them with torches and held them at gunpoint.

Jose had somehow managed to see all of this coming and tossed the offending substance into the bushes. Jeannie faked her best innocent look whilst holding up her arms, her horrified eyes fixated on the torch beam like an escaped prisoner caught in a spotlight. The police searched everywhere but couldn't find anything, leaving them with the only option of telling Jeannie and Jose off for possession of a joint, which they had found. If they had discovered Jose's larger stash, it would have meant jail for both of them. Jeannie was clearly shaken by the whole event.

"I though I was going to jail, Foz," she said. "The last thing my daughter said to me before I left was not to get into trouble because she couldn't bail me out."

Jeannie's good humour about the refuge lifted my spirits a little. I was still waiting for news from Trish, made all the more frustrating because I had no contact details for her. I found the work a little less monotonous and the conversations with Kylie and Warren always made me giggle. Warren especially was given to spouting stuff quite randomly.

"Did you ever get the feeling your ex is getting laid?" he offered one morning. Kylie looked at me and smiled.

"Yeah, I do," I replied. "It's weird, like you, well, you just know she's having sex with someone else at that precise moment. What's she doing having sex at eleven thirty in the morning anyway?"

"Huh?" Warren looked a little bemused.

"I said, what is she doing have sex at eleven thirty in the morning? You said you knew your ex was getting laid: how does she get sex at eleven thirty am?"

"How should I know? Does it matter?" he said uncomfortably.

"In fact, that's not strictly true," I added. "I take it she lives where you do in Portland. Therefore, they are around, what, ten hours behind us here. Therefore, she's having sex at roughly... two... three thirty am! Did you two normally get it on at irregular hours?"

"Well, no, not really. Sort of normal hours, really, in the evening and stuff."

Kylie had his back to both of us but I could tell by his shaking that he was quietly giggling.

"I think maybe her new man is giving her a rich and varied diet, Warren. Maybe this is why she left you in the first place. Maybe you weren't sugaring her coffee? You know, weren't buttering her baps?"

At this point, Kylie collapsed backwards in a fit of hysterics and promptly fell off the dirt heap, throwing up a cloud of dust.

"Do you think she knows when you're having sex?" I asked.

"Well, if she does, she probably knows I've been celibate for months."

"You two are weird," chipped in Kylie, who stood up looking like someone who had, well, just fallen off a dirt heap.

Sifting dirt was placed on hold the following day as Jato took us to a raised tomb in the graveyard right behind the refuge. He gave us each a wire brush, explained to Kylie what he wanted, and walked off.

"What's going on?" I asked.

"Well, he just wants us to clean off this tomb and then give it a couple of coats of emulsion."

So we spent the morning rubbing and inhaling a mixture of old paint, cement dust and the occasional bit of dried lichen. There was unusual bustle around the headstones. Half the village seemed to be pruning, placing flowers and doing a spot of DIY on their lost loved ones. There were tubs of white paint everywhere – it was like B&Q on a Sunday morning. The local florists must have done 80% of their yearly trade around that time of year. I never did discover what the occasion was, but by the time we had finished and trudged back to the refuge, the whole cemetery had been scrubbed, scraped, cleaned, given a lick of paint and polished. We did find out, however, that the tomb we had worked on belonged to his grandfather.

That evening the phone rang in the dining room whilst I was sitting outside enjoying a cigarette. Kylie answered it.

"Call for Keith." He paused, somewhat confused. "Do we have a Keith?"

"Who the hell's Keith?" Jato asked.

I was just walking back in.

"Last call for Keith, Trisha on the phone, KEITH!"

"Whoa! That's me!" Everyone looked at each other, surprised, and muttered in unison, "Keith?"

Trisha had managed to secure a flight for the Saturday morning, so on Friday, needing an excuse to get out for a couple of days, I headed towards Madrid on the 10:05am coach from Ponferrada. And what a coach it was! Forget the best of National Express, this thing was like Concorde. There was so much leg room that I had to squint to see the person in front. The seats reclined back so far that if I looked back I could see the woman behind looking at me; she looked a bit funny upside-down. The headrests even had little raised areas at the edge, so my head wouldn't roll off when we went around a corner. TV, video, radio... I half expected a flight attendant to announce when we would be landing.

I was looking forward to Madrid. Cities aren't really my thing, but after being in Villafranca for an eternity, I was looking forward to a strong dose of the twenty-first century. Unfortunately, it proved a little too much. I had inadvertently picked the weekend of the Real Madrid and Barcelona football match. The locals, wisely, had moved out and let the hordes in.

This included the football fans, the usual city workforce, some Christmas shoppers and a few general misfits. It was horrible. Oxford Street on Christmas Eve had nothing on this. After walking so far and not having to worry about anything getting in my way on the Camino, my brain was in turmoil trying to dodge everybody. It was like a human version of bumper cars. People were stressed, tempers frayed, and everyone was constantly apologising for getting in the way. I was completely out of my depth.

Accommodation was proving a problem as well. I would have liked to dump my bag in a room, have a quick shower and then get back into the fray to survey Madrid from the sheltered vantage point of a street-side café, but there were no rooms anywhere. I had never experienced a city or town being fully booked. I was in the middle of a city well past its population limit, with a tired friend flying in, expecting at least a bed for the night.

I used the last available option open to me, the tourist office. I was in a queue of about ten people and, as I moved closer, I realised that for once I had picked the correct attendant. Hearing what other people were asking him, I could see that he knew everything, and I mean *everything*. Not only could he give you several options for a barber, he could rattle off the opening and closing times and the exact address, all without checking any paperwork. If I'd asked where I could have a pint of Guinness while relaxing in a sauna with a leggy Danish masseuse fondling my steam settings, he could have given me the answer and told me the colour of the towels.

He provided me with three possible establishments within my budget. After trudging around Madrid central with a map, the first two were booked up. The third place I walked into had one room left and I was so tired that I agreed to take it without viewing it. I hoped the owner's appearance wasn't a clue to the condition of the rooms. Greasy black hair hung in his eyes. A week's worth of stubble protruded from his tired face and his eyelids were on the verge of closing. He wore jeans and a white vest with egg stains down the front, and kept brushing cigarette ash from his stomach.

The room wasn't as bad as I had feared. Two single beds took up most of the space. A forlorn-looking washbasin lurked in one corner, and a frosted window set three metres up the wall provided a little light. The bathroom was a shared affair with a few other rooms, but hey, when you're a budget traveller, you have to take what you can get.

I generally stay in Youth Hostels when I travel. They are usually basic but at least clean and cheap. I like the atmosphere and you meet like-minded people there. One of the best places I ever stayed was a cave in Cappadocia, Turkey, an area that is littered with caves that the local people have used as homes for generations. The particular one I stayed in was circular in shape with a fireplace, and a helping of rugs to take the coldness off a bare floor. It was unique and bursting with character, and cost the grand sum of £1.00 per night (a gas heater was an extra 20p). These places exist; you just have to know where to look for them.

As Trish was arriving in the evening, I decided to try out Madrid's tube network. There was a direct line straight to the airport but the train driver had other ideas. He stopped a few stations away from the terminal and then walked through the carriages announcing something I didn't understand. All I could get from him was that the train was stopping and another one was not forthcoming. I resorted to a cab for the rest of the journey and sat down in the airport bar waiting for the arrivals. My head was darting from side to side and up and down trying to see over people for Trish. She eventually came through and stopped in the terminal to try and fish something out of her bag. I executed my usual welcome by creeping up behind her and poking her hard in the side. She performed a flawless two-metre jump with contributory yelp, securing maximum scoring from the judges.

"Fozzie! Fuck! Hi, darling!" she squealed.

I can best describe Trish as someone who follows dreams and doesn't conform to society's expectations – like me, really, which is why we got on. She was in her late thirties. Long, curly, rustic-looking brown hair tumbled down her back and got in her eyes. Occasionally she would tie it back with a pink band kept on her wrist. It had been bleached by the Cretan sunshine over the summer, and her skin was tanned. Her dress sense was a little different but, no matter what the occasion, whether it be hiking, swimming, cooking or whatever, there would always be little feminine touches like a small bow here or a flower there. She also loved going clubbing in hiking boots. Try to mock her attire and she would just say, "But I'm a princess, Fozzie. Princesses are beautiful whatever they wear!"

She was a chef by trade, and a damn good one at that. We had spent the summer working at a yoga retreat on Crete and just clicked. She taught me a lot about the catering trade, food and nutrition, as well as how to moisturise correctly and dye my eyebrows.

On our days off, we would go out on adventures, as she clung to the back of my moped. We might climb a mountain, find the most out-of-the-way taverna possible, swim stupid distances or just get drunk in the local bar. Whatever it was, we had a great time. I had left because of a dispute with the owners in which Trish had been heavily involved. She had done the brave thing and seen it through to the end. No matter how bad the situation, that's what she did. She was one of the kindest and most sincere people I had ever met. It was refreshing. People always warmed to her and she never had a problem talking to strangers. She had an uncanny knack of having long conversations with me and sorting out my problems without my even realising what she was doing.

As usual, we ended up going out in the evening to catch up and the wine flowed. My budget was annihilated as glass after glass kept coming, but that was what we were like when we got together. Looking back after the walk I realised that most of the evenings during the last two or three weeks spent with Trish were an alcoholic blur. We must have tried every different type of Rioja available and kept the Spanish wine industry going single-handed.

We were accosted by three girls on a hen night from Manchester. I asked the bride-to-be what her intended was like.

"Oh, he's great, we have a really open relationship. It works because we both allow each other to flirt with other people and we can have sex with them as well, just not penetration," she explained.

"Oh, I see," I replied. "That's all right, then."

The Journey in Between

The next day we both headed back to Villafranca for one more final night's rest and then the summit push to Santiago de Compostela. I was now looking at the distance in terms of days instead of weeks. I felt happy to be on the cusp of walking again but the fear of finishing, and what would come after, still haunted me.

I was adamant that the final two to three weeks of the walk were going to be the best. I had met a few people who had walked the Camino previously and they all said the same about the last part. Beautiful scenery, a sense of anticipation and, if Galicia's weather held, the best chance to take it all in.

As it turned out, the rest of the Camino was to be the sternest test. The hills weren't enormous, but they certainly weren't small either. The countryside dipped and dived as the foothills warmed themselves in preparation for El Cebreiro, which, at 1,300m was neither the highest point on the Camino nor arguably a big mountain, but it did have a big reputation.

I always find walking so much better and more rewarding when I am at altitude. It doesn't have to be six thousand metres. My local hills in Sussex are probably only a few hundred metres high but that view from the top down on the rest of the world is enough for me. I feel free in the hills and mountains, where either I forget my problems or the solutions come to hand. For those few hours, I am not part of the world down there amongst everyone else. It is an escape that I thrive on. The air is cleaner, the wind fresher and the aromas more intense.

The day we left was perfect. An early morning mist wafted around Villafranca like ghosts, dying as the sun lifted. There was the tiniest of breezes which I could just feel on my face like the brush of a feather. The shadows were retreating and cowering.

A smell of damp stonework moved around in the village as we made our way through the rustic streets for possibly the last time. The chill of the damp walls in the tight alleys seemed to be trying to penetrate me. And then I walked with Trish out into the main square. It was different. Certainly more beautiful and charming. It had saved its best for last.

We passed the bar that had served me with numerous fry-ups, gave one last look at the photographs in the camera shop, took a quick, deep sniff of the bakers as I walked past, and glanced in at the hairdressers with all the usual customers gossiping and giggling. I felt the wonderful pressure of the cobbles on my heels and toes. We were both smiling.

El Cebreiro was thirty kilometres away. Not a huge distance, but on that sort of terrain we could be beat after fifteen. I had said my goodbyes to all the friends I had made at the refuge. Jeannie had left about three days earlier, and we hoped to meet in Santiago. Virginia gave me a pendant for my neck chain, which was touching. Slaps on the back from the chaps, Jose muttered *tranquil* and even Jato touched the peak of his cap and smiled.

It was sixteen kilometres to Vega de Valcarce and the next refuge. Bearing in mind I had not walked for nearly two weeks and Trish needed some gentle breaking in, we agreed it was a reasonable target. We crossed over the River Burbio and took a right fork. This was the steeper and harder of the two possible routes, but it was away from the main road. And boy, was it steep! We were both hunched forward, gasping for air and sweating profusely. It smoothed out after about thirty minutes and the climb mellowed out to a good incline. We caught our breath and lay by the trail trying to cool off, laughing and soaking up the sun.

It was now the first week of November but it still felt summery. Insects buzzed around my head, many plants were still green, the earth was dry and I smelt pollen. This was my eightieth day of walking and the total distance now under my boots was 1,317 kilometres. However, the signs of autumn were also all around us. Polished horse chestnuts peeked out from their spiky cases, shining like lacquered mahogany. Leaves hung in drifts against stone walls, while others spun and whipped skywards in wind flurries. Golds, reds, browns and greens blurred into nothingness as they flew around us.

Trish asked me how many footsteps I had taken, which we soon agreed would take too much working out. However, I started calculating the number of times I had done certain things. I estimated I had drunk 300 litres of water. Not surprisingly, taken a pee around 500 times. Eaten about 40 omelettes (even more worrying, that's about 100 eggs). I must have picked my nose a lot, maybe even three times a day, so that's about 240 pickings. Lifted my pack on and off – I had to spend a bit of time on this one – about 600 times. Sung a lot of songs, or at least hummed them, and taken around 20 wrong turns.

I was just compiling the options for tracks eleven and twelve for the Song of the Day album when I realised we were lost. Typical, I thought, on the first day of my new guide status and I'd already taken a wrong turn.

"Nice one, Fozzie," Trish commented. "Been reading the book properly, have we? How did you manage up until now, then? Not the best of starts, is it?"

"Yeah, right," I said. "Come on! It's all part of the adventure! We're still heading vaguely west, I think. We're not that far off. Where's your sense of spontane... spon... spontinuit... spon... you know, adventure?"

I ignored the heated rantings of four local people waving us back the other way and then had to eat a serious portion of humble pie when we returned later after I realised they were right. They shook their heads from side to side and smirked as we passed.

The countryside gave way to a main road and one of the most dangerous stretches of the Camino I had walked on. There was an occasional path on the side of the road, but most of the time we had to walk hemmed between crash barriers and the traffic. We eased into Vega de Valcarce at seven in the evening. It was cold, very dark and we were both tired. The refuge was a lacklustre affair with bunk beds made from wrought iron and mattresses looking as though they were full of potatoes. The shower was a cold trickle but I didn't care any more. My attitude towards these safe houses now was that, no matter how bad some were (and only a minority could be described as bad), I knew I would have a bed with a roof over my head. What more do you want at night?

The local bar provided us with soup, chips, an omelette and some half-decent beer. The food was getting tedious. Trish was fed up with the same options already. Invariably there were chips, bocadillos (sandwiches) with either cheese or chorizo (Spanish sausage), or the ubiquitous Spanish tortilla (omelette). My cholesterol quota for the year had been exceeded about three weeks before. But most places obliged when we asked for stuff that wasn't on the menu board such as a tuna sandwich, a mixed salad or soup. The only real food to be had was in the larger towns. It seemed an age ago that I was in a tapas bar like the ones in Pamplona. Some days when the culinary offerings were becoming too tedious I would drift off into a daydream about sitting in one of those bars: twelve metres of polished mahogany, supporting cabinets teeming with collections of taste bud heaven.

I awoke the following day after little sleep. My tortilla bocadillo the night before had been waging all-out war on my digestive tract. You could have set your watch by the cyclist in the bunk above, who would snore constantly for thirty minutes and then break into a coughing fit, which sounded as if he was trying to hack up a golf ball. Yet he never woke up. The 'selective noise recognition while asleep' phenomenon is truly astonishing. Why is it that someone can snore like a road drill and not wake up, yet if they hear a certain sound they come to? An ex-girlfriend used to snore pretty loudly while sleeping like a baby, yet she would reply as soon as I asked a question.

Inadvertently, Trish hadn't helped either. I had told her to bring a two or three-season sleeping bag. Some college leaver in the outdoors store had sold her a one–season bag with one of those marvellous cock-ups of design, a large sheet of tin foil otherwise known as a space blanket. I understand the theory, but the disadvantages far outweigh the benefits. They may reflect heat back on to your body, but they make a racket similar to several hyperactive chipmunks having a party in a pile of empty crisp packets.

We casually meandered through a Camino that was becoming more outstanding every step of the way, never failing to surprise me no matter how well I thought I knew it. The area approaching the climb to El Cebreiro was in full autumnal display. Grass a vivid shade of green looked almost edible, crisp and glistening with moisture. There always seemed to be the sound of gurgling water nearby and occasionally I would catch a glimpse of pure mountain water cascading over rocks and tree roots.

An old woman was standing at her front door in one of the many small hamlets we walked through. She looked really miserable and ready to snap off the head of any pilgrim who even dared look at her.

"I'm not going to say hello to her," I said. "She looks far too miserable."

"Maybe she's miserable because no one ever says hello to her," Trish replied, in her usual wise fashion.

I didn't really have an answer to that, but I did promise to try and smile at anyone that looked a little down for the rest of the day.

Trish was good to walk with, but then I wouldn't have asked her to come if I didn't think we would get along. Most of the day we would walk together, but occasionally I would get an adrenaline rush and go ahead for a couple of hours, usually checking behind me just to make sure she was following. Sometimes she would walk ahead. It was a great mixture of walking with company but having our own space as well. We got hungry at the same time, and after a while started buying more food at shops to carry with us so as not to have to rely on finding a suitable bar. We would get the freshest baguette possible and stuff it with maybe tuna, peppers and a pile of parsley, or cheese, rocket and onion and then sit on a stone wall, legs dangling, and stretch our mouths to cram in this ridiculously tall feast.

Trish sensed that I didn't want to finish and took everything at a sedate pace, which was fine with me. The last thing on my mind now was any form of schedule. I didn't want to be thinking about doing twenty kilometres before lunch or just making the next hamlet by three fifteen so I could push out another ten before dark. We would walk fifteen to twenty-five kilometres a day and take it easy. If we had walked only ten, and it was another sixteen to the next accommodation, we always considered that stopping was a viable option. Never had such a lack of planning worked so well.

"How you feeling, Trixy?" I would enquire at one in the afternoon.

"I'm OK, Fozzie. Little tired, darlin', but OK."

"There's a refuge two klicks away, sounds really nice."

And we would stop early in the afternoon just because we could. We were developing a blasé attitude, as though walking had become random roaming.

The sleepy collection of decaying buildings that was Herrerias signalled the start of the 680m ascent of El Cebreiro. It was reputedly the hardest climb of the whole Camino but it seemed much easier than the Route Napoléon out of St-Jean-Pied-de-Port. To my mind, it was also far superior. Once above the tree line, the hills opened out like a friend with outstretched arms to reveal boulder-shaped hills undulating all around us. We took regular rests, stopped at a couple of cafés and just eased our way up. At one point we felt so nonchalant that we had a cigarette break and lay back in the grass for a siesta. One of the few photos Trish took was of me at one such rest stop, with a look on my face of total contentment that summed up the whole day, possibly the whole adventure.

El Cebreiro commanded views in every direction. The assortment of dwellings and a few bars perched on top had entered winter earlier than expected. We booked in at the refuge and, once washed and changed, did our usual search for a bar and a couple of bottles of Rioja.

Sitting in the local bar we could see orange lights twinkling over the hills around us like candles at a concert. Occasionally the barmaid would come over, check our drinks were OK and carefully place another log on the fire. If this had been a plush ski resort, we would have been paying a small fortune for the privilege. We sank back into our chairs, smoked a lot of roll-ups and drank a lot of wine. Speech slurred, objects on the table doubled up and we giggled at the adventure so far.

Jennifer, a Canadian pilgrim we had got to know since Villafranca del Bierzo, joined us. She had taken a little persuading as she was sober and we clearly were not, but we enticed her over by raising and lowering our eyebrows in temptation and stroking a bottle of delicious '98.

She had been with her boyfriend but they had decided to be apart for a while. He had stayed behind at Jato's, taking advantage of the construction vacancy I had left. Whether they were planning on meeting up later I never did find out and she seemed content with her own company. She was tall, but she didn't appear imposing. Short blonde hair was tousled up over her ears and her eyes peered out from behind wiry glasses.

Luckily the bar closed up while she was still able to walk

because she had to assist both of us back. Clear stars gazed back at us from a blanket of the darkest black possible. The Milky Way splayed across the sky like a plume of faint mist. The air was biting but marvellously fresh. Winter was definitely arriving. As always, I was afraid of hitting snow before I finished, although, once down from El Cebreiro, the rest of the trail was at low altitude where the risk would be lower.

Chapter Fifteen

Closing in

Opening the refuge door in the morning, I saw a scene transformed. Snow had fallen overnight; the arrows left by birds' feet speckled the crisp, smooth layer. Only black, shiny roads interrupted the vast, white uniformity. As I had thought, the lower altitudes, easily visible, were untouched. I had timed my walk to absolute perfection. A couple of kilometres down the hill and we would be out of the fresh fall and back on firm footings. Fingers crossed, the snow would not fall on the lower levels for our remaining time on the Camino.

We digested El Cebreiro one last time, sitting in a bar over a leisurely two-hour breakfast, mainly because my diary was seriously behind. After the descent, the temperature soared and we found ourselves taking a warm siesta once again.

Trish had by now developed a pace quicker than mine and she was usually half a kilometre ahead of me, but then slowed down on the hills. At this stage, I was just ambling along, taking it all in. We met at the hill tops, sat down, had something to eat and rested. I remembered a message I had read in the visitor's book at El Cebreiro refuge: *I have just begun to realise that Santiago is only the destination.*

That pretty much summed it all up for me, as I began to understand its full meaning. I had approached the walk with the idea that there was a beginning and an end. You start at Le Puy en Velay and Santiago is your target. Well, it didn't work like that. The truth was that everything between those two points was where answers lay, where the challenges, events, people and life-changing events happened. It wasn't about getting from A to B. It was all about the experiences that in turn made the memories.

We passed the Alto de San Roque, where a huge bronze statue of St James dominates the road. Sitting on the grass, we made sandwiches from tomatoes and parsley that we had picked from the windowsill of a bar, while the owner looked on smilingly and gestured that it tasted good.

At day's end we found the refuge at Triacastella, which looked like a school building in the middle of a playing field. Jennifer was sitting on the stone wall outside and pointed us in the right direction. Inside, too, it seemed like some sort of school building. Polished lino on the floor gave way to bare breezeblock walls. The rooms echoed conversations and there was a strong smell of disinfectant.

The warden checked us in and we made our way to the designated room. As I pushed the swing door, it stopped abruptly and a hand appeared over the top and gently eased the door open. The hand's owner bore a striking resemblance to the actor Christopher Lloyd (the mad professor in the *Back to the Future* movies), only younger. Unfairly tall, he was bald except for a line of greying hairs clinging to the back of his head as though they had slipped from the top. I'd not seen him before and he didn't look very happy.

"You can't sleep in here, I'm afraid," he said. His voice was soft, an unexpected and striking contrast to his presence.

"Why?"

"Because I am—" He was cut off by the warden behind me, who moved me to one side apologetically.

"You have no reason to deny them a room. I have booked them in and I allocated them this room because there are two beds free. I am the warden here, not you. Let them in or I will let you out." He spoke with such authority that no one would have argued with him.

Although I wouldn't have minded finding another room, I was a little curious as to why he didn't want us in there. It soon became apparent. Jennifer had passed us checking in and was sitting on one of the beds, looking a little sheepish. It would appear that her ex-boyfriend back at Jato's had been well and truly dumped and she had taken up residence in the Mad Prof's bed. I gave her a nod and a wink as I passed.

After visiting town in the evening for a bite to eat, we returned to the refuge. Tucked up in our bunk beds, Trish was just kind of staring into space. Jennifer and the Prof were reading, still playing out the 'only friends' act by occupying separate beds.

"What you reading, Fozzie?" Trish asked.

"Er, *The Pilgrimage*, Paulo Coelho."

"Any good?"

"Not bad, I s'pose."

"Read us some, then."

"Yeah, OK. Huh? What you say?"

"Go on, read us all a story so we can get comfy and wind down to sleep."

So I did. There I was, in the middle of some big hills in north Spain, sleeping in a converted school, reading a story to my best mate, a cute Canadian and a mad Prof.

When I awoke the next morning, Jennifer had slipped into the Prof's bed at some point overnight and their heads were romantically nuzzled up together. So close, in fact, that he looked as if he had miraculously sprouted hair overnight.

I went outside to retrieve my clothes, left drying overnight on the washing line. It had been so cold that my T-shirt and other items had frozen solid, so instead of draping them over my arm I carried them under it, as one would a stack of large books.

Trish went on ahead as usual. I always revelled in my own company and Trish, although a sociable person, was using the time to figure out where she was in her life, in the big plan of things. Her job in Crete had proved hard work with long hours, high temperatures and many mouths to feed. It appeared she was taking to her newfound solitude and freedom with relish. Once in a while she would grab her long hair, push it out of the way and turn to check that I was still visible, and smile, just as confirmation she was comfortable and to let me know that, although we were walking apart, she was happy and wanted me to be too.

As the day moved on and the sun lifted higher, it warmed. The frost on the ground gradually darkened from whites to vivid greens as the grass came up for air. Light from a damp, shiny countryside twinkled back at us from a million different locations. We passed through San Cristobo do Real, a small hamlet forcing the River Oribio to split and flow either side of it, then we followed a muddy track through and passed stone dwellings covered in moss. Straw lay here and there, moving slightly in the breeze, and leaves floated down from side to side like someone swaying in a hammock.

The Benedictine monastery in Samos appeared at the end of a leafy lane, an imposing stone masterpiece which dominated the small village and still housed a few monks, but in its heyday was home to about five hundred of them. We walked around it but all the doors were closed and the windows tiny, leaving the whole place eerily lonely and like a closed book. A fine drizzle engulfed us as the sun disappeared, leaving us pulling on fleeces and waterproofs.

Spain had changed in a matter of days. Winter had sneaked up quickly and caught summer by surprise. It was difficult to get moving in the morning, but after half an hour our bodies had warmed up and we were removing gloves and hats, unzipping jackets and squinting at the low sun with rosy cheeks. We passed through an uninspiring Sarria and looked behind to a backdrop of white where we later learnt it had snowed in Samos also. Not only was it snowing higher up, where we had escaped from, it now seemed to be chasing us west as well.

"Fozzie! Fozzie!"

I spun round to see Tamar emerging from a small café in Cortinas.

"Who's that?" Trish enquired. I sighed, asking her how much time she had, so I could explain to her the paradox that was Tamar and I. Espe looked on and watched Tamar approach and hug me as though her life depended on it. When Trish saw the resigned look in my eyes, she realised our relationship was not as promising as Tamar's welcome might suggest.

We all shared a surprisingly light-hearted coffee and for the rest of the day I walked with Tamar; Trish seemed happy with Espe, who was no doubt filling her in on the previous weeks.

Before long we had slipped back into the old routine of trying to hold a conversation, becoming stressed and settling for a language that had no barriers – kissing. When we had originally met it had taken only half a day to realise there was a huge physical attraction and even less time to understand that it would prove difficult. It was all about desire, nothing more; I knew that now.

We reached Morgade, a simple collection of small, old buildings and Trish had found a little place capable of sleeping two pilgrims, with the option of some home cooking. Although we hadn't done much walking that day, it felt right to stay there. Tamar had never asked to stay with me at any of the places where we slept, but had always waited for me to ask her first. This time I felt I couldn't. Part of my reason was that I wanted to walk with Trish and if Tamar was with us then I knew she would demand all my time. More importantly, I realised at that point it was time to say goodbye, and although I somehow knew I wouldn't see her on the Camino again, something told me our paths would cross at some future date.

I explained as best I could but a resigned look crept over Tamar's face before I had said much. She said she understood and to some extent agreed but had hoped we could have spent more effort working on the conflicting areas. We hugged and kissed for an eternity and then she turned and left. I watched her slender figure becoming smaller with every step until eventually she vanished.

The rest of the day I was in a sombre mood. Trish sensed this and just did her own thing. I took a siesta and then went for a walk – of all things. It was quiet except for the odd call of a crow and the distant hum of a tractor. There was no wind, water trickled and wove around the stones on the path ferrying red leaves downhill. A tiny chapel barely big enough for one person sat about fifty metres from where we staying. Some pilgrims had left the usual notes for others, keeping the trail grapevine alive.

Hey Foz, steps at two, miss you. Jeannie x.

It was written on a piece of cloth, like a hanky, and was draped over the table's edge and kept there with a small stone. It was dated ten days earlier. *Steps at two* referred to our agreement that for as long as we stayed in Santiago, every day we would each go to the steps outside the cathedral at two o'clock and wait for ten minutes to see if the other showed up. I smiled; despite my low mood after dealing with Tamar, Jeannie still had an uncanny knack of cheering me up even though she was ten days distant.

I returned to find Trish tending a roaring fire that threw moving shadows everywhere and transformed our little hideaway into several shades of orange and red. The owners arrived with several dishes of delicious food and even threw in a bottle of Rioja. We drank toasts to open fires, little hideaways, comfort food, being lucky enough to be doing what we wanted to do, and to finishing the Camino. Retiring outside to watch a full moon, we pulling our jackets tightly around ourselves. Smoke from our cigarettes vanished and reappeared as it rose up and caught the light of the moon through gaps in the buildings. The episode with Tamar notwithstanding, it had turned into a day I knew I would remember with great fondness.

The following morning, as we were thanking the owner for her hospitality, she showed us a pair of huge hiking boots.

"These belonged to Andreas," she explained. "He didn't stay here but just stopped for a drink. We don't know whether he left them here by mistake or intentionally. We presume it wasn't intentionally – either that or he doesn't mind walking in his socks! Do you know him?"

I said we didn't know anyone by that name. "What did he look like?" I asked.

"Oh, he was very tall, all the hair was on the back of his head and he was with a lovely girl, Canadian I think. They seemed an odd couple."

"It's the Mad Prof!" cried Trish and I in unison, and we made it our mission for the next few days to return the boots to him. Renaming him Bigfoot, we tied a boot each to our rucksacks and set off to hunt him down.

The truth at this stage of the walk was that Bigfoot, although an interesting distraction, was the last thing on my mind. Each time I walked up a hill I half expected to come over the brow and see the spire of Santiago cathedral. We were only about eighty kilometres away now and the end of the walk was consuming most of my thinking. Of course I wanted to finish – I had to finish. My determination had surprised me over the last few weeks but a lot could happen in eighty kilometres and, although I felt confident, I never took it for granted. What I was struggling to deal with was that I had become settled into this way of life. I was comfortable walking twenty-five kilometres a day, in whatever weather. It made no difference if I stopped for lunch at one or two, if at all. I was grateful to have a roof over my head each night for the cost of a cup of coffee. I was completely at one with the trail and to stop what I was now doing was going to leave a very large void in my life. Everything else in the world was unimportant; I had become a nomad and could have carried on forever.

I had already considered turning round and walking back to Le Puy en Velay but knew that delaying the inevitable wasn't going to help. I would be returning home, with little in the way of funds, and that would mean looking for work until such a time as I could head off again somewhere to pick up with this walking thing that was engulfing me. I felt I could be completely happy if I could just carry on walking until I was too old to do it any more. I didn't care about finding a job, looking for somewhere to live, going food shopping, drinking on a Friday night, buying clothes or anything else. The Camino had completely taken over my life.

Of course the physical act of walking was only a tiny part of the journey. My legs just did their thing, which left me free to think about what I was doing, had done, and what the future held in store. I don't mean spending a few minutes on one area or another; I mean taking one aspect of my life and really getting involved in it. We seldom have time these days just to get into our own heads: mostly we're too busy working, looking after children, making a home or whatever. I always used those few minutes while falling asleep as thinking time, but on the Camino I had the day as well. I was becoming spoilt.

* * *

Most of the refuges were manned by part-time volunteers and, although many continued to stay open during the winter, some were shutting up shop. Many had phone numbers pinned to the door, so a quick phone call meant someone would arrive and open up for us. But we were caught out on numerous occasions and had to find lodging somewhere else, such as guesthouses, which were inconvenient financially. Shops and bars were opening later and closing earlier and we had to rearrange our days to take account of this.

Gonzar appeared to be shutting all its doors like an out-of-season seaside resort. We reached it late one evening after the sun had set, knowing there was a refuge there. We were both cold, hungry and trying to stave off the start of the winter blues. The school was doubling up as the refuge and there was a good kitchen to get some food going. The sleeping area consisted of several bunk beds crammed into a small and cold room. The place was empty apart from a solitary lady who looked a little depressed. I disappeared off to the local bar for a couple of warming whiskies while Trish did her best to cheer her up.

A fine mist hung in the air, refracting and absorbing what little light crept out from dim windows. I felt the moisture glance against my face and creep down between my jacket and neck. A couple of cars went past, their tyres hissing against the damp road. I shivered, stuffed my hands deeper into my pockets, tried to lower my head into the collar of my jacket and squinted through the gloom to try and locate the small illuminated beer sign I had seen earlier on our way in.

The place seemed homely enough. A handful of older guys were smoking and drinking an assortment of spirits. There was a small tapas display next to the beer pump and empty sugar sachets and matches littered the floor under the bar's steel footrest. A fish was sucking the inside of its bowl in search of some small morsel. I ordered a large whisky and small beer and raised the glass with a nod of my head to the locals, who returned the compliment. The TV flicked into life to show a weather guy becoming a little carried away with a few cloud symbols and some alarming-looking temperatures.

Trish arrived about an hour later with Ulrika, the other guest from the refuge. Trish's amenable character and infectious playfulness had rubbed off on the German woman and we sat at a corner table, giggling from the alcohol. It transpired that they had bonded over, of all things, face packs. Trish, for some bizarre reason, had thought it prudent to pack a small tub of some concoction to be spread over her face when she felt in need of some pampering. I discovered that we no longer needed to pursue Bigfoot. Ulrika had been in Morgade when he was there and witnessed him leaving his boots. Apparently they were simply not comfortable and he could not break them in. We left and made our way back for a cold night's sleep.

Santiago was less than five days away. We walked under canopies of overhanging trees, their branches forming tunnels over the trail which beckoned us to follow and go deeper, as if there were rewards at the other end. Sunlight filtered through, dappling the path, as we scrunched through piles of leaves. Shadows became longer, birdsong less frequent. The evenings and nights gave us opportunities to gaze up at cloudless skies and the Milky Way stretched over us, our guide westwards. The good weather was holding and the deep blue above us contrasted beautifully with the mellowing of the foliage.

We arrived in Melida too late for lunch and too early for dinner, so settled in to a bar and checked our emails. The latest news from back home remained unchanged from the usual. A mate advised me that lots of the women we knew were having babies and his wife was broody. *I don't understand it 'cause I'm a bloke*, he commented.

I had several emails from friends and family spurring me on and congratulating me on my achievement so far. I left with a warm feeling, as if I had just received a glowing school report.

The town of Melida is famous for its numerous eateries that serve *pulpo* (octopus), cooked the traditional way, boiled with a sprinkling of paprika and served on a wooden board with a little lemon. We had both been salivating all day at the prospect of a walker's portion (the largest available, twice for each of us) with chips. We were spoilt for choice but settled on a rustic bar filled with people laughing, eating and drinking. Although used to the enormous appetites of pilgrims, they watched astonished as we piled through plates of *pulpo*, only coming up for air to point at the next dish we wanted or for Rioja. We ate and ate without feeling full – although half an hour after finishing we had moved to a couple of chairs and there we sat, legs outstretched, hands on stomachs, blowing air through puffed cheeks.

The Journey in Between

Food is one of the most talked-about topics on the Camino and other long-distance walks. Food gets you going in the morning, carries you to a lunch stop and lures you through the afternoon. I was astonished during the first few weeks by how much I was tucking away and thought I had something wrong with me, until I saw all the other pilgrims consuming vast quantities of food in the evenings. Normally, 2,500 calories a day for a man and 2,000 for a woman is average. It's not unusual on long-distance walks to need double that quantity. In fact, 6,000 calories a day is not unusual for some trails, notably in America, where extreme changes in elevation and temperature force the body to burn fuel at an alarming rate.

It's a great feeling to be able to get through all that food every day and not put on weight – maybe even losing some. Food wasn't just a conversation piece, it was an all-consuming fixation and unless you have completed a long-distance walk it's a hard one to explain. We have all had days of physical exercise when we are preoccupied with what and when we are eating, but it goes deeper than that. Thoughts of carbohydrates were my vice. I would be ambling along minding my own business when all of a sudden my head would be full with visions of potatoes or rice. I would see risottos, chips, jacket spuds, and my mouth would quite literally start to drool. Either that or it was a craving for sugar: bottles of cold Coke, ice cream, pastries, the sicklier and stickier the better.

Many pilgrims mentioned to me that I was grumpy in the evening until I had eaten and then the transformation was immediate, but I had noticed this in others too. After a day's walk, the need to refuel is all that matters and woe betide anyone who comes between a hungry pilgrim and their plate. If you love eating but want to watch your waistline, then go on a long walk: you'll have an absolute ball!

In contrast to the previous night, the refuge at Melida was packed. We wondered where everyone had all come from, bearing in mind the refuges of late were either empty or had a couple of pilgrims at best. The washrooms were so filthy that we both decided to forsake a shower. About twenty people were piled into bunk beds in a windowless room. This did not bode well and at two in the morning the lack of air made me feel I was being asphyxiated. At two thirty I grabbed my sleeping bag and went to sleep in the common room, after an all-sides snorer started cranking up. I awoke on the sofa in the morning to see Trish sitting on the table-tennis table with her legs swinging beneath her. She had gone into town and returned with large espressos and an assortment of pastries. We giggled and stuffed our faces, wiping sugar from our mouths and licking our fingers like children.

The following morning we headed off, knowing that we would reach Santiago de Compostela that day. I had mixed emotions. Happiness, reflection, sombreness and expectation. Again, it was a beautiful morning, the sun rising over the hills battling some low, wispy cloud. There was a silence everywhere, like an early Sunday morning. A few birds sang and our boots crunched along quiet gravel roads.

We had walked through Monte del Gozo, where a collection of buildings resembling army barracks had been built to accommodate the crowds at an open-air mass when the Pope visited in 1989. We dropped down to a road and as we walked over a bridge Trish stopped and tugged me back. I looked at her smiling but confused. Her smile became wider and her eyes bigger as she nodded behind me and upwards, beckoning me to look in that direction. I turned to see a sign – *Santiago de Compostela*. At first I just stared at it, disbelieving; it didn't seem the right kind of sign or the right spot to place it. I stupidly expected something twenty metres high with lights, bells, whistles and *Well done, Fozzie* emblazoned across it. Trish was all smiles and hugs and we spent half an hour balancing cameras on self-timers to take shots of us doing stupid antics under the sign.

The further we made gains into the city, the more the architecture blended from mundane to inspiring. We entered through the Porto do Camino, the traditional point for the pilgrim, and walked down the Calle Azabacheria. Occasionally someone nodded at us and smiled, presumably in recognition of what we had done. People went about their business, shopping or conversing with others. Car horns beeped, mopeds whizzed by. I was excited but in a restrained way. Walking into the Plaza de Obradoiro, we came face to face with Santiago cathedral.

Almost as if it knew we had arrived, it tolled its bells to mark midday. It was a grand welcome that bought a tear to my eye.

We knelt down in the middle of the square to touch the single, solitary stone that marks the end of the Camino. I was beaming, for a multitude of reasons. Obviously, because I had reached Santiago. All those weeks of walking were coming to an end; we only had Finisterre to reach now. For once in my life I had battled against elements that conspired to defeat me and I had won. Nothing had beaten me and I had resisted my tendency to take the easy way out. We hugged and cried, laughed and took it all in. I didn't have a care in the world, as though my future could never falter. I had an overwhelming feeling as though my life were a jigsaw puzzle that had always been missing a piece, which I had just found. I felt complete, satisfied and immensely proud of what I had achieved.

We found a small guesthouse on the edge of the square and left our bags to find the office where we were officially supposed to check in and make claim to our certificate. I had no desire to take part in the religious practices that many of the pilgrims come here to do. I didn't need to go in the cathedral and kiss the feet of St James and I bypassed the queue winding back and forth. I felt a little different from other pilgrims who made the journey on religious grounds. Religion played no part in my life, and although I respect those who have a faith, my faith was in myself.

I leaned across the desk at the bored-looking clerk who processed the completion certificates.

"Hi, I've walked from Le Puy en Velay and have come for my certificate."

She stopped what she was doing and looked at me, smiling.

"Le Puy en Velay is a long walk. We do not get many pilgrims who have come from there. Congratulations. Did you walk all the way?"

I looked at Trish who motioned me to answer, almost as though giving me her blessing.

"Yes," I replied, looking into her eyes. "I walked it all. Every single step."

Chapter Sixteen

Finisterre

We spent a couple of days in Santiago just for the novelty of having two days with no walking, and to have a fix of the big city. We hung out in a small bar tucked away down a side street, drinking Rioja, smoking and talking to the local people. I waited on both days at two o'clock on the cathedral steps for Jeannie but she didn't show. She was a woman of her word and if she'd still been there I knew she would have met me, so it was with a heavy heart that I realised she was probably back in the States.

My mother had mailed me an English newspaper clipping detailing an article about the Parador Hotel on the square in Santiago, which apparently provided free meals for pilgrims. I made my way over with Trish to get some more information. The five-star hotel was indeed as grand inside as it was out. Polished wood framed sparkling glass, light bounced off immaculate surfaces and carpet cushioned our every step. We responded to a couple of disapproving looks from guests at our hiking attire with smiles and 'I don't really care how I look' expressions. There were two gentlemen standing alarmingly erect behind a metre of mahogany on reception, and both they and their suits appeared to have just been freshly pressed. Their expressions also suggested we should not have been there.

"Ola. We have heard that you offer pilgrims food in the evening," I said, smiling in the hope of deflecting their disapproval.

"Yes, you are correct," one replied. A resigned raise of his eyebrows suggested he had answered the question a thousand times before. "Please, you have to wait by the underground parking place outside, down the street at seven pm."

We left, wondering how we would be allowed in the restaurant. Our question was answered as we returned at seven to find a small group of pilgrims waiting by the car park, including Bigfoot and Jennifer who had finished the day earlier. We were led through back passages, through gardens and corridors and every possible route that avoided actually entering any of the hotel areas. A small room, barely big enough for ten people, lay just off the kitchen and we queued while a chef tended a vegetable stew with rice, and expertly adjusted several fried eggs spitting on the griddle. The food was good but we left with the feeling that the whole thing was a bit of a publicity stunt for the hotel, especially as they had gone out of their way to ensure none of the guests actually saw us. As grateful as I was for a good meal, I left feeling a little like a leper.

We left for Finisterre the following morning and for the first time I had real difficulty trying to find the route. Although the direction signs continued to the coast, we couldn't find them and ended up a long way off route. By nightfall we couldn't find anywhere to stay and ended up getting a bus back to Santiago to stay at the same place where we had spent the previous two nights. Trish said she knew things weren't auguring well in the morning when I started humming the tune to the *Mission Impossible*.

Finisterre was about seventy-five kilometres to the west. It was considered the end of the known world until Columbus came along and to have walked 1,600 kilometres to Santiago and not continue the meagre extra distance to get there seemed a waste, especially as the few reports I had heard painted a very promising picture. It was referred to as a peaceful waterside town with a beach not to be missed. I was, after all, in no hurry to get back home.

The second attempt proved more successful and we found the way. Eucalyptus trees hemmed us in on the path, which became sandy underfoot as we scrunched along. Occasionally it gave way to open heath, rolling along over small hills. We reached Puenta Maceira, which immediately welcomed us with open arms. It was extraordinarily peaceful; only the rush of water tumbling over a gracefully arced weir made any hint of sound. We walked on to the Capilla San Blas Bridge and watched the River Tambre glide beneath us. Stone houses appeared to be constructed from a light brown marble, contrasting with the vivid green of the grass framing the riverbanks. We sat on that bridge for what seemed like hours, amazed at how some places you stumble across immediately make you feel completely at peace with the world.

We reluctantly walked on to Negreira in the dark and stumbled around the edge of town trying to locate the refuge. A note pinned to the door advised it was closed, but again there was a number and a very un-Spanish-sounding contact named Andy. Andy seemed a little irritated on the phone and went out of his way to suggest a hotel would be better. I persevered and a few minutes later he arrived, unlocked the place, offered a feeble good night and left us in one of the nicest refuges I had stayed in. It appeared to have been built recently and everything seemed new, including a great kitchen. There were showers and even the heating was on. The local store was open and we stocked up on edibles, returning to revel in the open expanse of the refuge and walk around in shorts soaking up the heat. I dreamt of sandy beaches and hot summers.

We left by nine o'clock in a dense, swirling mist, needing to walk thirty kilometres to get to Olveiroa. There are only three refuges between Santiago and Finisterre and this stretch proved to be the longest between two of them. Trish was behind me by about five minutes and because the lie of the land was flat and open I could see her when I occasionally glanced round to check. The way forked right to skirt a small knoll or left to its summit. The guidebook was sketchy but appeared to point to the top. I placed both my trekking poles on the ground to form an arrow in the right direction so Trish would see them and pick them up. My idea was that I would wait at the top for her. I took in the views on the summit and waited five, ten, twenty and eventually thirty minutes with no sign of her. On my way back down I saw my poles were still on the ground and became concerned that perhaps she had become lost, as I appeared to be. I retraced my steps for ten minutes or so, with still no sign of her, and I figured she must have taken the wrong route.

I could make no sense of the guidebook at all and was struggling to find any signs by the path. All I could do was to follow the direction of the setting sun as darkness started to envelop me. Dogs howled in the distance and an eerie silence fell on the countryside. It appeared that I was the lost one, completely.

I knew Trish would head to Olveiroa and the refuge, so I followed the faint glimmers of an occasional car headlight and what I presumed to be one of the local roads. I stumbled aimlessly through lifeless farmyards until eventually I came across two men leaning on a wall chatting.

"Ola, direction Olveiroa, por favor," I said.

They pointed along the road. "Dos kilometres," one said.

It was now pitch black and I had to walk by the side of the road because it was the only way I could see. My head torch was dying by the second and I was constantly squeezing myself between the road and a hedge to stay out of the way of traffic. Asking another local in his garden how far it was to Olveiroa, he shouted back that it was five kilometres. At this point my distance for the day had crept into the thirty-kilometre bracket and I was feeling it. Eventually lights appeared and a welcome road sign announced I had found my destination.

I dumped my bag at the refuge and the only other pilgrim there, called Aslam, said he was under instructions from an attractive Englishwoman 'with great hair' to tell me that I should make my way to the bar. Sure enough, Trish was at the bar laughing with the other customers and gave me a big hug.

"Fozzie, you just sort of disappeared!" she said.

I explained what had happened. Trish had followed the signs and had assumed all the time that I was walking just ahead, spending some time on my own. When she arrived at the refuge her only major concern was for someone to get her backpack off. The straps had broken after a couple of days so each day I had to tie and untie them for her as they were out of reach. By the time she reached the refuge she had been strapped to her pack for most of the day and her back was killing her.

The three refuges on this stretch were fantastic. This one was a very old building with exposed timber frames and had been lovingly restored. On talking to Aslam, we realised that he had started from Le Puy en Velay a mere couple of days before me: it astounded us that in three months and 1,600 kilometres we had not met, but that was the way of the Camino. I felt a kinship with him immediately and we spent the evening swapping adventures. His finances had dwindled to nothing, yet he had made the decision to walk back to Le Puy en Velay on a tiny budget that would last most pilgrims two weeks.

He was in his mid-thirties although the creases around his eyes and his posture suggested older. He talked quietly, choosing his words carefully, and appeared very much at peace with himself. A shepherd by trade, he had found a dog on the trail which he had adopted. It would lie on the floor by his feet, occasionally glancing up to check he was still there. Although we wanted to give him money, we felt that cooking him a good meal would be a better idea, and I shared my tobacco. We left early the following morning and placed a bag of food near his backpack with a good luck message. I wonder about him to this day.

Emotions were running high. I knew it was my last day on the trail and I vacillated between elation and sadness. Although the way of life I had grown used to had lasted only three or so months, it felt like years. We walked slowly to make the most of it, to prolong the experience. It was a cloudless sky and we stripped down to shirts and shorts. Cresting a hill, we caught our first sight of the Atlantic Ocean and hills of fir trees tumbling down to meet it. The ocean stretched to the horizon, where it hazily blended into the sky. Our legs moaned as we made our way down fire tracks, our boots kicking up dust. The sun warmed us, as though summer was fighting back. Sweat ran down my back and I licked my salty lips.

Through the trees I glimpsed a huge sweeping beach, almost white and at least three kilometres long, and water that changed from turquoise to green as its depth alternated. At the far end buildings dotted the peninsula. With seagulls crying over us, we watched our feet sink into the sand as we stepped on to it. Gentle waves lapped the shore, which was littered with scallop shells.

Hand in hand, we walked into Finisterre. We dumped our bags by the harbour and for the last time I retracted my trekking poles. There we sat in silence, on a pile of fishing nets, looking out at thousands of miles of ocean and occasionally exchanging cheeky smiles. Colourful fishing boats swayed gently and pulled at their ropes.

Now there was no sense of elation, just immense satisfaction, pride and gratitude. I was grateful to the Camino for allowing me to follow her during those past few weeks. Grateful for all the friends I had met and still know to this day. Grateful for an experience that had changed me. The Camino had altered my outlook on life. I was a more patient man, humbler, more appreciative of the simpler things.

A peace washed over us that day by the port. There was no need for words. We both knew we had experienced one of the highlights of our entire lives.

Chapter Seventeen

Reconciliation

Trish and I returned to Santiago and booked flights back home to the UK, where I could stay at my parents' and figure out my next move. I looked out of the window as the plane taxied to a stop at Gatwick, sulking under a heavy sky of low cloud and drizzle, the wings reflected in pools of water. Ground crew moved about in orange waterproofs as the pilot thanked us for flying with them and announced a shocking-sounding outside temperature.

    I spent a couple of days with Trish in Brighton, where she had the use of a flat on the occasions she returned to England. We moped around for a day or so, moaning about the weather, missing the experience we had loved, until we realised it was time to snap out of it. I was eager to get out of the English winter and Trish was resigned to the fact that she had to stay and work until the spring, when she would no doubt head back to Crete.

    We were holed up in a small café nursing coffees and drawing symbols on the steamed-up windows.

    "Fozzie, what you going do?" Trish enquired.

    "I dunno, Trish," I said. "I don't want to stay here. The winter always depresses me. I've got a bit of money left to go somewhere warm. Maybe I can do some work abroad, even some voluntary stuff. What do you think?" I drew a smiley face on the window, as someone opened the door and a gust of cold wind blew in.

"There's an organisation called..." The features on her face tightened as she struggled to remember the name. "Woof, or woofing, something like that."

I gave her a puzzled look.

"It has a database of farms around the world, mostly organic, where you can go and work. Some do pay, but the majority offer simple food and board. You can check the website, Fozzie, put in a country that you fancy going to and look at which farms are advertising for help."

A week later I was staying on an organic farm just north of the Everglades in Florida, helping grow vegetables, salads and micro sprouts. I had the sun on my back, good company and a great boss.

It was the perfect place to reflect. I had spent most of my life trying to find answers to the usual meaning of life questions, if, indeed, there are any answers. One day on the farm I realised where my thinking had gone wrong. I had always believed I was heading towards some sort of defining moment, some life-changing event, which, in the aftermath, would make my purpose clear. My future would suddenly be mapped out, my goals visible and the whole reason why I was on this planet explained. I remembered the message I had seen while on the Camino: *Santiago is only the destination.*

It was then, while tending vegetables in the Florida sun that I understood. There was no defining moment, no end result, and no sudden enlightenment. I had waited for it in vain when I should have been living in the moment, enjoying a journey, my journey, my time on this planet.

The Camino had in effect been a condensed version of my life. I was born at the beginning, in Le Puy en Velay, raised along the way until I arrived at Santiago a man. It had drawn me towards it in the first place because of my love of walking and for the opportunity to spend some time away from modern life. But the Camino had guided me from Le Puy en Velay to Santiago de Compostela to teach me that all the valuable lessons and experiences lay between those points. The journey was all.

How does this new understanding play out in my life now? I may have a rough idea where I am heading and what I may be doing, but I do not concern myself with the day I get there any more. I try to appreciate life in the moment.

I returned to England at the beginning of the spring to meet Trisha again. As it happened, the chance to run the taverna on Crete had come up again and we spent the season there. It was hard work but enjoyable and I eventually returned to England again in the grip of winter.

Then, after a chance encounter with a childhood friend, I took a job with him as a labourer on a small building extension to a restaurant in Horsham, West Sussex. It was near my home village, I had friends dotted about and it was a pleasant enough town. I lodged with friends for a year or so and eventually became self-employed as a painter and decorator. I enjoyed working on my own, loved not having to answer to someone and became very good at what I did. Whenever I had the opportunity, I would try and go for a walk around the Sussex countryside and up on the South Downs. If finances allowed, I would head up to the Lake District, Wales or Scotland for long weekends, sometimes with company but more often on my own.

I had always considered the Camino would be my last extended expedition. I had spent most of my twenties and some of my thirties trying in vain to control a raging wanderlust that always seemed to get the better of me. Indeed, I have been running my business for a few years, quite content with the odd trip abroad and weekends away. However, the travel bug crept up on me once more, and I had a yearning to enter the next stage of my life: to hike even more, and to write about it.

* * *

The Pacific Crest Trail in America is arguably the greatest long-distance hiking trail on Earth. It's not the longest, but the PCT is not about length, it's about its diversity; it encompasses searing hot desert sections, the magnificent Sierra Nevada mountains, and the volcanic landscapes of Oregon and Washington. I decided to throw caution to the wind, and set out to hike the entire length in one season.

Double the distance of my Camino walk, plus another 650 miles, and grand total of some 2,650 miles, the PCT is a daunting challenge not to be taken lightly. However, I was confident in my abilities and the opportunity to experience pristine wilderness at its most magnificent proved a strong pull.

* * *

And finally…

One day, during my time in Crete with Trish, I was coming out of a shop with supplies for the taverna and thought I heard a cry of *Fozzie!* from behind me. I dismissed it because I was new in the village and didn't know anyone, so I carried on walking. It came again.

Fozzie?

I turned around. The face was familiar but I couldn't quite place it.

"Yes, that's me," I replied, hesitantly. "I'm sorry…"

"It's Louise! Remember? I met you with my husband Hans on the Camino in Saugues?" said the woman, coming towards me with arms outstretched. It suddenly came back to me: the couple who had brought me a coffee and suggested the campsite where I had holed up to try and deal with my blisters.

"Louise!" I exclaimed. "What are you doing here? What are the chances I'd meet you here?"

"I'm with a friend who lives here! This is amazing. Fozzie, did you finish?"

"Yes, I finished. I did it. You?"

"Yes, we both finished!"

She came to the taverna for a drink and we reminisced for a couple of hours before she had to leave to get a flight back to Holland.

After finishing the walk, Jeannie spent a month or so in Europe seeing friends and sights before heading back home. Her career as a painter had taken off and her work seemed to be making her a living. I visited her during my time at the farm in Florida and I still keep in touch with her.

Pierre returned to France. We email occasionally and have spoken on the phone. He goes off every year for a month's walking somewhere and even returned to the Camino one year to do a short section.

I have not seen Tamar since, but we have been in contact. She has met someone she calls a wonderful man and is very happy with him and her daughter. She too returned to the Camino for a short section a couple of years later with Espe.

John and Yetty Joose spend a lot of their time as church volunteers helping those in need, mainly in Africa. They also helped in a rebuilding programme in Louisiana after Hurricane Katrina.

Trish is the living embodiment of 'enjoying the journey'. She divides her time between England and Crete. Now a qualified yoga teacher and masseuse, she returns to the south coast of Crete to teach and work. Whenever she is in England, we catch up, invariably on a very long walk. She remains one of my good friends.

* * *

They say things happen for a reason. I like to think that the Camino made itself known to me at the precise time in my life that I needed it. It gave me the tools, the wherewithal, the people and the insights to make sense of my life.

To realise there is a journey in between, and to enjoy it.

Acknowledgements

In my preparation for El Camino and during the actual walk I made new friends, and they, along with existing friends, all helped me in various ways. Some steered me gently in a new direction, whilst others offered help and advice.

Some people come into your life for a fleeting moment, some you know for a few months or years and some are with you for life. The following are in no particular order but they all deserve a mention for assisting me in the walk, helping me write this book or for just being someone I value.

Thanks therefore to:

Mum, for never doubting anything I have done or aspired to do, no matter how crazy it was at the time, for always encouraging me to do what I wanted, and to realise my dreams.

Dad for 'eventually coming round' after a bit of persuasion, for his advice and concern and for passing on the hereditary walking gene in the first place.

My sister Tracy and nephews Thomas and Liam, who spurred me on with the well-worn question, "How's the book coming on?"

Gabriella for providing me with a paradise where I could write, and for her hours spent in front of my laptop digesting the drafts. "You only have to ask, and the universe will provide."

Ziena for her help, even if it meant that I couldn't quote her.

Trish, I have so much to thank you for, but that would be a book in itself.

Alex Roddie at Pinnacle Editorial for a sterling job with the editing and formatting.

Faye Fillingham for help with designing the front cover.

Ryn and Christina, who turned a simple request for assistance into a personal mission.

Mano for the translations.

Lesley, I hope you are happy where you are. Spencer Vignes from The Observer.

Obs the Blobs for his work on the photos and manuscript.

Nikki Johnson for her word-processing skills.

All my friends who proofread some of the work and gave me their views: Sparkers, Lotty Wotty, Agapi, Baz, Maggie Moo, Moneypenny, Mumfa, Amy Lou and Grovesy.

All the pilgrims I met and became friends with along the Camino: the French Canadians (Gérard, Chantal and the names I forget); Jeannie, Bernard, Gare, Reginald, Tania, Pascal, Antonio, Sean, Roberta, Pierre, John, Yetty, Warren and Kylie.

And apologies if I have missed anyone, but if I have, thanks anyway: you surely know who you are.

The Journey In Between

The Last Englishman

A 2,650-mile hiking adventure on the Pacific Crest Trail

In memory of my Nan

Chapter 1
Escaping Volcanoes

There's no sense in dreaming small, moderation is for monks.
Charlie 'HoJo' Mead

Few things in life are certain. I can tell you that the Pope is Catholic, that NASA did fake the moon landings and that Tottenham Hotspur is the greatest football team ever to grace the playing field. What's also certain is that I don't like cold weather and I get grouchy when it gets too hot. I have an aversion to rain and if there is even the slightest chance of snowfall, I head south. Getting dirty makes me uncomfortable and I become grumpy if I don't have enough to eat. Sleeping well in tents doesn't come naturally. I get scared in the woods after dark, too.

Hardly impressive credentials, then, to hike the 2,650 or so miles that make up America's Pacific Crest Trail, otherwise known as the PCT. So why attempt it? It was a question that I was asked many times before, during and after my hike and at some point later on in this book, I promise I'll tell you.

Before I explain why, allow me to explain what. The PCT is arguably the greatest long-distance hiking trail on Earth. It's not the longest, but the PCT is not about length, it's about variety. Starting under a searing Californian sun just south of a small cluster of houses known as Campo near the Mexican border, it winds its way north (and indeed east, west and frustratingly even south) through scorching desert, the magnificent Sierra Nevada Mountains, the volcanic landscapes of Oregon and Washington, the northern Cascade mountains and finishes at the border with

Canada. The route was first explored in the 1930s by members of the YMCA. Once its feasibility became apparent, Clinton Clarke and Warren Rogers lobbied the federal government. Because of the sheer amount of work involved, they had to settle for several trails that already existed but were disconnected. During the ensuing years, hikers and equestrians worked to link these routes together and fill in the gaps. Eventually, in 1968 it was designated a scenic trail by Congress and in 1993 it was dedicated.

A thru-hike of the PCT means an attempt to hike its entirety in one attempt. 40% of those drop out in the first month alone. As the months pass, those that are still on the trail dwindle further, until you are left with the small number who finish the challenge. Some sources claim 85% of those who start will not finish. Take it on and there is a very real chance that you will not make it.

I need to enlighten you all regarding the pitfalls and dangers because some of you reading this are probably stupid enough to go and try it, so it would be remiss of me if I didn't try and put you off.

First, more people have climbed Mount Everest than have hiked the PCT. That would suggest it is easier to climb the world's highest mountain. You have to negotiate over sixty major mountain passes. Think about that for a second. Most of us have not even been up a single mountain pass. At best, it involves at least a day's hard walking with an early start and a late finish. You'll probably get wet, undoubtedly get cold and spend most of the day cursing yourself for making the attempt in the first place. So, try and do it sixty times − and that just refers to the 'major' passes, not all of them.

If you like quality and variety in your diet then make the most of it before you go. You can still have the variety, sort of, it's just that everything you eat will probably be dehydrated. You can't just pop in the supermarket and do your usual shop of fresh meat, fruit, veg and some cans. It's more a case of preserved food where the water has been removed, which is necessary to lighten your load.

Alcohol will also be restricted by what you can carry. Forget your six-pack of beer and bottles of Chardonnay. Most walkers make do with spirits like whisky or rum that come in smaller and therefore lighter sizes and require less volume to produce the desired effect. We only ever left a town stop with one bottle, more often with none at all, given that we had to carry it.

Inseparable from your bathroom cabinet? Make do with a toothbrush and toothpaste, toilet paper and maybe a small piece of soap. It's pointless taking anything else. You won't be able to wash your hair in the wild and deodorant is begging for forgiveness mid-way through the first morning; you'll stink whether you spray or not.

I apologise for all the negatives but you need to be aware of what you're up against. Attempting a thru-hike of the PCT is no holiday; it is a physical and psychological minefield. OK, 95% of the time it's just a case of putting one foot in front of the other but the other 5% can beat you into submission. In truth, if you make it, or even make a half-decent attempt, you'll be rewarded with the most amazing experience of your life.

So, negatives aside, allow me lift you back up with the positives. The draw of being able to spend several months in the great outdoors and indeed pristine wilderness is what lures most people on to the trail. Leave your mundane job, kiss your bills goodbye and experience life at its simplest and most uncluttered. Trail life educates you. It becomes apparent that we don't need most of our luxuries, we can live without shopping, TV becomes a distant memory, and realising how uncomplicated life can truly be is an absolute revelation.

You rise on the trail when it feels right, crawl out of your tent, rub your eyes and acquaint yourself with a rough location. Put some water on the boil and sit down with a coffee and bowl of oats. The only sounds are those that nature has laid on: birdsong, the rustling of the pines as a gentle breeze negotiates a way through them and possibly the nearby tinkle and babble of a creek. No alarm clock, no mobile phone and no car horns.

I became detached – gladly separated from the life that I had become accustomed to. Detachment out on the trail is a good thing. It imparts an understanding and a yearning to learn more about the outdoors. At times I wanted to be back in civilisation for a day or so but in the main I relished being lucky enough to have witnessed the wilderness at its most pristine and for a duration that most people will only ever dream of.

Human beings have spent the vast majority of their existence in the wild – the *vast* majority. Towns and cities are a relatively recent concept and, although they make us feel secure, we are not meant to be there. They are not our natural surroundings. You will realise pretty quickly that the outdoors is where we were nurtured, where we spent our infancy and where we were raised. It is embedded in us and is as natural as it is comforting.

There's camaraderie on the trail that you won't find anywhere else. Don't be put off attempting this hike on your own; there are many others, a lot of them soloing. You'll soon find like-minded people you may want to walk with and will probably make friends for life. On the other hand, if you value your independence, you can spend time alone as well.

Having been raised to appreciate the outdoors and walking, it's always been part of my make-up. I have photos taken by my parents of my sister and I walking in the countryside when I was just a toddler: I was literally learning to walk before I could properly walk. Other activities have come and gone but heading out into the green open spaces has always been second nature to me. I have no need to question it. Walking seems as natural, enjoyable and instinctive as sipping a cup of Earl Grey.

The anticipation of throwing some gear into a backpack for the weekend and venturing out who knows where curls my mouth into a smile. Escaping the annoyances of everyday life and instead discovering the energising, invigorating quality of the countryside sends me into an ecstasy of contentment. The restless rush and needless stresses of the working week get trodden into a carpet of auburn-coloured softness, muted by a blanket of leaves.

In my life so far, I have explored a variety of interests and pastimes, by studying, training and taking part in them. If it turns out that they are not for me, I move on. Other interests and activities seem to come to us so easily, to require so little effort and to offer so much enjoyment that they seem to be made for us, and we for them.

I work to earn enough money to go and immerse myself in that wholly natural and familiar activity of putting one foot in front of the other. I usually receive one of two reactions to my lifestyle.

"Fozzie, you're weird," is a confused comment I hear regularly, usually after explaining my latest adventure. My reply is, "Really? Do you think so? Thanks!" Alternatively, people react with envy.

I do not subscribe to the idea that life is about leaving school, breaking my back to progress in a career, having two kids, accepting the standard four weeks' holiday a year (and pretending to be grateful) and handing over my hard-earned cash to a financial company to be put into an annuity that they deem profitable. It's just not for me, that's all. The statement that you either live to work or work to live holds great truth. I believe life is for living and to hell with the consequences; I'll deal with them when they occur.

I have a recurring dream in which I am 85 years old, sitting in my living room, swaying back and forth in a rocking chair, studying the newspaper. I pause, look up and think of all the adventures I could have experienced and say to myself, "Shit, I should have done that." That is a scene I am determined will not happen in real life.

So, a weekend camping and walking recharges my batteries. A week, maybe two, provides an opportunity to get lost in the outdoors and completely wind down. Occasionally, though, every two or three years, my yearning for something a little more rewarding starts to gnaw away at me. If I were your normal average bloke, I would probably ignore these feelings, but I'm not and so I don't. I sit up and take notice. I get excited about the prospect of what I could do. At any given moment, I have numerous plans rolling around upstairs: cycling around the world, taking a year out to explore the canals of Great Britain on a boat, restoring a campervan and travelling around Europe for the summer or – and this is always the idea that takes centre stage – walking a stupid distance through a part of the world that beckons to me.

The PCT grabbed my attention about five years before I made the decision to go and try it. I had completed a thousand-mile walk through France and Spain, and the long-distance hiking experience had not so much bitten me, more ripped out a healthy chunk of flesh. As with all challenges, we do one and then look at what we can do to surpass it. In walking terms, this usually means increasing the distance.

Apart from the length and difficulty of the PCT, the other factor nibbling away at my sanity was its location and with it my longing to let its remote wilderness engulf me. I love walking in the UK but it lacks large areas of backcountry – and, although it can, with some planning, provide routes of insane length, I couldn't have both distance and wilderness there.

Talk to anyone who has been involved in walking long distances and they will probably tell you that the three most renowned routes in the world are all in North America. The Appalachian Trail (2,181 miles), the Pacific Crest Trail (2,650 miles) and the Continental Divide Trail (3,100 miles) are fine objectives for any serious long-distance walker. Walk all three and you can call yourself a Triple Crowner.

There is no standard order of completing these three masterpieces but most attempts start with the AT because it is the shortest, progress to the PCT and finish with the CDT. To me, not known for conformity or following trends, the PCT appealed primarily because of its climate. You could quite possibly walk its entirety and never get rained on, although you will definitely experience extremes of heat and cold. I discounted the AT because of its reputation for high precipitation and also because I didn't want to be like most people and do it first. The CDT is a serious undertaking. It's obviously long, still not completely finished and it's not at all unlikely that, in spite of the scores of walkers who tackle the route each year, you could go for days without seeing a soul. I wouldn't have particularly minded this but I did feel the PCT was a more well-worn trail in terms of numbers of walkers attempting it, which could be an aid to logistical planning en route. The towns along the way are well accustomed to strange-looking people with backpacks, weird-looking footwear, crusty hair, soiled clothes and potentially lethal body odour aimlessly wandering around, muttering either 'food' or 'shower'. The vast majority of them always made us feel welcome and special.

Having made the decision to go a year in advance, I had spent the time playing an anxious waiting game. I had needed that year to nurture the bank balance into something a little healthier and, although I didn't realise it at first, also to plan. A year may seem a little excessive but I was surprised at how much preparation went into organising such an expedition.

I had spent most evenings glued to my PC trying to find equipment sponsors, start a blog of my trip and arrange flights, medical insurance, gear and logistics. I spent hours forming kit lists, looking at each piece of equipment that should be up to the task, noting weights, durability, reliability and recommendations. I did already own walking gear but most of it was either too old or too heavy.

As D-Day dawned, I had everything packed and was checking last-minute details when a newsreader on the radio caught my ear. 'Flights are being cancelled from the UK due to a volcanic eruption in Iceland...' I jumped at the radio and turned it up, hoping it was April Fool's Day. The news reports were sketchy at best and for the four days preceding my flight no-one in the UK, including the airlines, seemed to know what the hell was going on. The TV news either showed a plume of white ash rising from Eyjafjallajökull or pictures of Gordon Brown trying to remember to smile and wondering whether he'd win the next election or not. I remember posting on my blog:

Volcano – What volcano?

This is clearly a conspiracy theory. The English Tourist Board has dreamt this tale up to prevent us from flying to foreign destinations and thus force people to holiday in the UK. It's very frustrating and I was going to write to my MP about it but he's out all the time. Something to do with an election?

Eventually I received an email from the airline saying the flight had been cancelled. Now I was starting to get annoyed. Events were conspiring against me to end my hike before it had even begun. You may ask what the hurry was to get out to California. The answer is the ADZPCTKO. Before somebody thinks I've sneezed, this stands for Annual Day Zero Pacific Crest Trail Kick Off. Lake Morena campground, a short drive from the start of the PCT, is the destination for most of the year's thru-hikers, section hikers, previous hikers, organisers, equipment stalls and all manner of general misfits. It usually takes place around the end of April, which is generally considered to be the optimum time to start the hike, taking into account receding snow levels in the High Sierra and getting to Canada before the winter grips. No way in hell was I missing it.

In common with most people, I don't particularly like problems. I hate going through the mechanics of trying to solve something that has gone wrong, so I just sit down, look at the situation and spend as little time as possible coming up with an easy and logical solution. The reports from the media were advising that the dust cloud causing the problem to aircraft did not affect airports in southern Europe. Rome, Madrid, Athens and others were throwing up 747s like they were going out of fashion. 'Simple,' I thought, 'just get down to Madrid airport.'

I quickly flicked around the Eurostar web page and watched, amazed, as seats were disappearing every time I refreshed the page. It was time for a decision, so I made a reservation to leave that evening. The rest of the afternoon was spent running around the house saying goodbyes on my mobile, spilling coffee on the carpet, looking at my packing list in one hand and tripping over my sleeping bag that was dangling from the other. It wasn't quite panic, more a sketch from Laurel and Hardy who'd got themselves into a nice fix.

I arrived in Paris just past 9pm and took stock. Somehow I needed to get to Madrid overland and get a flight to San Diego, via my Uncle Tony and Aunty Jillian's place near San Francisco – my 'HQ' for the hike, where I was dumping excess gear. The Gare du Nord station was strangely tranquil. Coffee machines hissed from a couple of snack bars catering for insomniac late travellers. Damp footprints from the drizzle outside wove in from the entrance and gradually faded, the tannoy crackled occasionally and a sweeping machine hummed from a distant corner. I went outside for some air and sheltered under a shop front from the rain. Paris was alive, humid and noisy and as I returned to the station the cacophony of the city abruptly ceased, as though I had just closed the door on a crowded pub.

The only attendant I could find advised that I needed to get to the Gare de Lyon station to get a train to Madrid. I cringed when he added that the underground would be the best option. London Underground I can deal with but the Paris Métro is notoriously unreliable and confusing, not to mention being signposted in what was for me a foreign language.

A suspicious-looking character was loitering by the ticket machine, watching travellers buy their tickets and occasionally trying to make conversation. It transpired that he had made it his business to help those unfortunate souls, like me, decipher the train system and work the machine. Within two minutes he had provided a welcome tutorial on finding the correct route. He did not ask for payment nor indicate that he expected it, but I passed him a couple of Euros and a grateful 'Merci'.

The Gare de Lyon was deserted, save some homeless; and I ambled round a stark terminal, a prison of cold, lifeless white tiles. I decided against a hotel on the grounds of cost and that I needed to be at the ticket office as soon as it opened in case half the population of Europe had also decided to converge on Madrid. Seeing some unsavoury-looking men peering at me from behind pillars, I also decided against sleeping on a bench. For eight hours I tried to amuse myself, waiting for 6am, when I hoped to be able to buy an onward ticket. I eventually gave in to my drooping eyelids and curled up on the floor by a row of fourteen glass windows displaying 'Fermé' signs. Somehow I managed to get four hours' sleep, despite a hard floor half-crippling my left side. I woke up to the hum of chatter, cracked open my left eye and peered out at a student wearing, somewhat appropriately, a red T-shirt with the slogan 'All is not lost' contrasting in yellow across her chest. She was giggling at me – and for good reason. As I winched open the other eye, I realised I had been lovingly spooning my rucksack in my sleep, while a long string of drool stretched down to my shoulder.

As I queued, the omens did not look good. Ticket vendors shook their heads gravely and, although I spoke no French, I could tell from the pained expressions and outstretched palms that those queuing were discussing onward travel options. I inched forward to window number 7 and held my breath.

"Bonjour, madame," I stuttered anxiously. "Avez-vous une ticket to Madrid? Please ... I mean, sivous plaît."

She smiled shyly, displaying one tooth with an alarming slant trying to break free from the others, and pushed a pair of orange spectacles back up her nose.

"Please, I speak enough English to help you. Probably a little better than your French?"

It sounded like a question but her tone suggested otherwise, so I just smiled.

"Madrid is no problem; the next train is at ten."

I spilt my change on the counter in a rush to pay her before she either changed her mind or gave the ticket to someone else. Relieved, I made a beeline for the coffee shop.

After a long day sitting on trains watching a green countryside flash by, I eventually hit Madrid airport at 1am the following morning. This airport was deserted too, which I found confusing. I had expected hordes of people who had followed the same logic to get here, but it was not so. A solitary woman sat at a help desk and seemed glad of someone to talk to. Most of the airline desks, she told me, opened at 6am and she suggested I either wait until then or go to an internet terminal and try and book a ticket online. Not wanting to take any chances, as my progress to Madrid had been smooth, I went online but got irritated when the computer kept swallowing my money and its connection speed was slower than a tortoise taking a nap. I spent my time tapping my feet or fingers and growling at the screen.

Enter a chap called Adonis who was sitting nearby with his laptop, making the use of the free Wi-Fi.

"You need help?" he asked.

"I need to book a flight to the States for tomorrow, sorry, today. This connection speed is killing me," I replied, just on the verge of kicking the machine.

"Let me know what you need and I'll do the searching for you."

I paused, cautious as always about anyone offering me something when I haven't asked for it, especially whilst travelling. He couldn't exactly take anything from me, I thought, but the process would entail taking my credit card details. I decided to let him have a go and see what happened when it came to the booking stage.

For an hour we sat propped up against a vending machine. Adonis couldn't have been more helpful. He had page after page open and his hands floated over the keyboard so quickly I got tired just trying to keep up.

The Last Englishman

My initial flight that had been cancelled had cost me only £240, a favour from a friend who worked for one of the airlines. I winced when most of the opportunities for flights departing that morning were £800 but there was nothing I could do about it. It annoyed me that the carriers had obviously increased their fares in the aftermath of the volcano.

After we had whittled it down to one option, Adonis explained that he would erase the browsing history and left me for a minute while I entered my credit card details. He then showed me he had done what he had promised. I took him to McDonald's, the only place open, and told him to eat whatever he wanted. The poor bloke wolfed down three hamburgers, fries, a milkshake and an apple pie as if he hadn't eaten for days. He thanked me profusely and then wandered off to the machine again to help someone else.

Smiling contentedly, I felt the plane lurch as it hit the Californian tarmac and the tyres squealed the welcome confirmation that finally, 54 hours after leaving England, my destination was within striking distance. At least I was in the right country.

A bleary-eyed Uncle Tony completely missed me at Arrivals, as I did him, but we found each other and used the hour's drive to catch up. I had last seen him ten years earlier, when I had spent a few months bumming around America. After my head hit the pillow, I slept solidly for ten hours, emerging refreshed to hugs from Aunty Jillian and introductions to their grandchildren, Rudy and Hayley.

Several parcels were waiting for me, containing gear that I had ordered, and I spent the day organising final logistics. A shop for the first week's food on the trail was trial and error, as I could only guess how much I would need. This was followed by a ritual that I would repeat many times over the next few months to remove all excess packaging and decant the contents into Ziploc bags, discarding an astonishing amount of card and plastic. After a few weeks on the trail, I tired of this process because it wasted precious time on my day off. Some of the supermarkets sold provisions from stores in long plastic tubes, from which you just measured out your requirements and placed them into bags, saving the time of repacking and sparing the actual packaging as well.

That evening Tony and Rudy dropped me off at the San Jose Greyhound station for the final leg to San Diego and the ADZPCTKO, four days after leaving England. I was tired and not looking forward to an overnight bus ride but I was proud of the determination I had shown to get even this far. Determination and a stubborn refusal to quit were traits that I was to nurture during my time on the PCT, and I needed to.

***

The hardest part of the PCT, and indeed any long-distance path, is actually making the decision to attempt it in the first place. The second hardest is the waiting. Once you've made both commitments it becomes surprisingly obvious that you should have done it a long time ago. The apprehension you felt at making such a big decision suddenly becomes insignificant and your goal becomes clear and lucid. Make the choice and everything starts to fall into place.

Chapter 2
The Five-Minute Hobble

The time you spend out here is worth more than the time it takes, so take your time.
Michael Thomas 'Lion King' Daniel

I walked aimlessly out of the San Diego Greyhound station, confused about where I was and what my intentions were. It was 5.30am; beams of sunlight from a cloudless blue sky sliced and ricocheted among the glass buildings all around me. A cluster of birds took flight, startled by a passing lorry, and I watched as they lifted skyward, swerving and changing direction quickly as if calculating the best bearing. A street cleaner stopped and cupped his hands to light his cigarette, illuminating his face as he propped himself on his broom. A shop door rattled open rudely, startling me as a businessman hurried out, trying to balance a briefcase, laptop, coffee and bagel, and promptly dropped the coffee. Like me, the city was struggling to wake up, a bit scruffy but full of potential.

I rubbed my eyes, tired from having endured the overnight bus ride from San Jose, and looked around for possible onward transport options to Lake Morena. Being Sunday and early morning, public transport was a little limited.

A driver was leaning against his cab with his arms folded on the roof, resting his chin on his hands. He looked bored and lost in his own thoughts.

"Hi," I offered, becoming distracted by the smell of coffee from a nearby café. "I need a ride to Lake Morena."

"Where?" he asked, looking bemused and scratching his chin

with one hand while the cigarette in the other hovered hesitantly near his mouth.

"Lake Morena. It's east on the main highway out of town."

"Donny!" he called over to his mate. "You heard of ... what was it called again?"

"Lake Morena," I reminded him. I had a familiar feeling of unease in the pit of my stomach that bubbles up sometimes when events are not going to pan out too well.

"Where?" replied Donny.

"Lake Morena," I answered, almost shouting so they both heard me. "It's about thirty miles east out of town on the main highway, I think."

"Never heard of it, but I can try the satnav. We can get you there."

"How much?" I asked. Wise from previous travel experience, I had learned to agree a price before accepting a service, especially with taxis.

"Thirty miles you say, about a hundred bucks."

Previous experience had also taught me never, ever, to accept the first price.

"How does $60 sound, for cash? I don't need a receipt."

Donny walked over and had a short discussion with his mate while I kept peering over at the café, longing to taste the espresso that a woman had just walked by with.

"We can take you there for $80, cash." The look on Donny's face suggested that the money would end up in his back pocket.

"Fine, let's go. Give me five minutes to grab a coffee."

We headed east on the 94. Donny slouched in the driver's seat, one hand on the wheel, the other switching between a breakfast burrito and the satnav. The highway was quiet as we left the city but became gridlocked on the other side. Glum-faced commuters stuck in the jam tried to peer round the car in front of them to see what the holdup was. I didn't envy them – despondent people with another day at work ahead of them – but realised that just two weeks earlier I'd been one of them, gazing out of my car on the dull and frustrating commute. The odd car horn sounded. This was my first inkling that I was leaving the fast pace of life behind and winding down for the backcountry.

"How far did you say this place was?" Donny asked. His

narrowed eyes in the mirror suggested distrust.

"I think it's about thirty miles, but I'm not sure."

"Well, we're on thirty-five now and I haven't seen the turn-off yet."

I grimaced as I saw the meter hit $120 but remembered our agreed deal.

"You mean that turn-off there?" I replied, smiling, as I pointed to the right at a blurred sign displaying 'Lake Morena'.

"Oh, shit," Donny said and then cursed again as he dropped the last portion of breakfast burrito on his trousers. "I got another five miles before I can turn around ... shit."

Thirty minutes later we pulled up at the campsite at Lake Morena.

"$225 please."

"You gotta be having a laugh or something! We agreed on $80."

"Yeah, but it was more mileage than you said it was. Man, I gotta charge you or I'm in trouble with the office."

"Don't feed me a line, Donny," I said, that little feeling creeping back into the pit of my stomach. "We agreed on $80, a deal is a deal where I come from and the money's going in your back pocket anyway. You're the bloody cab driver with the satnav here – why are you asking me the mileage? You can sing for the other $145."

I handed him four twenty-dollar bills, which he counted.

"I gotta charge you as the meter says," he sneered. "Pay or your backpack stays in the trunk."

Ah yes. I cursed myself silently for not keeping my pack with me. After ten minutes of arguing, we settled on $120 and Donny roared off in a cloud of gravel.

The ADZPCTKO is held at the Lake Morena campground towards the end of April each year. The entire place is devoted to the registration, entertainment, feeding and watering of many potential thru-hikers, plus a lot of others associated with the PCT as well.

The place was buzzing and hikers had crammed the area to bursting point. Tents were jammed into plots too small for them, guy lines were tripped over, marshals milled around. The atmosphere was one of anticipation and excitement. Strangers said hi and smiled at me. I felt at ease straight away.

I made my way towards the registration area, winding along the track and taking it all in. Past volunteers who had hiked the trail in previous seasons had returned to give something back. Some of them toiled away in the numerous food preparation areas, peeling spuds, lighting barbecues and chopping vegetables. Gear manufacturers were setting up their stalls and placing their tantalising merchandise on view. Brand-new sleeping bags hung from canopies and the latest tents lined up in rows from the tallest to the smallest, resembling a mountain ridge. Boxes were strewn everywhere waiting to be unpacked.

"Hi, good morning," said the elderly woman in the checking-in tent. "Have you registered?"

"Yes," I replied. "The name is Foskett. Keith Foskett."

"Oh, we dispense with formalities here. What's your trail name?"

"Oh, sorry, it's Fozzie."

Over the next few months, I'd hardly ever use my real name. Everyone on the PCT goes by their trail name. This is usually pinned on you by other hikers and reflects how you look, what you have done or how you act. Each trail name has a story behind it, often humorous in nature, and if you are offered a trail name then you usually have to accept it, although not everyone does. I had registered with the nickname that stretched back to my school days, which was derived loosely from my surname. This was partly because I was fond of it and also because I did not want to be landed with some bizarre label such as 'Irregular Banana', 'Curtains', 'Shits Skyward' or 'Shave your arse and walk backwards', as some had. You can understand my eagerness to nip this one in the bud quickly.

"OK, Fozzie, I have you down as a thru-hiker from England and you're camping. You're one of only a handful of English here this year," she said, checking the long list of names on the desk in front of her.

She handed me a name badge, which she insisted I pin on my shirt, and gave me the much sought-after PCT bandana. The bestowing of the bandana was started by the PCT class of 2002, who made the first design available to hikers in 2003 and the tradition has continued every year since. It sports the same layout each time, namely a map of the route with major place names, the year and the phrases 'Hiker to Town' and 'Hiker to Trail' printed boldly near the edges, to be used when hitching a ride. The only change each year was the colour of the material. I cringed when she handed me the latest incarnation in a rather fetching shade of pink.

There was so much going on that I didn't know where to turn. A waft of bacon floated over and I made a beeline for the food area. One of the many advantages of a being a thru-hiking virgin at the kick-off each year is that all the food is free. Hungry souls formed an orderly line, licking their lips in anticipation and getting into practice for the next few months, when everyone would be trying to increase their energy intake to catch up with their energy expenditure. I took more coffee than I needed and slurped it up, in between mouthfuls of scrambled egg, tomatoes and bacon, while trying to maintain a conversation with Bob, one of the organisers.

I found my tent plot squeezed between three others who had nabbed more than their fair share of ground space, then went about setting up what was to be home for the next couple of nights.

"Hey, this plot was for someone who isn't showing after all, so you can set up here if you like." John, one of the volunteers gestured to a far more spacious area with a look that suggested I should take it before someone else did.

"Thanks, I would have struggled to get in there." I shook his hand and we exchanged a few pleasantries.

One of the few items of gear that I had not sorted out before leaving was a backpack. Logic and experience suggest this is the one piece of equipment that is vital to try on before you buy. I had tried but had not managed to find anything suitable. The volume was either too big or too small, some were uncomfortable, some too heavy and some just basically rubbish. During my research, I had heard good things about a company called ÜLA. I needed a light pack but also with a built-in frame to stiffen the whole unit. Many of the packs available shed the frame to save weight and the end result is a limp sack that dangles off the shoulders like a half-full sack of potatoes. ÜLA's proprietor, Chris, turned down my request for sponsorship.

"I don't need the advertising, Fozzie. Nearly half the hikers this year have my packs."

He was right; the familiar green fabric models named Catalyst and Circuit were bobbing around on shoulders all over the campground. He had, however, told me to make sure I went over to see him, as he had made the trip down to set up stall.

"Chris, Fozzie from…"

"Fozzie!" He interjected and started laughing. "This guy sends me email after email from England wanting a freebie," he said, motioning others to look at me. "You're a persistent guy, Fozzie. You get the pack OK?"

"Yeah, fine, thanks. It seems to fit well but I said I'd come over to meet you and get that expert fitting you offered."

"Sure, hoist her up and let's take a look." He studied the pack and me for a while, suggesting I lift the hip belt up a touch. We talked shop for a while and as I walked away I turned to him again and said, chuckling,

"I still want the next one for free, though!"

I woke the following morning to the realisation that this was the day my PCT thru-hike was to start. I opened one eye and peered out through a slit in my sleeping bag at the dim light struggling to illuminate the green tent fly sheet. It was cold, moisture clung to the roof of my little haven and I could see the ground outside was white with a crisp frost; not the sort of temperature I had associated with southern California. Escaping the confines of a warm sleeping bag and getting into cold clothing is not one of my favourite experiences and I shivered as I slid on my hiking gear and jumped out of the tent, flapping my arms and jumping up and down, trying to warm up.

"I definitely don't recommend this."

I looked over at the guy next to me: yes, he was talking to me, his face contorted into an expression of sheer disgust.

"Don't recommend what?" I asked.

"Well, I thought I'd save time and washing up by putting coffee in with the porridge. I don't recommend it."

A few hikers were already up and the steam from boiling water atop cooking stoves looked like chimneys puffing smoke in an industrial landscape. People cocooned in hats and gloves stood around waiting for hot water to make a brew, while chatting and smiling at the prospect of their virgin day on the PCT. Grass peeped through where footprints had broken the frost. The atmosphere was so full of an intoxicating enthusiasm I could almost smell it.

Lake Morena looked glorious, having apparently saved her best for the day. A weak mist covered her, but as a gentle breeze wafted past I glimpsed pockets of clear air and sunlight bouncing off her waters, as if she were a birthday surprise gently unwrapping herself.

The start point at the Mexican border actually lies a few miles south and several visitors to the kick-off were laying on transport. I jumped into Shrek's car with Gabe and Cara, two hikers I had become acquainted with the previous day. The familiar sight of the PCT start monument appeared, flanked by an imposing black steel fence separating us from Mexico. It was a view I had seen countless times in photos. A few hikers were leaving, having had their starting snaps taken; and we did the same, handing our cameras to Trailbird, who obligingly clicked away for us.

I watched as those hikers set off and wondered how many of them would make the cut. Four or five out of every ten potential thru-hikers quit in the first month alone and even more would not last the distance. I looked at Cara and Gabe, who both looked confident and fit. Were they wondering the same about me? Averages dictated that one or two of us would not make the finish. As it transpired, in the ensuing weeks both of them unfortunately fell foul of the drop-out statistics.

The morning cold soon surrendered to a magnificent day. This was to become the norm for California, as one would expect. The sky was a flawless blue; winds occasionally ruffled my hair, and before long I had replaced my down jacket with shorts and T-shirt as sweat trickled down the valley between my back and pack. We found our own pace that first morning, sometimes walking with others and sometimes on our own. Space Blanket and Dicentra joined me and we idly chatted away most of the twenty-odd miles back to Lake Morena, itself situated right on the trail. I was surprised at the abundance of plants. The first 700 miles are classed as desert, although not the typical sand dunes and searing heat that one might imagine.

Strictly, it is known as chaparral, consisting of waist-high scrubby vegetation clinging on to a mix of grit and rock, which gives a satisfying crunch underfoot. An occasional yucca plant towered over me, its flowers looking like a thousand dangling white bells. Over time I learned these flowers were edible and regularly grabbed a handful to supplement my dried provisions. They provided a satisfying crispness in the mouth and tasted a bit like lettuce leaves. I made my way through sections of lush grass that moistened my legs from the lingering dew. Memories of England entered my head as I pulled off pieces of rye grass and threw them like darts.

Gabe and I stopped under a low tree for lunch, trying to squeeze back in the shade. Dicentra soon joined us and sat down next to me. Her long hair was tucked under a green sun hat with her white-rimmed sunglasses perched on the brim. The dust gaiters on her shoes were made from a colourful fabric and I had watched her modelling them to admirers earlier. She seemed happy-go-lucky, smiled a lot and made frequent arm gestures when excited about a topic, her favourite being nutrition. I learned she had written a book extolling the tricks, virtues and delights of eating well on the trail. This book, *One Pan Wonders*, was proving a success with those who were looking for something more exciting than the usual supermarket offerings. I thought I was doing pretty well with some tuna and tomato stuffed in a tortilla, until saliva started trickling from the corner of my mouth as I watched her prepare her lunch. Gabe's eyes were also twitching enviously in her direction. She placed three tortillas on her lap and prepared the fillings. She rehydrated fried beans with cold water, added fresh avocado and topped it all off with taco sauce.

I'm quite proud of the fact that I can convey hunger, admiration and envy, all in one facial expression. Once they have seen it, recipients generally relent and are forced to offer me some of whatever they're having. If I could also display what meagre rations I had into the bargain, I generally didn't even have to trade for anything – although I should say that I suffer from a karmic guilt complex and would always repay any favour when I could, such as buying them a beer in the next town.

Gabe was also in on the act and doing splendidly, but

Dicentra, being a kind-hearted soul, merely made us a tortilla each without blinking an eye and smiled.

"I'm happy to make you one," she said. "There's more stuff in my book."

I walked on my own for most of the afternoon and stopped at Hauser Creek for water. The desert had been blessed with abundant rainfall over the winter and I had several opportunities each day to re-stock, which in the temperatures was a godsend. Motor joined me as I filtered a couple of litres for the remaining five or so miles back to Lake Morena. She asked if I had seen any snakes, which I hadn't, and went on to tell me she had encountered three already.

"How many?! Where?" I enquired, gulping.

"Well, the last one was only about five minutes back up the trail. I saw it slide off as I came round a corner. It was a rattler, for sure. I saw its tail."

I grimaced. I have a deep fear, bordering on a phobia, of snakes and bears – hardly ideal for the PCT, which boasts a varied selection of both. The rattlesnake was the most common. I think I inherited my anxiety from my father, whom I have seen executing six-foot jumps on sighting a grass snake, one of our completely harmless native English varieties.

"You know, there is a simple way of dealing with snakes," Motor said.

"I'm all ears."

"Well, you have to make sure you're walking with two others and you're not the last in line."

"Uh-huh."

"Well, the first person wakes the rattler up. The second one pisses it off and the third one gets the bite."

"Right, thanks for that," I said drily, raising my eyebrows slightly to let her know I had been hoping for better.

For the first few weeks I walked in perpetual fear of *Crotalus atrox*, the western diamond-backed rattlesnake, and other species. It scared me because it ticked all the right boxes – or, rather, all the wrong boxes. First, it grew to silly sizes. Second, its bite was pretty nasty, although not lethal if one received medical attention. Mainly, however, it scared the crap out of me because it just looked terrifying. I'm not suggesting any snake looks exactly 'cuddly', but the rattler's eyes are just evil. Its brows slant diagonally from a high point of the outside of the eye to a low point on the inside, giving the appearance that it is relentlessly pissed off, which, if you come across one, it generally is.

I had received a lot of advice about snakes. I was told that I probably wouldn't see one, which always makes me nervous because it's a sure-fire way of ensuring that I will. Others told me that it can only strike as far as its body length and I read that if you do get bitten the best thing to do is lie down! This priceless piece of wisdom originates from the Aborigines. The theory is that lying down relaxes the victim, slows the blood flow and hence delays the poison getting into the bloodstream. Excuse me, but if I did get bitten by a reptile, I would be more likely to be screaming my bloody head off, jumping around like someone who had just stepped on a campfire and screaming, "I'm gonna die, somebody help me!"

I also read somewhere that the bite is rarely fatal and at worst I would only experience the most excruciating pain, similar to liquid fire being pumped around my arteries. Right, then, thanks for that.

I was on 'rattler alert' when I thought I was in prime snake territory, which in California is pretty much everywhere except the local 7 Eleven. I would scan the trail up to fifty feet ahead of me, making visual and mental notes of anything that could be a snake. From a short distance, sticks that scattered the trail could easily resemble one. I imagined myself sweeping the environment through the eyes of a Terminator machine: anything that looked potentially dangerous would be flashed up in red with three alert beeps and margined over the left-hand side of my vision for verification as I moved closer.

As there was such a lot of natural debris scattered about, my head beeped like a microwave with a short circuit and so many potentially lethal objects were margined in my eye that my left field of vision reduced to a hazy shade of crimson.

As with most natural predators, however, once I had actually seen a few, I started to evaluate and eventually understand what little danger they actually posed. The positive thing about rattlers is that they let you know where they are by rattling (which incidentally sounds something like air escaping under high pressure from a pipe) and then all you have to do is give them a wide berth. I saw many during my hike and came to have a healthy respect for them.

Snake count: 1
False alarms: 27

    I walked the final five miles back to Lake Morena on my own. Gabe was behind me because I had increased my speed to get away from a local called Andrew, out for a day hike and intent on holding a conversation with anyone who would last more than five minutes in his dreary company.
    Twenty-one miles is not a huge distance by thru-hiking standards, but for a first day, with a full pack and in those temperatures, those final miles seemed to last an eternity – but an enjoyable eternity it was. The temperature fell a little with the approach of another cold night and the sinking sun painted stripes of shadow across the trail. With the last high point of 3,000 feet under my belt, I descended the two miles back to camp just as dusk was falling, almost willing Lake Morena to appear before me. Eventually I saw countless head torches moving around like fireflies and the laughter and chatter of happy hikers.
    As I crossed over the last dirt track towards the others, I was met by a standing ovation and around a hundred people cheering. At first I looked around, expecting to see someone famous behind me, but then realised they were cheering me, just as they welcomed back every successful hiker on that first day. It honestly brought a tear to my eye and I cockily bowed and then raised my trekking poles above my head in salute.
    As I stumbled in, I was greeted by Terrie Anderson. I was to meet her later in my hike – she and her husband Joe open their house to hikers every year. Thrusting a gigantic plate of Mexican stew into my hand and a beer in the other, she kissed me on the cheek and said, "Sit, stay!"
    The hikers were in good spirits that evening thanks to good food, beer and great company. I ate, rested, chatted and laughed for a couple of hours and then, succumbing to tired limbs and

too much beer, wove my way through the rolling mist back to my tent.

Sliding into my sleeping bag and placing a weary head on my rolled-up jacket, I smiled, took a very big breath and told myself that all I had to do to become a Pacific Crest Trail thru-hiker was to repeat that first day ... about another 180 times.

***

I have never had any problems with my own company and can happily spend a whole week, or longer, walking on my own. This obviously is a positive attribute for a thru-hiker. I hadn't expected to have company straight away, preferring to find my own feet and socialise in small bouts as I met different hikers each day to figure out which ones I clicked with. So, it goes to show what a sterling bloke Gabe is that we ended up walking together for most of the first week.

We were both pretty laid back and preferred to take it easy those first few days, so we had no problems agreeing on when to take breaks, where to camp and how far to walk. On the final few miles of the approach to Mt Laguna campground at 6,000 feet, we were taking lunch and comparing our food supplies. Hikers experiment a lot with mixing food. We have to, as our favourite stuff depletes quickly, leaving the less tempting options, which get livened up by being mixed in with something else. Gabe proudly offered me his simple concoction of a flour tortilla generously smeared with Nutella and scattered with banana chips, exclaiming:

"Foz, it tastes just like a pastry!"

He declined my offer of a fair trade, turning his nose up at my tortilla with peanut butter, shaved parmesan and chocolate M&M's. I can't say I blamed him.

Gabe was 26 and attempting the PCT "to try something exciting before I start medical school". He hailed from Orange County and was also keen to escape the hustle and grind of city life. A little taller than me and well-built, he was someone you wouldn't pick an argument with, but if you ever did, he'd probably shrug it off and make a joke of it anyway.

For the first week we concentrated on finding our feet. All

our gear was being worn in and we were still learning how to use it. We honed our skills in packing and unpacking our bags, pitching our tents, cooking our food, hygiene (or rather lack of it) and finding water to treat. Searing heat meant that this was one area we could not skimp on: we had to drink or become dehydrated. Our maps indicated where the sources were and thankfully most of them were flowing well. Gabe carried a gravity filter, which entailed filling a small bag, hanging it on a branch or something similar and letting the fluid seep through an attached hose at the bottom and through a filter. Other than lifting the bag, it required no effort; but it took a little longer than my water filter, which looked something like a small bicycle pump that I pulled out to suck in water and then forced back in again to filter. It kept clogging up, so it had to be dismantled, the rubber valves reversed and water forced through again to wash out any dirt and debris. It seemed for every two litres I was treating, I needed to backwash a further litre, a process I soon found frustrating. There was Gabe, sitting and munching on a snack while his bag did all the work, grinning as I crouched, elbows stretched out to my sides, exerting so much effort that my face looked as if someone was pumping air into my head and it was about to explode.

The gurgle and splutter of sweet, cold water was a beautiful sound to hear as we rounded a corner or topped out on a hill. Not only could we drink but we could also down our packs and sit for a while. To save weight in my pack, I usually treated a litre and drank it straight away, feeling the cool liquid tumble down my throat. Then I would take another litre with me to last an hour or two until the next creek. On one particularly hot day I worked my way through seven litres, as well as all the confrontation with my filter that went hand in hand with it.

As we walked the half mile or so on the road to the store at the summit of Mount Laguna, we could see several hikers sitting outside in the shade eating ice cream. Mojave and Cheeks, whom I was to encounter many times on my hike, told us that the store owner was forecasting a fierce storm. After quickly discussing the options, we decided to hunker down for the night in a cabin at the rear of the store. Mojave and Cheeks, being a married couple, took the separate room, Gabe got the main single bed and I was lumbered with the famous 'cot'. This American institution, common in motels, hotels and other establishments, is what we English refer to as a 'put-you-up' or fold-away bed. It is stored vertically and folds down, usually leaving some sort of uncomfortable ridge in the middle. The hard frame sinks into your arms (so by morning my biceps had red stripes across them), the twanging springs keep you awake, and one particular model even tried to spring back upright with me still in it.

At 3am I parted the curtains and peered out to see horizontal rain whipping debris across the parking lot. By the time we rose, it had subsided a little and the store owner persuaded us to stay put till lunch, when he assured us it would die down.

Gabe and I left shortly after and bumped into a steady stream of hikers backtracking to the store to dry out and get warm, a couple of them borderline hypothermic. We later learnt that, before the first week had even finished, nine people had decided enough was enough and got off trail that day.

We continued on through vicious gusts of wind to the water supply at Penny Pines, where Ben, glad of some company, joined us. Being constantly blown back, forwards or sideways, we stumbled into the picnic site at the Pioneer Mail Trail Head late afternoon and decided that we should camp there – mainly on my insistence, because there were picnic tables. The availability of tables may seem a strange reason for choosing a camping spot, but they were high on my checklist on the trail. After spending days sitting on the ground to eat and do simple tasks such as journal writing, they were a blessing. An occasional added bonus was meeting a family who had stopped off during a long drive, with whom I could perfect my 'I want your food' expression, usually producing excellent results.

We all helped pitch the others' tents, two sitting on the canvas while the other went round and pegged them out. Despite some great tables, we couldn't help noticing that we had camped a hundred or so feet down from a col, which was funnelling the wind through with frightening ferocity. Mojave and Cheeks arrived an hour later and retreated back to a more sheltered position to set up their camp.

The wind howled frighteningly all night, making my tent

billow and shake. I unzipped and poked my head through the opening in the morning to take stock of the mayhem. Twigs and large branches scattered the area and upturned litter cans spilled refuse. I laughed as I looked over at Ben's tent: at some point during the night, he'd cleverly anchored two of his guy lines to an adjacent table that was firmly cemented to the ground. The warden arrived and surveyed the scene, taking off his hat with one hand and scratching his head with the other, amazed we had managed to ride out the storm. In theory, camping is not allowed at picnic sites but after we promised to pack up and be on our way quickly, he accepted that the circumstances were unusual. Mojave and Cheeks sauntered in, looking slightly battered, and explained their tent was wrecked and they had to get a new one or at least a replacement under guarantee.

We were soon joined by the Mad Hatter, an English guy living and working in Saudi Arabia. I had seen him at the kick-off with an impressive top hat straight out of Alice in Wonderland, which he told us he had ditched as it kept blowing off in the wind. Having bought a house in Oregon, he was essentially walking 'home'. Up to the point where we met him, he had been walking with a guy called Upchuck and sharing a tent, as he hadn't thought it necessary to bring his own, but a personality clash meant he had left him behind.

"Upchuck is like herpes," he said, grinning. "I can deal with him but only in very small doses."

At that precise moment, Upchuck came careering round the corner like a runaway train. Mojave and Cheeks had to jump off trail as he ploughed straight through our group, with a feeble 'excuse me' and muttering something about a forty-mile day.

After the storm, the trail – strewn with pine needles and cones – alternated between dry and damp sections, which I started to refer to as either a milk or plain chocolate path. We dipped in and out of shade before returning to the chaparral as we descended. Gabe and I were suffering from blisters, which subsided as usual when we were walking but were excruciating for the first ten minutes or so after we had sat down to rest.

"It's called the five-minute hobble," I explained.

"Yeah," he replied. "So this is how it feels to be ninety!"

I used to think about how my body was dealing with the

onslaught. I conjured up an imaginary woman called Angela in my feet, sending signals up to the nerve centre HQ, run by a chap called Reginald.

"We've got problems down here," Angela would say. "I don't know what the hell is going on but I'm trying to deal with three blisters, impact problems, muscle sprains and a potential abrasion on the third toe of the right foot. You gotta send me some backup; I can't hold it together much longer!"

"You idiot!" Reginald replied. "We've got six months of this! He's on another one of his walking adventures, isn't he? You think I haven't got other problems up here? There's lower backache, sunburn to the ears, I'm trying to sort out grit in the left eye and if we don't take on board more water, we're in for some serious overtime tonight! I've got no resources! You hear me? No resources to work with! I'm in desperate need of nutrients up here and I can't get those from chicken ramen! Just pray he stops in the fruit and veg aisle in the next supermarket. You'll just have to shore up the defences in the meantime and work with what you got!"

We hobbled on down to the Rodriguez Spur road, where a local called Wayne had set up camp with some welcome amenities for hikers. I got very excited when I saw some chairs and even a table. Solar showers provided an unexpected but sorely needed wash. The Mad Hatter set up camp in one of the shower tents (as he still didn't have a tent of his own) and soon began to realise that the uneven floor and cramped space weren't boding well for a good night's sleep. When he then spilled most of the contents of his water bottle, he wasn't in the best of moods.

The blisters were really troubling Gabe. I knew how he felt; no matter what action or precautions I took, I always fell foul to them. I had a few but was managing to cope. Trying my best to lift his spirits, I kept reminding him that the first month on the trail was always going to be the hardest and blisters were inevitable, but he was despondent and a little withdrawn. Before we turned in, I urged him to get to the next town stop, Julian, and maybe take a day's rest. Good food and a warm bed always worked wonders for morale.

***

"A life has to have purpose. A life with no purpose is meaningless and a meaningless life has no purpose." The Mad Hatter was lavishing profound sayings on me as we worked our way down from the hills towards Road 78, where we hoped to get a lift into the town of Julian. He was hankering after a hotel bed and I for the pie shops that I had heard so much about. Zigzagging down the switchbacks, I could already feel the slight crunch of pastry in my mouth as the crust gave way and my teeth sank into the coolness of a cherry pie. I also needed meat, chips, ice cream, beer and coffee. I think Reginald, up in nerve centre HQ, was getting a little stressed out when he realised that the fruit and veg aisle may not be a high priority.

We stumbled on to our first water cache. These are maintained by local people and are found especially in dry areas or sections of trail where there is a long distance between water sources. This first one set a high standard. There must have been 160 litres nestling in wooden shelving, along with several cool boxes harbouring Cokes and other soft drinks. Even though the road was only a quarter of a mile away and a lift to Julian beckoned, we sat in the shade for thirty minutes and drank our fill.

Julian impressed me the moment I arrived, but I was not planning on staying. I needed only to re-stock on food and get a couple of good meals inside me. My walking was going well and progress seemed positive, so I wanted to make the most of it. I left Hatter at the hotel and got a quick ride back to the trailhead to put in some more miles as the sun began to sink.

I was barely 50 feet up the 2,000-foot climb that led into the San Felipe Hills when I noticed someone waving at me from a couple of hundred feet away. I didn't recognise her but she kept waving, so I waved back.

"Hi," I said, upon reaching her.

"I'm a bit freaked out," she greeted me with. "There's a couple of Mexicans and I'm sure they're following me. Every time I look round, they duck behind a bush. I'm walking on my own and it's making me uncomfortable. Sorry, hi, I'm Brittany."

We shook hands.

"I'm Fozzie. Look, it's getting dark," I said. "There are some trees with cover from the road down there and I think a creek as well. If you like, we can set up camp there. I think Ben is literally just behind me as well, so I'm sure he'd join us."

"I'd like that, thanks."

We intercepted Ben on the way, who again was glad of some company for the night, and we pitched tents. We cooked and I hopped about on one leg for a while trying to wash one foot at a time.

"I killed a scorpion!" screamed Ben triumphantly. "I killed a scorpion!"

So far, I had become fond of every single person I had walked with. Such a mix of characters, but with a common love and respect for the outdoors. I nodded off with a contented smile and an ear cocked for escaped Mexicans.

Journal entry:

All good! The ADZPCTKO party is fantastic; lots of like-minded people there to give and exchange advice. 350 or so thru-hikers registered this year, lots of free food, great people and great fun.

I start at 7am on Sunday 25 April, at the Mexican border. Blue skies, temperature around 25C and a cool breeze. I am with two thru-hikers, Cara and Gabe. We sign the register at the official start monument, take photos, pause for a moment to contemplate what we are about to do, and start to walk north 2,650 miles.

The first 400 miles (about three to four weeks) is essentially desert walking. Not as hot as I expected. For a thru-hiker, long sleeves, trousers, sun hat and a bandana over the neck are the norm. The PCT gains in elevation, from 2,200 feet at the start to 6,000 feet in the Laguna mountains, in the first few days. Very few trees, but generous rainfall over the winter means that there is greenery, including spring flowers.

Occasional shade is welcome, and I can feel the sometimes-damp ground on my skin and smell its sweetness. There is more than the average amount of water for this time of year, but it's not much. Most of the water sources are flowing; little creeks and streams of clear, sweet water gurgle past. I have to use the water filter to drink, but it's tempting just to dunk my head in. Now and again I soak my bandana and squeeze it under my hat, to give some respite.

Within two hours Gabe and I receive our first greeting from the resident rattlesnake population. We round a bend in the trail, and suddenly this chap rears back. The rattler is coiled and ready to strike, tasting the air and shaking its tail. A few well-aimed sticks fail to move it on its way, so we skirt around it, about twelve feet away. Twenty minutes later – another one! "Great," I think. Two snakes in as many hours. Now I've encountered them, though, I think my phobia has been cured. Rattlesnakes just do their own thing and won't strike unless you get too close.

We climb slowly up to Mt Laguna at 6,000 feet, and arrive late on Tuesday 27th. Awe-inspiring panoramas all around, and this is only the first few days. There is still the occasional small patch of snow, and we have been warned there is more to come.

The wind is so strong sometimes that we can't move forward. Ben joins us and together we somehow reach the Pioneer Mail trailhead. Forced to a halt by the worsening wind and cold, we hastily cook a hot meal and pitch tents. Slightly to our surprise, we survive the night, albeit without any sleep. I have never experienced such winds, and the way they slammed into my tent and buffeted me all night was frightening.

Physically I'm good. The knee is solid and no problem at all. My right calf aches from time to time, though, and I massage it each night. I have some minor blisters, but nothing compared to what I experienced on El Camino a few years ago, so I'm happy. Every night I pierce each blister with a needle, squeeze out the fluid and sterilise with alcohol. My face is a little dry, though that's to be expected, and I smell like a skunk who's taken a vacation in the local sewer. I am now in a charming little village called Julian, having hitched a ride from a local lady called Sandra. I am in the company of the only other English man on the trail, who goes by the name of the Mad Hatter. We have eaten at Buffalo Bills Burgers, and I have a few things to buy before heading back out on the trail later today. I will camp again tonight, unlike the Mad Hatter who can't resist the lure of the hotel.

Having the time of my life!

Chapter 3
The Art of Hitching a Ride

Spam; it's pure energy condensed to a slow vibration.
Mahmood 'Cedar Elk' Mokhayesh

Sweltering under the Californian sun, I continued to knock miles off the desert section. Unlike some trails such as the Appalachian, the PCT deals with hills by employing switchbacks like you would find driving a car up a mountain pass. The Appalachian Trail takes the direct approach, steep but straight up and over. I often thought about which I'd prefer. Switchbacks drive you insane: a direct two-mile up and over can increase to six when all the twists and turns are taken into account. On the other hand, because the incline is kinder, generally the ascent is not too severe. I kept reminding myself of this but it still became a little frustrating. Imagine your hand laid flat on a table, fingers apart. Take a line directly over the knuckles, go up and down four times and you're over the hills. Fingers represent foothills decreasing in height from the knuckles down to the fingertips, or the valley floor. The PCT would climb up the base of the first finger, work its way down to the nail, back again to the knuckle and then up the second finger and so on and so forth, until reaching the base of the little finger. Every time I saw the elevation increase in my handbook, I would be met by images of countless hands and fingers stretching as far as the eye could see.

I surveyed valley floors and saw green lines of trees meandering as they kept in touch with a creek for a drink. Minerals would glisten and wink at me as I looked down at the trail, like infinite stars splattering a night sky. Dead trees dotted the way, bleached stark and white by the sun and long since stripped of bark. The branch remnants towered over me, clawing and grasping at me like a giant's hands. Hummingbirds would occasionally buzz around my head, at times stopping a mere couple of feet away from my face, and hover miraculously, almost motionless, their wings humming, their iridescent plumage changing colour in a pearlescent blur. They seemed to be watching me, trying to work me out. I was absolutely mesmerised and bewitched, awestruck at their sheer beauty. I passed the 100-mile mark, where someone had carefully laid out '100' in a neat stone pile. Most major mileage targets were signified this way and I praised myself for making it this far. "Just do all that again twenty-six times," I thought.

At another water cache I found hikers contorted and squeezed in any morsel of shade they could find. Bob was sitting under his umbrella and I was introduced to Stumbling Norwegian, Sugar Moma, Dinosaur and Swayze. As I sat down and reversed, cheek by cheek on my bum, until I was under a low hanging bush among them, the conversation picked up from where it had left off.

"Did you go today?" Dinosaur's remark was aimed at Bob.

"Yeah," he replied, smirking.

"Are we already on the poo topic?" Sugar Moma enquired.

"It would appear so," I joined in, thinking it was like my first day at school when I wanted to be part of everything.

"How about you, Fozzie, you keepin' regular?"

"Very much so. I may miss the odd day but that's to be expected with a lack of fruit and veg out here. M&M's, jerky and cheese have a habit of bunging me up a little. You know? A lack of fibre?"

"I agree," Bob offered. "Nevertheless, a good colour, nice consistency?"

"Yes, I didn't have any complaints, thanks."

Apart from Julian, the small town of Warner Springs heralds the first main stop. There's not an awful lot there save a petrol station with some meagre rations to restock, a golf club serving a great breakfast and the actual Warner Springs Resort. PCT hikers enjoy a reasonable discount at the thermal hot spring, which can be reduced even further by pitching in with a few others to share the cost of a cabin. I had agreed en route to split with Brittany and Ben and in anticipation of a rest day had left myself merely thirteen miles to walk before I arrived. I often left small distances to arrive at a town stop. Arriving late means that as soon as you have checked in it's time for bed, and as most establishments chuck guests out at around 10am, you don't get much chance to enjoy the room. At the latest I aimed to arrive at midday but usually I would camp a couple of miles from town, get in early morning and have the whole day to chill out.

After a night when I'd camped in a dry stream bed at 5,000 feet, the PCT descended to 2,000 feet on the approach to Warner Springs. From a damp, misty and cold start, the trail welcomed me with open arms at the end of an extraordinary first week. I spent the day weaving through woods that provided dappled shade, passed Eagle Rock and listened to the tinkle of the San Ysidro Creek as it kept the trail company for a short while. Trees merged into meadows bursting and overflowing with spring flowers in all shades of lilac, blue, red, and pink. Vibrant orange poppies peered over tall grass. Mice peeked at me from their burrows; lizards ran for cover; rabbits hopped about. After the cold, the wind, the aches, the blisters and the hunger, it felt as though I had proven myself over week one and in return the PCT just gave me a huge welcome hug.

I passed Hojo, Jess and Tradja and admired the way they had camped the previous night, 'cowboy-style', as the Americans call it, in a sleeping bag but no tent. It's a great way to save time pitching and taking down your tent but the real reward is gazing up at beautiful skies every night and feeling the breeze tickle your cheeks. I regularly used this method back home in England but was reluctant out here because of the large variety of wildlife that could bite, sting, claw or just plain kill me. OK, so a flimsy piece of tent canvas isn't going to save you from a bear or mountain lion, but when you are inside that little haven, it feels like a castle. There's something remarkably (if falsely) comforting about being cocooned in a tent: you think you're safe from anything. I vowed to cowboy-camp more often regardless.

Hojo caught up with me as I was checking in and took up my offer of sharing, as there was a spare bed in the room. Ben and

Brittany were already there, revelling in the opportunity to take a shower, lie on a bed and walk barefoot on a carpet. The resort was well cared for and, although old, very well run.

The others left earlier than I did the following morning and I made the most of the great American breakfast with Tradja, Jess, Brittany and Burnie.

"How would you like your eggs, sir?" the waiter enquired.

"Er ... erm..." I looked at the others. "How the hell do you order eggs over here?"

The table giggled.

"Fozzie, I'll give you the American breakfast tutorial," Tradja replied, sounding as though it was going to take much longer than it actually did.

"First, eggs. Sunny side up, just cooked on the bottom and not flipped over. Tends to be somewhat raw on the top. Next, over easy. Flipped for a few seconds to cook out those raw bits. Finally, well done. As the name suggests, turned over until the yolk is cooked through. Potatoes, either hash browns, which are shredded and cooked on a hot plate, or home fries, little cubes, sometimes with onion and garlic. Finally, toast. You can have white, which is self explanatory, wheat, which I believe is the same as your brown bread, and finally rye, which is kinda like sourdough with rye seeds in it."

"Thanks very much," I said. "I feel fully confident now."

The waiter hovered as I perused the menu.

"OK, two eggs over easy. Bacon, well done, hash browns, also well done and wheat toast. Orange marmalade if you have it, orange juice, no ice, and coffee, strong, black and keep it coming."

There was silence around the table and heads nodded in approval, confirming I had passed the breakfast-ordering initiation ceremony.

I headed out just before midday, taking advantage of the lower, flatter terrain. It was hotter down there and the grass was turning from greens to browns as the summer strolled on. I passed Cheeks resting under a tree, who explained that Mojave had returned to Warner Springs to check if their new tent had arrived at the Post Office. I stopped and chatted with Alex, who was from Scotland, although his accent had been diluted a little with what sounded like English private school overtones. He walked in a white, collared shirt, soiled as one would expect after days of grime and sweat. He had removed the hip belt from his pack, to save weight, and I was astonished to learn that his budget for the entire PCT was £400.

I have the fondest memories of the camp spot that evening at Lost Valley Spring. Water was on hand, albeit half a mile down a side track. A small plateau commanded a great view over the valley below us and the blue of the sky merged into maturing reds and oranges. Stumbling Norwegian, Sugar Moma, Bob, Brittany, Elk and Burnie were in various stages of setting up camp, cooking or playing impromptu guitar. Giggles floated through the air and aromas of mac and cheese, coffee and Elk's pop tarts mingled with the scent of spring flowers. Burnie was eyeing my hot sauce to spice up her dinner and Elk was trying to sell the benefits of spam to me as he made inroads into his fourth pop tart. Early starts and early bedtimes, or 'hiker midnight', meant we went to bed at dark and got up at light. Most of us were therefore asleep just after 9pm.

The food topic continued over breakfast. Porridge, or just plain 'oatmeal' as it is called in America, took pride of place. I go through phases with porridge: sometimes it turns my nose and at other times I can merrily knock it back for weeks. I researched our friendly grain and among the information I managed to gather was the suggestion to cook it for at least eight hours. I regularly did this at home although not, I hasten to add, every morning. I would knock up a pot to keep in the fridge and just reheat what I required each time. The lengthy cooking time really brings out the flavour and the consistency is wonderful. Additions of sultanas or other dried fruit, nuts, spices such as cinnamon and nutmeg and even chocolate had me experimenting for weeks. I became an oataholic.

The trail limits your food options but I usually settled on adding powdered milk to the mix, water obviously, sultanas and honey powder, which I found in a hiker box (I'll come on to hiker boxes later). I would mix this all up in the evening and let it steep overnight, which meant less cooking time and a superior texture once cooked for a couple of minutes.

"They're a good respite from depression," claimed Cedar Elk

(referred to by everyone as 'Elk'), watching my recipe as he cooked his.

"Does that explain why you're so freakin' happy all the time?" Brittany asked.

Pop tarts were also a heated subject of debate. I'm not a fan: there are too many ingredients, for starters, which always makes me suspicious; they're heavy; but mainly I didn't think they tasted very nice. Cedar Elk was converted, along with a few others, and he used to munch on a couple to solve the immediate hunger crisis before his main cooked meal was ready. Marshall Walker Lee referred to eating pop tarts as his 'morning ritual of self-loathing'.

The San Jacinto Mountains started peeking at me every time I crested a high point, their flanks still dressed in snow. I was becoming acclimatised to the high temperatures more quickly than I had imagined and the heat wasn't affecting me greatly. As long as I concentrated on drinking at least half to one litre of water an hour on average, and covering any bare skin with trousers, long sleeves and a Sahara hat, then I was OK. This made me sweat more but my Smartwool layers remained comfortable. The ascents produced more perspiration as my body strained and my breathing rate increased, and as I wiped my hand over my forehead, a mixture of SPF50, sweat, sand and grit grated and rasped against my brow. I was working towards my next stop and re-supply at Idyllwild, a regular haunt of hikers due to relatively good hitching chances on a busy road, a variety of eating establishments, a half-decent store and a gear shop. There was also a good campsite with showers. I had camped near the highway in the company of Hojo, Charmin, Stumbling Norwegian and Sugar Moma. Hojo and I were on the road at 7.30am in the hope of hitching a ride, a ritual I was to repeat many times over the following months.

Sometimes there is no rhyme or reason to getting a ride, but I did try to follow some basic tips I had picked up over the years to increase my chances. First, always put your pack by the side of the road where drivers can see it. This advertises the fact that you're a hiker and not an axe-wielding madman. Choose a straight stretch of road so you can be seen, but preferably a short stretch so vehicles can't pick up much speed; a speeding car is less likely to stop than one moving more slowly. Try finding a layby so any potential rides can pull in off the road, and stand a good couple of hundred feet before it so it presents an opportunity for them to get off the road quickly. If this is just before a corner, even better as they have to slow down. Junctions were perfect spots as vehicles had to actually stop and then be faced with my wry smile and well-honed pleading look. Any driver caught in my foolproof gaze would be rendered completely helpless.

My worst effort at hitching a ride was when I waited by the roadside just outside Etna for three hours. I eventually resorted to collaring a day-hiker who came off trail to his parked car. The best? Reaching a dead-end road just outside Wrightwood, where cars had to turn around to go back down the hill. I approached, still on trail, as a car was doing just this and as I stuck out my thumb, the driver came out of the manoeuvre and started to accelerate. She saw me, stopped, reached round and opened her back door, which enabled me to walk straight off the trail without so much as breaking my stride. It couldn't have been quicker or easier. Being with a female increases your odds substantially, presumable because motorists find a woman less intimidating. Sometimes, to improve our prospects, I would hide off road in a bush and shout advice.

"Pull your skirt up a bit," or "Toss your hair about. SMILE."

The expression of many blokes changed from delight at having picked up a good-looking girl to disappointment as they saw me walk out from my hiding place.

"Oh, fancy that," I used to exclaim as I emerged from the bushes. "I mean, what are the chances of reaching the road just as you stopped? Thanks very much."

Lastly, if just standing there isn't producing good results then do something stupid. I used to jump up and down, dance or open my umbrella and spin it round in front of me. This makes drivers slow down and look because it's different. Once you have their attention, get eye contact, then smile and look sorry for yourself. If the driver is female, a quick, suggestive rise of the eyebrows also works wonders.

After an hour outside Idyllwild of dancing, umbrella spinning and enough eyebrow raises to make my forehead ache,

I eventually received a reciprocal smile from a young lady and she took us both into town.

The campsite was excellent and I set about my day-off routine. First came my body and the important task of ridding it of dirt, grime, sweat and odour. I cringed at the violent stench that assaulted my nose as I removed my shoes, leaving a clear sock line between a white ankle and a brown mix of congealed dust on my lower legs. I gingerly peeled off my socks with two fingers and placed them with other soiled clothing in a bag as I put on the only spare clothing I had that wasn't heading for the tumble drier: waterproofs. You can always spot a thru-hiker in the launderette because they will be sitting there, waiting for the machine to run its course whilst they drip inside a Gore-Tex jacket and bottoms. I liked to wash my clothes first because it meant I had something clean to wear when I emerged from the shower later.

While waiting, I would sit and read a magazine, lifting the machine lid now and then to see just how brown the water actually was. A quick tumble dry and back to the showers.

Never before in my life had I been so grateful to take a wash. Watching a tawny-coloured murk swirl down the plug hole, I loved the invigorating feeling of water and soap against skin.

I hadn't been bothering with shaving as there was no need for it. Most of the male hikers also dispensed with this chore and, as the walk progressed, so did our beards. After a few months there were some impressive clumps of hair adorning most of our faces. My ability to grow bristles doesn't rank up there with the greats such as Grizzly Adams. I end up with a nice goatee merging into my cheeks, where it just sort of gives up. That said, further into the PCT, even I was proud of my beard. The amount of facial hair is a sure way to distinguish a thru-hiker from a day-tripper.

Washed and laundered, I'd catch up with emails, update my blog, check all my gear was OK, and replace, repair or upgrade if necessary. The main call, however, was food. American breakfasts are incredible affairs and I was salivating at the thought of them, even days before hitting town. Eggs, bacon, pancakes, hash browns, beans, mushrooms, sausages, patties, toast and coffee. Not necessarily in that order. I made my way over to the Red Kettle, which was teeming with hikers, and was invited over to a corner table with Elk and Brittany.

Elk was a true outdoorsman and completely at home in the wild. He knew a lot about plants and was soon to provide me with my first taste of rattlesnake, which he had dispatched after it had been hit by a car. I aspired to match his enviable beard. He strode effortlessly along on two tree trunks for legs. He smoked a pipe and the conversations I enjoyed with him always made me laugh, often to the point of hysterics, thanks to the sheer preposterousness of his obscure angles on various subjects. If you look at the quote at the beginning of this chapter, you'll get the idea.

Brittany was married with a daughter and was only attempting part of the PCT but loving it. She had shaved off her long hair before starting and it framed an attractive face, which was always dressed in a big, cheeky smile, whether she was battling or not. I was immensely fond of her; her infectious cheer rubbed off on me every time I spent time with her, and she always lifted my day.

I returned to the campsite, pondering lunch options on the way, and found Burnie had set up her tent near to mine. She was my other favourite girl, although at first I was unsure of her. She had a sweet voice with the slightest hint of a squeak and when she laughed it made her sound like a seven-year-old witch, if you can imagine such a tone. I often tried to amuse her just so I could hear her giggle. She also had some sinus problems, which meant she had to blow her nose loudly and often. I remember one particular night camped with her and a few others in the forest and she had gone off for a pee. As she returned, she was clearing her nose.

"What the hell is that noise? Is that a moose?" I had asked the others, who were also listening intently, trying to figure out what sort of creature could produce such a bellowing. Closer and closer it got, to the point where torches came out to illuminate the scene. Most of camp fell about laughing as Burnie eventually emerged from behind a bush with a handkerchief in one hand. After a few days, tired of carrying an endless supply of tissues, she started employing the method most of us used: holding one nostril shut with a finger and blowing out hard to remove any debris, and then repeating on the other side. Burnie referred to this as 'snot rocketing out my boogers'.

Burnie was in her mid-twenties. She already had the Appalachian Trail under her belt and the long-distance walking bug had taken hold. When trying to use her MSR WhisperLite stove during the early days of the AT, she couldn't seem to get the timing right and the burner kept going up in flames (anyone who has owned a WhisperLite can surely relate to this). After melting the sleeve of her synthetic jacket, burning a hole in her wool hat and nearly burning down Springer Mountain shelter, she was issued her trail name. With me, she seemed at first unsure and hesitant; for that reason I tended not to spend time with her, but then realised that I exhibited the same trait. People often find me difficult to get to know and perhaps unapproachable. This is not something I do intentionally; I think it's just some sort of subconscious warning signal. The result is that I find the people who do make the effort are genuinely worth knowing. So, after we had both broken down each other's barriers, I enjoyed her company.

"Apache Peak still has snow, apparently," she said to me.

"Yes, I heard."

"My ice axe and crampons have been mailed up trail for the Sierras, so I don't have them."

"I don't think there'll be that much up there," I said, trying to reassure her. "Even if there is, I'm sure it's negotiable with care."

"Hmm," she said uncertainly. She looked worried.

"Look, if it will make you feel safer you can walk with me and we can watch each other's back."

"No, it's fine – I don't want to impose."

"Burnie, you're not imposing. If you want me to walk with you, then it's not a problem, really."

"But I don't walk very fast, I'll hold you up."

"Look, think about it. It makes sense. I don't want to force you into something you don't want to do, but I don't mind. Really, I don't mind. I leave tomorrow, so give it some thought."

In the morning I got an easy ride back to the trailhead with her, employing the road junction tactic, coupled with female company. Twenty feet back on trail and we stopped before we had even properly got moving, thanks to some trail magic in the car park. Trail magic is the term used to describe an act of kindness or generosity taking place – usually by the side of the trail or where it crosses a road. It normally takes the form of food and drink in abundance or somewhere to rest in shade, and is laid on by previous thru-hikers who realise its value, having been on the PCT themselves. Meat was grilling, cold drinks adorned the interior of the coolers and I met Grey Fox, Spiller, Flashlight, Vader and Pyjamas all taking a well-earned break in the shade.

We passed Upchuck sitting by a pile of beer cans on the trailside and smoking something that made him talk at speed about nothing interesting for ten minutes. We didn't sit down but just leaned on our trekking poles, pretending to be interested, and made our escape as quickly as possible.

"What's he going to do?" Burnie asked afterwards. "Hallucinate his way to Canada?"

Burnie did walk more slowly than me, but remembering my reasons for taking on the PCT in the first place, namely to be completely open to events and circumstances, I didn't mind. I was to walk with several others during the hike and rarely found someone who walked naturally at my pace, or I at theirs. One had to consciously slow down, speed up or just walk ahead and rest once in a while for them to catch up, which is what I did with Burnie. Having offered to accompany her, I felt I had a duty to see her safely over Apache Peak – or at least the snow-bound sections – and it was equally reassuring to have her watch my back as well.

In any case, she was good company, in no hurry and had a relaxed aura about her that rubbed off on me. There were, again, rumours of storms coming in and we were both aware that we could be up there in the thick of it between 6,000 and 7,000 feet. On reaching Fobes Saddle (in America they refer to a col, which is a pass or depression in a mountain range or ridge, as a saddle), I noticed a side trail marking a water source half a mile down and decided it would make a suitable early camp spot, mindful of the imminent storm. A quick scout down the trail proved a good idea: there was indeed a well-flowing spring and a flat area to set up tent, it was 500 feet below the saddle and abundant trees should provide some wind break. I remembered how Gabe and I had wisely chosen to shelter on Mount Laguna, and as the trail went up to 9,000 feet I was keen not to increase our altitude any more. I walked back up and left a note for Burnie, who was catching up, by the side of the trail:

"Storm coming in. Camped half mile down track in good shelter with water. Take side trail and turn immediately right and follow down. Fozzie."

She arrived shortly after and we both started to set up camp. It was still only 4pm but the winds were increasing. The spring provided excellent water and there was also miner's lettuce growing in abundance. Also known as winter purslane, it is named after the Gold Rush miners who used to eat it to stave off scurvy. Brittany had shown me this edible plant a few days earlier and it was common in shade and near water. As the name suggests, it tastes just like a salad leaf and I used to fill up my pan with it and sprinkle with grated parmesan, olive oil and pepper for a tasty starter. Several people had warned me not to make a habit of eating too much because it has a reputation for – how shall I say? – loosening up one's movements a little. Burnie was very excited to find a free food source and tucked in as well.

By dusk, the storm seemed to be racing over our heads a mere hundred feet up. There was no rain but sand was being kicked about, blasting everything in its path, including us. As each successive deafening blast ripped across the valley below, we braced ourselves for the impact. As soon as we could, we retreated to our tents, where I spent most of the night unable to sleep until it abated around 2am. Frustrated by the lack of rest, I resorted to snacking after a raging hunger kicked in and worked my way through a large proportion of my supplies. Despite restocking in Idyllwild, I would have to go down the Devil's Slide, another exit point down a steep ascent and long walk, to make up the food deficit.

We climbed up the following day, hoping to reach Saddle Junction and the Devil's Slide. The early morning heat melted the last remnants of snow clinging to branches over the trail and I felt the occasional slap of meltwater on my head. Little puffs of dust erupted on the trail as the drips landed. Eventually we rounded the north side of Apache Peak, where we had been warned about lingering snow. It was worse than I had anticipated but by no means impassable. Sections of the trail were still obscured by snow banks covering the steep sides of the hill but there were plenty of dry sections poking through. It was vital to keep an eye on the track and a firm footing, as it kept disappearing and reappearing. One slip would have sent us tumbling down an infinite Andreas Canyon Gorge. Post-holing was also a problem. I had heard a lot about post-holing – it doesn't sound that dangerous but can end a hike. The first souls to walk over fresh snow on the PCT each year leave footprints for others to follow, assuming they are going in the right direction. The best way is to follow these prints as the snow under them is compacted and therefore more solid; also, breaking trail is hard work where sinking up to your waist is not uncommon. The problems start as the summer wears on and the snow becomes slushy and unstable; then, hikers can break through the surface and a stray leg can hit the ground underneath, which is often rock. It usually results in nothing more than a graze but bruises, sprains, breaks and cuts are common. The worst scenario is if you are walking quickly downhill and a whole leg breaks through. The momentum carries you forward while the leg stays in place, leading to inevitable horrors.

We climbed and dipped relentlessly like leaves on a fluctuating breeze, one minute gasping and sweating, the next pulling on extra clothing because of the cold. From Fobes Saddle to Saddle Junction, we tentatively made our way through the six-foot snow drifts that littered the trail, making an average of a mile an hour (normal walking speed is three miles per hour). I, too, had mailed my ice axe and spikes up to the start of the Sierra, so it was a balancing act as we gingerly tiptoed through, supported by our trekking poles.

By the time we had got to the bottom of the Devil's Slide, it was getting dark and we still had three miles further to go on the road to town, the previous twelve miles having taken us eleven hours. I stumbled into the campsite again, too tired from effort and lack of sleep after the storm even to cook or shower, and fell immediately into a deep slumber.

Journal entry:

Vistas to die for. I was expecting hot, arid and dry desert in southern California, but it continues to surprise me. Sand gives way to scrub, surrendering to rocky outcrops, which remind me of old Western movies. Then, I climb to 8,000 feet and walk through pine forest resplendent with flowers. I strain to make out a horizon that is many days away. Heat that I have never experienced before changes to a chill in the mountains, as I put on a hat, gloves and a down jacket and wake up to ice on the tent. It's a constantly changing scene that continues to catch me out.

For the last two days I have walked from highway 74 (not the most romantic of locations; I apologise for that), to a place called Saddle Junction in the San Jacinto mountains. I have been warned by some of the park rangers that there is still snow in places, mainly on the north-facing slopes.

However, some fellow hikers and I decide to walk, rather than wait three or so days for my ice axe and crampons to be sent here. The first night at Fobes Saddles (around 6,000 feet), I am with an American woman called Burnie and several other guys as we watch a cloud bank roll towards us like a charging bull. The guys decide (foolishly) to continue on and up. Burnie and I retreated down a couple of hundred feet, to the relative safety of a woodland clearing.

At 8pm I stand outside the tent and watch, dumbstruck at the roaring storm flying past a few hundred feet above me, like a torrent of water at rapids. At 2am it finally abates and I manage to get some sleep. Surveying my tent and equipment that I had left under the fly sheet, in the morning I find everything covered in a fine layer of dust and grit. Storms, it would appear, are part of the deal here.

I walk eleven miles the following day, climbing and dipping. One minute I gasp and sweat in heat, the next I pull on extra clothing to ward off the cold. From Fobes Saddle to Saddle Junction, I tentatively make my way through six-foot snow drifts that litter the trail. For the last two miles the PCT appears and vanishes under the snow as the sun begins to set. Twelve miles take eleven hours. At 8pm I finally stagger down the Devil's

Slide Trail to Idyllwild, somehow managing to erect my tent and climb, exhausted, filthy and too tired even to wash, into my sleeping bag.

I'm loving every single second of it.

Chapter 4
Blisters

Hiking is my addiction. The PCT is my dealer.
Patti 'Sugar Moma' Kulesz

I hadn't seen Gabe for days but at breakfast the following morning I learnt he had ended his hike shortly after I last saw him at the Rodriguez Spur Road. He sent me an email citing blisters as the main problem but also saying that he felt he should have prepared more in terms of fitness and gear. "I wasn't ready for a thru-hike, Fozzie," it read.

The Red Kettle was buzzing and I sat with Brittany, Burnie and Elk. Brittany, wearing an orange top with white trousers, was bouncing up and down to the piped music, looking like a bobbing buoy lost on choppy seas. She also had an alarming habit of smothering everything she ate with tomato ketchup, so that her breakfast looked as if she had lost a limb in some freak accident.

I was never too fond of ketchup but I did have a small bag where I kept condiments to spice up my trail food. Salt and pepper were staples, along with a few herbs (curry powder, cumin and oregano) and sugar. I would occasionally buy a cup of tea at a petrol station and 'accidentally' slip a couple of tea bags in my pocket as well; after all, an Englishman must have his Earl Grey. I was also developing a fondness for hot sauce, which is commonplace on American restaurant tables. It's uneconomical to buy these items because they are packaged in large quantities, so I used to procure them in eating establishments along the route. I didn't class it as stealing, as I was eating there anyway, so my conscience was untroubled. Elk always said 'stolen condiments taste better'.

Once the attention of the waiting staff was diverted (the perfect time was just after the food was delivered, because they'd then leave us alone for a while), I used to unscrew the top of the salt and pepper shakers and pour some into a little receptacle kindly given to me by Hojo at Warner Springs. I also added to my sugar container and tipped some hot sauce into a little screw-top plastic bottle with a flip-top spout. This top-up would see me through a week or so.

My favourite was a brand called Cholula but I was also partial to Tapatio, the ever-popular Tabasco and lots of other varieties. The further I made inroads into the PCT, the more different types of hot sauce found their way into my bottle, which varied in taste from one week to the next. Sometimes it was a little sweet, sometimes salty, on occasion really fiery, at other times mellow. I used to say, when others teased me about refilling, that at some point the taste would be perfect and I would have found the ideal hot sauce. When, after a few weeks, I eventually realised that I had reached that moment, it dawned on me that the secret was lost forever, as I had only a rough idea of which brands were in the bottle and in what quantities. I had reached hot sauce enlightenment, but was unable to preserve it for posterity.

The Red Kettle chatter centred on Fuller Ridge, which we would be crossing that day. It was still covered in snow and known for often being the first snow section encountered on the route. I got a lift back to the bottom of Devil's Slide, where a group had formed, keen to have company and reassurance over this section. Stumbling Norwegian, Sugar Moma, Burnie and Pigpen were all there, checking packs and preparing for the slog up the slide and then Fuller itself. A couple of day-hikers sporting beer bellies smiled at us as they passed us on the way up, remarking that it was easier to walk with a day pack than our loads bursting with several days' food supply. Twenty minutes later, we caught up with them sitting beside the trail in a pool of sweat and trying to catch their breath.

"It's also far easier to walk when you're fit," I remarked and winked at them as I passed.

The Last Englishman

Pony and Your Mom joined us and we all teamed up to navigate our way over Fuller. As I have mentioned, one of the problems over snow was navigation. With the trail buried a few feet under us and, at times, the actual PCT signs buried as well, it wasn't easy. Occasionally we could pick up footprints but this was no guarantee we were on the correct trail. Obviously we couldn't go too far off course as we were walking on a ridge, so we only needed to keep on or near the top, but it involved a lot of GPS checking, scouting around and general discussion. Slips, slides and falls were the order of the day as we picked a route through the white. Trying to obtain some sort of purchase on angled banks of snow meant that our walking speed plummeted. Every step was taken gingerly and with a healthy fear that at any moment our feet could be whipped from underneath us as if someone had tied a rope to our ankle and pulled sharply sideways.

I was bringing up the rear of the pack at one point and watched in horror as Pony slipped and started falling down the slope to our right, gaining momentum quickly towards a steepening drop-off. Under other circumstances she could have self-arrested (plunged an ice axe into the snow to stop the slide). However, none of us had our ice axes with us, as we had not been expecting snow this early in the hike. In a flash, Pigpen dived over the side and slid down to catch her up, arresting both of them with his feet and any other part that would bring them to a stop. I wouldn't have attempted such a risky manoeuvre, but Pigpen threw caution to one side and acted completely on impulse. Having only known Pigpen for one morning, I already had a strong respect for him. Pony was understandably thankful, as well as shaken.

I expect a few of you are shaking your heads at this point because we were negotiating a snow ridge with no ice axe, no crampons and no rope. In mountaineering terms this is a no-no and I have to say I agree with you, but allow me some defence, albeit a weak one. If a thru-hiker had to carry every piece of equipment that was needed, we would all be struggling under a towering rucksack weighing 50 kilos. It's just not possible. Also, we put weight a long way before safety. If we can get through a section with 100ml of stove fuel, then we risk it. If we're buying a jacket, the first thing we check is not whether it's waterproof but how many grams it weighs. One pair of socks is fine for a week because two pairs would make our packs heavier.

Lightening the load is a series of small steps that make an overall improvement. We would not notice whether we were carrying one pair of socks instead of two, but if you make several small improvements, the bigger picture emerges. Buy the lightest gear possible you know will work, carry the smallest amount you're comfortable with and make a lot of minor sacrifices.

Failing that, learn the hard way. Take more and then walk for a week. Every year, somewhere around Warner Springs, you'll see a lot of hikers throwing stuff out of their packs and mailing it back home.

When we arrived at Black Mountain Road, we were all fatigued although in good spirits. We also realised that not one of us had remembered to fill up with water for camp, and had it not been for Your Mom, Pigpen and Pony, who graciously offered to walk two miles back up trail and then back, we would have gone thirsty and hungry.

The following morning, I walked with Stumbling Norwegian down the endless switchbacks on Fuller Ridge's east side. We stopped for a break and some shade under an overhanging rock. I reached for my spork (a plastic eating utensil with a spoon one end and a fork the other), only to discover it had somehow disintegrated into four little pieces. Norwegian laughed at my forlorn expression as I realised I had nothing to spoon out my peanut butter with.

"Don't worry, Fozzie, the trail will provide," he said reassuringly.

I reached the bottom on my own and made my way across a dry, featureless flatland to a promised water cache under the bridge where the trail met Interstate 10. Marker poles stuck in the sand every quarter mile or so guided me through. Dry creek beds crossed the trail, their surfaces etched with ripple patterns that looked like tree bark where the water had once flowed. A huge gopher snake whipped out from beneath a bush, making me stop abruptly in mortal terror. It was longer than I was tall and flew across the terrain at a speed faster than any human could run.

I reached the underpass and water cache just as the local trail angel who looked after it came sliding down on his quad bike. Dr No stopped in front of me and, without even asking, reached round to the cooler strapped on the bike and handed me the coldest beer ever. As I took the bottle, a sliver of ice gently slid off the top and glided down the side, where it melted and dripped down my finger.

"Thanks," I said. "Great timing."

"No problem, here to help," he replied.

We chatted for a while, and as I put my rubbish in the bin, I noticed something sticking out of the sand. Bending down to pick it up, I couldn't believe my luck. An antique spoon, black with tarnish, nestled in my hand. On the handle it bore the inscription 'MBL' and on the underside there was a silver hallmark and the engraved letters 'Pat 1907'.

Dr No explained that the highway had been built over a hundred years ago and, although he doubted if it was a worker's spoon, as they would not have eaten with silver cutlery, it may have been left by someone picnicking under the bridge to get some shade. I remembered Stumbling Norwegian saying, "The trail will provide", and smiled. I spent a few minutes rubbing it in the sand, which removed the tarnish, and it came up like new. That spoon stayed with me for the rest of the PCT and I still use it when I go hiking now. Despite weight penalties, we all have to have one item of luxury.

I was tempted to get a ride into Cabazon for a hot meal, five miles up the Interstate, but mileage was not meeting my expectations. I was managing around fifteen miles a day and I wanted to be putting in twenties. Besides, hitching a ride on the Interstate is nigh on impossible, as the vehicles are travelling too fast – and it's also illegal. Not that this would have stopped me trying. "I'm sorry, I'm English, I had no idea" got me out of a few scrapes with the authorities.

I carried on through knee-high grass to get to the Mesa Wind Farm. Lizards ran for cover and startled me after my snake encounter earlier. Even my trekking poles kept catching the grass and rustling, so I was a bit of a nervous wreck. Stumbling Norwegian had told me that the workers at the wind farm welcome hikers into their canteen and even keep their freezers stocked full of goodies, asking no more than the actual cost of what is eaten by way of payment. It was shut when I arrived and I hoped some of them would be working overtime the next day, as it was Sunday. Burnie, Stumbling Norwegian, Pigpen, Your Mom and Pony arrived shortly afterwards with the same plan.

Excited by the rare opportunity to get a hot breakfast on trail, most of us were up and in the canteen by 7.30am, rummaging through the freezer and microwaving burritos, burgers and croissants, drinking loads of coffee and washing it all down with ice cream. I said I'd cover the cost to return the favour of the water collection mission the previous evening.

The heat was intense which, coupled with the ups and downs of the trail, left us all dripping. I still couldn't believe how much water was about. It wasn't exactly abundant, but there was a creek every five miles or so. It made me laugh when I remembered back in England that we get a drought warning after two weeks of sunshine. Out here they rarely see rain for weeks, even months, but still we could fill up.

We made the steep descent through the Whitewater Canyon to the Whitewater River. It was only midday but everyone was so hot that the chance to cool down was irresistible. For two hours we splashed about, did some laundry, built dams to create pools and washed off our accumulated grime. The canyon walls plunged diagonally into the ground, striped in different shades of brown, like a huge slice of chocolate layer cake that had been rammed into the earth. It felt wonderful to be clean again and I took a short siesta in the shade. Keen for a little solitude, I left before the others, progressed over to the next valley and picked up the trail weaving from one side to the other of Mission Creek. Blisters were still plaguing me and I figured it must have been the sand and grit working through the mesh on my shoes.

I jumped down on to the banks of the creek, ready for another crossing, and as I landed another blister burst, making me shout and hobble to a painful halt. Enough was enough for one day. I pitched tent among some scary-looking holes in the ground that I hoped did not house a tarantula or something equally creepy. I checked the tent for holes and made sure my zip was well and truly sealed before sleeping.

I woke early, cooked some porridge and was just on the verge of leaving when I noticed someone approaching from downstream, jumping nimbly from one side of the creek to the other like a mountain goat. Yvo had started on the trail at 6.30am and I walked with him for most of the day. He hailed from Switzerland and bore a striking resemblance to John Lennon, with scruffy hair meeting an unkempt beard, interrupted only by wiry spectacles. I half expected him to whip out a guitar and play a rendition of Hey Jude or similar. He walked quickly and apparently effortlessly. Gliding along without even breaking sweat, he would stop every thirty minutes, comment on the view and carry on, with me gasping somewhere behind him, leaving a trail of perspiration in the grit. It was like trying to keep up with a pacemaker. If you needed to be somewhere quickly, and if you could keep up, Yvo was the man to stick with.

We fumbled our way aimlessly along Mission Creek, hemmed in by towering cliffs either side of us as they narrowed like a huge funnel, feeling the heat of the sun when we walked out of the shade and a chill when we returned to it. With the constant gurgle of water as a companion, we must have crossed the creek thirty times, hopping from one side to the other. Sometimes we balanced our feet on one side ready to leap over and the weak soil gave way beneath us, the icy water chilling our toes. Straining our eyes, we tried, sometimes in vain, to locate an elusive trail. A rattlesnake glided casually across the path, startling me. Normally they would signal a warning but this one was silent, seemingly without malice or intent to confront, and my fear subsided. A forest fire had left trees stark and white, stripped of their bark and twisted into bizarre shapes at the trail edge. We climbed up, and up, and up, praying for an end to unrelenting hills.

The end did not come until ten hours later. Yvo, who had long since pulled away from me, had camped under the fir trees at 8,000 feet. I nodded a greeting and gestured I was carrying on, and he signalled that he understood. Two miles further on, after walking twenty-one miles and climbing 4,500 feet that day, I pulled off the trail. It was 7.30pm. I laid down my pack, set up the tent and watched the sun sink over the mountains to the west and a crescent moon rise. Stars slowly began to pierce the black as my saucepan lid rattled, letting me know that my food was ready. It was the only sound in the mountains.

I reached Onyx Summit the following morning and managed to get a ride into Big Bear with a fireman after just a couple of minutes. I was planning on staying at the hostel, which I'd heard good things about; and after a bus ride, which I swore circled the same route twice, I finally arrived. Grayson, a very hospitable host, checked me in and told me to make myself at home. A sombre Sugar Moma was already there, explaining that she had got off the trail at the top of Devil's Slide because of fatigue and some dietary problems. She didn't look happy and I sensed something a little deeper was simmering.

I wasn't taken with Big Bear. It was just far too spaced out, a phenomenon I encountered a few times at town stops. It sounds crazy that you're walking from Mexico to Canada and then complaining about having to walk everywhere once in town, but rest was important to me on my days off. I concentrated on the usual tasks of showering, laundry, food shopping and emails as quickly as I could so I could just sit down, grab a beer and chill out. But it never happened that way. My plan to take one day a week out always extended to a day and a half or, more often, two days, just to fit everything in that I wanted to do.

The main time drain was sitting at the computer. My hike was gaining momentum. I was receiving more and more communications from people I had never heard of and the blog was doing well. Most were wishing me well, which was heartening, but it took an ever-increasing amount of time to answer them all, which I felt obliged to do. I was constantly frustrated as well by the lack of internet facilities. The library usually had several computers but they came with a stingy one-hour time limit, which was nowhere near enough.

My appetite in town was massive. On the trail I was hungry, but no more than I would be on a normal day at home. Once I was resting, however, my body seemed to sense I had time on my hands and decided it should be spent making inroads into my calorie deficit. I always had a huge breakfast and the wait for lunch was so long that I had to eat mid-morning as well. By the time I had eaten again just after midday, I had already put away 4,000 calories and I would snack mid-afternoon and then indulge in a huge feast in the evening. Of course, ice cream was a must an hour or so before bedtime as well. I estimated I was packing away 6,000 to 7,000 calories a day and was still constantly thinking about where and when I was going to eat next.

Grayson took me back to the trailhead after two days and I set off again alone. Classic single-track had me wishing I was on my mountain bike. The way was dusted with pine needles, which cushioned the feet and suppressed the dust. The air was ripe with the sweet smell of butterscotch leaching from the trees and I kicked the occasional pine cone, pretending I was taking the winning penalty in the World Cup. Huge fallen tree trunks sometimes blocked my passage and as I approached I would size them up, calculating whether it was best to climb over, squeeze under or walk round.

I fell into daydreams and miles would pass without my realising it. I sometimes missed turns or splits in the path and I had to remind myself to concentrate more on where I was going, as well as watching the surface for rocks, snakes and obstacles that could result in a twisted ankle. I felt angry at having to scan the ground immediately in front of me, because it denied me the chance to look up and around at my surroundings, so I would stop once in a while and just gaze about. I tried to look behind me as well – sometimes the best views were staring me in the back. Some days went by in a blurred trance as the repetitive rhythm of footfall lured me into another world. Hours passed without seeing another soul or even hearing another sound except the crunch of my feet on the ground, the regular stab of my poles either side and my breathing.

Passing some hot springs, I was tempted to plunge in but it was Friday evening and they were teeming with people from town. Beers cans littered the banks and hoarse shouts disturbed me as I walked past graffiti scrawled on the rocks. Fairly innocuous slogans like 'I love Kate' or 'Alcohol forever' were interspersed with lewd sexual suggestions, which reminded me why I had come to the PCT in the first place.

The peace and ambience of the wilderness were often rudely shattered on the approach to civilisation and I started to resent the human race, sometimes retreating further into myself and forgoing company for fear of being dragged out of the very solace I had discovered, and savoured. To preserve my selfish tranquillity, I often waited if I saw hikers ahead so I could remain alone, or if I knew people were behind me I might speed up. I camped well off trail to prevent being disturbed. For days I just yearned for nothing more than to get lost in the desert, pretending I was a sole apocalyptic survivor and could roam at will. I begrudged roads, cars and buildings their existence and even aircraft started to grate.

I became addicted to a self-imposed loneliness and started to savour the prospect of the remote Sierra Nevada, where I could indulge my desire to become even more detached from the life I had become used to. I tried to berate myself for allowing such feelings, convincing myself they were too negative, but I couldn't. I was happy in my solitary meanderings and dreamt up ways to stay infinitely detached.

Then, suddenly, I would snap out of it and be eager to walk with others. I liked company but equally I relished being on my own and I used to flit between the two according to my mood changes.

Snake count: 3
False alarms: 62

After 350 miles I was already in need of new shoes. The trail surface was rasping away my footwear like sandpaper, but even taking that into account I was surprised. On that sort of average I would be getting through eight pairs by the end of the hike. An English company called Inov-8 had sponsored me with Gore-Tex boots but I had only intended using them when and if the weather became wet or cold. In the desert, as comfortable as they were, my feet would have fried. Philip Carcia, otherwise known as Lo, pointed me in the direction of some Montrails, which he swore by. I had discovered that my feet were wide and suited to this type of fit. After a day of wearing them they also appeared to be blocking out much more of the sand, as the fabric was a tighter weave, but my blisters still persisted regardless.

Wrightwood, better known as a ski resort, immediately made a good impression on me. It was compact and everywhere was in walking distance. The Evergreen and Grizzly cafés knocked out an admirable breakfast, the large supermarket made my re-supply easy and the Evergreen Bar was popular with hikers in the evening.

Many had stopped here for a few days waiting for snow to clear on top of Baden-Powell, which, at 9,400 feet, was still sporting an impressive coating. A similar backlog was due to occur at the start of the Sierras but I did not want to linger waiting for snow to melt. An extra day or so would make no discernible difference and I was still not happy with my mileage. I had pulled in a few twenty to twenty-five-milers but, after taking town stops into account, the actual daily average over a week was a dismal fifteen. I had to get moving; less time in town and more hours on the trail.

The main problem with this was that my blisters were limiting my mileage. If I pushed too hard, then either I made the existing ones worse or new ones appeared, so I had no choice than to stick below twenty a day. The days I had exceeded this I, or rather my feet, ended up paying for it.

It was to be weeks before my feet eventually sorted themselves out. The body is the best judge of what to do during a thru-hike and will generally heal itself, albeit over time. I had always suffered from blisters, whether on the PCT or shorter adventures. They normally appear after a couple of days, which makes a week's walking a somewhat painful experience. I had learnt over the years to accept them as part of the walking deal but I had to pay them attention to make sure infection didn't take hold.

Every night I religiously washed my feet in a creek (trying to make sure I was downstream of anyone else!). Then I would dry and inspect them. I didn't enjoy having to look after them because it made inroads into my time chilling out in the evening, but I had little choice. The new ones required the most attention: this entailed sterilising my pen knife and needle in a lighter flame and piercing them to squeeze out the liquid, then cutting the loose skin away. The excruciating part of the proceedings was dabbing rubbing alcohol on the exposed, raw skin underneath, which had me rocking back and forth like a baby, gritting my teeth and stifling a scream that would probably have been heard over in the next valley. I never dressed them, preferring instead to let the air do its work and, although this proved painful the following day, my feet got the message and they healed more quickly.

Despite this care, I did get an infection near the town of Agua Dulce. The soft pad at the base of the big toe was looking alarmingly red under the skin and a little tender. I had tried to pierce it several times but the soles of my feet were becoming astonishingly hard (when hiking the skin eventually toughens to the point where it is so thick it can be tapped like a piece of wood). I couldn't get the needle to penetrate but on the third evening I decided enough was enough: the pain was getting worse and the red area was changing to white and even shades of blue. I inserted the needle, broke through the hard skin and kept pushing, probing and testing each area and pushing as one would a toothpaste tube. I eventually watched, disgusted, as a thick, congealed mixture of pus and blood oozed out and a nasty smell hit me. Even Stumbling Norwegian held his nose, and he was twenty feet away.

I have tried nylon socks, wool socks, sock liners (a thin pair worn under the main pair), waterproof boots, non-waterproof boots, washing, not washing and wearing blister patches, but nothing seems to work. However, I become immune to the pain and once I am on the move it disappears anyway after the first ten hobble-inducing minutes.

The grit wasn't helping but neither was the heat, which was making my feet sweat. I used to remove my shoes at breaks and lunch to air them out but my feet still looked all wrinkled, as though I had been sitting in a hot bath for thirty minutes. I hadn't done my research properly to start with either. I had always walked in Gore-Tex (or similar) lined footwear because I don't like getting wet feet, but in the desert this was inviting problems; so, just a week before leaving, I switched to a low-cut trail runner with mesh inserts for ventilation, which is what was recommended. However, I had not had a chance to wear them in. That, I figured, was the main cause of my problems. Now that the first pair had worn out, I had to trust Lo's advice and buy a pair from a manufacturer that I had not tried before, although he did say they were ideal for wider feet and his Hardrocks, amazingly, had covered 2,500 miles. They weren't too pretty to look at, though.

Stumbling Norwegian walked in shoes that were designed to be used and get wet during water sports. They were open to the air and highly breathable. Elk used full-blown leather boots, Burnie the same but fabric, some wore sandals and I even saw a couple of pairs of Crocs. Blisters healed at different times for different people and some were lucky not to suffer at all. After the first few weeks, the complaints and moans died down as the feet healed or their owners dealt with the problem psychologically.

I was downing a couple of espressos in Mountain Grinds Coffee Shop the morning of my departure from Wrightwood. A sign on the wall made me chuckle: 'Unattended children will be given an espresso and a free kitten.' Stocking up on breakfast afterwards at the Grizzly Café with Borders, we discussed our plans for tackling Mount Baden-Powell. Hojo, Vicki and Dennis had retreated from their attempt, having nearly been blown off trail again, as well as wet from what turned out to be the last of the bad weather. This was due to clear, so I left shortly after with Borders, Grey Fox, Spiller, Jake and Upchuck. Despite the weather, those who had made it were reporting that, despite lots of snow higher up, it was easier than Fuller Ridge.

For the early part of the day I walked with Jake, who proved to be good company. Descending down to the road at Vincent Gap, we were suddenly face to face with an apparently never-ending stream of Japanese walkers out on a day hike. Trail etiquette suggests that you should give way to those ascending a hill, so we stepped to one side. Patiently, time after time, we waited on the edge as they filed up, one by one, ignoring us, making no eye contact and offering no thanks.

After about forty had passed us, displaying no manners whatsoever, we decided to throw politeness to the winds, increased our throttles and stormed down the hill, making each climber yelp and jump off the trail to get out of our way.

We snacked with the rest of the group at the car park while several tourists came over to us and offered congratulations for our endeavours to date and wished us well for Baden-Powell and the rest of our thru-hike. Some were back from the summit and left us their surplus food, which we gladly wolfed down.

Switchback after switchback coiled up the north flank of the mountain. Despite the elevation and the snow, we were all sweating copiously and drinking water to stay hydrated. It was four miles, all uphill, and on each turn in the path the snow became deeper until eventually we lost it altogether. From there on, we drifted apart, finding our own pace. Before long I was playing a guessing game as to my location. I did not have a GPS but the map told me the gradient was steady, if steep, to the top, with no serious contours that suggested dangerous drop-offs. I followed a compass bearing north and aimed for the high point. Snow eventually came up to my thighs and, gasping for air, I took one lunging step at a time, breathed deeply and then repeated the manoeuvre. The sun glared from the crisp, white surface, reducing my eyes to narrow slits behind my sunglasses. Eventually I stumbled onto the path, saw the crest of a hill and then heard laughter. The group had all made it to the summit, apart from Upchuck, who was nowhere to be seen. I assumed he was catching up with his beer hydration therapy.

The views were stunning. To the north the mountain sloped down to meet flat plateaus as far as I could see. The east, south and west were a collection of more mountains and ridges, some capped with snow and some not. We looked back to Fuller Ridge where we had been eight days earlier, its classic triangular silhouette still visible, commanding the surrounding hills.

I left the others, vaguely suggesting we may meet again at camp, and followed a rollercoaster ridge, skipping around and over snow banks, trying to stay away from the edge and surveying the best line to take. Somehow I inadvertently veered right at Dawson's Saddle before realising my mistake when the trail filtered into nothing and started to steepen. I could hear traffic on a road and decided to aim for that, as it would give a better indication of my position and the chance to correct my direction, as opposed to wasting energy returning to the top. The loose soil and steep slope made any sort of purchase extremely difficult and I spent the best part of two hours either sliding or falling on my arse. Finally I reached a creek at the bottom as dusk moved in and the highway finally appeared. Camping near to this was not ideal but the availability of water, my fatigue and the chance to get a bearing in the morning from the road decided the spot for me.

As I looked back up towards Dawson's Saddle, I could make out several figures at varying positions progressing down. I figured it must have been Jake, Spiller, Grey Fox and Borders, who had either followed me down or made the same mistake themselves. With daylight fading fast, I placed my head torch on a rock pointing towards them and turned it on to the flashing strobe setting, while I hurriedly built a fire to act as a homing beacon. Either side of me, rock faces shot up from the road. I didn't want any of them falling over the edge.

One by one they emerged, glad to have a fire already going and water at hand. They too had all somehow made the same navigational error as I had. We commandeered a corner of a small off-road parking area and busied ourselves making evening meals, rehydrating and relaxing. A car pulled in and an anxious-looking guy came over to us.

"Have you lost a hiker?" he asked.

We all looked at each other and replied in unison, "No?"

"Well, some guy called Upchuck damn near fell in the road in front of us after falling down a slope and we nearly ran him over!"

We had all forgotten about Upchuck. The last we saw of him had been an hour into the climb up Baden-Powell. He too had made the same mistake and ended up coming down Dawson's Saddle, although his final bearings must have gone a little astray and he found an unexpected drop-off. Minutes later he stumbled into camp a sweaty mess, with blood oozing from several lacerations to his legs.

"You OK, Upchuck?" I asked.

"Yeah, man, just lost the trail."

He started to unpack his sleeping bag and then slid inside.

"You going to eat anything, dude?" enquired Jake.

"Nah, too tired. I'll have a beer. I'm doing OK."

You couldn't really reason with Upchuck; he just did his own thing regardless. He could have arrived with one leg, an eyeball hanging out, two branches through his chest and a case of diarrhoea but he still would have drunk a beer and turned in. We all smiled and just shrugged our shoulders.

Chapter 5
Eat

I've never seen skinny people eat so much.
Unknown

Food is an obsession when you are long-distance hiking. As soon as I woke, I was thinking about breakfast; once on the move it was the mid-morning snack; then I yearned for lunch; my afternoon snack loomed and the evening meal couldn't come soon enough. It is the most hotly debated subject on trail bar none.

I resupplied roughly once a week from the store or supermarket in the town where I was resting. After a month or so I got my rations down to a fine art and could judge quantities fairly accurately. How much to take was important: too much and your pack is unnecessarily heavy; too little and you run out of food. If in doubt I took more than I needed, despite the weight penalty, as running out of food was sheer misery. I have mentioned porridge, which became a staple, although sometimes I had granola. Lunch consisted of tortillas in which I would vary the fillings: often salami or cheese, both of which lasted well, tuna, peanut butter, mayonnaise and fresh vegetables such as onions, avocados and peppers, which would keep for three or four days before they started to turn. My evening meals provided the most calories and I relied on pre-made rice and pasta meals with sauces such as cheese, spicy Mexican and Spanish vegetable. I tried to keep my snacks as healthy as possible, so nuts and dried fruit kept me company, as well as providing valuable fats and protein. Extras included a small bottle of olive oil (procured from restaurants), hot sauce, cookies, grated parmesan, some spices, stock powder and a favourite – dark chocolate-covered almonds. To drink, I usually had coffee and tea, as well as a product called Emergen-C, which provided valuable electrolytes and salts lost from perspiration, and during the later stages I carried a protein powder mixed with water. A few people carried protein powder but I only became familiar with it later on. If I had known earlier then I'm sure it would have been a staple: a little heavy but with no trapped air it packed small and was one of the richest forms of protein available. The chocolate varieties were filling and even when mixed with water tasted like a milkshake. With powdered milk it was a revelation.

When I tired of the packet meals, I experimented with my own concoctions. A favourite was powdered French onion soup with added rice, peanuts and hot sauce. The result tasted like a takeout Chinese meal.

I craved meat and ate my fill when I was in town, but carried jerky, which developed into an addiction; I consumed mountains of the stuff, especially the peppered and teriyaki varieties. Although expensive, the camping stores carried a varied selection of freeze-dried meals and I treated myself occasionally to bacon and eggs or beef stew. Chocolate cheesecake and even freeze-dried ice cream were available.

My weekly shopping totalled around £50, sometimes more, occasionally less. One way to keep the cost down was to buy the cheaper brands, make my own mixes or plunder the hiker boxes. Hiker boxes were found in various places but usually in the camping stores, hostels or at trail angels' houses. They contained items that others no longer required, including old footwear, clothing, repair kits and a lot of food. The sell-by dates had to be checked, but with the amount of rubbish most of us were eating, our stomachs could handle anything. I tended to stick to unopened packets, so I knew the quality should be good, and I did find some excellent stuff.

Some hikers were on extremely strict budgets, to the point that they walked the entire PCT using only what food they found in the boxes. Scorpion was a prime example. I met her in Tehachapi and walked with her on occasion. Her pack was huge, mainly because she carried a lot of food, not knowing when she would find the next box or how well stocked it would be. There was a standing joke that you should always get to a hiker box before Scorpion or there wouldn't be much left in it. She would also trade her surplus with others.

Camping one evening, I offered her some coffee and she reciprocated with some sun-dried tomatoes. I accepted the offer, but as soon as I put one in my mouth, I wished I hadn't. The dry, grainy, gritty morsel with the texture of dried leather told me that the sell-by date must have expired a couple of years earlier. I tried to look pleased with the gift and finish chewing it, forcing it down as you would a pill that's too big to swallow, then I rinsed the aftertaste away with a couple of swigs of whisky.

In the latter stages of my hike, I became acquainted with Nick Levy, one of only two other English guys on the trail that year, who was a source of many food stories. Nick had been travelling on and off for most of his life and had become used to existing on meagre budgets, which drove him to drastic measures in his search for food. Over the years he had become skilled – if you can call it that – at judging if food from some bizarre sources was edible.

His first and favourite stop was actually rubbish bins in the street. Yes, that's what I said: rubbish bins. Many times in town, walking down the street, I used to wait for him to reply to a question, only to turn and find him twenty feet behind me with his nose and arms in a trash bin, smelling the offerings. Half-eaten hamburgers were his most cherished procurements and he would carefully unwrap them (if they were still indeed wrapped), offer them up to his nose and greet them with either an expression of disgust or sheer delight as he merrily tucked in. I was shocked the first time I saw him doing this but after a while I came to accept it as normal.

For Nick, rubbish skips – or dumpsters, as they are known in the States – were further horns of plenty. These scored highly because the quantities were usually greater and the quality superior. He had learnt that supermarkets regularly got rid of food even before the sell-by date. Bakeries were prized for their dumpster-diving opportunities, because any unsold goods were thrown away daily. Sometimes the swing doors on the side were locked, but if not, Nick would disappear for alarmingly long periods, to the accompaniment of the rustle of plastic bags being torn open. He would resurface, grinning, with a bag of bagels or even a cake clutched in his hand.

He recalled one situation when a friend had found an unlocked skip outside McDonalds. The fast food chain treats dumpster divers seriously, even with arrest, and to stumble across an unlocked one was a treat. This trip scored well with his friend locating some fried eggs. I was under the misguided impression that an expert egg chef merrily nurtured several of these to order; the reality is somewhat different. The skip housed a large, plastic 'condom' (as Nick called it), with twenty-four compartments, four along the top and six down the side. Housed in each one was a perfectly cooked egg which presumably was then just microwaved or maybe heated in hot water. His friend knocked back the lot and probably got his protein allocation for a couple of weeks in one hit.

Some people had to deal with dietary issues such as coeliac disease, intolerances to certain foodstuffs and being vegetarian or vegan, although the latter could re-supply pretty well without too many problems. The only way to deal with intolerances and allergies was to prepare, dehydrate and post all supplies out at various points, to be picked up along the trail. Food boxes were used by a lot of hikers, not just those with specific dietary requirements, but I never quite saw their appeal. The sheer amount of effort to source, dry, mix, pack and post up to seven months' worth of food was mind-boggling and it constrained the hiker to stop at certain points to collect packages, where they often encountered delays because the post office was closed. I did have a 'bounce box' – a term used to describe a package that we mailed ahead of ourselves and caught up with once in a while. It contained things that we needed occasionally but were not worth carrying because of their infrequent use, for example shaving equipment, batteries, toothpicks, spare pens and recharging equipment for cameras and mobile phones. If I had surplus food that I didn't want to throw away or leave in a hiker box, I would sometimes leave it in my bounce box, but this was as near as I got to posting food ahead.

Trooper, whom I first met in the Sierras, was vegetarian and posted most of his food along the trail, a total of twenty-six boxes. His main meal was a dehydrated vegan soup, which he used to supplement with cheese from town to add to his fat intake. His lunch staple was tortilla with vegan jerky, cheese and mayonnaise.

Sugar Moma was hypoglycaemic (low blood glucose levels), protein deficient, low in iron and a vegetarian. Hell, why make life easy? She mixed and pre-packed most of her food and organised mail drops. She had to scrutinise everything in the supermarket to check the ingredients and survived mostly on protein shakes for breakfast. She also added powdered milk and TVP (textured vegetable protein) to most of her meals.

Others survived on simpler rations. Ryan 'Steve Climber' Bishop Ashby told me his success in Oregon was down to Snickers and the McDonald's Dollar Menu.

Fat intake – or, rather, lack of it – was responsible for weight loss among hikers. Dehydrated food is generally severely lacking in fat, and because most fat sources were heavy, they took a back seat until we realised our bodies were becoming way too skinny. Carbohydrates were the staple energy source; after these deplete, the body turns to its fat reserves for energy. If these were not topped up, then it could quite possibly end a thru-hike. My main sources of fat were peanut butter, which I was pretty much weaned on from an early age and still crave, along with nuts, olive oil and cheese. I, too, neglected these at the start until I realised after a few weeks I was losing body mass.

An average week's re-supply consisted of oats supplemented with raisins, sugar, dried milk and maybe some nuts for breakfast, plus of course coffee and tea. Snacks were mainly crunchy oat bars of various flavours (chocolate, honey, maple syrup, etc.), nuts, a bag of crisps or tortilla chips, jerky, chocolate, M&M's, Snickers or similar and some boiled sweets. Tortillas provided lunch, filled with cheese, tuna, salami, peanut butter or spam, and a tube of mayonnaise to moisten it a little and provide some extra fat. Dinner was a packet of rice or pasta of varying flavours. Despite the weight penalty I tried to leave town with a few items of fresh fruit and vegetables. Apples, peppers and onions all kept well for a few days and even avocados, if treated carefully, could go for three days. I also took a couple of bananas.

I then had to remove all the packaging and decant the contents into Ziploc bags. This prevented the build-up of unnecessary rubbish, saved a little weight and made access easier. The whole process could take an hour.

A staple with hikers was macaroni and cheese, known simply as mac 'n' cheese. Kraft seemed to be the preferred brand but it never appealed to me. Firstly, I try not to mix protein and carbohydrate because the body digests them differently, and secondly it looked and smelt disgusting. The cheese sauce was inside a plastic bag and once opened, when the pasta had cooked, it had to be squeezed in to heat up. It looked like liquid plastic in a disgusting, lurid yellow.

By far the most popular hiker staple, and most famous, is ramen noodles. These are thin, dried noodles shaped into a block, sealed in a packet with a foil sachet containing the flavoured powder. Choose from staples such as pork, beef, shrimp, mushroom and chili or venture into California vegetable, oriental, creamy chicken and Cajun shrimp to name a few. Ramen gets a bad press amongst hikers but you'll probably find those complaining have a pack in their supplies. It does have a lot going for it; it's light, small, incredibly cheap and reasonably filling. I wouldn't say it was particularly healthy but if you think eating on a thru-hike can be, you've been misled. It also contains a lot of salt but even that could be considered a bonus in the hotter sections.

Most stores sell them for about 60 pence and this is even cheaper if you buy in bulk and mail out, reducing the cost to an incredible 30 pence per meal. I did buy them but found one was not enough for a main meal. They were tasty but the salt was very evident and each meal was usually followed by drinking lots of water.

And lastly, allow me to introduce you all to GORP. Good old raisins and peanuts was apparently invented by a couple of surfers in the 60s. Since then it has been changed, added to, messed with but remains a staple amongst hikers. Other ingredients have found their way into the mix such as soya beans, cranberries, apricots, pretzels, banana chips, you name it. I like raisins, peanuts and all of the above but put them all together and it just doesn't do it for me. One manufacturer had even invented a salty and sweet version consisting of peanuts and chocolate covered raisins; it was pretty dire.

I remember watching a video detailing how one hiker put together enough GORP to mail out for their entire thru-hike. A large bucket was filled with huge quantities of various dried fruits and nuts, all mixed together, then divided into twenty-four generous-sized bags for mail drops along the trail. After four weeks she hated the stuff. Enough said.

***

After the mishap coming down Dawson's Saddle, I followed the highway for only a mile and reconnected with the PCT. There was a toilet near a small parking area, which gave me the rare opportunity to sit down for my number twos. I emerged, a couple of kilos lighter, and met Bigfoot, Wide Angle and Stanimal. We descended to Cooper Canyon campground, which was busy with people enjoying themselves, and set about practising our hungry looks and wisely choosing to sit at a table next to someone laden with a large amount of food wantonly on display. Before long, after hearing of our hiking exploits, the family seated there were greeting us with respect and admiration, plying us with cold cans and firing up the barbecue. We were soon stuffing ourselves with burgers, chicken and even a large rack of sticky ribs. There were smiles all round and a licking of honey-glazed fingers rounded off a very successful lunch.

The temperature was now climbing at night as well as by day. My research on sleeping bags had advised on taking one rated to minus seven degrees centigrade (about twenty degrees Fahrenheit). This was fine at the start, when the nights hovered around freezing point, but now it was far too warm. I climbed into my bag with the zip undone a little and over the course of the night I kept opening the bag up more, until eventually I climbed out and just slept underneath, using it like a duvet. Before long I was going to need a cooler bag.

At some stage on the PCT each year, it is pretty much a foregone conclusion that there will be a detour off trail. Usually this is because of a forest fire, either one still burning or another that has raged in the past, where the area is cordoned off to encourage regrowth. I was coming to the end of a forty-seven-mile detour, all redirected on roads, and my feet were taking a hammering. Trail cushions feet somewhat but tarmac is harsh. The constant pounding meant several new blisters had flared up and most of my leg muscles were retaliating. Motorists used to ask me what I was doing and when I explained I was walking forty-seven miles to get back on trail I was met with looks of bewilderment. Most could not comprehend walking this distance, so when I then added that I was walking 2,650 miles to Canada, their looks changed to complete confusion and disbelief. To them it was completely incomprehensible.

As cars approached, I used to look at the occupants; and in those split seconds when I made eye contact, I tried to guess at their lives. The smart executive models such as BMWs and Accords were mostly driven by businessmen on their way to meetings or back to the office. Elderly couples in sun hats and sunglasses, most likely just out for day trips, drove more cautiously, peering out through windows at the scenery. Larger cars with a couple of kids in the back and roof boxes suggested the holiday season was on the way. Attractive women drove past in convertibles and I used to smile, look tired and put on my hungry expression, hoping they would stop. Judging by the complete lack of success, this needed more work.

Unbearable heat recoiled back off jet-black bitumen and assaulted me. The sun glared down, almost forcing me to back off. Sweat ran off my forehead, wove around my eyebrows and occasionally into my eyes, stinging. I would instinctively wipe them with the back of my hand, only to make matters worse, as the sunscreen burnt them even further. Despite my frantic arm-waving, insects buzzed relentlessly, like someone constantly poking me in the side to try and raise a reaction.

I reached a KOA (Kamp Ground of America), where a few hikers had holed up for the day to take advantage of a small shop, swimming pool and showers. Elk, Brittany, Mojave, Cheeks, Stanimal, Bigfoot, Wide Angle, Vicky, Dennis and Hojo had cordoned off several picnic tables. Elk was busying himself preparing a rattlesnake for dinner. He had witnessed it being run over by a car and put it out of its misery. I had not tried rattlesnake before but I was very impressed. It tasted somewhat like chicken, with a hint of a fish aftertaste. Elk prepared a few separate dishes, spiced up with various herbs and spices including curry powder. Rattlesnake curry, I thought, could definitely catch on.

Elk also had a staple recipe for the trail that I saw him make on several occasions in preparation for the week's hike. He called it Raw Dawg and it consisted of an onion, an avocado, a can of pork and beans, one bulb of garlic, a can of spam or corned beef, some packets of hot sauce and ketchup. Elk used to obtain these, as I did, from restaurants, saying, "Stolen condiments taste better." He put all of these in a Ziploc, shook it and then left it in the sun for twenty-four hours (if he was walking, this presumably meant he would leave it on the outside of his pack). It would keep for a few days on the trail, I think because the garlic and hot sauce fended off any bacteria.

That night, while trying to doze off, I hoped that my ears were deceiving me. Then I heard the sound again. I sat up in my tent, momentarily comforted by the notion that the flimsy piece of canvas around me would keep me safe. It wouldn't – well, maybe it would protect me from the odd snake or spider, unable to find its way in – but from a mountain lion? I hoped I had been dreaming, but then it roared again and this time it seemed closer. I looked at my watch; it was just after 3am. Mountain lions hunt their prey mainly at night and this one seemed to be creeping closer. I drifted off but woke up again at 6.30am, dressed quickly and got out of the tent. Bigfoot was outside in his sleeping bag but awake.

"Mate, did you hear that roaring last night? I thought I was a gonner. Sounded like a mountain lion or something," I said.

"Oh, yeah," he replied. "There's a farm up the way that keeps a couple of lions and a bear. They use them in the movies." He rolled over and started snoozing again, while I stood there feeling like a prat.

I left the KOA to pull in some miles. After taking a wrong turn as I tried to cross the railway line, I began to climb. Nothing too serious, but with the ever-increasing heat of the past couple of days, I was dripping with sweat. It rolled down my nose and caught the edge of my mouth, where I could taste the salt. My arms shone and I gulped down more water. I passed Elk, Brittany (who had now been given a trail name of Logic, in acknowledgement of her simplistic problem solving), Mojave and Cheeks, who had made camp on a small ridge, and listened as Logic recounted how she had woken the previous night and watched two coyotes sniffing around camp before she shooed them off. I walked further, steering a course around a bee's nest in the middle of the trail. The PCT wound down a few switchbacks, across a level section and then under the highway via a tunnel, perhaps 200 feet long. It was dark, pleasingly damp and I walked to one side to avoid a small stream of water in the middle. As the circle of light at the other end grew bigger, I could make out the silhouette of someone sitting by the exit. The familiar features of Tomer came into focus as I reached the end. He looked up at me casually.

"Welcome to the other side," he offered.

After the wide space of the trail in the morning, a canyon suddenly narrowed and enclosed me. Rocks, outcrops and cliffs loomed up to either side towering over the course of a small creek, which I was forced to hop over several times. Layers of different-coloured rock, millions of years old, streaked across the cliff face. I spilled out onto the road, a mile or so from the town of Agua Dulce. Suddenly to be swept out of wilderness into 'reality' always caught me off guard after days on the trail. I reached the intersection of Darling Road and made a left for the last mile as I approached what is fondly referred to as Hiker Haven. This house on the hill is home to the Saufley family, who every year offer the grounds and outbuildings to all thru-hikers who wisely choose to stay there. While I was given the guided tour by John, my laundry disappeared, to emerge later smelling of lemons. I collected the packages that they had held for me and found an empty camp bed in one of the outside tents.

The Saufleys' proved a great place to unwind. There must have been fifty others scattered about the place, relaxing, collecting mail, resupplying, eating or listening to music. There were too many for my comfort after the previous days spent on my own and I made plans to move on the following day, still keen to increase my mileage tally. I picked up a new water filter and sent my old one back, wrapped in a complaint letter.

The café in town cooked up an excellent breakfast and I concentrated on consuming as much fat as I could handle after the scales confirmed I had lost a couple of kilos. In the store, excitement got the better of me when I wandered down the condiments aisle and stumbled across a hoard of hot sauces. With the local café devoid of any, and not knowing which of the many brands to choose, I settled on the lightest choice: a bottle of ever-reliable Tabasco.

I was enjoying myself and becoming more immersed in the PCT experience. My camp routine was becoming honed, resupplies were proving well-judged and my body was coping well. I was, however, tiring of the desert. The constant battle with heat and dust had me yearning for the High Sierra, another 250 miles away. Some had already made it to Kennedy Meadows, a small town at the foot of the mountains that was considered the start of the higher elevations, cooler temperatures, abundant water and stunning scenery. I longed for it as for an ice lolly. Others were feeling it too: the sand was wearing us all down, insects buzzed around us and the temperature continued to climb. Kennedy Meadows started to be my focus of attention. Everything between Agua Dulce and there needed to be wrapped up so that the next stage of my adventure could begin.

Trying in vain to find somewhere to camp one evening, I became more and more frustrated. In mountainous areas, the trail is often cut into the side of a hill, so a slope climbs above and drops away below. Locating a flat area to pitch tent is nigh on impossible. Many times I walked for miles waiting to find a small patch of suitable ground but never did. Thwarted by the terrain and, at the end of the day, tired and hungry, I often just put down my pack and pitched on the path itself. The chance of another hiker coming along that late was unlikely, and even if they did, there was enough space to step round. It is not advisable to pitch on trail because wild animals use it as well. They're not stupid and pick routes that require the least effort; a clear path saves them tramping through undergrowth.

Having set up camp, I was descended on by an airborne squadron of biting flies. They looked like house flies but these predators came equipped with a nasty ability to nip. Flapping and jumping around as if I had just caught fire was futile; strangely enough, even swearing seemed to have no effect. Eventually, as twilight set in, they gave up and went to bed, only to be replaced by onslaught number two in the form of mosquitoes. Mozzies love me, for some reason. They say some people fare worse than others, maybe because of the smell of their blood, and if there is a mozzie within a mile of me, it sends out a general invitation to all of its mates that there's good eating in the area. My flapping routine started again in earnest and, stifled by the intense heat, I was sinking lower into a foul mood.

After I called surrender, I quickly cooked my meal and dived into the tent, zipping up frantically and settling down to eat in peace. The temperature inside was overwhelming and damp blotches of sweat appeared on my trousers. It was only then that I remembered I had not exactly cooked the ideal meal in the circumstances – curry with an extra helping of hot sauce. I sat there like a customer in a Turkish steam bath.

News was filtering back from hikers already gathered at Kennedy Meadows that the snow levels had not receded as far as expected and much of the Sierra was still under a lot of snow. My ice axe, crampons and some colder weather gear were waiting for me at the post office, and I hoped that by the time I reached them, the snow would have dwindled enough for the backlog of people to start pushing up.

Before then, and only seventeen miles or so away, came the Andersons. I had met Terrie and Joe at Lake Morena and they too opened their house for hikers each year. The Saufleys have a two-night maximum stay; the Andersons have a two-night *minimum* stay. I was met with a slow clap as I walked up the drive, part of the arrival ritual. I was instructed to pick a Hawaiian shirt from a rack, as this was strict dress protocol, and given a guided tour by a bloke who was too drunk to even remember his own name. Familiar faces came into view among bins mainly full of beer cans. Laughter filled the air and the whole atmosphere was laid back and relaxed. It was a case of pitch your tent, grab some alcohol and chill.

I spent two days at the Andersons in an alcoholic daze. All the food was laid on and everyone chipped in with cooking and cleaning up, drinking in between. There was only one shower for everyone, which proved interesting: as soon as the bathroom door clicked open, there was a rush towards it of dusty hikers, eager to grab a wash, but invariably someone had held vigil outside and nipped in before everyone else. The slow-clapping routine continued every time a new face arrived, as did the guided tour and choosing of the Hawaiian shirt.

I left with my hangover at 5pm on the third day with Hojo, Swayze and Dinosaur, who were also keen to get going. Walking late into the night was a new experience for me and an enjoyable one. It was far cooler and the glow from the setting sun was mesmerising. The mosquitoes were out again, however, and the stillness was disturbed occasionally by the howl of a coyote.

Hojo was forty-two. When he wasn't hiking he was an emergency medical technician, preferring to spend his winters as a member of the National Ski Patrol. He had completed the Appalachian Trail a few years previously and had been in remission from cancer some eight years earlier. When you have such a close brush with death, life seems that much more valuable. That, I believe, is why he walked the AT and now the PCT: you never know what's around the corner. His trail name came about after his second day on the AT, when he arrived at a shelter for the night. As he removed his hat, another hiker noticed his ginger hair and commented that it was the same colour as found on the roofs of a US motel chain called Howard Johnson's. The name stuck.

He was good company, easy-going, with no plans or schedules that ever seemed to put him in a rush. Fair-skinned, he took care in the sun and regardless of the temperatures he always covered himself up, head to foot, including wearing a modern-day hiking variant of the cowboy hat. He liked his kit and was looking forward to settling down to cook that evening.

"I sent my old stove back, Fozzie," he announced while preparing camp.

"Why?" I said. "No good?"

"No, it was OK, just too slow. I bought a Jetboil."

Jetboils, about two years on the market, were gas cylinder-based stoves renowned for a fierce heat and super-quick cooking times.

"I demand more immediate gratification," he explained.

He walked with his water bag strapped to one side of his pack exterior, which made refilling easier. Once it was full, one side of his pack was naturally heavier than the other and he had to counteract this by placing more weight on his other side. He joked that he always knew when he was getting short of water because he had to start leaning more to the other side.

We passed the 500-mile mark, which someone had marked on the trail in an artistic cluster of pine cones. Hojo and I shook hands and he congratulated me.

"Well done, Canadian."

He referred to me as the Canadian because I was not from the US. Despite my initial protestations and reminders that I was English, I eventually realised it was not his memory failing him but his weird sense of humour.

At mile 519 we arrived at the Hiker Hostel. I can only describe the place as bizarre. It was situated in the middle of nowhere, the nearest sign of life being a store about a mile down the road. Bob, the owner, used to work in the film industry and the area was littered with props. There was a mock-Western shop front with post office and store, vehicles dotted around, an old police car and even a Rolls-Royce. Mannequins peered at me creepily through sand storms.

Having just spent some quality time nursing more blisters and watching a toenail drop off, I went to check my email but on the way stubbed my foot sharply against a chair. After a good minute of hopping around stifling a shriek and enough swearing to make my mother cringe, I looked down and saw my hands covered in blood and my little toe dripping all over the floor. Leaving a red-dotted trail behind me, I hopped to the kitchen, where Hojo reviewed the damage and pronounced it was not serious but a nasty cut nevertheless. I cleaned the mess up and surveyed a flap of skin, which lifted up and down like a submarine hatch. Not wanting my mileage to suffer any further, I left the following day with the Stumbling Norwegian and several layers of Elastoplast wound round my toe. Trying to keep up with him, my leg buckled every time the wound rubbed.

We followed the Los Angeles Aqueduct for seventeen miles.

Sourcing water from the mountains and carrying it all the way to the big city, it was covered in a layer of grey concrete and just looked like a road. Norwegian had devised an ingenious method of obtaining water, despite the fact it was apparently inaccessible. To indulge my curiosity, he unclipped his pack and rummaged around for his filter, attached an extra length of plastic tubing and lowered this through a hole in the surface of the aqueduct into the raging torrent below. Sure enough, as he pumped and I held the water bottle, a steady stream of fluid dribbled out. We celebrated by taking a break and seeking shade squeezed under a bridge, itself only about a foot above the aqueduct.

Snake count: 5
False alarms: 117

Magnificent cloud formations decorated the sky around us. One elongated specimen stretching up from the horizon looked like a giant lava lamp bubble. The wind intensified, blowing us about like litter in a storm. We reached Cottonwood Creek at dusk but decided to carry on a further six miles to possible shelter at Tylerhorse Canyon. Turning round to check Norwegian was still keeping up with me (which was a wasted exercise, as I could have been riding a trial bike and he still would have been gliding smoothly behind), I smirked as a furious gust caught him and carried him sideways. He had to execute a brisk jump over a low bush and just managed to keep his footing as he landed. Occasionally, I thought, the Norwegian does indeed stumble.

We descended into the canyon in darkness, our head torches navigating a slim trail to the bottom, where a creek tinkled past us. It was too windy to pitch my tent, so I followed Norwegian's lead and spent my first night cowboy-style, lying back studying the skies above and listening to a howling gale rip through the canyon.

***

After reaching the town of Tehachapi, I rested for a day and caught up on England's progress (or rather lack of it) in the World Cup. Mocking Stumbling Norwegian and Jake, both avid USA supporters, with the taunt that they didn't stand a chance, I had to eat my words after a 1-1 draw.

My distance targets over the next couple of weeks and planning for town stops were based solely on when England were next playing. I noted the date of the games and worked out a plan to hole up in a bar or motel. After their first lacklustre performance, adjusting my routine to make town for the next disappointment may not have been the best of ideas.

A few hours out of Tehachapi, I realised that my calculations were a day out. To get to Ridgecrest I needed to walk two days of twenty-eight miles and one of fifteen. This was not impossible, but bearing in mind the Mojave Desert, with its searing temperatures, was over the adjacent ridge and water was in very short supply, the going was painful. I stopped at Bird Spring Pass water cache, where Burnie, Cheeks and Elk were sheltering from a fierce midday sun. Elk had a mild case of Giardiasis and boasted about recently scoring a thirty-second fart.

"Fozzie, did I tell you about my trout fantasy?" he asked.

"No, but I'm in the mood, so go," I replied, looking at him expectantly.

"Well, I'm on the trail and suddenly come across a bear pulling fish from a pristine mountain stream. It has caught a golden trout about the size of my forearm. Now, what I will do in this fantasy is scare the bear away, purely with my anger, and steal the trout from it." He laughs. "Then I will take a quart-size Ziploc bag, half-fill it with lemon juice, section the trout up so it fits inside the bag and hike with it for fifteen to twenty minutes. Then I will take it out, build a fire and sprinkle it with salt and pepper. I will then let out a huge roar of triumph and eat the meal."

"Elk, do you walk with your shrink or just make regular phone calls?"

I walked with him that afternoon, finding him interesting company as always. We sweated profusely as we climbed up the 2,000 or so feet that make up Skinner's Pass. Elk slipped behind a little and I threw boiled sweets down to him as an incentive as

I rounded a switchback. We crested the top and were met with our first views of the Sierra Nevada: ridge after ridge stretching away to infinity, most still covered in snow.

Elk was homing in on one of his geocaches and getting more excited by the minute. A geocache is an item or items hidden in a specific location and most often buried, so that others cannot take it or wild animals happen across it. The coordinates are saved, usually by means of a GPS, so the owner can find it whenever they choose to. Elk had buried many of these along the length of the PCT the previous year, with staple contents that included canned meat, alcohol and pipe tobacco. Checking his GPS and beaming, he went off to home in on his prize, saying he would meet me at camp.

It was busy that evening and I had Burnie, Littlebit, Bigfoot, Stanimal, Wild Angle, Cheeks and Mojave for company. The talk was of bears and I cringed when I learned of three sightings in the last three days.

Little did I know then that I would be the one witnessing the next.

Chapter 6
Bears

Not all who wander are lost. But, to be perfectly honest, most of them are.
Shane 'Jester' O'Donnell

I left the others sleeping just after 6am, eager to hit the road early at Highway 178 and get a lift to Ridgecrest. I couldn't find any trail signs and came across McIvers Spring, which according to my map was about 500 feet too far east of the trail. I walked back to camp, still unable to find the route, and then back to the spring, increasingly frustrated. I sat down by the water, filtered and brewed a coffee to calm down.

Twigs cracked and snapped from a small wood behind me but, having become accustomed to sounds from the trees, I ignored them, losing myself in the taste of my coffee and the morning stillness.

Suddenly, I sensed a tense environment. The hairs on my arms stood up and I felt that something was behind me, something that made me fear turning around. Then I heard a loud animal noise, somewhere between a snort and an aggravated sigh. I knew it was a bear – it couldn't have been anything else. I turned around slowly, and as my peripheral vision focused, I saw something I really didn't want to see.

A black bear was standing a good eight feet tall on its hind legs, and holding its nose up, smelling the air and, presumably, me. It dropped to all fours and most of southern California shuddered as it landed. It looked at me; I returned the gaze and then remembered everything I had read about these creatures, the first being don't look them in the eye but bow your head and avert your gaze. Eye contact can be threatening, so I focused at the ground a few feet in front of the bear and rapidly planned who I was going to leave my limited estate to.

My natural and initial reaction was one of sheer terror. Confusingly, I also felt it was an honour to be witness to such a beautiful and commanding creature. Its very presence demanded respect. These feelings vanished quickly as it started to hesitantly walk towards me, still holding up its nose to find a scent. I also knew not to back off or run from an approaching bear. However, putting that advice into practice when a bulk of hungry muscle weighing several hundred kilos is coming towards you is quite another story. I stood up and started to feel real fear. The others were just two minutes back down the path, probably still waking up and completely oblivious to my situation.

I had never been so scared. I was shaking, confused and felt completely helpless. Then I remembered to make a noise. Lifting my arms up to make myself look bigger, I screamed, "Get out of here, bear. Oi geezer! Go on! Sod off! GO!"

Immediately the bear bolted back into the forest. I was astonished at how fast it covered ground. I crouched down to get a better view through the trees as it galloped away. Any hiker walking through the forest at that precise moment in the opposite direction would probably have jumped off the nearest cliff.

I eventually stopped shaking, calmed down and congratulated myself for at least remembering my bear research and reacting accordingly.

The black bear − *Ursus americanus* − is the smallest and most common type of bear in the USA. The other species, the grizzly, with the far more appropriate Latin name of *Ursus arctos horribilis*, is mainly confined to Canada and Washington, the northernmost state on the PCT. I was scared of snakes, though beginning to accept them, but bears terrified me. Their sheer size doesn't do much for one's confidence. Bears, however, are misunderstood. The 'friendly' encounters are rarely reported, the media preferring to concentrate on incidents where people are attacked, as this makes for better reading. So, we are regaled with stories of this attack, that person getting killed, this particular bear causing havoc, etc.

Bears are pretty docile creatures. They go about their business quietly, concentrating on eating over the course of the warmer months to build up enough fat reserves for hibernation, and then the process repeats itself. Attacks are rare and there has not been a reported case of anyone being killed on the PCT by a bear, a fact I recalled in earnest during my encounter.

Because the media tend to report only the attacks, and because of their size, capacity to intimidate and the fact that they have been mercilessly hunted for decades, bears are portrayed as a dangerous menace. This is a huge shame and could not be further from the truth.

I saw around eight bears on my hike but heard many more. Usually they came sniffing around my tent after I had turned in. It's not just food that attracts them – toiletries also smell tasty to a bear. I always cleaned my teeth a good fifty feet away from the tent, although this was probably not far enough and is what usually acted as a homing beacon. I would just be falling asleep and I would hear that familiar snort or maybe some scratching. A shout would normally suffice to send the bear thundering off into the night.

In areas where many people were out enjoying the outdoors, bears were more common. They're not stupid; they know where food is, and rubbish bins (even if bear-proof) act as magnets. Yosemite is a classic example and one of a few places where hikers are required, by law, to carry the renowned bear canister.

Simply put, a bear canister is a bucket with a lid that a bear cannot gain access to. The plastic is super-tough and the screw lid has a mechanism that locks it shut unless a finger is pressed on a small lug. The theory is that all food and anything else with a strong smell is placed in one of these and left away from tents and sleeping areas. Any curious bears will smell the canister but will not be able to gain entry. After some inspiringly strenuous efforts, some of which can be seen on the internet, they generally cave in and search for something a little easier. A pot or pan placed on top can help because of the sound made when disturbed. Many a hiker has woken in the morning to find their canister a fair distance from where they had left it, dripping with bear saliva. The standing joke is that a group of bears find one and then have a game of hockey for half an hour.

I hauled my canister around through the designated areas, resenting the fact that it easily took up half my pack. Outside the danger areas, most people kept their food in or near their tent or they hung it in a tree. Suspending your food bag from a tree has long been the most common form of protecting it. I often used this method. Pick a branch around twenty-five feet high. Tie a fifty-foot length of parachute cord to the bag and wrap the other end round a stone. Throw the rock over the branch as far away from the tree trunk as possible to prevent bears climbing up and along the branch. Watch as the stone misses the branch, falls back down and unravels the cord. Repeat attempt. Repeat again. Once a successful throw has been made and you manage to duck past the falling stone, hoist the bag up over fifteen feet and watch as the branch either snaps or bows down so low that your food bag is swinging in front of your face. Pick another, stronger branch and, amid cursing and stomping around, once the stone with cord drops down, remove the stone and tie this end to another tree or suitable anchor point.

The bear canister was introduced because our friends in the forest learnt the trick and used to climb up and retrieve poorly stowed bags. I hated that canister, as did most of us. In fact, a few just stuck with their usual bags, taking their chances that rangers wouldn't perform a spot check. I don't know if rangers have a legal right to search rucksacks. I met perhaps three on my trip, all of them respectful of our mission and polite. When I confirmed I was carrying a canister, none of them asked to check my bag and had they done so I would have refused on the grounds of privacy and fundamental human rights, whatever the legalities.

I did hear of an encounter at Lost Lakes, just south of Lake Tahoe, where Elk, Your Mom and some others had camped. Just after they had settled down for the night, Your Mom called out to Elk to put a light on, as she thought something was in the camp. Elk initially discounted this as he was only a few feet from her and he thought he would have heard any movement. However, he turned on his light and got out of his tent. The first thing he noticed was that his medical kit and backpack were covered in drool. Your Mom was uneasy and it was decided that they should hang their bags, except for Elk, who had a bear canister, and a couple of others who placed their bags by their tents because they were too heavy to hoist into the trees. Everyone settled down again.

Elk's bear canister fell over, the clatter of the pot and mug resting on the top causing one hell of a commotion in camp and scaring the life out of him. Everyone woke up but Elk saw the culprit first.

"He must have been 300 pounds, Fozzie," Elk told me afterwards. "The ground shook when he ran away."

Elk shouted and caused as much noise as he could to scare the intruder off, which worked, but the villain made three further visits that night. Your Mom found her food bag in the morning minus all the contents except, perhaps not surprisingly, a packet of chicken ramen. They named the bear Two Socks after the wolf in Dances with Wolves because he kept returning.

After my bear encounter, I walked down to Highway 178 with Bigfoot. His trail name was obviously derived from his large feet, which made it difficult for him to find big enough shoes for the hike – in fact, he ordered several pairs of the same trainers before starting. He was also tall and towered above me but, to use a cliché, he was a gentle giant, very amenable and easy-going. Bigfoot chose his words carefully and was a pleasure to chat with. He was also one of the most easily identifiable characters on trail – apart from his size, his standard apparel was a hiking kilt and the kind of white cotton shirt that one might wear to a black tie occasion.

We reached the road, where a couple of locals had set up some trail magic. Hojo was there, along with Your Mom and Elk. I knocked back a swift Coke and made off for the road to catch a ride to Ridgecrest, as the football game between England and Algeria beckoned. In the other direction lay Lake Isabella, which I would have opted for had I known what a disappointment Ridgecrest would prove to be.

It took five hours to get there as the hitchhiking was poor. The town was steaming hot; in fact, almost unbearable for someone who'd just dropped down from the mountains. The main drag seemed to stretch for miles. Jet-black bitumen disappeared off to the horizon as a lazy heat haze hovered. I thanked Brian, who had brought me in his gravel lorry, and started walking through the endless monotony looking for a cheap motel. The lurid red, yellow, blue and white logos of the fast-food chains assaulted me from both sides, only to be interrupted by hotels or supermarkets. The occupants of passing vehicles stared at me rudely as if I were a caged animal.

Judging from its appearance, the Budget Motel had been built in the 1950s and glossed over with several years' worth of emulsion. I figured the price would be acceptable.

Ridgecrest reminds me now of a holiday destination that looks gorgeous in a catalogue but doesn't deliver. At the launderette, which was a thirty-minute walk away, litter spilled out of rubbish bins onto the floor and a meagre selection of magazines draped an old wooden table. The detergent machine ate my money, as did the first washing machine. I found a nearby barber and had my beard removed while my clothes dried.

I spent most of my time in the motel room, as it was the coolest place I could find – coolest in temperature, not reputation, that is. My nose had now been added to the list of bodily functions that were breaking down. It was itchy, incredibly dry and kept bleeding. The pharmacist at Walgreens told me it was a common problem caused by the dry heat and he gave me a tube of moisturising gel. A sore, red rash had appeared on the soles of my feet, which looked like prickly heat and was extremely tender. Thankfully my blisters were receding but the rash took three days to disappear after several Epsom salt foot baths and some good old fresh air. I occupied myself with the World Cup, slept a lot, chastised myself for not going to Lake Isabella and worked my way through several tubs of Ben & Jerry's Cherry Garcia.

It was good to get back on the trail again but I was depressed. My body wasn't behaving; I felt lethargic, tired, lacking in enthusiasm and I cursed the constant heat. My nose was worsening: in the morning I would hold one nostril shut and blow out the contents of the other. A mix of blood, snot, dust and other dried debris shot out with a very unpleasant crackle. It wasn't pretty to look at and after a few minutes I had to repeat the process.

It was day 65 and I was approaching Kennedy Meadows, around the 700-mile mark. My mood sank deeper and everything was taking its toll. I started to sleep later in the morning and the only things that motivated me were food breaks. I longed for the next town stop where I could just hide in a motel room and swim in self-pity. I had spoken several times to my girlfriend back in England and frustration had resulted in arguments, which upset me. I was plummeting over a precipice of misery into a raging river of despair. Now I was missing my daily targets and my finish date based on average mileage was looking like December, a whole three months over schedule.

At lunch I sat by Fox Mill spring, the sun relentlessly beating down on me. I started to cry, holding my head in my hands, ashamed of my weakness. Trying to muster some morsel of energy, I convinced myself I was on the verge of throwing in a threadbare towel and quitting the PCT.

***

Kennedy Meadows is the sort of place that you would miss if you weren't paying attention. A few mobile homes appeared along the roadside as I rounded the corner and the General Store came into view. Hikers sprawled everywhere; tents peered from among trees in the back yard. A few familiar faces greeted me – Stumbling Norwegian, Cheeks and Mojave, Walker Texas Ranger, Flannel and Elk. This unassuming place in the middle of the desert was to prove the proverbial iced tonic.

My mood lifted, everyone was in good cheer, there was food and beer, and the prospect of the Sierra Nevada's cooler climate, abundance of water and stunning scenery gave me a boost. I relaxed and concentrated on what I needed to do to make my hike the experience I wanted it to be. I called my girlfriend and we lifted each other's spirits back up. Knowing she was fine always made everything else seem OK. I ate some good food, drank lots of water, caught up with everyone, made some new friends and told myself to stop being a miserable little shit.

The following morning, I walked out of Kennedy Meadows a new man. I joined up with Chad and Justin, who had just started, and were simply planning to get where they could before money and time ran out. They were both in their early twenties but Chad was more dominant, making them seem, at times, like father and son.

Just before midday I exited a clump of pine trees and was presented with one of the best views, no, surely *the* best view on the entire trail. Monache Meadow at 7,800 feet didn't just suggestively wink at me; more grabbed me firmly by the arse and snogged the living daylights out of me. It was ludicrously stunning. Cumuli wafted over me from horizon to horizon and the Kern River wiggled along between sandy banks cradled by a wide, gently sloping valley, speckled with pine trees, which rose into the surrounding hills. I sat down, feeling very humbled and in awe of what spread out before me.

Several times Chad, Justin and I stopped, speechless with wonder. It was as though we all knew that with any step Monache Meadow would vanish from view and we might never see her again. We just didn't want it to end. My only regret was not camping next to the river and enjoying her exquisite company for an afternoon and night.

Snake count: 9
False alarms: 347

My pack was heavier now. I had posted mountain equipment to Kennedy Meadows. I was carrying an ice axe, some Kahtoola spikes (devices that stretch over the soles of shoes and have spikes for grip in snow, a lighter version of crampons), a mosquito head net and the formidably bulky bear canister. I had managed to balance the weight out by not carrying much water; the mountain creeks and rivers were flowing well, so I would filter and drink one litre and carry just a further litre, if that. The mosquitoes were proving a big problem, especially in the evenings, when they were relentless. I hate them and can barely think of anything as annoying.

Mosquitoes love me. I don't know what it is that attracts them to me but I clearly have a load of it. If I get bitten in Europe I suffer the usual annoyance of a swollen, red, itchy bite. American mosquitoes seemed larger and more numerous but the bites bothered me less – the need to scratch was negligible and my physical reaction was milder. Their onslaught was enough to make even the strongest person crumble, though. They didn't party much during the day. The only time I really saw them was when I was near water. Come evening, however, all hell broke loose.

I camped in the forest with Chad and Justin, just off the trail in a comforting spot with water nearby, plenty of firewood and flat areas for the tents. Before we had put our packs down, the mosquitoes were all over us. I put on my head net for the first time and immediately discovered a major design flaw that had somehow slipped through quality control: I couldn't see a thing out of it. I had to move my head up and down to find a sweet spot in the mesh. The three of us spent most of the evening slapping ourselves, shaking our heads, scratching and sitting in fire smoke coughing to repel the critters.

My colleagues left before me in the morning with similar plans in mind. I needed to re-supply – the increasing elevations and colder nights meant I was getting through my food bag more quickly. As I rolled down Trail Pass Trail on to Cotton Wood Trail, I reached the parking lot. Chad and Justin were already there, along with Farm Boy and Splints, who had camped there in the hope of getting an early ride into Lone Pine. The road finished at the car park, so there was no through traffic, or indeed any traffic at all to speak of. Two cars came and went in as many hours and we reluctantly succumbed to the 'we may as well walk it, we could be there before the next ride stops' theory.

Just as we started the plod, a minibus rolled by and we flagged it down. Bill, the driver, said he ran a taxi service up to the car park and so couldn't take us down for free, but it would cost ten dollars each, a nominal amount given the distance involved. He insisted on giving us the guided tour as well, making the journey probably thirty minutes longer than I had hoped for.

We stumbled into the Alabama Hills Café and bakery. Regardless of how hungry I was, I always tried to take some time to find a good, independent breakfast place. The usual giveaway was that they were busy – which this little gem certainly was.

We all sat down, long overdue a good feed. The waitress

ambled over, eyeing us up: six soiled, aromatic and undesirable-looking hikers covered in insect bites. She was also a gem, and took it in her stride. I never checked the menu; every breakfast place I have ever visited in America has what I need and they cook my food exactly how I like it.

"Two eggs, over easy. Hash browns, crisped on *both* sides please; bacon, also crispy. Toast, rye if you have it, wheat if not, butter on the side. Orange juice and coffee, black, strong and keep it coming," I requested, scratching my right forearm.

And they do it! One thing you have to give the Americans: they know how to do a bloody good breakfast.

I enjoyed Lone Pine. The place had a long history, it felt good to walk around, it had pretty much everything a thru-hiker would need, and it commanded a spectacular view of the High Sierra, with Mt Whitney grinning at you. As usual it was tempting to stay in town just that one extra day, to see if anyone else showed up, or just to visit that café one more time.

I pulled myself away and found Trooper hitching on the same road to the same destination. I had met him a few days earlier; he was walking with an Australian woman called Vader who made me (unintentionally and rudely) laugh, because her face was covered in mud. I saw her in town afterwards and the first thing she demanded to know was why I, or Trooper, hadn't told her. She only discovered upon looking in the motel mirror.

Trooper was a cracking geezer in his mid-forties and said 'Ain't that the truth' a lot. Always calm, he would apologise if he swore, was unassuming and solid. He had attempted the PCT before, getting agonisingly close to Canada before being blown off trail by a storm. Trooper didn't merely go back to that point, but started again from Mexico. He loved it out there as much as any of us and, boy, did he want to finish.

I walked with him for only about half a day, and I asked if he'd like to camp, but he said he needed to push on another five miles, so on he went. I just knew I would be seeing a lot more of Trooper.

The following day I met Flyboxer, Indie and Answerman, sitting at the trailside and smiling in the sun. We exchanged a quick greeting and I continued.

The Sierra Nevada was wonderful. It was wild, and its

remoteness was a reminder that the nearest help was a long way away. This element of danger and detachment added to the excitement.

It was also drop-dead stunning, pristine mountain wilderness, shimmering lakes, slithering creeks and majestic forests. It was tough going, probably the hardest section of the entire trail, but because it rewarded me with so many visual treats I couldn't blame it for anything.

I camped that night at Crabtree Meadow for two reasons. First, I just wanted to see it; and second, there was a side trail that ran up to the summit of Mt Whitney at 14,505 feet, the highest mountain in the contiguous United States. When someone first told me this, I had to look up 'contiguous' in the dictionary. Once I discovered its meaning, I felt it would have been rude not to climb her.

Humming Bird and Flashback had left a good two hours ahead of me the following morning and Indie, Flyboxer and Answerman were behind me. The trail climbed steadily at first, dipping in and out of pine trees, and I glimpsed the night sky, a rising sun and the dark silhouettes of the mountains far above. As the sun started to light a way up, more of my surroundings came into view.

Snow-clad upper reaches capped a long, wide valley that eased itself up to the left turn-off to Mt Whitney itself. Marmots peeked at me curiously. They made me laugh because they studied me but ran off when I got too close, which could be just a couple of feet. Glance back, however, and you could guarantee that they would poke their faces out from their hiding place to have a last peek.

After just over four hours, at 12.50pm, I reached the top of Mt Whitney. It was Independence Day, which made my Englishness somehow more satisfying.

As if Whitney weren't enough to whet a hiker's appetite, shortly afterwards begins the ascent of Forester Pass, the highest point of the PCT at 13,200 feet. The final section to the pass is one of the most feared areas of the PCT because it involves crossing a snow chute, which can be too slippery or too mushy depending on the time of year, and it's a long way down. I had seen it countless times on video, and must confess it gave me the willies. None of us had ropes; they were considered unnecessary and bulky.

I struggled over Tyndall Creek, which a ranger had warned me to treat with respect owing to high water. I rose through the warmth of the lower elevations, passing and being passed by Flyboxer, Indie and Answerman.

A call of nature forced me off trail to the only tree for miles that offered any privacy. As I assumed position, I looked a short way downhill and saw a squall rapidly approaching me. I disregarded it at first, but it was on top of me with shocking speed. The wind slammed me first, then the rain. I watched in horror with flailing, outstretched arms as my bog roll took flight. My soap catapulted skywards and I fell flat on my arse. The squall passed as quickly as it had arrived and I carefully waddled off, looking like a penguin, to retrieve my toilet roll.

I met up with Indie and others just before the final hour-long push to the pass. Grinder also joined us as we were attempting to save time by taking a direct route up and avoiding the switchbacks. Heaving in lungfuls of oxygen, we sank into the snow and hauled ourselves up, bent double, sweating, then resting to catch our breath. When we topped out on the last switchback, all five of us lay down on the trail, our chests rising and falling quickly.

The snow chute had a clear track carved into it by those who had gingerly stepped across before. Indie was nervous, as was I, but one by one we made it across, hugging the nearest rock in gratitude. To the north, more of the Sierra stretched away to infinity. The mountain passes were like turning pages in a book – each one seemed to make a mere dent in the bigger picture, an unnoticeable gain on an immense journey. At times it reminded me of the journey yet to be conquered. These were pleasurable moments, though. Instead of becoming disillusioned with my modest progress, I smiled. I knew I was being gifted a generous time span in which to experience what the PCT yet had to offer.

Coming off Forester Pass was quite possibly the hardest and longest alpine descent I have ever made. It wasn't too technical, although in parts my pulse was racing, but it seemed to go on and on. I post-holed severely several times, and, as usual, navigation was difficult because of the snow. The valley bottom mocked me. Grinder and I reached the end of a relatively flat-topped ridge, which abruptly ceased and fell away. We checked the map and, after deliberating, decided to negotiate a steep face to get back on track. We began stumbling, toppling and sliding down the face. I gripped my ice axe firmly and concentrated on foot placement. Looking up, I saw Indie and the others peering over at us, and they followed us down. Grinder pulled away from me and became a mere dot. I crossed Bubbs Creek and again lost the trail, so had to improvise a route over rock and then snow fields. Tentatively I picked my way over Bubbs Creek again, which, a couple of thousand feet lower, had matured into a crazy, raging cascade of ice-cold water. My legs numbed and started to shake from the force and chill of the water as I cautiously placed each foot on the next rock, trying to ignore the hundred-foot drop to my left that was waiting to gobble me up with the slightest mistake.

As dusk fell and the incline became kinder, I started to search for a suitable spot to camp. I pulled off trail into a flat area circled by a few trees, then lit some twigs and placed larger sticks on top before pitching the tent. Crouching to push through a small gap in the trees, I was surprised to see another tent.

"Hey," I called. "Anyone at home?"

There was silence, so I presumed the occupant was either asleep or looking for firewood. About ten minutes later the reply came.

"Fozzie?"

"Yeah! How the hell did you know it was me? Who is that? Trooper? That sounds like you."

"Yeah, it's me. Man, am I ill." His voice was somewhere between sleep and sickness. The tent's zip gently glided down, two hands stretched the canvas back and a forlorn, pale face squeezed through the flap and offered a weak smile.

"Trooper, you look bloody terrible. What's going on?"

"Giardia. Fozzie, I got the shits big time. See that clump of trees down there?"

"Yeah."

"Don't go looking for firewood there, that's my toilet."

Giardiasis is an infection of the small intestine, caused by a microscopic organism (protozoa), *Giardia lamblia*. Giardiasis outbreaks can occur in both developed and developing countries where water supplies become contaminated and, more importantly, are untreated. Beaver droppings are a common contaminant and the biggest culprit on the PCT, but the infection can also be spread from person to person through poor hygiene. While not fatal, the symptoms are nasty and include vomiting, diarrhoea, bloating, abnormal amounts of gas (as Elk would testify to), headache, appetite loss, fever, nausea and a swollen abdomen. I met several people on the hike who had Giardia, and it was not a happy experience being in their company. It was enough to make me filter all of my water.

I had spoken to Stumbling Norwegian about it. He had been infected the previous year, and enlightened me as to what he considered the worst symptom, *sharting*. Sharting, he informed me, was essentially a mix of a shit and a fart. I feel that I need explain this no further. The accepted course of treatment is a drug called Flagyl, which will cure the majority of cases. I had tried to obtain this at a couple of pharmacies as a precaution, but was unsuccessful because it was not prescribed unless one actually had Giardia; it was also expensive. Several hikers did carry the drug, however, and luckily Trooper had started a course of it. Generally it clears up in a week to ten days, but it may persist longer and can flare up again later in life.

Trooper spent all of that evening sleeping, interrupted occasionally by a sprint to the 'toilet'. I offered to make him food and help out, but he was too tired even to eat or get out of his tent.

Indie, Answerman and Flyboxer appeared shortly thereafter and, although lured by the fire, said they were going to get another couple of miles in before pitching camp. I left Trooper in the morning. My conscience nibbled away at me because you don't leave someone sick in the mountains, but he insisted he would be fine.

After the pain of coming down Forester Pass the previous day, the next challenge of Glen Pass beckoned, as well as countless others. I was consuming food quickly and needed to find a way to re-supply. However, in the High Sierra, access to the outside world is not exactly forthcoming.

Chapter 7
Dealing with Natural Obstacles

As long as I live, I will hear the birds and the winds and the waterfalls sing. I'll interpret the rocks and learn the language of flood, of storm and avalanche. I'll make the acquaintance of the wild gardens and the glaciers and get as near to the heart of this world as I can.
John Muir

John Muir was born in 1838 in Dunbar, Scotland. His parents, and father in particular, were deeply religious and considered anything that distracted from the Bible as frivolous. The family emigrated to the United States in 1849 and set up a farm near Portage in Wisconsin.

Aged 22, Muir enrolled at the University of Wisconsin-Madison. Although he only ever achieved average grades, geology and botany kindled his interest. In 1864 he went to Canada to avoid the military draft, returning two years later to Minneapolis, where he worked for a factory making wagon wheels. Many argue that the turning point in his life came after he was struck in the eye by a tool that had slipped. He was confined to a darkened room for six weeks, fearing he would never regain his sight.

"This affliction has driven me to the sweet fields. God has to nearly kill us sometimes, to teach us lessons," he said.

He promised thereafter to be true to himself and follow his dreams of exploration and the study of plants.

His legacy is the John Muir Trail, a route better described as a work of wilderness art. Starting near Mount Whitney, it continues 215 miles to Yosemite National Park and offers quite possibly the best example of American wilderness. Its path is shared by the PCT, and its status as a designated trail needs no explanation, The John Muir Trail is also ludicrously difficult; the elevation losses and gains are perhaps the most punishing on the whole PCT.

It was, however, proving to be enjoyable punishment. A regular pattern started to emerge – a mountain pass had to be conquered each and every day. For three weeks I had to climb the equivalent of Ben Nevis daily, often in snow, at altitudes of up to 13,200 feet. The novelty of getting out of the desert and into the mountains was soon replaced by fatigue and an insatiable craving for food. Some would regard this environment as scary or intimidating. Is it dangerous? Absolutely. If it all goes wrong, you're in trouble. You don't get an ambulance in ten minutes out there; you don't even get mobile reception.

I took the Bullfrog Lake Trail up to Kearsarge Pass, intending to get a ride into a town called Independence to buy food for the coming section. The trail disappeared off my PCT map, so I had to wing it a little, but the way was well worn. I walked past lakes so deeply blue they were almost black. Occasionally, the sun wouldn't rise far enough over the surrounding peaks to melt all the ice on the waters. I marvelled at a vision of ice merging to turquoise and the stark contrast between both. Brown trout darted this way and that in the creeks, jumping now and then to catch a fly. I dangled a line into the water, hoping for fresh breakfast, but the fish seemed to scatter as soon as they sensed a presence.

It was nearly a day's hike just to get to the parking lot at Onion Valley, where I sought a ride into Independence. As I reached the top of Kearsarge Pass, a long series of switchbacks appeared, winding downwards. As much as I loved the PCT, I didn't love its miles of trail to towns and highways. It seemed that other hikers had followed in my footsteps, and I passed Cheeks, Mojave, Burnie, Brakelight, Splints, Farmboy, Uncle Gary and the two other English hikers Nick and Chris on the way down. They told me to catch a ride back into Lone Pine, as re-supplying in Independence would be difficult.

I reached the parking area mid-afternoon, and stuck my thumb out at the first car leaving. It stopped, and Damon and Renee Rockwell offered to take me all the way back to Lone Pine. I felt suitably rewarded for my hard work that day – until the car broke down in stifling heat on the highway.

"Don't worry," said Renee. "Damon can fix anything."

And fix it he did.

I have mentioned my inability to remember people's names. I listen, but my brain doesn't seem to register, so invariably I have to apologise and ask again. After some thought on the trail, I thought it was perhaps a memory confidence problem. I decided to follow my instinct, be positive and go with what I thought.

I entered the Mount Whitney Hostel where I had stayed a few days before, and checked in for two nights. The same receptionist was there.

"Thanks, Teresa," I said.

"It's Jessica, actually," she replied, smiling, raising her eyebrows.

I didn't really need two days in Lone Pine, but filled the time with eating, drinking coffee and answering many emails. The World Cup was still on, although without England, and I settled down in the Dow Villa Hotel to watch Spain play Germany. Being English, any country taking on the Germans got my vote, so I was cheering on the Spanish. Three German guys in the room looked at me strangely.

"You are supporting the Spanish side?" one of them enquired, puzzled. "Why is this so?"

"I'm English," I replied, looking him straight in the eye. "Do you really need me to explain?"

I felt guilty about being off trail, so I decided to move out the following day. I visited the Alabama Café for one last breakfast. The place was buzzing as usual, and a guy stopped by my table.

"You doing the PCT?" he asked, looking me up and down and scratching his stubble.

"Yes, I am," I said, swallowing my last mouthful.

"Well, God will be with you."

Feeling a bit belligerent, possibly because of the heat, I replied, "Actually, bearing in mind I don't believe in God, and with due respect, I don't think he will be."

He looked momentarily flummoxed and slightly shocked.

"How can you say that?" he retorted. "I find that offensive."

"Actually," I said, "I find the fact that you think God *can* help me offensive, bearing in mind I don't believe he even exists. However, thank you for your support."

I left rapidly, not wanting to clean up the can of worms I'd opened and making a note to work on my tact.

I took a bus back to Independence and got a quick ride back up to the Onion Valley parking area. Making short work of Kearsarge Pass, I was soon back on trail with a full pack of food and a spring in my step. It was about seven days to the next town stop, so I steeled myself and got going.

This section of the Sierra was hard. Leaving the trail was tricky, and the passes were brutal. Glen Pass (12,000ft), Pinchot Pass (12,150ft), Mather Pass (12,100ft), Muir Pass (11,950ft), Selden Pass (10,900ft) and Silver Pass (10,900ft) all loomed ahead of me like a huge obstacle course. The descents were more difficult than the ascents. Knees ached and the valley bottoms teased me from miles away. The uphill sections required more exertion, but I coped with them better. I had more purchase in the snow and found more of a rhythm. Downhill was a series of leg-breaking jolts and gravity caused me to post-hole alarmingly.

Coming off Glen Pass, I lost the trail, as usual, but I knew the approximate direction. The entire route was laid out in front of me like a gigantic version of my map. I simply had to pick the easiest and least dangerous line to reach my destination. I followed a fast-flowing creek to Rae Lake, easily identifiable because the trail hopped straight through a land bridge in the middle. The snow was soft near the creek edge about thirty feet below me, so I stayed back, but still sank worryingly easily. Reaching the end of a stretch of snow, I blithely rushed to solid ground. My right leg went through the snow and bent back at a right angle. My shin smashed into the rock and I screamed in agony. I couldn't push myself up and out; the snow around me was too loose. The pain was excruciating. Fearing that a broken leg or fracture would spell the end of my hike, I pummelled the snow, screaming in frustration.

Eventually the pain subsided a little, and I relaxed and took stock. I placed my pack on the snow and used it to pull myself out, a red streak of blood smearing the stark white surface. With some trepidation, I peeled back a blood-soaked trouser leg to inspect the wound. A cut, perhaps three inches long, was starting to congeal and swell. I cleaned the wound with snow, prising it open to remove any debris. I applied some antibiotic cream, dressed the wound and swallowed a couple of ibuprofen. I hoped, against my better judgement perhaps, that I hadn't suffered a broken leg. I brewed some tea and tried to calm down, concentrating on my breathing. After half an hour I hobbled carefully away, figuring that unless bones started to protrude or I heard a nasty grating sound coming from my leg, that the prognosis was good.

This part of the PCT has numerous rivers and creeks, all swollen with an angry, foaming froth of meltwater cascading from the mountains above. While some waters were only ankle-deep, others presented more of an obstacle.

Through summer, the upper Sierra Nevada warms up and a huge amount of snow melts. Small trickles of meltwater work their way under the snow, join larger trickles which run into creeks and merge into rivers. It's a massive amount of water which has to channel somewhere, and the further into summer I ventured, the more the levels rose.

Water crossings appeared often and each had to be sized up carefully. I considered three factors: depth, width and current. Some creeks were only a few feet across yet were speeding along; others were impressively wide but flowed smoothly. Tyndall Creek, at the base of Forester Pass, was the first crossing to catch me out. As I drew near, I saw why the ranger had warned me about this particular creek. It was perhaps only twenty feet wide and three feet deep, but it was flowing fast. The real problem in crossing water is the possibility of being swept away; with forty pounds strapped to your back, you're all but helpless.

Elk had told me about a creek that had given him trouble. It was waist-deep, but relatively slow-moving, so maybe he was lulled into a false sense of security. Two steps in, and he was whipped downstream for fifty feet before managing to clamber out. Once you lose your footing, all you can do is try and work to the shore and grab anything solid to haul yourself out.

I approached each crossing the same way. I didn't assume that the point at which the PCT met the bank was the best place to cross. I walked a couple of hundred feet upstream and the same downstream, sometimes more, looking for alternative spots. I learnt some things this way. If the river narrowed, obviously the other side was closer, but by the same token the water was squeezed tighter and therefore the current was usually stronger. So a wider crossing was sometimes the better option, because the current was kinder. On occasion, the river widened but the current remained the same. This usually meant that the water was deeper, the extra water being accommodated by the depth. The main prize sometimes to be found when scanning downstream and upstream, especially in forest, was a natural bridge in the form of a fallen tree, possibly manoeuvred into place by kindly hikers. A tree bridge got me out of many a scrape.

Tyndall didn't look that threatening. It wasn't particularly wide, but there was plenty of water between its banks, so I pulled off my boots, slipped on my Crocs and put my socks over the top. This was a trick I had picked up from countless internet video clips – socks over footwear provide better grip on the creek bed. Three steps in, and the freezing water hit my feet and legs, numbing them immediately and painfully. Wanting to escape, I made the mistake of speeding up. As the current then hit me, I strained to stay upright, leaning in to the flow of the water and using my trekking poles for balance. The deafening roar was all I could hear as the torrent gushed around me as far up as my waist. I glanced downstream at the fate that would befall me should I slip. Rocks poked out from the froth, the water hurtled downwards; there would be no chance of getting out if I stumbled. I tried to ignore the pain and take slow, steady steps nearer the bank. Scanning the creek bed for a decent foothold was almost useless, given the force of the current smashing into my legs. By the time I reached the rocks on the opposite bank, I was a wreck. My legs were screaming from the cold and I was heaving in great lungfuls of air. Still, I was thrilled to have made it safely across.

Reginald at Nerve Centre HQ was getting messages from Nancy in my right leg. Gertrude, responsible for the left leg, was having a fit and good old Angela down at foot level was going into hypothermic shock.

"What the hell is going on down there?" Reginald screamed. "I got a sudden drop in temperature, severe force to the right side of both legs, and I hear rumours that he's got his socks on over his Crocs. Is this correct?"

"I think we just did a river crossing!" Angela shouted back. "I definitely felt the socks peel off, and then he put his Crocs on; I'm not sure about the socks, I mean, why the hell would he do that? I think we're out now, though; the temperature is slowly going up. Forget Gertrude and Nancy, they'll bloody complain about anything."

I continued to tackle water crossings, sometimes as many as fifteen in a day. The more I crossed, the better I got at it. At first I resented getting my shoes and socks wet, but it was quicker to wade in with them on than stop constantly to change. At the end of the day I could dry the shoes and socks by the fire and they generally dried overnight anyway. I began to think I had mastered the art of crossing water – until, that is, Evolution Creek spoiled an otherwise typically pleasant Sierra Nevada morning.

Evolution Creek takes the overspill from Wanda Lake. I was woken from my daydreaming when the trees cleared to reveal a stretch of water that seemed at least a hundred feet wide. Because of its width, the current had backed off a little, but was certainly strong enough to get my attention. I made two mistakes: first, I had become complacent about crossing water, and second, I decided it would be a good idea to capture the crossing on video to post on the blog. Filming entailed losing the use of one trekking pole for the duration, because my camera was mounted on the end, with the aid of a nifty gadget called a StickPic. I could hold the pole in front with the camera facing back at me; the resulting film gave the impression that the camera operator was walking a few feet in front of me.

I did the usual scout for a suitable crossing place but decided the PCT had already found it right by the creek. I guessed the water was about waist height, though in one short section it seemed deeper and the current stronger. I checked that my gear was securely ensconced in waterproof liners and commenced what I hoped would be a quick but safe traverse. All was well, until I sank up to my armpits in freezing water and then felt the current hit me like a freight train. I had difficulty lifting my foot for the next step, as the water threatened to send me flailing downstream. Helplessly stuck, I was gripped by fear; yet, somewhat taking leave of my senses, I carried on filming, not wishing to lose either the camera or such potentially great blog material.

I gritted my teeth, leaned into the current and decided that the next step would either see me through the deep section or send me tumbling downriver. With the water rushing up over my neck, I couldn't read the creek bed to find my next step. After a few seconds that seemed an eternity, I powered through to the far bank, exhausted.

Peeling off my soaked clothes, I sat on a warm rock and grabbed my camera, eager to review what must have been great footage. I cried at the sombre message blinking at me on the screen: 'memory card full'.

***

The Sierra was certainly providing me with all the solitude I wanted, if not more. Now 800 miles in, and having covered a third of the PCT, I was seeing fewer of my fellow hikers. Some forty per cent of those who attempt the PCT fail to get through the first month. For days, a landscape of surreal beauty, pristine wilderness and indescribable vistas was all mine to enjoy. My body was becoming a powerhouse; despite the altitude, I felt as fit as I had ever been as I stormed up passes and whipped along the trail. Forest opened up into meadows and merged with rocky, snow-covered higher lands.

It became a daily routine to tackle a pass, descend to a lower, warmer, more oxygen-rich elevation and prepare myself for more of the same in the morning. My fear of bears was under control too – I almost relished the prospect of an encounter.

I liked the evenings. After the vast effort of a twenty to twenty-five-mile day, including getting up and over another pass, having a few hours to wind down was bliss. I would look for a suitable rest spot once I had reached my distance target for the day. My preference was for forest, mainly because I could get a fire going using scattered wood. My first goal was a flat patch of ground to sleep on; my second was a nearby creek to use for water but not too close to attract mosquitoes. I would filter a few litres and give my back and neck a stretch. Next, I made arrangements for sleeping, which were by now second nature. I'd lay out a piece of Tyvek (a building material used to 'wrap' houses in, acting as a breathable membrane). Tyvek is ideal as a sleeping platform or to lay under a tent groundsheet as added protection. I would then inflate my sleeping mat and hang my sleeping bag from a tree to aid the lofting. Every couple of days I would wash my feet and socks in the creek and then sit down to cook. A litre of water was enough to give me a hot cup of tea and to hydrate whatever culinary concoction my food bag offered. I would update my journal and might then, time allowing, do a little reading.

One of my most enjoyable experiences was listening to the wind rush through the forest. It struck me several times how simple this phenomenon was. It transported me to an almost primitive era, before technology took over the free time of collective society. No other sounds intruded, and for a few minutes I would actively listen to the wind, appreciating and then studying it.

Sometimes it was a mere breeze, which barely glanced against my face. Stronger gusts, however, played a game of cat and mouse with the forest. Myriad currents and flows wove their way through the trees. The pines occasionally parted like theatrical curtains to reveal a tantalising glimpse of the night sky before closing in again. I could hear stronger torrents coming from hundreds of feet away, faintly at first, then building in intensity as they drew closer. At times they would pass behind me with a roar, leaving my little haven calm and undisturbed. Other times they would slam into me, a cool and exhilarating blast that ruffled my hair and clothing. The forest around me came alive when the wind came out to play. Whirls and eddies whipping around me made my whole body tingle.

Mather Pass, however, took the wind out of me. Forester was

the highest but not necessarily the hardest. Mather was a stiff climb up and a long and harsh ascent. I had to work my way around several fallen trees, and water crossings were abundant.

Having reached the bottom, I was enveloped in thick forest once more. At 6pm I reached the Middle Fork Kings River, where three mighty rivers violently converged. Indie and Flyboxer had settled down to cook their evening meals before venturing off for a few more miles. They introduced me to Stacks, who was cooking mac 'n' cheese over a fire. It transpired that Stacks had walked the Camino de Santiago in Spain the same year as I had, but we had never met. He seemed extremely relaxed, and when I enquired about the green plant he was chopping, he said it was wild onion. I was aware that this existed but had no idea how to identify it. He had used up all of his, and we tried in vain to find some more for my future use. I left after he did, and lo and behold, two miles up the track, a neat bundle of wild onions took pride of place on a boulder in the middle of the trail.

I walked a little with Indie past Grouse Meadow, which shone in the early evening sun as insects danced on its surface. Now and then the river would steer a course close to the trail and thunder past us, crashing and slamming its way downstream. I pulled off trail for an early night as Indie walked off to catch up with Flyboxer, and we agreed to meet in the morning for the assault on Muir Pass.

We had heard a lot from other hikers and some of the rangers about Muir Pass. It was acquiring quite a reputation. The main hurdle was a seven-mile stretch of snow, which made postholing a real danger, and some of the creeks were still snow-covered, necessitating walking over snow bridges.

From my elevation at camp, I had a 4,000-foot climb to the top and then some difficult miles back down past the snow line to solid ground. I started early, at 7am, to make the most of what I knew it would be a brutal day. I soon met up with Indie once more, along with Flyboxer and Answerman, and we formed a team to tackle Muir and be safe in numbers. Stax, Black Gum and Ursa Major were also packing up camp but soon passed us.

I crossed the Kings River again and scrambled up a rocky outcrop, where the river mockingly blocked my path again.

Cautiously crossing using boulders, I reached the other side to discover the path was blocked by a steep outcrop. I had to retrace my route back down to join the others coming up.

As we hit the first of the snow and glanced up, things appeared worse than we had anticipated. The gradient was steep, there was snow all the way to the top, the river forced us to make several crossings and we soon lost the trail. Other tracks in the snow were always a clue but could not be trusted; after all, they were not necessarily heading up to Muir Pass. I met a woman coming down, who confirmed it was hard going, but that a day's work should see us up and over. She also warned me that the snow was soft and would get even softer as the sun became hotter. She pointed out a dangerous snow bridge a mile away and advised taking a safer route. I thanked her and adjusted my course to take this into account, while signalling the others to veer up and follow me.

We all tried to balance ourselves on the slope, which steepened down to the river. I was wearing my spikes and steadying myself with one trekking pole, my ice axe ready in the other hand. The snow alternated between soft and firm, broken up with damp, slippery rock sections that demanded the use of my hands. We targeted a small col at the base of a lake, descended to the river and followed its course up to the col. As we crested, a turquoise lake dotted with floating islands of ice met our eyes. We plodded on, our breathing becoming heavier as we surveyed the pass, still two miles ahead. Using well-trodden footprints where the snow had become firmer, we descended to a narrow creek and crossed over a snow bridge that creaked beneath us. Flyboxer veered off, preferring a more direct but steeper approach, while Indie, Answerman and I took the longer but kinder route. At 3pm we reached the round stone shelter perched on the summit of Muir Pass. We ate a late lunch, took photos and mocked each other's appearance. After several days on trail, we were all completely filthy.

We went back down at our own pace and spaced out within sight of each other. Clouds billowed up around me as a few raindrops fell, the first rain I had encountered in weeks. The snow gradually thinned. I removed my spikes and wove a way over rocks and meltwater until Evolution Lake appeared below.

One last crossing and I stopped for the day at the edge of the lake, after twelve hours and twelve miles of particularly gruelling hiking. Gradually the others limped in and set up camp nearby. We all watched the sun set poetically between two mountains that tumbled down to form a V shape at the end of the lake. Oranges and reds streaked the sky, reflected in the waters as the clouds slowly dispersed. We were exhausted but smiling, gradually relaxing as steam rose from our stoves. We ate like wolves.

It was 110 miles between my last, and next, town stops. I had seriously misjudged both my food and alcohol supplies. I only had a day's food at best and my alcohol was a mere dribble. That's stove alcohol, not Jack Daniels. Shit, if I had been running low on JD, then things really would have been serious. I knew there was a cut-off trail heading to Muir Trail Ranch, a remote lodging miles from anywhere, and hoped I could re-supply there.

I made my way further down from Muir Pass, past ferocious, tumbling, emerald rivers cascading into waterfalls. Immense granite rock-faces towered above me and small watercourses trickled down them like streaked tears.

I was miles from civilisation, completely hemmed in on all sides by wilderness. No intrusion from buildings, no noise from roads, and the only light at night was the moon and stars. Many people find this sort of environment uncomfortable, unnatural. It never bothered me or anyone I was walking with. Far from it: the sense of detachment was one of the primary reasons why we were out walking the PCT. I remembered coming down Forester Pass and stopping to admire the peaks around me, the lakes glistening below, the clouds floating above me and the welcoming silence. Dangerous it could be, but that was the price one paid to experience the serenity of a place like this.

I met Frank and his horse, Chief, out for an afternoon ride. He was the blacksmith at Muir Trail ranch and as we chatted for a few minutes, he showed me a fabulously intricate and detailed key ring he had forged. According to him, I would definitely get food at the ranch, as there were several hiker boxes and the owner, Pat, kept stocks of stove fuel.

The ranch lay less than a mile off the PCT, and as I walked

down the track it became clear that others had also made a beeline for it. A sign on the gate said 'Please ring the bell'. I nodded to Answerman, who was sitting there, relaxing.

"Don't worry, Fozzie," he advised. "Just come on in."

As I walked through and clicked the gate shut, a voice broke the silence.

"Did you ring the bell?"

It was Pat, the proprietor. I had heard a few stories about this elderly lady's fearsome manner, so I was half expecting a Doberman to come charging out from somewhere.

"Er ... no. Sorry?"

"It's OK," Answerman offered. "It's my fault. I told him to come in."

"Please ring the bell," she ordered.

Despite her reputation, Pat proved to be a little angel. She gave me a quick rundown of what was where, and confirmed that she could supply me with stove fuel. There was not one, but five hiker boxes. Signs politely requested hikers to take no more than they required, as food was in high demand. I needed about two days' worth of sustenance and scored some excellent results: dehydrated bacon and eggs, chocolate-coated sesame crackers, powdered milk, oats and a couple of evening meals. Pat sold me some alcohol fuel, and after chatting to a few hikers, I was on my way.

My next re-supply was in a large town called Mammoth. After a twenty-miler from the ranch, I had left myself another twenty miles to camp; then, the following day, a short five to reach the trailhead and catch a ride to town. After I'd knocked off the twenty by mid-afternoon, my stomach got the better of me and I pushed out the remaining mileage, calculating that the incentive of an imminent cooked breakfast increased my speed by an average of 0.2 miles per hour. If I had a cooked breakfast every morning, I could therefore walk an extra two miles a day. If only.

My second water filter had now packed up and I was using a Steripen. This little unit was essentially an ultraviolet tube which treats water when immersed in it, destroying the reproductive capability of any organisms. It was fragile but its simplicity attracted me. Just wave it in a litre of water for about a minute, and job done. I passed a group of hikers at lunch and stopped to chat. One of them asked me what water purification method I was using, and when I told him, he said he was also using a Steripen and his batteries had run out. I offered him my spares and refused payment, saying I would reach Mammoth that evening and could buy some more. He thanked me profusely as I walked off. A couple of hours later I stopped by a creek to treat a few litres of water to get me to town – and saw with frustration that my batteries were dead. So much for karma!

Chapter 8
Washed Away by the Tuolumne River

Shake your water, it makes the Giardia dizzy.
Cary 'Borders' Hart

I walked out on to the trailhead at Reds Meadow late afternoon and made a beeline for the café, with nothing more important on my mind than bacon and eggs. Once re-fuelled, I caught the bus that made regular trips to Mammoth, and sat behind a guy near the front. After a couple of minutes he spoke to me.

"Are you a thru-hiker?" he enquired, turning his nose up slightly.

"Yes, I am," I replied, smiling pleasantly.

"I thought so, you smell like shit." He then got out of his seat and moved to the back of the bus.

I would normally retort in such situations but I was so amazed by such outright rudeness that my tongue was tied. He was right, though; no denying it. After several days on trail, a cheesy odour rising from my feet was enough to make even me grimace.

Mammoth earned its living from the winter ski season trade. During the summer, it was a mecca for mountain bikers and hikers and was well equipped in every way for a thru-hiker. It was not, however, my kind of town. The amenities, again, were too spaced out, which meant time wasted trying to find the launderette, the supermarket, a breakfast place and, more importantly, a motel. There was a jazz festival in town and everything was booked up. I called at several motels, but no luck. On my way to the KOA, I called in on the off-chance at the

Motel 6. A register in reception was filled with messages from PCT hikers that had a spare bed available.

'Hey, Grey Fox in Room 6. Give us a call.'

I dialled the number.

"Hello?"

"Grey Fox, how you doing? Says here you may have a spare bed?" I said.

"Er, who is this?"

"It's Fozzie."

"Fozzie, hi. Yeah, er, a spare bed? No, sorry."

I got the distinct impression he did but for some reason didn't want me to take it.

"Right," I replied. "Well, you might want to change the message in the book to reflect that?"

I hadn't seen Grey Fox for a couple of weeks. He walked with Spiller, who I had originally assumed was his girlfriend; so when I learnt that she wasn't and that he was engaged to someone else, I was intrigued. The Grey Fox and Spiller saga was bread-and-butter gossip for most of the thru-hikers. They acted as if they were together and I guess you could have classed them as inseparable. Grey Fox had driven back home when he reached Kennedy Meadows because his fiancée apparently demanded they sort some things out. Whether Spiller was part of this I never found out, but they kept most people guessing for the length of the PCT. I had never quite managed to read him, and got the impression he had a problem with me, which I suppose was verified when he rejected my interest in his spare bed.

Continuing to scan through the register, I saw a note from Pockets.

'Hey. Got chicken pox! Come say hello!'

Having gone through my chicken pox phase aged seven, I called his room. I had met Pockets briefly at Kennedy Meadows but had not seen him since.

"Fozzie! Hey! What's up?"

"Pockets, how you feeling? I'm looking for a spare bed for a couple of nights. Any chance?"

"Man, I feel like shit, not good company at the moment. Tell you what, though, come back tomorrow and I think I'll be through the worst of it. You're welcome to grab the bed then if

The Last Englishman

you like."

"Thanks, mate. I'll give you a shout in the morning."

I plodded on down to the KOA, confident that I could at least get a spot to pitch and grab a shower. The warden told me she was absolutely full up because of the festival.

"I only need a space seven feet long by three feet wide," I explained, outlining a rectangle with my hands.

"You have to stay at a designated spot and I don't have anywhere, sorry."

After she had driven off in her golf cart, I ducked up one of the tracks, disappeared into the trees and could have picked a spot among hundreds. If they weren't specific camping areas, with a nice little drive to park your SUV and a space big enough to accommodate the average American motor home, i.e. about half an acre, then you couldn't stay there. I walked a little way into the trees to hide me from the warden, and pitched.

Walking down to the shower area, I heard the familiar cackle of Burnie's witch laugh through the trees, and went to investigate. She was with Cheeks and Mojave, and they too had experienced similar problems finding a camp spot until a kind couple had let them pitch near their motor home. It seemed funny that in the wild we had millions of acres to pitch a tent, but when we reached town there was no availability and, even if there was, we would have to pay for it. To top off the day, the shower block was closed, so I walked to the nearest eatery, McDonald's, with my lingering foot odour in hot pursuit.

I admit it couldn't have been pleasant for anyone near me, but I couldn't help but be amused by the insulting looks I got in McDonald's that evening and the way people moved away once they'd got a whiff of me. My clothing had dirt marks, my hands looked as though I had just done an oil change, and my hair was so sticky it was vertical. Even I baulked at the strange character peering back at me in the mirror.

What I found peculiar was that to me, and most other hikers, the townsfolk were the ones who stank. After being out in the woods for a while, you lose touch with how people smell. Perfume, deodorant and hair products suddenly become offensive. Even on trail, we could tell a casual day-hiker from a hard-core thru-hiker just by the body odour.

I went to the Black Stove with Burnie in the morning for breakfast, and set about the usual 'zero' tasks (a day when no hiking is done is called a zero). On my return to Motel 6, Pockets invited me up and said I could stay as long as needed.

I would have trouble describing Pockets in under fifty pages, but I'll give it a shot. His trail name came about from a thru-hike he completed on the Appalachian Trail a few years before. He had reached a small outdoors store and agreed that the owner would give him a gear shakedown (someone goes through your pack contents and advises what you do and do not need). After having the contents of his pack scrutinised, Pockets was doing well, until he was asked to empty his pockets – at which point all manner of items spilled out, and the trail name was born.

Pockets was 27, and his home was a small town called Paw Paw in Michigan. He sported an impressive beard the like of which I could only ever dream of growing. His eyes were a piercing blue that he claimed drove the women wild, and his passion was photography. Having only picked up a camera a few years before, he showed an uncanny knack for taking beautiful pictures. So much so that he had already managed to get published in National Geographic, the holy grail of any budding photographer.

We went for a meal in the evening and Burnie joined us. There were only two beds in the room, and as she had left the campsite, she took up Pockets's offer of a place to stay. I offered her my bed, saying I could take the floor, but she declined and laid out her sleeping bag on the carpet.

"Yeah, so, I got this unusual problem when I sleep," Pockets said. "I figure I should really warn you both in case something happens."

"Something happening? Like what?" asked Burnie, sitting up and raising her eyebrows.

"Well, I dream a lot and sometimes sleepwalk. It's nothing to worry about; I don't turn into a werewolf or anything. They hooked me up to some measuring machine a while back and apparently my brain is ten times more active at night than most people's during the day. If I start making noises and talking just ignore it. I've been doing it like forever. I was born in Germany but left when I was about two. I can't speak German but in my sleep I'm fluent. I also speak a little French and Spanish when I sleep. Most of the time I'm just incoherent and ramble on. My parents always had to watch me when I was little because I would get up and move around the house."

Burnie and I looked at each other in silent astonishment. Pockets carried on.

"When I was walking the Appalachian Trail, I was sleeping in the bottom bunk of one of the shelters. I dreamt that I was walking up a hill and suddenly all these logs started rolling down, so I tried to stop them. This woke most of the other hikers up and, although still dreaming, I could sense a lot of head torches shining at me. In the morning everyone said that they had woken up with me screaming to get out and I was leaning hard against one of the wooden shelter supports, slipping back on the floor in my socks. 'Get out of the shelter!' I was screaming. 'You could at least look a little appreciative, I'm trying to save you all!'"

With that, Pockets turned over and went to sleep, as if he'd said nothing unusual. Burnie looked at me and shrugged her shoulders and we both nodded off, keeping half an ear open for a German-speaking, crazed thru-hiker bracing himself against the motel wall.

Pockets was quiet that night, save a few mumbles. He had skipped a section, so the following day he went south to Kearsarge Pass to complete the missing miles. I had a funny feeling we would be meeting again.

I caught the bus back to Reds Meadow, and couldn't resist a slice of cherry pie with a chocolate milkshake to set me up for the afternoon. I was shocked when the waitress handed me the bill for $12.02. I paid at the counter.

"Would you mind filling up my water bottle for me, please?" I asked, holding up my grubby-looking bottle.

She took a step back.

"There's a spigot round the back for hikers," she said.

"Would you have given me a glass of water with my pie had I asked?" I said, becoming a little assertive now.

"Yes, of course." The look on her face suggested she had got my point before I had made it.

"Good. Because I've just spent twelve bucks on a meagre

piece of pie and a milkshake. Now, please could you walk the four paces to that tap over there and fill my water bottle for me?"

I put in a few miles that afternoon and eventually stopped near the Vogelsang Trailhead. A pleasant breeze kept the mosquitoes at bay for once, and I camped just a few feet off trail near the river. It was a beautiful evening, the sun seemed to take longer than usual to say her goodbyes and the forest was silent except for the river whispering to me as it slid gently past. I sat on the bank and dangled my sore feet in the water, watching some trout manoeuvre around the shallows. Lush, deep green grass banked up gently from the far side before disappearing into the trees, which in turn surrendered to the towering granite outcrops above them, an orange brushed sky providing the finale. A doe and two fawns circled me cautiously, grazing the undergrowth and occasionally glancing my way. They came within a few feet, and it reminded me of how lucky I was to be experiencing the wilderness. I heard a twig break perhaps a hundred feet behind me, and looked round to see a wolf skulking through the trees. It stopped and looked at me, seeming to chastise itself, annoyed, for making its presence known. We locked eyes for a few seconds, its nose testing the air for a scent, and off it went.

The following day I made a beeline for the café at Tuolumne Meadows. This was a popular spot for tourists exploring the Ansel Adams Wilderness, the John Muir Trail and a huge rock-face known as Half Dome, down the road. I crested a hill in the trail and came face to face with Wyoming, whom I had not seen since Idyllwild. I was momentarily taken aback, thinking she, or I, must be going the wrong way. We had a big hug.

"What … where, er, why are you walking the wrong way?" I stammered.

"I'm not, Fozzie! I skipped up to Ashland in Oregon because of the snow in the Sierras. Now I'm walking back to where I skipped from, Kennedy Meadows."

"That's a big skip!" I exclaimed. "How was it from there to here?"

"There's snow in the Marble Mountains down to 6,000 feet, other than that it's fine. Oregon is kinder, the trail is smooth and the elevation loss and gain are minimal. You can crack out some good mileage there. How are the Sierras?"

"Difficult!" I said, smiling to try to lighten the news. "There are a lot of hard passes and still plenty of snow. You can get through all of them if you're careful. Take extra food: the altitude and temperature will increase your appetite. Oh, and watch out for Mather Pass, it's a bitch."

We hugged again and I watched her trudge off south. It was strange meeting my first SoBo (south-bounder). I couldn't get my head around it. I also felt a tinge of sadness. I had first met Wyoming on only the second day, at a campsite off Fred Canyon Road, when I was walking with Gabe. She was an extraordinarily unassuming and gentle woman. She spoke quietly; I had to listen closely to what she was saying. She was slight, and her hair was cut short, perhaps as the sort of low-maintenance approach many hikers adopted. I dearly wished I could see her again, but I knew I probably wouldn't.

SoBos thru-hike the PCT from Canada to Mexico. The norm is to do it north-bound, NoBo-style. Because Canada and Washington State receive more snowfall over the winter, which does not clear until later in the season, a south-bounder starts and finishes later than a north-bounder. There are pros and cons for the SoBo, but the main advantage I could see was that you walk away from the bad weather towards California, which stays warm long after the northern states are under several feet of the white stuff. NoBos are always caught in a game of chase-the-weather, trying to reach Canada before the snow hits them. Wyoming was not a true SoBo as such; she was just south-bounding one section. I met more of them the further north I walked. Generally a SoBo starts around June and finishes around November.

The track dipped out at around 8,700 feet from Donahue Pass, and kept a close friendship with the Lyle River on my right for a good eight miles. Occasionally, winter overspill from the river had crept over the trail and softened the ground into a rich, deep brown mud which clung to my shoes. I stopped several times to talk to other walkers, who congratulated me on attempting the PCT. The area is easily accessible from the road that runs through Tuolumne Meadows and attracts many a visiting hiker. That morning, it was easy to see why; as I walked through the meadows that stretch out from the river, the flat terrain made for contemplative meandering. I felt at ease there. I ate a good meal at the café and got in a few supplies at the well-stocked store. Holidaymakers, hikers and climbers dotted the area, and the air was busy with the chitter-chatter of people anticipating a day in the wild. I had thought about catching a ride down to see the famous Half Dome, a hugely impressive rock-face. I was putting in good mileage at this stage, around twenty-five a day, and I also felt that though undoubtedly awe-inspiring, Half Dome would be no more spectacular than the sights I had become used to seeing every day. Supposedly the inspiration for the logo of well-known outdoor equipment manufacturer The North Face, Half Dome is the centrepiece of countless photos taken over the years, perhaps most famously by Ansel Adams, whose work adorns many an outdoor-themed calendar.

I walked along the road briefly and then followed the PCT as it turned up a side road scattered with parked cars and screaming kids. Holiday-makers sat in air-conditioned cars, eating ice creams, and I wondered why they were there. Many people just sit behind their steering wheel, scared to venture into the wilderness. I found the place annoying, and I quickened my pace, leaving the cars behind and disappearing into the forest again. The woods were now my home, my comfort zone. A quick meal was always a morale booster, but everyday distractions had started to irritate me. I became frustrated at people asking me what I thought were stupid questions, which in turn made me feel guilty for not being more approachable. "What are you doing?" they would ask me. "Why are you so dirty? Why is your pack so big? You're just wearing shoes; where are your hiking boots? Don't you miss the TV? Where do you wash your hair?"

Before long, though, such things were a distant memory, replaced by the tumbling rage of the Tuolumne River cascading past me on my left. I approached Dingley Creek slowly, and saw the boulders peeking above the surface, acting as stepping stones.

Maybe I just wasn't paying attention at this point, or maybe my familiarity with river crossings had bred contempt. Dingley Creek seemed innocent enough: the tributary was flowing fast, but it wasn't deep, and a good assortment of stones and boulders should have spelt an easy crossing. And it was, apart from one unfortunate casualty.

My trekking poles, Click and Clack, named after the sound they make when they strike the ground, had been with me some ten years, since my walk on El Camino de Santiago in Spain. These constant companions gave me a feeling of security as they eased me up the ascents and stabilised me on the descents. Out here, they were a blessing on river crossings – walking without Click and Clack would have been unimaginable.

I jumped and hopped from one boulder to the next. Sometimes the water would find a way into a split in my shoes, making me shiver. Mid-jump, I sensed hesitation with Clack, who had become stuck in the creek bed. I let him go; I had to, the momentum carried me forward, and I figured that, as he was firmly rooted, I could just hop back and retrieve him. To my horror, as I looked behind me, I saw the current tearing at him. Like a boxer on the receiving end of a last, devastating punch, Clack slowly started to slump sideways, picking up speed as the current took hold.

"No! Clack!" I screamed.

It was too late; as I jumped back and held out a flailing hand to rescue him, he succumbed to the flow and started to float off. Dingley Creek travelled a mere fifty feet before joining the Tuolumne River. I ran along the bank, dropping my pack while trying to dodge fallen trees and other obstacles. I closed the gap, but the river was getting closer, Clack's speed was increasing and he seemed to be looking at me pleadingly. Then he was engulfed by the Tuolumne and torn away in an instant. With only a small part of his stem and handle protruding above the river, he swayed from side to side like a waving friend on a departing train. I waved back and swore I heard him say:

"Don't be sad, you still have Click! It'll be fine, I'll wash up downriver somewhere and a hiker will find me. I'll hike on. I will hike on!"

Click and I watched despondently as our companion bobbed into the distance. Our hearts sank. We turned north, paused for one last glimpse and began plodding up the trail.

I got lost trying to navigate over a section of granite. Such areas were few and far between, but because of their hard surface, the trail was not easily distinguishable. A few cairns marked the way, but they dwindled to nothing. Had it not been for a tent just visible through the trees ahead, it would have taken longer to find a way through.

Steve Climber, Borders, Jolly Green Giant, Dan and Splizzard were stretched across the trail, enjoying the afternoon sun. Borders had erected his tent and was relishing a few minutes free of mosquitoes. I sat with my fellow hikers for a while, before moving on.

It was now the last week of July, but in the higher elevations of the mountains, it was still spring. Elder shrubs were dressed in white, meadow flowers splattered the grass with hundreds of colours, and squadrons of dragonflies hovered in formation over the lakes. A sandy trail carved its way through grass, and brown trout were still feasting.

I walked with Chrissie and Dodge for a morning. We were all wrapped in our mosquito head nets and I, as usual, was struggling to see through mine; but wearing it was the lesser of two evils. Click was doing his best to keep me company, but I felt off-balance without Clack. The major passes were now behind me, and although there was still a lot of altitude variation, I felt that I'd accomplished the hardest part of the Sierras.

The splits in my second pair of shoes, running from the soles to the laces, were now widening. I had tried to repair them by squeezing a rubber paste over the outside, but this had only made matters worse. It had dried, leaving rough lumps on the insides which were rubbing on my toes, so I tried to pull and cut the worst of it off. This only made the holes bigger. After 990 miles, I was due my third pair of footwear. I was at the tail end of the pack because of the time I had lost resting my bad feet. I had completed just over a third of the route, but it had taken 91 days, which put me on course to finish around January! This was four months after a typical end date of September, and frankly, the ferocity of winter in the northern states would make a January finish all but impossible in any case. I needed to increase my mileage, and try to keep town stops to one day a week at most.

On the plus side, the water crossings were less of a challenge now that I was through the big passes. Oregon was 700 miles ahead; a long way off, but the terrain was supposedly easier going. I was strong, my feet were in good shape, but I knew that unless I started to step up the pace, I wasn't going to make my thru-hike. After all the planning and hard work to get this far, the thought of failing gnawed at me. My daily mileage totals were good going for the Sierras, but not easy to sustain.

I had also received some good news from Chrissie and Dodge. We were apparently coming to the end of the worst mosquito areas. The familiar granite outcrops were soon to be replaced by a more porous, volcanic rock. Less water meant fewer mosquitoes.

I reached the end of a hard day and started to look for a camping spot. I saw smoke wafting through trees up ahead, near to a creek and a potential place to pitch up. Sure enough, as I hopped over the water, Mojave and Cheeks waved me over from just off the trail. A new face, Mr Green, was sitting in the smoke from his fire, seeking refuge from the dreaded mosquitoes. The surrounding rock-faces were turning from a granite grey to a pinkish hue, which I took to be the start of the transition Chrissie and Dodge had mentioned. Unfortunately, the mosquitoes hadn't seemed to notice, and by sundown we were all engulfed. Cheeks seemed to be coping quite well, but Mojave had retreated to their tent, so I chatted with her through the canvas. By the time I too had sat down to cook, I was being attacked from every angle. I boiled my water quickly, re-hydrated my meal and dived into my tent, quickly closing the zip after me. I stayed there for the rest of the evening, unwilling to get out to brush my teeth, and had to make a brisk dash for the quickest pee ever. I had decided to go to a town called Bridgeport, which meant an eleven-mile morning walk to the road at Sonora Pass and, then, with luck, a ride into town. Conscious of my need to start putting more miles in, I set the alarm for 4am.

The 1,700-foot gain stated on the elevation graph before the descent to Sonora Pass seemed kind, but after a couple of miles I realised it was wrong. The route climbed from the campsite. After walking in darkness for the first hour, I gradually became familiar with my environment as the sun crept over the peaks and bathed my world in a gentle light. The forest faded into a gritty soil as the mountains came down to meet me. To my left was a huge valley with snow-capped, towering peaks as a backdrop. The PCT wound and coiled its way up to the right, heading for a pass just south of Leavitt Lake. I assumed I would be able to see Highway 108 as I crested, but I couldn't. Not only did the elevation figures seem wrong, the distance did too. I walked along a wide ridge towards a notch, where I would cross over to the other side of the mountain flank and weave my way down to the road.

I passed a figure huddled in a sleeping bag a few feet from a 1,000-foot drop over the edge of Leavitt Peak, and walked up to say hello.

"Morning," I said softly.

"Morning! Who's that? Is that Fozzie?" came the muffled reply.

I recognised the scruffy, early-morning face of Swayze as he rubbed his eyes.

"Swayze!"

We exchanged a hearty handshake, as it was a few weeks since we had last met. Back then he was with Dinosaur, who I assumed originally was his girlfriend, and Scorpion had joined them at Tehachapi. However, he was camping alone.

"I heard Scorpion was not with you any more?" I said, prying for information.

"Yeah, she only wanted to do six-mile days, which obviously wasn't enough for us. Good to see you! I haven't seen you since Tehachapi. No! That's wrong! It was that spring around the 600-mile mark."

"It was the spring," I confirmed, having to think for a second. "There were a lot of people there. That's the last time I saw Stumbling Norwegian, Jake, the Israelis and a few others as well."

"You seemed in a hurry, Fozzie? You ate your lunch real quick and moved on."

I thought for a second.

"I was! I was trying to get to Ridgecrest to see a World Cup game. Big mistake. I did fifty-eight miles in two days and shredded my feet. I had to hole up for four days. That's probably where you got ahead of me. Where's Dinosaur?"

"She's camped up ahead maybe five miles, you should see her."

We shook hands again. I liked Swayze. He was laid back and never seemed in a hurry. I was curious about his trail name but never got around to asking him about it.

Indie was also in his sleeping bag by the side of the trail, a mile further on (it was still only around 5.30am at this point). I stopped and chatted to him also. He seemed in good spirits. I had a lot of time for him too.

It was great to constantly see familiar faces on the trail, and indeed new ones. I assumed I would always meet fellow hikers on the trail, or that they would catch me up, and so I had a certain expectation of who was where. I could, however, never rely on seeing someone again. For example, when I took the four days out in Ridgecrest, I imagined that perhaps those who had been near to me on the trail would thereafter be four days ahead, and I wouldn't bump into them again. It didn't work exactly like that; people took time out, some more than others, and so we were all always overlapping each other. Because these meetings were by chance, I tried to make the most of them; it could be the last time I saw that person. Swayze and Indie were classic examples. This would prove, regrettably, to be the last time I saw either of them.

I followed the ridge towards the notch and started to descend in the direction of the road, still a long way down. I could just make out Sardine Creek, teasing the back of my throat, as I was out of water. My thirst worsened, and I longed to reach the creek and drink from it. I crossed a couple of slushy snow banks, and finally reached the highway. I had done eleven miles, which felt more like twenty.

A few cars were scattered along the edge of the road, and Boy Scouts spilled out and formed a group on the other side, where their leader drilled them about the hike they were undertaking. I dropped my pack by the side of the road and tried to catch a ride, just before a blind summit. I figured vehicles would have to slow down here and I'd have a better chance. After an hour, my theory hadn't borne fruit, and I looked back at the Scout group moving up the trail to start the hike. The parents were slowly getting back into their cars, so I walked over.

"Hi," I said, trying my best to look tired, hungry and expectant. "I'm walking the Pacific Crest Trail and need to get to Bridgeport to re-supply and grab a shower. Is there any chance of a ride if you're going that way? But I should warn you that I stink." A little humour sometimes greased the wheels of kindness.

"Always happy to help someone who's walking the PCT," one of the mothers said. "If you can bear with me for five minutes then one of us can help you out. How bad exactly do you smell?" She smiled.

"It's pretty bad," I replied, shrugging my shoulders. "I can open the window, though."

An hour later, I was sitting in the Sportsman Inn tucking into breakfast. I made my way to the Bridgeport Inn and passed a small snack bar, where Nick and Chris, the other English guys on the PCT, were cramming in as many calories as possible. Cheeks and Mojave were also there, grinning cheekily, because they knew I was trying to figure out how they beat me there after leaving the campsite later than I had.

With all good intentions come a few surprises. I had intended to spend the day, as usual, re-supplying, eating and checking emails before getting back on trail the following day. If someone had told me then that the following day I would be sitting on the patio at my Uncle Tony's in San Jose with a cold beer, I would have shrugged off the suggestion as crazy.

Chapter 9
Light, Heat and Duff

Town? If I wanted to hang out in town, I could have stayed at home.
John 'Tradja' Drollette

My mobile service provider in the United States constantly claimed that their reception covered '97 per cent of all Americans.' I therefore put my almost total lack of signal strength down to the fact that I was English. I barely turned my mobile on; I didn't really need to. It was ready and waiting for me should I need it to call the emergency services, send an occasional message to another hiker or friend back home or, as I frequently did, call my service provider to top up.

Bridgeport didn't have any reception, but I had come to expect that. It was a sweet little place, though; walking from one end of town to the other took five minutes, and a smattering of history gave it some sort of purpose. It had some good eateries and a half-decent supermarket too. The Bridgeport Inn did need a touch more refinement, though, as there was no air conditioning, no TV and a shared bathroom, all for the princely sum of $73 per night including tax. There were other places to stay, but they cost even more, so I accepted the Inn for what it was.

I bumped into Steve Climber, Splizzard, Mr Green and Borders having breakfast at the Sportsman Inn. The conversation hovered around the prospect of thunderstorms lasting for four days. I peered out of the window and saw blue skies.

"Are you sure?" I asked Splizzard, who was twisting the

ends of his moustache to try to look like Hercule Poirot – as, for some reason, were the others.

"That's the forecast, coming in tomorrow. We're going up north to rest for a few days so we can ride it out."

Despite my eagerness to get some miles in, it did make sense to avoid the coming storm. I was accustomed to walking in the rain; I lived in England after all. However, I was due to meet Uncle Tony at Lake Tahoe, about seventy-six miles further on. The plan was for him to take me back to San Jose so that I could rest for a few days, have a good sort-out of my gear and get hold of a new, cooler sleeping bag. I reasoned that I may as well do all of that while the rain was pelting down. I called Tony who, bless him, said he'd leave the next morning and pick me up. This left me with a day to chill out and, for once, forget about the usual chores.

I bumped into a rather shaken-looking Burnie, who said she had walked to the highway at Sonora Pass in a thunderstorm.

"I've never been so scared, Fozzie," she said, still looking a little worse the wear from her experience. "Lightning was striking the ground all over the place. I thought I was finished."

She also told me that Cheeks and Mojave had left to face the bad weather, come what may. I felt a little guilty for taking time out and continued to worry about the distance I still had to walk. Going to San Jose was a big gamble; I had planned it from the outset, as a sort of mini-holiday to lighten my load, both physically and mentally. My ice axe would have been useful, but the worst of the snow was now behind me and I no longer needed my shoe spikes. My bear canister was still required for a few more miles, but I decided to ditch that as well and deal with questions from rangers if and when they arose. My new sleeping bag would make me a few grams lighter, too. New shoes were also on the list, and I was toying with switching to full-blown ankle-high hiking boots, which I hoped might see me through to the end and cope with any bad weather further north.

I returned to the Sportsman Bar in the evening, taking a seat behind a couple of feet of mahogany, with the sole intention of severe inebriation.

"Jack Daniels with ice, please," I said to Gordon, the owner.

"Can I see some ID, please?"

I looked at him, then at Brad and Steve, who were drinking next to me. They smiled, I sighed.

"I'm English; the only ID I have is my passport, which is back at the hotel. I would be more than happy to go and get it for you, but let me ask you a question first. I'm 43 years old. Why do you think I may be 21 or under?"

"I have to card virtually everyone in case there is an undercover agent in the bar," he replied.

This made me laugh, which probably didn't help my chances, but the idea that a sinister agent was lurking somewhere in the bar, checking up on drinkers, was funny. It was like Mulder and Scully were casting a wary eye over the place. I turned to Brad and Steve.

"Do I look under 21?"

They replied in unison to the negative. I turned back to Gordon.

"OK, if you really want me to go back and get my passport, then I can do that for you. I'm just here for some food, to watch some sport on the TV and enjoy the atmosphere. I will be drinking, probably too much but not enough to cause you any trouble. Do you want me to go and get my ID or can I please have a drink?"

"Gordon, give the English guy a drink, he's OK," Brad jumped in. Gordon sighed and poured me a JD with ice.

"Thanks," I said. "I'm an undercover agent and ... just kidding!"

He narrowed his eyes at me and sucked in some air, then smiled.

Brad continued to educate me about Californian drinking law. It is illegal to have an open bottle of alcohol in a vehicle; however, it is legal to have it in the boot. You can't take alcohol out of the bar, but it is OK to drink in the street on Independence Day or if the bottle is in a brown paper bag. This was familiar to me from the movies. The strange part was that if you do see someone in the street drinking from a container in a brown paper bag, then it's obviously alcohol! On the plus side, at least the law in California allows you to drink until 2am. In England people still get chucked out at 11pm.

This got me thinking – what other ridiculous laws had been

passed? After a little research, I can offer you these classic American laws. Don't feel left out if you want some English ones though; they're coming as well.

In New Mexico, females are strictly forbidden to appear unshaven in public. West Virginia states that children cannot attend school with their breath smelling of wild onions. In Oklahoma people can be fined, arrested or jailed for making ugly faces at a dog. If an elephant in Florida is left tied to a parking meter, the parking fee has to be paid just as it would for a vehicle. Citizens in Indiana are not allowed to attend a movie house or ride in a public streetcar within four hours of eating garlic. Finally, my personal favourite: in Louisiana it is illegal to rob a bank and then shoot at the bank teller with a water pistol.

As for Englanders like me? Well, we can offer some similarly bizarre rules. It *is* legal for a male to urinate in public, as long as it is on the rear wheel of his motor vehicle and his right hand is on that vehicle. Ladies can be arrested for eating chocolate on a public conveyance. Believe it or not, it is illegal to eat mince pies on the 25th of December (this is true!). It's said that a member of parliament may not enter the House of Commons wearing a full suit of armour. In Chester you can shoot a Welsh person with a bow and arrow inside the city walls if it's after midnight. Lastly, in London, a Hackney Carriage (otherwise known as a taxi) must carry a bale of hay and a sack of oats (this dates back to the days when taxis were drawn by horses).

Apparently there is a government department solely dedicated to scrutinising laws going back centuries, in order to revise or abolish them. Due to the sheer number of such idiosyncrasies still in existence, the task is supposedly huge, and this is why some of these classics are still actually enshrined in law.

***

Uncle Tony collected me the following day for the long drive back to San Jose. It was weird being in a car again for that length of time. We must have covered 600 miles that day. A distance that had taken me fifty-five days to walk flashed by in a few hours. I watched the scenery change as we travelled further north, and with the sun in my eyes I fell asleep.

I discovered the following day that Western Mountaineering, who made my sleeping bag, were actually based in San Jose. This was too good an opportunity to miss, so I called Gary Peterson, whom I had unsuccessfully emailed from England about sponsorship. He agreed to loan me a summer sleeping bag until I needed to revert to the warmer winter one again. I asked if I could come down to collect it, meet him and have a look around the factory, and he agreed.

It took a while for me to find the place, which was tucked up a back street in the older part of town, but Gary came out to meet me and took me through the manufacturing process. There were skilfully operated sewing machines everywhere, and rolls of material teetered on the end of benches for use in the finished articles. Western Mountaineering has an enviable reputation, not just in the United States, but worldwide. Best known for their down-filled insulation products, they produce sleeping bags, jackets, down trousers and a few other accessories. As I strolled around, the air was filled with escaping fluffs of down, floating around me like snow.

We discussed the options and settled on the Summerlite model, which was good down to freezing point and weighed a scant 539 grams. Western Mountaineering's Ultralite bag, which I had purchased in England, was a dedicated winter bag, good to around minus seven degrees Celsius and weighing in at 822 grams. Gary also presented me with a Flash Vest as a gift. This was a waistcoat filled with down, perfect for keeping the chill out. At a superlight 100 grams, I couldn't even feel the weight in my hand.

Three days whizzed past in San Jose, and before I knew it Uncle Tony was driving me back to Sonora Pass, with Rudy coming along for the ride. At the pass, as I strode off waving at them, I shouted that I'd see them in October. How wrong I would be!

My pack felt light; I estimated I was travelling about two kilos lighter. I tried to carry just one litre of water where possible. I had also left Click, my walking pole, behind as I now had a new pair of poles. My full-blown leather boots were heavy, but I hoped they would last the distance. It was great to be back on the trail again and I smiled as I made short work of the 600-foot climb. It was now late July and I knew I was bringing up the rear. While I never thought of the PCT as a race, I was painfully aware that I had to get moving. Imagining I was a middle-distance runner, I was just over halfway and the other athletes were pulling away from me. It was time to make my move and ease up the field.

The attacks from mosquitoes appeared to be fading away, as I had been told they would. The prevalence of granite was also decreasing, and a pinkish-grey rock tumbled down rolling green hills of lush grass. Meadow flowers were still painting their colours, and many lakes, rivers and creeks dotted the landscape.

Walker Texas Ranger and Dozer, taking a nap by the side of the trail, were startled when I rounded the corner. To be honest, I had forgotten Dozer's name, which is no reflection on him but on my failing memory. I didn't recognise Walker, as he was horizontal and his beard had sprouted alarmingly since we last saw each other at Kennedy Meadows.

"Hey, Fozzie, it's Dozer," he said helpfully, as he stood up to shake my hand.

"Good to see you again," I said. "Sorry, not good with names."

"Fozzie, it's Walker!"

"Mate, I didn't recognise you," I said apologetically, offering my hand. He refused it, which immediately made me think I had offended him at some point.

"Dude, I think I got Giardia," he said, with a resigned look on his face that suggested it was bound to happen at some point. I drew my palm back faster than England's exit from the World Cup. Walker admitted he had consumed untreated water from creeks high in the Sierras, thinking they would be safe. We all walked together for maybe ten minutes, before Walker stopped, opened his mouth and emptied out most of his stomach's contents. I hadn't seen so much vomit since Margaret Holloway threw up on the school canteen table when I was five years old.

"Dude, I think I just purged a demon," he said, wiping sick from his beard.

In spite of ourselves, Dozer and I couldn't hold back our

laughs. Unsympathetic, I know, but Walker was smirking as well.

"No, I'm serious," he continued. "I just performed an exorcism." He smiled as he tried to clear his nose as well.

"If you got a sense of humour, Walker, you're halfway through it," I suggested.

We walked slowly to the highway at Ebbetts Pass, where we sat by the side of the road cooking an evening meal. Dozer fired up his Jetboil and had his water boiling while I was still pouring alcohol into my stove. He knew I was a little envious of the speed of his stove, and smirked at me. By the time I was pouring a dehydrated chicken stew into my saucepan, he was clearing up.

Dozer and I tried to catch a lift for Walker, so that he could see a doctor in Lake Tahoe, but the road was empty. One guy did stop, but explained that he was going the other way. He offered to call someone who could help but Walker insisted that he could walk the twenty-four miles to town. We carried on, but after two miles he was finished. We camped together and somehow he managed to get some sleep. In the morning I again tried to get a ride to Lake Tahoe but failed so carried on walking. Walker, Dozer and I had all agreed to share a motel room there.

The morning was cold. I pulled up the zip around my neck, shivered and walked quickly to try to warm up. The meagre 400-foot ascent over a ridge known as the Nipple soon had me sweating, so I stopped at the summit and laid my head down for five minutes.

"This," I thought, "is the closest I've been to a nipple for some time."

I usually timed my sections during the day so that I could see my progress and, more importantly, keep tabs on my position. Here, though, I let that go. I knew it would be a long day getting to Highway 50 and maybe then catching a ride into town, and I didn't want to be reminded of it. The days pass more quickly when you don't know where you are and purposely losing track of mileage has the same effect.

I stopped for a break mid-morning and discovered that I only had one snack bar. I then realised I couldn't even cook rice, as my fuel had run out the previous evening. A walker travelling south tried to reassure me that I might at least get some water from the Carson Pass visitor centre, at the next road crossing.

"They don't have any food, though," he added, with a resigned look and outstretched palms.

I practiced my best hungry-and-thirsty expression as I entered the parking area, hoping that maybe someone would hand me a cold coke or something, but there were only cars and no people. I dejectedly slumped on a chair outside the visitor centre and started to rummage through my pack, in the hope of finding some long-forgotten morsel of peppered jerky cowering in the bottom. It was not to be.

"PCT hiker?"

I looked up to see a kind face belonging, I later learned, to a lady called Peggy Geelhaar, a volunteer at the centre.

"I am, yes," I said, smiling, but still looking sorry for myself.

"You want a soda, maybe something to eat?"

Before I could answer, she disappeared and came back with grapes and two apples. Perhaps my wide-open eyes, coupled with my tongue resting somewhere around my ankles, had already suggested I craved nourishment. She told me to help myself to a soda from the cool box and gave me some cheese. Her companion, Dan Quayle, sauntered down to the car and returned with a bear-sized pack of crisps. He apologised because the bag was swollen from the change in altitude it had suffered in its journey up the pass. As if I needed an apology.

"Don't forget to sign the visitors' book," Peggy said.

I wolfed down the goodies and looked at the visitors' book. Familiar hikers' names were scrawled, with the date and messages next to them. It was good to see that many of my friends were just a few days ahead, and I felt that I was making progress. I scanned the entries: Burnie had passed through three days previously, Answerman just before, Mojave and Cheeks were five days ahead, Bigfoot about a week, Jake was still in the mix and Stumbling Norwegian and HoJo were a good nine days in front.

'The trail will provide' was ringing in my ears as I carried on towards Lake Tahoe, thanking Peggy and Dan for their well-timed gifts.

However, during the afternoon, my spirits gradually fell back down, as I felt my new boots rubbing alarmingly on my left

The Last Englishman

small toe. The road to Lake Tahoe was about three hours further ahead, so I had little choice other than to push on. I thought that I needed to remove the offending boot and check my toe, but also knew it would be difficult getting it back on and having to endure the five-minute hobble. It hurt like hell. Although in the grand scheme of things it was a minor problem, I let it get to me and ended up surprising myself by crying. Such a swing of emotions, from positive at lunchtime to negative a couple of hours down the trail! My feet had returned to shipshape, only for blisters to rear their ugly heads again. I would probably have to stop for longer than I had hoped in Tahoe to deal with them. This would in turn put me further behind schedule.

Full-blown leather hiking boots are notoriously difficult to break in and are best worn for many short walks, slowly building up to longer distances. Of course, I did not have that luxury, and I'd given my choice much deliberation. I decided to send the boots back when I reached Tahoe and secure a new pair of Montrails, which seemed to suit my feet.

I eventually reached the highway and hobbled to a halt. Easing off the left boot, I saw a blister, filled with blood and on the verge of bursting, on the top of my little toe, and another nasty one on the next toe. I switched to my Crocs, and stuck out a hopeful thumb at passing vehicles. After thirty minutes watching cars zoom past, I saw a familiar yellow taxi cruising up the hill with its light on and virtually stood in the middle of the road to hail it.

I turned on my mobile when we reached the outskirts and heard a voicemail from Dozer saying he and Walker were both in the Best Western. Walker was lying on the bed looking quite pale, having seen a doctor and had confirmation that he was suffering from Giardiasis. He was on medication and was confident he would be back on the trail in a couple of days.

I slowly peeled off my boots, closed one eye and pushed a needle into the blister. A yellow and red liquid oozed out and dribbled down my toe. I cut off the surrounding skin to reveal a tender wound, which I knew would take a couple of days just to dry out. Less severe blisters wouldn't have stopped me, but this one needed time to heal at least a little, and that meant getting air to it. I bathed the toes in a strong Epsom salt solution and hoped for a rapid recovery.

For a while, I relaxed with Dozer and Walker. Jack Straw knocked on the door, followed by Scorpion, Crow and Dundee, who also made themselves at home. With the room getting crowded, I limped up to town and went to the local outdoor store to look at the footwear options. The Montrails I had worn before were not available, but there was another version, which were lighter, more cushioned and seemed more of a running shoe. They felt wonderful, so I bought them and sent the other boots back to REI in San Jose. REI is the major outdoor retailer in the United States and they have a brilliant returns policy. They will refund anything purchased from them with absolutely no questions asked. That system might be abused at times, but presumably REI are big enough to swallow the odd return. A few days later I received a full credit to my bank account.

Pockets was in the room when I returned. I was surprised that he had made up the time so fast, which also reminded me of my own slow progress. It was great to see him again, though. He was with a woman called Courtney, whom he had met in Wrightwood, and who had driven up to see him and to walk a section of the PCT. The five of us relaxed in the evening watching movies and eating as much Ben and Jerry's as our stomachs would allow.

I spent a further three days in Lake Tahoe allowing my blister to heal as much as possible. Walker, amazingly, left two days after he had arrived, so I moved to a different motel. Dozer had left me the number of a guy who had given them both a ride back to the trailhead, and when I called him he said he would be happy to take me back too.

Back on trail I reached Echo Lake, stopped for a quick drink and carried on skirting the water. A ranger coming the other way stopped me. He struck me as quite young, and had an air of authority.

"You hiking the PCT?" he said, looking me up and down.

"Yes, I am."

"Do you have your permit, please?"

All thru-hikers on the PCT have to carry a thru-hiking permit. As many of the areas and national parks en route require separate permits, the PCT Association offers one permit that covers the entire length. I had applied for mine at the kick-off party in Lake Morena. I duly handed it over. He asked me if I was carrying my bear canister. I wasn't; I had left it in San Jose because I wouldn't need it much longer.

"Yes," I lied, tapping the side of my rucksack where I knew a hard plastic bottle was lurking, hoping this would fool him.

"Be sure to use it, please," he ordered, and walked off.

I hate being told what to do, almost as much as I hate being told what I can't do. I do have a problem with authority. I don't know where it stems from, but I treat anyone in uniform with suspicion and perhaps unfair disdain. I don't get on with the police and customs officers are my worst nightmare. I had met several rangers thus far, many of them living at ranger huts in the forest. All were welcoming, pleasant to converse with and helpful. If it had not been for their uniform, I would have probably not even have known they were rangers. This guy was different, though. He seemed to revel in his position and almost look down on me, which riled me and made me a little short with him. In any case, I resented having to carry a permit, even though it was free. From what I gleaned from other hikers, permits were introduced so that the United States Forestry Service could monitor the number of people in certain parks and areas, and make some money. This land, although owned by someone, I regarded as free. To have to register and pay to venture in to it annoyed me.

Hikers also had to apply for a Fire Permit before starting. This particular ranger checked for that too. The online application process included a few simple questions about what and what not to do when having a campfire. Passing the test was easy; information containing the answers was supplied with the test. But I did learn a few things. For one, all flammable material should be cleared around the fire, to a distance of five feet (this assumes there is not an existing fire ring, which is quite often the case; if so, this should be utilised to prevent further scarring). A shovel is to be used for clearing, and said shovel also helps with extinguishing campfires. A 'responsible' (other multiple choice descriptions were 'happy', 'reputable' and 'busy') person should be in attendance at all times. To put the fire out, separate any burning pieces of wood with the shovel, then drown the fire with water, stirring with the shovels to produce a sticky mess. This is known as the 'drown, stir and feel' method (other answers were 'shake, rattle and roll,' 'hit or miss' and 'cut and run'). Once we had answered the questions correctly, we could print off a permit.

The main cause of camp fires was something known as duff. Duff, I learned, is the decomposing layer of vegetation under the leaves and on top off the dirt. It isn't highly flammable and its air supply is restricted by the leaves, so it can smoulder for days from a stray ember. Once enough heat has built up, it can break free and start a fire. One thing I always tried to do was clear an area around the fire, removing the duff by getting down to the dirt underneath, and I always poured water over the finished fire and stirred with a stick. I never met a hiker or indeed anyone else who had a shovel; they were simply too bulky, and besides, we could use our feet to clear the area and a stick to stir in the water.

I never had a fire in desert land; there was no need, as it was warm enough already and there wasn't anything to burn. Once in the forest, and especially at elevation, a fire provides warmth, light, some mosquito protection, heat for cooking, a signal to others if they need company, and – maybe most of all – a boost to morale. To sit and watch a fire burn is a great way to relax. It also dries out wet shoes and clothes (and indeed sometimes burns them!) Often I would be camping with a few others when a strong smell of burning plastic would waft over, followed by a stampede of hikers converging on the fire and pulling their shoes away from the flames.

The warmth factor was what appealed most to me. Up in the Sierras, and during the latter stages of my hike, the temperature would drop many degrees below freezing. I was always warm in my sleeping bag, but sitting around before bedtime was a chilly affair. I would perhaps write my journal in the light, and often just sit and stare into the flames. There is something deeply mesmerising about looking into a fire, watching the oranges fluctuate with reds and the ambers blend into the greys, and seeing patterns or sometimes even faces.

Mosquitoes dislike the smoke from fires and they're not fond of the wind either. The only true way of using smoke to ward them off was to sit properly in the smoke, eye-watering though that could be. And naturally enough, wind direction would always have a habit of wafting the smoke over you when you didn't want it to. It was amusing watching others around a fire as they ducked, stooped and leant to avoid the pesky fumes.

Natural light from a fire allowed us hikers to chat without shining our head torches into each other's faces. The beams were only a few feet long, but they were bright enough.

Obvious though it is, many, myself included, didn't cook on a fire until we saw others doing so. One disadvantage is the tendency of the cooking pot to get caked in a sticky mix of soot, small pieces of twig and pine resin. This put me off at first, and I used my alcohol stove; but the more fires I lit, the more often I cooked over them. It saved weight, to the tune of maybe 500 grams of stove fuel per week. I could also cook more adventurous meals with the almost limitless heat available from a fire. For example, I could make several cups of tea instead of just one (an Englishman must have his tea) and still have plenty of hot water to clean up with afterwards. After a re-supply in town, I would often treat myself to fresh meat or a jacket potato. A couple of sausages suspended over the embers with a potato wrapped in some tin foil (I always kept a small piece of foil somewhere), or some corn, would round off the day splendidly.

Fire is a real danger on the trail, though. On the PCT, we were at times reminded of the power of fire – several sections are merely burnt-out shells. Fires dating back to the eighties still leave their scar on the land. The trees have yet to fully grow back and wide expanses of shorter vegetation remain. More recent blazes have resulted in a stark landscape of black soil and white trees where the bark has burnt away to reveal the trunks underneath. These fire-ravaged places were like a bizarre fantasy land, where no life existed except for mythical, lurking creatures. One severe forest fire over a couple of days can take years to recover from. Although it was educational to see such sights, I longed for the greener spaces.

Many fires are started by lightning strikes, and little can be done to prevent those. Careless hikers can also cause fires; at Apache Peak in southern California, for example, I learnt of a fire accidently started by a thru-hiker who spilt some fuel.

I was camped one evening with HoJo and Ben on a plateau in the desert. I cleared a bit of grass away to set my stove on the ground. As I held my lighter over the fuel, a trickle that I had unwittingly spilled also ignited. In a second, the grass had caught fire. I didn't panic, but I screamed to the others a couple of seconds later when the fire began spreading like, well, wildfire. They sprinted over and we dowsed the flames. They both then realised in dismay that their carefully filtered two litres or so of water would have to be replenished.

Chapter 10
Ghosts on the Trail

*This world is too cynical, greedy and self-serving for me.
I'd rather be poor and work from trip to trip than die rich.
We take none of our possessions to the grave, but
hopefully God grants us our memories.*
David 'Walker Texas Ranger' Allen

I made quick progress from Lake Tahoe and awoke to a chilly morning and a tent damp from overnight rain. As I peered through the hills, I could just make out the lake flanked by mountains. She glinted back at me as an upturned feather of mist floated above. It was quiet, vegetation glistened from the rain as it caught the rising sun, and drops gently plopped from trees on to my head. I had managed an early start at 7am, eager as before to make up for lost time.

I concentrated on my breathing, as I had learnt from yoga. Expanding the abdomen muscles when I inhaled and pulling them in on the exhale forced more air into my lungs. As I gingerly walked along tight ridges, I marvelled at the beauty of the vista below me. Even after 110 days walking, my environment still had the capacity to pleasantly surprise me. The mountains and forests I saw every day made me feel honoured.

It was now the second week of August. The first thru-hikers were about a month away from finishing, but from Canada down through Washington, Oregon and northern California, a long line of walkers stretched out before me. It was amazing to think that I was still in California. The Californian section of the PCT is around 1,700 miles long. That is a full 500 miles more than Land's End to John O'Groats. My current target was Oregon, another 530 miles distant. Soon I might reach that little solitary tree, by the trailside, with a wooden sign nailed to its trunk marking the state line. Then, I thought, I'd know I was on my way. After that, I had a mere 455 miles to my next goal, Washington State, and then a paltry 495 miles until the end of my journey. I wasn't even halfway; completing the PCT was a daunting thought. Nevertheless, this is what I had come out here to do, and I was excited to be doing it. Many people, after all, can only dream of being so connected to the beautiful outdoors for that period of time.

I reached the Peter Grubb Hut, a haven for those caught out in the elements. It was vast inside, with a large kitchen and eating area, a smaller, cosier room to the side with an open fire and a sleeping room upstairs. For the very first time, I tucked into a peanut butter and jam sandwich, which met with my full approval. Given my love for peanut butter I was amazed I had not sampled this mix before. I perused the trail register and saw that Pockets had left a message the day before.

"Foz! Catch up. I wrecked my tent, got a great story for you!"

I was intrigued, so I wolfed down the rest of my lunch and set off, hoping to catch him that day. Steve Climber had also stayed at the hut, with a few others. It would have made a great place to spend the night, but it was only midday so I kept moving.

I saw no-one for the rest of the day, so I set up tent on a flat spot to one side of the trail, just below the pinnacle of a long ascent. A builder working down in the valley stopped on his quad bike and chatted for a while. He had to come all the way up to the top of the hill for reception to make a mobile call. I optimistically turned my phone on to check for messages, to be greeted with the familiar sight of 'No Service' on the screen.

I made a fire, cooked and turned in for the night. Much later, I recognised the grunting and sniffing of a bear. I had brushed my teeth perhaps fifty feet from my tent, but evidently the scent had been detected. I slammed the ground and shouted, and heard the bear thunder off into the forest. From the reverberations, I thought it must have been a fair size. Thirty minutes later it was back, in the same area, and again I made some noise and again it charged off. It returned once more, and this time a hard blow on my emergency whistle seemed to do the trick. I lay still, listening. I looked at my watch, which said 4am. The forest was deathly quiet; no wind, no animals stirring, and I was miles from the nearest road.

"What are you doing here?!" a woman's voice screamed at me, from literally three feet to one side of the tent. Still awake listening for the bear, I sat bolt upright, my heart pulling at my chest. I started shaking, and tried to focus on the weak moonlight coming through the canvas to get my bearings.

"What do you mean what am I doing here?" I shouted. "What are *you* doing here!?"

It was silent again. I unzipped the tent and peered out. There was no-one there. I didn't sleep at all until the sun rose, when I emerged from the tent. The first thing I noticed was the amount of twigs and sticks on the ground. It struck me that nobody could have approached the tent without making a noise. What the hell was a woman doing at that time of morning, creeping up on hikers? The man from the previous evening stopped again on his bike, and I told him what had happened, feeling rather stupid.

"Oh, I'm not surprised," he replied. "Depends on your beliefs really, but this area is littered with old and derelict homesteads from the first pioneers who tried to make a living here. It's not the first time someone has told me that they have heard voices in the forest at night."

"You mean a ghost?" I asked, astonished.

"Like I say, it depends on your beliefs." We shook hands, he wished me good luck and sped to the summit to make another phone call.

I walked for a couple of hours, and filled up with water at Haypress Creek. I knew Pockets was ahead of me – unlikely as it may seem, hikers can recognise each other's footprints. Crossing a small logging track, I stopped to adjust my pack and was startled, not for the first time that day, by footsteps behind me. I spun round to see Courtney standing there, smiling at me.

"Where the hell did you come from?" she asked, laughing.

"Where the hell did *you* come from?" I replied.

"I just stopped for water back there. Pockets is up ahead – he said if he stopped he would leave his trekking poles by the side of the trail."

"Let's go catch him, then."

Only a few hundred feet further, the poles were indeed by the trail.

"Pockets!" I cried out.

"Fozzie! Up here, mate!"

I ducked through the trees to an opening, and saw him on top of a small rise. His camera was set up on a tripod and he was taking a time lapse of the passing clouds.

"Hey mate, how's it going?"

"Good, didn't expect to catch you so quick. I was only at the Peter Grubb Hut yesterday."

"Yeah, I've been taking a lot of photos; great clouds about, and Courtney walks a little slower, so I've been keeping with her."

"What the hell did you do to your tent?" I asked.

"Dude, you will not believe the story I got for you!"

Courtney arrived, smiling as she had already heard his version, and shook her head.

"It's so far out that you *have* to believe it!"

I took out my Dictaphone to record the conversation, and settled down on the ground.

"Pockets, go."

"OK, just as a sort of intro, a few years back I had camped in a slot canyon, a flash flood hit me and the tent and washed us away. I was OK but a bit shaken. Anyway, erm, after I went over Barkers Pass and I was hiking along that big ridgeline by the ski lifts and everything – you know where I mean?"

"I do," I said, adjusting my position to get more comfortable. When Pockets told a story it went on forever. This was a good thing, though.

"Well, this storm was rolling in and it looked bad, really bad. I started to run along the ridgeline until it began to drop off. There was switchback after switchback and I also needed water. So, I get all the way to the bottom and set up my tent just before it starts to rain. I eat, chill out a bit and take it easy. I go to sleep right about eight thirty. At nine it starts to pour, lightning and thunder, it was going crazy. I dozed off somehow and started to dream."

"No shit?" I said. "You, dreaming?" I looked over at

Courtney, who started giggling.

"I know! What must have happened was that I put my hand down on the groundsheet and there was a small puddle from the rain. This started me dreaming that I was back at the slot canyon in the flash flood and I must have started to try and get out of the tent. In the process I think I must have knocked the pole over and the tent collapsed on me. The canvas was right on my face so I started biting it to get out."

"Are you serious?" I asked.

"Yes! I can piece this shit together after the event. So I keep biting and biting until I finally make a hole in it, grab this with both hands, tear it open wider until I can get my upper body through it. Remember, I'm still dreaming here, I'm still asleep. I grab the ground because I think I'm going to get washed away. Then the rain wakes me up. It's pitch black and I'm in the woods. I'm like, 'What the fuck?' I look down and see what I've done to the tent and I'm just sitting there with my torso poking through the hole in the canvas with the rest of the tent lying on the ground around me."

Courtney was now shaking with the giggles, and I was laughing hard at the absurdity of it all. Pockets continued.

"I had to spend the rest of the night poking out with my umbrella up! I had done a thirty-four-mile day and was really tired, didn't sleep at all. I even called the guys at Tarptent and they believed me! He's sending out a new tent!"

Pockets's story was so unimaginable that I could do little else but believe it. He ran off to Highway 49 to get a ride into Sierra City, where he needed to find the post office before it closed, so I carried on with Courtney and we agreed to meet him there. We had heard great things about the Red Moose Café, run by Bill and Margaret Price. Camping was free in their back yard, and the food was apparently not to be missed.

Courtney was twenty-eight and came from Troy, Michigan. She claimed she could trace part of her ancestry back to the First Nations, and her features gave some indication of this: black hair braided in pigtails, skin a subtle brown. She was taking the summer off before starting as a Ski Patrol member in September, back in Wrightwood. She was tall and attractive, and I could see why Pockets had taken a shine to her. It was not going as smoothly as she would have liked, however. Pockets was also beginning to realise that he needed to put in some miles before the snow fell up north. He walked quickly anyway, a little faster than my usual coasting speed, but it didn't bother me; in fact, I liked it because I also clocked up more miles when we walked together. Courtney, though, was becoming a little frustrated, not to mention fatigued, trying to keep up. She had only joined him for a short section, and we were now in great physical shape, which wasn't helping her. I think there was also some friction because she didn't know where she stood in the relationship; I got the impression she didn't even know if there *was* a relationship.

We reached the highway, and I did my usual chivalrous act: I placed Courtney by the side of the road, suggested she show a little leg and I loitered by the bushes. She started signalling to cars going in the opposite direction to Sierra City.

"It's that way!" I pointed.

"I know!" she retorted. "But you never know, there's no harm in trying!"

I watched, amazed, as a BMW driving out of town pulled up, turned round and offered her a lift. I went over and got in as well, thanking him and congratulating her on a job well done. I made a mental note to keep a skirt handy for my own future hitchhiking attempts.

We peered cautiously into the Red Moose and Bill looked over.

"Come in!" he said. "Upstairs, everyone is upstairs."

We walked into the lounge on the first floor.

"Fozzie! Dude!" Dozer came over, and hugs were dispensed all round. Walker Texas Ranger was also there, along with Jack Straw and Pockets, who had somehow made it to the post office in time.

Sierra City was a small village with a population of just over 200. First settled in 1850, it was destroyed during the winter of 1852-53 by an avalanche. It remained in this state for several years, before being rebuilt and earning a crust from several gold mines established in the area. I look back on the place with fond memories. There wasn't much there: the Red Moose Café, opposite it the Buckhorn restaurant and down the road the local store, providing us with a reasonable re-supply and some substantial burgers. The town was surrounded by pine forest and the sheer, looming Sierra Buttes. It was relaxed, quiet and a super place to hang out.

We all went down to the bar in the evening. Bill and Margaret revealed a little about the Red Moose, how they ran things and a bit of local gossip to boot.

First we learnt that we couldn't camp in the garden. Some of the residents had complained about the tents and hikers, whom they referred to as 'vagrants'. True, many thru-hikers had given up their homes, so could be considered as homeless, unemployed wanderers. But we didn't wander idly, I felt; nor did we deserve the stigma attached to the word 'vagrant' in the minds of many people, especially town folk, who simply don't understand the appeal of walking 2,650 miles. As for the notion that PCT thru-hikers are a bunch of soiled misfits who smell, drink too much and demand unreasonable discounts on accommodation and food, well, I agree wholeheartedly!

The local paper, the *Mountain Messenger*, had printed a reader's letter, in the Sheriff's Blotter column, in a typically complaining vein:

'Monday August 22nd. A transient was seen hanging around the campground.'

The sheriff's office had replied by saying:

'In our experience most of those in campgrounds are transient.'

This made me laugh. The reader had clearly used the word 'transient' for emotive effect; like 'vagrant', the word has negative connotations, perhaps unfair. I emailed the paper to point this out; Don Russell, the editor, said that he was just having a cheap shot at the sheriff's description.

Trying at least for now to placate their neighbours, Bill and Margaret asked us not to camp, instead offering their lounge and balcony. They were a terrific couple; welcoming and helpful to a fault. Karma and Detective Bubbles, a couple of thru-hikers who had ended their hike in Sierra City, were also staying at the place on a permanent basis and helping to run it.

Margaret explained that she and Bill had a small claim to land, and that they indulged their hobby for gold mining;

although by 'mining' she meant a filtering machine that they placed in the creek bed. She asked me if I knew how heavy gold was. I replied that I had never really given it much thought. She opened an envelope containing some small fragments they had found, and placed a piece about the size of half a peanut in my hand. I was taken aback at its mass, and handed it round to the others.

She also filled me in on who had already passed through. Cheeks and Mojave had visited, departed, consequently returned and then finished their hike. I was despondent when I heard this as they were some of the first hikers I had become acquainted with. Apparently, Mojave had stepped on a nail which went in about an inch on her instep. Veering on the side of caution they went to Reno where a doctor advised the wound was fine but would take about three weeks to heal, which turned out to be a pretty accurate estimate. They both decided this was too long to wait, would put them too far behind schedule and deplete their funds sitting and waiting. They cut their losses and went home.

Dinner at the Red Moose Café was an absolute feast. We lined the bar, waiting in anticipation, as plate after plate of ribs kept coming. Mashed potato and sweet corn made up any spare room on our plates, and there was complete silence for thirty minutes as the six of us demolished an obscene amount of food. We were charged only a modest fee, which I remember thinking could have barely covered the cost of the ingredients. Afterwards we went to the Buckhorn Restaurant for some drinks.

We had been warned about the Buckhorn. The proprietor was not too fond of thru-hikers, and although we would be served, the welcome may not be too generous. We ventured over out of curiosity, and because we were all dying for a drink.

The owner, Joanne, said hello as we entered, and provided the first confirmation that the rumours were correct.

"Perhaps you would all like to sit outside?" she offered. I took this as a hint rather than an invitation. We all declined and once again lined up at the bar, ordering a good amount of alcohol, but drinking sensibly and behaving ourselves. Joanne remained pleasant enough for the rest of the evening, but a certain noticeable tension remained.

The following day, Courtney, Pockets and I went back to the Buckhorn for lunch. To be fair to the place, the garden was a great place to hang out. We were served by Joanne's daughter, Sierra, and we all went for the good old-fashioned hiker staple of burger and fries. Sierra was polite, the service was prompt and the food excellent. The three of us were beginning to wonder where the bad rumours had come from; until we asked for the bill, that is.

"Can we have separate bills, please?" Courtney asked.

Sierra sighed and looked rudely skyward.

"Well, no. You should have told me at the start. I'm not going to rewrite the bill now, so you can't."

She stormed off to the kitchen. We all looked at each other in astonishment. I had to go back to the Red Moose to send some emails. I left my share of the bill, and the others returned shortly afterwards and filled me in on what happened.

"It was unbelievable," Pockets said. "We went into the bar and I asked her nicely if we could have separate bills because we wanted to pay separately. She did her huffy puffy routine again and said, 'I don't have time for this, I really don't have time for this.' Joanne took over and sorted it for us."

Despite the PCT sign on the window suggesting hikers were welcome, I think a better idea would have been 'Hikers *not* welcome'. The staff obviously harboured a dislike for us, and we would have been better off going to the store for lunch.

I slept on the balcony that night, but awoke in the morning to a little sweet return. Snoozing occasionally, I rolled over and peered through the wooden railings towards the Buckhorn. Joanne had just arrived for work and was unlocking the door. Sierra slowly plodded along the path in her footsteps and, thinking no-one could see her, proceeded to pick her nose and scratch her arse in one beautiful, synced unison. Imminent revenge was a joy to behold.

"Morning Sierra!" I called out, motioning to her nose. "Anything good up there?"

To say she gave the most evil glare ever dished out in northern California would be a big understatement. She gave me the finger and disappeared inside. It took ten minutes for me to stop giggling.

Pockets was waiting for some new trekking poles to be delivered to the post office, so he had to take a zero. I followed suit, as Sierra City was nice and relaxing. Brains, another thru-hiker, arrived; and Hawkeye, who was walking the PCT in sections, also turned up to sample the delights of the Red Moose.

Walker, Dozer and Jack Straw had already left, so Courtney, Brains, Hawkeye, Pockets and I chilled out in the lounge that evening. Hawkeye was full of stories, especially about Sasquatch. Also known as Bigfoot, this huge, hairy biped is the subject of countless stories. Thought to be between six and ten feet high, ape-like in appearance and weighing an estimated 230 kilos, this beast is most commonly thought to lurk in the Pacific Northwest, where we were heading. The legend fascinated me. Pockets was also riveted, and he admitted to me later that it was his ambition to photograph the creature.

Scientists claim Bigfoot is a mixture of folklore, misidentification and hoax. This is standard practice for the scientific world, to assume the non-existence of something if it can't be proved. In my book, though, if something can't be proved, it's intriguing. Scientists argue that a species must exist in numbers sufficient to sustain a breeding population. Or, put simply, if Sasquatch does exist, there must be more of them; and if there are, then there would have to be more evidence. I fully understand the sceptical view, but I'm also a sucker for a legend, myth or story that the scientific world can't explain.

Before the 1950s the Bigfoot phenomenon was just a series of stories. However, in 1951, the British mountaineer Eric Shipton photographed what he described as a Yeti footprint. The public's interest was then captured, and the legend started to grow. In 1958, in the area of a road construction site at Bluff Creek in California, several large footprints were reported. Gerald Crew, a bulldozer operator, decided the prints warranted further examination, especially given the lack of interest in their discovery. A cast was made of the prints, and the subsequent photographs appeared in the *Humboldt Times*. This, in turn, fuelled speculation until the story was picked up by the Associated Press.

The most famous film footage allegedly of the beast surfaced in 1967, when Roger Patterson and Robert Gimlin released what they claimed was decisive proof of Bigfoot, taken near Bluff Creek in California. However, the two later admitted that Bob Heironimus, a friend of Patterson, had worn an ape costume.

In 2007, Rick Jacobs, a hunter, captured an image triggered by a motion camera he had left in the Allegheny National Forest, Pennsylvania. He claimed this was Sasquatch, although experts thought it showed nothing more sinister than 'a bear with a severe case of mange'.

Many cryptozoologists claim that up to eighty or ninety per cent of sightings are not real. This raises the obvious and interesting implication that ten to twenty per cent *are* real. Another possibility is that Bigfoot was a close relative of Gigantopithecus, whose fossils have been found in China. Migration across the Bering land bridge from China to America could have taken place, but no fossils of a biped similar to Bigfoot have ever been found in America.

After discussing the topic with Pockets and Brains, we decided that our next adventure after the PCT would be a Sasquatch hunt. Pockets would do photography, Brains would be responsible for securing and flying a radio-controlled helicopter with an infra-red camera, while I would document and write about the expedition.

To fuel my Sasquatch appetite in the morning, I surfed the web for more information. I had also received an email from a company called Backpackinglight in Denmark. The owner, Niels Overgaard Blok, had been reading my blog and noticed my alarming habit of damaging sunglasses: I dropped them, sat on them, and on one occasion just plain forgot them. Niels was the Danish distributor for a company called Numa Sports Optics, based in Arizona. They claimed their shades were unbreakable. Niels said he'd be happy to send me a pair in return for a little advertising space, and I readily agreed. We arranged for them to be shipped ahead. As for the chances of my losing them, I figured that I'd take a lot more care with them than with an average-price pair of shades. As it turned out, they stayed with me for the rest of my hike, and I still use them now.

I also gained another sponsor. Brains had been walking in a kilt made by a company called Sportkilt in California. In fact, I had seen several guys walking in them. Pockets had started from

Mexico wearing one, but lost a waist size, so switched to shorts. Everyone spoke highly of kilts; the air circulation around one's undercarriage was reason enough to try one. Brains had suggested Sportkilt the previous day, so I tried my luck and emailed them. They arranged for one to be sent to me in a fabric pattern called Blackwatch. I was excited; it's always great to get stuff for free.

Courtney had decided to return to Wrightwood. She had discussed the situation with Pockets and thought it best if she went back. I reluctantly left Sierra City with him and Brains, and we formed a loose group over the ensuing days. Sometimes we walked together, sometimes one of us had a burst of speed and went ahead, but we usually ended up camping together. They both walked faster than I did, but I was comfortable with their pace, and it meant I could cover a couple more miles in a day.

I cautiously peered down at the Feather River a couple of hundred feet below me, from a bridge spanning a chasm. It was good to camp near water; the mosquitoes were not as prolific as in previous weeks, so we could hang around a river or creek in the evening without fear of too many bites. Hawkeye had left a note on the trail saying that he had found a nice camp spot by the bank, so I ducked and weaved through the undergrowth until I found him. I stripped off and lowered myself into calm waters, sheltered by a few boulders above the surface. I washed some clothes, took half an hour to appreciate the opportunity to get clean and then sat on a rock drying off.

"Fozzie! Fozzie! Look what I got!"

I turned my head to see Pockets skipping over rocks like a nine-year-old, with something wrapped around his forearm. I couldn't make it out.

"What you got, Pockets?"

"Look mate, it's a rattler!"

In the split second that it took my eyes to send a signal to my brain, Reginald at Nerve Centre HQ decided to have a severe fit. In a matter of milliseconds he had discarded a few first-responses, ranging from "Back off quickly" to "Keep a safe distance" and eventually let rip with a simple but effective "Get the fuck out of there".

At first I didn't believe Pockets, but as the reptile merged into focus, Reginald's advice hit home.

"Pockets, get that thing away from me! Are you nuts?!"

"Fozzie! It's OK, I killed it! Look, no head!"

Sure enough, a bloody stump was all that remained. The eerie part was that the body was still writhing about and curling around his wrist. It made me cringe just to look.

I found Pockets's behaviour curious. One minute he was merrily hopping along like a kid, the next he was mischievously creeping up behind me. And at first he seemed happy to have scared me, but when he saw that I was genuinely soiling myself, he showed real concern.

Pockets explained later that, as he stepped over a log, the snake had struck the sole of his shoe. Taking exception to this, he turned round, waved his hand to get the culprit's attention and then punched it on the head with his other hand. Having stunned it, he picked it up and killed it with a quick slice of his knife behind the critter's head. I watched as he skinned, gutted and prepared the beast for the fire. Even when we placed the meat over some embers, it was still moving. My second taste of rattlesnake was just as delicious as the first.

Pockets had a seemingly bottomless pit of energy. The way he chomped at the bit and then tried to rein himself back was hilarious. He was the last to get up in the morning, but bloody hell, when he was up, he really was up.

His pace was faster than mine, but he never looked in a hurry. He often had to stop for photographic work; he had a PCT photo-story deal with *Backpacker* magazine. He sometimes stayed in one spot for an hour or so. He would see artistic potential in trees, skies, water, snow; places that wouldn't even occur to me as good photo opportunities. After burning off extra energy this way, he'd run off a few more calories by upping the pace to catch up with me or Brains.

Then he'd play his games. I think, in retrospect, Pockets just came up with the most simplistic idea that would amuse him, and offload a little more of that energy. Sometimes, Brains and I would be walking through a forest and he'd jump out, growling loudly. Most of the time I found it funny, but if I was tired, it annoyed me.

And to this day I still can't figure out how, when I was

convinced I was ahead of him, he would appear in front of me, and when I was sure he was in front of me he'd pop out from a tree behind me. He did this several times in one day, too; I started to think he was some sort of PCT ninja.

In town he just went crazy. We didn't usually need a TV in our hotel rooms: Pockets laid on his own cabaret. A regular act consisted of him opening the back window and barking. Within seconds, half of the canine population within a mile would go completely bananas. After a while they'd calm down a little, leaving just a couple of dogs still yapping. Then, trying different types of bark, Pockets would try to have a genuine conversation with them. Seriously.

Then he'd start with the cats...

At one motel I was sitting on the outside porch with Brains, having a cigarette and supping on a Pale Ale, when the door was flung open. Pockets stepped out completely naked, hands covering his genitals, and cried:

"Come on boys, get inside! I haven't finished with you yet!"

Brains's normal reaction, as was mine, was to hold his head in his hands and deny any association with him.

His other favourite prank was to wait until Brains or I were asleep and get the other person to take a photo of the slumbering one, while he stood in the frame, his back towards the camera, flexing his muscles, with his shorts dropped. And using someone else's camera. I can't tell you how many times I checked my shots at day's end to find a picture of me or Brains fast asleep with two buttocks in clear view.

Alluringly insane, Pockets was certainly the wild card of the group, and perhaps of the entire PCT.

Brains, on the other hand, was a little more laid back, very intelligent and usually had an interesting point of view to share. He seemed to know a lot about everything, which kept me on my intellectual guard.

We would regularly sit outside smoking when we stayed at a motel, and a ten-minute cigarette break quite often became a thirty-minute chat.

Brains was originally from Long Island, New York. He grew up in a suburb of New York City and used to ride the train into Manhattan, Queens or Brooklyn whenever he could. He moved west when he was eighteen, and had been moving ever since. Illinois, Utah, Nevada, California, Colorado and North Carolina all lured him, and he would find work, stay for a while and then move on.

Sitting outside a motel during one of our smoking sessions, I asked Brains why he was hiking the PCT. I didn't normally ask that; it was too common a question. Something told me he had a different story to tell, though.

"Fozzie, there are two main reasons why I am on the trail," he began. "First, I wasn't comfortable with where my life had taken me, and I was utterly bored with it. Exactly the same thing day after day. Get up, go to work, come home, watch TV, go to sleep, wake up and do it all over again. I wanted a challenge, the bigger the better."

"And the second reason?" I pushed him.

"Well, that could be classed as a little controversial, I guess. I am expecting Western civilisation to crumble. The greed, corruption and graft displayed by the ruling powers is astonishing. I have been paying attention for a while and noticed things were getting in a terrible state, so I started to save money. Sure enough, the financial sector melted and then brought the whole world to the brink. I figure it's just a matter of time until someone, somewhere, makes an irreversible decision and then the banks, corporations and governments will fall."

"I feel that way sometimes as well, mate. Do you really think we're heading that way?" I asked.

"Yes, I'm sure. Anyway, this leads me to why I am hiking the PCT. I thought that if I hiked the trail, it would give me some skills that I would need in the future. Skills like wood lore, hunting and trapping, orienteering, weather reading and so on. I grew up in and have lived in cities my whole life, so I know nothing about camping; the last time I ventured into the woods was twenty years ago. I thought then, as I do now, that it would be smart to get a jump start on the skill set I would need in the future. I would learn to live a meagre existence, move quickly over long distances and be able to find water, food and shelter when needed.

"So," he continued, "I wanted to make a change in my life to test myself, and I sure have. I haven't really learnt much of what

I thought I would. I can read a map better but I haven't learnt to hunt, yet. I have learnt endurance, though."

It was an unusual view but one I could relate to. I often found myself wondering when, not if, Western civilisation would collapse. Being in the wilderness and not seeing a building for days, let alone another human being, only fed those thoughts. I agreed with Brains; we are becoming too greedy, we supposedly live in a democracy but our voices are not heard. We elect leaders on the basis of promises that are then broken. What can we do about it? Not much – write a letter to our MP or post about it on Facebook. It's frustrating to feel so helpless. Democracy is not democracy any more.

As for living in a so-called free society, that too is being eroded. In America you can be arrested for standing on a street corner. In the UK, we are filmed while walking down the street, entering a shop or driving our car. We have our retinas scanned at the airport. The extent of information-gathering is astonishing, but where is it all going?

My opinion is that society as we know it is moving towards a point where everyone says 'enough'. I think we are tired of restrictions on the way we live, of rules and regulations and of being ignored. History shows that if people are not heard, they revolt. At that point, when everything comes tumbling down and society collapses, I, too, will escape the riots, meltdown, disorder and disarray – and disappear into the woods.

***

Hawkeye had already left as Brains and I climbed from the river the following morning. The 3,500-foot ascent seemed surprisingly easy; we both steamed up it like raging locomotives. Leaves from the previous autumn still carpeted the trail, cushioning our feet, and poison ivy reached out from the undergrowth.

Poison ivy is not to be taken lightly. Although not life-threatening, even the slightest brush against a leaf will set the plant oil on an all-out war with your skin. The plant alkaloid urushiol causes severe itching, inflammation, colourless bumps and blistering in four out of five people who come into contact with it. I learnt from other hikers how to recognise the plant, as it is not found in my native British Isles.

The plant only grows to perhaps a couple of feet on average, but was commonplace along the trail. 'The Poison Oak Dance', as I heard several others refer to it, was the name given to the contortions one had to perform to avoid contact. I was perhaps complacent at times, but I remained unscathed. Maybe I was one of the lucky individuals who had some resistance to the effects of the plant. Hiking at night was a little precarious; my head torch picked out the small plants and shiny leaves, and I had to exercise a tad more caution.

The air cooled as we rose, affording a welcome respite from a sweaty night at the river. Stunted oak trees occasionally allowed shafts of sunlight through, which patterned the ground. Brains surged ahead and I let him go. An hour later I saw another hiker approaching. We both stopped and chatted whilst resting.

"I'm about a month behind where I should be at this stage," I said to a solo SoBo called Peacemaker.

"No," he replied with a wry smile and a glint in his eye. "You're *exactly* where you should be."

Peacemaker looked like a lost hippie. I had watched him climbing the hill that I was working my way down. He strolled up calmly, taking his time. Stopping in the middle of the trail usually suggested that someone wanted a chat; if not, they would generally keep up the pace and step to one side to let you pass. If someone removed their backpack it meant they had decided to take a break, and this was something of an open invitation to the other to do the same. I sat and talked with Peacemaker for about ten minutes, glad to be resting and eating. He was hiking a stage of the PCT, though he said that if he found it enjoyable, he may keep going further. The expression on his face was of someone completely at ease with himself. As I left him, his words reverberated in my mind: "You are exactly where you're supposed to be, Fozzie."

It made me feel happy and secure. Regardless of my limited progress, hearing those words validated my position and reminded me the PCT was not a race.

I passed Brains who was taking a break. We had split off

again into our different day paces, and I tried to catch Hawkeye to camp with him, but he clearly wanted to get some miles in. Approaching twenty-seven miles for the day, I was still alone as I left a note for Brains telling him I intended to camp in another couple of miles. Sure enough, he joined me an hour or so later. I had become grateful for the company at camp. During the day we each had our own routines; sometimes we spent the whole day together, other times we criss-crossed or walked alone. Neither of us knew where Pockets was, but as night fell, I left my poles at trailside in case he should pass by.

I stood outside the tent listening to the wind rip through the forest around me, marvelling at the sheer energy of the night. I crawled into my tent and updated my journal, and contemplated something Hawkeye had mentioned in passing earlier. I had heard him, but was not really listening. However, if I knew then the repercussions of his words during the latter stages of my hike, I would have taken more notice.

"Bad weather up north forecast later in the year, Fozzie. They say it could be one of the worst winters for years."

Chapter 11
Setting the Limits

I found things in the woods that I didn't know I was looking for ... and now I'll never be the same.
Jennifer Pharr Davies, 2011 record holder for the fastest ever thru-hike of the Appalachian Trail

I left Brains to snooze in the morning and made quick progress down to Belden, a small community established when the railroad was built. Hemmed in to one side of the surrounding hills by the familiar sight of the Feather River, it was a sleepy little place with a population of just twenty-two. The original iron bridge spanning the river was a useful reference point as I made my way down from the hills. The few people I had spoken to about Belden were none too enamoured with the place and told me it wasn't worth stopping there. I was glad I did, though.

I was under the impression that a diner and store could be found two miles down the highway, so I was excited to find a restaurant, bar and simple shop in Belden proper. Resting on the bench outside, I was surprised to see Pockets emerge.

"Where the hell did you come from?" I said.

"Got in last night, me ol' mucker. Walked through most of the morning and slept in that old rock-crushing building over the road." He pointed to a restored structure on the far side of the river.

Pockets had taken my accent to heart and by now had a string of English words and phrases to his bow. "Me ol' mucker" was his favourite; he'd also come up with bizarre concoctions like "You gonna 'ave a bacon buttie, then, mate? Wiv sum, yer know, braaawn sauce and a cuppa tea?"

Brains strolled in shortly thereafter, and we all settled down for breakfast, which became lunch. Before we knew it, it was afternoon. We swam in the river and I thanked the Feather for giving me two good baths in as many days. The old monument provided us with some secluded shelter for the night.

***

I often pondered the juxtaposition of technology and the outdoors. Certain gizmos were carried by most hikers: head torch, mobile phone, iPod or similar musical device, perhaps a GPS. All designed to make our lives more comfortable, and some, like the head torch, could be considered necessities. I wondered how far this kind of technology might advance, and what equipment would be around twenty years from now. Tents with solar panels in the fabric? Body implants that monitor temperature, energy, pulse and other functions and give advice on improving performance? Kinetic-energy trekking poles or shoes that produce electricity from movement? (I think I might copyright that one, so don't tell anyone.)

The need for gadgets on the trail can be considerable, but is always balanced against their usefulness, weight and energy consumption.

Escaping computers, mobile phones and other annoyances was a motivation for me to do the PCT. Although I would find life difficult without my computer or my mobile, especially as I use them for my business, retreating to nature was a beautiful and enlightening way of realising what I actually needed. I never missed the computer, and even though I carried a phone, I rarely turned it on more than a couple of times a week. TV was a novelty in towns, and I spent many a night in a motel catching up, but I never missed television when I was on the trail.

Experiencing the outdoors or – even better, the untamed wilderness – imparts a certain wisdom about what is truly needed to be happy. Though material pleasures do provide a sense of achievement, a feel-good factor if you like, I worked out many moons ago that the feeling is only ever temporary. Two weeks after buying a car it's just a car. Your bright, shiny new mobile phone is exciting for a couple of days and then you look for the improved version. It's only a fake pleasure. If you're after true fulfilment, I say take a walk in the wilderness.

We started the 5,000-foot climb out of Belden the following morning, and bumped into Billy Goat on his way down. Perhaps the most famous face on the PCT over the past few years, he has walked the route many times and each year ventures out for the summer to do a section. Wispy white hair and a long beard earned him his nickname. This was the third time I had met him; first at the kick-off party and again coming down Fuller Ridge. We all spent a few minutes chatting and taking photos, and wished each other well.

The talk turned to mileage. We were knocking out around twenty-five-mile days on average now. This was a comfortable distance for a day and respectable progress. We discussed how far we each thought we could walk in one day. Thirty-milers should be easily achievable, we thought; mid-thirties likewise. Silly mileage was anything over forty, fifty-plus miles was classed as mad, and in the unlikely event that any of us managed a sixty, this was simply 'insane'. I had not reached the thirties thus far, at least not on the PCT, and neither had Brains or Pockets, but it was a tempting prospect.

As with most sports, there are a few die-hards who set out to break records. Andrew Skurka is one of them. In 2006 he walked a 1,744-mile section of the PCT in 45 days and 16 hours, an average of 38.2 miles per day. To put this in perspective, it was three times quicker than my average.

On the 3rd of November 2007, Skurka became the first person to complete the 6,875-mile Great Western Loop, averaging 33 miles per day for 208 consecutive days. On the 19th of July 2005, he completed a coast-to-coast walk starting from Cape Gaspe in Quebec and finishing at Cape Alava in Washington State, some 7,800 miles and 373 days later. He said of his section of the PCT:

"I was successful in doing what I set out to do. I dropped 25 pounds and am currently a little leaner than I was at the end of my sea-to-sea hike. I now think of a 40-mile day as hardly unusual; hiking 45-50 miles a day successively presents a more notable, but entirely doable challenge. And I have a much greater understanding of how I must manage my mind and my body while I'm pushing it to this level. Yeah, I only spent an afternoon at Kennedy Meadows; but I am a much better and more enlightened backpacker as a result, who is now in a much better position to succeed in some of the challenging hikes I have planned over the next few years."

In 2004, Scott Williamson, on his fourth attempt, became the first person to 'yo-yo' the PCT. A yo-yo entails reaching the end of a long-distance route, then walking back to the beginning again. He took 205 days to complete the 5,280 miles, an average of 25.8 miles per day. In 2011, he set the record for completing the PCT, in an astonishing 64 days, 11 hours and 19 minutes, an average of about 41.1 miles per day. His pack base weight (without food or water) was 3.9 kilos. This was well under half of mine, which was around 9 kilos. It was his *thirteenth* thru-hike of the PCT!

He didn't carry a stove, water treatment or a bear canister. He slept under a tarpaulin and used a quilt (made famous by a designer of lightweight backpacking equipment called Ray Jardine) instead of a sleeping bag. He hiked without a waist belt and sternum strap on his pack, and did not use trekking poles. Rising at 5.30am, he would be walking by 6am. His breakfast consisted of what he called a 'green shake', containing a powdered protein, a green supplement which had all the greens he would need for the day, spirulina, soy milk powder and of course water. Lunch was a swift fifteen-minute affair utilising homemade 'Phat Doug' bars, and dinner was simply dehydrated refried bean powder, crumbled organic corn tortilla chips and a generous splash of olive oil.

"That may sound very unappealing to you," he once said during a presentation. "Actually, right now I'd agree, but it gets to be delicious and satisfying after several weeks on the trail."

If you feel the urge to do a long-distance thru-hike and can't make up your mind which one, how about doing all three? Walk the Appalachian Trail, the Pacific Crest Trail and the Continental Divide Trail and you earn the accolade of a Triple

Crowner. Several hikers have completed this feat and many, myself included, wish to.

On the 31st of December 2000 Brian Robinson walked eight miles to reach Springer Mountain, the southern terminus of the Appalachian Trail in Georgia. On New Year's Day 2001 he started hiking north. Nine months and twenty-seven days later he had not only walked the Appalachian Trail, but also the Pacific Crest Trail *and* the Continental Divide Trail. He was the first person ever to walk all the three long-distance trails in America in one year, a total of 7,371 miles.

The Appalachian Trail has also seen its fair share of record-breakers. In 2008, Jennifer Pharr Davies set the women's record for a thru-hike with a remarkable 57 days, 8 hours and 35 minutes for the 2,175-mile trail.

If that weren't enough, in 2011 she vowed to do even better and also to beat the men's record of 47 days, 13 hours and 31 minutes set by Andrew Thompson in 2005. Having averaged around 38 miles per day every day for her 2008 record, she now somehow had to pull off the same feat ten days faster. Forty-six days, 11 hours and 20 minutes later she set the AT thru-hike record for both men and women. This equates to a leg-numbing 47.2 miles per day. My personal best for a day's hike on the PCT was 38.5 miles, 8.7 miles short of what Jennifer was cracking out each day, every day.

"The first two weeks were a physical challenge," she said afterwards. "Adjusting to back-to-back 30- to 45-mile days is brutal, especially on New England terrain. The weather was bad, the trail was slick, and hiking in New England usually involves using your hands or butt to overcome significant grades. I would finish each day looking like I had come from a war zone: muddied, bloodied and bruised. After the first two weeks, the remaining hurdles were mental and emotional. Mentally, it was hard because I never had a break. It is really difficult to maintain mental focus for 57 days."

The latest, unsupported, PCT record was set on August 7th, 2013, when hiker Heather 'Anish' Anderson of Bellingham, Washington truly smashed it. Having averaged around 44 miles each day and beating the previous record by almost four days, she reached Canada in 60 days, 17 hours, and 12 minutes.

The Appalachian Trail record set by Jennifer Pharr Davies was improved upon again in August 2015 by Matt Kirk, who registered a time of 58 days, 9 hours, and 38 minutes. That is, until Heather romped home a month later in 54 days, 7 hours, and 48 minutes. I'm betting good money she has her eye on the CDT next.

It is worth noting that there are two types of hikers who take on these challenges: those who hike with all their possessions with them, known as unsupported, and those who have help, such as a support vehicle so they carry little equipment. Pharr Davies was supported by her husband, Drew, on her record-breaking attempt, but both Matt and Heather deserve respect by setting their records unsupported.

And the guy that's currently breaking all the records? His name is Karl Bushby, and he's from England (of course!). Karl is making Scott, Brian, Jennifer, Andrew, me and every other walker on the planet look like we are taking our first, tentative steps in kindergarten. Allow me to explain.

Karl is attempting to be the first person ever to walk around the world entirely on foot, with no transport. And before you question whether this is actually possible in light of a small problem known as 'the sea', he's figured that one out as well.

Karl started this mammoth undertaking from Punta Arenas, Chile, on the 1st of November 1998, and he estimates the journey will take him fourteen years by the time he arrives back at home in Hull. If the timespan doesn't grab your attention, then consider the mileage: 36,000! This is about fourteen Pacific Crest Trails!

He has walked the entire length of South America, through America itself, into Canada and Alaska – and this is where I come back to the ocean problem. Believe it or not, to walk around the world one only encounters about seventy-six miles of ocean. His first water obstacle was the infamous Bering Strait, a fifty-six-mile stretch of water separating the USA from Russia. During the winter, the sea freezes here, sometimes completely, but usually partially. In 2006, Karl and a French explorer called Dimitri Kieffer walked (where possible), crawled and stumbled over ice and water to arrive in Russia some fifteen days later. When he reaches the French coast, he has permission from the

English and French authorities to walk through the channel tunnel.

Currently, Karl is involved in a battle with the Russian authorities, who have allowed him only a ninety-day visa. In 2008, as a result of the first delay in obtaining this permission, he managed to walk for three weeks to reach Bilibino. This area is essentially swamp and can only be traversed in the winter when the surface has frozen solid. He had to leave after his visa ran out.

From late 2008 to 2010, Karl spent most of the time in Mexico, for reasons to do with costs and funding. Because of the Russian delays, he lost valuable sponsors.

In 2011 he reached Srednekolymsk, again having to leave because of his visa. He needs to complete another 560 miles to reach roads and not have to rely on crossing frozen earth. The last I heard he's still going.

People such as Andrew, Scott, Brian and Jennifer fire the imagination. Physical boundaries are then pushed further, records are smashed and extreme feats of endurance are set. I never set out to break any records on the PCT; my goal was purely completion, but reading about what others have achieved makes me want to better myself. Distance is the obvious target; 2,650 miles is a hell of a long way even by car, let alone on foot. As I walked the PCT, the Continental Divide Trail was starting to seem viable to me, as was the Appalachian Trail and indeed the whole Triple Crown. But I also found myself thinking about other, more original goals. Approaching mid-way on the PCT, I was already planning my next thru-hike.

There are several 'E' routes in Europe that I thought would make good targets. The E8 starts in Ireland and finishes 2,920 miles further on in Turkey. The E4 begins in south-west Spain and stretches through Europe some 6,250 miles to Greece. Or perhaps I could attempt a round-the-coast walk of the UK? I could immerse myself in my home country over the course of a year and improve my hiking total by a healthy 6,500 miles. I started to walk a little faster in anticipation of these challenges.

Dozer told me after his thru-hike how he had pulled in a sixty-two-mile day. I didn't believe him at first, but he enlightened me.

"I had not planned the day," he began. "But I was trying to catch Crow, Dundee and Walker. I had been pushing hard doing a four-mile-per-hour pace when darkness settled in. I stumbled across the Pro from Dover who was also hiking in the dark, and we startled each other. We decided to push on and try to catch them but figured they must have camped off trail somewhere. Looking at the map we realised we were only about twenty-five miles from Mount Hood, the Timberline Lodge and that famous breakfast buffet. We carried on with that in mind, only stopping for water and a couple of ibuprofen. We were hiking fast but by now I was hurting. My feet were blistered, I had chafing and my knee was painful and swollen. The hardest part was the 2,000-foot climb to the lodge and some of it was on sandy soil and very steep; we kept slipping. We took turns leading, which motivated us a lot, and we made the lodge as the sun came up. It was epic! Twenty-one hours of hiking took its toll on me but after breakfast and a hot tub I was happy that we had pushed and made it."

I also contacted the Pro from Dover who furnished me with his version of events:

"I never set out to do a huge day. I did plan to do about fifty miles which, although big, was something I had done before. I have completed at least a half dozen forties and I think one fifty to get across the Oregon border. I was a strong hiker and the draw of doing big days was attractive to me. I liked to bust it out every once in a while and prove my own mettle.

"The motivation for this one day might be misplaced but it was really centred around getting to Timberline Lodge on Mt Hood in time for the breakfast buffet. My initial plan was set up by a forty-miler I did to put myself sixty-five miles away from the destination. I figured I could hike a fifty and then wake up early and crush another fifteen in the early morning, and make it to the buffet some time in the middle of it. That would allow near a couple hours of feasting and gorging.

"The day didn't start off too well. I woke up and got moving before sunrise but I just wasn't moving fast and it was a little chilly. So naturally I found a spot to get water, with a view, and I took a long break. Surprisingly, Dozer, Pajamas, Uncle Gary and JC found me. I hadn't seen these guys since Kennedy Meadows, so I was extremely surprised and happy to see them, especially Dozer, because I had done a fair amount of hiking with him: we started the same day way back in Campo. I still wanted to make the buffet the next day but these guys were talking about the morning after that. I was stubborn and wasn't backing down from my plan.

"So I hiked on and on, still firmly bent on doing fifty. Dozer caught back up with me when it was about to become headlamp time. He was looking for Crow, Dundee and Walker and wanted to camp with them for the night. We kept hiking together but still couldn't find them. By this point, I had a forty in place, whereas I think he'd done five miles less, based on where we had started. After thinking hard about where they would have camped and not finding them, Dozer decided that he would just keep going with me. Big days are better with someone to go through them with.

"The thought of doing a big day was enticing to Dozer, but his head had started to churn. I remember saying to him at one point, 'I will hike with you as far as you are willing to go.' I wanted to get as close to Timberline as I could, and his support was making this hike a lot better. It became Dozer's golden carrot as well. The prospect of the morning breakfast buffet had got him excited too. He had never done a monster day of forty or more miles and now was his chance. So we kept going and as we neared the fifty-mile mark for me, we both just decided that this was going to be the day of all days and we were going to make it to Timberline Lodge come hell or high water. So we did. Once Dozer made that leap mentally, we were both going to push ourselves to the end.

"The late night and early morning portion took a while. Our bodies got tired and slowed down. We used instant coffee every five or so miles to give us that recharge for the next leg. Rest for twenty minutes, make coffee, eat something and then get moving again. The last stretch was the longest; it seemed as if it would never end. Time moved slower, miles weren't clicking off as they had been earlier in the day. We were mentally tired too, from pushing our bodies all day. I would have loved a nap but knew I would never wake up. We had to keep going all night; sleep was not on the cards at all. The overnight portion was methodical. I had been going for three-quarters of a day already and my legs just kept moving, step after step; not really physically sore or tired, to the point where I couldn't possibly take another step, just tired from over-exertion, but the muscle memory was there and they just kept going. There was one point on the last climb where I just closed my eyes and my legs kept moving. I could keep my eyes closed for a minute at a time and still be on trail. It was weird; I sort of knew where I was going. I also just wanted to see the door of the lodge within my sights.

"The sun was starting to lighten up the sky faintly but we were basically there. Nothing could stop us now; maybe another half mile and that was it. The joy of accomplishment was awesome. We had just done this stupendous hike and pushed ourselves further than we ever had before. I don't really know how to describe that feeling. It was intense: we felt invincible mentally, though exhausted physically. I loved it.

"As it turned out, I never recovered from that superlative effort until my thru-hike was done. That run of miles left my legs beaten up and devoid of any real strength. I lost all my speed. I could still hike long days but they were mentally exhausting and from then on I began to hate long days, even thirties. I simply couldn't push myself as I had before. With the speed in the legs wiped out, all I had left was endurance. I continued to enjoy the hike but the physical aspect of it depressed me. As a result, my hiking style changed a bit. Although I still did the miles, I switched to a new pace. It was another one of those things that I learned about myself, and I am much wiser and stronger for it."

Talk of a forty-mile day ebbed away, and after 25.8 miles we reached a small clearing by the side of the trail just before Humboldt Summit. It was a beautiful evening and tents were left in our packs as we laid out our sleeping bags beneath a wonderful, inky-black sky embedded with millions of crystals. Trees around our clearing framed the night sky perfectly, and as our eyes became accustomed to the light, the Milky Way appeared like a vapour of mist. It was so vast and clear that I felt as if I could just let go and fall away into infinity.

I woke at first light, around 5am; feeling rested, I got up and put some water on the boil. Brains was still snoozing but began

The Last Englishman

to wake and then Pockets, who I thought was still in his sleeping bag, appeared from behind a rock carrying his camera equipment.

"Morning!" he cried, as though he had been awake for half a day. "Got a great time lapse of the sun coming up, what a great morning!"

It was another perfect day. We left to knock off the remaining twenty-two miles to Highway 36 and hopefully get a quick ride to Chester. Over the past few days the track had been covered in a layer of fine dirt, roughly the consistency of sieved flour. Each footstep made clouds of powdery soil stick to the sweat on our legs and cover them in a dirty mess. As we walked into the night with our head torches on, the air was obscured and glistened with seemingly billions of dust particles. Brains had taken to wearing his bandana over his mouth to stop choking. Even our feet were brown with a congealed mix of muck at the end of the day. I had by now stopped washing my feet at day's end, because I couldn't be bothered – and I also felt a minor sense of achievement at coming to terms with my filth. Brains and Pockets also embraced the dirt, and after a week on trail we would emerge from the woods looking as if we had put in a shift down the local coal mine.

"I can't stop thinking about getting into town," said Pockets, breaking the silence mid-afternoon. "I'm gonna get some Ben and Jerry's, you know, buy four and get four free? Then I'm gonna empty them all in the bath, lie in it and roll around till I'm completely covered. And, *and*, you two are going to watch me."

"I won't be there, Pockets," I told him, noticing Brains up ahead catching drift of the conversation and shaking with the giggles.

Before the highway, and catching us completely off guard, we came across a granite marker by the side of the trail. I was bringing up the rear, and when I emerged, the guys had dropped their packs and Pockets was grinning as though he had just found a hidden café serving free, all-you-can-eat food complete with naked Singaporean waitresses making themselves at home on our laps while offering 'extras'. Or something like that.

"What you smirking at?" I asked.

"Dude, we're halfway!"

I did a double-take at the small obelisk-shaped monument with its engraved gold inscription.

'PCT mid-point, Canada 1325 miles, Mexico 1325 miles.'

Suddenly, everything focused and became very, very lucid. I had completed half the distance I needed to get to Canada. It was the 20th of August, 119 days since I started back down in Campo. This meant that at my current pace I would finish just before Christmas. That would be too late. I had another two months at best to get there before the winter hit. Immediately, Hawkeye's words whispered to me.

"Bad weather up north forecast later in the year, Fozzie. They say it could be one of the worst winters for years."

I looked at Pockets and then Brains. They were both beaming, as was I, but I could see the underlying worry in their faces as they realised what I too had realised. We pushed our fears to one side, shook hands, jumped about, captured some photos and video and set off to celebrate in Chester.

"Guys, do you know the name of the town that's famous for being the place where most thru-hikers quit and end their hike?" asked Pockets, after we had walked in silent contemplation for a couple of miles. Neither Brains nor I responded.

"Chester," he added. "The town we're heading for now."

Chapter 12
Paw Fall would be Awful

You will never make it to Canada.
Billy Goat

I did make it to Canada.
Patrick 'Wideangle' Pöndl

Pockets was right. A lot of hikers crash out after reaching Chester. When the euphoria abates, the full extent of the situation smashes into them. They now know what it entails to walk 1,325 miles and with shock realise that they have to do the same distance again. After many celebrate their achievement to date in Chester, a few are unable to cope and comprehend what then faces them. It was a sobering thought that none of us was entertaining but mind games like that can creep up on you. Feel fine one minute but slowly it starts to sink in, fears surface and doubts start to crumble one's resolve. We walked in silence to the highway and caught an easy and quick ride into Chester with Rick, a passing builder.

"I always stop if I see you guys," he said. "I take my hat off to all of you."

Reaching town after dark, we decided against getting a motel, but planned to get one early the following morning to make the most of a full day and night in comfort. We wolfed down a burger at the Kopper Kettle café, and after a quick scout for suitable sleeping areas we crashed out on an open-air stage in the park, tucking ourselves near the back, away from prying eyes. A few kids kicked a ball around, smoke rose from a family barbecue and as dusk fell the park gradually emptied.

We stayed in Chester the following day and moved out after one night at the motel. I think Pockets's words were ringing in our ears, and we were keen not to quit our adventure here as many others had before. Trooper had also arrived at the motel and, while Brains and I ate a speedy lunch at the Kopper Kettle, he caught a ride with Pockets eight miles back to the trailhead.

Trooper had walked on by the time we caught up with Pockets, and we made our way to the Drakesbad guest ranch. We were on a bit of a roll in terms of food availability. Our stomachs were groaning from Chester, the ranch was looming and Hat Creek resort, home to trail angels Georgi and Dennis Heitman, was a day's walk away. None of us were entertaining any thoughts of quitting. In fact it was quite the reverse; getting away from Chester quickly had proved a good move and the prospect of food always put a smile on our faces.

We set a good pace through intermittent forest dotted with open spaces and stopped at Boiling Spring Lake. A warning sign advised not to approach the small expanse of water that happily bubbled and steamed about fifty feet from the trail.

I treat signs telling me not to do something the same as I treat someone in authority. Albeit with some caution, I walked a few feet from the banks as Pockets took some photos and Brains smoked. Being near volcanic activity gives me the willies so I was glad when Pockets finished so we could get to the ranch.

The forest cleared and opened out into a lush, green strip stretching away either side of us. Despite the breaks in the trees that afternoon it was almost a relief to emerge into the open. We had barely dropped our packs when the front door opened and a waiter appeared.

"Guys! You thru-hikers? It's the end of August, you're late!"

We laughed nervously, all aware of the situation.

"Come in! Sit!"

Drakesbad ranch was in the middle of nowhere. I couldn't even see a road leading to it. Paying guests are made to feel welcome at this forest nirvana and can relax in the hot springs, eat great food and forget about the nine-to-five routine. We were given some water and our waiter came over again.

The Last Englishman

"Guys, what you wanna eat? You're a little late, kitchen is closing but we have leftover quiche and plenty broccoli." Smiling a lot, his grasp of English was amusing as he left out the occasional, unimportant word. I tried to guess where he was from.

We looked at each other and paused.

"I'm not actually hungry," Brains offered first.

"Strangely, neither am I," I added, before Pockets also agreed.

The waiter looked momentarily perplexed. During the course of a season, hikers appear at the ranch in a steady stream and proceed to demolish obscene quantities of food. Now all of a sudden three of them turn up and aren't hungry. He was as confused as we were. Whispers starting coming from the other waitresses, the kitchen door twitched and eyes peered out from nooks and crannies. All was silent.

"Don't want any food?!" said Billie, the proprietor, leaning against the kitchen door. "First time in ten years that I've heard a hiker saying they don't want any food. Is it a money thing?"

"No," Brains replied. "We have money, just not much of an appetite."

"Well," Billie continued, "You're all eating and I don't want to hear another word about not being hungry!"

We fell silent as though the headmaster had just rapped our knuckles. Billie was jesting, of course, but we weren't about to argue with her. Said food arrived, followed by chocolate mousse, and we all realised how hungry we actually were. Pockets was trying to eat but becoming distracted by several lovely Slovenian waitresses.

"I'm moving to Slovenia after my hike," he said.

We thanked them all profusely for the food. Upon discovering that they didn't even want payment, we left them a thirty-dollar tip, which they only reluctantly took. They handed us each a towel and gave us directions down to the hot springs.

For an hour we floated about laughing and relaxing, the water soothing tired muscles as steam rose away from the surface, catching the beams from a full moon. If it were not for one of the ranch staff who arrived to close off the spring, we would have stayed for another hour. Walking a mile down a rough track away from Drakesbad I kept glancing back as the forest slowly engulfed the building and finally it disappeared completely.

Four miles in to the following day, we emerged at a campground by a road.

"Guys, this isn't right," I said sheepishly, as I had been leading the way and therefore, following an unwritten rule, was responsible for navigation.

"It's not, no," Brains confirmed, checking his map.

We eventually managed to pinpoint our location, and lethargy set in. Having put in four miles on the wrong track, and needing to walk another four to get back, we decided the obvious and natural solution was beer. We managed a quick hitchhike to the angelic Heitmans at Hat Creek. Georgi and Dennis, in their welcoming and helpful way, showed us round and fed us.

Brains pitched tent in the grounds with Pockets and I grabbed a spare bed in the tree house, complete with TV, ageing video recorder and wonderful selection of 80s movies.

I had learnt the hard way when trying to secure sponsorship from gear manufactures never to give up; persistence pays off. Before embarking on my journey I'd contacted Matt Swaine, editor of *Trail* magazine, the biggest hiking publication in England. I asked whether the magazine would like to publish an article. They politely said it was a good idea but not at the current time. I had spoken to Pockets and he was keen to have some of his photos published too, so I tried again.

We sent *Trail* six of the best shots. I made our adventure sound as enticing as I could, mentioning that Pockets's work had featured in *National Geographic*. Two hours later I received a reply to my email.

"Hi Keith. I am about to head out on my wedding for a couple of weeks but I am actually interested in this and I've forwarded it for someone here for discussion. Will try to get back to you before I leave on Wednesday. All the best. Matt."

Two days later a big smile rippled across my face when I saw another email from Matt. I took a deep breath and opened it.

"Hi Keith. We will run with something but the current issue is looking very busy, so might have to wait until the following one. I've forwarded to the editorial people and will get back. Hope all's going well with you! Matt."

I went nuts when I read it.

"Pockets! POCKETS!" I cried.

"Mucker, wassup?"

"We got in *Trail*, they're gonna run it!"

We jumped around for a couple of minutes, and then realised we had to catch a ride to Burney. The internet connection at the Heitmans was slow, and Pockets's photos were on his laptop, which was in his bounce box on a shelf at the post office. Georgi kindly drove us into town, with Brains accompanying us, and before long we were guests at the Shasta Pines Motel. I had to write the piece for *Trail* in a couple of days, and Pockets started sorting out which photos would show the PCT and us in their best light. Each photo took an hour to send (the motel's internet wasn't much better than the Heitmans'), because the magazine wanted high resolution. Eventually we sent all the pictures, and cracked open a case of Pale Ale.

I was keen to get going the following morning, but the guys wanted an extra day. I pondered for a while, but guilt got the better of me. I told them I'd see them up trail and waited by McDonald's to get a ride out of town. After giving in to temptation in the form of chicken nuggets I went outside to try again, promptly returning for another portion. It would prove to be difficult getting back to the wrong turn off the PCT at Kings Creek. My first ride dropped me five miles up the road. I stuck my thumb out, hoping that another willing soul would put on the brakes. Steve, a plumber, stopped and said he could take me part of the way to the entrance of the Lassen Volcanic National Park, which he duly did. Next, Marjorie stopped and said she could take me to the Park entrance but no further, as she would have to pay to get in.

"You have to pay the entrance fee if you want to come into the park," the woman at the gate told me.

"I'm hiking the PCT," I replied. "Just took a day out to re-supply." I gave her my thru-hiking permit and she waved me through, wishing me good luck.

I was still ten miles from the car park where Pockets, Brains and I had found ourselves after straying off the trail. I walked to the visitor centre and grabbed a cold Coke from the machine. I then went to catch ride number four of a long day. A police SUV pulled up alongside me, tyres crunching on the gravel. A smoky window lowered.

"You know you can't hitch a ride here, don't you?" said a most attractive female officer.

"Really?" I asked.

"Yes. I'm afraid it's illegal to try to hitch a ride in a national park."

I was aware of this as several hikers had told me before. Figuring it was only a very minor misdemeanour, I decided to try anyway – I was hardly likely to be arrested at gunpoint and thrown in the local slammer. I decided flirting was the best option. I flashed a cheeky grin, looked her in the eye and plumped for the innocent English tourist routine.

"I'm English," I said. "Sorry, I didn't realise. Shit, how the hell am I gonna get back up to the park at Kings Creek?"

"I don't know, but I think you may be walking. What are you doing here anyway?"

"I'm walking the PCT."

"Oh, really?" Her eyebrows raised a little and she started to loosen up. "Well done for getting this far but you still can't hitch a ride, I'm afraid."

"What are you up to now?" I decided to go for the big sell, hardened the accent slightly and tried to look forlorn.

"No way!" she exclaimed. "I just finished work, I'm going home to have a long, hot bath and to relax. Don't even think about asking me for a ride."

"Come on. You're gonna get home, slip into your bath, lie there and then you're gonna start to feel guilty because you know you should have given me a ride instead of leaving me out here helpless in the middle of nowhere. Do you want that on your conscience? Please? It's just a few miles up the road."

She sighed, looked skyward and smiled again.

"Hang on," she said, reaching for the radio. "Guys, where are you, are you due down at the entrance at all?"

The radio crackled but I couldn't make out the reply.

"OK," she continued. "You're in luck, Mr Englishman. My buddies are just starting their shift. If you can wait for thirty minutes, they will grab some lunch and be here shortly after. They can give you a ride."

"Sure you won't let me ride with you? I'll buy you a drink," I said, making one more throw of the dice.

"Don't push your luck. Good luck with your hike; I'm going for that bath minus any guilt complex. And don't hitch in the national parks!"

With that she flashed me a cheeky smile, tossed her hair back, slipped on her sunglasses and drove off.

Sitting in the back of my first American cop car, I quizzed her mates on why they needed five guns between them. There were two big shotguns, a couple of guns that looked a bit more familiar, and something resembling a sniper rifle. They also had a pistol each. For a moment I was Rambo in the back of that car, being taken back to the town outskirts before being told not to return. I felt like letting their tyres down, sticking my tongue out, flicking one of them in the ear and running off into the forest taunting, "Catch me if you can!"

Finding the same track down to Kings Creek easily enough I soon came to the junction with the PCT where we had gone wrong. It was late afternoon and I felt I needed to put in some miles to make up for a lost day. We'd missed the section from there up to Burney a couple of days earlier, so I had around sixty miles to reach Highway 299 from where I had begun that day. I thought the Heitmans' would make a good place to get a quick rest and a bite to eat. I started walking into fading light. The forest was dense, so long before sunset I needed my head torch. I did my best not to remind myself that I was walking in the woods after dark. Bird shrieks startled me and twigs snapped in the darkness, amid an eerie, enveloping silence.

I turned my light up brighter and looked up trail. Two yellow eyes appeared from the forest and stopped about fifty feet ahead of me. They paused for a few seconds and then disappeared again. I couldn't stop thinking about the scene in *The Amityville Horror* where Margot Kidder's son says his invisible, imaginary friend has just gone out of the window and, as she looks out, a pair of menacing white eyes flash at her and disappear. My mind was certainly not helping the situation. I was convinced those eyes belonged to a hungry wolf that by now had crept through the undergrowth to my left, flanked me and at any moment was going to jump on my neck – and it wasn't for a tummy scratch.

Eventually, after ten miles, I left the forest and entered a large, moonlit clearing. I walked for a further half mile to the next section of forest and camped just inside, with faint light for company.

It was strange being separated from the guys, and I was starting to miss their company at evening camp. For the next few days at least, I had to accept it.

Hiking a long-distance trail is not about giving up six months of your life. It's about having six months to live. The harshest days, when everything seems to be going wrong, when you doubt the whole idea of hiking the PCT, when the rain is flying horizontally into your face and you realise you've run out of stove fuel – these are only ever that, just days. Whenever I was in my sleeping bag after a brutal few miles where I thought the world was against me, I would relax in the knowledge that tomorrow would be kinder. And really, the bad days rarely come; on the whole, a thru-hike is a heart-warming experience that nurtures the soul and makes you feel glad to be alive to experience it.

I woke at 5am to light rain tickling my face and catapulting leaves a few inches skyward. Weak sunlight filtered through the pines and I peered up at dark clouds racing overhead. It was the 1st of September, and my surroundings were looking distinctly autumnal. Foliage was withering and changing colour: even California could be cold. My watch showed nine degrees Celsius, and I shivered, wondering why the temperature had plummeted from the mid-twenties yesterday. Skipping breakfast, I set off quickly to warm up.

I reached Hat Creek where I had been dropped off with Brains and Pockets a few days earlier. I decided against calling the Heitmans again because I knew, especially given the cold weather, that I would struggle to move on if I stopped there. I went into the café and ordered the biggest breakfast they cooked, plus a few extras. I nurtured my miniscule celebrity status as two day-hikers chatted to me outside, eager to hear about my hike, but eventually headed off to make some inroads into one of the hardest sections of the PCT.

The Last Englishman

Hat Creek Rim is a notoriously hot and dry twenty-six-mile stretch out of Hat Creek, so hot that it's more typical of southern California. The Heitmans maintained a water cache at the start. After a short climb to the top of the rim, I filled up. The clouds had dispersed and the temperature was already rising alarmingly. I had twenty-six miles to the next cache – about eight hours' walking plus breaks – so I filled up my litre bottle and pulled out a two-litre bag, which I normally used to fill up for camp. As I balanced a four-litre plastic jug and poured into the bag, a small jet of water sprang out from the side; it had a hole.

"Shit," I mumbled. I pulled out a clear, waterproof compression sack and emptied the contents back into my pack. Filling the sack up with another two litres, I strapped it securely on and strode off. Three miles further on, stopping again to rest, I saw that the sack had also punctured and had deposited most of the water on the trail behind me. I now had only one litre in my bottle, but rather than return to the cache, I decided to press on: perhaps not the most sensible of decisions, but any thru-hiker will tell you that making miles is far more important than safety.

It was now ludicrously hot, and the rim was starting to earn its reputation. Walking in that temperature I should have been carrying an absolute minimum of two litres, ideally four; I had one. To my left the rim dropped down and away to the flatter lands below. The grass was scorched and blond; a heat haze made the horizon seem like an apparition. Stunted trees appeared ill and withered. I felt as though I was in the African bush.

Three hours and nine miles in, I stopped for lunch. My throat was rough. I coaxed the last few trickles from my water bottle. It was so hot that I started longing for the desert. Popping a couple of boiled sweets into my mouth to elicit some sort of moisture response, I picked up my pack and carried on. I had no choice but to walk the entire rim; there was no water until the next cache, and that was still another seventeen miles away.

I passed through a fence and a reflection caught my eye, to the right. A group of cattle had gathered round a water hole. They dispersed as I approached. The water was black, with the consistency of sludge, and strange green organisms floated on its surface. Flies buzzed round my head. I pulled out my water filter and sat by the edge. It stank, cattle dung littered the area, and one of the cows was eyeing me up suspiciously. I relented, putting my filter away, and walked away. Even at this stage, I was contemplating turning back to the water cache; it was still only ten miles behind me, whereas the next one was still sixteen miles distant. I had visions of diners in the café the following morning, tutting and shaking their heads as they read the *Hat Creek Herald* running a headline "English hiker found with no water on Creek Rim."

Reginald at Nerve Centre HQ was in a mess. While trying to cope with borderline dehydration, heatstroke and sunburn, he was sending out orders faster than a thru-hiker's mouth in a burger bar. His centre of attention was Nancy, responsible for the main chest organs. Normally faultlessly efficient, she too was overheating.

"I'm running way above normal temperature down here, Reginald. He must know he needs water; I need a good two litres just to maintain stability. Anything above that is a bonus."

"Do what you can," Reginald replied. "I think we're in some sort of dry zone. His field of vision is only showing parched, dusty soil. I don't think any fluids are forthcoming, so you'll just have to shore up the defences and wait."

Five hot hours later, I came across a white sign by the side of the trail:

"Cache down here!"

In the shelter of a few trees was a solitary chair.

"Don't rely on the cache twenty-six miles in," Georgi Heitman had told me a few days earlier. "It is maintained but not often; there's a good chance it could be empty."

About ten large water bottles were tied to a tree (this is often done to prevent the empty bottles blowing away). As I gingerly lifted each one, my hopes fell further and further.

"There's a good chance it could be empty..."

They were all empty. I was still coherent but not in good shape. I had a pounding headache and felt tired and lethargic. My throat was so dry that I couldn't even muster a swallow. Then I noticed a cool box nestled under a bush. I didn't open it but lifted it from one corner; it felt heavy and my hopes rose. I pried open one corner of the lid and peered in. One jug of water sat lonely in the corner, and two Coke cans slid down and rested next to it. The writing on the cans was speckled with thousands of little condensation bubbles. They were still cold! I literally poured one can straight down my throat; the fluid was so frigid it almost hurt. I had never drunk a can of anything that quickly. I drank a further two litres from the water bottle, and left one Coke and two litres of water in case someone was behind me. From there on, the situation, according to my maps, was due to improve anyway.

From the searing heat of the rim, I descended quickly and camped near Lake Britton amid the gentle hum of a nearby waterworks. The scenery in the morning was transformed, and reminded me of home. Lush green grass, lakes idling in hills, familiar trees such as oak and elm, and a heron fishing. A low mist hovered over the water, and it even rained a little.

After some barren weeks, the rain caught me off guard. I felt restricted in my waterproofs, so I removed them and carried on regardless, dodging a few light showers. The undergrowth was damp as I brushed against wet leaves, chilling me even further. I wondered whether Pockets and Brains had overtaken me somewhere, and I started to check footprints, as I was familiar with their tread patterns, but I couldn't see any.

The temperature had dropped, and this combined with the moisture in the air attracted a multitude of gnats. They drove me insane, constantly buzzing round my face and following me in formation for miles. I had long since ditched the mosquito head net because I just couldn't see through it, so I had to resort to waving my trekking pole handle to and fro across my face.

Encountering a hiker going south, I learnt he had seen Brains by himself the previous evening. I was now walking through dense forest and felt constrained, hemmed in. I had mail in Castella, a few miles down the road from Shasta which I figured would make a good place to rest and re-supply; the town had a good reputation with thru-hikers. I reached the road a couple of miles down from Castella and ducked into some woods, squeezing past a gate with a sign saying 'no camping'. I settled down for the night. Writing my journal that evening and tallying up my mileage, I was pleased to see I had knocked off 150 miles in only 5 days – an average of 30 miles per day, including a 33, the most I had done in one day.

I walked up to Castella in the morning. It consisted of a post office and a garage. No Pain was sitting on a bench outside, cramming a breakfast burrito into his mouth. He got up and shook my hand when I arrived. It had been a while since I had seen him, and we chatted for an hour while I too munched some food.

"You won't make it to Canada now, Fozzie," he said, matter-of-factly.

"Really? What makes you say that?"

"You're way too late. The snow will hit Washington and you won't get through."

It was clear from his unfaltering voice that he was certain of his ground and there was not even a whiff of doubt in his mind.

"Are you going to carry on from here?" I asked.

"I will, but I know I won't make it all the way. I'll carry on until it gets too cold or wintry and then go home."

"You're wrong, No Pain," I said. "I am late, yes, but I'm not backing off now. I've come too far. I will hit snow but I've put in too much work just to presume I won't be successful. Good luck with the rest of your hike."

I shook his hand again and walked back to the highway. There was a very good chance that No Pain was right, I knew that; but I didn't want to entertain it. A little into September and I had completed 1,509 miles; there were still 1,131 left to go. Assuming I put in six-day weeks with twenty-five miles each day, I still had seven to eight weeks left. This meant finishing in the beginning of November, a good month over target if I was to beat the weather. I respected No Pain's opinion; he had been walking this trail and the Appalachian Trail for several years and he knew the seasons. Emphatic as he was, though, when someone tells me I can't do something, that's all the incentive I need *to* do it.

When I finally managed to get a signal on my phone, during a fifty-metre stretch on the road out of Castella, I listened to a voicemail from Pockets.

"Mucker, I'm in Shasta, call when you get in."

I got a quick ride in and we agreed to meet outside the local supermarket. Many shoppers stopped to talk to me as I sat outside; spotting my pack and soiled appearance, they guessed I was on the PCT. They were pleasant enough, but they kept reminding me of the obvious.

"You're a bit late, aren't you?" or "Most thru-hikers passed through a few weeks ago."

With Pockets, whom I now referred to as 'Rockets' on account of his walking speed, I went off to find a motel. How had he overtaken me, I wondered? It transpired that he had camped at Ash camp, perhaps a quarter of a mile further on from where I had spent the night in a clearing. I had even walked into Ash camp in the morning to get water from the river, but somehow missed him. Brains was holed up in a motel in Dunsmuir about seven miles away, with the flu or something similar.

Shasta was an excellent little town, with a good selection of re-supply shops and plenty of restaurants. Rockets had found an Italian place already, so we went for lunch. It was all-you-can-eat, unlimited pasta dishes and salad of your choice, so we settled down for a feast. I watched as he picked up the glass jar of grated parmesan. It was full, but he unscrewed the top, proceeded to pour the entire contents over his dish and then called the waitress over. He showed her that the jar was empty and she duly went off and returned with another. He unscrewed that and finished it off as well. He ended up with not so much pasta with parmesan, but parmesan with pasta.

We left the following day, eager to move on and make inroads into a 5,000-foot, eighteen-mile climb out of the highway near Castella. Halfway up, in the late afternoon, we were both tired, so we camped early and made a fire. Rockets darted around the forest taking photos.

Although we were keen to make up for lost miles in the morning, we had only managed twelve by lunch, so we ate a quick snack and Rockets set a four-miles-per-hour pace through the afternoon.

"I hate puds," he said.

"What, as in puddings?"

"No, puds. You never heard of a pud before? A pud is a pointless up and down, p, u and d."

"Oh," I replied and then thought for a while. "Does that make this bit of trail a paular then?"

"What the hell is a paular?"

"A pointless and useless left and right."

Once in the groove, we were steaming up the hills, and pulled up at 6pm, having clocked thirty-three miles for the day. The site we chose to camp on was stunning: a small, open plateau offering views for miles until the earth suddenly shot skywards and finished on the summit of Mt Shasta. As the sun set, streaking her white flanks with orange, she rose supreme over all she surveyed.

Four days from Shasta and we had both run out of food. Having purposely only re-supplied with a smaller amount, to keep the weight down, we had agreed to get more supplies at Etna, but had not properly considered the distance. There were two possible locations from which to catch a ride in, and the first one we stumbled to was Carter Meadows summit and Highway 93. We could either try to get a ride or else camp and push out a twenty-one-miler in the morning to a smaller road without any food. It was a no-brainer. We set down our packs and stuck out a thumb.

About three forestry trucks passed within ten minutes and then it all went quiet. An hour passed and we saw no-one. Finally, we heard the groan of an engine approaching from the other side of the pass. Both standing in the middle of the road, we started waving and pretty much forced the car to stop.

The window lowered and an attractive woman stuck her head out. She had a cigarette dangling from her mouth and one foot was contorted into a sort of yoga position on the dashboard.

"You two are going to get run down! You hiking the PCT?"

"Yep," we replied simultaneously. "Any chance of a ride into Etna?"

"No way!" she replied. "I've just come from there, it's twenty miles down the highway, I ain't going all the way back again!"

We hung our arms limply and said we were out of food, hoping it might swing things in our favour.

"Listen," she continued, "I live six miles down in the valley. If you want to come with me, I can feed you and give you somewhere to sleep tonight. There's not many houses where I live, it's in the middle of nowhere, but maybe someone can give you a ride to Etna to re-supply in the morning."

It was a good offer and certainly the best we would hope to get.

Laurissa's place, tucked away from a cluster of other houses, was wonderful. Walking into her garden, you could have been in the middle of the wilderness. She grew many fruits and vegetables and was more or less self-sufficient; she had even stopped off en route to fill up several bottles from a local spring. The house was off grid, generated its own electricity and must have been a beautiful place to live. It looked as if it had been constructed with materials found somewhere in the local vicinity. Different types of wood formed the outside shell, their naturally differing colours enlivening the walls. A hotchpotch of mismatched tiles clung to the roof, and there was a sizeable porch where we could sit outside while a little gentle rain fell.

The interior wrapped us in a warm feeling as soon as we entered. A wood stove provided most of the heat, shelves groaned under books and rugs decorated a wooden floor.

Laurissa disappeared into the garden and returned with home-grown tomatoes, onions and herbs. She boiled some rice, pan-fried some tempeh and mixed it all together in a bowl with a generous dash of olive oil. It was one of the best meals I had eaten on the entire trail, and even Rockets, who wasn't much of a health-food fan, was raving about it for days afterwards.

One of Laurissa's neighbours gave us a ride into Etna in the morning, and we grabbed some breakfast at Bob's Ranch House.

The only motel in Etna was full, so we were forced to get a bus to Yreka, where we stayed for the day. Rockets had been suffering with toothache and it was becoming unbearable. He kept holding his jaw. He phoned around trying to find a dentist in the area and eventually a family friend pointed him in the direction of Portland, Oregon. I naturally couldn't wait for him, so we parted the following morning and he said he would catch me somehow. After a long series of rides back to the trailhead, I started walking in the hope of putting in a few miles before sunset.

As dusk fell, I tried in vain to find somewhere flat to camp. The trail fell away to my left and rose to my right, where it had been cut into the slope, and eventually I accepted that I wouldn't find anywhere; the contours on my map were only getting worse.

It was a clear night but in the forest my environment was a dark, inky black. There was no wind, not even a breeze. If a mouse scurried home fifty feet from me, I could hear it. Cowboy camping was normal for me now; it put me in touch with the woods, and I looked forward to falling asleep every night waiting for a shooting star or two. Also, I saved a little time by not pitching the tent or taking it down in the morning. After laying out my ground mat, sleeping pad and bag on the trail, I settled down to cook and write my journal.

After a few minutes I heard wood cracking in the trees, maybe a hundred feet away up the hill. Ignoring this as I normally did, I continued writing, but then I heard bushes swishing and springing back to make way for something. Whatever it was, it was big, no mistake. The closer it got, the more I could hear footsteps – or indeed hoofs, maybe even paws. I pleaded with whoever was listening not to make it paws; paw fall would be just awful. The intruder seemed to be making a beeline for me – certainly heading too close for comfort.

"Please let that be a deer," I thought. "Please, don't make it a bear."

Closer and closer it slowly crept. I could almost feel the reverberation as it came closer. I stood up, heart thumping, as I waited for some fearsome beast to emerge on the trail.

However, thankfully adjusting its course, it veered off slightly and thundered down the trail about twenty feet away. I could hear it, but couldn't see a thing. I turned on my head torch. The beam immediately picked out two big, menacing eyes which bored a hole right through me. It was a bear.

Chapter 13
Into Oregon

If everyone in the world treated each other as we treat each other on the trail, the world would be a far, far better place.
Unknown

Size, we are told, is not important. This maxim is not applicable to bears. The size of a bear is in fact directly proportional to the fear it strikes into one's heart. It had been weeks since my last bear encounter, and perhaps I had been lulled into a false sense of security.

I didn't know what to do. The mere thought of facing a bear, let alone being in the middle of nowhere with such a creature, was the one situation (along with falling down a crevasse, maybe) that had haunted me in the months before my hike. I must admit that I very nearly decided against going to America because of the possibility of encountering a bear.

I had seen several since my last close call at McIvers Spring some three months earlier. I had become comfortable in their presence, purely because they had all been some distance off or were happily munching away on berries and preoccupied. If they were aware of me, they usually ran off anyway. This one was different; it scared me. Unpredictability and bears are not a good match.

Not wanting to shine my light in its eyes, I kept the beam directed at the shoulders. It was dark and I avoided eye contact. Fear kept me frozen to the spot, unable to act, make a move or process even the simplest of thoughts, though I knew I should do something. I waited for the beast to react, like a cowboy facing his arch-rival across a dusty street, guns at the ready. It was waiting for me, and I was waiting for it. A standoff with a bear; great.

The bear stood still, eyes glinting. I glimpsed my dinner-smeared pot lying a few feet from its nose, and other culinary items dotted the camp. If this bear was on the hunt for food, it must have thought it had lucked upon a supermarket aisle. I half expected it to disappear amongst the trees and emerge with a shopping trolley and grocery list.

It then moved a few feet towards me, slowly, deliberately and confidently; perhaps it was following a new smell. The animal's sheer bulk cleared aside some overhanging branches which had kept it in the shadows, and it emerged on to the trail as the moon bathed it in a weak, silvery light. I could almost make out the hairs on its back, shimmering as its nose moved up and down, testing for scents.

I started shaking, and then kicked into self-preservation mode. If, I thought, it was moving closer to see if I would react, then it would probably do so again, as I hadn't twitched a muscle.

"Hey, bear! Get outta here! Go! Go on!"

It didn't wince, and merely carried on staring at me. Now I really was in trouble. Bears are supposedly more scared of us than we are of them, but this one was not conforming to the rules.

"Go! Get out! GO!"

Nothing. I was a comedian having delivered my lines and no-one was laughing. I definitely wasn't amused, and was in fact becoming ever more convinced that dinner was on the agenda and I could be the main course.

I wondered if the bear sensed my fear; was I giving off a scent? Perhaps it could see my anxiety, or maybe it was picking up on my unease through its other senses.

So far I was simply behaving as I should have done in this situation, though fear had prevented me from revealing myself a little earlier by making noise. I had, however, stood my ground. When the beast crept a few paces closer, my instinct was to retreat, but I knew that would have been a big mistake. Retreating is a sign of weakness, and all the excuse a bear needs. It's like sizing up to the bloke in a pub when you've just knocked his pint of Guinness over. You don't run – you attempt to resolve the situation rationally and if things turn grim, you stand your ground and square up.

Bears communicate with each other by establishing a pecking order, a hierarchy. They fight only as a last resort, wary of sustaining an injury. The hierarchy is about dominance and submission; territorial disputes are usually solved by the alpha male. If nothing else, I knew that in this encounter, I had to continue to stand my ground. All this guy was looking for was a weakness, a chink in my armour. I was slap bang in the middle of a very serious game of chicken.

"All or nothing," I thought. I raised my arms over my head, puffed out what chest I had, and screamed.

"Hey! Bear! Get the hell out of here! MOVE!"

Still it remained rooted to the spot. Then, slowly, it turned its head to one side, looked down the hill and sniffed the bushes. It took one last look at me, appeared bored, and sloped slowly off. I felt exhausted, as though I had just run five miles. I looked skyward and thanked whoever had helped me, and lay down. I didn't sleep at all that night; every time a twig snapped, I shot bolt upright like a jack in the box, torch at the ready.

Preparing breakfast in the morning, I had more bad luck – my Steripen had packed up. I had been using it since Mammoth because my second water filter had broken. When it worked it was brilliant, but it was temperamental. The batteries were not standard so I had to carry not only a spare pair but another pair on top of that just in case. A green LED on the side lit when the purifying had worked but there was also a red LED that blinked if there was a problem, which more often than not was nothing to do with the batteries. Every time I used the device, I really dreaded that red light. It was like turning the key in your car's ignition and hoping the spanner symbol doesn't illuminate. To be fair, Steripen had sent me a new unit when the first one failed, but that had also been sent back for repair. I looked in dismay as, sure enough, the red LED started to blink mockingly and furthermore, nothing I tried corrected the issue.

I had only been back on trail for an afternoon and a night and my next re-supply was six days away. A few purification tablets were my sole backup, which would at best see me through a couple of days. I resigned myself to the fact that I had to walk back to the highway, get another ride into Etna, find a motel and locate the nearest decent hiking shop to buy another piece of water treatment equipment. Dejected, I plodded back to the road and stuck my thumb out.

Etna is a beautiful little town with much to recommend, but it lacks a dedicated shop for outdoor enthusiasts. I tried the pharmacy, desperately hoping for some purification tablets, but it was not to be. The owner of the hardware store shrugged his shoulders when I asked him, and said my only option was to reach Yreka again and catch a connecting bus all the way back to Shasta. I started to wander off to the motel but then remembered a cheaper alternative at Alderbrook Manor.

The Manor had converted a large garage to one side for the use of PCT hikers during the season. The owner, Dave, showed me around and made me welcome. I dumped my gear and hurried to the bus stop for the 10.30am ride to Yreka. As the bus trundled into the Walmart car park, I took a gamble by missing the next connecting service, and went into the store. The camping section was limited, but there was a small bottle of iodine tablets. This purple chemical kills any nasty organisms but I didn't like using it. Iodine has a reputation for being unkind to the body; in fact, some research suggests it should only be used as a backup and never for long periods of time. However, this particular brand came with another small bottle of tablets that neutralised the iodine after it had worked its magic. Besides, I only had six days until my next stop in Ashland. So I bought them and caught the next bus back to Etna. I made a quick phone call to a camping store in Ashland, some miles up the trail, who confirmed they had the filter I was looking for and kindly agreed to put it aside for me. Dave took me the few miles up the hill, and I was back on trail five hours after I had left.

A mental calculation confirmed that I still needed twenty-five-mile days, with one zero a week, to finish the walk by the 31st of October. I remained behind schedule, but if the winter held off a little, it was certainly achievable. Oregon was also approaching, which meant two positives. First, I would finally be out of California. That would be a huge morale boost, and tangible proof of progress. Second, Oregon is known for being a little more hiker-friendly. Elevation loss and gain are less severe than in California and Washington, and generally the terrain is easier. On the negative side, the temperatures were dropping at night, and dusk was now falling not in the evening, but late afternoon. I put my head down, increased my pace a touch and became stricter about leaving camp early, taking fewer and shorter breaks and meeting my target each day. I tried to stick to this plan; it was easy, surely? All I had to do was make sure I walked at least fifteen miles by lunch, and put in a brisk three hours in the afternoon to make up the miles. Anything on top of that would be a bonus.

Journal entry:

The weather is changing. It's getting cold, clouds appear more often and become more threatening each time I look up. Climbing out of my cosy sleeping bag in the morning is now something of a chore. Tentatively I reach out and pull down the zip, groping around for my clothes. I cringe as I slide into cold trousers and a frigid top. I crawl out of my warm little haven, squint into a rising sun and decide whether to fire up the stove or jump-start my body. My brain sputters grains of a battle plan for the day. Come the evenings, I'm stopping a little earlier because of the diminishing sunlight. Fire is the first priority; food and erecting tents take a back seat compared to warming my tired and aching body. A cup of hot chocolate brings a glow to my face and the pain begins to melt a little. I know that food is close at hand; the portions seem to increase as the temperatures drop. I sit by the orange glow of the fire, and warm my front as my back chills. Twigs cracking and snapping in the forest around me bring thoughts of bears and Sasquatch.

They say the PCT really starts to take its physical toll after the halfway point. They're right. I am tired, the aches take longer to fade and new ones appear. It hurts just a little more each day, and the ibuprofen supply seems to run out a bit earlier each week. However, none of this really matters. The PCT continues to astound, surprise and welcome me. New views greet me each day, different panoramas and vistas bringing a smile to my face. The relentless California stretch that I have been eating away at for the past 138 days is coming to an end. Oregon is in sight, maybe about five days away, and in about three days I will have 1,000 miles left to walk. These things are huge confidence-boosters. My morale needs little lifting, but targets help to keep me focused and positive.

My mileage has gone up from around fifteen per day at the start to around twenty-five now. On a recent stretch I managed to complete 150 miles in five days, and I maxed out at thirty-three in one day. I need to keep moving at that kind of tempo, because a finish in late October means walking nearly twice as far each day as I did during the first half. I continue to walk with Rockets, a fine companion. Brains left us a few days ago but we spoke on the phone recently. We expect to catch him because he had to rest for a couple of days owing to illness. Rockets is the crazy wild card. A veteran of the Appalachian Trail in 2006, he continues to make me smile with his larking around and mischievous antics. A true outdoorsman, he is at one with his surroundings and regales me with his adventures in walking, climbing and mountaineering. He stops often to pull out his Nikon when he sees something worthy of his photographic eye. He is one of perhaps a handful of people that I can see myself walking all the way to the end of the PCT with. A thousand miles is still a long way, but I know it is the start of the home stretch. Mexico, all those weeks behind me, seems an age ago. Time has little meaning out here; I get up when it feels right and stop when I'm tired. One day melts into another, and I don't even know what day it is; but a small part of me knows that I am within striking distance of Canada. Though the elements may grow restless, winter draws its sword and I find myself at the tail end of the pack, I walk with delight in my eyes and success in my heart.

***

I wandered off trail into a meadow to locate Buckhorn Spring

The Last Englishman

and fill up with water. A small clear pool tinkled as the spring trickled in, and I scooped up a litre, added an iodine tablet and sat down to wait for it to take effect. Despite being at 6,500 feet, it still felt like the middle of summer. A heat haze shimmered in the valley below, insects hovered and butterflies floated past. Cicada hummed a gentle, reassuring melody, the meadow grass waved as a breeze wandered through and flowers splashed colour everywhere. Long grass tickled my bare skin as I sat there.

Downing the first litre in one go, I filled up again and dropped in another tablet so that I was set for another couple of hours.

I checked the PCT atlas to ascertain my route and general plan for the day. I had twenty miles to go to Seiad Valley, descending 5,000 feet in the process. I planned to ingest some fat at the famous café there. The elevation graph included a 4,500-foot climb, which normally wouldn't be a problem for me, but it stretched out over only eight miles. That would make for a steep and tiring end to the day.

I met Colin, a SoBo, on the downhill into Seiad. He agreed that I should be able to crack out some good mileage in Oregon. He also confirmed that the climb out of Seiad up to the summit at Devils Peak was long and steep. I was glad I was going down and he was going up but that situation would soon be reversed.

I reached Highway 96 and made quick work of the couple of miles to the café, store and small post office. Seiad Valley Café is renowned among hikers for its pancake challenge: eat five inch-thick, 500-gram, dinner-plate-sized pancakes in less than two hours. A complimentary drizzle of syrup and trickle of butter finish off the dish. This innocuous-sounding test has laid out most of those who have taken it. In fact, only a handful have succeeded since its inception. The only reward for success is that the food is free.

This was, however, the last thing on my mind. Not being too fond of American pancakes, and with the climb out of the valley on my mind, I settled for delicious bacon and eggs as I chatted to a couple of locals.

"You're late," said Brian, a local decorator having lunch. "Most hikers have come through by now."

I didn't need reminding again.

"There's a hiker holed up in the campground next door, by the way. He had Giardia but has more or less recovered. I think his name is Cash."

I had bumped into Cash a couple of times and wasn't too fond of him; there was just something I couldn't put my finger on. I didn't want to see him again, so cautiously peered out of the window to see if he was loitering. The coast appeared clear so I grabbed my pack and walked out.

"Fozzie!"

"Shit!" I thought. "He's seen me."

Cash came over, looking very much the worse for wear.

"Are you with anyone?" he asked.

"On my own, trying to make tracks and still aiming to finish," I replied.

"Wait for me? I'm just getting over Giardia but think I'm OK to walk, so let me pack up camp, get something to eat and I'll come with you."

I made some excuses and said I couldn't wait. It may have been harsh to leave an ill hiker, but something about Cash didn't ring true to me. He went back to the campsite and said he'd catch me up.

Another SoBo called Two Dog stopped me, and told me whom she'd met. To my surprise, she had bumped into Rockets two days earlier.

"What the hell?" I thought. "Where does that guy get his energy from? I leave him in Yreka to sort his tooth out and now, somehow, he's passed me?"

I called his mobile.

"How the hell did you get ahead of me, Rockets?"

He laughed.

"I don't know, mucker," he replied. "I got the tooth sorted and didn't have to go to Portland, so put my head down and ground out some miles. I walked late a couple of evenings, so guess I must have passed you while you were sleeping."

He was with Brains in Ashland and said he would wait for me there although Brains was moving on.

I walked along the road for a mile and then turned right back into the forest to take on the Devils Peak climb. It was hot and humid. The hill was steeper than I would have liked, but it maintained a steady gradient, so at least I knew what to expect and could adjust my pace accordingly. Stopping only briefly at Lookout Spring, I gritted my teeth and let fly, reaching the top in one go. As I eased on to flatter terrain, my legs gently relaxed after their efforts. I battled on, trying to put some distance between Cash and me.

"Everyone I meet is walking south," I thought, as I glimpsed another hiker descending towards me. As he came into view, I realised I had met him before.

"Patch!" I exclaimed. "I haven't seen you since Wrightwood!"

I had camped in the back yard of a trail angel's house with Patch some three and a half months earlier. He was having a bad time there; on the approach to town, he had left his pack by trailside and taken a side route to fill up with water at a spring, and on his return found that someone had stolen his pack. Apparently this had happened to several hikers; the rumour was that someone was lying in wait at the trail junction. The culprit presumably knew that the route to the spring was downhill and a fair distance and that most hikers slipped off their packs so as not to be burdened on the climb back up.

This was a major blow. The cost of equipment for a thru-hike can run from £700 to £1,300 and over. My main essentials – namely pack, camping mat, sleeping bag and tent – totalled around £800 on their own. If you are on a tight budget, having your gear stolen can end your hike.

I'd watched Patch at his computer ordering replacements for all his gear, and then play the waiting game with the postman, but he managed it.

He'd skipped up to Canada from the Heitmans' and was now walking back, on course to complete the PCT in two more weeks. Somehow, he had managed to walk 800 miles more than I had in the same amount of time. I feared it was more my slow pace that was to blame.

"In anticipation of becoming a thru-hiker," I offered, "let me be the first to congratulate you," and I shook his hand.

"Go, Fozzie!" he shouted after me as we went separate ways. "You can do it!"

Fuelled by good progress since Etna, I rose early. I downed a litre of water, threw my only remaining snack, a handful of parmesan shavings, into my mouth and sped off.

Perhaps two hours into my fifteen-mile morning shift, I approached a couple of signs nailed to a pine tree. I assumed it was a 'distance to Canada' reminder, so I took no notice. I dropped my pack and rested for a few minutes. Curiosity got the better of me, though, as I got up, and a broad smile rippled across my chops as I checked the sign:

'Welcome to Oregon
'Interstate 5 – 28
'Hyatt Lake – 51
'Washington Border – 498
'Canadian Border – 962'

I felt a fire in my belly, a mixture of achievement, pride and determination. At last I was out of California and into Oregon! It was well under 1,000 miles now until the finish, and I could in theory get through this next state in a month. Finally, after four and a half months, I felt as though I was on the home stretch.

"YES!" I screamed, as I literally ran off. "Get in there!"

I spent the next hour kicking pine cones into the back of an imaginary goal past an imaginary, helpless German goalkeeper in an imaginary World Cup final.

I walked well into the night, and took a short rest before vowing to walk a few more miles. The lights of Ashland twinkled below me a few miles away and a full moon cast a soft, silvery light. I called Rockets and said I would get to him by lunch the following day.

Searching for a good place to camp for the night, I came across a four-way intersection on the trail. A sign pointed to my right:

'Grouse Gap Shelter – 0.25 miles'

Shelters on the PCT are few and far between. The Appalachian Trail, by contrast, is strewn with three-sided buildings where hikers spend the night in the dry; a hiker will pass one or more each day. I turned right, anticipating the simple prospect of a picnic table where I could eat and chill.

I reached my goal at 10pm after a long day. Lights from a couple of recreational vehicles penetrated the darkness and

The Last Englishman

Steve, who ran the shelter, came out to meet me as he saw my head torch scanning the area.

"You walking the PCT?" he enquired.

"Yes I am, glad to come across the shelter."

"You're a bit late, aren't you? Sure you'll make it?"

This was becoming somewhat regular, but I didn't mind. The look of surprise on most people's faces was all that I needed to prove them wrong. I settled down, cooked the last remaining meal in my food bag and tallied up the mileage. I arrived at the figure of 38.6. I was happy, but also chastised myself for not keeping tabs on my progress and pushing on for another 30 minutes to achieve my first 40-miler. To my delight, I also discovered I had walked 95.4 miles in three days, an average of 31.8 miles per day. Finally, the need to crush some miles was starting to sink in.

I woke early, sat up and peered through the slit in my sleeping bag. The sun was just under the horizon of a distant hill but casting enough light to see by. A low mist had settled on the field by the shelter and seemed in no hurry to disperse. I was just about to light my stove when Steve appeared smiling and handed me a coffee. We sat and took in the calm environment for a few minutes and he left, bidding me good luck.

I set off, eager to get to the highway ten miles away. There was also the prospect of breakfast at Callahan's Restaurant and maybe a ride to Ashland. I startled a huge bear in the forest, and watched in awe as it thundered off up the hill like a runaway goods train. Passing under Interstate 5, I entered the restaurant. Callahan's is also a hotel with a great reputation among hikers; it's a little upmarket for the likes of us, but we are made to feel more than welcome there.

Callahan's burnt down in September 2006, but the owners Donna and Ron Bergquist bounced back, re-opening bigger and better in August 2008. In order to keep attracting business from PCT hikers, they have kept their mid-week prices flexible. The place also now has showers and laundry, and allows camping on the back lawn, as well as offering one of the best breakfasts I had eaten.

I felt slightly self-conscious, but the receptionist didn't bat an eyelid. I explained I was heading to Ashland and so, despite my appearance, didn't need a wash or laundry. She led me into the dining room, introduced me to my waitress and wished me well on my hike. An immaculate waitress called Angela floated over, poured freshly squeezed orange juice, asked me how I liked my coffee and gently placed a menu in my hands.

"You're running a little late for a thru-hike, aren't you?" she asked, looking me directly in the eye and smiling so sweetly that I considered proposing to her there and then.

"Not enough decent breakfasts," I replied, feeling a little bashful.

Making quick work of the meal, I got a ride into Ashland from a member of staff named James. I knocked on the door of room five at the Ashland Motel, and Courtney answered.

"What are you doing?" I smiled as she hugged me.

"Came up to see Pockets and chill out for a couple of days."

"Mucker!" came a voice from inside the bedroom, as Rockets strode out and gave me another hug.

"You seen anyone in town?" I asked.

"Nope, we're the last of the pack, I think. Brains left a couple of days ago with Lone Ginger. You?"

"Saw Patch south-bound and due to finish soon, someone called Two Dog, who said she had bumped into you, and also Cash."

His face dropped.

"Cash is here?"

"Well, I don't think he's in Ashland," I continued. "I left him at Seiad and I've put in some good miles since then but he's probably not far behind."

Rockets was not too fond of Cash, since they had nearly come to blows in Mammoth. Apparently Cash was slightly the worse for wear after a few drinks, and tried to pick a fight and grab Rockets's camera. Rockets, a former nightclub bouncer, said that Cash had backed down with a little gentle persuasion.

We were all in good spirits. I was still on a high from my mileage, Courtney was just happy to be with Rockets and he was full of his usual energy. We went down to the post office to pick up mail and as we parked Cash strolled over, surprising me at how he had caught up so quickly.

When he asked us if we had found somewhere to stay, we

confirmed we had but there was no space. We drove him to the hostel, also full, and eventually two miles out of town to a motel where he found a spare bed.

We spent two days in Ashland. As usual, I tried but failed to get everything done in a day. I had to update my blog, answer emails, download photos, re-supply, clean myself up, do laundry and eat a lot of food. It rained on and off, and was getting colder. I had a raging hunger, for which the café next door was a godsend come breakfast. I worked my way through a pile of hash browns, eggs, bacon, toast and sausage every morning. I drifted around in a caffeine-induced high after discovering an abundance of good coffee houses, and finished off pizzas so big that I normally would have surrendered after three slices.

The camping shop had indeed put a Katadyn Hiker filter to one side. I hoped that this, my fourth water treatment device of the trip, would see me through to Canada. My waterproof pack liner had also reached the end of its life, so I replaced it. All my other gear was faring well, although I was resigned to the fact that I might need a new tent soon. What with the impending wetter weather and possibly snow, I knew I'd need the Gore-Tex lined boots that Inov-8 had sponsored me with. I called Aunty Jillian and she arranged to post them up trail.

Rockets and I zoomed off in the late morning, constantly aware now that the weather could close in. Winter was almost upon us and snow was all but inevitable. Hikers up the trail had said that Washington hadn't had snow, but was wet. The forecast bad winter was, so far at least, late.

We stopped briefly so that Rockets could take photos. Before long we spotted a hiker snoozing by the side of the trail, his gear drying out on branches. It was Cash.

"Hey guys! Wassup?"

We stopped briefly to exchange pleasantries but carried on as soon as we could. Cash appeared in no hurry. As we looked back, we expected to see him packing up and coming after us, but he just lay down and went back to sleep. However, two hours later when we had stopped for lunch, he rounded the corner and sat with us, opening his food bag. He shared some of his food, which I thought was a nice gesture, and I started to think that maybe he wasn't so bad after all. Rockets raised his eyebrows at me, suggesting that he thought the same.

Cash appeared to be taking the trail lightly, and again stayed behind when we strode off. Reaching Hyatt Lake road, we spotted Keene Creek reservoir down the hill and camped on the bank so as to have access to a supply of water. It was a still evening; I watched the sun slide down behind a hill and the moon rise, reflecting in the Keene's waters. Car headlights flashed on a nearby road as the driver negotiated the hairpin turns.

I sloped off a few feet just before hiker midnight for a pee. There's something immensely satisfying about peeing outdoors. Sprinkling in a toilet doesn't come close. I often pondered this as I stood, legs astride, in the woods. I think it stems back to our caveman days, when it was the norm. It's territorial too, I think; the marking of one's patch of land. Dogs and cats still do it, as do wild animals. I'm sure that before humans lost their evolved, heightened sense of smell, they knew when they were encroaching on someone else's area. Even in motels, I still had the urge to go outside to pee. At home, I nearly always go in the garden. I feel the need to mark my dominion, and will tinkle in various spots to spread the scent around. It's an enlightening experience to relieve yourself outside; try it, you'll be pleasantly surprised.

We woke to damp gear and ice crusting the outside of the tents. It had rained again during the night, and we knew it wouldn't be long before plunging temperatures turned rain to snow. Clouds streamed overhead and didn't disperse all day. We discussed tactics. Rockets had a friend in a town called Corvallis, accessible by a road about eighty-five miles up trail. We debated getting a ride from there, re-supplying and then finding transport to Cascade Locks and the Bridge of the Gods.

This impressively engineered bridge spans the Columbia River and separates Oregon from Washington. Our plan was to skip up to the border before the snow hit, knock off Washington, get transport back to the bridge and then south-bound to Oregon, where we had left the trail. It made a lot of sense; we were keenly aware of the game of dice we were playing.

Oregon was living up to its reputation. Instead of a rollercoaster of hills, now the altitude graph had settled into a kinder, flatter line. We did twenty-seven miles the next day, nearing Brown Mountain shelter, most likely nearby water and a useful stock of firewood. Taking the 0.1-mile side track to the shelter, we were lucky on both counts. A hand pump provided access to clean well water and inside the hut we found not only wood but also a huge, cast-iron stove in the middle of the single room. By the time we had fired it up, it was so hot that we were walking around in shirts and shorts. We cooked on the stove and settled down to read and write journals. Just as I was just dozing off around 11pm, I heard, "Hey, Fozzie."

I turned over to see Rockets with his nose pressed to the window, looking outside.

"Hmm. Wassup?"

"I think there's someone coming."

Chapter 14
Jekyll and Hyde

The long trail can change us if we listen and let it. The longer we are on the journey, the deeper the truth penetrates and the deceptions of modern life vanish away.
Ned Tibbits (Director of Mountain Education, a free service to educate hikers on winter skills)

Rockets peered out of the window and spotted a head torch bouncing along towards us.

"I think it may be Cash."

Sure enough, Cash poked his head through the door. I sat upright and acknowledged him as he walked in.

"Sorry, mate," I said, "our stuff is everywhere, we weren't expecting anyone. Hang on and I'll make some space for you."

"No, it's fine," he replied. "I can sleep on the trail."

Before I could answer, he left and I watched through the window as he sat at the table outside and started to read. Thirty minutes later he stormed back in, a changed man.

"This is disgusting!" he screamed.

Surprised at such an outburst, I looked at Rockets, who raised his eyebrows in amazement.

"Your stuff is everywhere, there's no room! What's this trash doing on the floor?"

"It's our trash, which we'll take with us in the morning, Cash," Rockets said. "We can make room for you. We weren't

The Last Englishman

expecting anyone, which is why our stuff is spread out. We *can* make room for you. Where do you want to sleep?"

"This is fucking disgusting!" he screamed. To say Cash was angry was a huge understatement. Rockets sensed something amiss, as did I, as Cash carried on with his Jekyll and Hyde tirade.

"What is this?!" he cried, and began to throw our gear about. He approached Rockets, who was zipped up in his sleeping bag, and shouted at him. Rockets glanced at me and narrowed his eyes. It was a warning that the situation could turn dangerous, a fact I was already very well aware of. He gently unzipped his bag as Cash threw a torrent of abuse at both of us and encroached threateningly on Rockets's space.

"Cash! We can make room for you!"

"You're both scum! Look at this shit!"

I broke in. "Cash, you're being a prick. Shut the fuck up and piss off."

"Fuck you!"

Then he started with our gear again. I began to get out of my bag. Rockets stood up and confronted him. Holding his ground, he pleaded with Cash to calm down, but also told him in no uncertain terms to stop or else get thrown out. Cash motioned to throw another piece of equipment, but Rockets stepped in, and held him with a firm gaze.

"Cash, I'm going to say this once. Leave our stuff alone, get the fuck out of here or I'll throw you out."

Cash paused, glared at me and then at Rockets. The atmosphere was tense. Rockets was standing tall and ready for anything, his body rigid and primed. I got up and stood staring at Cash. His fists were clenched, his stance suggesting violence. In the momentary ensuing pause, I was convinced all hell was about to be unleashed, but then he appeared to relax and retreated a few steps. Picking up his bag, he thundered off into the night.

"What the hell was all that about?" I exclaimed.

"I don't know," Rockets replied, "but I never want to see that guy again."

We slept fitfully, half expecting Cash to storm back in. Although he didn't, we knew that at some point we would bump into him again. Sure enough, a couple of hours into the following day, Cash's familiar frame appeared ahead of us, seated by the side of the trail.

"What you wanna do?" I asked Rockets.

"I don't know about you, mate, but I don't even want to look at him."

I made eye contact a good ten seconds before we passed Cash and locked his gaze. He showed no remorse, didn't move and said nothing. We left him and sped up to put some distance between us.

"I got a message from him," Rockets said, checking his phone as we were finishing lunch. "He's apologised and said he was out of order."

"It's a nice gesture but it doesn't excuse his behaviour," I said.

Rockets nodded.

"Too little, too late. Good of him to apologise but I still never want to see him again."

Just then my mobile beeped with the same message.

We hurried up, agreeing that mileage was the priority, and also with any luck we'd leave Cash behind. For once I was ahead, and had stopped near a spring, which was reduced to a small trickle. Rockets arrived a few minutes later, sweat staining both his top and the trail behind him.

"Where's water?" he asked.

"Down that trail," I replied, motioning for him. "Ignore the first creek bed, it's empty. There's another one a few yards further that's just about running."

Rockets sweated more than a Taliban member trying to get through customs at Heathrow with a fake passport and an AK47. He literally dripped his way along. We discussed our intake when he returned. I drank about two to three litres a day, more or less regardless of the temperature, while he apparently knocked back between six and seven litres. We timed our rest breaks around creeks or springs that we located on our maps, so when I got there first he would stroll in and the first words out of his mouth would be, "Where's water?"

The Oregon trails were indeed kinder and we found ourselves finishing our daily twenty-five-mile target earlier than previously. The trail itself, dark, sandy soil with a smattering of pine cones, felt softer and cushioned each strike of our feet on the ground. The temperature was warm during the day but chilled rapidly in the evening, and mist often wafted around us.

We reached Highway 62 and got a ride with John, who was heading for Mazama village. This small cluster of buildings included a store, restaurant and post office. As we pulled up, I noticed a familiar figure leaning against a wall.

"Cash is here," I said, pointing towards the restaurant.

"Great."

I walked over and completely ignored Cash but as I looked back, I saw Rockets talking to him.

"I'm sorry, Pockets," Cash began.

"We appreciate you sending the messages apologising," Rockets said, "but what you did was completely out of order. You don't go crazy at people in the middle of nowhere. You threatened both of us."

"Where's Fozzie gone?"

"He's inside, and he doesn't want to speak to you. In fact, he never wants to see you again and neither do I. Good luck with your hike, Cash."

After downing a few hot dogs, John asked if we could use a lift somewhere. We checked the map and realised we were right on top of Crater Lake. One of the finest sights on the PCT, the lake was formed around 7,700 years ago when Mount Mazama collapsed and formed the caldera now filled with water. At 1,943 feet deep, it is the deepest lake in the United States and the seventh deepest in the world.

"Why don't we try to get a ride to Corvallis from here?" I asked Rockets. "Imagine walking back and finishing at Crater Lake: it would make one hell of a finale."

He agreed and we jumped in the car with John, who took us all the way to Benton. Dancing on the slip road to the highway to attract attention, we were quickly picked up again and dropped off at Grants Pass. It was now dark, so we looked for somewhere to sleep in town and passed the Greyhound station. A bus to Corvallis was scheduled to leave at 3am. After grabbing a bite to eat, we slept round the back of a factory – or tried to. Rockets didn't sleep well.

"Your feet smell like a dead rat in a rotting, musky basement," he said.

"Thanks," I replied, laughing.

"And what is it with your Neoair?" (A Neoair is an inflatable sleeping mattress which has a habit of squeaking when the user shifts position.)

"What do you mean?"

"It's noisy! Every night you sound like you're wrestling a dolphin."

"Have you not met my mate Flipper yet?"

We arrived in Corvallis early morning and found Rockets's mate Brett in his kitchen.

"Guys, if you're hungry, we can go down the local café and maybe you can try the Beaver Buster!"

Tommy's 4th Street Bar & Grill was responsible for the Beaver Buster. It's a breakfast named after the local American Football team, the Beavers, and to call it monumental is something of an understatement. When I first read the menu, I decided that just good old eggs, hash browns and bacon would do; but Rockets, who can put away abnormally large amounts of food, was tempted by the challenge.

Said challenge was to eat the calorie-loaded mound of gluten and cholesterol in under an hour. The diner must sit alone – I believe this rule stems from an incident when someone discreetly passed some of the food to a friend on the same table – and a timer is placed near the diner. You can only start when the waitress gives the nod, and the reward for success is a free meal. Otherwise, it's a $24 bill. In the four years since Tommy's had offered the challenge, only four people had succeeded.

Rockets looked at the menu, then at Brett, checked the menu again, looked at me and scratched his chin.

"I'll give it a go, me old mucker!"

A waitress appeared fifteen minutes later, struggling to keep hold of a plate groaning with an obscene amount of food. She placed it carefully in front of Rockets, who had sat at an empty table. He raised his eyebrows slightly, picked up his cutlery, looked at me, then at Brett and finally at the waitress.

"Good luck, go!" she said, starting the timer.

We had discussed tactics. I advised making the most of the

seven-minute rule – that it takes seven minutes for the brain to register that the stomach is full. Therefore, Rockets needed to put away as much food as possible before his brain had a chance to react. I also told him to eat the wheat products such as bread and pancakes first, because these are the most filling; the sooner he got those out of the way, the easier it would be to finish the rest of the plate.

This, I thought, was all good advice. The problem was the actual contents of the plate. When I first laid eyes on it, I couldn't believe what I was seeing. Two six-egg omelettes (that's an astonishing *twelve eggs*), a mound of hash browns, piles of home fries (sautéed potatoes), five pancakes, two biscuits (in America a biscuit is similar to a savoury scone in England), strips of bacon, sausages, ham, gravy, and eight pieces of toast!

As Brett and I tucked in to our modest servings, Rockets dived in, piling in the food as fast as he could. However, a mere ten minutes in, he puffed out his cheeks and raised his eyebrows. The poor chap had barely made it through half the plate before giving up and holding his stomach, groaning. Brad and I just sniggered.

We stayed in Corvallis for two days and then caught the Greyhound to Cascade Locks. Arriving late, we found a cheap motel. We were both eager to get back on the trail and tackle Washington.

We bumped into Uncle Gary the following morning. I hadn't seen him since Independence, where he was hiking with the two Brits, Nick and Chris. I was keen to hear where my fellow countrymen were. He thought they were about seventy miles up the way. They had gone to England for a wedding and returned to finish off the trail.

We set off late but walked until Panther Creek, still only managing nine miles. Gary told us in the morning that Flannel, Walker Texas Ranger, Crow and Dundee were close behind. It was Rockets's birthday, so we got a swift ride back to town, secured some beer and snacks and sat by the creek, slowly getting drunk. Sure enough, at midday the others rolled in. They were surprised to see us, as they had heard through the hiker grapevine how far behind we were. We explained we had skipped up to Cascade Locks and were planning to finish Washington and return to complete the section we had missed. We set off, and I felt good being among familiar faces.

Uncle Gary was from Petaluma, California and was studying outdoor education. He sported an impressive beard and mound of hair and, despite the sunshine over the previous few months, he had somehow managed to stay as white as a sheet. We all walked together for most of the day, until Rockets, Uncle Gary and I descended a series of switchbacks to camp by a creek.

Journal entry:

The bears know when it's time. So do the mountain lions, the squirrels and the snakes. They sense when the snows are coming and they prepare for the winter. I can see the obvious signs, like the leaves painted in reds, oranges and yellows. When the wind catches the trees, we walk through thousands of leaves cascading down, floating from side to side like a mother cradling her baby. The mornings are colder and frost clings to our tents. We watch a cloud of warm mist rise as we exhale. Gaggles of geese fly overhead calling out, perhaps warning us of what to expect.

The vibe of autumn approaching is hard to explain. It's more than merely visual signals, as mesmerising as they are. This is my favourite time of year: the temperature is perfect for hiking, the sunsets are magical and sitting in camp with a blazing fire is comforting. Something in my body makes me aware that summer has ended. It's more than the smell of musty leaves; it goes deeper than the mist banks swirling around me with beams of sunlight slicing through.

Rockets and I have been joined by Uncle Gary. At twenty-six years old, he is an interesting guy to walk with. A powerful hiker with thighs like tree trunks, he walks a good-but-not-quick pace, and reels off a series of jokes. Many times he stops to study fungi poking through the soil and we feast on the forest's bountiful supply. His knowledge in this area is impressive, and adds to my modest memory bank of information regarding edible shrooms. Our food stocks are well supplemented by the likes of cauliflower fungus, boletes, chanterelles and white matsutake. Throw in some leftover bacon, fresh garlic and possibly some 'past-its-best parsley', and the finest restaurants would be hard pressed to come up with anything this tasty.

Washington State is providing great walking. We meander between pine trees towering above us so high that we strain to see the tops. The trail is dampened with occasional rain, which cushions our steps and puts a stop to the clouds of dust we normally kick up. Occasionally we glimpse valleys below us. Lakes peek through gaps, and peaks such as Mt Adams and Mt Hood tower imposingly above us, capped with fresh snow. Tough going after our brief Oregon entrée, Washington has the dips and crests we had become used to in California. Climbs of 3,000 feet or more, and four-hour ascents, make our thighs and calves scream.

***

Progress was good but I was concerned about Rockets; he wasn't behaving in his normal, mischievous manner. I'd noticed this over the course of a week and had broached the subject of whether anything was wrong a couple of times. He was more despondent and said he was tired of walking, was unhappy with his photos and had no motivation. He seemed too blasé about taking zeros, and the threat of possible snowfall didn't bother him. It was a strange departure from the carefree, positive and crazy friend I had come to know, and it was threatening to demotivate me, too. I never needed an excuse to take a zero, and I enjoyed a more sedate pace than some, covering fewer miles than I should. I was, however, painfully aware of the changing season, and, unlike my mate, was desperate to get moving.

I rose early with Uncle Gary and we tried to rouse Rockets. He grunted and said he'd catch us up.

Reaching a dirt track, we decided to clean up and re-supply in the small village at Trout Lake. We tried for thirty minutes to get a ride, but no-one passed so we started walking the thirteen miles. After two hours, a ranger truck came by, and I saw Rockets sitting in the back, grinning and waving. The ranger pulled over and took us into the village.

Rockets admitted he hadn't risen until 2pm. He complained that he felt constantly tired. That night he threw up on several occasions. He was getting worse and was again unable to get up in the morning. I told him he should see a doctor but he shrugged it off and said it would pass.

Walker, Flannel, Crow and Dundee showed up, re-supplied and left. They were late like me, but I could see in their eyes their determination to finish. They kept their rest breaks as short as possible, and I was envious of that attitude – I was still struggling to get out of Trout Lake. The usual diversions of the café and hot food had made me stay too long.

It was a constant battle to get moving, and difficult to find motivation, especially when surrounded by town comforts. It was cold and wet in the woods; though I could stay warm when moving, stopping for camp meant fighting the cold. I also felt a sense of duty towards Rockets – you don't abandon your hiking partner unless by agreement or illness. He was clearly ill, and I felt obliged to be there for him. He stayed in bed for most of the day.

Uncle Gary had found some matsutake fungi in the woods. He was confident that's what they were; he'd picked them before. They can be elusive, but in the woods around Trout Lake we spotted them a few times. We discussed lunching on this expensive treat. I went into the Trout Lake Store Grocery where we had rented the room above and asked Greg, the owner, if he had a frying pan we could borrow.

His ears pricked up when I told him what we were cooking.

"Really?" he said. "I haven't had matsutake for a while. How many you got?"

"Enough to let you have some, if you'd like. I'd trade for some bacon and garlic."

"I like!" His eyes lit up. I soon found out how highly prized our fungi were when he also threw in some chanterelles and a slab of steak each.

We fired up Uncle Gary's stove, let it heat up nice and hot, dropped in some butter and watched it become a layer of liquid fat, coating the bottom of the pan. We carefully added the steak with a little seasoning, seared it for a couple of minutes each side and then took it out to rest. We had trimmed and prepared the fungi, and they hissed as they hit the hot butter. Then, in went the bacon, and we cooked both to a golden brown, finally throwing in some chopped garlic. The resulting dish was one of the best I had eaten on the entire trip. Dundee appeared.

"What are you cooking? It smells amazing!" she exclaimed.

We let her try it. Her face contorted into ecstasy as she looked gratefully skyward and made approving noises. Even Mike and Murray, the two local cats, came over to see what was going on.

Uncle Gary left in the morning and I was keen to move on as well. Rockets was still unwell, and seemed grumpy; he was annoyed at a couple of things I had done, and he moved out of the room because I apparently made too much noise in the morning. He had always let stuff like that slide before; when you hike with someone day in and day out, you let the little things go because it's just not worth the tension. If you don't get along with another thru-hiker, then you don't walk together. I didn't blame Rockets – I knew it wasn't him, it was his illness. I asked if he wanted me to do anything for him, and he said no.

"I have to hit the trail, Rockets, I have to finish. I can help you out but you have to make a decision: stay and find out what's wrong with you, or come with me."

"Go, Fozzie, I'll catch you up."

Greg dropped me back on the trail. It was cold, a low mist lingered and moisture dripped all around me. I looked at the track and watched water trickling around tree roots, trying to find the path of least resistance. It worked its way into creeks and streams, which in turn fed the rivers, all the way to the Pacific Ocean. Water never took a zero, didn't fall ill and never quit until the goal was reached. It's funny, the comparison we make between nature and walking, I thought, as I skipped along the trail trying to keep my feet dry.

I camped in a small clearing circled by trees, which made me feel like the centre of focus in a large arena. The melancholy mist had lowered and thickened, and my head torch struggled to make an impression against a random mix of eddies, fluctuations and billions of water droplets twinkling at me. Somehow I managed to start a fire in the dampness, to warm up and dry out my shoes. The glow from the fire arched out as far as it could before being forced back by the mist. An orange dome formed around the flames, gently tickling the trees around me and illuminating the patterns on the bark. Beyond that, the light was engulfed by the forest void. It felt oppressive, as though several giant hands were smothering me.

The murkiness had subsided a little in the morning, just clearing the treetops. Sunlight occasionally lit solitary trees around me like a spotlight in a crowd of people. Silence was broken by the occasional creak and groan from the forest, and huckleberry bushes hemmed me in on a trail so worn that it was more of a shallow trench. Barely a thing stirred or made a sound all day. My only company as I walked was the gentle crunch of my boots on crispy, volcanic soil.

At 8pm, before the ascent to Goat Rocks Wilderness, I stopped for the day. It was late, and from the map I saw that the contour lines were about to have a party. I was approaching a climb and a knife-edge ridge walk. There was no way I was going to attempt that in the dark, especially with ominous clouds rolling in. I tucked my tent into a tiny gap at the forest's edge for some extra protection, lit a fire and cooked over the flames. A log offered a seat and, as I sat, I reached out to the fire for warmth. A faint light from the moon bounced around the camp, but not enough to see by, so I switched on my head torch and supped hot chocolate.

The beam began to pick out something falling, reflecting thousands of tiny particles winking at me. I assumed it was light rain, but then noticed that the particles were floating rather than falling. It was the first snowfall, and though only a light dusting, I knew then that the Washington winter was beginning. It threw me into a few seconds of mild panic, which subsided but left a deep feeling of fear and failure in the pit of my stomach. All those zeros, all those days I could have walked a few more miles. Why didn't I get up a little earlier or walk a little further? Now, all my mistakes had snowballed, as it were, into one. My PCT hike was in very real danger of faltering on the home stretch. I had 336 miles left in Washington, and then I had to travel back down to Cascade Locks and south-bound the section I had missed to Crater Lake, a further distance of 322 miles. This 658-mile effort would equate to about 26 days of walking, or a month, to be safe. I was looking at completion around the second week of November, a good two months over schedule.

The Last Englishman

The mornings and nights were cold, the days chilly. I woke again to ice on the tent and on the trail. My boots crunched on the frozen dirt as they broke through the crust into small puddles. Icicles protruded horizontally from bushes where the wind had forced them sideways. I drank from my water bottle, and a mix of water and slush slid down my throat.

Entering the Goat Rocks Wilderness area, I climbed for what seemed an eternity towards the ridge at 7,150 feet. I crested the ridge and was dumbstruck as I was confronted with the best view in the world. The trail followed the ridge as it descended and I walked carefully as my boots tried to gain purchase on shiny, slick, icy rock as smooth as glass. I was in the middle of a gigantic arena; the ridge fell away to green lowlands and then rose again, dipping and diving all around me as it disappeared to infinity. White peaks merged into grey rock and plummeted into valleys, where the silver ribbons of a river wove their way along the bottom. Mt Rainier stood majestically, like a king perched on his throne, as low cloud whipped past and occasionally obscured my own personal panorama.

I negotiated the rollercoaster like a feather caught in the breeze, straining up hills and relaxing a little on the downs. Early afternoon I spilled out on to Highway 12 and turned left towards White Pass, where a small store stood by the side of the road. Walker Texas Ranger, Crow, Dundee, Flannel and Uncle Gary sat outside opening mail boxes and cramming new supplies into their packs. I grabbed a quick coffee, and the assistant told me that my mail had not arrived but had probably ended up in Packwood, a small town nineteen miles down in the valley. I wished the others luck and caught a quick ride into town. The Packwood Inn had a reasonable room for me, and the owner, a creepy and untrustworthy-looking guy, took my laundry away. I reached the post office just before it closed, and picked up a package from Dicentra. I had sent her a copy of my last book in exchange for a food box. I opened it eagerly, and smiled as I found several dehydrated meals from her own recipes, proper coffee, almond and peanut butter sachets and a host of other goodies. My other packages contained a new tent, my winter sleeping bag, down jacket, warmer socks and a neck buff. My mood brightened at the thought of being a little warmer and better fed over the coming days. I sent my tent back to HQ in San Jose, and my summer bag to Western Mountaineering.

The soles of my feet were in bad shape. Although blisters were a thing of the distant past, I had painful and tender areas of red skin. I had no idea what caused them, but they had slowed my progress over recent days and I pondered resting for a day more. I secured some comfort food from the store, along with Epsom salts. I sat with my feet in a strong solution while working my way through a tub of ice cream and occasionally pausing to take in some Pale Ale.

Later, as I wandered aimlessly around town, I caught the aroma of coffee drifting up from a little side street. Following my nose, I found the Butter Butte coffee shop. Not content with making wonderful espressos, they also ground and roast their own beans. I returned several times, and sat in the corner reading and contemplating my hike thus far and the challenges still ahead. I can reliably inform you that the Butter Butte coffee shop served me the best coffee on the entire Pacific Crest Trail.

Rockets called me the following day and told me to hold on; he was due in Packwood that day. Although he had seen a doctor, who had diagnosed possible E. coli poisoning, he sounded upbeat and eager to get going. He arrived shortly afterwards and we moved over to a twin room at the Hotel Packwood. The hotel was empty save the owner and her dog.

The doctor had told Rockets to get off trail. Most thru-hikers don't consult doctors, regardless of the ailment. The advice, nine times out of ten, is to 'get off trail', and nine times out of ten hikers don't need to. Rockets simply said "You can't keep Pockets down."

He was, however, not well. Apart from the physical problems associated with E. coli, it was his psychological state that troubled me. He was despondent, still sleeping a lot, and reluctant to move on. He was constantly tired and struggling, but would not admit it. I looked up to him in some ways, and was thankful for his lead when we walked together. But maybe because of my admiration for him, I let his disinclination rub off on me, and I became too comfortable also doing nothing. Rain had covered Packwood for two days, only adding to the gloom, and I found myself repeating a mantra several times a day to try

The Last Englishman

to generate some self-motivation:

"I will finish the PCT and I will enjoy it. Foz, you have to move. YOU HAVE TO MOVE."

On the third day, despite the rain, I left Rockets again and caught a quick ride back up to White Pass. He wanted to wait for clearer weather, but I couldn't. Recoiling from the spray of passing trucks, I found the trailhead and disappeared back into the damp forest. My shoes, now worn out, slipped on the mud, but they had to last until Snoqualmie Pass, ninety-nine miles away, where HQ had mailed my Gore-Tex boots. Water seeped through the mesh as I squelched unceremoniously along. When dusk crept in, I pulled off trail to a flat area near the shore of Snow Lake. I dropped my pack as drizzle started falling, and was two minutes into erecting my tent when I heard what sounded like the call of an eagle behind me. I swung round to see Rockets peering out from behind a tree, smiling.

We spent the rainy evening in separate tents, eating and reading. We discussed plans, our conversation somewhat drowned in the pitter-patter of water falling and trickling off our tents.

"I have to get going, mate," I said. "I know you're ill but it's your head that worries me: it's holding you back and, in turn, me as well. I *need* to finish this. I've got way too much resting on it to consider failing. I'm late as it is, I have to move. I'd love you to walk with me, but you do have to start walking."

"I know, me old mucker, I know."

The inevitable happened: rain turned to snow at higher elevations early afternoon the following day. Venturing upwards, we hit dark, damp, sticky soil, which turned white with a couple of inches of snow. The cone-shaped hills around us were topped with a sprinkling of the white magic like huge iced buns. Rockets was ahead of me as I stopped for water at a creek which crossed the trail. A voice from behind startled me.

"How's it going?"

I spun round to see a very damp Trooper grinning at me.

"Trooper! Where the hell did you come from?"

Pleased though I was to see him, I was again reminded of my slow progress. Trooper had walked from Chester, where we had last met. He had made it through Oregon and the section from

Crater Lake, which I hadn't. I couldn't help feeling a little jealous of how far he'd walked. He already knew what it was like to falter at the last hurdle, after his previous PCT attempt had ended a few years earlier. He was determined to succeed this time, and he was 313 miles away from doing so. He was putting in some miles to reach Stehekin, 251 miles away. That was the last place to re-supply before the end, and lay eleven miles off trail. A bus service runs through the summer, taking hikers to this small settlement on the banks of Lake Chelan. There, they can rest and stock up for the final sixty-five-mile section to the Canadian border. However, the buses had usually stopped by the middle of October, so time was running out. Anyway, Trooper was in good spirits and seemed glad to have company, as were we.

We camped that night and dried gear by the fire. Through the day, we stayed reasonably dry in our waterproofs; it was really only our socks and shoes that were damp. We tried to build a fire every evening, but the damp conditions were making life difficult. Usually finding shelter in the forest gave us some drier wood, but we constantly had to check and feed the fire before it spluttered to a moist death.

Trooper had left when I started the following morning, leaving Rockets taking photos of the appropriately named Dewey Lake. The target for the day lay twenty-six miles away: a cabin called the Urich Shelter by the edge of a meadow, where we could dry out in comfort and, for once, get warm. I descended towards Highway 410 and Chinook Pass, where the sun had emerged. A curling vapour rose from Trooper's gear, which he'd spread out over a wall by the roadside. Rockets arrived shortly afterwards and I left ahead of both of them, eager to conquer a series of small passes between me and the shelter. I crested Sourdough Pass, Bluebell Pass and Scout Pass, the thought of a warm night spurring me ever onward. Rockets caught me after a couple of hours, and we finished the day off with two fast-paced two-hour stints. He pulled away from me with a couple of miles left, and said he'd start a fire.

Daylight was fading as I emerged from the forest and crossed a wooden bridge over Meadow Creek. I homed in on the cabin, seeing a window glowing a faint orange in the murk.

"How is it in there?" I called out as I approached the large, impressive-looking shelter.

"Awesome!" came the muffled reply. "There's a stack of firewood, a good stove and seating. Come on in!"

Rockets's head torch struggled to illuminate the back wall. I turned on my torch too, and found a few tea lights. The fire caught and before long the gloomy cold was warming up nicely, as the flames cast a flickering light, which played a game of shadows and silhouettes on the walls. Trooper strolled in after dark, and we spent the evening drying out, warming up and eating in comfort. I updated my journal and looked down to a see a mouse sitting next to me, patiently waiting for a crumb or two.

Trooper had already set off by the time I left at 9am. Rockets had said he wanted to take a zero at the cabin and take more photos. I crunched my way along an icy trail, guided by Trooper's footprints. A solitary jet plane screamed over me, perhaps twenty minutes from Canada at that speed. Reaching Tacoma Pass, I was sitting down munching on some snacks, when two motorbikes pulled up and the bikers came over. They congratulated me on my story, and gave me apples, pears and a pack of my favourite dark chocolate-covered almonds, before zipping off home.

My body was in reasonable shape after 173 days. I did have an aching right elbow, and a right calf muscle which always made itself known at some point wherever I walked. Otherwise, though, my only slight concern was a sore throat. I could handle a cold, but I sincerely hoped it wasn't the onset of flu. The weather had turned somewhat and, for the time being at least, I enjoyed sunshine and rising temperatures. Fungi poked through the ground, topped with clods of earth, and announced themselves in vivid reds, browns, greens and whites. Sunset foliage decorated the bushes, and leaves clung on with their last hope.

A hum of traffic intruded on my solitude as I reached the brow of a hill and looked down on Snoqualmie Pass and Interstate 90. Ski lifts crawled up from the small cluster of buildings by the roadside, and beyond I grimaced as a series of peaks and passes spread away to the horizon. I followed a collection of tracks downwards, crossed the road and walked through an area shivering between the lost season of summer's end and the start of the ski season. The Howard Johnson Motel beckoned me over and Trooper was there in reception, washed and laundered.

"Pockets is here," he said.

"What? What the hell!" I spluttered. "I left him at the cabin and he said he was resting for a day. How the hell does that guy do it?"

"Well, he didn't say much," Trooper continued, "but he didn't walk in. I think he got picked up by a couple of hunters slightly the worse for wear."

"Do you know what room he's in?"

"No, but Reception may tell you, providing the receptionist has cheered up a little and finished with his arsehole routine."

I approached the desk and looked at the PCT book, which was often left at reception. It included comments about the establishment as well as messages for other hikers. To my surprise, most of the writing was covered in Tipp-Ex.

"Hi," I said to Dominic, seeing the name etched on to his shiny brass badge. "What's with all the Tipp-Ex in the PCT book?"

"I use it to block out the negative comments," he replied matter-of-factly. "I don't want other customers reading them."

"Aren't you missing the point?" I asked. "That's what they are there for, so you can take note and do something about the complaints."

Ignoring me, he said: "Is there something I can help you with?"

I looked at Trooper, who, in turn, raised his gaze skyward.

"I need to check in but will be sharing a room with Josh Myers."

"I'll need to speak to him about that." He checked the records, picked up the phone and called the room.

"There's a gentleman in Reception who says he will sharing with you. I need you to come to Reception and verify this will be OK." He replaced the receiver, and continued to ignore me while shuffling some paperwork. Trooper disappeared off to his room.

Rockets appeared, looking somewhat dishevelled and

The Last Englishman

annoyed at being disturbed.

"I'll fill you in shortly," he said to me and then turned to Dominic.

"Wassup?" he asked.

"The room is booked under your credit card, so I need your permission to book this guy in."

Rockets glared at him. "Can you make my stay here any more unpleasant than it already is?"

After checking in, I collapsed on the bed, and he filled me in on what had happened.

"I'm feeling shit," he said. "I stayed at the shelter until midday and then started to walk. I had no energy and was really struggling. I was stopping every few minutes to take a shit and then I virtually fell on to a forest road and had resigned myself to putting up the tent, when a couple of hunters stopped in their truck. They drove me here; I got a bus to Seattle, where a doctor took a stool sample. He thinks it's E. coli but I have to wait for him to call."

"What are you going to do?"

"I'm not stopping now, Fozzie. I have to make the hike."

"And what's the deal with the guy on reception?"

"That guy is an arsehole. He wouldn't let me check in till three thirty despite the place being empty. All I wanted to do was sleep; he wouldn't give me the Wi-Fi passcode, wouldn't give me my package he was holding, wouldn't let me change the channel on TV in reception, wouldn't let me lie on the couch even though I made sure my feet were hanging off the end and wouldn't let me use the PC. He wouldn't let me do anything!"

The situation cooled a little in the evening as Dominic finished his shift and was replaced by a more accommodating lady. All three of us ventured out into the rain to a local bar, which had laid on a midweek all-you-can-eat Mexican feast. We ate heartily, including Rockets, whose hunger was alternating between non-existent and insatiable, despite his condition.

To my dismay, my boots had not arrived in the morning, so I left a note to return them to HQ and went online to order a pair for delivery up the trail. My existing footwear was splitting alarmingly, and the sole flapped around as I walked. Rockets also had to wait for new shoes and for the doctor to call, so as usual, he said he'd catch Trooper and I up.

We huffed and puffed up the steep 3,000-foot climb from the pass into the Alpine Lakes Wilderness, and camped in a little dip, which offered some shelter from the cold wind whipping through the mountains. Trooper walked at a pace identical to mine. After slipping over a couple of times on icy ground, he was fast earning himself the new nickname of 'Tripper'.

It was now 255 miles to the Canadian border and the end of the PCT, for Trooper, at least. Before the finish line were two re-supply points: 75 miles away lay trail angels the Dinsmores, just down from Skykomish, and another 99 miles would take us to Stehekin and the last chance to re-supply for the final 81 miles to the border. A further eight miles into Canada was Manning Park, where a solitary hotel stood by a main road, and from there Trooper could get transport home, and I could travel back to the Bridge of the Gods.

At our lunch stop, a succession of hikers heading back to Snoqualmie Pass came by. Instead of the familiar "You won't make it" comments, they were full of praise for us and fed us titbits from their packs. I felt like a duck in a pond waiting for bread to be thrown at me.

The weather forecast was promising, with no rain predicted, but I knew that weather patterns in the mountains were notoriously temperamental. The ice was also becoming more of a nuisance. Rounding a corner cut into a steep incline, I gingerly placed each foot on a solid sheet of ice glued to the rock. Knowing Trooper was immediately behind me, as I reached safety I waited for him to round the bend and called out a warning:

"Trooper, watch the ice, it's..."

It was too late. His legs slipped out from under him and he came crashing down. I grimaced as he fell, hoping he'd grab the nearest lump of something solid to stop him careering over the edge. This was the third time I had seen him fall. He would always laugh it off, dust himself down, check nothing had fallen off him or his equipment, and carry on. He surveyed his trekking pole, which had snapped, and performed a spot of emergency repair with the aid of that good old hiker staple, duct tape.

We all carried duct tape. The wide, silver material is easy to tear off yet extremely strong. To save space in our packs, large rolls were often wound around trekking poles. We used it for pack repairs, broken sunglasses, ripped clothing and even taped it to our ankles. The strong consistency and slippery surface were ideal for blister prevention. I would consider it one of a few truly necessary items.

Our hunger was raging. The mix of mountainous terrain and cold weather was playing havoc with our systems. In extreme conditions of cold, the body prioritises and conserves fuel to look after the main organs and to increase bodily warmth. This is its basic survival instinct. Remaining calories are used for energy expenditure and motion. Fat reserves also take a hammering when the temperature drops, and consequently I found myself craving sugary sweets and oils, nuts, cheese and the like.

During the summer my sweet tooth was satisfied by crunchy oat bars, and I could get by on a couple a day. Now when re-supplying I would allow for no fewer than seven sweet candies per day. On a typical day, I'd polish off four bags of M&M's, a couple of munchy bars and a Snickers or two. I was eating double portions of oats in the morning, laced with sultanas, nuts, powdered milk and sugar. My evening meal, usually a packet of pre-mixed rice with various flavours, was supplemented with pools of olive oil, chunks of cheese and bacon bits. My jerky consumption was alarming, and expensive. Five hundred grams used to see me through the week: now I was eating three times this amount. In the rare event of finding a butcher that made their own jerky, I was like a kid in a toy shop. I'd taste everything and then buy 500 grams each of the best three.

My hands never fared well in cold weather. They'd started to crack, bleed and were very dry, despite taking care and using my gloves. My feet were permanently wet, and the cold was almost painful when I stopped, although once moving it subsided. The rest of my body was coping well with the cold. I walked in a long-sleeved wool top with my waterproof jacket over the top, wool leggings and waterproof trousers. My wool hat stayed in place all day, and once at evening camp I put another wool T-shirt on and replaced my jacket with my down alternative. Despite advice from sleeping bag manufacturers to wear nothing inside the bag, as the body heat warms it more quickly, I wore most of my day clothes in the bag. I knew it was getting colder because I was waking to ice on the inside of the tent as well as the outside.

The Glacier Peak Wilderness was stunning, a mix of all terrains. In places it was flat, but more often than not it dipped, dived and wiggled its way through Washington. We clung to ridges, walked along a trail cut into the hillside, relaxed on soft soil and slipped on rock. Enjoying the sun in the exposed sections, we shivered when we returned to the forest. Once the sun was up it was pleasantly warm, and even Trooper commented on how lucky we were for this time of year. The landscape was taking its toll at times, though, and twenty-five-mile days meant twelve hours' walking.

Knee-jarring descents levelled out and rose into formidable ascents. It was a repeating pattern of bottoming out and then getting stuck into the uphill stretches. After five minutes, lungs were heaving, legs were screaming and calf muscles were ready to burst. Thereafter, however, the physical conditioning we'd acquired over the past few months came into its own, the adrenaline surged and we settled into a good rhythm.

We left the Waptus River intending to cover twenty-nine miles, leave nine miles for the following day to reach Highway 2, and catch a ride to the Dinsmores'. Fallen trees littered our path, the remnants of a major storm a few years earlier. We regularly had to clamber over slippery, moss-covered tree limbs, or duck underneath them. Trooper laughed as I spent ages figuring out how to surmount one particular tree, only to find, upon rounding a switchback, the same culprit blocking that as well.

Access to this remote part of the world was difficult, but the forestry service had cleared the area to a large extent over many years and the work was slowly paying dividends. The forestry teams must have put in a mammoth effort. One huge trunk had been sawn off revealing growth rings dating back to the Middle Ages or further. Someone had marked notable dates on the rings, such as the world wars, Declaration of Independence and so forth.

Trooper was walking behind me. He had a metal mug

strapped to the outside of his pack, which kept banging against the metal buckle. It was like walking in front of a Swiss cow.

"You like your coffee in the morning, huh, Fozzie?" Trooper said, breaking a spell of contemplative walking.

"Coffee in the morning should be made compulsory," I answered, smiling.

"I agree. But what is the fashion these days for putting other stuff in with it and ruining the whole drink?"

"Like syrups and stuff?" I asked.

"Yep. Vanilla flavour, hazelnut, cream, sprinkles, hell, even milk should be left out."

"Strong, thick and black, one sugar," I continued. "Just like motor oil."

"I've given up smoking and gambling but never, ever, coffee," he added.

"At least it's natural. I know it gets a bad rap sometimes but I think there's nothing wrong with it at all."

"And Fozzie, you know when you've found a coffee shop with good coffee?"

"They roast and grind it themselves?"

"Apart from that. They charge for refills. Free refills don't necessarily mean bad coffee, but if they're charging, it means it's the real thing."

I was contemplating a serious caffeine top-up in town when I approached Deception Creek. It tumbled down through a slice of mountain and, although not particularly wide, was flowing quickly. The stepping stones looked slippery and the first one meant a leap of perhaps four feet. I eyed the route across the creek and crouched a little, ready to spring up to the first safe haven. Once there, it would be a balancing act to jump to the next boulder, and then a final vault to the far bank. I reached the other side and, aware of Trooper's propensity to fall, I dropped my pack in case I needed to rescue him from the currents.

Trooper eyed up the first and hardest boulder for an eternity. He kept making false starts and then backing down. I glanced around as I waited patiently, until I looked back to see him in mid-flight. His right foot landed on the boulder but didn't grip and he did the splits. A four-point plan rushed into my head. First, drag him out; second, dry him out; third, get him comfortable and warm; and fourth, run back to the two equestrians we had passed earlier and have them ride back and call mountain rescue. I rushed to the bank, where he had managed to curtail his fall. His face suggested he was in pain. I gestured as though to grab him.

"No, Fozzie! I'm good, I can get over!"

Feet now wet, he cautiously made it to my side and rubbed his shin.

"All OK?" I asked hopefully.

"Yeah, I thought I'd broken something when I landed but it feels OK."

We struggled through to Trap Lake and camped by the shore. We were taking a hammering. Exhaustion set in when we stopped in the evening. After getting into warm clothes, erecting shelters, building a fire and eating, all we were fit for was sleep. I watched the moon reflecting in the lake; a slight wind rippled the water's surface and blurred the reflection into a huge serpent. The tops of the pine trees painted an irregular border to the night sky above them. I watched the fire fade and the last, weak wafts of smoke rise and disappear as they left the light from the orange embers.

We reached Highway 2 late the following morning and spent a frustrating hour trying to catch a ride. Roadworks spilled on to the hard shoulder, leaving nowhere for vehicles to pull over, so we walked for a mile down the hill and tried again. A young guy soon stopped, eager to show off his new silver Mustang. We reached Skykomish and picked up our bounce boxes from the post office. An extra, warmer top and gaiters had also arrived.

"You're a bit late to be thru-hiking, aren't you?" came a voice from behind us. We turned round and Trooper recognised Jerry Dinsmore from his previous hike.

"If you can wait until two o'clock, I can give you a ride when I finish work," Jerry continued. "Come down to the school when you're ready and I'll wait there."

We thanked him and sat outside the brilliant deli by the junction. It was a beautiful day and we warmed ourselves on the deck while wolfing down delicious, homemade breakfast muffins. So good were they, in fact, that we each ordered the same again, washed down of course by a couple of mugs of

The Last Englishman

excellent coffee, refills extra.

I'd not found much internet access in this remote stretch of Washington. I sat hopefully with my iPod outside the library; it was closed but the Wi-Fi was on, so I was able to rattle off a few emails and update my blog. There was no news from Rockets and, strangely enough, I had no reception on my phone with which to check on him.

The Dinsmores' home, River Haven, lay eight miles down from Skykomish. Jerry, puffing on a cigar, gave us a brief description of how he ran things with his wife, Andrea. They had converted a large garage for the benefit of PCT hikers and there was ample room. We were the only ones there. We did our laundry, fired up the stove and brought provisions from the store. Several hiker boxes were filled with surplus food; if it were not for these, our cuisine for the section to Stehekin would have been a little limited.

"You're English, Fozzie, yes?" Andrea said when she came over to check we were comfortable.

"Yes, I am."

"Two English guys passed through last week and stayed for a few days to help build the new deck."

"They did?" I exclaimed, wondering who it could have been. "What were their names?"

"Nick and Chris. They've been walking since the start but missed a section between Crater Lake and the Bridge of the Gods. They said they intended to go back and finish this section to complete their thru-hike."

I couldn't believe my luck and this was a coincidence too good to miss out on. Not only had they missed the same section as I had, but they were returning to walk it, and they were fellow countrymen. I emailed Rockets the news, saying I intended to catch them and that he should join us. I asked Uncle Gary, who had walked for many weeks with them, if he could forward their contact details.

We ate well at the café over the road and slept like fallen logs. We woke in darkness to pack our bags and prepare for the ninety-nine-mile section to Stehekin. After giving our thanks and farewells to the Dinsmores, we went back to the café for breakfast.

"Be careful," Andrea called out after us, "the weather's turning for the worse. They say storms are rolling in."

Chapter 15
Monument 78

A hiker whose desires stray from being on the PCT becomes an empty vessel stumbling across beauty without ever touching it.
Jake Nead

We tucked into a quick breakfast at the café, and were lucky enough to catch a ride back to Skykomish with the deli owner. Seizing the opportunity to stock up on more fat, I promptly ordered four breakfast muffins wrapped in foil to take out, figuring the cold climate would preserve them as well as any fridge. I paid a brief visit to the library once more to see if there was any news from Rockets. There wasn't, so I emailed him our plans and returned to the deli. Trooper looked suitably pleased with himself as he introduced me to a local called Kathleen, who had offered to take us back to the highway at Stevens Pass.

"I need to walk my dogs and would love to come with you for a few miles, if that's OK," she offered.

"No problem," Trooper replied. He seemed a bit smitten, I thought from the look on his face.

"She's nice," he said, as we reached the highway and we adjusted our packs ready for the next stage.

"Then get her number," I said. "I think she likes you too."

Kathleen kept us company for an hour, and then kissed us both, wishing us good luck.

We had ninety-nine miles to Stehekin. After some discussion, we decided that allowing four days for the journey would be more achievable than three, bearing in mind the terrain and weather. Also the Stehekin post office, where we had mail, would be shut on the Sunday. We therefore adjusted our plan to knock out four twenty-five-mile days, arrive Saturday afternoon, take a zero on Sunday and pick up the mail on Monday morning.

The terrain was gruelling but beautiful. A pattern emerged – uphill, then flat, then downhill. At the end of the ascents we often glimpsed, through breaks in the trees, the land and lakes below. I wondered who had first discovered and named the waters. Some were obviously christened because of their shape – Heart Lake and Pear Lake to name just two. Other names mimicked the appearance, such as Mirror Lake and Glass Lake. The origin of other, more curious names kept me guessing: Lake Janus, Sally Ann, Valhalla.

We reminisced about wrong turns we'd made and the time we'd wasted as a result. I proudly boasted that I'd only slipped up once, with Brains and Rockets at Kings Creek. Feeling well pleased with my natural navigation skills, I soon found myself munching on humble pie as Trooper called out from a couple of hundred yards behind me:

"Fozzie! You're going the wrong way! That's Cady Trail! The PCT is down here!"

I backtracked rather sheepishly, and watched with amusement as Trooper swung his pack on to his back – and fell backwards, caught off guard by its weight.

Looking down from Fire Creek Pass, we saw a huge storm front rolling in from the west. By the time we had descended a couple of hundred feet, it had cleared the ridge line to our left, the clouds whipping ferociously over the rock. We sped down the pass towards Mica Creek, where we'd spotted flatter ground nestling in the forest. It was dark as we filtered water and camped, just in time for the rain to fall and another mist bank to engulf us.

It was gloomy the following day, although the rain had stopped. Trooper was perhaps only a hundred feet ahead of me, yet had disappeared into the mist. As I passed Vista Creek, menacing skeletal trees appeared in the murk, like huge Grim Reapers. Occasionally a sign reassured us that we were on the right track. I pulled my jacket collar tighter and shivered, trying to fend off a chill that seemed to penetrate everything. The storm had passed, creating an eerie, oppressive environment, like the opening sequence to a 1950s horror movie. I longed to be warm. We spent most of our time cold and damp, only warming up around a fire at camp or in our sleeping bags. Waking up in the mornings, I opened the mesh panel to my tent vestibule and stayed in my bag while I boiled water for porridge and coffee, to stay warm as long as possible. Packing most of my gear away, I emerged only to take down my tent, and then we were off, using movement to generate body heat.

Making our way down the 3,000 feet from Dolly Vista to the Suiattle River, we again clambered unceremoniously over and under fallen trees, emerging at a wide expanse of sand and rock stretching out from the river. Shielding our eyes from the sunlight, we scanned the opposite bank for any hint of the trail, while following the occasional pile of stones left by others to signal the way through. Trooper said that the last time he had passed through, the bridge had been washed away, and we hoped it had been rebuilt since. Unfortunately it hadn't. We wandered up and down the river bank, our feet sinking into the waterlogged soil, trying to find a place to cross. Eventually a fallen tree offered a slippery crossing point, and I cringed as Trooper cautiously stepped across and then decided to run the last few feet to safety. One slip would send him plunging twenty feet to a raging, icy torrent beneath him.

We raced up the incline as night fell, collecting water from Miners Creek. On reaching flatter ground, we turned on our head torches. For an hour we walked, turning our heads sideways to let the beams illuminate the forest around us, in the hope of spotting a flat clearing to make camp. Eventually we pulled up at the best option available, a meagre space in the trees, where somehow we managed to squeeze in both our tents. We talked of making the twenty-two miles into Stehekin the following day, and looked forward to drying out and getting warm.

Trooper had stumbled four times in as many days. We reached High Bridge mid-afternoon after good progress, but my right ankle was aching; after six months' walking, I feared I could have picked up an injury. We turned right over the bridge and hoped the Ranger station was occupied, for a possible ride into Stehekin. A padlocked door suggested otherwise, so we plodded off down the eleven-mile track to town.

After a couple of hours, a house appeared to our left, with several buildings resembling holiday cabins. No-one was at the house and the cabins were all locked, following the end of the season. Just as we were dejectedly walking back down the drive, a car pulled in and approached us. The window lowered and Martha stuck her head out.

"You PCTers?" she enquired. "You're a bit late, aren't you?!"

I looked at Trooper and smiled. If I had a dollar for every time I'd heard that over the previous few weeks, I'd definitely have a healthier bank balance.

"Yes, we are," I replied, smiling and trying to look cold and needy. "We were looking for somewhere to stay. Are the cabins still available or do we have to carry on to Stehekin?"

Her husband, Martin, leaned over from the driver's side.

"Follow us, we can help you out."

We trailed the car up to a beautiful log cabin in an expanse of grass, with a vegetable patch to one side. Martin led us to the rear and a two-bed room in an outhouse above the log store.

"You're welcome to stay here," he said. "Give me a minute to turn on the hot water. There are showers next door and I'll bring you some logs for the fire. If you come to the house in about an hour, we can feed you."

I looked at Trooper, who looked speechless, as was I. We thanked Martin, and Trooper agreed to light the fire as I sat under a hot shower for ten minutes, letting the steaming hot water warm my chilled bones.

As we walked to the house, Tip, a border collie, intercepted us and demanded I play ball, which I obligingly did. We knocked on the back door and it creaked open, revealing Martha's kind face as she beckoned us in.

"Please, sit by the table. Coffee?"

"Yes, please," we replied in unison.

As she placed popcorn and vegetable nibbles on the table, her daughter, Misha, chatted to us. I thought how open the Americans were, compared to the typically reserved English. There were only a few occasions back in my home country when

I had been so graciously offered somewhere to stay, a plate of hot food and good company. It's not that we English are unfriendly, we just don't take people in off the street and give them a bed for the night. I had experienced similar hospitality in other countries, and always made a point, when I returned to England, of doing the same if I saw a couple of wet cycle tourists or hikers. Americans, you cannot fault their affability.

Trooper, being vegetarian, winced as Martha placed a deer heart on the chopping board and started to cut it into bite-sized pieces.

"You both OK with deer heart?"

"I've never eaten the heart from anything but am more than willing to try it," I said. I looked at Trooper.

"I'm vegetarian," he said, shrugging his shoulders. "But by the look of that salad and rice you're making, I'll be fine."

She dusted the heart chunks with flour and carefully tipped them into a hot pan, the meat sizzling and spitting as it hit the oil. Having lit the fire and settled comfortably in a chair, Martin explained how he had lived in the cabin all his life; his father had built the place years earlier.

The table groaned underneath Martha's pan, salad, rice, vegetables and homemade bread. We wolfed it all down. The deer was excellent: not tough, as I'd feared, it melted in my mouth like a perfectly cooked steak. Martha didn't let us help clear up. She turned on the radio to contact people in town.

"Martin can take you down in the morning," she said, turning to us. "I'm trying to arrange a ride back to the trailhead for you and I can probably get the postmistress to open up for you as well. If you come down around eight thirty and eat some breakfast, then we can leave."

We thanked them profusely and returned to our little warm haven with full stomachs and warm limbs.

"Unbelievable," Trooper exclaimed as we relaxed a little and read. "Incredible hospitality, I've never experienced anything like it."

"I know," I agreed. "If we hadn't walked up that drive, we would probably be shivering in the woods again."

As Martha dished out a breakfast of homemade pancakes consisting of buttermilk and rolled oats that had soaked overnight, maple syrup from their own trees, eggs and a fruit smoothie, I began wondering about the whole karma thing. Believe what you will, but I feel that whether you take someone in from a storm, such as we had experienced here, or do some work free of charge for someone in need, or even buy a friend a coffee or give your finished newspaper to someone else, the goodwill returns. Those that give freely in this life will be looked after.

The karma issue rolled around in my head for a few more minutes. How, I wondered, were our karma 'points' recorded? After all, to use an extreme scenario, if I were to stand on a street corner for a week handing out £10 notes to everyone who passed me, inviting them round to dinner, offering to clean their houses and do their shopping, then surely I'd rack up a fair-sized karma bank balance? I never expect karma to be directly returned from the recipient, that would be missing the point; I realise that it comes round in another form at some later time. However, would my altruism on the street corner earn me a set amount of points? Ten points for making someone dinner, fifteen for cleaning their house? Who was keeping the records? Could I expect my balance of, say, 235 points to be returned in equal value? Martha's karma balance must be running into the thousands, I thought. Mother Teresa must have done pretty well too, and all those who volunteer their time for good causes. I made a note to try harder in the future; what goes around comes around.

Martin took us to Stehekin, via the bumpy road. We passed the famous bakery, which to our dismay was closed, and saw Lake Chelan through gaps in the trees. He dropped us at the boat landing. He said he would see us again, as it was a small town, and we thanked him. We checked in at a cabin overlooking the lake, and ventured to the post office where the postmistress had indeed opened up. Inside a package she handed to me was a cigar – or 'stogie', as they are called – from Elk. He had written a short note:

"Fozzie, three requests, please. Firstly, smoke this stogie at the Canadian border for me. Secondly, send me a postcard from Stehekin, and thirdly, please sign the book at the monument for me. I was a dumbass and couldn't find it! Lastly, you are a savage badass, congrats on your accomplishment. Stay in touch, please – Elk."

It made me smile. I wrote him a postcard (he'd even left a stamp), tucked the stogie safely in my pack and went off to do some laundry.

Trooper was snoozing as I returned to the cabin. I quietly made myself a cup of tea (an Englishman must have his tea), grabbed my journal and sat outside on the deck. A gaggle of geese glided over the lake, and a solitary fisherman rowed out from the dock with his line in tow. I thought of the distance I had come and the distance still ahead. Four or five days to Canada and then a further two or three weeks in Oregon. I remembered an email I had received from a friend: "Don't worry, you'll breeze the last section and soon it will all be a distant memory." That was when I was in Packwood, feeling depressed. Still, I didn't want my quest to be over; I was sure I'd cherish the memories, and wouldn't want them to become faded and distant. I was among only a handful of hikers still on trail. Perhaps my companions were the last few left. I had come to the PCT to experience the adventure of a lifetime, a dream ten years in the making, and despite the hardships, I was still happy to be here, still marvelling at the adventure, still proud to be living it. I recalled that a man in the launderette had said earlier, "Rain for the rest of the week, snow at higher elevations, ninety per cent chance," and that Trooper had replied that the weather will do what it will – we can't change it – but we would make it.

I was reminded of a quote I had read in a book called *Zorba the Greek* some years earlier, that when we are happy we sometimes fail to recognise it, and it's only when we look back that we fully realise how happy we had been. Sitting on that deck in Stehekin, I was happy; but, more importantly, I was aware of my happiness.

I was interrupted by my phone beeping. A message from Rockets read: "Mucker, in Chelan, three hours' ferry ride from Stehekin. Will get in late morning."

Trooper was awake and I told him the news. After much discussion, we reluctantly agreed that we couldn't wait. Time was now very much against us, storms were forecast with snowfall, and we had to get up in the mountains before it hit. I replied to Rockets: "Mate, we have to move early. Heading for Rainy Pass at day's end, catch us up, you always do."

I felt guilty, like a mountaineer abandoning his partner, but my goal was clear and I needed to move.

Journal entry:

I'm writing this from a cabin overlooking Lake Chelan at Stehekin, the last chance to get off trail and re-supply before Canada.

I look at what lies above me. There is a clear snow line down to 4,000 feet; the tops of the mountains are sprinkled with a fine layer before the clouds obscure the upper elevations. Solitary spectres of fine mist float across the lake and geese call to me to move. The hill flanks are coated in the greens of pine trees, the uniformity broken by the occasional gold of a lost maple. It is eerily quiet save for the occasional rustle of leaves as a gentle breeze toys with them.

I think about how far I have come, and how far I have still to go. The last two weeks with Trooper have been terrific; he's a fine walking companion. Tomorrow we leave at 7am for the final eighty-nine-mile stretch, whereupon he finishes his PCT thru-hike. Rockets has a confirmed case of E. coli and has been told by the doctor to leave the trail. He is ignoring this, telling me, "You can't keep Pockets down."

We stumble in here on Saturday the 23rd of October. Trooper has fallen four times today, a habit that is earning him the revised nickname of 'Tripper'. I have also picked up an injury. We are increasing our speed noticeably because we hear that snow is on the way, and we have one last section in Washington, but it's a tough one through the North Cascades. It's a case of when, not if, it snows. A few miles from Stehekin, my ankle started to ache, but I just put it down to over-exertion and figure a couple of days' rest and a re-supply will sort it out.

***

Martin and Martha had offered to collect us and take us back to the trailhead at High Bridge. We met in the café. Martha returned my gaze as we entered, looking concerned.

"Fozzie, there's bad weather rolling in. Forecast says four feet of snow will fall." Martin said nothing but his face suggested he was worried too. They both knew from experience how fruitless it was to warn us, though, stubborn as we thru-hikers were.

"The weather will do what it will," Trooper said. "We have to move."

"We'll call you from Canada," I added. "If you don't hear from us within seven days then we may be in trouble."

Martha smiled weakly. As we bounced back up the road, I wiped the condensation from the window and peered out at the mountains above us. It had snowed already.

If either of us had known then what the next few days had in store, I doubt we would have even left.

In my PCT research, I saw a series of videos made by two brothers who had hiked the PCT some years earlier. One of them had been plagued by blisters and foot problems since day one, and these never eased up for the entire hike. The brothers arrived at Rainy Pass, nothing more than a picnic area by the side of Highway 20. It was at mile 2,595, just 61 miles from the end of the PCT. After several months on trail, and with perhaps only two or three days to go before becoming a PCT thru-hiker, the guy quit, stuck out a thumb and got off trail. He was simply tired of nursing his feet.

I was dumbstruck; yes, I felt sympathy, but also disbelief. Little did I realise at the time how similar my own experience would be.

The day started innocently enough. Trooper and I both made slow progress up the 3,500-foot climb to the pass. Rain fell constantly, and a chill seeped through to our skin. Negotiating streams that had spilled on to the track, we concentrated on our breathing and focused on our target. Hunting the best route through a shallow creek, I placed my right foot on the ground and came to a shuddering halt. Pain shot up from my ankle, my leg buckled beneath me, and I fell. Trooper, tucked into his jacket, hadn't heard me fall, so I picked myself up and carefully placed my foot back down. My ankle screamed again.

"Trooper!" I cried.

"You OK? What's up?"

"My ankle. Think I've done something to it."

We sat under a tree and ate lunch in the rain. I had not experienced joint or muscle pain like it before. At first I was convinced that I'd somehow broken the ankle, and then remembered the ache I had experienced on the approach to Stehekin. I was worried. Trooper said little, letting me deal with it in my own way. We set off again, but as soon as I put weight on my ankle, I felt a searing pain. Trooper looked on anxiously, pausing and giving me time. I let the trekking pole take the strain and carried on hobbling, fighting the urge to return to safety. The rain turned to snow as we climbed, covering our heads and packs in a white powder. The temperature dropped further.

Two miles from Rainy Pass, I made the decision to get off trail and finish my thru-hike; I'd had enough. I thought about the brother who'd quit. For all that it made little logical sense, I now understood his decision to give up; his patience, worn unendurably thin, had finally run out. I said nothing to Trooper, but plodded on, looking up at the stark white landscape that lay between us and Canada. This was no mere dusting – it was deep snow. For whatever reason, I just wasn't in the frame of mind to carry on any more. I'll come back next year and finish off this section, I thought. I can be in a warm motel in a couple of hours.

"Trooper, I'm quitting here."

"You're what?!"

"My ankle is excruciating. I've had enough, and I can't go on any more."

"Fozzie, hold on. Give it time. Get in your tent, get warm, eat some food and think. Don't make a rash decision, you're four days from Canada and then you have Oregon, it will be a little warmer down there. See how your ankle is in the morning and then decide."

We smashed the ice covering a puddle and filtered its water. Snow continued to fall around us as we set up our tents, inflated our mattresses and puffed up our sleeping bags. I checked my watch for the temperature – minus seven degrees Celsius. I climbed into my bag with all the clothing I could wear, and cupped my hands round a mug of tea, idly observing a lump of powdered milk that had floated to the surface. Tapping the roof of the tent occasionally to let the accumulated snow slide off, I read until my eyes were too heavy. Then I zipped up my bag and drew the hood string tightly around my head.

Waking early, I called over to Trooper.

"You awake, Troop?"

"My mind is, I'm just waiting for my body to catch up. Go in thirty?"

"OK."

We hauled ourselves up to Cutthroat Pass at 7,000 feet. The snow got ever deeper, at times up to our knees. By some miracle, my ankle never gave out even a twinge during those four hours. However, what greeted us at the top made me grimace – the PCT had all but disappeared. The snow had settled on the trail, leaving, at best, the faintest of indentations, a cupped line of settled snow. An icy wooden sign directed us further onwards. I checked my map and tried to picture the contours of the terrain ahead. My navigation, normally sound, isn't so great in the dark or the snow. Trooper asked if we should carry on.

"I can get us through but you'll have to bear with me and give me some space for the occasional error," I said, trying to sound confident. "I'm not good at navigation in these conditions, Troop, but you can pick out the trail occasionally." I pointed to the dip in the snow and showed him the map. "We have to keep this side of that ridge, about 200 feet down; look, you can just pick it out."

A faint trail cut through the side of the hill and disappeared off to one side.

"If we both concentrate, keep an eye on the dip and check the GPS occasionally, let's see how we go. We've got twenty-five miles to Harts Pass, there's a Ranger Station there and a road. I don't think we'll make it today but hopefully we can stay on the trail. If we're really struggling, then we have a get-out clause there, at least."

The weather had cleared and showed no signs of the forecast stormy weather. Through ever-deepening snow we pushed onwards, at times up to our waists. On the west-facing slopes, we guessed our way through drifts that had obliterated not only the trail but everything around it. My ankle continued to hold, and I figured the snow was cushioning my foot somewhat and also acting as a huge ice pack to numb the pain and reduce any swelling. We kept our down jackets on, rubbed our hands and blew into them to keep them warm and quickly put our gloves back on. Sunlight bounced off the snow and blinded us and we fumbled to find our sunglasses. We saw no-one, there were no footprints, and at that point I realised we were the last hikers on the PCT that year.

We carefully made our way down to Methow Creek, keeping away from the edge of the trail, where the land dropped away steeply. Pausing to take in water and calories, we shivered as our clothing struggled to keep in our body heat. Huge expanses opened out below us, green valleys dotted with forest and creeks tumbling down the hillside.

I slept badly, curled up in a foetal position with my hat and gloves on and my bag wrapped tightly around me. We were now nine miles from Harts Pass and progressing slowly, as we had done the previous day. Constantly comparing the map to my field of view, I regularly checked the GPS and my compass. Somehow we were still on the PCT.

We stumbled in to Harts Pass and startled a couple of hikers sitting in their car, who looked as surprised to see us as we were to see them. We sat on the steps by the Ranger Station, which was closed for the winter, and took stock. The hikers came over and we filled them in on what we were doing. Offering us bananas, apples and cups of tea, they apologised for having eaten all the chocolate brownies. They looked genuinely worried for our welfare. They insisted on giving us their phone number, and pleaded with us to call them when we reached Canada. The weather, they informed us, was a mixed bag; sunny at times but with a fierce wind and low cloud.

We surveyed the area around us. There were a few picnic tables, some fire pits, a latrine and enough firewood to see us through the evening. It was now 5pm and nearly dark, the wind had picked up and the clouds were indeed hampering visibility. There were still thirty-one miles until monument 78, which comprised three wooden pillars marking the end of the PCT, and then another couple of hours to Manning Park. Trooper was a couple of days away from being a PCT thru-hiker.

The Last Englishman

We dragged a log near to a fire pit, to sit on, and spent some time stocking up the wood pile. As the flames came alive, I felt my body respond in kind, and we sat huddled with our palms facing the fire. I drank endless cups of tea and hot chocolate, ate my dinner and then cooked another to battle my hunger pangs. Trooper retired for the night early, and we agreed to also start early next morning; it was likely to be a difficult day.

At 4am I was rudely kicked into consciousness by my alarm. I peered under the fly sheet into the darkness, and could just make out snow falling and low cloud reducing visibility again. Staying in my sleeping bag, I drank some coffee and cooked an extra-large helping of porridge. I heard Trooper moving around and the clink of his spoon on a pot as he also readied himself for the rigours of the day. We emerged, rubbed our eyes, smiled at each other nervously and started to pack our gear away.

Merely one minute into the day's walk, we were in trouble. Visibility was down to about fifty feet, a hard wind slammed into us from the east and snow streaked across our faces, forcing us to turn our heads and pull our hoods tighter. Low cloud whipped past and we strained to pick up a trail that was vanishing by the second. We could barely hear each other through the noise as we tried to pick up the dip in the snow where the PCT lay concealed underneath. It was exhausting just concentrating. Trooper said that he would never have attempted this on his own, and that it was my navigation that had brought us this far. I put it more down to luck than skill, and was glad he was with me for company – since walking with him, I had never heard him complain, despite the battering we were taking.

It seemed to take forever for the sun to break through, and at one point I swore it would stay permanently dark. We were up at 7,000 feet, the cloud was at 5,000 feet and doing its utmost to block out any light. As sunlight slowly came, our field of vision improved a touch. I attempted to record a video, but the batteries failed within seconds in the cold, even though my camera had been snugly in my inside pocket.

We battled up hills and I waited for Trooper at the summits, while scanning the lie of the land and finding our position and route. Trooper was struggling, but I needed the time to navigate and rest myself. Simple tasks, such as reaching for my map or unwrapping a snack, were hampered by the cold that attacked our hands when we removed our gloves. Snow clung to our gaiters and boots and accumulated to form a solid coating of ice. Whenever we stopped, the cold sank in further, so we kept moving, even strolling around when we ate to keep from seizing up.

My sweet rations were depleting quickly. I'd calculated my allowance to see me through to Canada, but I was becoming so hungry and had developed something of a sugar addiction. I kept borrowing more than my allowance, so the next break or meal would be one or two candy bars short. Candy loans, as I called them, were becoming dangerous. At this rate, I thought, I'd be entering into negotiations for a food overdraft at breakfast.

"Trooper!" I called out through the wind.

"Fozzie?"

"If we get through this, then I'll buy you a beer."

"I don't drink."

"Oh, yeah. OK, I'll treat you to a huge steak dinner."

"Fozzie, I'm vegetarian."

We settled on a meat-free breakfast, the thought of which had me salivating for hours.

At mile 2,644 (for Trooper, at least), and near the top of a climb getting icier by the minute, we saw a suitable flat spot to camp, down in a small dip. I was getting fed up with the unremitting cold. My gloves were struggling, my hands cracked and bleeding. No matter what clothing I wore, the cold penetrated through the layers and wore away at my resolve. The wood was too wet for a fire now, so the only heat we experienced was from food and drink. Over a mug of tea one evening, I calculated it must have been the warmest thing for a twenty-mile radius. We scraped back the snow to solid ground so we could drive in our tent pegs, and then made plans for Trooper's final day before trying to get some sleep.

We had 12.2 miles to the PCT finish and then eight miles further to Manning Park in Canada. Once we had surmounted Devils Stairway, a couple of miles away, it was all downhill to the border. The problem was one section called Lakeview. The two hikers at Harts Pass had warned us that there was a quarter-mile-long west-facing slope, renowned for accumulating snow.

The Last Englishman

It was the last hurdle. As I rounded the corner, I realised they were right. A steep slope plunged down from my right to my left, the trail was non-existent and neither of us had our ice axes or crampons. The only saving grace was that the snow was soft, offering a certain amount of grip; if it had been ice, we'd have been faced with an angled traverse, like walking on a slanting mirror. We took slow, deliberate steps across, the snow up to our thighs, and cautiously glanced to our left at the 1,500-or-so-foot drop to the rocks below. The wind intensified once more and snow began to fall. Even the cloud lowered, as if some higher power were trying every mean trick to make us quit at the last stretch.

We reached the top of the staircase and sat on our packs. A lump of snow and ice encased each boot. I looked at Trooper; he grinned, and for good reason. In eight miles he would become a PCT thru-hiker, and it was all downhill now. After admitting he was not good in snow and had never camped in it, I was initially worried that he might come to grief. Barring some ascents where he fell behind a little, I could have not wished for a better companion through the toughest and most extreme conditions I had ever walked through. Upbeat to a fault, he had managed to make me smile even in the direst circumstances.

As we made our way down, the snow slowly disintegrated, the temperature rose a little and we peeled off our jackets. Water dripped from the trees above us and we skidded on wet mud and rock.

"There it is," Trooper said, stopping abruptly.

"There's what?"

"Monument 78. That's the finish of the PCT."

I moved my head from side to side, trying to look through the foliage. Trooper handed me his camera and asked me to film his moment. He sped up in anticipation, finally reaching a small clearing with three wooden pillars on one side. He let it all go.

"Yes!" he cried. "YES!"

He looked briefly skywards and raised his arms above his head.

"Well done, mate," I said.

"Thanks, Fozzie. Could not have done that without you."

"Nor I you."

We spent an hour relaxing. There was no border control here, simply a clear-cut line of trees perhaps forty feet wide, stretching from one horizon to the other. It made me wonder if it was necessary to fell thousands of trees just to mark a boundary.

We found the trail register in a metal obelisk, and I duly signed my name as well as Elk's. Trooper scanned back through the pages to see who else had finished. I watched him beam as I lit the ceremonial stogie Elk had given me. After his successful second attempt, and unsuccessful first, Trooper had walked around 5,300 miles to be at that monument. I could only admire his resolve, and hoped mine would get me through the 300 or so miles I still had left in Oregon.

We followed forestry tracks for another two hours and emerged on to a road where we turned right. A mile further on, we pulled in to the most welcoming Manning Park Hotel. We ate heartily, and Trooper kept his promise of buying me a celebratory meal and a bottle of wine. We chuckled as the waitress asked us if we would like any water.

"Yes, please," I replied. "But no ice, I've had enough of that stuff to last a lifetime."

For the first time in days I was warm and well fed. I looked forward to getting back to Crater Lake to knock off my final section in Oregon and also earn my place as a Pacific Crest Trail thru-hiker. It had been the hardest week of my life, with my ankle nearly ending my adventure and in those violent conditions; but I was proud to have pushed through. I was on an immense high, buzzing with excitement.

I had no inkling then that the news I would receive in the morning would send my world crashing down around me.

Chapter 16
A New Strength

How can we return to our normal lives and ever hope to achieve the high we have experienced out here?
Nick 'The Brit' De Bairacli Levy

I woke early and picked up the phone to call my parents.

"Dad, I made it to Canada, just have to do that section in Oregon. Is Mum there?"

"She's at your nan's. Well done."

I detected something unusual in his voice and dialled my nan's house. My mother answered and immediately broke down in tears as she handed the phone to my sister.

"Sis, what's going on? What's wrong?"

"Keith, Nan died this morning. She had a stroke a couple of weeks ago and has been in hospital since. She couldn't really talk but understood what we were saying and nodded her answers. We didn't want to worry you with it, which is why we didn't call; we thought she would be OK. Bruv, we asked her if she wanted you to finish the walk for her and everyone. You will probably miss the funeral but she nodded that she wants you to complete it – she definitely wants you to finish."

My sister was also trying to hold back the tears and then I broke down too. My mum came back on the line.

"Keith, you must finish the walk now for Nan – she wanted you to finish. Go and complete it for her."

I choked back a few tears, trying to come to terms with the news. My high had come down to earth with a thump.

"OK, I will," I said. "I'll do it for Nan."

Replacing the receiver, I fought back more tears. I had enough reasons of my own to finish the walk, but now I was walking for my nan's memory. After a couple of hours I had calmed down and felt strangely uplifted, even managing to smile. The shock and grief had abated and I somehow felt a new strength within. Before I'd left, I'd said goodbye to her.

"See you when I get back," I had said to her as she kissed me on the cheek.

"Bye, Keify."

Initially it felt as though I had broken a promise to her, that I had lied, but I took comfort in knowing that she would never have held that against me. Now I had her strength with me, and I could feel it. In a moment of clarity, I felt she would be right there by my side as I attempted to finish off the PCT.

Nan and I had never shared a word in anger in all of the years I had known her. She had struggled to bring up three children through a world war, scraping together enough money to live on. My walk seemed to pale in comparison to her toil, and I reminded myself that, if it were not for her, I wouldn't even be doing the PCT. A new determination surged through me; an invigorating feeling. I took a deep breath and watched the snow float down outside.

"OK, Nan, let's go finish this thing."

Apart from the usual thru-hike niggles such as the expense of the trip, occasional cold and constant hunger, I'd always had this additional anxiety: what would I do if someone back home, especially immediate family, died? If my mother, father or sister fell ill or died, and I didn't make it back to them in time, my world would collapse. I worry about it before I leave and it troubles me when I walk. I hate saying farewell to loved ones for fear that it could be the last goodbye.

Now I finally knew how it felt to lose someone and not be there to bid farewell.

Uncle Gary had sent an email with the contact details of Nick Levy. Nick was walking with his mate, Chris, and they were the only other Englishmen on the trail that year. I knew they had missed the same section, from Crater Lake to the Bridge of the Gods, as I had, and I hoped they were returning to finish it off. I sent Nick an email.

"Nick, rumour has it you and Chris missed a section from Crater Lake to Cascade Locks. By some coincidence, so did I and I am looking to finish it off. Fancy some company?"

My phone beeped a few minutes later.

"Fozzie! We're in Vancouver, heading to Seattle soon. Definitely doing the final stretch, come join us!"

Trooper and I packed and caught the Greyhound to Vancouver, the nearest transport hub. I slept most of the way until we arrived mid-afternoon.

Vancouver was bustling, but when I left the station to find some food, I found downtown depressing. Light rain was falling and leaves carpeted the park like a giant Turkish rug. Concrete hemmed me in, traffic hooted, sirens blared, people shouted, dubious-looking characters lurked on street corners. I grabbed a sandwich and sought solace back in the park, sitting on a bench and trying to feel at home among the trees. Civilisation felt somehow wrong after months in the woods. Smoking a cigarette outside the station, I broke wind out of habit, and smiled as people turned round.

"Sorry," I offered. "Been out of touch for a while."

The 7pm to Seattle hissed as it pulled up, and Trooper and I boarded. Water trickled down the windows separating me from an alien world. I was way out of my depth, and longed to be back on the PCT. Seattle, a more affable city perhaps, seemed to welcome us both as we walked from the station. It was Halloween, so finding a room might not be easy. We walked into a well-known hotel and leant on the reception desk.

"Hi," Trooper said. "We need a room for one night, how much are you charging?"

The receptionist looked us up and down rudely.

"180 dollars for the night."

I interjected.

"You're taking the piss, mate; don't judge people because they have a rucksack."

We walked off and found a Best Western; in my experience, they usually charged a little more but they were well-run establishments. We were both pleasantly surprised by the very reasonable $70 room price. Trooper was leaving in the morning to return to California. I called Nick and agreed to meet him and

Chris in a couple of days for the early morning bus to Portland, and then onward transport to Cascade Locks. I had a day to get organised, replace some gear from REI, clean myself up and find some coffee houses.

"Fozzie, give me a call when you get to Crater Lake," Trooper said, as he left by taxi early in the morning. "My sister lives in Oregon and I plan on coming back to visit in a couple of weeks. There's a good chance I can collect you from there."

It was a nice gesture on his part. Crater Lake was in the middle of nowhere, and the thought that we might not have to try to get a ride out of there in the middle of autumn was a small comfort.

"Thanks, Trooper, it's been a blast. Thanks for the company."

I returned to the hotel and was lying on the bed when my phone rang. 'Rockets' flashed up on the screen.

"Mucker!" he said. "Where are you?"

"Seattle, heading out tomorrow with Nick and Chris," I replied.

"Stay there! I'm coming down."

A block from the hotel, I stumbled across a great health food store, where I gorged on salads, beans, pulses, grains and fruit, drank a load of water and rested as best I could. I re-supplied, bought warmer gloves and socks and prepared for the final 330 miles.

Rockets arrived in the afternoon and I laid out my plans. He seemed eager to join us, but was still lethargic from the E. coli.

"I have to leave in the morning, mate," I said. "Come with us but I have to leave tomorrow. I've cut it fine as it is. I shouldn't have made it through Washington but somehow I did; now I need to polish off Oregon before the winter strikes down there as well."

When I left in the morning, he wasn't ready. I shook his hand and walked up to the Greyhound station with his familiar words ringing in my ears:

"Go, I'll catch you up."

Despite their rucksacks and typical thru-hiker appearance, Nick and Chris walked straight by me in the waiting room, and I failed to recognise them, too. We shook hands and briefly discussed our plans for the final section with renewed excitement.

They both lived near me, in Sussex, south England. Nick, the more outgoing of the two, basically lived for his next adventure. He was thirty-three and worked as carpenter. A Mohican adorned his head, two fat rings pierced his ears and countless tattoos decorated his stringy frame. Conventional this man was not. He looked like a cross between a benefits scrounger and the sort of bloke you wouldn't buy a used car from. Appearances are deceptive, however, and contrary to my snap character judgment, Nick turned out to be priceless. Born to a Jewish mother and Moroccan father, he nurtured a love and respect for the outdoors, and was highly intellectual. Nick would not only have an opinion on any topic you cared to mention, but he'd also reel off a string of facts and statistics to back his view up. Whether it was the cooking habits of ancient Greeks, how to repair fridges in the African bush, or where to rent a hedge trimmer in Mongolia, Nick knew something about it. His erudition showed up my comparative ignorance. Sometimes I thought he was just making stuff up, but he spoke with a confidence that suggested otherwise.

Chris had joined Nick for the adventure. He was younger, at twenty-four, and less of a conversationalist than Nick (not that that would be difficult). He had never even been out for a day hike back home; the PCT was his first hiking adventure, and one hell of a baptism it was too. He was stockier than Nick, but still slim, and his stomach had a tendency to inflate alarmingly when he ate. And, boy, did he know how to eat!

After a series of bus journeys and local rides, we arrived at Cascade Locks late in the afternoon. It seemed warmer, and as I looked up I saw that snow had not yet fallen on the higher ground. We crammed in some last-minute calories at the supermarket; I stocked up on candy for fear of running out again. We left the Bridge of the Gods south-bound, heading for the woods and our final 330-mile section of the PCT. With darkness falling we hiked a couple of miles only and set up camp by the promisingly named Not Dry Creek.

Nick and Chris made a well-oiled team, and I admired their organisational skills as they set about their respective camp tasks. Chris treated water while Nick prepared their food. Together they set up their two-man tent, and as light rain fell, we all chipped in to start a fire. Campfires, I was soon to learn, were a regular staple for them both. It took a little planning every evening, but I soon warmed, as it were, to the reward of a crackling fire. I thought I was a pretty accomplished pyromaniac, but Nick was quite the expert. As we gently fed a smouldering pile of damp wood, the flames would flicker occasionally and then go out, with only a weak puff of smoke for our efforts. I would have given up after ten minutes, but Nick and Chris persisted, spurring me on, until eventually a small fire burst into life. With the rain still falling, we sat near the warmth and I marvelled at Nick's persistence. Every couple of minutes he glanced over to check the fire was still burning. Occasionally he'd feed in some more fuel, blow a little life into it and generally nurse it as one would a sick relative. As the skies cleared a little, stars flickered into life, and we decided to risk the elements and sleep cowboy-style.

At 3am the forest around us reverberated from a huge crash. All three of us sat bolt upright as if we were Jacks and someone had just opened our boxes.

"What the hell was that?" we cried in unison.

Being half-asleep, my immediate thought was that a bear had charged through the forest, but as I came around, I realised no bear could ever make such a thundering noise. We shone our lights around but, seeing nothing, cautiously fell back to sleep. I woke thinking I had dreamt the whole event, but soon saw it was very real.

Walking around the camp, we found a freshly fallen tree that we had not seen the previous evening. We suspected it had been hit by lightning, but the skies had been clear and storm-free. Maybe the tree's time had simply come. Nick, deepening the mystery, said he'd seen something that looked like an asteroid, complete with blazing green tail, shortly after the event. We all also recalled hearing a crash in the next valley over, just after the tree fell. Maybe I was reading too much into this, but we all agreed that something weird had happened that night. My time with Nick and Chris was off to an interesting start.

Over the next few days we got to know each other better,

having gelled pretty well from day one. We walked at around the same pace, required a similar amount of time before we rested and were happy with our mileage totals for each day. The weather held, and I looked forward to the evenings most of all – round a fire, relaxing.

We left Salvation Camp Spring, hoping to make Timberline Lodge twenty miles away. The exterior of this huge hotel was used in the movie *The Shining*, and it attracted a lot of outdoors folk who hiked or skied in the area. It was also renowned for laying on one of the best breakfast buffets on the entire trail. However, our hopes of getting there by the evening were disappointed. Some days on the PCT, one can reel in a twenty-mile day in what seems like no time at all. Other times the same distance seems to take an eternity. That day was in the latter category.

Mt Hood, with its near-perfect symmetry, completely dominated the skyline. The contours on my map were fairly regular until they reached the base of the mountain, and then all hell broke loose. Ridges, ravines, glaciers and cols jostled for position amid a jumble of lines. It was a cartographer's nightmare.

We also hit snow. Oregon had received its first fall a couple of weeks before, but thankfully it was only up to a couple of feet deep and receding; the lower elevations seemed untouched. However, it made navigation difficult and although we walked for nearly ten hours, we were frustrated at every turn. As night fell, we unanimously agreed that we were off course, albeit somewhere in the approximate vicinity. My journal at the end of the day simply said 'lost'.

We agreed to camp and wait for sunrise to get a better fix on our position. However, even finding somewhere flat to sleep was a battle. The foothills of Mt Hood rose and fell all around us like a rumpled carpet, but eventually we came upon a couple of level areas sheltered by trees. Our spirits lifted momentarily, before Nick brought them down again.

"Shit, we forgot to get water."

None of us even remembered having seen water in the previous few miles, so we built a fire and began melting snow. This is not as easy as it sounds; it has to be collected away from overhanging branches, to avoid detritus from the trees such as bark pieces and pine resin. The top surface is no good because it may have collected contaminants, so we used the lower layers. Melting snow also requires a lot of fuel. We didn't have enough alcohol, so we continued to gather as much wood as we could, and before long we had enough for all of us. The water then had to be strained to remove the last of the impurities. Finally we sat around the fire warming ourselves and watching our dinners bubble.

My sleeping area was so small that if I turned to my left I went uphill, and a little too far to my right and I'd have rolled about fifty feet down a snow slope. On the plus side, I did have a natural pillow where the ground rose slightly, and my feet were a little elevated. It was like sleeping in a hammock.

We packed quickly as the sun rose, eager to get to the lodge and have a feast. We spotted the cables of a ski lift and followed them until suddenly the lodge loomed into view. I had spoken to Logic a few days earlier; she lived nearby and had asked me to call when we reached Timberline so that she could come and join us. When she pulled into the car park I barely recognised her in civilian clothes, but she greeted me with a welcome hug.

Retreating inside we found the buffet, one that could have fed an army, and I watched in amazement as Chris demonstrated his eating capabilities. He ladled a generous portion of batter into the waffle machine and, when cooked, spooned some fresh fruit on top and added a large dollop of cream. Having wolfed that down, he went back for another helping. And then another one. 'Dessert' followed: a huge plate brimming with bacon, sausage, hash browns, scrambled eggs and toast. Then another one of those as well. I was struggling after just one plate. Nick merely raised his eyebrows at the display of gluttony; he'd seen it all before. Chris would have made a prime candidate for the beaver buster. Logic demanded we stay with her that night and agreed to meet us at Highway 26 a few miles further on.

As we lost altitude, the temperature rose, and we found ourselves stripping down to T-shirts. It was like summer again. Oregon was hitting us hard, though. We'd been lulled into thinking this beautiful state was easier going, and some of the time it was, but at other times it was punishing, especially with the snow. I sensed a change in the air also; the temperature was fluctuating. The days were a mixed bag of cool and warm, the nights cold. Winter was clearly imminent, and we were playing a dangerous game with the autumn. Hikers were enjoying the last days before the snow, while skiers impatiently waited for the first powder.

We emerged from the forest to find Logic by her car, reading some pages from her studies.

"Slight problem," she announced. "I locked my keys in the car!"

She had called her boyfriend, Ben, but he couldn't make it for a couple of hours, so we all scanned the area for pieces of discarded wire. Nick spent thirty minutes prodding, pushing and pulling, and eventually he earned his car thief wings. We returned to Logic's house a few miles away, where she made us feel more than welcome. She'd only ever intended to complete a portion of the PCT, and returned home shortly after. Her house sat on a quiet road with beautiful views of the Oregon mountains.

I wonder how I would have coped without trail angels. Whether simply providing a water cache or offering their house as a free hotel, they demonstrated overwhelming generosity.

Trail angels were fewer and farther between now, as the thru-hiker season was over. During the first couple of months, water caches had been a regular sight. I topped up on calories many times from previous hikers and locals who'd taken time out to sit in the heat for a weekend, dishing out food. The Saufleys, Andersons, Heitmans, Dinsmores and others – all wonderful people who simply offered hospitality for a small donation or often free, and expected nothing else in return. I couldn't do what they do. If I had twenty hikers staying at my house every night, fond as I am of them, I'd go nuts.

Ben dropped us back at the trailhead the following day and wished us luck. The clocks had gone back an hour, so darkness was falling at 5.30pm, which meant stopping around 4.30pm to make camp in the fading light. Compared with the height of the summer, when we could walk till past 8pm, we now had four hours less to make any headway. Now, twenty-mile days were excellent progress.

We passed a south-bounder who had enough gear to support all three of us, including a rifle. His pack, he told us, weighed a hefty thirty-seven kilos; twice ours, which were around eighteen kilos. Most of the weight came from his food supplies, consisting of heavy army surplus packs. His rifle was for protection against bears, although they were mostly preparing for hibernation. We chatted with him for five minutes and suggested politely that he could halve his pack weight just by getting off trail every week or so to re-supply, and by losing the gun. I left him wondering how the hell he was going to get to the Sierras, let alone make it over them.

During the afternoon, it started to snow as we climbed steadily to our target for the day, Skyline Road, where I had a shelter symbol marked on my map. We eventually located it: a simple, three-sided hut with a huge fire pit on the exposed wall. Piles of wood lay around the area as though the last of the campers had left in a hurry. A lonely picnic table had been squeezed inside. We set about making a fire and restoring some life into our feet.

There were perhaps four inches of snow around us and it was still falling. The following day we needed to ascend to 6,500 feet, a climb of about 1,000 feet. Normally this wouldn't be particularly daunting, but we were concerned about the snow conditions higher up.

I rose early, despite the cold, and took a short stroll around the area. More snow had fallen, and there were numerous frozen puddles, which I had to break through to gain access to water. Surrounded by forest, Breitenbush Lake had frozen over. The cone-shaped Campbell Butte rose from the far shore. Animal tracks littered the snow in a maze of crisscrossing lines. All was silent.

I was now in similar territory and conditions to those I had experienced in Washington with Trooper. We did not know what lay above us, but the situation was not likely to improve with altitude. Again I scolded myself for leaving my hike so late. Discussing the timings of our adventure, Nick and Chris put forward the intriguing notion that we had come out to experience the PCT and live in the woods for a few months – everyone else had finished, but we were still out here, so in a way we were the winners.

But ... to win, we still had to finish. And to finish, we still had to beat the winter and conquer another 217 miles.

We left at 7am. Three miles in, winning seemed a rather distant notion. As we climbed, the snow became deeper and continued to fall. Snowdrifts were up to our thighs, we lost the trail numerous times and the three miles took three hours. We put our packs down and took stock. This wasn't like Washington. There was far more snow, the temperature had plummeted and we were still climbing. At this point, a mile an hour would be good going, and we were facing long, tiring days where ten miles would have been excellent progress.

Not only that but also the PCT had, to all intents and purposes, disappeared off the face of the earth, even though I took regular GPS readings to try and find it. We unanimously agreed to return to the hut, where we built another roaring fire and ate, to try to restore some morale and re-group. We were in a bit of a pickle, though, if we couldn't even find the trail. With plenty of concentration, map reading, GPS checks and observation, we might have been able to cover ten miles in a day if we were lucky. It was almost mid-November, however, and at that rate we'd be walking until the middle of December – assuming conditions remained the same, that is, which they wouldn't.

"We could road walk it," I said.

"How do you mean?" they replied in unison.

"There's a rough track leading up to this campsite so vehicles can get here. That track must at some point spill out on to a road; once we get our bearings we can road walk all the way to Crater Lake. OK, so it's not the PCT; but as far as I'm concerned, it still means we can walk from Mexico to Canada. We won't have to worry about navigation, and the road will be at a lower elevation so should be snow-free. The surface will be harsher but we can crack out some serious mileage. We'll be passing plenty of places to eat, so we can carry less food, there'll be more motels and, of course, more chances to drink coffee."

The guys looked at me and then at each other for a few seconds. Nick scratched his beard and Chris raised his eyebrows. Slowly, they smiled.

"Road walk!" Chris piped up, and Nick nodded in agreement.

I had become fond of these guys. Many hikers would have given up and gone home by now; indeed, many had. It is said that eighty-five per cent of thru-hikes aren't completed. We were still there, though: the last PCTers of the year. It made me proud to be English, proud of my stubbornness and proud to be walking with two like-minded fellow countrymen.

Nick was used to hardship on adventures. In previous travels, he'd survived winters and existed on a budget so meagre that I wouldn't have even attempted the journey. As I got to know Nick and Chris, I developed a strong respect for both of them. Living with other hikers for twenty-four hours a day is not easy, requiring patience, diplomacy and forgiveness. Not a single bad word passed between us. It was an English team effort – the British bulldog fighting spirit.

I was also becoming used to their habits. Nick was the talker. I joked that he held records not just for long-distance walking, but also long-distance talking. I enjoyed solitary walking in silence, but after a few days of being with Nick, that became something of a distant memory. We took things easy, with regular cigarette and snack breaks, and sometimes we just sat and talked for an hour. We didn't know when we would get to Crater Lake, but we knew we would get there.

The first obstacle was finding the actual road, to even attempt the road walk. We hiked down the track, as we lost altitude, the snow turned to rain, the surface gradually thawed and we put on our waterproofs. The guys had jackets and trousers made of a waterproof material that was excellent at shedding water, but none too durable. Over time, their waterproofs had been snagged on bushes and the seat had worn where they sat down, with hilarious results. Chris's waterproof trousers had so many rips and tears that, as he put one leg forward, it would emerge from the material, which, a second or so later, attempted to catch his leg. Nick's jacket was in no better state, sliced and slit as though he had been mugged by someone with a very sharp knife. Various pieces of yellow duct tape were unsuccessfully trying to hold the garments together, and as I walked behind them I laughed at the strips of tape and material blowing around aimlessly in the wind. The guys were also wearing running shoes – ideal for the drier, hotter sections, but now they had permanently cold and wet feet. I had been wearing my waterproof boots for a while, and even they were struggling to keep out the moisture.

Nick's violent phase, as I called it, kicked in around 2pm. "He does it every day, sometimes several times," Chris commented. Nick seemed to need constant mental stimulation, and if he didn't get it, he got comically angry. To vent his frustration, he would suddenly lash out with his trekking pole at innocent bushes and branches that he had taken an irrational dislike to. In between blows, he'd use his pole as a spear as though he was hunting a fleeing gazelle in the African bush. The whole display lasted for some minutes.

Sometimes Nick would speed off to dissipate some excess energy, so Chris and I spent many an hour chatting. He never appeared stressed, took each day at a time and just did what needed to be done. He walked a solid and steady pace, had good stamina and never, to my knowledge, complained about anything.

After two hours descending the track, we hit tarmac. A country road intersected us but we had no way of knowing where it went or where it had come from. Following the compass, we continued south through the pouring rain. Though we moaned about the snow, at least it merely settled on our bodies, whereas the constant rain soaked through us with a mighty chill.

We passed a sign saying that Detroit was eighteen miles away, which lifted our mood a little. The thought of at least drying out at a motel and getting some decent food inside us edged our speed up. A ranger truck passed and stopped, and the two occupants got out to chat with us for a few minutes. They confirmed the mileage to Detroit, offered us a ride, which we declined, and described the little town. A good motel, a couple of nice eateries and a store, they said. We also learnt that it was on the main road down to Crater Lake, with a few towns along the way. On we went, cowering from passing vehicles as they sent up showers of spray.

Road signs constantly reminded us of the remaining mileage.

On those flat roads, we knew our average speed, and it was easy to calculate our arrival time. As we reached the highway, Detroit appeared through the rain and mist, and we huddled under a shelter outside the store. A hot dog and coffee solved the immediate hunger and thirst crisis, and we smoked a cigarette outside, discussing the next move. The motel, we were assured by the store owner, had recently been refurbished and was excellent. The bar was friendly and served basic but filling grub. There was also the café, which came similarly highly recommended. None of us needed much persuading to get inside the motel, dry out and warm up.

As we checked in, the motel owner strolled off to prepare the room and I called after her.

"Can you please switch on any item capable of producing heat and turn it up to the maximum?"

Chris laughed as she waved back in acknowledgement, and by the time we entered the room, a wall heater was firing out a welcome blast of heat. As we took off our wet items of gear and hung them on anything resembling a hook, the windows rapidly steamed up. I collapsed into a hot bath and slowly felt the warmth penetrate my limbs and drive out a stubborn chill. After days outdoors in the winter, we were tiptoeing around on the floor complaining about the cold tiles!

Spirits restored, we ventured over to the bar to revive them further, by that marvel of pick-me-ups, alcohol. A line of perhaps fifteen guys stretched along the bar, and Nick had to politely squeeze between two of them to get some drinks.

"You guys doing the PCT?" said Brad, one of the locals. "You're a bit late aren't you?"

The eight blokes to Nick's left shifted along the bar, and the other seven to his right did the same. Brad brought three stools over and we jostled in. The bartender placed a pitcher of beer in front of us.

"On the house," he said, smiling.

We spent a couple of hours in the bar that evening, and I have fond memories of the occasion. Ensconced in classic American hospitality, we felt the stress of the previous few days melt away in a sea of Pale Ale. We felt like minor celebrities, amid the compliments and encouragement from the other patrons.

"I take my hat off to you three," said Brad. "I live here and I'm lucky if I get one day a month to go for a walk. You guys come to my country and experience the woods for six months, something I'll probably never be able to do. It makes me proud to live in this country when people like you travel a huge distance not just to get here, but to hike. Best of luck to all of you, I'm truly inspired."

People left, and others arrived. The cook dished up an admirable burger and chips, as the whole focus of attention in the bar centred on us and what we were doing. Later we staggered back to the motel, half expecting to sign autographs.

Our gear was still wet the following day, and the newsreader looked depressed as she informed us, and Oregon, that the day would be a washout. We decided to take a zero. Returning to Cedars Bar once more, we were fed an excellent breakfast. Oliver, the owner, offered to take our laundry away to wash. I must admit that I didn't envy him opening the contents of that bag.

A lazy day ensued, checking emails, keeping warm (something of a novelty at this point), eating and sleeping. The weather forecast changed from 'occasional rain' to the slightly perkier 'occasional showers'.

Journal entry:

Wet! Resting in the Lodge Motel in Detroit. Been thrown out of the mountains! Too much snow to carry on any further. We discuss the options, settling on a road walk to Crater Lake, and then the few miles further to where we left the trail at Mazama Village. There is no other option really. We now have 157 miles to walk on the road, which means only one thing: blisters. I know this from my experience on previous road detours. I'm looking forward to it, though. I think it will be a novelty not to worry about navigation, and we should pass plenty of places that serve real food.

Nick and Chris are good company. We laugh a lot, and we need to laugh to maintain morale; the weather is either wet or cold. I think about, among other things, the desert; it was brutal at the time, but now I yearn for the warmth, and have fond memories of those days in a T-shirt. The sun rose early and set late. The spring flowers burst into bloom to survive another season before the heat finally made them retreat underground for another year. It reminded me of my hike; it was never intended to be a race against the weather, but it became one. I remember that hummingbird hovering two feet from me. The beauty of it was mesmerising.

My friends have finished the adventure, some many weeks ago. They are back to their normal lives, and I hope they're planning their next thru-hike. I miss them, in particular Stumbling Norwegian, Sugar Moma, Hojo, Logic, Burnie, Your Mom, Pony, Pigpen, Evo, Gabe; really, everyone I shared time with. The messages I receive from them and from friends and family back home are encouraging – they spur me on. Only a few more days left and we can call ourselves thru-hikers.

Chapter 17
Crater Lake

It's more than just walking. There's a whole culture that goes along with the people. You know how you want the world to be? It's like that on the Pacific Crest Trail. People are helping people.
Monty 'Warner Springs Monty' Tam

We set off on Highway 22 south-bound. A quick look at a map in the supermarket confirmed we needed to stick on that road until it merged with the 20, then the 97 for most of the way before we took a small side road on the final approach to Crater Lake. A few towns and smaller settlements clung to the road such as Sisters, Bend, La Pine and Chemult. They were well spaced and made good, two-day targets. We hoped to reach Sisters, fifty-eight miles away, the following day. We lost a small amount of weight from our packs by taking less food, hoping to supply as we travelled.

Our morale was high and we felt cheerful. We knew we were closing in on our target, that all the hard physical effort over the previous months was going to pay off. Very soon we could call ourselves thru-hikers. The rain had cleared and we walked in sunshine. An occasional cloud wandered past, the air was lush with the smell of fallen leaves, and steam rose from the tarmac as water evaporated, catching chinks of sunlight filtering through the trees.

We warmed up, peeled off a layer, put on sunglasses and started to get used to this new environment. The road was not busy but we had to pay attention to what was approaching. It was too easy to feel safe there, a dangerous attitude when road walking. Every few seconds we'd check oncoming traffic just in case a lorry forced us on to the verge. The road started to play games with us. Sometimes we walked on a softer, gritty surface to the side, which cushioned the feet somewhat and crunched nicely. More often than not, we had to walk on the asphalt, as grit was in short supply. Crash barriers sheltered cars from drops or bridges and these squeezed us dangerously between their steel surface and passing traffic, so we usually tried to get on the other side. Painted white lines became mesmerising and I would slip into a trance, just letting them flash by one by one across my field of vision.

Bends were few and far between. Often we faced a long stretch of road disappearing over the next horizon, which never seemed to get any closer until finally we hit it, crested the hill and saw more of the same. Trees dripped water, which plinked on our heads, and we splashed through the occasional puddle. At last we stopped for a coffee in Idanha.

"What are you guys up to?" asked the waitress.

"Walking the Pacific Crest Trail," Chris said. "We're on the road to Crater Lake because of too much snow up there." He nodded up towards the hills.

"Awesome!" she replied, scratching her head and nodding. I could tell she had absolutely no idea what we were talking about.

Making good progress on a road isn't difficult, as roads always follow the path of least resistance and we didn't have to descend to rivers and ascend again because bridges took them out of the equation. We skirted mountains, rather than going up to the top and down again. We had no need for maps; road signs calculated distances for us and there were few uneven surfaces on which to twist a misplaced ankle.

It is, however, monotonous. Pleading for even a small morsel of stimulation, I played my old trick of getting a brief glimpse of drivers as they flashed by and trying to guess who they were and where they were going. I smiled at the attractive women and awarded myself bonus points for a reciprocated grin. I tried my best to look mischievous when the police approached, just so I might be questioned. If I was struggling mentally, Nick must have been near breaking point: his violent phase kicked in a little earlier each day and lasted just that little longer.

We walked at different paces, which meant we were usually well spaced out. Whenever Chris reached the brow of a hill half a mile ahead of me, or Nick disappeared round a corner, I wondered if I was walking too slowly. Equally, if I was ahead, I thought I was walking too fast or perhaps the others had slowed down. The person up front pretty much dictated breaks so the other two could catch up, but we generally walked for two hours, covering six to eight miles, and then rested. During one section, five miles passed in no time and I felt as if I had glided along with absolutely no effort whatsoever. Had I reached walking enlightenment?

In an attempt to make our situation more acceptable, Nick rigged his iPod inside a small case with a built-in speaker and we sang along to some Kate Bush or Nick Cave, our voices occasionally drowned out by a passing lorry. His other method of not going mad was indulging in a little trekking pole balancing. He pulled this off admirably, even in the forest, but on the smoother and uninterrupted road where there were no obstacles he was flying. The challenge was to balance the tip of the pole on one finger and keep it upright for as long as possible while still walking. He had developed ingenious tactics, which we borrowed: keep the eye focused on one part of the pole (I stuck a small piece of duct tape just below the handle for the purpose) and block out your surrounding field of vision. Dangerous though this doubtless was, the risk of collision with a car was sometimes deemed necessary in the pursuit of a record.

A couple of walking hours had usually elapsed before the first event took place. Nick would steadily keep an outstretched arm in front, delicately balancing the pole, often for many minutes on end. Occasionally he would experience a loss of concentration or a slight breeze would throw him off – and then the fun started. At times he would have to stop dead in his tracks or hit reverse to prevent the pole from tipping back. Then he might have to speed up to catch up with it as it threatened to fall to the front. I lost count of the times Chris and I observed and laughed as we watched Nick break into a sprint and disappear down the road, trying in vain to stave off defeat. If a sideways tilt caught him off guard he'd think nothing of running sideways into the forest, down an embankment or over scrub. All would go quiet for a minute as he vanished into the pines, before a simple "Bollocks" floating out of the trees confirmed that the game was over.

I reflected on the previous 202 days. All the excitement at the beginning, meeting my fellow hikers at the kick-off party, those hot few weeks in the desert or standing at the top of the world. Fondly remembering all the people I had become acquainted with, I wondered where they were now. Hojo, Stumbling Norwegian, Your Mom, Burnie, Elk and a few others had sent me texts saying they had finished. I caught up with the others through their blogs or email.

We drifted up hills and walked through occasional shallow snow before descending to a wet, shiny road again. The light faded, we donned head torches, the last in the line wearing his so the light shone behind us, just in case, and we started to search for somewhere to sleep. Dense forest lined both sides of the highway, dropping down into a dank darkness. We passed a campsite, now closed, but ventured further to make some miles and then took a side track to get away from the traffic noise. This offered no flat areas, so we returned to the turn-off, walked over to the other side and dipped down the bank. Fallen trees and leaves hampered the search but eventually we squeezed into the best area we could find. I pitched my tent between two fallen limbs and, on opening the vestibule, was confronted with a bright orange fungus with a patterned head that looked like a face winking at me; it watched me all evening. Tyres hissed from the road and slowly the traffic faded.

We had done well the first day on the road and pulled in twenty-eight miles. This left thirty-one to Sisters, a long day but achievable despite shortening daylight hours. However, by 3pm we calculated a dismal seventeen miles had passed under our boots. We ate a late lunch sitting on a solitary bench by a panoramic point overlooking the mountains. Occasionally a car pulled in and the occupants spilled out with cameras to admire the view. Some eyed us warily; others ventured over and made conversation or tentatively offered us food, as though we were

The Last Englishman

wild animals. One elderly couple spent a good fifteen minutes chatting, showing apparent, genuine interest. As they walked off, I overheard the wife say,

"What are they doing?"

"I have absolutely no idea," the man replied.

Lights started to blink ahead of us as we approached the final section to Sisters but it took an hour to reach them. Traffic slowed on the approach to the town and we began to see pedestrians from time to time. In a burger bar, we took advantage of the 'buy one, get one free' option, warming our backs against a radiator as we ate.

Our feet were on fire. Walk half a mile to work every day on concrete and it would never bother you. Do it for ten hours, however, and it's a different story. Similarly, slapping a wall with your palm doesn't hurt, but do it for hours on end and you'll feel it. Despite all our conditioning over hundreds of miles, the blister was making an unwelcome comeback – and as we sat in the burger bar, we grimaced as we stretched out a sore limb. It was like being back at the start. Calves, tendons and thighs all ached and the pain shot up into our backs. Thank God for ibuprofen.

Reginald at nerve centre HQ had only just got on top of dealing with the temperature drop from the mountains before a long string of messages from Angela down in the feet arrived.

"I think he must be walking on concrete or something," she started. "I thought it would be temporary but I'm experiencing hours and miles of shock to the feet, the soles are getting tender and I've got to deal with the first blisters for 780 miles. Anything you can give me down here?"

"They're on a road walk, apparently," Reginald answered, "and we've got another few days of it as well. It's temporary, don't worry; the diet is a little better, so take what you need from the minerals and nutrients cupboard."

Sisters Inn and Suites was just down the road next to the supermarket, so we checked in for the night. We did a small resupply and Nick and Chris prepared meals for the coming section. They usually concocted their own recipes by buying a staple such as rice or couscous, then adding spices such as garlic powder, cumin or nuts. At camp they might add a cured meat or empty in a can of fish. Nick sat by the window with five Ziploc bags, carefully measuring the same amount of each ingredient for them, while Chris sat on the bed chopping various additions and every now and then handing Nick more for each bag. They offered to do the same for me but I declined because I enjoyed my little cooking ritual each evening.

Later, I went for a wander around Sisters, a place well regarded by thru-hikers. Towards the centre of town, I came upon older buildings and an assortment of restaurants and curious little shops. Christmas lights were already up and tinsel hung from window displays. A few late holidaymakers strolled around and chatter spilled out from bar windows. I reached the end of town and looked south, thinking the mountains around Crater Lake would be visible, but they were hiding 127 miles distant below an orange horizon.

Temperatures had risen slightly as we left Sisters and set off to cover the twenty-three miles to Bend, also held in high hiker esteem. We walked in T-shirts through flat, agricultural land, where fields dotted with cows or horses and pale yellow dry grass met the roadside. Cars started to honk and a couple of motorists stopped, asking if we needed anything.

"My sister met you at the motel back in Sisters and told me what you three are doing. That's amazing!"

Word was circulating that three mad Englishman were road-walking to Crater Lake. We entered a few bars and the waiting staff welcomed us before we had opened our mouths.

"You're the three Englishman! Come in, sit down, you must be starving!" She flapped around us like a worried mother hen looking after her brood. We just lapped it all up; if nowhere else, we were famous along a small ribbon of tarmac in Oregon.

At another roadside café, we were shown to a table in the corner and customers nudged each other and nodded our way, returning our smiles.

"You're doing what?" exclaimed one guy as we brought him up to speed, a section of rump steak hanging from his startled mouth. "What ... er, how, why, no, wait, you've walked from Mexico? That's impossible!"

Most of the clientele got busy discussing our plans, the road options and the weather outlook. The waiter came over with the

The Last Englishman

bill and placed it on the table. A red pen had crossed through it, with the words 'paid' underneath.

"Guys, it's your lucky day. Your bill's been paid."

We abruptly stopped eating our apple pie.

"Huh?" Chris said.

"One of the locals was listening to your story. He used to hike but can't any more because of a bad injury. He asked me to tell you that it was his pleasure listening to you and he would be honoured if you would allow him to meet your bill. He's left; he didn't want to be known."

I sat back in my chair, feeling a little humbled and emotional. 'He can't hike any more' echoed in my mind over and over again and I realised how lucky I was. Lucky to even have two legs that worked. We thanked the waiter and left in a grateful, contemplative silence.

We had received good reports about Bend from other hikers, but as we entered the outskirts, it was hard to see what all the fuss was about. A nondescript collection of garages, one or two food stores and supermarkets – hardly enough to justify the claim that it was one of the best trail towns. We had stopped at an intersection, not knowing which way to head, when a woman appeared next to us, waiting for the lights to change so she could cross. It was a rarity to see a pedestrian; most people didn't venture out without their cars.

"Do you know where the town centre is?" asked Nick.

"Yes, it's about a mile, I can show you the way if you like."

We followed her for a short distance and she directed us left at another intersection.

"You can't miss it," she said. "It goes straight to town."

Slowly the out-of-town shopping areas dwindled, to be replaced by houses. The Deschutes river curled up to the road and turned back to run along the rear of some houses at the town's edge. The ugly duckling started to turn into a swan and our town expectations were slowly met.

Nick stopped to chat to a local, who immediately offered us a place to stay and get cleaned up. I needed to write and send an email to *Country Walking* magazine who had requested a piece on El Camino de Santiago in Spain, a walk I had completed some years earlier. Kelly insisted we stay with him, so we all bundled in the back of his van.

"Don't worry, Fozzie," he said. "There's a great café with internet just around the corner from me."

He showed us his home, which turned out to be one of the houses that backed on to the river. There was a small jetty where we sat with a beer, watching the sun go down. Kelly apologised because he had to go out, but left us a key and told us to make ourselves at home.

We ate at the café, where the owners took a keen interest in our adventure and amid the cacophony of rowdy drinkers I somehow managed to concentrate and spent two hours writing the magazine piece. Even the barman asked them to keep the noise down a little.

"There's an English writer in here trying to work," he said. "Keep the noise down a little, guys!"

Returning to Kelly's, I joined Nick and Chris on the jetty for more beer and we idled away an hour just watching the river drift past.

We never did see Kelly again, as he returned in the early hours, but we left him a thank-you note. Oregon hospitality was turning out to be priceless. Word seemed to be getting around about our mission and more and more cars were hooting at us as they sped past, to which we would raise a trekking pole in recognition.

We were detained in Bend by my coffee habit and the proliferation of establishments serving an excellent espresso; I think I stopped at three of them, much to the bemusement of the guys. We scrambled up a steep embankment by the railway to reach Highway 97 and continue our road walk. A long, straight road disappeared over the horizon some three miles away but the 97 was kind. There was less traffic and a soft soil stretched right up to the verge, which made for easy walking.

The amount of litter and discarded items was astonishing. Nick was like a radar and would regularly stop to examine an object to see if it was worth keeping; frankly, I never managed to fathom why such items appealed to him. We came across numerous lighters (most of them working), food scraps, old mobile phones, CDs and quite a few plastic bottles filled with a dubious-looking liquid we assumed was urine. Passing

The Last Englishman

roadworks, the construction team stopped to chat and offered us hot drinks from their flasks.

Nick was also strangely drawn to abandoned buildings. If he spotted anything in the forest that appeared to be manmade out of concrete or wood, he'd disappear to investigate. If this happened near the end of the day, I'd groan because I knew he'd want to sleep in it. I reckon his fondness for such buildings went back to his budget travelling days without a tent, so anything with a roof meant shelter and a dry night's sleep. We often queried why he'd want to sleep in an abandoned building, with perhaps a dead animal or a pile of excrement sitting in the corner, when he could pitch his tent. I guess it was too hard a habit to break.

We had fifty miles left to Mazama Village, Crater Lake and the end of our hike. Word had reached us of an impending storm. The trail by the lake itself topped out at around 7,700 feet, so we knew that if it rained where we were, then it would be sure to snow up there. We hoped to reach our finishing point before the snow did. A cold wind was already blowing down from the mountains but as we looked to our right we could see no sign of the white stuff on the peaks. Fresh from my triumph against the elements in Washington, I had begun to regard myself as invincible. Snow didn't scare me any more; I didn't particularly enjoy it, but I knew it shouldn't be a problem.

After a brief cigarette and M&M's break, we continued walking. The guys were in front by a short distance and I took a cursory look behind to see if any lorries were approaching and also to see how far we had come. A sheriff's car was not so much approaching as apparently, slowly, tailing us. A bear dashed across the road behind him. At least drivers had some entertainment, I thought. Those coming from the opposite direction would have first seen three English guys with backpacks being followed by a police escort and then a bear scampering across the road. When the police car driver caught my eye, he accelerated past and pulled in a few yards ahead of Nick, who was in front. The sheriff stopped, got out and started talking to Nick and Chris. I arrived half a minute later.

"What's going on?" I enquired.

"Apparently," Nick explained, "we've had an altercation

with a gentleman back down the road."

I looked at him, then at Chris. I don't know which one of us looked more perplexed; even the sheriff started to look puzzled.

"Huh?" was all I could think of saying, but then added, "We haven't seen anyone for at least an hour."

The sheriff attempted to shed some light on the situation.

"We received a call from a gentleman saying you had shouted abuse at him a couple of miles back. Do you know anything about this? His dog was going crazy."

"Oh, the dog!" I said, as realisation suddenly dawned. "We passed a house and there was a dog looking through the gate at us, so we whistled at it, but not out of aggression or anything. You know, you see a dog in the park and you sometimes whistle at it. We didn't even see anyone else."

The sheriff scribbled on a pad and had a quick conversation with someone on the radio.

"What are you guys doing anyway?"

"We're walking the Pacific Crest Trail, but got snowed out of the mountains above Detroit, so we're finishing it off by road walking the section down to Crater Lake," Chris explained.

"You know there's a storm blowing in, don't you? Snow higher up." We said we had heard. "Our phone call," the sheriff said, "was obviously a misunderstanding; I'll go see the guy and ask him to stop wasting our time. Guys, good luck, I wish you well."

Generally I don't get on well with those in authority but I do, strangely, enjoy encounters with the American police. There's the odd officer who thinks he rules the world, but on the whole they're a reasonable bunch, and this guy was no exception.

We were making better progress than expected and suddenly La Pine looked within reach as long as we could do thirty miles that day. We put our heads down, forgoing breaks, and cracked out nine miles in two and a half hours. La Pine was basically a trucker stop. An old-fashioned motel in a rather fetching shade of pink bordered the highway, and Gordy's restaurant and bar over the road looked like it might serve up a decent dinner. Nick charmed the woman on reception into giving a healthy discount for cash and we holed up in our art deco-styled room as a frost crept up to the front door. The push-button TV needed several

The Last Englishman

minutes to reach operating temperature but there were gallons of steaming hot water with which to have a bath.

A couple of drinkers propped up Gordy's bar, and an empty dining room didn't bode too well. Stuffed animals hung on all the walls and I wondered if the owner had more of a penchant for taxidermy than for cooking. As I perused the menu, an elk was eyeing me cautiously, two raccoons seemed to be sizing me up and a very large black bear held his paws by his head in a posture of surrender. It was a little creepy. Thankfully, the owner was a good cook and we tucked into 'breakfast' at dinner.

We had calculated just forty-four miles left to Mazama Village, which we knew was achievable in two days providing the weather held. However, after a quick check on our road map, I announced my maths needed a little adjustment and in fact the figure was nearer sixty-eight. Highway 97 carried on a further thirty-eight miles to an intersection, where we needed to turn right on to the 138. Fifteen miles up this road the entrance to Crater Lake would appear, and from there it was a further fifteen miles to Mazama Village. Two days suddenly seemed a little ambitious, even with easy walking on the road; moreover, once we hit the Crater Lake National Park turn-off, there was a good chance it would be covered in snow. The snow plough, we were told by a local, only clears the highway, not the park roads, which were now closed for the season.

The side turning on to the 138 also apparently housed a motel and another restaurant. Although the finances were taking a bit of a battering, our stomachs were full and we were warm at night. Sleeping in a tent in freezing temperatures, however, does condition you to the cold. Snuggling up under blankets in a warm motel room doesn't. As we emerged from our haven, we shivered and jumped up and down. Ice covered the car windows and dusted long blades of grass, making them curl downwards like white talons. Postponing our exercise in warming up to operating temperature, we ducked into Gordy's again for breakfast.

The adventure I had hoped for did not consist of road walking, but sometimes plans have to be altered to fit circumstances. In an ideal world, my hike would have been in total wilderness, all conveniences necessary for re-supply and food would be clustered around a road crossing every week and then I'd be back in the hills. My hike would have started at Mexico and weaved north to finish at the Canadian border. Skipping a section to return and complete it wasn't part of the plan either. I had wanted to do a pure hike, start at the start and finish at the finish, and the other guys had had the same ambition. We were confident of completion, but we would rather have followed the natural course of the PCT and not been snowed off. Yet, aware that a very small proportion of our hike was off trail, we never once considered reaching Mazama and not calling ourselves PCT thru-hikers.

Although Highway 97 had never even crossed my mind before, I didn't begrudge her company. She was looking after us, keeping us warm at night and filling our stomachs. By now we had become known on the highway, and were waved at, beeped at, given the thumbs-up out of windows, fed for free, not charged for coffee and offered a roof for the night. It may not have been the wilderness, but it was pure entertainment.

After finally emerging from Gordy's, we crunched along on ice and grit. It had turned much colder, perhaps a sign of the imminent storm. Cloud blocked out any hope of warmth, the wind was increasing and leaves flew across the road as if trying to escape.

After a disappointing seventeen miles that seemed to last an eternity, we reached Chemult, essentially a garage and a drive-in coffee shop. I walked up to the window in search of an espresso and startled the woman inside.

"You're supposed to be in a car!" she joked.

"I wish," I replied.

"What are you guys doing?"

After I'd given her the shortened version, she handed us each a coffee, gave me a hand-crocheted beanie and called her husband.

"Wait five minutes and you two can have one as well," she added, pointing to Nick and Chris.

We had only managed another three miles by the time we reached the turn-off for Highway 138 and the Whispering Pines Motel. 'Whispering' was a bit weak as a description; 'howling' was more appropriate. We checked in, relaxed a little and then ventured through the gale to the diner on the opposite side of the road. Although about to shut up shop, the cook knocked us up a quick burger and chips.

According to the owners at Whispering Pines, this was the storm that had been forecast; the snow was pretty certain to start in the early hours, and Crater Lake, higher up, would already have received a plentiful coating. We got our heads down for an early start and the final 30 miles to our finish.

At 4.45am, Nick hesitantly drew the curtain back and pressed his nose to the glass.

"Raining," he announced.

As I did the same, all I could make out was a solitary street light illuminating the road junction. The rain came in waves and water trickled down the cold window. An occasional car speeding past sent a fine spray skywards, obscuring the street light. We all harboured mixed feelings: anticipation at finishing together with hesitation about going out in the rain and probably snow. My stomach fluttered with butterflies. We wrapped up in waterproofs, made sure our pack contents were protected and gingerly stepped out. It was still dark and noticeably colder. We had fifteen miles before the turn-off for Crater Lake Park, all of it on a slight incline. I pulled the draw cord on my jacket hood tighter and slapped my arms to warm up. Gradually, the slick, shiny, black bitumen began to change. Rain slowly stopped falling and instead started floating around us as snow, which settled on our shoulders. The moisture from the rain on my jacket started to freeze and I found myself encased in a coating of ice, which cracked as I bent my arm. The splashing of feet turned to crunching as black faded to white. The higher we ventured, the colder and whiter it became, until everything was virgin silver. It had taken just an hour to walk straight into winter. Ice crystals formed on my beard and flakes rested on my eyelashes. There were no tyre tracks until a snow plough suddenly came towards us, sending up a huge arc of snow on to the verge. It was barely light but he saw us and graciously stopped until we had passed, puzzlement plain to see in his face.

When we eventually reached the Crater Lake Park entrance, our ploughed road ceased and we encountered a strip of pure white powder stretching away through the trees. A solitary latrine offered us some shelter for a few minutes as we ate some food and smoked cigarettes. Cringing, we drank some water, which was barely still liquid. It was already painfully cold and we had further still to climb.

The road was our main focus of attention. Our road map lacked detail, so we clung to this fast-disappearing black strip. On the short sections where the road cut through some sheltering trees, we could see it well enough, but once we emerged it took all our concentration to pick out the narrow, black ribbon that wound up to the lake. The snow was starting to drift, and our only clue that we were still on tarmac came from tufts of grass and vegetation poking through the surface at the sides. It was now about a foot deep and the clouds had merged into a grey mist, cloaking the tops of the trees. Nick's knee was troubling him; he had taken a week out right back at the start to rest it and it had not really troubled him since. Now, though, having to pull his legs out of the snow with every step, it was becoming painful and he was lagging behind Chris and me.

Finally, we reached the crater. What greeted us took our breath away. A giant caldera six miles wide, flanked by peaks and filled with the purest blue water, glittered and sparkled. The blue was beginning to recede as an ice sheet spread. Below us, the conical symmetry of Wizard Island broke the surface. We sat on the cold, hard ground for an age and just looked, speechless, a hint of a smile cracking our frozen faces. There was no need for words, nor could I have found the right ones to describe the vision that I had been dreaming about for months. We were nearly at the end. Nearly.

The last few miles down to Mazama Village couldn't be that difficult, we thought. The western side of the lake, however, had received the full brunt of both wind and snow. Only the occasional morsel of open road peeped out of the drifting snow, which came up to our waists. We constantly checked ahead to try and catch a glimpse of black poking through white, sometimes walking at the side, but the ground sloped away from us and threatened to whip away our feet.

Nick was having a rough time. He spent most of the afternoon hobbling, in between fairly frequent stops to try and rest his knee. Either Chris or I shadowed him as the other walked

The Last Englishman

ahead and pushed through a route. He didn't complain, just told us how it was and got on with it, albeit slowly. Several months of solid walking and then his knee gives up on the last day! He had no choice; he had to struggle on or be left in the freezing cold. It was painful progress and we were all exhausted. You don't walk through snow, you plough through. Most of the time we were knee to waist deep. We'd take a step forward and guess whether the snow would compact and hold the foot or whether we would sink further, as invariably we did. Drag the trailing leg out of the hole, keep it bent to clear the surface, place it down and repeat the whole process. We were at the edge of energy reserves, dangerously cold, disheartened and on the verge of calling it a day. The only solace was that we were expecting to see Trooper at Mazama after I had arranged for him to meet us. Being an Englishman, I was not part of the 'we cover 90% of all Americans' promise by my mobile provider, so I had no way now of contacting him. I had only known Trooper for a few weeks; the guys were worried whether he would turn up.

"Trooper will be there," I told them. "And, if he has to go back to his motel, he'll be there waiting in the morning."

We knew Mazama Village would be a ghost town; it shuts down out of season, so there would be no chance of food or board. After thirty miles in these conditions, our only reward would be sleeping out in them.

Gradually we descended, too tired to even rest and eat. Slowly the snow thinned out, until we were back hopping from one section of road to another. We stamped our feet to dislodge ice encrusted on our boots, brushed the snow off our shoulders and somehow staggered the last few miles to a small cluster of buildings. It was dark as we stood by the road intersection where I had been with Rockets some weeks earlier. I was startled at how everything had changed. On my last visit, I had been sweating in shorts and a T-shirt. Now I was wearing most of what I was carrying. Trooper was nowhere to be seen but it was now 9pm. A few tyre tracks ribboned and swirled around the intersection and then a ranger pulled up.

"You Fozzie?"

I raised my eyebrows in surprise and smiled.

"Yes!"

"Guy called Trooper wants you to know that he was here waiting for you. He said he'll come back at nine tomorrow. Where you guys going to sleep? Will you be OK?"

"We'll be fine," I replied. "Thanks for the message."

In better spirits, we put up the tents, fluffed up our bags and blew up our mattresses for the last time that year. Before long, we were huddled in our tents, watching steam rise from our stoves as I had done way back down on the first morning in the desert chill. Cupping my mug, I sipped delicately at the hot chocolate. There had been no celebration. We were so tired we had completely forgotten we had even finished.

Chapter 18
The Original Question

Days like today I'm a half step from putting on my pack and wrapping my hands around those trekking poles. I just want to go back to what makes sense to me. Back to where I'm happy. Back to where I'm the best me I've ever known.
Dave 'Upchuck' Ferber

I woke up grinning. After completely forgetting to celebrate our finish, the realisation dawned that I was now a Pacific Crest Trail thru-hiker. I poked my head out of the tent to bright sunlight bouncing off fresh, crisp snow. I didn't care about the cold any more, the exhaustion or the hunger; I had beaten all of the odds. California couldn't stop me, Washington didn't hold me back and Oregon tried but failed. I felt like a seven-year-old waking up on Christmas day, eager to get out of bed and open my presents.

The guys were up before me, and after a quick breakfast and breaking camp we strolled down to the road junction where I needed to organise a quick task before Trooper arrived.

At the beginning of my trek I had continued to hound Chris, the proprietor at ÜLA, for pack sponsorship. I knew it was a futile exercise; it just turned out to be a bit of a joke between us. Attached to the last email I had received from him was a photo of a woman carrying one of his packs. It was taken from behind and she was naked. The email message was simple: "She gets one, you don't."

From time to time during the hike, this email flashed into my mind and made me smile; walking 2,650 miles also gave me ample time to plot a little revenge. The guys agreed with my plan. After setting Nick's camera up on his tripod, we stood in line with our backs to the camera and dropped our trousers. The lens clicked and we checked the photo: it was perfect. Three guys wearing ÜLA packs and displaying three pairs of butt cheeks. A few days later I sent this to Chris, again asking for a free pack. I heard nothing for a week, so I sent him another email asking if he had received it.

"Yes, Fozzie, I received your message," he replied. "I've just got out of therapy and no, you still don't get a freebie."

What Chris does not yet realise is the more he resists, the more of a challenge it is. One day…

True to his promise, Trooper came sliding down the road and skidded to a halt in front of us, beaming.

"I told you you'd make it!" he cried. "You must have been through hell and back!"

"I think hell would have been a little warmer," I replied with a satisfied grin.

I introduced him to Nick and Chris and we bundled in to his car and headed for Ashland, the nearest transport hub, from where we could continue our journeys. In England we don't know how to drive in snow because we rarely receive any snowfall. Trooper took off down the hill as if he were on a rally stage, while I held firmly on to the door and looked skywards for help.

Chris had chosen to travel down to Los Angeles and Nick to San Diego for different reasons but both decided that sun was the major factor. I had to get back to San Jose, collect my belongings from my relatives, wind down for a couple of days and get a flight back home. We stopped at the first diner and ate like wolves, treating Trooper to his meal, as he wouldn't accept any money for fuel. Chris needed to get to a different bus station and, as Trooper had agreed to take him there, it was time to say our farewells. Chris lived a few miles from me back home – as did Nick – so I knew I would see him again. I gave heartfelt thanks to Trooper, who lives near Campo; we said we would see each other at the next kick-off party. Nick and I waited for our bus to Sacramento, where we would go our separate ways.

Too tired to talk but not tired enough to sleep, I gazed out of the bus window as darkness fell and city lights appeared. While Nick slept, I answered a few voicemails from friends demanding news and watched the world flash by. Sacramento was uninspiring, especially in the middle of the night; and after an hour's waiting, Nick boarded his onward bus with a thumbs-up and a smile. Before I knew it I was back at the home of Aunty Jillian and Uncle Tony, booking a flight back home to the UK.

Journal entry:

Back home.

Nearly four weeks back in England now. I still sleep with my head torch by the bed. I'm way too hot in the house and have to open the windows, even in this weather. I still wake up for a brief moment, thinking I have to walk twenty-five miles, and feel strange when I'm not wearing my trail gear.

On the plus side, it's great not to be cold for seven days at a time. I love not being restricted in a sleeping bag, I can have a coffee pretty much whenever I want and I don't have to filter my water. When I go for a walk in my local woods, I still take a mental note of where the water is and find myself looking at clearings between the trees sussing out suitable places to camp. Without my pack, I walk quickly and have to remind myself to slow down, that I'm in no rush.

The transition back to 'normal' life is going relatively smoothly. I don't appear to be suffering from the post-travel depression that usually dogs me when I return from such an adventure. However, I do miss the trail. Being out there in the wild has left a mark on me. Leaving my humdrum life behind was easy. OK, sometimes I yearned to be back in civilisation, but in the main, I relished being lucky enough to have witnessed the wilderness at its best.

I am more patient now. Few things are worth becoming stressed about, and after a trip of this kind you realise that most situations in life are not as bad as they appear. Spending time outside nurtures you; it seizes hold of you and lures you to a peaceful, serene, natural-feeling environment. The logistics of the PCT can be complex, but once you are out there, they are all worth the effort.

So, what now? I'm back doing my decorating, which is bearable, but I daydream between brush strokes. I think about the next walk; and there *will* be a next walk. All the national trails in Great Britain in one attempt? A walk around the coast of Great Britain, maybe? Or how about all 3,200 miles of the classic European E1 hike from Italy to Norway (or the other way round)? There are also numerous other long-distance paths in Europe I have my eye on, with a possible 2012 start date. My thoughts also return to America: the Appalachian Trail and the Continental Divide Trail beckon, along with the prospect of becoming a Triple Crowner. I may not be walking at the moment but life's good when you're planning the next adventure. Or I think about the Himalayas, the Far East, Scotland. Each has its own unique perspective, and each should be experienced. This isn't a competition, though; it's an education.

***

The transition back to everyday life goes well for some hikers. Others struggle with it. Flyboxer revealed his post-hike experience:

"In some ways, I felt like my post-PCT experience was more interesting than my actual hike. I could probably write a small book about it but I will try and summarise it in a couple of paragraphs.

"I finished my actual hike on 3 November after hiking southbound from Idyllwild to Campo. I had hiked from Idyllwild to Manning Park from May 22 to October 13. I thought I had done a pretty good job budgeting my trip. I tried to keep zeros to a minimum, didn't waste a lot of time in town and didn't go overboard staying in motels. However, I had a couple of unforeseen expenses that basically wiped out the money I hoped to have saved for my post-hike transition. I found myself unemployed, almost broke and homeless in San Diego. A good friend of mine lived there, but I didn't want to crash at his place while I was looking for work. I got the vibe that I wasn't welcome to do that anyhow, so I decided to live in my car. I missed how the trail seemed to consume my day, physically, mentally and emotionally. I found this gaping hole screaming to be filled once I finished. For the first few days in San Diego, I felt lost. I was spending most of my time walking all over the city because I still wanted and needed to walk. I was a wanderer. I felt more akin to the homeless than my working peers. I found myself hanging out naturally in places where most homeless people hang out. In parks, near the water and on benches. I was still in survival mode, I guess, and my eyes were constantly looking for natural shelters and places to sleep in the city. It felt very strange, something I had never done before. I still had my beard, didn't have access to a regular shower and people began talking to me who never used to before, mostly homeless folks."

I felt lucky when I first read this experience – at least I had a room to stay in. Flyboxer continued:

"I knew that I needed structure, so I tried to set up a daily routine. My day seemed to revolve around the toilet. It's amazing what a person can take for granted when they have a place to live. On the trail, I tried to stay hydrated, almost over-hydrated; it didn't matter. You stop and pee wherever you want. Now I found myself keeping my liquid intake to a minimum, because I got tired of having to look all over for a public toilet. The park restrooms were always filled with creeps, and weird stuff seemed to be taking place in them all the time, which was very disheartening. I started drawing a lot. I'd just hang out in the park and draw for hours; it was very therapeutic and gave me something tangible to look at when the day was over. My computer was in my storage unit in Los Angeles, so I had to use the library computers in the city to look for work. The city's libraries felt more like a mental institution than a library.

"My car's brakes were completely shot, so I had to spend $600 to get them fixed, just so I could drive up to LA to get my computer and look for jobs. A trip up there and back would cost another $100. Driving was the only thing that helped me feel normal, but I had to keep it to an absolute minimum. For a start, gas was expensive. Also, having found a good parking spot where I felt relatively safe to sleep at night, I didn't want to lose it and have to find another place to sleep. I was keeping an eagle eye on my bank account, watching the numbers fall day after day. I was in a race against my account.

"I started going to daily mass at the Catholic church in Little Italy. It forced me to wake up early, was predictable and so gave me a feeling of normality, and that I was starting the day right. After one morning mass, I watched a homeless man exit the church in a front side door no-one else used. Why did he take that exit? I wondered. I decided to do the same, and discovered a sparklingly clean private restroom in a courtyard along the side of the church. Hallelujah!

"Once I got my computer back, I started going every day to a café, where I could take full advantage of the free Wi-Fi to start looking for work. My life fell into a routine. Each day I went to mass in the morning, then drew in the park for a couple of hours. I looked for jobs, went for a long walk around the city, went back to a different café in the afternoon, allowing myself a cup of coffee or two, looked for more jobs or wasted time online, went for another long walk in the evening and then called it a day. It was amazing how hard it was to fill my day. I craved normality.

"Often I would walk down by the waterfront at night and look at the people eating in the restaurants. It was a life that seemed almost unattainable at this point. My heart ached, wondering what I had become. I would see my peers who were going to work, eating lunch. That too seemed out of my reach. It was as if I had fallen. At the same time, paradoxically, I carried this fire within, this wholly satisfying feeling of accomplishment, knowing that I had completed the PCT. It was pure *1984*-style doublethink: carrying two contradictory notions in my mind at the same time.

"I had been living in my car for a month in San Diego and experienced a new low when a homeless man actually gave me a dollar. I couldn't believe it. What was happening? It was almost comical. I tried to refuse it, but the man had collected $45 that day, begging down by the waterfront, and was going to sleep in a hotel room for the night. 'I have everything I need for today,' the man said. 'Take the dollar.'

"A few days afterwards, I received good news. I got a job

offer. Although I wanted to live in San Diego, the job was in northern California. Unable to wait any longer, I took it. By the time I left San Diego, picked up the rest of my belongings in LA and arrived, I was down to my last few hundred bucks. I was in a completely new town, didn't know a soul, and for the first couple of weeks was unbelievably lonely. I tried to keep my situation to myself. I put my things in storage, applied for membership of a gym in order to access the showers and opened a PO box. My monthly expenses were $80. I started work immediately, worked out and showered at the gym in the morning, went to work during the day and ate at a café at night. I didn't have enough money to rent a room, so I continued to live in my car. When my first paycheck arrived, I cried with relief and a sense of achievement. Now my routine became solid, like hiking the trail, but naturally different in many ways. The PCT had given me the knowledge and confidence to survive, the patience to work towards a goal and the determination to face difficult circumstances.

"Four months later, I was finally able to get out of my car and back under a proper roof. I'll never forget how it felt to sleep in my own room again, to use my own toilet and shower, to cook on a stove with gas! It was all luxury to me – anything other than a meal and shelter was sheer indulgence.

"Despite it all, I'm hoping to hike another long trail soon. I am currently planning an attempt on the CDT. Hopefully this time, I will be in a better place financially post-trail."

Most hikers' post-trail experience is not as hard as Flyboxer's. I had given up my rented house, my possessions were split between two friends' garages and I had a little money left, though not enough to rent anywhere, so I moved back with my parents. My work picked up quickly and, despite my fears that my business might have suffered after I'd left it for seven months, I enjoyed the busiest year of work ever.

The problem with this successful period of work ever was that I wasn't doing a long-distance walk. Putting by funds for a walk is a necessary evil, unless you're rich or have financial sponsors. To save money you have to work: it's a terribly unfair arrangement. I often wonder who invented money, and what idiot thought up the notion of exchanging money for goods and services. Did they have the remotest idea what they were getting us into?

It's a common pattern among hikers. Do a long-distance walk, live free (in spirit) for a few months, forget about your worries and then return. Realise just how many useless possessions you actually own, find somewhere to live, get a job and then the process starts over again. I don't dislike my life back in town; I would just rather be up in the hills. Post-trail depression is also intensified by the weather, as most hikes take place in the summer months, bringing you back to the comfortless gloom of autumn or winter. Daylight recedes, the cold sets in and you're not where you want to be.

We carry on cooking our meals in one pot over one burner, the heating gets turned off and the bedroom window stays open. Except possibly for the occasional reunion with a favourite pair of jeans, we continue to wear our hiking clothes because we know they are the most comfortable. We take a shower when we think we smell enough and wash our clothes when they look undeniably grubby. Rising in the morning, we try reluctantly to come to terms with the fact that there is no trail waiting for us.

It's a long, slow transition, or perhaps more of a reluctant acceptance until gradually we get back into the nine-to-five and settle grudgingly back into society.

"What has changed me most is that I am way simpler than I ever was, although I was pretty simple to begin with," Sugar Moma explains. She continues:

"I can still live off 200 to 300 bucks a month and I sleep in my sleeping bag almost every night. I shower no more than two or three times a week and only when I'm in a city! I still cook and eat out of my one pot. I'm always longing to hike, and when I'm in the city I walk everywhere. Poor Kharma (her dog) doesn't get driven much any more.

"My feelings after getting off the trail? Oh my God, so mixed. Sad because it's over, happy not to have to get up every day and plan my miles, missing my hiker friends a lot (they're the ones who know how I'm really feeling), confused about what to do next, where to go, do I want a real job with a home or do I want to gypsy everywhere and keep on adventuring?

"I've always loved nature and what Mom gives us. I respect it more now and appreciate every moment I have with her; rain, snow, sunshine. I keep a smile on my face always, even when I'm sad or angry. It not only makes me feel better, it makes everyone around me feel good too!

"Did I learn anything on the trail? So many things: be creative with your food, drink lots of water, smile always even when your feet are killing you, stop and smell the roses, don't sweat the small stuff, be grateful for the big stuff, which is usually little anyways. Relish the moments you have simple things that most people don't appreciate every day: a soft bed, long hot showers, a real meal that someone else cooked! The company of someone you haven't seen in a long time, transport, a chair to sit on, pretty dresses, heater when it's cold out, fresh clean laundry – shall I go on?

"Getting off the trail made it difficult for me to go back into the city and be a part of so-called society again. People that haven't hiked a long trail just don't understand. I've been called lazy, a runaway from society and the real world. I look at it differently. I hiked 2,650 miles, with everything I needed on my back – that's hardly lazy. It took a lot of planning, configuring and mental drainage, not to mention the physical part of actually walking and carrying everything all that way. Sleeping in the rain and the snow, wondering if the bears and mountain lions would be attacking me for food at night, finding scorpions in my bag in the morning, dealing with sore feet and running out of important items, knowing I still had fifty miles to the next town before I could do anything about it. I have learned to appreciate every day as it comes and as it is; not too many people can accept that. I'd rather be in the mountains, with nothing but necessities, than in the city with the hustle and bustle. People too busy to stop and see what's around them, too stressed out to notice the beautiful flowers growing right in their yard or people sleeping on the sidewalk in the cold or homeless children hungry on the streets. Things I didn't see before, I see it all now, *all* of it."

It's interesting that Sugar Moma picks up on others calling

her lazy and a runaway from society and the real world. Long-distance hiking or any adventure of long duration tends to confuse people who don't take part in it or may even make them bitter. We seem to be brainwashed into thinking that there is an acceptable way of living our lives, and anyone that moves off that path or makes their own choices against the grain is not normal.

I've experienced it myself. Even though most of my family and friends now accept my wanderings and encourage them, nearly all of them struggled at first. I, too, was often labelled as lazy and accused of running away from my problems. As Sugar Moma says, the one thing you cannot accuse a thru-hiker of is being lazy. One year of planning, logistics, securing sponsorship, saying goodbye to people you love and then *walking* 2,650 miles with everything strapped to your back? Anyone who can put forward a good argument for labelling this as lazy I would love to hear from.

I suspect that underneath the accusations lie the difficulties many people have in grasping the notion of leaving their everyday lives to go and do something they really want to do. OK, so hiking isn't to everyone's taste but we all have passions, loves, fixations and pastimes that need feeding, whether it's mountaineering, fishing, yoga, cooking or riding a horse.

I fully appreciate that most of us are perfectly happy in our careers, bringing up children, paying the mortgage and not ever wanting to leave for several months, regardless of the reasons. I have no argument with this choice (in fact, I'm a little jealous) and equally I understand that some of us can't (or feel they can't) leave because of these commitments. I am not married (probably never will be), do not have kids (that I know of), don't have a mortgage and I am my own boss. These weren't conscious decisions I made so as to free me to fulfil my adventurous instincts, but they worked out perfectly for me. I can't get married because I'm terrible in a relationship, I don't like the tie of a mortgage, kids drive me nuts and I became my own boss because I hate people telling me what to do.

Elk summed his hike up from a different angle:

"Shortly after the PCT, I returned to Utah and I tried to get a job with a wilderness therapy program I had worked for previously. My old boss strung me along for a few months until I realised this wasn't going to happen.

"I had a little money left over, so I scrounged and saved while putting resumes together to try and get another job. After near on a hundred attempts, I got a job with my current employer. Now I'm OK.

"However, between the time I was unemployed and when I found a job, I had some realisations about my old job, my life and the period I took off for the trail. It sounds basic but I understood, finally, that it doesn't matter how much energy you put into something, the return you want is not guaranteed. It's important to be proactive but, even then, one needs to understand that it's how you react to certain situations that counts. This is sometimes even more important when you decide to not react at all.

"In short, I finally realised the importance of making a timely decision and not allowing my emotions to make my choices.

"Currently I'm working with the commercial fishing industry as an oceanic observer. I have short hair and I shaved my beard. In other words, I'm really lame but I'm no longer hungry. I can't begin to describe how great the trail was for me."

Elk, Sugar Moma, Flyboxer and most of the others I met on trail realise where their hearts belong: out in the wild. They will work for a while until the bugs hit them again (if, indeed, it ever leaves) and then they'll set off on another hike. At some point, probably when our knees give out, we'll call it a day and then we can all look back and be proud at what we have achieved. No sitting in that rocking chair I mentioned and regretting what we didn't do.

Like some of the others, I also began to resent my life back in town. When I made the decision to tackle the PCT, one of my goals was to be completely open to circumstance. Let me elaborate. None of us is truly free; we only ever attain steps towards freedom, some more than others. In our everyday lives it's extraordinarily difficult to live freely. We follow familiar patterns: wake up, have breakfast, go to work, get back, chill out and go to bed. Imagine being able to get out of bed, look out of the window, be met with a beautiful day and decide to discard your normal pattern and simply follow whatever course you want – just for one, short day.

Perhaps you decide to go for a stroll in the park? You see an old man sitting on a bench looking a little sad. Instead of walking by, you think about sitting next to him and trying to cheer him up, so you do. You chat for a while and leave him smiling, feeling better about the day. He has told you about a path leading off into the woods that you don't remember even being there. You take it. It leads to a stream winding through a copse bursting to life in the early spring. Flowers poke through the soil, you smell onions and then discover a huge swath of wild garlic. Picking a few leaves, you decide to cook some soup with them later. And so it carries on…

I wanted to nurture this freedom, take advantage of random events on the trail, and for the most part I did, making as few plans as possible. Even then, of course, I wasn't completely free. I was entertaining one big, overall plan after all; to walk from Mexico to Canada. But in between those two points, I tried to pander to random events. Walking the PCT I came as close as I ever will to being truly free.

I'll leave the last post-hike word to Hojo:

"I remember getting back to my folks and being kind of a zombie. I was exhausted physically, mentally, emotionally and I think I slept for a full day. It took a couple of months for me to recover physically, and when I did, the enormity of what I had just accomplished began to set in. I also remember getting up at 5.30am every morning for a few months, feeling like I had to break camp, make breakfast and put some miles in!

"When I see a map of the United States these days it makes me smile. I've always been patriotic but I think I have a bit more national pride these days. Having walked both coasts of this great nation (I did the Appalachian Trail in 1998), I know it to be an amazing place filled with incredible people and spectacular scenery.

"I remain grateful for the opportunity to pursue my dream of hiking the Pacific Crest Trail. Sharing the experience with family and friends (I hiked three days and thirty-three miles with my father near Lake Tahoe) and making new friends along the journey remains a highlight of my thru-hike. It's an incredible accomplishment, made extra special by the fact that I'm a cancer survivor.

"Since finishing the PCT, I've been fortunate enough to give a presentation on my thru-hike and led a college-level backpacking course in West Virginia.

"As I write this, I'm sitting in my ski patrol dispatch building. It's thirty-five degrees and raining outside (essentially the weather I hiked through Oregon in). I didn't particularly like it then and I don't care for it now. It remains my least favourite weather to be outside in!"

Hojo, Sugar Moma, Elk, Flyboxer and 99% of the people I met on trail will be friends for the rest of my life. Most of them live in the States, so I won't get to see them regularly, but I shared a strong connection with them. They were all there for their own different reasons, apart from walking the PCT, but I felt as close to them after just a day in their company as I am to people I have known for years. Hiking makes for the strongest bond I know.

I'm asked many times why I hike. People wait for my answer with an expectant look on their face, as if they think I have discovered the meaning of life or have reached some sort of enlightenment. Of course I haven't; if only it were that simple. However, spending so much time in the wild does change a person. It doesn't matter if the challenge is the Pacific Crest Trail, the Appalachian Trail, sailing around the world, climbing Everest or crossing the Sahara – adventuring for an extended period of time opens one's eyes. When we look back as an outsider to the lives we left, we can act as an impartial observer and see what we are doing wrong, what we can improve on and what we are doing right. Call it a reality check, if you like. Sometimes we are aware of how we can improve our lives, but when we are actually embroiled in them, changes are difficult to make. An escape to nature is a perfect time to take one step back and study the situation we have left. Invariably we return as improved individuals with passionate ideas on how to be better people.

So, I shall take you back to the beginning and the promise I made to answer, as best I can, *that* original question: why?

Be free
Eat as much as you like
Become super-fit
Meet like-minded people
Meet some idiots
Give up alcohol on trail
Make up for lack of alcohol in town
Experience pristine wilderness
Don't pay rent
Appreciate people more
Have no time for losers
Live by what you carry
Realise just how much of what you own is completely pointless
Not have to wake up to an alarm clock
Forget about TV
Leave your phone turned off for days
Sleep under the stars every night
Sleep under the sun during the day
Go and do it in reply to people saying "You can't do that!"
Take a bath in a lake
Lie under the sky at night and feel yourself fall away into infinity
Because you can
Know exactly what you want for breakfast, and how you want it, without looking at the menu
Lose weight
Gain muscle
Laugh at the confused expressions of people in town when you tell them what you're doing
Figure out what you actually want to do for work
Have the guts to go and do it
Make up stupid names for other people
Have other people make up stupid names for you
Cleanse your body by drinking loads of water
Accept and be at one with your stink
Realise how bad town people stink

Learn perseverance
Learn stubbornness
Learn how to never, ever, ever give up
Implore others to never, ever, ever give up
Actually enjoy a McDonald's
Wear one pair of underwear and socks for a week
Watch your hair do amazing and crazy things without products
Grow a beard
Be amazed at the hospitality of others
Be a shoulder to cry on
Find a shoulder to cry on
Be a shrink
Be a super-human, indestructible hiking machine
Have time to think
Cook a filling meal for £1
Be at one with and learn to respect wildlife
Scare yourself shitless by meeting a bear for the first time
Be the furthest you've ever been from anyone else
Make genuine friends for life
Become mildly famous
Gain respect
Sleep outside more times in a year than you slept indoors
Become hypnotised by camp fires
Breathe clean air
Experience being speechless at a view
Sit in a public place having not washed for nine days and snigger to yourself at other people's reactions
Get asked to leave public places
Enjoy bananas
Appreciate stuff you haven't seen for ages
Don't look at your inbox for a week
Try and catch up with your inbox after a week
Get to wear tights and be accepted
Get to wear a kilt and be accepted
Get to wear tights and a kilt at the same time
Shop for a lot of gear and for once be confident that it will all get used
Get sponsored with free gear
Become a porridge expert

Avoid relationship commitments for six months
Meet the person of your dreams
Pinpoint who always has chocolate and quickly make friends with them
Discover wild food
Repair anything with nothing
Realise what it's like to be homeless
Understand why our fixation with money is the root of all evil
Be at one with yourself
Don't work for six months
Actually have the time to read your camera manual
Sing at the top of your voice
Read a book a week
Run away from your problems
Discover the pleasures of dark chocolate-covered almonds
Learn to accept ramen noodles
Escape from ramen noodles
Do gear comparisons
Have a genuine excuse to make a video of yourself
Accept being cold
Accept being wet
Accept being too hot
Moan at how cold, wet or hot you are
Sleep outside at well below freezing
Drink two litres of water in one go and still be thirsty
Escape from the media
Believe in conspiracy theories
Make up your own and scare people
Accept anything offered to you
Give freely
Hug people and mean it
Be hugged and know they mean it
Invent disgusting new recipes based on the food you carry
Have others confirm it
Feel alive in a forest with the wind around you
Realise the outdoors is where you are supposed to be
Nurture a deep loathing for batteries
Miss your favourite beer, discover new ones and get a new favourite

The Last Englishman

Learn how to push just that little but further
Play frisbee at 12,000 feet with drops all around you
Instigate longest frisbee flight ever recorded from same place
Make your dreams come true
Have others appreciate and accept you for who you are
No reason at all except you wanted to
Be as free as you will ever hope to be
And, finally, be at one with yourself

Any questions?

Acknowledgements

Writing a book and attempting a thru-hike are similar in many ways. They are both long journeys involving some heartache, lots of persistence and patience. Both require little steps to reach a far-distant goal, covering a little ground each day until eventually the finish is in sight. However, a writer has many allies fighting with him to make that journey a little smoother and it's a pleasure to be able to give them credit here.

Apart from acknowledging individuals who helped me with the actual writing, I also need to express gratitude to those who put up with my unsociable lifestyle but are proud, I hope, of what I have become. Thanks therefore to:

Mum and Dad, for their continued support and understanding of my raging wanderlust since I first realised it was too strong to resist (not that I ever wanted to). Ideally, from their point of view, I'd be married with two kids and a solid job but I think they've accepted that this is what I'm happy doing.

My sister Tracey and nephews Thomas and Liam, whom I don't get to see often enough.

For work on the book:

My editors Ingrid and Adam Cranfield, who again have taken a raw rock and honed it into a far more polished stone. I will remember where the apostrophes go in the next book, I promise.

I enlisted the voluntary help of a few proofreaders who deserve recognition: Katie Bryant, Big Foot, Tradja, Chris Partridge, Mumfa, Obs the Blobs, Sugar Moma and Amy Lou.

Spencer Vignes, Rosie Fuller of Adventure Travel magazine, Ingrid Cranfield, Chris Townsend, Jennifer Pharr Davis, Andrew Skurka and Kimberlie Dame for supplying endorsements.

Those who helped out with the words of wisdom at the beginning of each chapter – Charlie 'Hojo' Mead, Michael

Thomas 'Lion King' Daniel, Mahmood 'Cedar Elk' Mokhayesh, Patti 'Sugar Moma' Kulesz, Shane 'Jester' O'Donnell, John 'Tradja' Drollette, David 'Walker Texas Ranger' Allen, Jennifer Pharr Davies, Patrick 'Wideangle' Pöndl, Ned Tibbits, Jake Nead, Nick 'The Brit' De Bairacli Levy, Monty 'Warner Springs Monty' Tam, and Dave 'Upchuck' Ferber.

Jennifer Pharr Davies and Andrew Skurka for permission to use their quotes.

Rockets for the photo on the front cover and all his photographic work on the website.

Faye Fillingham for help with the front cover design.

For all the people who made the hike possible and enjoyable:

All the trail angels en route who took time out to help the thru-hikers and smooth their passage.

Alex Johnson for at least trying to get me a discounted flight.

Uncle Tony, Aunty Jillian, Rudy, Hayley and all my relatives over in the US for feeding me, giving me somewhere to stay, running me on errands and generally acting as a first-class HQ.

The countless drivers who picked up a dirty, smelly hiker and went out of their way to take me to a shower.

My hike may not have even happened had it not been for the generosity of my sponsors, who ask nothing except for a little recognition and advertising space:

Shane Ohly at Inov-8, Niels Overgaard Blok at Backpackinglight.dk, Richard Codgbrook at Smartwool, Francesca Sanchez at Olympus, Aimee Gasparre at Nalgene, Rand Lindsley at Trail Designs, Jake Bennett at Numa Sport Optics, Road Java at Stickpic, Erik Asorson at Blackwoods Press for the *Pacific Crest Trail Atlas* and Seamus at Sportkilt.

Not least, my heartfelt thanks go to all the thru-hikers I met. You are very much a part of my Pacific Crest Trail memories, as well as honorary members of Hiker Trash! I feel privileged both to have met you and to continue to know you:

Dicentra, Space Blanket, Kara, Gabe, Mojave, Cheeks, Ben, Mad Hatter, Upchuck, Wyoming, Bob, Logic, Stumbling Norwegian, Sugar Moma, Dinosaur, Swayze, Hojo, Jess, Tradja, Burnie, Alex, Elk, Charmin, Grey Fox, Spiller, Flashlight, Vadar, Pyjamas, Pigpen, Pony, Your Mom, Yvo, Lo, Bones, Borders, Professor, Vicki, Dennis, Jake, Scorpion, Trooper,

Steve Climber, Turbo, Stanimal, Big Foot, Wideangle, Tomer, Littlebit, Walker Texas Ranger, Flannel, Chad, Justin, Flyboxer, Indie, Answerman, Humming Bird, Flashback, Grinder, Uncle Gary, Stax, Black Gum, Ursa Major, Pockets (aka Rockets), Brains, Jolly Green Giant, Dan, Splizzard, Chrissie, Dodge, Mr Green, Dozer, Jack Straw, The Pro from Dover, Spartan, Wreckless, Crow, Dundee, Karma, Detective Bubbles, No Pain, Chris and Nick.

And, lastly, an apology if I have missed anyone out. If that's you, please let me know, but in the meantime consider yourself thanked.

CANADA
FINISH - Manning Park (2664)
Stehekin (2575)
Stevens Pass (2472)
Seattle
Snoqualmie Pass (2403)
WASHINGTON
Portland
Cascade Locks (2155)
OREGON
Sisters (1993)
Crater Lake NP
Ashland (1731)
Etna (1611)
THE PACIFIC CREST TRAIL
Old Station (1382)
Belden (1294)
Sierra City (1201)
2656 Miles from Mexico to Canada
CALIFORNIA
Tuolumne Meadows (945)
NORTH
Mt. Whitney
Kennedy Meadows (704)
Mojave (560)
Agua Dulce (455)
Wrightwood (370)
Big Bear (265)
PACIFIC OCEAN
Warner Springs (109)
START - Campo (0)
MEXICO

Keith Foskett

Balancing on Blue

A Dromomaniac Hiking

This book is dedicated to the Appalachian Trail Class of 2012.

And – to those who didn't come home:

Dwight Cope, Dagan Cope, Thomas Andersen,
Carmen Kotula and Paul Bernhardt.

Thru-Hiker
Someone who hikes a long-distance trail end to end, usually in one, continuous attempt.

The Appalachian Trail
The Appalachian National Scenic Trail, known simply as the AT, is a 2,180 mile hiking route in the eastern United States. Starting at Springer Mountain in Georgia and passing through fourteen states to finish on Mount Katahdin in Maine.

Dromomania
From the Latin dromas (runner) and mania (excessive or unreasonable desire, even insanity) is an uncontrollable impulse to wander.

Chapter 1

The Converging

Peter 'PJ' Semo

I had to tell her, but every time my mouth opened in anticipation, I fell silent. The plan of confronting her when she returned from work had been delayed. At each attempt to break the news that I was leaving in the morning, I clammed up and put it off for another ten minutes, which in turn never arrived.

Just tell her PJ, get it out of the way.

I can't.

You have to tell her, there's not much time.

I know.

Just do it!

Enough! I'm going to tell her when we go to bed!

I looked over at my wife, who was just falling asleep. I had only minutes left, but still I kept delaying the inevitable.

You have to tell her now.

I know.

This is your last chance; you won't get another one. You have to leave soon.

I know!

Turning my head towards her and fighting back some tears, I finally broke the silence.

"I didn't tell you, but I have to catch a train. I'm leaving to hike the Appalachian Trail in the morning."

Jess shot up in bed.

"What?"

I explained as calmly as possible, foolishly thinking that this would make the situation acceptable.

"And you were going to just, to just, leave me?"

"Yes."

"And not say anything? When were you going to tell me?"

I looked sheepishly into her eyes, felt her anger and sensed her sadness. Feeling a slight pang of guilt, I quickly realized it was hollow.

"I'm telling you now."

With that, I went to the closet where my backpack was stored. Most of the packing had been done in preparation for a quick departure.

"So you have a new backpack too?"

"Yeah."

She hovered; I felt her staring and it made me nervous.

If you turn back now, if you wait, you won't do it.

It took just ten minutes to finish getting my stuff together, which was ten minutes too long. I told her I loved her but that this was goodbye. Was it possible to love someone and leave them for good?

"When will you be back?"

Why was she asking me this when I thought she had realized it was permanent? I paused to think of an answer. Not wanting to remind her in case she had misunderstood, I replied simply.

"I don't know. The trail should take six months tops."

Avoiding any further eye contact, I grabbed my trekking poles, opened the door and started to walk to the Amtrak station.

***

I was born Peter John Semo, but my neighbour, Tom, nicknamed me 'PJ' when I was a baby. As my father was also called Peter, the nickname helped avoid confusion. I suppose I'm grateful for it; it has always felt more fitting for me.

I had decided to hike the Appalachian Trail, or the AT for short, when I was sixteen. I had just returned from a camping trip with my family and was experiencing my first real taste of life dissatisfaction. On one side was Jess, my girlfriend back then, trying to persuade me to move to South Dakota once I had finished high school, and she often made phone calls to my family's house to try and persuade them to let me go. My family, in particular my father, were pulling me in the opposite direction and urging me to move to Pennsylvania to attend college, as my sister and brother had done before me. Neither side was shy about expressing their opinions. My father would take the opportunity to lecture me during long drives to go fishing. Being trapped in the car, I had no choice but to listen. It infuriated me.

Jess and my family loved me dearly, which was comforting but also the problem. I had been presented with plan A and plan B but sorely needed a plan of my own, a different plan, a plan that I wanted, not one that everyone else had in mind for me. This was plan C.

I knew what plan C entailed: I just didn't know where it would be. Plan C was to hike, to hike for miles, to hike for such a distance that people would deem it impossible to go that far. For whatever reason, I didn't make the choice then, but instead chose to go and live with Jess in South Dakota.

My family treated my decision with disdain and, on the day before my departure, some hostility. I ended up in a fight with my brother, and my father cried for one of the first times in his life.

"I just don't want you to go," he sobbed.

They drove me to the airport. We were all in tears as I got my luggage from the car. I can't remember my last words to my father, but I do remember him holding me, feeling his bristly chin, his strong, wide chest and the way he patted my back in a silly rhythm. That was the last time I ever saw him.

I was still clueless, not knowing whether to stay with Jess on arrival, go back to Pennsylvania after a couple of weeks or do some more work on plan C. Landing at Detroit to change planes, I pondered fleeing, going somewhere, anywhere.

It's Detroit, for God's sake, you'll get killed.

The closer my plane got to Jess, the more urgent plan C became. Her parents picked me up at the airport, leaving no time for another getaway or a last-ditch attempt at fleeing by going to Wal-Mart, kitting myself out with hiking gear and escaping to the American Discovery Trail.

We got married on July 9th, 2010. My family wasn't invited, as we had stopped speaking by that point, still down to the aftermath of my decision to move. It was so bad that the last words I had said to my father over the phone were "Fuck you." Those proved to be the last words we ever shared.

I started working in retail, which became bearable, my good-spirited co-workers making up for any career disappointments. Having received news that my father was suffering from pancreatic cancer, which could be terminal, I applied for a leave of absence to see him. Owing to misunderstandings between my employer and my father's doctor, I never received the paperwork in time. It arrived on September 2nd, 2011, the day after my father passed away.

***

The train lurched, brakes squealing as I awoke from another sleep. Harpers Ferry in West Virginia is considered the halfway mark of the AT. Nestled at the confluence of the Potomac and Shenandoah Rivers, it is a hugely important target for thru-hikers. I had dozed off several times on the train but smiled as I saw the Harpers Ferry sign. I knew its significance and thought it was a good omen that I had woken there.

Making a final change in Gainsville, I knew I had eventually arrived in the state of Georgia and disembarked. It was late, dark, I was tired and confused as to my next step. Looking around for inspiration, I spotted another guy with a large backpack and we got to talking. His name was Adam. I put my faith in him and we decided to share a taxi to Amicalola Falls State Park, where an approach trail leads nine miles to Springer Mountain and the true start of the AT.

I spent my first night in a hostel and in the morning I trod carefully. I had researched a method of running and walking called POSE, which reduces injuries. I guess I was taking it easy in order to find my feet and break my body in for the mammoth task I was asking of it. People passed me but I didn't care, it wasn't a race. Some guy with a silver umbrella came by me and nodded a greeting, smiling.

"You walk carefully. It's interesting to watch! What's your

name?" His accent sounded British.

"PJ," I replied. "And yours?"

"Fozzie, nice to meet you."

"Are you British?"

His stride slowed as though he was going to stop but he didn't.

"Yes, English to be exact. See you up the trail I expect?"

"For sure, it's all good."

I rested a while, drank some water, took stock of the events of the past few days and looked skyward, silently saying, "I don't ask for much from the universe but I'm grateful to be here. Please accept me for my faults and mistakes and let me make something right. Let me do something that makes my father proud of me, wherever he is now. Let me finish this trip, every step. Please, world, just give me a shot and lead my footsteps in the right direction."

Phillip 'Lazagne' Colelli

I was well qualified in fort and dam construction. It was hard work digging with shovels, chopping with hatchets, moving fallen trees and amassing a pile of sticks into a fortress, but I enjoyed it. From my present standpoint, my early career as an engineer obviously didn't amount to much. But when you're a kid, surveying the small reservoir, flanked by your impregnable garrison, your achievement seems huge and life feels rich and rewarding.

My father had also taken me camping during those times. Not exactly in the remote wilderness, but to me, a flat area of gravel next to the parked car with a fire ring was just as exciting. We'd unpack a huge tent, coolers packed with ice and drinks, hot dogs, hamburgers, condiments, eggs, bacon and oatmeal. I had the time of my life, all the comforts and luxuries a boy needs, right on his own private camping spot.

I was too young then to know what the AT was, but my father and uncle occasionally used to spend a few days there. It was years before curiosity got the better of me. Dad had guidebooks for the North Carolina and Pennsylvania sections of the trail and I would pull them out and study them. I was especially intrigued by the maps: the trail was a series of red dashes playing with black contour lines, passing by the blue outlines of rivers, lakes and occasionally meeting a road.

I was still a kid when Dad agreed to a short hike on the trail and we parked at Trent's Grocery near where the trail crossed the road, a few miles from Bland, Virginia. The instant we left the road, the beauty of the woods enveloped me, and I felt I was in another world that was peaceful, quiet and leisurely. We just slowed down and walked.

Passing the Kimberling Creek Suspension Bridge and Dismal Falls, we continued up steep hills until we were too tired to carry on. We hastily pitched our tent as a storm threatened, then cooked a simple dinner on the camp stove and read the books we had each brought. I fell asleep quickly, tired from the hiking.

Wonderful though that trip was, it was years before I set foot back on the AT. It was as if I'd read one chapter from a great book and then put it aside. I was working a miserable job at a burger bar and became good friends with a guy called Sam Ridge, who spoke of his plans to thru-hike the entire trail the following year. Before long, Sam and I were planning a trial trip to see if our hopes had any chance of being realised.

We planned on hiking into the Great Smoky Mountains National Park and trying out a forty mile section of the AT from Newfound Gap to Davenport Gap. Again I became immersed in the woods: spotting all the different types of wildlife was mesmerising, even smelling that mountain air validated my being there and reawakened lost memories.

We reached Ice Water Spring shelter and set up our sleeping mats and bags inside. Again, after eating and chatting to some of the other hikers, I fell asleep quickly, but I remember waking in the early hours, astonished at the clarity and brightness of the night sky away from the lights of town. The stars were simply incredible. Reinvigorated in both body and mind, we hit the ridge of the Smoky Mountains the next day, with Tennessee on our left, North Carolina to the right and with epic views in all directions. That book from long ago had been opened again and I loved what I was reading.

It didn't take long for me to decide that I wanted to thru-hike the AT and Sam encouraged me. Soon, all I could focus on was the trip. Work became even more mundane and I ended up quitting a full month before we planned to start because I couldn't deal with it any longer. I stayed in touch with Sam; we had decided to start together but agreed we were each free to make our own plans on the trail. We spoke daily on the phone, making arrangements, discussing gear and took various day hikes around the area. I repeated a five-mile loop on a local trail three times a day to gain some fitness. It was repetitive and tiresome sometimes, especially in the rain, but I persevered to get in shape and also to test my mind and resolve further. I wanted to know that I could push on when the going got tough.

The final week dragged and I feared I would go nuts just waiting. I don't like wishing my life away but I wanted that week gone. I longed for that feeling of being cradled in the woods once more.

We arrived at Amicalola Falls and hiked a few miles before camping, completing the short distance to Springer Mountain the following day.

At last, I was back in the woods.

Sam 'Daffy' Ridge

Many people hike the Appalachian Trail to see some of the world. I wanted to hike to get away from it.

Needing to be different and break out of a conventional life, I wanted to experience and appreciate an adventure that I could call my own. I had just been arrested and kicked out of school for selling weed in my dorm room. Having blacked out, which is how I got caught, I only remembered tiny parts, like being cuffed and led away. I don't remember them taking my mug shot but when I saw it, my face was streaked from crying. I'd been selling weed and getting into trouble, or dodging trouble, since I was fifteen. I'm not proud of it, that's just how things turned out. Every time I got into hot water, I chastised myself and told myself to stop dealing but I never did.

I came to in a prison cell with a bunch of smelly drunks. Everyone looked terrible, which is exactly how I felt. It was 5 a.m; I called my Dad. Naturally I didn't want him to know, but he was probably the only one who could bail me out. I must have called him thirty times before he eventually picked up. Twelve hours later I was out, on a crash course to reconstruct the pieces of my life laying on the ground. I was in debt from the bail and my grandmother had lent me $3,000 to pay for school, which I had spent on weed. I was ashamed I had let her down and lost my father's trust in one stupid moment of madness, or at least one stupid moment of madness where I'd been caught.

I began to question my motive for selling, namely money. Why the hell did I need it? To buy stuff because I thought it made me look cool which in turn, I thought, would make others think I was a better person? I thought that money and status should be my highest priorities; that's what we are led to believe anyway. The only redeeming factor was that I had no clue as to what I would have spent it on, let alone what I actually needed.

I began working in a burger bar, but apart from earning money, I questioned why I was working at all. As no good reason was forthcoming I became disillusioned and decided to escape from the frustration and the discontentment. I figured I wouldn't be angry about how much money I didn't have when I died, but I would care if I wasted my life making it my number one priority.

I began to approach life from the opposite angle: simplifying and abandoning all ambition to gain financial status. In retrospect, this was the period in which I acquired the knowledge that set me up for life on the trail. I read *Walden* by H. D. Thoreau and *Dead Poets Society* by N. H. Kleinbaum, to name but two. I found a one-room place with a shared bathroom. I made do with one fork, one spoon and one plate. Far from striving to have as much as possible, I sought to get rid of what I didn't need. It was fun, enlightening and even now, after the AT, I still try to live this way. It gives me a pleasant feeling as though I'm still on the trail.

I love the outdoors, so it seemed the best environment for doing something different. While I was planning the hike, I had the idea that I needed to escape from people. I soon learnt it was actually the people who made the trail in the end. Without everyone else, I couldn't have hiked the AT, nor would I have had such an extraordinary experience on it.

Balancing on Blue

With all that time out, all that space to think, I believed that I would figure my life out — in fact, figure life itself out. However, does anyone really achieve this? Things ebb and flow but it's rare that we come up with any answers. All I wanted to do, at its most basic level, was to have fun. I knew that for the most part it would be great, but hard in places. I knew there would be tough moments, rough days. I knew it would be versatile and dynamic; at times it was to prove even hallucinogenic.

It was giddy groundlessness that kept me so alive. I knew that at any time I could meet anyone, from anywhere, and do anything. Everyone wants to get to the same final mountain on the same trail but everyone has different reasons for doing it.

I had figured out that conformity was dangerous and that the police, school and authorities had done me much more harm than I had ever done to anyone else. I did need to get away from urban areas so I could be myself and not be crucified for it. Call it hiding, if you will.

The only real dread I felt while I was out there was meeting someone else who was there for the same reasons as I.

John 'Thirsty' Beshara

A Bachelor of Arts, as far as I could tell, was a fancy piece of paper telling me nothing more than I had just spent seven years of my life and an obscene amount of money 'earning' it. Of course, there were great experiences and personal development along the way, but it wasn't nearly as satisfying as I had hoped. All that effort and I had no career prospects, which actually suited me, because the last thing I wanted was a career.

The only awakening that recognition impressed on me was that I desperately needed to do something different, maybe outrageous, and possibly even stupid. I considered several options: walk out of my front door with nothing but a little money and see where the wind blew me, devise some master plan to organise a criminal conspiracy, continue working my comfortable but insanely boring job, or go hike the AT. Option one lacked structure: there was a good chance I wouldn't even make it out of the city and the entire romanticised adventure would fail before it ever started. Option two was attractive but I had no real plan or experience in such matters. Work was definitely out of the question, as it didn't even come within the outrageous, different or stupid bracket. That left the AT.

I couldn't say for sure when the seed was planted. A guy at work had hiked for a couple of months on the AT. We talked about it occasionally and I kept toying with the prospect. Starting to do some research, I found that the more I discovered, the more the idea appealed.

Before I knew it, I had booked a flight to Atlanta and was working sixty-hour weeks to get the money together. I stayed up all night sometimes to fiddle with alcohol stoves and other homemade gear projects. I read everything I could find about long-distance hiking and began walking to work with a sixty-pound cinder block in my pack. In short, I was obsessed.

This carried on for six months. My buddy and I made weekend trips to every state park we could get to in a few hours. It was great luck that we got to experience just about every kind of weather on those weekend trips: the pouring rain at Lake Mariah, freight train winds coming off Lake Superior and a raging blizzard in Duluth to ring in the New Year.

The idea of hiking the AT appealed to me because it seemed so random, even pointless. I had spent the first twenty five years of my life doing more or less what my parents expected of me, because they had an eye on my future. In my estimation, thru-hiking was the direct opposite of that. It certainly wasn't, by any stretch of the imagination, required, and there was ostensibly little benefit to be gained from it that could have any bearing on my future plans. It was socially and professionally frowned upon by most people. I wanted to hike the AT for the sole purpose of doing it.

I flew into Atlanta with nothing, not even a small bag. I had sent all of my gear to the hostel I was staying at and didn't want to be burdened with shipping anything back. There were six other hikers in the hostel shuttle and a further sixteen at the hostel when I got there. The excitement and anticipation was huge, a culmination of all the training, the research and hard work was about to come to fruition. Sleep didn't come easily.

Balancing on Blue

I elected to start my hike at Amicalola Falls, where many begin, as it is the official thru-hiker register point. On my way across the parking lot, someone caught my eye. A wide-eyed, cheerful-looking guy who was wearing a Packers hat and a University of Minnesota athletic shirt. I smiled, as I had just come from Minneapolis. Small world.

I didn't see that kid again until Fontana Dam, some 182 miles in. His trail name was Bush Goggles and we ended up becoming great friends, hiking a lot of the trail together. Holed up in the Fontana shelter with a couple of others, we enjoyed some beer and spoke animatedly about heading into the Smoky Mountains. We all partied that night and had a raging fire next to the reservoir. Bush Goggles left the next morning with a couple of other guys. I had some chores to do in town and didn't get going until the afternoon.

It rained solidly the next day so in order to get dry, a few of us decided to take an offer that the local church had posted on a tree for lodging. We stood around waiting by the road for a ride, wet and miserable, repeatedly failing to roll a cigarette in the damp conditions. Some British guy whom I had also met at Fontana called Fozzie came strolling by under his umbrella — casually smoking a cigarette, as if he was walking the dog on a Sunday morning — and headed off into the woods.

"Fozzie!" I cried after him.

"Yeah?"

"A guy called Bush Goggles is down the trail. We're staying at the church place. Tell him we ain't gonna make camp tonight!"

There was a momentary pause as if he was digesting my statement.

"Who?" came a muffled reply from the trees.

I shouted once more.

"Bush Goggles!"

"OK, I'll tell him!"

Dallas 'Bush Goggles' Nustvold

My Grandpa spent his retirement scrapping and junking, which meant he would get old lawnmowers, refrigerators, bikes and the like and salvage the valuable metals. Spending lots of time helping him as a young boy, I thought it was so cool, like finding old treasure in trash. Occasionally he would take me to one of his friends' houses, where we would go through their junk and sometimes find valuable antiques. It was this initial grounding that gave me an eye to spot 'treasure'. I used to watch shows like Time Team and nurtured the ambition to become Indiana Jones when I grew up.

I was also very adventurous and loved exploring the woods. Spotting animals such as a deer, watching an eagle soar or even just playing with plants were my other treasures. I was, and still am, awed by nature. When I was too young to get involved in any major adventure, I lived vicariously through some of the classics like *Robinson Crusoe* and *The Count of Monte Cristo* to feed my passion.

In high school my life changed somewhat after my Mum became sick. The doctors had no clue of a diagnosis for a long time but eventually they discovered she had lupus. It made me think about my life plans: did I just want to work until I became ill or died, or should I defy conformity and have some fun?

I read Bill Bryson's *A Walk in the Woods* , which introduced me to the AT. The seed was planted but not watered, as I spent most of my time in college with my friends experimenting with drink, dabbling a little in drugs but mostly chasing women. I was lucky to be one of those annoying students who could skip class, barely do any reading and still get an A.

Between semesters, I worked for my uncle's environmental contracting company as a general labourer, busting down walls with a sledgehammer, removing hazardous waste and making some money. As I had no idea what to do after graduating, when he offered me a supervisory role running jobs and managing workers for a better salary, I jumped at the chance.

It was like being a kid again sometimes. Often I was the first into old buildings that had lain dormant for years, like dusty time capsules. As the guys worked, I went off exploring and found old beer bottles, newspapers, pictures and great items like electric fans from the 1920s. I'd take out the scrap copper and

Balancing on Blue

aluminium to make some extra cash. After nine months, I'd had enough and the desire to sprinkle a little water on that AT seed crept back into my imagination.

I really had no idea what I was getting into. I was familiar with the woods, having camped on short trips occasionally but never for more than a week. As at college, I did little research; in fact, my only preparation was to buy the gear I thought would do the trick and then ask my Mum if she could drive me the eighteen-hour trip to Georgia.

Her lupus was under control but she still fought daily battles against it. She was a huge inspiration in my life, and I had always appreciated what she had done, especially the encouragement she offered me to walk the AT.

It was to be the start of the most extraordinary journey of my life.

Chris 'Juggles' Chiappini

It was August 3rd, 2000, and two minutes before I was due on stage at the World Juggling Championships in Montreal, Canada. My Dad was with me and I was nervous — of course I was nervous. I had competed the previous year at the same competition, hosted nearby at Niagara Falls, and earned bronze.

Part of my act was to close my hand around a juggling ball and wave a hand fan underneath, thereby releasing thousands of pieces of confetti. This entailed taping an extremely delicate cellophane ball filled with the confetti to the fan. It was ludicrously fragile; I felt that I needed only look in its vague direction and the cellophane would split, spilling the contents. I was sweating, shaking and aware that I shouldn't grip the ball too tightly, and yet I needed to or it wouldn't stick.

"Chris, do you need some help?"

"No, Dad. I got it!"

Eventually, with seconds to spare, I was ready.

I was ten years old when I first started juggling. I have no comprehension of what life can be like without this passion, it's so ingrained in me. As a boy, I soon glimpsed where it could take me and it became my identity. It's exceptionally difficult to learn but I picked it up quickly and realised that others enjoyed watching me. The praise I received made me feel great. Hearing applause as a kid feels marvellous, and the pleasure doesn't diminish as an adult.

My dad always encouraged me, I think because he is an artist also (a musician). He is aware how tough carving a career in the arts can be, especially doing something as out of the ordinary as juggling, but at the same time it's also hugely rewarding. Although he always inspired me, he never forced me to do anything, leaving me free to make my own choices.

Juggling is a solitary pastime. To achieve anything in the field requires thousands upon thousands of hours on your own, in a high-ceilinged room, constantly repeating the same trick until it becomes second nature. You have to push yourself mentally and physically to learn a new skill, or hold a trick for a long period of time. I never had a coach; I simply adhered to common practice principles and listened to those who were better than I was.

Josiah Jones finished his act and walked off stage towards me. He looked unhappy and rightly so, as his act had gone badly. In fact, it would have been better described as a train wreck: he dropped a lot of props. My name was announced and I looked at Dad, who just gave this smile that suggested he knew something that I didn't. My heart was pounding so hard, and my breathing quickened as I wiped away more sweat. The audience applauded and time seemed to slow down as I walked, confidently, on to the stage.

Dad and I had taken advantage of every trick we could to gain a head start, even down to my costume of polished black shoes, smart pants and a red sequined shirt. I looked like a young version of Elton John. He had hired a local dance teacher to choreograph my movements through the eight-minute routine to three different songs. She also taught me little tricks that could make all the difference, like taking a comb from my pocket and running it through my hair while winking at the audience. I worked with balls, rings and clubs and varied the quantity of each.

It went well, the audience responded and my Dad smiled as I walked off behind the curtain. I was confident but not blasé, feeling I had given a better display than all the other acts. I had the least number of drops (two) and the highest skill technique. It had to be gold.

It may seem like a strange comparison, but juggling has much in common with thru-hiking: it demands physical and psychological strength and dedication, hours of repetitive action to arrive at a distant goal and toleration of a solitary existence. I have always loved the outdoors but, to be honest, it was the chance to be alone that appealed. Dedication and repetition I had already mastered.

I lived thirty minutes away from where the AT wanders through Harriman State Park in New York State. I had walked some sections many times, as well as making a failed attempt on the Long Trail in Vermont, which is 272 miles long. The AT was familiar, close to home and on the East Coast. I just felt as though I would be safe there.

Several times in my life elders have said to me, 'Do what you want before you get married and have kids.' We're brought up to think that you can go on an adventure if you're still alive when the kids have grown up. I wasn't buying any of it.

I did win gold at the World Juggling Championships that year, and now I'm 28, juggling for a living. As much as I love what I do, I had never known anything else, never taken up any other passion and milked it for all that it was worth.

So in the summer of 2011, needing a break from throwing balls in the air, I made the decision to thru-hike the AT, and in the spring of 2012 I found myself looking at a bronze plaque embedded in a rock on top of Springer Mountain, the start of the trail.

I knew there were no medals for coming first. The only gold you achieve on the AT is for finishing.

Keith 'Fozzie' Foskett

The 1970s was a fantastic decade for interior design. Legendary wallpaper, majestic flooring and any item of furniture you longed for could be procured in bright orange. I was just a kid at the time but later in life, around 2008, I dove headlong into a

1970s revival for my lounge. The centrepiece was an old British Telecom phone complete with rotary dial, and even the small piece of card displaying the phone number and 'Dial 999 Fire Police Ambulance' was still intact. Pop a finger in the right hole for each number and push it round to an unassuming chrome lip, where it wound back to position with a hissing sound I remembered from my childhood. The two-tone chocolate-coloured body and receiver were immaculate. The phone lived on a white plastic table with an orange lamp, which completed my retro look.

The only drawback was that the ringing was incredibly loud; it used to startle the hell out of me and my cat absolutely detested it. Invariably he was asleep on my lap if someone called and in a nanosecond he would flip over, look at me with insane, crazed eyes, then glare at the phone and arch his back ready to pounce upon and subsequently kill it.

One afternoon I arrived home, walked into the lounge, and found him fast asleep. This was not unusual, as you can imagine for a cat, but his location was. To my surprise, he had snuggled up on my white table, lovingly spooning the telephone. Now, I'm an animal lover, make no mistake, but it was just too good a chance to miss. I quietly reached into my pocket, pulled out my mobile phone and dialled the house number ...

I'm telling you this to try and paint a picture, which in turn, I hope, will make a point. Great opportunities come along rarely. We don't necessarily have to grab them when they do; indeed, it may not be the right time and they may present themselves again later. More often than not, we don't take them because we are scared of what will happen if that path does not work out, despite somehow knowing that it will. Many of us go about our daily lives with no quibbles: we have accepted our lot, are happy with what we have and, fair enough, have no desire to change anything. On the flip side, many of us do feel stuck and lack the courage to change how we live. Paying a mortgage, feeding the kids and holding down a job are big enough challenges in themselves without taking the risk of attempting something that may not work.

Travelling, adventuring, undertaking an expedition, finding yourself, escaping, call it what you will, the number of people who are fleeing from the system has rocketed in recent years. The last generation's acceptance of how we live is now being questioned and many don't want any part of it. Thus, getting away from it, often into the wilderness, provides a chance for us to breathe, re-evaluate and make changes in our life.

Allow me to explain further. Let's assume that, when you pop out into this world, aged just a few minutes, you are able to read and possess the intelligence of an average adult. The swing doors of the delivery room squeak open and someone enters, dressed immaculately in a subtly-striped grey suit. I always imagine this individual as a woman. Her shirt is as smooth and white as copier paper, ironed to a crisp finish, with edges so precise you could cut a finger on them. Her hair is greased and visible comb lines appear like a furrowed field, which reflect the lights on the ceiling, before being pulled back hard into a tight ponytail, making her eyebrows lift somewhat. She wears little makeup save a weak, gothic white foundation and lurid red lipstick. Everything about this person screams perfection. Intimidated, you sense a feeling of authority that is about to impose restrictions on your life forever.

Instinctively, you accept the several sheets of paper she hands over and you notice the main header: Life Contract.

She places a clenched hand over her mouth and clears her throat delicately, a little apologetically.

"I'm from Life Planning. This is all pretty standard stuff. I just need you to read through it quickly and sign at the bottom."

She sits by your bed, a little too close for comfort, and shifts her stern gaze between you and the contract. You start to read, or rather to scan to get the gist of the content. You begin to feel uncomfortable and yet you start to presume it's all acceptable, like the terms of motor insurance. You summarise the content:

At five years of age you will start school, where you will stay until age 16. You may wish to choose further education, which we encourage. You will strive to achieve the best grades possible.

You will obey your teachers, peers and elders at all times.

Education complete, you will begin employment. This will last around forty-five years; however, there are concessions such as four weeks' holiday a year, a company pension and possibly other incentives such as a subsidised cafeteria. You are expected to work hard for your employer, be punctual, work late at your own cost and get along with your colleagues. Moving jobs is frowned upon.

The country where you live is under control of a government, which passes laws you are expected to abide by, regardless of whether you or anyone else think them fair or not. You live in a democratic society but will have little input into how it is run. Every four years, you may vote for the incumbent party or other options that will be presented to you.

The government will deduct something called tax from your earnings. Depending on your salary, this could be as much as 45%. Goods and some services are also taxed. You have no real say in how these taxes are calculated, invested or spent.

In your early to mid-sixties, assuming you have accrued enough pension funds, you may retire. It may well be possible that any annuity offered to you will not be sufficient to live on, in which case you will have to make your own arrangements to deal with the shortfall or possibly continue to work.

You are encouraged to get married and start a family. This will occupy a large proportion of your life, around twenty to thirty years as you bring up your children.

And so it goes on, and on, and on.

I ignore her eyes drilling into my side and her hovering hand offering a pen. I return her gaze, smile and hand the papers back.

"Nah, it's OK, thanks. I'll do my own thing."

And 'do my own thing' is pretty much what I have done. Of course I did my time at school and I have a day job when I'm not hiking. A lot of aspects associated with a conventional life I don't care for and have little choice in, but I make changes constantly. I do what I have to. Work, for example, is solely a means to earn enough money to go and get lost in the great outdoors.

Some years ago I discovered thru-hiking and a monumental void in my life suddenly filled. Almost instantly, I found a freedom that had been missing. I could travel to a part of the world that appealed and disappear into the wilds for a few months, with everything I needed strapped to my back. My concerns in life during those months faded to nothing; the rules and regulations that I had constantly endured and battled with vanished.

Away from civilisation, I discovered a new pathway. Far from being oppressive, my surroundings were invigorating. I felt no restrictions but revelled in immunity. I felt energised, my thoughts became clear and precise, my direction in life clarified and my goals focused.

I felt liberated.

Chapter 2

The Steaks are High

"Sir, would you like anything for lunch? Can I offer you a menu?"

"You actually have menus?" I replied, scratching my head, perplexed.

She giggled sheepishly.

"Yes sir, we have menus."

With that she handed me a leather-bound example and also a wine list. I couldn't believe it, a wine list as well.

"An aperitif, perhaps?"

That was far too much and I started laughing nervously. I turned away, momentarily embarrassed and looked out the window at the Atlantic some 35,000 feet below.

"A gin and tonic would be smashing," I said, smiling to dissipate any offence I might have caused.

I perused the options. Tender Fillet of Beef Steak, Dover Sole, Roast Chicken Breast and numerous other dishes were neatly presented, spaced evenly, with succinct descriptions on slightly marbled paper. I paused briefly as she returned with stainless steel cutlery cushioned in a navy blue napkin with 'Delta Airways' embroidered along one edge. She placed it delicately in front of me with a wine glass and my gin and tonic, ice clinking as it bobbed up and down.

"You have proper cutlery as well? None of that plastic stuff up front, huh? I'd like the steak please, medium, thank you."

Balancing on Blue

Business class was a whole new world: an inner sanctum, an oasis in an aluminium cage, and something way beyond my previous experience. A good friend in the business had managed somehow to get me a discount ticket.

"Just ask for an upgrade when you check in," she had told me. "They always have room in Business on that route. You'll get it for sure."

At one point, I just had to take a walk back to the Economy section. I gently pulled the curtain to one side and peeked round. There they all were, livestock in an overcrowded pen, knees under their chins, looking somewhat cramped and prodding their catering option with puzzled expressions. I coughed loudly and some of them looked up. Smiling somewhat mockingly, I nodded a silent hello, coupled with an expression that said, 'I got a Business class seat, restaurant quality cuisine, a very quaffable Rioja, a better movie choice than the National Film Archive, a fully reclining option and more leg room than a ski lift'. Then I went back to my seat for a slice of chocolate cake.

***

In the spring of 1948, a 29-year-old carpenter called Earl Shaffer started hiking north from Mt Oglethorpe in Georgia, which in those days was the start of the Appalachian Trail. One hundred and twenty four days later he became the first person to complete the entire trail in one attempt and unintentionally coined the term thru-hiking. His journey and subsequent book *Walking with Spring* have since inspired thousands of others to do the same.

Taking just over four months to complete the trail is an admirable time, even by today's standards, but back then it was met with derision. Not solely because of the time itself but because someone had claimed to have hiked the entire trail in one attempt. It was unheard of. Even the Appalachian Trail Conservancy initially deemed his claim to be 'obviously fraudulent'. His feat earned him the name 'The Crazy One'.

Compared to the equipment we have today, his was sparse and inadequate. He carried no tent or shelter, no stove, wore simple boots that lasted until the end and an army rucksack. I sometimes wonder whether in sixty-five years' time others will look back on the thru-hiking gear of today in similar disbelief.

Shaffer was born in York, Pennsylvania, on November 8th, 1918. His family moved to a small farm near the village of Shiloh when he was five years old. His mother died when he was a teenager but had instilled in him an appreciation of poetry and literature. He graduated from high school in 1935 and during the Depression found work on neighbouring farms. In the winter he hunted and trapped for furs before eventually becoming a carpenter.

With his close friend and regular hiking companion, Walter Winemiller, he discussed and subsequently planned a thru-hike of the AT before their idea was put on hold by the outbreak of World War Two. Shaffer enlisted in 1941 and served as a radioman in the South Pacific until well into 1945. Winemiller was killed in action during a beach landing at Iwo Jima, a small island south of Japan. Shaffer's subsequent reasons to hike the trail stemmed from a desire to walk the army out of his system and to mitigate his feelings of sorrow at the loss of his friends who had died during the war.

The AT had been completed some eleven years before Shaffer's attempt but, owing to labour shortages and other factors brought about by the war, it was overgrown and neglected in many sections. With trail guides not yet in existence, he had only road maps and a compass, meaning navigation and bushwhacking were the order of the day.

In 1965 he thru-hiked again, this time starting from Mt Katahdin, the northern terminus, and travelled south to Springer Mountain, which had replaced Mt. Oglethorpe as the official southern start point. He became the first person to complete the hike in both directions. In 1998 he made another successful northbound hike at the age of 79, at the time the oldest person to do so. He succumbed to cancer and died on May 5th, 2002.

To this day, Earl Shaffer remains a hero and an inspiration to many.

***

Atlanta is the nearest major airport to Springer Mountain, but

Balancing on Blue

Delta flight 261 was bound for Miami. An hour or so south of the city lies a small town called Homestead, where I had spent three months volunteering on an organic farm some years before. I had kept in touch with the owner, Gabriele, who had kindly agreed to act as base HQ for my adventure. Essentially this meant somewhere I could leave gear that might be needed at some point, along with food supplies and other requirements to be mailed out should I need them. For example, the weather can still be cold when most start their AT hike, in late March or early April. A warmer sleeping bag is required until the weather warms and spring takes hold. A cooler bag would then be needed during the summer months. Food requirements vary for everyone; for me, most was procured from stores along the way. However, some items I bought in bulk because they were cheaper or hard to obtain, in my case several kilos of my favourite chocolate protein powder to be mailed as I needed it.

A good HQ and someone who is willing to give a little of their time to help you out are invaluable when thru-hiking. I was also able to mail some new gear from American companies to Gabriele which saved on postage costs, as opposed to shipping them to England. In the coming months, I was to appreciate just how good a job Gabriele performed.

***

Amicalola Falls State Park is where most thru-hikers start their journey, following a nine-mile approach trail that links up to the actual start point of the AT on Springer Mountain. Getting to Amicalola Falls from Homestead involved a fifteen hour Greyhound trip to Atlanta, the prospect of which I wasn't exactly relishing. To tie up a few loose ends in Atlanta such as last-minute gear supplies, accommodation and a ride to the trailhead, I had emailed a thru-hiker distress call to friends I knew from my previous hiking adventures in the States. Hiker hospitality is amazing; American hiker hospitality is legendary. Within a couple of days of sending out my plea, I had offers of everything I'd asked for.

Keith 'Hiker X' Baitsell and his girlfriend Sarah 'Sami' Van Vliet both lived and worked in Atlanta. Keith had the 2,640-odd miles of the Pacific Crest Trail (PCT) already under his boots and understood the importance of offering assistance to hikers, especially those from a foreign country. My call for help had been forwarded to them via Kathryn 'Dinosaur' Herndon, also a PCT hiker whom I had met during my time on that trail, and they offered me somewhere to stay for a couple of days to get myself sorted. The delectable Lauren 'Swiss Miss' Moran volunteered as an excellent taxi service for the errands and a ride to the trailhead.

Nicknames such as 'Hiker X' and 'Dinosaur' are known as trail names. Not many use their real names on a thru-hike; most go by their trail name and often we still refer to one another by this name after the hike has finished. If you don't have a trail name, you can think of one yourself, but, more often than not, it is bestowed on you by another hiker. The name usually refers to your appearance, mannerisms or behaviour, and it is generally understood that if someone offers to name you, you have to accept it. However, this is not always so. My trail name, Fozzie, loosely derived from my surname, I had used since school.

I stepped off the Greyhound in Atlanta at 3.30 in the morning and looked around. I was hungry and secretly hoped to spot the neon lights of a roadside diner but it was not to be. A few passengers stood outside the terminal sucking on cigarettes, and warm air from the exhausts of a shallow queue of taxis rose up to meet the chill of late winter. A street light flickered annoyingly, revealing brief glimpses in the shadows of two men lurking underneath, occasionally glancing over in my direction.

"Downtown Atlanta at that time of the morning is not somewhere you should hang about," Hiker X had warned me a few days earlier. "Get a cab, come here and knock on the door. Don't screw around down there, it can be dangerous."

"But the Greyhound arrives at 3.30. I don't want to be knocking on your door at 4.00 in the morning!" I had replied, not wanting to impose even further.

"It's fine, I'll hear the door. I don't mind."

I walked over as the cab window slid smoothly down.

"You need a ride somewhere?" asked the driver, who bore an uncanny likeness to James Brown. I opened the door, got in and started humming Living in America.

I checked the piece of paper on which I had written Hiker X and Sami's address and repeated it to him. The cab lurched forward and we journeyed through empty streets that were barely contemplating waking up. He slowed to read the house numbers in a dim light and pulled over, offering a weak, "It's around here somewhere."

It was quieter away from the centre. I sat down on the doorstep and lit a cigarette, trying to delay knocking on the door to assuage my guilt. Bare trees were outlined starkly against a bright moon. A cat ran past, startling me, closely pursued by another. Finally I knocked gently on the door. No answer. I looked up; there were no signs of life. I knocked harder and then heard footsteps coming down the stairs and saw the hall light illuminate.

"Hiker X?" I asked, tentatively.

"Fozzie, come in."

"Look, I'm really sorry. I feel bad for getting you up. I really appreciate you doing this."

"It's fine, really. Sami is still asleep. Do you want a drink or maybe you wanna catch a couple of hours' sleep?"

"I could do with some shut-eye."

"OK, there's just the couch, I'm afraid, but it's very comfortable. You still want that breakfast?"

I'm a sucker for a good breakfast and nowhere delivers breakfast better than America. I had mentioned this to Hiker X in an email and was pleased he had remembered.

"Oh hell, yeah," I answered, no doubt with a greedy glint in my eye.

I slept for three hours, waking briefly as I found myself running through a planning list and final logistics. After a few minutes, the practicalities faded away and my mind settled, as it always did, on one, very simple question: why?

It is the standard query from people who don't understand the lure of thru-hiking. The stock answer you will get from most thru-hikers investing many months of their time, a few thousand dollars of their money and several thousand miles of walking is something along the lines of enjoying hiking and the freedom the outdoors bestows. Others may go into a little more depth but, to be honest, we tire of answering because one answer merely invites more questions. Most people cannot relate to spending around six months eating crap food, getting filthy, being too hot or too cold and smelling like an overburdened trash bin two weeks past a collection date in the heat of midsummer. Despite all of this, we live for it.

I spent many years trying to solve this question and it wasn't until I was writing this book that a definitive answer suddenly surfaced. Of course I love hiking and to be in the great outdoors is wonderfully nourishing. It is time-out from a conventional lifestyle that I don't particularly enjoy. I revel both in the solitude and the company on the trail and always return refreshed, recharged and energised.

However, when I really went into my reasons in depth, I discovered that I had felt the same need for escape many years before my first thru-hike, which was a thousand mile walk on El Camino de Santiago in 2002. But the appeal wasn't found in thru-hiking as such; this was just the means to try and placate a wanderlust. Even in my teens, I had a yearning — a deep-rooted desire to wander, to be nomadic. At first I thought there was something wrong with me. All my friends were concentrating on school, choosing a college or career path, debating where they would live and, later, in their early twenties, their thoughts turned to marriage and kids. All I wanted to do was get the hell out. I wasn't comfortable living conventionally and I'm still not.

I battled with it for years. I fought it, argued with it and became frustrated. Why was I different? Why couldn't I just get a decent job, find a house, make trips to IKEA, buy a better car than next door, get married and watch the wife pop out a couple of kids?

I finished education, dropped out of the extra year at school I had committed to and bounced around a series of jobs, none of which I enjoyed. I went into sales because I thought the meaning of success was having an office job. Back in the 1980s, if you had a white shirt with a silk paisley tie, a Prince of Wales check suit and a briefcase (even if it did only contain a round of sandwiches), everyone thought you had arrived. Appearance was everything. Surely if you looked successful, then that was the whole point, wasn't it? I was trying to conform, to fit in with a lifestyle that apparently we were supposed to follow because I

Balancing on Blue

didn't know any different or ask any questions.

In my mid-twenties during a stint as a financial advisor offering minimally shrewd advice to a lot of very boring people, I began seriously questioning my life route. Moreover, I was miserable and exhausted, constantly fighting my desires to travel and wander because they weren't accepted by the mainstream. I'd been led to believe that travelling was wrong, or at least spending more time travelling than working. Although travel was experiencing an upsurge, it was frowned upon as a way of life.

I loved praise, enjoyed being told I had done a good job, like a dog that comes when it is called, wagging its tail, and thrived on pleasing people and winning their approval. However, I also began to understand that receiving recognition for performing a meaningless job was a waste of a life. Surely, to go wandering without praise must be more rewarding than doing something I hated?

Disillusioned with trying to forge any career at all, I became angry with society, lost any interest with fitting in and instead I rebelled. I started smoking, drinking and chasing women to distract me from the urge to travel because, first, I didn't know how to escape the system and, second, I was scared that people would chastise me for being different.

To begin feeding my peripatetic desires while at the same time maintaining a semblance of being in the workforce, I joined employment agencies because I could work one job for a few months until the contract ran out and then escape somewhere. Being a temp didn't affect my CV (not that I really cared) and it was completely acceptable to work many jobs without any thought of future advancement. I made my first, tentative escape to Greece, where I spent a few months hopping round the islands by boat, testing my resolve. Even there, the drifter in me demanded further gratification by not staying in one place too long. A couple of days here, a short layover there, then move on — feed the craving, go somewhere new, anywhere. Keep moving, you must keep moving.

For the first time in my life, I felt peace during those times in Greece. I was happy because I was doing what I loved, roaming, but, more importantly, I was happy because I had stopped battling the desire and finally realised that wandering was what I was supposed to do. I didn't need to fight it any more. I embraced my life.

***

Dromomania, from the Latin dromas (runner) and mania (excessive or unreasonable desire, even insanity) is an uncontrollable impulse to wander, the kind that is appeased often at the expense of careers, relationships and maintains a blithe disregard for mortgages and pensions. When I first saw the word, though it sounded somewhat like an ailment, it struck a chord with me.

In extreme cases, a dromomaniac may have no memory of his travels. One such was Jean-Albert Dadas, a Frenchman from Bordeaux, who would suddenly start walking and find himself far from home in cities such as Moscow.

The fact that mania is tagged on the end of this word is unfair. Let's face it: most of us consider anyone with a mania to have something wrong with them. And yet, indulging dromomania, far from being frowned upon, should be embraced.

I don't care about the reasons for my wandering. I'm not one for understanding the mechanics of anything. I expect my car to start when I turn the key and I care as much about the periodic table as to why these letters appear as I type. Now, I cherish it. It is the one aspect of my life that takes precedence over pretty much everything. I deal with being stationary because most of the time I must, but I'm only truly happy when I indulge, and thru-hiking is my chosen method. The world is a wonderful place when experienced at walking pace.

Some say our desire to wander goes back thousands of years to when we had little choice in the matter. Seasonal changes drove us to the cooler mountains in the summer and back down to the plains in winter. We searched for more hospitable environments to live in. If food became scarce in one area, we moved on to where it was plentiful. In the Ice Age we fled south to escape; in times of drought we moved on in search of water. Cook, Magellan, Columbus and others were perhaps not so much mapping a new world as indulging their appetites to move ever onwards.

As far as romantic relationships go, forget them. My history of getting involved with women is not a happy one. It's not something that bothers me. I have come to accept it easily because, again, relationships don't fit with my wandering instincts. If I occasionally meet someone I like then I'm honest about my ways. If it's a night of pleasure or a week of fun, I'm grateful but then I move on.

Most of my friends have accepted my ways and many admit to being a little envious, while others treat it with confusion or derision. Some people even become confrontational and demand to know why I should get six months out at a time. It's just not fair that I should be seeing this marvellous world when they are staring at a computer screen for eight hours a day.

Such reactions do puzzle me. I wouldn't aggressively challenge anyone who works a nine-to-five job. I struggle with their choice but respect those who have consciously made it.

For many it all boils down to fear. The standard life charter is comfortable for most, although an increasing number are beginning to cast it aside. We're an intelligent race but, for some reason, we choose to work for forty-eight weeks of the year and accept four weeks' holiday. Some, especially in America, don't even get that and are made to feel guilty for even asking for time out.

Many of you out there have dreams, a desire to do something different, but are perhaps hesitant to follow them because they are a little dangerous, perhaps risky. OK, some dreams fail, but I would urge you to at least attempt whatever it is you dream about. Persistence and desire can conquer any gaps in skill, knowledge and qualifications. If you want something strongly enough and are prepared to chase it as you've never chased anything before in your life, you can succeed in doing what you truly want to do. Whether that choice is hiking a few thousand miles in the wilderness or forging a career as a graphic designer, it makes no difference. Henry Ford once said that whether you think you can, or you think you can't, you're right.

There is another reason I thru-hike or, as I mentioned before, use thru-hiking as a means of escape. During my second walk on El Camino de Santiago, I met a French hiker called Pierre. He travelled with his delightful dog, Flo, and as we talked, the inevitable question of why we were walking naturally cropped up. One evening I ate dinner with Pierre and Patrick, from Belgium, whom I was walking with at the time and who translated for us.

Pierre said that he walked often and preferred to camp or sleep rough, partly because of limited funds and partly because of how he looked. The sides of his head were shaved and his appearance, which most would call scruffy, attracted the attention of the police. He had been arrested for sleeping in a park a year before with his previous dog, which, wanting to protect him, began barking and growling at the police when Pierre was placed in handcuffs. Much to his anguish, they shot his dog. Even now, a year later, his eyes welled up as he spoke and he pulled Flo closer.

He went on to explain his lack of faith in how we are governed, controlled, taxed and how he is treated unfairly by the police because of his appearance. His words resonated with me. Here was a man following a life he loved. Like me, he worked to earn some money and, when he had enough, he would take his devoted dog for a long hike, sometimes for months. Occasionally he slept under a bridge, discreetly, or camped out of view. He would perhaps stay in a cheap hotel once a week, get cleaned up and do some laundry. His appearance suffered, as does a thru-hiker's.

He disliked rules, regulations and hated being told what to do. He didn't understand why we need insurance and mortgages, why everyone's voice isn't heard; why the government doesn't really consult us, despite many people believing it does. He thinks we have lost our freedom and he hikes to gain his, and to escape.

Patrick stopped the translation. It was clear to us all that this dishevelled, wiry little Frenchman's thoughts had connected with me.

Was I an anarchist, as Pierre claimed to be? Do thru-hikers and other adventurers undertake their long trips to escape the system?

I consulted the dictionary:
Anarchy:

1 – State of disorder due to absence or non-recognition of authority or other controlling systems:
2 – Absence of government and absolute freedom of the individual, regarded as a political ideal.

I wouldn't want a state of disorder but to have absolute freedom as an individual, if that is indeed possible in our society, is an idea I do relish. Perhaps there is a little of the anarchist in me. Perhaps there is a little of the anarchist in all of us?

***

Having finally understood and embraced my roaming ways, I turned from Greece to other destinations. After El Camino de Santiago, I began looking for longer hikes in remoter regions, in pristine wilderness, where it would be possible to walk further without encountering civilisation. I also wanted to experience solitude more. Solitude is a great leveller and I love it. Not that I don't enjoy company, but being on my own feeds the nomad.

My attention turned to America because they have an enviable collection of ridiculously long trails in remote regions. The three main routes are the Appalachian Trail (2,184 miles), running vertically through the eastern states; the Pacific Crest Trail (2,640 miles), which runs, again vertically, through the western states; and the Continental Divide Trail (distances vary as it is not yet fully complete, but the average is around 3,000 miles), following the Continental Divide along the Rocky Mountains and also south to north or vice versa, depending on your inclination. The AT is by far the most popular virgin hike, mainly because it is the shortest; it passes through many towns for re-supply and there is safety in numbers. It also has many shelters, usually simple, three-sided wooden constructions, sleeping on average around eight hikers, conveniently located near water sources and spaced along the length of the AT so you would normally pass perhaps three each day. Having completed a successful thru-hike of the AT, most turn their attention to the PCT and finally the CDT. Hike all three and you earn yourself the accolade of a 'Triple Crowner'.

Every autumn, the ALDHA West (American Long Distance Hiking Association) honours those who have walked the 8,000 or so miles to complete all three. As of October 2012, only 174 people had been successful.

Not one for conformity, I discounted the AT as a first choice, mainly because at the time, I thought I might get the chance to do only one of the big three and the other two appealed more. The AT has a reputation for being wet. It clings to the Appalachian chain of mountains, which receive more than their fair share of rainfall. Being English and familiar, if not necessarily comfortable, with being damp on hiking trips, my attention turned to either the PCT or the CDT. The CDT is a serious undertaking for which I wasn't ready: it's the longest, the most remote, has fewer chances of regular re-supply and skilful navigation is a must, as some of the trail is not yet complete. By elimination, the PCT was the obvious choice. It had a fantastic reputation, and encompassed a variety of geographical areas such as desert, high alpine mountains and dense forest. Moreover, it boasted a fantastic climate.

I completed the PCT in 2010, albeit taking slightly longer than I had planned for and developed an incurable case of the thru-hiking bug in the process. The AT was still in the back of my mind, along with the CDT, and in January of 2012 I had the possibility of taking on the AT that March, which is exactly what I did.

***

Long-distance trails are life-changing events. However, they're not easy. The impression most have of us thru-hikers is that we get a vastly extended holiday, eat only sweet treats, do lots of sunbathing, drink a lot, go wild swimming, smell terrible and generally muck around in the woods. Admittedly some of this is true but make no mistake: it is a huge physical effort and is about as far from easy as you can get.

If you attempt a long-distance hike, the chances are heavily stacked against you and there is a very real chance that you will fail. Most quit in the first month. They were not as fit as they thought, new gear is chafing everywhere, red-raw blisters make walking excruciating or it's too cold, too hot, too dry or too wet, sometimes for days on end. I always say push through that first month and if you come out the other side, chances are you will be successful. Above everything else, you have to be single-minded and totally fixed on your goal to succeed. If you are mentally strong, can persuade yourself that you're not in pain and can push another mile out, that your hunger and thirst are imaginary, that it really isn't the seventh straight day of being wet and the fact that you badly misjudged your food supply doesn't really matter, then you just may succeed.

The AT forges a path through fourteen states: Georgia, North Carolina, Tennessee, Virginia, West Virginia, Maryland, Pennsylvania, New Jersey, New York, Connecticut, Massachusetts, Vermont, New Hampshire and Maine. Just the prospect of walking through so many states may be enough to deter most, but a thru-hiker views this with a glass-half-full approach, seeing the crossing of thirteen state lines as an indication of progress. On the PCT you cross just two. Currently around 2,700 prospective thru-hikers set out to conquer the route each year, in addition to section hikers. These walk a piece of the trail each year, or perhaps may miss a year and take several years to complete a thru-hike. Then there are the day hikers, or weekenders, who make regular visits to the AT, usually living in the vicinity of it. Some day hikers will accumulate more trail mileage in their lifetimes than most thru-hikers. In fact some two to three million visit the AT each year. Virginia boasts the longest section, at 550 miles, whereas the trail in West Virginia just clips the state corner and is a mere four miles long. Maryland and West Virginia are considered the easiest sections, New Hampshire and Maine the hardest.

By the time a successful thru-hiker stands on top of Mt Katahdin (or Springer Mountain for a south bounder), he or she will have gained the equivalent altitude of climbing Mount Everest sixteen times, consumed around 900,000 calories and drunk approximately 600 litres of water. Most will have camped for more nights than in their entire life to date, and probably more than they ever will again. A few will have worn out just one pair of shoes; others will be finishing off their sixth. Many will have spent as little as a thousand dollars, others eight thousand or more. A small proportion will be injured and some, sadly, may even die.

Most hikers start the AT in Georgia and head north. They are known as north-bounders, or Nobos. A small percentage start later in the season after the snows have subsided further north and head south from Maine. These are the south-bounders, or Sobos. North-bounding is by far the most popular, thanks to a thru-hikers' eagerness to begin earlier.

An average hike in either direction takes around four to six months, and in that time it is possible to experience all four seasons. Most start in March or April, just after the tail end of winter, and continue through spring and summer, finishing in autumn.

Spring is the logical start time; it makes best use of the impending finer weather. But a hike starting late March or early April means the seasons are not just times of the year, but an experience. Instead of getting out in the woods every weekend, or worse, not at all, we *lived* the seasons, which revealed themselves in ways we could never hope to see. We shared the changing face of the year every single day. We saw the trees change from emaciated skeletons to bearers of tiny leaves. We noticed those leaves become more abundant as time rolled on, watched them burst from their buds and unfold, splaying outward to catch the light, changing from a translucent pale green to an opaque depth, becoming the best they would ever be. And then we observed them attain middle age and decline to old age. Deep greens gradually lost their sheen and resignedly faded to yellows, reds and browns, clinging to their twilight years far from gracefully but more in a final, riotous flourish of an artist's palette. Then they died, fell and fed the children of the following season.

I felt privileged to encounter not just the leaves but the whole gift that the woods offered me. During the early stages of my hike, I would often stop at high points and look down. Up there it was still stark winter but witnessing the blossoming of spring in the valleys below and watching it slowly creep up the hillside was a season's tease. However dark and unfriendly my immediate surroundings, the energy of the changing season below me was abundant and unstoppable. Every day, as it grew warmer, that energy crept uphill to meet me, and every day I would look down to urge it ever upwards. I was completely in

Balancing on Blue

awe.

I watched creeks, streams and rivers burst from the snowmelt and, as the summer strode on, raging torrents weakened to calmer waters, rivers slowed to a more sedate pace, streams become shallower and creeks turned to mere trickles. Ponds and lakes receded, their banks becoming dry and crusty, emaciated weeds strewn on their shores.

I saw a damp, cocoa-coloured trail lighten to beige as a warming sun drew out the moisture. I observed snakes hesitantly checking the temperature to see if it was warm enough and then glissade back through dry leaves, unexpectedly silent.

I observed storms raging miles distant, gliding along the horizon casting rain shadows. Lightning forks cracked and struck the ground, followed by ominous rumbles. I felt the wind on my face to gauge its direction and sat, even longer, counting seconds between enraged flashes and angry claps. Holding up a dry leaf and letting it go, I watched it fall as the wind caught it. Sometimes I wished the storm would come to me so I could experience the anger right above.

I walked in downpours, snow, the unbearable heat of summer and sapping humidity. The roar of rain on foliage behind me was startling at times, and I would flee through the woods trying to outrun storms, giggling like a child at the craziness of it all. Paths became sodden until puddles formed, which in turn overflowed until trickles tumbled over tree roots and matured to streams themselves, soaking my feet.

I stood in silent forests late at night, trying to catch teasing glimpses of stars through branches. I strained my ears to hear nothing but absolute silence, waiting for a wind to travel up the west side of the Appalachian Mountains and censor the calm. Sometimes it merely stroked my face or ruffled my tent wall; at other times I would struggle to hold myself upright against it. Its energy was invigorating, so intense I felt as though it was filling me.

I sat on rock shelves, legs dangling over precipices, and peered down, feeling my stomach clench. Over a hundred sunsets gifted sapphire skies which melted into brilliant ambers, touched by rose pinks. And at dawn too, the sun first peeked shyly over distant hills, then worked a route through the trees around me until I felt its warmth on my grateful face.

I sat on logs around campfires with others who shared the love of this trail, and as we talked, their faces flickered in an orange glow, bright one second, dark the next. They spoke animatedly of their lives and what the trail meant to them, with moving honesty and authenticity.

I walked with children, the retired and every age in between. I befriended soldiers, conversed with teachers, laughed alongside builders, shared food with writers, drank in the company of artists, sang along next to musicians, enjoyed the scenery with truck drivers and camped in the company of forest rangers.

***

Dromomania. That's what I have, and if you're reading this, it's very possible that you do too. Don't fight it ...

Balancing on Blue

Chapter 3

Privy Sitting

March 28th to April 1st
The Start — Mile 0 to 51

I have few expectations in life. A mandatory prison sentence seems only fair for those annoying individuals who insist on relaying their life story to the cashier whilst we wait patiently in the queue behind them. Secondly, it's obvious that *The Great Escape,* a 1963 movie starring, amongst others, Steve McQueen, should have its own dedicated TV channel and be broadcast on a permanent loop. Finally, coffee should be officially recognized as the saviour of the human race and be made accessible, mandatory and free for all. This is my world vision, and with it in mind I duly helped myself to a cup of joe and ambled over to the desk inside the Amicalola Falls Visitor Center.

Whilst filling in the hiker registry form, a man emerged from the back office.

"A group of British started about three weeks ago. You are British, right?" he enquired after noticing my passport. He was amiable enough, but his question annoyed me, as it always does.

"I'm English," I replied in a polite, but corrective tone.

"There's a difference?"

"Yes. England is part of Great Britain, and it is true that I am British but I'm patriotic enough to consider myself not British, but English. If the politicians have their way, before long I'll be known as European along with everyone else in the EEC. It's just my way of trying to save my nationality."

He looked at me somewhat confusedly, nodded, smiled weakly and wished me a good hike.

I circled the room once, checking information, looking at maps and studying a stuffed snake, my nose pressed against the tank to get a better angle. It soon became clear that it wasn't a dead exhibit as it reared up, forcing me to fall backwards onto my arse in surprise. Quickly checking that Swiss Miss, who had given me a ride to the centre, hadn't played witness along with anyone else, I exited through the back door to save any loss of face.

Nice one, Fozzie. You haven't even made the approach trail yet, let alone the actual AT, snake encounter number one is already under your belt, and you've bloody fallen over. Great start mate, really. Way to go.

Swiss Miss followed me out and asked for my camera, suggesting I go and stand by the AT sign. I looked at the writing that I had seen countless times in photos:

Appalachian Trail Approach. Springer Mountain, GA, 8.5 miles. Mt. Katahdin, Maine 2108.5 miles.

She took a few snaps to ensure the second most important photo of the trip had been recorded, wished me luck, and gave me a hug and a peck on the cheek for good measure. This ensured I was grinning for the rest of the day.

I'm not an avid planner, so my hiking strategy was loose except for one aspect: begin slowly. The main intention over the first couple of weeks was to avoid blisters, which had plagued me on El Camino and the PCT. I figured a slower-than-average pace, regular breaks and short daily distances would be the key. I would doubtless have to reign in a little over-enthusiasm at times but the mileage deficit could always be turned around later.

The hum of the road faded and the visitor centre was gradually lost in a sea of trees. My environment had been simplified from a bustling, crowded and noisy town to the simple browns of late winter. A sand-tinted trail cut a clear path and was sprinkled with dry, crisp, umber leaves. I was surrounded by trees stretching upwards, attempting to touch a fading, weak mist. A clear sky was barely visible, and it was quiet, serene and already very, very beautiful.

The temperature was a surprise: unexpectedly warm. I peeled off my jacket. Amicalola Creek curved in to join me, offering a hushed gurgle as company, seemingly almost aware of the quiet. The falls themselves, at 729 feet high, were originally named by the Cherokee, 'Amicalola' meaning 'tumbling waters'. The ascent from the creek to the top of the falls entailed climbing up an impressive 604 steps on a wooden staircase. There was a smattering of overweight tourists in varying states of decay littering the climb, some grasping the handrail, bent over trying to catch their breath, others sitting on the steps chucking water down their throats wondering why they hadn't brought another six bottles. I felt good. I wasn't as fit as I could have been, but I had spent a couple of months getting into shape with several hour-long runs and a couple of fifteen-mile walks each week. I breathed easy and sped up all 729 feet like a sprightly teenager.

I knew Springer Mountain was a mere 8.5 miles from the visitor centre, but it seemed to take ages to arrive. A mix of anticipation and eagerness to sit by one of the most renowned hiking spots in the world forced my pace up. After each bend and turn in the trail I thought it would arrive, teasing me all the way until eventually, some ten years after I first promised myself to walk the AT, the climb mellowed and flattened into a clearing. A small gap in the trees facing north gave me what was soon to be a familiar view of round-topped, tree-cloaked hills fading away to the horizon. I set down my pack gently against a rock embellished with an embedded bronze plaque. A figure of a hiker stood proud and I ran my hands along the cold surface and felt my fingers ripple over the raised words:

Appalachian Trail
Georgia to Maine
A Footpath for Those who seek Fellowship with the Wilderness
AT 1934
The Georgia Appalachian Trail Club

I smiled. It was just a sign, but it could have been cast just for me, and indeed most attempting to thru-hike. The most significant words I had ever read about the AT sat right in the middle: 'A Footpath for Those who seek Fellowship with the Wilderness'. Just one line, but incredibly profound. I read the words again and again. I did seek fellowship with the wilderness: I wanted to be part of it again, to learn from it, to allow it to let me in and banish all the negative feelings and emotions that I was harbouring from two years spent in society since the PCT.

This was the moment I had dreamt about for so many years, a scene I had pictured when my mood was low, a moment I longed for that had finally arrived. Content at last, I had around six months to follow a classic trail through prime areas of the American countryside. I was free to roam: there were no schedules, no phone calls or alarm clocks, and a collection of other like-minded people willing to indulge themselves for similar reasons with whom I could connect and share the experience. Again, for a few short months I had escaped from society, and the relief was overwhelming. I sat down, cupped my face in my hands, gave in to emotions and completely unashamed, I cried.

Voices signalled people were coming, and I hastily wrote in the register behind the plaque and left, partly due to embarrassment and partly due to my need to be alone. The path worked its way down from Springer and I passed Springer Mountain shelter, the first of many over the next few months, but felt no need to rest so early.

I did have a guidebook, but no map. The AT is so well-marked that a map is not really needed. Mine, written by a previous thru-hiker called David 'AWOL' Miller, supplied all the information I needed without one. It detailed mileage both completed and left to walk, an altitude graph, distances to the next shelter or campsite, water sources, other trails and notable features for positional reference plus town layout maps.

Further route clarification was provided by white blazes, or trail markers. These are thought to be scaled to the size of a dollar bill and regularly dot the AT. Most are painted on trees, some on rocks, fences or other mediums, and they signify that you are on the right track. Dinosaur had told me that apparently they are spaced so frequently that the next blaze should be

Balancing on Blue

visible from the preceding one. I didn't always find this to be the case but it was true a lot of the time. These simple white rectangles led all the way to Maine; one couldn't possibly get lost. They were even painted on the opposing side of the trees so those heading south were guided also. Side trails, such as those to shelters, water sources and other trails were painted in blue.

The trees narrowed. Clumps of rhododendrons encroached and formed tunnels around me: a small piece of green paradise breaking up the brown. I skipped and jumped over small creeks, sometimes using stones to get across.

I saw my first hiker up ahead: a thru-hiker for sure. Simple giveaways like the size of his pack and his short hair signified he was Maine-bound (many thru-hikers cut their hair short at the start and leave it untouched for the rest of the journey). I slowed and studied him; his gait and stride were different from normal. He trod carefully, seeming to concentrate on each step and foot placement. Walking on eggshells would be too strong a comparison but that's what it reminded me of. Occasionally one arm rose slightly to steady him as though he was balancing on a tightrope and he walked slowly. I caught him quickly, and before passing, so as not to startle, I spoke.

"You walk carefully. It's interesting to watch! What's your name?"

"PJ, and yours?"

"Fozzie. Nice to meet you."

Noticing my accent he asked, "Are you British?"

Oh crap, here we go again.

I slowed a little, intending to stop, but couldn't be bothered to explain twice in one day so I offered the simplified version.

"Yes, English to be exact. See you up the trail I expect?"

"For sure, it's all good."

After twelve miles or so it was already late afternoon and a blue blaze marked a side trail to Stover Creek Shelter. Hearing voices from that direction and eager to see my first shelter I veered off towards it.

With no plans to use the shelters that much, I had packed everything required to do without them: tent, sleeping bag, air mat, cooking equipment and the like. I had heard much about these simple, three-sided wooden constructions that dot the trail.

Usually a focal point for hikers at the end of the day, they not only offer shelter from the rain and wind, but more often the lure of company. A wooden floor is usually built into the structure to elevate hikers off the ground. Simple additions like a fire pit, composting toilet or privy and perhaps a picnic table are occasionally found outside. There is no running water, electric, heating or plumbing. Shelters are purely that: sanctuary from the elements. They also help to minimise the impact on the environment; traffic is concentrated around one area instead of many tent sites so erosion is more limited, if somewhat heavy.

Occupied on a first-come, first-serve basis, they fill quickly, sometimes even by mid-afternoon. Hiker capacity is usually posted on one wall or by reference in our guidebooks but many times, especially in wet conditions, this is ignored and often exceeded.

The downside, for me at least, is that staying in a space with several others was not conducive to a decent night's kip. Snoring, passing wind, fidgeting, people holding conversations when others were trying to sleep didn't appeal. They are also renowned for sheltering other occupants: mice.

The main lure to our rodent friends isn't shelter, although that may be a bonus, but food, and plenty of it. Just above head height near shelter entrances are invariably several pieces of string or cordage, about a foot or so in length, with a stick tied horizontally at the bottom end. Most also have an empty food tin half way down, suspended by means of a hole in the tin and a knot in the cord. The purpose of the stick was to thread through the carrying loop on the top of backpacks and suspend them off the floor, away from mice. The can was there because although any mouse is capable of climbing down a line, they often find it difficult to negotiate the tin.

The food wasn't too much of a concern to me; at best, one could expect to find a nibbled pack of crackers, or perhaps some inroads into a loaf of bread. What worried me was the damage inflicted to equipment. It was not uncommon for hikers to wake in the morning and find several strayed holes in their packs or other accessories. With packs costing upwards of £100, you can imagine my concern.

I did stay in a few shelters, usually when they were quiet,

and I became used to our little friends. Come sundown, the shelter would echo with the scurrying sounds of our guests, checking out what was on the menu, carrying out some route surveillance and holding planning meetings to discuss the best line of attack. I didn't mind; mice never bothered me. They were just like us, trying to survive and looking for something to eat.

As it transpired, I did usually home in on shelters come the end of day, purely for the company and in the hope that any bears would take a liking to another hiker before me. I'm quite considerate like that. They were great places to socialise when I was in the mood, catch up with whoever was staying there, get the weather reports from whoever had reception on the mobile, swap or share food and go sit by anyone who had dark chocolate.

Stover Creek was certainly one of the better offerings. It was actually split into two levels with a stated capacity of ten, although more could have comfortably slept there. Twelve other hikers were occupying themselves with varying tasks such as journal writing, cooking or setting up their beds for the night. I chatted to Eric, Bridget and Josh before heading over to a flat spot to set up camp for the night.

I was gone by the time the others were up in the morning, being keen to put in a good shift and get an early finish. I was amazed at how warm it was: I had been too hot in my sleeping bag overnight and, after a short-lived morning chill, it wasn't long before I was down to shorts and a T-shirt. Spring was waking up as if it had just realised that there was much work to be done. However, I tried not to become complacent about the weather. The AT has a reputation for changeable conditions, and apart from the rain, there are plenty of places, especially at higher elevations, where we could still get snowed on. The Smoky Mountains, some 165 miles down the trail, are famed for throwing in a little late winter snowfall. For the time being at least, I was relishing being out of the English winter and enjoying a premature start to the summer season.

I stopped to chat to a couple of guys carrying out some forestry work. They were eager to talk about their home state of Georgia and the woods. They pointed out the early flowers of the Trillium plant with its three virgin-white petals, and also

Mayapple, sporting a simple, more delicate, single flower head. I asked whether there were any Ramps (wild onions) growing, but was disappointed when they told me that it was still too early.

I passed Eric sitting by Blackwell Creek collecting water for the evening camp.

"Hey Fozzie, the shelter is just up the way there. You staying there tonight?"

"Anyone there yet?" I enquired.

"Most of those from last night and some new faces."

"I'll see you up there."

Gooch Mountain Shelter signalled around thirteen miles for the day, pretty much the small target I had set myself so I took the side trail. Still hesitant to use the shelter, I found a suitable spot for my tent.

Bridget, Eric, Josh and another Josh were in the shelter along with PJ who seemed in a jovial mood. Noticing that there were now two Joshes and the confusion that this could cause, I decided that the bestowing of trail names should be implemented as soon as possible. For the interim period I referred to them as 'Josh Long Hair' and 'Josh Short Hair'. Highly unoriginal, I know, but I was taking the assignation of trail names seriously, and needed time to come up with some impressive suggestions.

I was surprised that everyone was still using their real names, but realised that the AT is the first route that many attempt, and trail customs were perhaps not yet familiar. Therefore, I made my feelings about trail names known to the group as we sat around the shelter, and the idea of bestowing them was proposed, albeit with a grace period for suitable names to be thought of, and either accepted or rejected.

I had chatted to PJ and Bridget, and I was curious about both of them. I'm not the most sociable person and I tend to reserve my communications to those with whom I think I would share an affinity. There are certain aspects of a person's character that suggest how devoted or focused to the adventure they are: from their hiking style, either lazy or purposeful, to whether they talk about the experience with excitement or an air of nonchalance, even to their organisation at camp, slapdash or orderly. All these aspects hold clues; indeed, I wondered how others may perceive my character.

Balancing on Blue

Bridget was a classic example. She was twenty-four and hailed from Madison, Wisconsin. She had been making noises about hiking the AT for years, as she put it. After a year in the AmeriCorps (sort of a domestic version of the Peace Corps), she had done a little travelling down in South America, then returned three months prior in December. The next two months were spent as a special education assistant. With spring looming, she decided that career advancement wasn't at the top of her list. However, spiritual progression was, and the AT seemed the ideal place to nurture that desire.

She wore a grey T-shirt with 'Madison' emblazoned across the front and sometimes tied her hair back with a pink headband. Appearing much younger than her years suggested, a pair of oval black-rimmed glasses advanced those years somewhat, and she had a propensity to giggle, making her very endearing.

She was relaxed, but I noticed from day one that she was utterly focused on the task. Out for a month to see how she did was not on her agenda. Her short frame was not totally suited for hiking but just from the way she walked, how she went about her tasks in camp and from the positive way she conversed, I just knew Bridget would make it all the way to Katahdin.

PJ had quite possibly the shortest trail name I had ever encountered. A head of dark hair flopped around randomly but always seemed to look tidy, and he already sported a beard to get him into the thru-hiker spirit. He was 22, fresh-faced, and bright-eyed. I could tell by the frequency with which he smiled that already he was having the time of his life. He sounded a little effeminate when he spoke, and hugged the guys and the girls freely, but by the way he commented on members of the fairer sex, I figured he was straight.

I politely asked him about his character and he laughed, saying he preferred the description of avant-garde or eccentric. His character was, however, infectious, and would always brighten up any situation. He also confided in me that he had left his wife the day before travelling to the trail and how difficult it had been not only to tell her, but to pluck up the courage to actually do it. As he explained, he showed a little remorse and sadness as he stared off into space, then quickly snapped back to the present, smiled, and offered his usual catchphrase: it's all good!

There were bear cables some 200 feet from the shelter, and after dinner I went over to hang my food bag. Two new faces, Krista and her mother, were added to the list of those needing trail names.

Most shelters have bear cables somewhere in the vicinity. The idea is simple: after eating, pack all your food and smelly toiletries into a waterproof bag and hoist it up. Cables were usually stretched between two trees, high enough from the ground so as to be out of a bear's reach, with any bags at the two ends also far enough away from the trees themselves that they couldn't climb up and reach out to the bags from there either.

Apart from keeping a hiker's food safe and away from sleeping areas where a bear could encroach, the main purpose of these steel wires was to educate our furry forest friends. Bears are very intelligent wild animals with three main instincts: survival, eating and procreation.

Over the years they have learnt that humans, especially where they congregate, bring food. If these supplies are easily accessible, they make an association between people and an opportunity to eat. This is why there have been instances where bears have ventured into towns and usually, unfortunately, have been shot. Cables are simply a way of teaching bears that just because humans and food are in the same vicinity, it doesn't mean there is good eating to be had.

Black Bears are common on the AT and chances are a thru-hiker will at some point see one, if not several. They usually go about their business without bothering anyone, are reclusive and will keep away from humans. The best deterrent is to make your presence known; in a group this becomes easier because of conversation. Solo hikers generally take their chances, but may shout something every few minutes; I used to simply bang my trekking poles together once in a while.

If you find yourself in proximity to a Black Bear, first give it the chance to move away so it doesn't feel threatened. If that doesn't work, then the general options become numerous. Some say to back off slowly, still talking and avoiding eye contact. Others, including me, are a little more gung ho. If I see a Black Bear, I will give it the opportunity to move away, but I will

Balancing on Blue

make my presence known vocally. In my experience, most bears will run away when they hear us. Unfortunately, and I can vouch for this, some bears don't, and this is where potentially you could, for want of a better description, be in the shit.

As far as I understand them, a few, rogue bears share similarities with that drunk guy in the pub who just wants to have a fight. He'll glare at you for a while, and when he decides he really doesn't like you, may advance in a threatening manner, look angry and clench his fists. You then have two choices: stand your ground, or get the hell out of the pub. Fleeing is a sign of weakness; it displays vulnerability, fear, and is the only excuse he needs. It's the same with bears.

However, very rarely will a bear act aggressively. When it does, against all your natural instincts, you have to stand your ground. Run, and not only do they see you as a mid-morning snack but they get a game of chase to boot. Even scarier is what is known as a bluff charge, where a bear will literally charge to test you. Stay put, and this indicates that you are strong, which hopefully should do the trick. Bluff charges are exactly that: a bluff. Unfortunately, we have no way of knowing in such circumstances whether the bear is testing you or genuinely — rarely — intending to attack. Either way, don't move. Shout, hold your arms aloft, and pray.

I battled a phobia of bears for many years, to the point where I nearly decided not to hike the Pacific Crest Trail because of it. After a few encounters in California and Oregon, including two very scary situations in close proximity, I now hold a deep respect for them. The chances are a hiker may never see a bear on a thru-hike or be in a threatening situation. Encounters are uncommon, attacks extremely rare, and fatalities virtually non-existent. Bears are beautiful creatures that are misunderstood. Having encountered them and experienced their behaviour, I now understand that they are not the problem. We are.

***

Ask a thru-hiker what they find difficult on trail and you will get various replies. Some may say they hate the heat; some can't deal with the cold. Others will complain about blisters, that their gear is not performing, or the lack of alcohol is too much. For me, it's an addiction to American cooked breakfasts. Reaching road crossings before 11 a.m. where a ride to town could be obtained always presented a battle of wills, and the AT, especially in Georgia, was riddled with roads. I always made sure I had enough food for the trail, but the lure of bacon and eggs was sometimes just too much to ignore.

For example, mid-morning on day three, I reached the road crossing at Woody Gap and my thoughts immediately turned to hash browns. I don't mean those triangular blocks of compressed potato we have in England; I refer to a pile of prime, shredded potato crisped up on a griddle. After only two-and-a-half days I considered this pretty weak, but in my meagre defence there were mitigating circumstances. Firstly, I was hungry. Secondly, rain was imminent, and thirdly, hitchhiking options were on blatant display in the car park across the road. Obviously, the situation had to be taken full advantage of.

Hitchhiking and asking for a ride are two separate skill sets. Some people who live near the major trails in the USA are used to not only seeing thru-hikers, but also being asked for a lift. Never one to assume this, I walked over to the car park and placed my backpack on the ground, near to a guy who had just arrived back at his car after walking his dog. I made sure I was in earshot and looked in his direction to obtain eye contact. Sure enough, he looked over, nodded and smiled.

"How's it going?" he enquired.

"Great," I said, casually strolling over. "Do you happen to know which town is near here?"

An open question generally makes an individual feel obliged to answer with anything but a "yes" or a "no". It also invites conversation.

"None of them are that close. Is there something you need?" he replied, towelling some dirt off his dog.

"Nothing more than a decent breakfast; I'm starving."

"The Wagon Wheel restaurant is just down the road. I'm heading down that way. Happy to give you a ride?"

With that, I thanked him profusely and climbed in the front seat of his ancient Volvo. Lucy the Dalmatian seemed somewhat surprised that someone got her front seat whilst she got relegated

Balancing on Blue

to the rear. I chatted with Jim during the brief ride to the Wagon Wheel, and he explained he was visiting relatives and taking time in the woods with Lucy. He decided to eat with me, and whilst declining my offer to get his bill, he in fact paid for both of us when I made a visit to the toilet. He even gave me a ride back to the trailhead. Southern Hospitality was alive and kicking in Georgia.

While I got over the shock of seeing my second snake that day, albeit a harmless rat snake sliding into a pile of leaves, I noticed two hikers approaching as I geared up to move from Woody Gap. They walked straight over to me and introduced themselves.

Thru-hikers look different from other hikers. Our gear veers more towards what we know works, as opposed to being slaves to fashion. You may see us walking in lime-green shorts with black tights on for warmth, orange running shoes and a light blue balaclava. Our appearance is often soiled, even filthy. The guys grow beards and have long hair (at least during the latter stages of a hike); the girls don't consider makeup necessary and sport hairy legs. This is how we distinguish ourselves from other walkers, and we tend to be drawn to other thru-hikers so we can share our experiences.

There was never any doubt that Phillip Colelli and Sam Ridge were thru-hikers. We had all just started so excessive hair growth wasn't yet apparent, but Phillip and Sam's equipment gave them away. They appeared more like a couple of joggers with tiny packs and we chatted momentarily before making inroads into the four miles to the campsite at Lance Creek. There was talk of a storm rolling in which made the shelter at Woods Hole more sensible, but it was seven miles further. We were all keeping our mileage low so Lance Creek seemed the better choice.

The site was busy. Bridget and PJ were setting up their tents, Krista and her mother arrived, and some new faces, Bill and Cassie, were cooking their dinner. Phillip and Sam had arrived just before me. AT campsites do not come equipped with such distractions as swimming pools, restaurants or bars. In fact the only facilities most laid on were level areas for tents and possibly a privy. Like the shelters, they were usually situated conveniently near water.

I looked up to menacing skies. The storm was not forecast until the early hours, but I decided to pitch my tent first, just in case. I was soon to discover that designated tent platforms, designed to conserve the surrounding area, left a lot to be desired. The obvious initial problem was the size. I grabbed one of the last plots and quickly realised that even my meagre one-man tent was too big for the space provided. I played around with various positions, but the best pitch I could muster involved hanging one side slightly off the edge. The guy lines stretched off the platform, which resulted in less-than-acceptable staking-out points. Then, I discovered the soil was rock-hard anyway, so had to resort to tying the lines to nearby trees.

***

Appalachian storms are legendary. Rain is common, and in the summer, fierce weather patterns scare the crap out of hikers. The other problem is the altitude of the trail. The highest point on the AT is Clingmans Dome at 6643 feet, but generally the trail merrily skips along at around four to five thousand feet, which coincidentally always seems to be the same height as the cloud level. Basically, if you're caught out in inclement weather on the AT, the chances are you're not under the storm, but actually in it.

For example, during Thanksgiving weekend in 1950, an area of severe low pressure pulled down a mass of cold, arctic air from the north whilst forcing warmer air up from the south. The result was catastrophic. One of the biggest storms ever along the Appalachian chain dumped several feet of snow in some parts whilst others in the warmer air suffered flooding. Wind speeds of 140mph were recorded on Bear Mountain in New York, and Mount Washington in New Hampshire, famous for documenting the strongest wind speed ever, anywhere, recorded gusts of up to 160mph. Extremes of temperature ranged from 50°F before the storm down to the teens behind it, and a low of -5°F was recorded. It cost insurance companies $66.7 million (or, more than $650 million adjusted for inflation) in claims, and was known simply as 'The Great Appalachian Storm'.

Balancing on Blue

***

Mountain Crossings Outfitter at Neel Gap, thirty two miles into the AT, has a fantastic reputation amongst hikers and wasn't far from Lance Creek. Food is a big draw and I had heard great reports about the fully-stocked equipment store and hostel. It was regarded as the premier outfitter in Georgia and was right on the trail.

I climbed with Arne from Maine, Bridget, Bill and Cassie up the 1500 feet to Blood Mountain, passing a group of hikers at Slaughter Creek. We briefly chatted to one guy, and learnt that a bear had actually ripped down the cables near his camp and made off with his food bag. He had heard the commotion and said it was like being in the middle of a horror movie.

Great. Slaughter Creek, Blood Mountain and a rampant bear. How about being a little more positive with the place names around here?

We were looking forward to Neel Gap where Mountain Crossings Outfitter was situated, and we made light work of the seven miles before hearing the occasional vehicle somewhere on the road below us. We spilled out onto US-19, crossed over and entered the shop, eager for sustenance. Several of us also needed to dry out gear, so as the sun flooded the outside deck, wet tents, bags and waterproofs were draped about. When I heard that there was a tumble dryer somewhere, I took the opportunity to try drying out my sleeping bag. I enquired inside and was helpfully pointed to a flight of stairs up the front of the building where said dryer was located. Sam also needed to use the machine, and we found it easily enough. I was just about to place my bag in the top loader when I heard someone running up the steps. One of the staff appeared at the door and glared at me.

"What are you doing?" he demanded.

"I'm about to dry out my sleeping bag," I answered, thinking that looked plainly obvious.

"Do not put your dirty bag in the dryer!"

"Excuse me? My bag is not dirty." I was a little taken aback by his behaviour.

"I don't care; do not put your dirty-ass bag in the dryer!"

This offended me. Not only was I acutely aware that my bag was not dirty because it was brand-new, I knew my bottom was also relatively clean.

"My bag is not dirty, it's just damp. It's brand-new; I have only slept it in twice. I just need to dry it out."

"You are not putting your dirty-ass bag in the dryer!"

I was trying to keep my cool. At this point we were exchanging comments rapidly, and Sam's head was flicking back and forth between us quicker than at a Wimbledon final.

I was about to retort again when he interrupted me.

"Get out of here!" he demanded.

"Excuse me?"

"Leave. Get out."

"I'm not going anywhere; I haven't done anything wrong."

Sam's head, fatigued from the side-to-side motion, exchanged to nodding in agreement instead.

"You're not putting your dirty-ass bag in the dryer without a cotton cover bag!"

"Listen mate, do you want to tell me exactly what the bloody problem is here? I just want to dry my bag. It's wet, not dirty. If you want me to use a cotton bag over the top then I'm happy to do so. Where can I get one?"

"You can borrow one from the shop downstairs."

With that, Sam and I backed off gently, as one would with a bear encounter, and ventured back to the shop.

"Why didn't he just bloody say that in the first place?" I said to Sam as we went back to the shop.

"I have no idea," he replied.

I dried the bag successfully and bought a couple of snacks before returning to the deck, which had been transformed by a collection of thru-hikers drying out their gear. A few others had arrived, including Bridget, and I took the opportunity to return inside to buy her a little gift. Her preference for pink-coloured equipment was evidenced by various items hanging off her person and pack. I returned, and handed her a small karabiner in a subtle shade of flamingo.

"It will go with the rest of your collection," I pointed out. "By the way, I have your new trail name."

"You do?" Her eyes narrowed.

"Yep. In relation to your penchant for pink-coloured gear, I thought that 'Pink Bits' would be perfect." I raised my eyebrows in anticipation of her reply, and was convinced she would accept without hesitation. After all, it was a brilliant, amusing and highly original trail name.

"Pink Bits?!" she replied, in a tone which hinted she wasn't exactly enamoured with the suggestion. She repeated again, "Pink Bits?!"

"Yeah. It's good, innit?"

"No! You can't call me that!" She did see the funny side, but her refusal was firm.

"Why not?"

She paused momentarily with a slight hint of embarrassment.

"Because it's got sexual undertones."

This was a fair point. To be honest, I did realise that others could possibly perceive the name as having connections with various sections of the anatomy, but had ignored this slight problem in hopes that firstly, Bridget wouldn't catch on, and secondly, I thought the double meaning was kind of clever.

"So, that's a 'no' then, is it?" I sought final clarification, to which she merely raised her eyebrows.

"OK. I'll give it some more thought. See you later."

I packed and was making inroads into leaving with Sam when I spotted the same staff member who had confronted me by the dryer. A little despondent about the situation, which I knew would play on me, I took the opportunity to disperse any friction. I walked over and gently placed a hand on his shoulder. He turned around.

"Hey, look, sorry about the misunderstanding with the dryer," I said.

"Yeah, it's OK, but I'm ex-military. I tell people what to do and they do it."

On the defensive, and a little miffed that he still had an attitude despite my taking the initiative to approach him, I replied.

"Well I hate to state the bloody obvious mate, but you're not in the Army anymore. You're back on Civvy Street and serving customers. A little attitude adjustment would go a long way," and I walked off, back into the woods.

Sam kept me company, and we chatted away the seven-odd miles to Whitley Gap Shelter that afternoon. There were numerous others relaxing after the day's walk, most in the shelter or cooking on the table outside. I walked about a hundred feet away from them and noticed a faint trail through some trees, which lured me in. The woodland thinned and opened out to a narrow, flat area just before the ridge dropped away. The view was immense. I pitched my tent between two trees that creaked and groaned in a subtle wind, and afforded me a contemplative view. My short distance from the others meant the noise and chatter was less obtrusive but still comforting, and after setting up my camp I went over for some company and to eat.

Desperado, a new face, sat opposite me as I ate. It was refreshing to at last find someone who actually had a trail name, but our conversation seemed more like an interview. I enquired about her name and she told me it originated from the song Desperado, which she used to sing at karaoke. I tried to eat as she fired question after question at me, in between jotting down what I could only presume were my answers. She didn't participate nor converse a great deal, but merely muttered an 'um' after I answered each question. Then she let rip with my favourite.

"So, Fozzie, you're British right?"

I stared into my pot, seeking savoury rice salvation.

Please, not again.

"I'm English, yeah."

She nodded and scribbled on her pad whilst I tried to peek, unsuccessfully, at what she was writing. She cupped her hand around the notepad.

"Um, why do you say you're English?"

"Because I am English? Look, it doesn't matter. Are you a reporter or something? You ask a lot of questions."

"No, it's just for my journal."

With my hint received, she stopped. We made some small talk about the trail before my company fix for the evening was satiated and I sloped off to the solitude of my camp. I stood near my tent, just before the ground fell away, and let an Appalachian breeze touch me and lift the weaker branches of the trees, still bare. A Georgia moon picked out low clouds drifting lazily across distant mountains, white ghosts surfing silhouetted ridgelines. To the west, a faint yellow glimmer was the only reminder of sunset as it merged into a sombre sky. I crept into my little haven, wrapped my sleeping bag around me and gazed through the open door until, too weak to resist any longer, I shut my eyes.

Chatter floated over from the shelter, waking me in the morning. There were twelve miles to Blue Mountain Shelter and I decided again, on route, to address the lack of trail names.

Hiker names, Fozzie — you have to spread the word, get them named!

I arrived early, having eaten up the distance quickly, still keeping my daily targets around the ten to fifteen-mile mark. The place was empty. It seemed strange to have a shelter to myself, and the lack of conversation lent a solemn air to my surroundings: a solitary woodpecker made the only sound. I sat near the entrance and studied the data book, checked my day's progress, and looked at what tomorrow would bring.

After ten minutes or so, I happened to look to my left and saw Jerry sitting a mere ten feet away reading his Kindle.

"Bloody hell, Jerry!" I exclaimed. "How the hell do you do that? You scared the crap out of me!"

"Do what?" he replied, smirking.

"One minute you just appear out of nowhere; you're like some sort of Ninja! Wait a minute, that's it!"

"What's what?" He lifted his eyebrows.

"I got your trail name! People need to be named, dammit, and I got another one!"

He looked somewhat dubious, as most hikers do when someone informs them they are about to be christened.

"Go on, I'm listening."

"I hereby bestoweth the trail name of Kindle Ninja upon thee. What sayeth you?"

I had never given anyone a trail name that had been accepted, but I thought it was pretty damned good. His eyebrows rose contemplatively and he scratched his chin, smiling.

"Fozzie, I like it. Seriously, I do."

That was it. Confidence boosted, I set up camp whilst studying everyone's mannerisms, behaviour, appearance, and other important criteria for clues to trail names. This was no half-arsed effort: day five into my hike, and I felt I had accrued more than enough information. Slowly, the mob arrived, and Blue Mountain came to life.

I ventured off down a vague track in the direction of the privy.

"Fozzie, it's taken! Queue's here!" Phillip shouted from behind the shelter.

I retreated and sat to join him, Sam, Little Josh and a guy who actually did have a trail name called Central Booking. The privy occupied just one place so as people slowly emerged from the woods clutching their toilet paper, someone would disappear off for the next allocated spot. Occasionally others would join the line, so numbers remained fairly constant. Of all the places to get to know other characters, waiting in line for the toilet proved a priceless location, and privy sitting, as it became known, caught on.

Firstly, if you got bored with one person, it was only a matter of time before they left anyway. Secondly, the new arrivals changed the atmosphere a little and implemented subject changes, making for varied conversations. Time was limited in the privy queue so topics were discussed animatedly as people realised they didn't have very long, and the result was a little taster, a snapshot of the character. Plus, we jokingly chastised those who came back from their business that had either taken too long, or made impressive noises. One such culprit was Jonathan, whose faltering head torch heralded his return from the darkness some fifteen minutes after his departure.

"Bloody hell, mate," I began, "That must have been some dump."

Little Josh covered his mouth and giggled, I think a little embarrassed at my forwardness.

Jonathan paused just before us, and looking somewhat confused, said, "Man, you have no idea the amount of shi ..."

Most of the group fell about in fits, and as I glanced over at Sam, it suddenly became apparent that trail name number two of the evening was beckoning.

"Phillip, I think I have Sam's trail name. You know that face he pulls when he's taken too much on a cigarette, and he doesn't want to breathe in case he coughs?"

"Yup?"

"Daffy Duck? It has to be Daffy Duck, doesn't it?"

Sam's lower lip receded whilst his upper lip extended somewhat, giving the impression of a beak. Phillip started laughing in confirmation, and Sam held no objections although we did shorten it to just plain Daffy.

Two new trail names out of three proposals; I figured that was a pretty good hit ratio. I chuckled my way back to my tent and knew I was happy. Not just at that precise moment, but my life in general thus far on the AT, and I still have fond memories of that evening on Blue Mountain.

Chapter 4

A Feast in the Forest

April 2nd to April 11th
Mile 51 to 153

One bonus of the AT, as opposed to other, remoter trails, is that it never warrants too much planning. As far as logistics go, or rather in my case, lack of them, it is a deliciously random affair to see what happens and deal with it then. The frequency of amenities along the AT's length means that if a food resupply is misjudged, it is only a matter of time before the next opportunity comes along. Apart from remoter sections found further up the AT, such as in Maine, towns are relatively frequent.

Organising overnight stops was easy, with a tent camping places were numerous and, if I decided to sleep in a shelter only to discover it was full, there was always another one a few miles up the track or somewhere to pitch in the woods. Apart from town stops, and getting to the roads that led to them, planning was loose and usually based on when food supplies would likely run out. Re-supply in town, check the data book, search for a road crossing three, four or five days up trail that provided access to the next town with decent amenities, confer with your buddies and the planning was complete. With logistics taken care of easily, I could concentrate on hiking and the trail was that much more enjoyable.

Planning and thru-hiking do lend themselves to each other,

some hikers are diligent in their approach, others not so. Most have an overall strategy and some stick to it religiously but this, to me, defeats the overall objective. My planning arrangements for a thru-hike are usually limited to asking myself two questions: do I want to do it and do I think I can? If a hiker draws up plans for an entire route, pinpoints certain towns to resupply, allows a set number of days in between to hike those stages and other criteria then the very essence of why they are undertaking such an expedition is undermined. As the explorer Roald Amundsen once said, "Adventure is just bad planning."

Take a wrong trail for half a day before realising and the whole plan for the ensuing few months would then be out of sync, and it wouldn't just happen once either. Travelling through a country on a bipedal adventure should be primarily about freedom, an escape. Getting too involved with logistics hampers my enjoyment of the actual trip. I relish uncertainty and one should always be open to a little serendipity. Margins of error are not things I generally concern myself with because my overall plan is adaptable anyway — I can always readjust after. A lot of flexibility is demanded when a trip is several months in duration. I know the distance I ideally need to hike each day and generally that's what I do, but I'm not religious about it.

My scheme when researching a thru-hike is common sense and revolves primarily around the distance to be covered and the time available to do it. The rest of the plan happens when I start hiking. Most who attempt to travel north on one of the big three routes in America will be concentrating on one aspect: getting to the finish before the weather turns. The AT, PCT and CDT all run vertically through the country and most hikers walk south to north. It is only a matter of time before the wet autumn weather arrives, perhaps around September, and shortly after the temperature starts to decrease. That's when snow enters the equation.

My calculations focus on the distance required, the time span I have, factor in one rest day every week as a zero (a *zero* is a day when no walking is done) and perhaps one day a month off as a buffer. The buffer is there if I were to drop behind a little — a get out clause, but more importantly it's to indulge in a little randomness. If your schedule is too strict then when you pass that turquoise lake, cupped in a flower meadow between snow-capped peaks then you either have to pass it by, or at best have a quick dip, which then makes you feel guilty because you've stopped and are now behind schedule. Want a lazy extra couple of hours in your tent because you're taking in a view of the Sierra Nevada? Make your strategy adaptable. The strict planners will miss out but you won't.

The main culprits on the thru-hikes responsible for altering plans, and especially the AT, are events known as trail magic. Usually found at road crossings with vehicular access, trail magic consists of some kind-hearted soul, often an ex thru-hiker, who has surrendered their time and money to provide assistance to hikers. Basic trail magic could just be a can of pop and a bag of crisps left by the trailside. Others may have several tables and chairs under cover; kegs of beer, coffee, cooking equipment with fresh meat and vegetables, all the condiments one could ever hope for, electrical charging equipment and even rides to a local town. Thru-hikers would generally leave a donation to at least cover costs, or offer assistance where it is required.

Word normally spread along the route if trail magic was ahead. Sometimes we caught wind from a day hiker or a sobo and, conversely, us nobos would return the favour. The best encounters were the ones I didn't know anything about, perhaps because they had only set up that morning and word had not yet swept around about the location. Being blissfully unaware that trail magic lurked up ahead was my preference. There were few greater pleasures than catching a wayward waft of a quarter pounder grilling 200 feet below and looking skyward to pray that trail magic was imminent, then popping out of the woods to discover it. It was wonderfully ambiguous and one such example was *The Feast in the Forest.*

Deep Gap shelter was around sixteen miles from Blue Mountain shelter. I was starting to base most of my days around walking from one shelter to another. There was nearly always water available, sometimes a view, usually a fire and other hikers gathering promised company if needed. Sixteen miles was not a lot to walk in a day but keeping to my principle of starting slowly it made sense. There was also a 957 foot descent from Blue Mountain to Unico Gap, a 1068-foot climb to Rocky

Mountain, a further 904 feet down to Indian Grave Gap and finally a three-mile, 1317-foot slog up to Deep Gap. Two months into a thru-hike and at peak fitness I could have knocked all of that off in less than a morning but I was determined to stick to my no blister plan.

As the day panned out, it became clear that Deep Gap was never meant to happen when randomness stole an opportunity. I walked on my own, revelling in the solitude and the chance to just think.

I descended steeply to Indian Grave Gap, turning and twisting down the bends, letting my legs go freely and then arresting the run. I thought I heard laughter and a few seconds later there it was again. I stopped, listened, and sure enough there were people below me and they sounded happy. A minute later and I caught wind of meat grilling.

Trail magic! Yeah! Trail Magic!

I broke into a jog, weaving around stones, hopping over tree roots and before long I was singing, then I started skipping. This merged into a jogging dance; two skips on the left foot with a right tilt of the head, two steps on the other side and an opposite tilt. My arms joined in and then an imaginary drum beat surfaced. I started giggling and singing.

Bacon's a'coming, it's not far below. Eggs? Well they're a'grilling, maybe hash browns to go? Coffee, oh coffee! I'm having some of that and ...

I rounded a corner to see a day hiker stationary in the middle of the trail looking at me strangely. You can always differentiate a day hiker from a thru-hiker because they look spotless and smell of shampoo. I pondered stopping but felt absolutely marvellous so pushed a little embarrassment of the trail and waltzed onward.

There's a day hiker on the trail. I'm in the groove, do you think he'll move? Maybe so, maybe so ...

"Bloody fantastic morning!" I yelled as I danced past taking full advantage of a banked corner and arresting a tad of over steer I careered past to take him on the outside. Open-mouthed with a deadpan expression, he raised his right hand slightly in recognition as his eyes followed me and then I was gone.

I bottomed out at Indian Grave Gap still laughing and

sweating, although not, I hasten to add, still dancing or singing.

"Fozzie!"

I turned to my right to see PJ walking very quickly towards me.

"PJ!"

"Fozzie, it's so good to see you!"

He didn't seem in any rush to arrest his momentum, crashed into me, put his arms around my waist and there he stayed.

"It's so good to see you!" he repeated.

I'm not particularly forward with giving out love until I get to know someone so PJ's forwardness caught me off guard. I casually peered around me; no one was taking much notice except for two rather attractive women over by the fire pit.

This looks like we're lovers. Fozzie, I think you may have blown your chances with those two.

I would consider around two seconds more than ample for a man hug; anything longer makes me suspicious, and nervous.

PJ's hug tolerance was obviously far more liberal and there he stayed like a frightened bear cub stranded halfway up a tree. He eventually relinquished his grip after what seemed like an eternity.

"PJ, I only saw you the day before yesterday!"

"I know, but I missed you and everyone else. I lost all of you. Where are they?"

"I dunno mate. I think Phillip and Sam, sorry Daffy, aren't far behind. Sam's trail name is Daffy now by the way." I became distracted by people eating. "I'll explain later, I need bacon. And coffee, where's the bloody coffee?"

I wandered off with a vacant expression that only caffeine withdrawal could impart, homed in on the aroma of coffee and found Moo. Moo was running the show with a couple of helpers. The deal was eat and drink whatever you fancied and in return maybe wash some dishes, wipe a table, take some logs to the fire, anything to share the karma.

"Moo, hi. I'm Fozzie."

"Hi! What can I get ya?"

She seemed busy cooking but relaxed with it.

"Er, I don't s'pose there's any chance of some bacon and eggs, please?" I offered.

"Sure, hell yeah! You want some home fries with that?"
"That would be fantastic!"

Moo was an angel in the woods and thirty minutes later she handed me a plate dangerously overloaded with one of the best trail breakfasts ever. I had only been hiking for six days but my appetite was borderline dangerous. I went back for more and then spied the beer keg. Ever aware that my destination, Deep Gap Shelter, was still three miles up a 1317-foot climb, that I hadn't had a beer for about eight days, was probably a little dehydrated and tired, I figured I should take it easy and drink one or possibly two.

Daffy found me about two hours later lying down in the middle of a track which I had no recollection of going to.

"Fozzie? Fozzie! You OK?"

I heard him but couldn't move; despite the gravel it felt comfortable. I only drank five beers and being English, champion of beer drinkers, needed to sleep it off. I raised one arm weakly skyward in recognition of his concern and waved him on with a thumbs up. I just about managed a weak "I'll see you at the shelter."

Half an hour later I managed to get up, said a heartfelt thank you to Moo with a kiss on the cheek and stumbled my way up towards Deep Gap. A few cheers greeted my arrival and familiar faces were scattered in and around the shelter: Phillip, Daffy, Josh Long Hair, PJ, Bridget and some other new faces.

I sat resting against an oak tree and chatted to Phillip. He had the perfect build for a thru-hiker — a decent height and slim, some would say lanky. It was his first thru-hike but he had done his research, at least in terms of his gear which was super-light. His pack was so small that it if you faced him head on, you couldn't actually see any of it. Daffy and I joked about his pursuit of the ultra-light (even though Daffy and I were just as guilty), and teased him, suggesting he removed every alternate page in his data book, memorised it and threw it away to save more weight — the only repercussion being that every alternate day his chances of getting lost increased.

He was hiking with and had planned the trip with Sam although each had agreed they were free to do their own thing, such as walk alone or with others if they felt the need. Mild-mannered, he seemed a little quiet when we first met but even over the course of a day had opened up. I got the impression he needed a little time to get to know others, albeit just an afternoon. His southern accent hailed from Raleigh, North Carolina and after getting to know him, he too, along with Bridget, struck me as the sort of person who would make a successful thru-hiker.

Daffy offset him a little by being more of an extrovert. He, too, was 22 and had a fiery sparkle of adventure in his eyes, tinged with a little mischief. His hair sometimes flopped over his eyes so when he tired of squinting he'd flick his head to see properly. He had a propensity to sound like an unoiled door opening when he passed wind and his favourite sentences were "Yeah, I hear yer" and "Yeah, no, oh I dunno."

Talk turned to getting to town the following morning for a re-supply and the luxury of a shower and bed. Hiawassee lay eleven miles down US-76 which the AT intersected at Dicks Creek Gap. It was the first major stop since the start and hence others were also planning to get a ride, which meant hitching could be difficult. Josh Long Hair, Daffy, Phillip and I agreed to get an early start to beat the crowds.

"We could always call the cops," Daffy suggested.

"And?" I prodded.

"Just tell them something that will make them drive up so we can get a ride with them."

"Oh, I get it," I added. "Like telling them that all cops are corrupt and they can kiss my arse? By the way there's a gun fight at Dicks Creek Gap."

He laughed. "Dang, yeah, that'll do it!"

Josh Long Hair had suggested on several occasions that he needed a trail name but rejected our proposal of Tom Petty based purely on his similar looks to the rock star. He had voiced a preference for something connected to his profession (he was a writer and journalist) and a hiker called Rollin' had suggested *Byline,* which he duly accepted. This just left Josh Short Hair, amongst others.

"Oh, we got that," Bridget chipped in. "Josh Short Hair is now Chatterbox."

Josh Short Hair wasn't exactly renowned for being the

Balancing on Blue

conversationalist. Despite this I thought that he may find Chatterbox offensive.

I cringed. "You can't call him that!"

"Well we did and he's accepted it! He likes it!"

We managed an early getaway the following morning but despite this there were about twelve hikers at Dicks Creek Gap trying to look presentable for the passing motorists, which after a week in the woods was no mean feat. I wasn't in a hurry so sat on the grass enjoying the spring sunshine and smoking a cigarette. Slowly the numbers depleted until just PJ, Phillip, Byline and I were left. I decided to do a shift with my thumb raised and a police car promptly pulled in the layby.

Great, I stick my thumb out and the first car is a cop.

It is illegal to hitch in some areas of America. Because it varied from state to state I never bothered checking and, on the few occasions I had been questioned, I just put on a heavy English accent and played the dumb tourist. I prepared myself for a brush with the authorities but was pleasantly surprised.

"Howdy! You guys need a ride?" said Georgia's finest as he squeezed himself out of the patrol car.

I looked at the others, raised my eyebrows and offered upturned palms with a cheeky grin, revelling in my own success.

"We're heading to Hiawassee if you're going that way?"

"Sure am, I'll be five minutes, just need to check on something."

He walked a little down the road to check on a road sign and returned, requesting we all jump in. We got a guided tour of the local sights on route and thanked him profusely as he dropped us off at The Budget Motel, regarded by thru-hikers as the place to stay.

I did look forward to town stops but they usually ended up as rushed and sometimes stressful affairs, mainly because there was so much to be done. By the time a day was over I was glad to get back in the woods to chill out.

The process went along the lines of firstly, obviously, get a coffee. Then find a motel, preferably with another hiker or two to share the bill. Walk for ages to the launderette and back, take a shower, eat as much breakfast as stomach will allow and walk for ages to the supermarket to re-supply. Eat snacks, discard all food packaging and decant contents to zip lock bags, eat as much lunch as stomach will allow and walk for ages to find an Internet café. Check emails and update blog, eat more snacks, take power nap, eat snacks and find out who had the beer and where they had hidden it. Take an hour to chat to roommates, go to dinner and eat as much as stomach will allow, return to motel to eat ice cream, watch some TV, eat more snacks and then go to bed.

Calorie intake is the priority. It is rarely possible on a thru-hiker diet to replace the amount of energy expended. Trail food is limited to what is the lightest to carry, with some exceptions. Some sources state that thru-hikers eat 6,000 calories day (the recommended daily intake for a male is 2,500 and a woman 2,000). Although I have never calculated my intake, I would guess it is nearer to 3,000 simply because I never actually get that hungry whilst hiking.

However, by the time I hit town, I am starving and my body demands prompt gratification. During a day in civilisation I can quite happily eat up to 8,000 calories; I am constantly hungry and fat is the fuel of choice. Meat, eggs, ice cream, crisps, milk, cheese and oils are not the healthiest of foods but I have learned to listen to what my body wants on a hike, and bad fat is its preference.

My trail diet, on the other hand, is pretty healthy whereas most hikers suffer. I always try to leave town with an avocado, perhaps a pepper and a couple of bananas. My main evening meal is usually a dried rice dinner in various flavours. Snacks, which form the main calorific intake, consist of nuts, dried fruit, oat type crunchy bars and some granola for breakfast, possibly with some dried milk and a little sugar. Protein powder packs some good muscle repair and my drink of choice, apart from coffee, is some Earl Grey tea. I am English after all.

Having finally ticked off the chore list, the Budget Motel shrank as I sped away in the back of Andy's pickup truck the following afternoon. He had seen my outstretched thumb and pulled over. Phillip, Daffy and PJ had left in the morning but I had some errands to run around town. We had agreed a rendezvous at Plum Orchard Shelter for that evening.

Few leave for the trail in the afternoon so I had it all to

myself for the four miles up a gentle 500-foot incline to the shelter. It was blissfully quiet. The hum of the traffic faded away and, enjoying my surroundings and the solitude, I took my time.

Tunnels of rhododendron bushes funnelled me through, sunlight catching the sheen of their leaves as rocks appeared randomly speckled with sage coloured lichen; they seemed out of place amongst a thousand shades of brown. It was strange being in the woods wearing light clothing as they still appeared to be in winter. The weather was still glorious and, although the sky was only just visible, again it shone blue. Birds chirped, perhaps my favourite sound of a new season, and I felt at home — not as in feeling close to England, but feeling as though the woods were where I belonged.

I do experience a deep-rooted sense of comfort when I walk through woodland, almost as though it is protecting me, and on the AT I was being well and truly spoilt. It is sometimes referred to as 'the long green tunnel'. It can be too much for some, months spent hemmed in on all sides by trees with little sunlight and no views but I revelled in it. I ran my hands along the bark as I passed; sometimes I stopped and placed my chin on the trunk to look skyward. Roots crossed the trail, worn in sections from millions of pairs of boots and all the while a sweet-smelling mustiness surrounded me.

In places young growth was splashing the ground with vibrant greens: grass, some young leaves and an occasional evergreen. Cooler air currents climbed up the Appalachians from the west giving me goose bumps and then vanished as I returned to the warmth.

Arriving at Plum Orchard, I opted to sleep in the shelter for two reasons. Firstly there was only PJ, Phillip and Daffy, along with section hikers George and Laura so it wasn't crowded and provided a good chance to experience one for the first time. Secondly, there was a note in the shelter logbook advising hikers to be aware of a Copperhead nest in the vicinity. The Copperhead is one of three venomous snakes found on the AT, the other two being various species of Rattlesnake and the Cottonmouth.

This was all the prompting I needed; I stayed near the shelter and kept a close eye on the ground in front of me when I went for a pee. Fortunately nothing slithered that night and I enjoyed a good night's sleep in my first shelter.

Another storm had been forecast the following day and I was due to spend my second night undercover at Standing Indian Shelter. I was still sleeping in my tent but if the weather was due to turn, and there was room, it made sense to sleep in a shelter. Good progress was confirmed as Daffy, Phillip and I posed for a photo at the state line between Georgia and North Carolina. We were already into our second state.

Phillip had gone ahead and I was enjoying some conversation with Daffy when we spotted a discarded bagel on the ground. We invented an imaginary scenario whereby they were in fact rare, wild animals.

We joked that these elusive creatures were naturally shy but renowned for being fiercely territorial and would attack if threatened or cornered. Daffy stopped dead in his tracks with his finger against his mouth as a signal for silence. We observed it for a good five minutes on the grass as it enjoyed a little warmth from the sun.

"I think it's the Plain White Bagel," he eventually whispered.

"How do you know?"

"Note the markings, or rather lack of them. It's the prominent breed in Georgia but there's also the Brown Bagel, no explanation needed, the Seeded Bagel with spots on its upper coat or the Spinach Bagel."

"Spinach?"

"Yeah, it's got a green tint."

Wild bagels were rarely seen but were, apparently, great eating: tasty raw, even better toasted over a camp fire and they had a natural affinity to spreads, particularly peanut butter, jam, or cottage cheese.

Sam, having hunted the Plain before, bent his knees slightly into a crouch and silently approached his prey. He somehow managed to get a mere forty feet before unleashing his trekking pole. I watched it soar in a perfect arc, like a flawless javelin throw, striking the ground directly in the Bagel's hole.

"Great Shot!" I cried.

Helpless and unable to escape, the Bagel was dispatched with a single thrust of Daffy's knife. He told me that anywhere in the main ring of the body will pierce the brain for a swift and humane kill. No gutting or skinning was necessary; every part of a Wild Bagel was edible and, hunger getting the better of us, we built a fire and toasted it right there and then with some peanut butter. I have to say it was delicious.

Standing Indian Shelter heralded my second night under a roof in a row but, again, there was good reason. The forecast storm was a sure sign that the shelter would fill quickly so in the company of PJ, Daffy and Phillip we arrived at 3 p.m. The middle of the afternoon was a little frustrating for me because it was simply too early to stop. I then had around six hours to kill before hiker midnight, as it was called, otherwise known as sleep.

I looked forward to a couple more weeks when my body would be in good shape, particularly my feet, and I would be capable of pushing out twenty or twenty-five mile days, even more. These normally meant a finish of around 6 p.m. which left an ideal space of three hours to set up camp, cook diner and update my journal. For the time being I was sticking to my no blister regime which still seemed to be working well.

An older lady called Susan had already staked a claim to one corner of the shelter, Bill showed up citing a case of flu for his recent absence, and with Eastwood as well the shelter was up to its capacity of eight hikers. Ninja and Shakespeare arrived and shared the fire with us before announcing around 8 p.m. that they were going to push on to Carter Gap shelter, some seven miles further on. Despite our best efforts at trying to convince them otherwise — due to the imminent storm, the fading light and the fact that the shelter would probably be full as well — they enjoyed the fire for a little longer but took off about 9 p.m.

Hiker midnight is whenever the sun goes down and, generally being a courteous bunch of people, thru-hikers would tend to get in their sleeping bags so others could get some sleep. Some may read by torchlight and perhaps some may stay by the fire, talking quietly.

I sat in the undercover lean-to area because I could sense the rain was imminent and wanted to experience my second, legendary, Appalachian storm. The wind had intensified, there was a damp smell to the air and, well, just that sense you get that it's going to rain. All hell broke loose about 9.30 when the skies erupted in a torrential downpour and the noise, oh my god, the *noise!*

I stood and surveyed the carnage from my haven, in awe of the deafening roar as rain tore through the trees and smashed into the ground. I would have been unable to hold a conversation with someone right next to me. Despite a fading light the wall of water obscured everything, and the trees disappeared in a silver deluge as the fire remnants hissed and spat in one last, brave effort. The wind slammed into the shelter. I looked back to see head torches flicker on and the rest of the group sat upright to experience the anger. The tin roof shuddered and cried a metallic shriek as it fought back against the elements. We all became concerned about Shakespeare and Ninja but there was nothing we could do. Eventually the cacophony subsided and we all got some sleep.

***

The 100-mile mark was heralded by a few whoops the following day as Daffy, Phillip and I made short work of the 1000-foot descent before pulling into Carter Gap shelter for a rest. It was the middle of the morning so we were a little surprised to see two hikers still wrapped in their sleeping bags. One of the lumps stirred and Shakespeare's familiar features appeared from the depths looking a little the worse for wear.

"Did you get caught in the storm?" I asked.

"We got about a mile from here when it started. We were soaked." He said, rubbing his eyes to get accustomed to the light. Ninja woke up and confirmed this, adding that they also got cold and were sleeping late because they didn't get any rest when they reached the shelter — partly due to the noise of the storm, but mainly because the shelter was full and they had to squeeze onto an uncomfortable dirt floor. They looked pretty miserable as we left them to catch up on some sleep.

Becoming increasingly frustrated with fifteen-mile days and finishing in the middle of the afternoon, I was eager to stretch my hiking muscles a little. Convincing Daffy and Phillip to also follow suit, we covered the twenty miles to Rock Gap Shelter

Balancing on Blue

which was located four miles from the US-64 road crossing. There we planned to get a ride to Franklin, some ten miles east for a decent meal and quick re-supply the following day.

It was April 6th, the day before Easter and as we unwound at Rock Gap a steady dribble of familiar hiker faces rolled in. Shakespeare and Ninja arrived, now dried out and joking about their damp adventure. A straw cowboy hat bobbing down the track signalled Eastwood's entrance and before long, the ambience of the shelter was transformed by laughing, conversation, steam rising from meals being cooked and also the arrival of the Easter trail angel. The local Ranger had taken it upon herself to boil enough eggs to feed an army, decorate them with bright paint, carefully place them on a cotton towel in a wicker basket and come up all the way from Franklin to feed us, as well as walking the four-odd miles from the road. She was greeted with obvious good cheer at the unexpected protein treat and chatter subsided as we stuffed eggs into our mouths with vigour and made repeated enquiries about second helpings. The net effect of our unexpected feast was that the shelter and immediate surroundings resonated rudely for a couple of hours to the tune of hikers passing wind. I was glad I was in my tent.

Phillip, Daffy, PJ and I were eager to get to Franklin quickly — not, as you might think, because of the lure of good food, coffee or perhaps even to see a little of the town, but because we needed to get back out the same day. The reason was our first *bald* (a high point clear of trees, affording great views) called Siler Bald, where we had decided to camp.

Catching a ride quickly but only to a junction outside of the town, we opted to walk the remaining two miles and pulled into the first, and most important, port of call, the Motor Co. Grill. Goose bumps had us reaching for warmer tops as we entered the air-conditioned chill and we cordoned off a large circular table in one corner. I offered an apology to the waitress for our slightly less-than-savoury aroma after a few days on trail with no shower. Most eating establishments along the AT are used to hikers and the waft of sweat, filth and general unpleasantness that follows them but she took it in her stride.

Having eaten, I left with PJ to search for an Internet facility, our stomachs groaning, and quickly realised we had both been caught off guard. After only eleven days and 114 miles, already we were becoming detached from society. Everywhere seemed alien; our wooded sanctuary was now concrete. The path was hard with traffic to our sides, not soft and shaded. This is common on trail. Experiencing the outdoors for even that amount of time, let alone several months, changes your perception of society and towns suddenly become unfamiliar.

I quickly became uptight — there was only one Internet café which was closed, people got in my way and the noise and general mayhem annoyed me. I retreated to Ingles, the supermarket, re-supplied as quickly as I could and got the hell out. It made me even more aware of my difficulties living in society and after enjoying the solitude of the woods, my problems seemed magnified.

Siler Bald, almost sensing my mood, did its best to calm me. We made short work of the 1000-foot climb from where our ride back dropped us and ignored the sign to Siler Bald shelter. The woods thinned; we stepped out into a clearing and made a short final climb through grass to the summit. We had high expectations of our first bald and Siler didn't disappoint.

The grassy dome peeked out from the woodland below us. Alone and isolated, this was our hotel for the night. An emerald desert island lost in a vast ocean of trees.

I had heard that the Appalachian balds, more common on the southern part of the trail, were originally cleared by the Cherokee or early settlers, but subsequent research makes this theory unlikely. It is argued that man may have been responsible for some, and it is accepted that isolated trees on the summits were cleared and further felling around the tree-line provided materials for fencing and pens where livestock were grazed, but the actual reason for their presence still remains a mystery. Cattle or sheep herds would be driven to the summits between early April and May, depending on the weather. In extreme years snow could still fall during this period and some herds would move back down to the relative safety of the woods and lower, warmer elevations. Even so, some animals, hot from the journey up, died from the sudden, cold exposure. Bone Valley creek, a branch of Hazel creek which drains off Siler itself, is so named after the bones of cattle that died there in the spring of

1902.

We loved the open air and wide space on Siler. We pitched our tents, played a little Frisbee and made friends with a family who were camping there for the night. We enjoyed a second hearty meal of the day as they were kind enough to share some of their food with us.

360-degree views of the land surrounded us. Gentle, round, tree cloaked hilltops stretched away to the horizon in every direction. A two-toned land of green down below ascended to the browns of the higher ground, still waiting for spring to creep up.

As dusk fell we stood and watched the sun sink and an orange sky gradually succumbed to darkness. From our perch and with no obstructions we gazed at a star-splattered canvas above us coming to life. I felt miniscule, humbled to accept my small seat in an infinite theatre. The universe was putting on the show and I was merely content to just sit, be silent and study the extravaganza.

Up above and all around me the play unfolded and the storyline began, changing by the minute. Clouds drifted past in no hurry, lighting varied, shadows stretched and, gradually, North Carolina turned silver as a rising moon chased away the remnants of reds. Subtle breezes stroked my face and the trees rustled. I stayed awake as long as I could muster the energy but eventually closed my eyes, sighed and drifted off, only to wake several times during the night to experience it all again.

Several encores didn't disappoint and although I now had a small idea of what the AT was capable of, that night was a mere prelude to the ensuing months. A canapé if you will to the feast, the prelude to the main show that had yet to unfold.

***

The Nantahala Outdoor Center, or NOC, situated on the Nantahala River itself, is a mecca for outdoor enthusiasts. It attracts hikers, bikers and those keen to learn rafting, canoeing as well as other diverse subjects such as wilderness medicine. It is a draw to AT hikers. The trail itself goes straight through the centre and what with the promise of some cheap accommodation, a decent restaurant and other amenities, it is on everyone's to do list. Dinosaur had also been kind enough to mail a package there for me to collect containing what she promised was a load of goodies.

I continued to walk with Phillip, Daffy and PJ as our pace was similar; we had also gelled well and were relaxed and loose with planning. That said, we often spent most of the day on our own, albeit a short distance apart as we settled into our own pace and rhythms. Meeting up at the end of the day we would usually camp together, discuss the day's events and make arrangements as to where the next day's destination would be. It was the perfect arrangement and just how I liked hiking: a little solitude during the day and the pleasure of some great company in the evenings.

The temperature had cooled somewhat, which wasn't unusual. It was that unpredictable no man's land between the end of winter and the beginning of spring. Couple that with the AT's changeable elevation and unsettled mountain weather, and we were constantly either adding warmer clothing or peeling off a layer. The Great Smoky Mountains — perhaps one of the best-known sections of the trail and home to Clingman's Dome which at 6643 feet was the highest point on the entire AT — was around eighty miles ahead and famed for its changing weather patterns, especially at that time of year. Once through the Smokies we hoped winter would well and truly have given up.

Spring was not the only thing blossoming; it had transpired that there was a little romance doing the same. PJ, having become used to a little affection during his brief marriage, was now suffering from a lack of it and it appeared to be hitting him hard. His testosterone levels were running riot and cracks in his celibacy, albeit not voluntary, were surfacing in frustration with a lack of female tenderness. Struggling to deal with his rampant hormones he confided in me as we approached the NOC.

PJ had started to leave notes announcing his undying affection for a hiker known as Firefox in the trail registers. These were books left in the shelters, and other places where hikers left notes on anything they felt like writing. They also made great communication tools and messages often reliably worked their way back to the intended recipient.

I never did read any of PJ's remarks and he was a little shy about revealing his comments. Despite them being public and the ease of reading his notes, he often only revealed he had left Firefox a message the day after so his declarations of love were all behind us.

Conversely, remarks and rumours also found their way back up the trail and when it transpired that Firefox had no intention of catching PJ, or indeed pursuing any romantic liaisons, he spent a day in a slight love depression but quickly moved on.

I had never thought to ask how Firefox had earned her trail name, and subsequently never did. I assumed it was connected to the Web browser and her ginger hair. After all, Google Chrome, Safari or Internet Explorer didn't have quite the same ring about it.

Trail romance isn't unusual and, indeed, some hikers who meet on the trail go on to get married and start families. If you're single, however, being out in the woods for months on end naturally can become a little frustrating. My sex drive could never be described as exactly raging. Sexual abstinence was not something that really bothered me so I just dealt with it. In fact, I did my best to steer clear of romantic liaisons, or a little fun, because of the complications that could arise in the aftermath of such encounters.

A little harmless trail fun between two consenting individuals quite often turns sour post encounter when one subsequently demands more than the other is prepared to give. Intimate misunderstandings, as in real life, create confusion whereby one individual is under the impression that a quick foray into the bushes, or testing the overnight condensation capabilities of their tent interiors, is mistaken by the other as the beginning of a relationship.

Arguments quite often ensue and accusations of being used, betrayals of trust or worse are levied. The situation rapidly turns sour and one of the party may storm off, suddenly increasing their mileage and speed to escape the situation.

For many the appeal of trail sex is tempered by the thought of what happens to the body after a few weeks on trail. The most off-putting aspect is bodily deterioration. Many male hikers complain that the sweet-smelling females they encountered at the start were now sporting hairy legs and armpits. On the flip side of the coin, the ladies struggled with guys who looked well-groomed and clean-shaven on Springer Mountain, but now had lips that had vanished from sight behind an unkempt beard harbouring various food debris. Bodily odour from both sexes and soiled clothing didn't exactly grease the wheels of romance either.

***

We camped at Cold Spring Shelter, leaving a brief twelve miles to the NOC the following morning. This became common practice the day before a zero or a *nero* (a nero is a day where little hiking is done), because it meant we could get into town early. Arrive in the evening and most motels state you have to vacate before 11 a.m., leaving little time to run the errands demanded. Arrive in the middle of the day however, and full use of the room could be utilised for most of the day.

Phillip disappeared behind some bushes and busied himself with erecting his tent, sounding somewhat like a burrowing creature as he cleared away the leaves. Daffy was sitting down scraping the dirt out of his toenails and PJ was trying to decide whether to sleep in the shelter or pitch his tent.

Phillip's tent wasn't in fact a tent at all — it was a poncho that could be erected by means of a trekking pole into something resembling a tent. True to his lightweight philosophy, this piece of gear not only doubled as rain wear and shelter meaning he saved weight by not carrying both, but it weighed around the same as a pair of socks.

The only problem was that one side was open to the elements so critters and mosquitos had free access, not so much a problem during the early stages of the hike as our blood-sucking friends didn't really wake up until the weather warmed. What it did mean was the rain could work its way in if Phillip gauged the wind direction incorrectly, or if it changed. We had been lucky with the rain so far but I remember talking to him at our previous camp at Lance Creek when a little rain had started to fall in prelude to the storm. Phillip had to gradually wiggle his way to the back of his shelter as the rain made inroads under the tarp until he was wedged somewhere in the depths at the rear, desperately trying to keep dry. Not surprisingly the conversation had centred on a new shelter, possibly a hammock so he could look forward to a decent night's rest.

***

The trail plummeted sharply from Cold Spring shelter and, despite a little 1000 foot ascent from Tellico Gap up to Wesser Bald, it was a knee-jarring 4200 feet drop all the way down to the NOC. With a mile to go we passed the A. Rufus Morgan shelter and spilled out onto the US-19 just in time for lunch at The River's End Restaurant.

Steep descents on the approach to towns were common on the AT, and indeed other trails. Because of the inhospitable climate in the mountains, the lower elevations were deemed more friendly and, especially during the early settler migration stretching west in the States, most towns sprang up around these locations, often known in America as 'gaps'. More often than not they were in the proximity of rivers to supply water. Roads and train lines could be constructed taking advantage of the kinder terrain.

Phillip, Daffy, PJ and I managed to rent one of the cabins for a night. The rate was very reasonable and, as usual, split between the four of us it proved even cheaper. I sat on my bed eagerly ripping open Dinosaur's care package which, being a thru-hiker herself, contained a well thought-out array of goodies such as sachets of electrolyte drink mixes, necessary to replace the salts and minerals lost during sweating, some sweet treats and a very welcome addition of some Earl Grey, luring me into making a quick brew.

We only managed a few chores in the afternoon so agreed a zero in the morning made sense. I watched a brown swirl of water disappear down the sink and shower as I washed both my clothes and myself. I updated my journal and secured a few supplies from the sparsely-stocked store to see me through to Fontana and the guys occupied themselves with similar tasks.

An alarming number of tourists disembarked from the morning train and suddenly the NOC was brimming with camera-laden, sunburnt day trippers who — from their appearance at least — had no intention of even getting in a boat, let alone learn the relative merits of healing with wild plants. I did what I could to scare them off by picking my nose, coughing loudly and plucking imaginary fleas from my beard to eat.

There was no computer to use at the NOC so I spent some time wandering around aimlessly waving my phone about trying to locate a decent Wi-Fi signal. I managed to order a power pack which would allow me to recharge my phone on trail, a poncho and a Sawyer water filter. The poncho also doubled as a groundsheet for my tent, saving me some weight as I could also send my rain jacket back home.

Phillip and Daffy set off at 6.15 a.m. but after giving into temptation for a decent breakfast I started making inroads into the 3000-foot climb to Cheoah Bald which seemed surprisingly easy.

Having gained a respectable altitude on the climb up to Cheoah Bald, as usual the AT rewarded me by promptly losing it all on a 2000-foot descent to Stecoah Gap. It was like being handed a bag of sweets which was then promptly snatched back again before you could take one. This was to become standard practice on the AT, and the constant dipping and diving caused frustration for some.

There were a few hikers enjoying some simple, but welcome, trail magic at Stecoah Gap where a cooler had been left stocked with cold drinks. As I sat down with a Coke, a truck pulled up with Eastwood yelping for joy in the back as he emerged clutching a triple cheeseburger and onion rings from a diner a few miles down the road.

Eastwood made me laugh. Even his name made me think of cowboys and what with a deep southern drawl and his cowboy hat, the image was almost complete. All that was missing was a couple of gun holsters and a horse, and every time I saw him I half expected a procession of wagons and early settlers to arrive behind. I never saw him down or unhappy; he always seemed to be smiling, cracking a joke or two and lifting the spirits of those he was in the company of. He was also tremendously thoughtful, especially with food. If eating, or preparing food, I lost count of the times he offered me a share and this was no exception as he wandered over stuffing his burger on one corner of his mouth and his outstretched arm clutching his onion rings in the other offering me a couple.

"Got a quick ride, Fozzie," he said, waving his burger in circles and struggling to speak as his triple cheeseburger took up most of the room in his mouth. "Great diner just down the way there, couldn't resist a burger. Here, have an onion ring," he offered as we hiked up to Brown Fork Gap Shelter.

Fontana Dam and the small store lay a few miles ahead and marked the start of the stretch which went up into the Smoky Mountains. I was relishing the prospect. One of the highest sections of the AT and famed for its scenery, abundance of shelters and fantastic reputation, I had heard much about it during my research.

Despite the chilly night at Brown Fork Gap Shelter, spring was slowly making inroads and the weather had been great up to that point. I had not experienced the famous Appalachian rains I had been expecting, except for a couple of nights, so if anything I was looking forward to warmer climes. Perhaps I had become a little complacent towards the elements.

Little did any of us know that the weather, and Mother Nature, had other ideas in store.

Chapter 5

The Smokies

April 12th to April 23rd
Mile 153 to 309

Most Americans I meet on my travels admit, when they discover I am English, to being a little jealous of our European history and wished their country boasted a similar heritage. They mostly refer to our visual architecture in Great Britain and Europe, the old castles, cathedrals and other such examples — even further back to periods thousands of years ago have left us wonderful reminders such as Stonehenge.

However, I would have to disagree with them because America does have its own, enviable history. Visually perhaps we are more spoilt for choice but indigenous people lived in the US for thousands of years before the first European settlers arrived. They may not have left much evidence but they have made their mark in the history books. It wasn't until Christopher Columbus's arrival in 1492 and his subsequent trips that buildings started to materialise which still serve as a reminder now.

Columbus's claim to be the first European to land in the US is debatable. Research and theories now suggest the Vikings may well have been before him. Bjarni Herjólfsson, a Viking sailor blown off course on a voyage to Greenland around 985 could have been the first to sight America, although it is thought

Balancing on Blue

he didn't land but headed to Greenland when the winds allowed him to do so.

Herjólfsson described his trip to Lief Ericson who set off around the year 1000 to see for himself. He did land on American soil and is thought to be the first European, some 500 years before Columbus to do so. Spending the winter of that year as well as 1001 and 1002, he then returned to Greenland. Several more forays ensued until he attempted to establish the first settlement in 1009. Accompanied by around 200 men, women and livestock, initially amenable relations with the Native Americans broke down and they were driven back out of America.

In 1960 a site now known as L'Anse aux Meadows in the northern tip of Newfoundland was discovered. It has been suggested that this site may have been Ericson's first settlement. It shares similarities to Viking sites found in Greenland, Iceland and remains the only non-indigenous settlement in America. Of course there are more, we just haven't discovered them yet.

Despite North America having a lack of ancient architecture compared to the rest of the world, they are fiercely proud of what they do have. The AT does have a wonderful sense of history behind it and passes through many historical sites especially those associated with the Civil War of 1861 to 1865. Harpers Ferry, considered the half-way point of the trail is a classic example, having some poignant old buildings and reminders of the war.

The Smoky Mountains are home to some seventy-eight structures within the park, remnants of bygone Appalachian communities. Even out in the middle of the woods, miles from anywhere, I passed old stonework — perhaps a ruined building or wall that once served as a livestock enclosure. Many places have historical associations and their names have wonderful stories behind them, hinting at an even greater sense of mystery, interest and curiosity. Much has long since gone but these names serve as a lasting reminder that rouses the curiosity.

I have mentioned Slaughter Creek which is so named after a battle between the Cherokee and Creek Indians during the late 1600s. Near to Slaughter Creek is Blood Mountain which some say is named after a bloody battle between the same two Indian tribes; others say it is the red-coloured lichen growing near the summit that is responsible.

Recent history has also left its mark on place names. Charlie Connor who, along with his friend Horace Kephart, were out hiking when they rested on a rocky outcrop then known as Fodderstack. Connor, upon removing one of his boots discovered he had a bunion which shared similarities to the shape of the rock. Kephart declared he was going to get the place on a government map and subsequently did. It is now known as Charlie's Bunion.

Lost Spectacles Gap, approaching the 700-mile mark in Virginia, is named after Tom Campbell, a member of the Roanoke Appalachian Trail Club who misplaced his glasses there on a work hike.

The recent past also served as a reminder. I was following the writers that had trodden the path I was now taking: Earl Shaffer, David Brill and David AWOL Miller to name just a few. I wondered if, in a hundred, or maybe a thousand years' time that these inspirations would be remembered, preserved for eternity as a name associated to a part of the trail.

These legends had all thru-hiked here and I had devoured their words in gusto as preparation for my hike, and years before when I had first heard of the AT.

All the mental pictures they had given me — their thoughts, observations and feelings that were up until then, just images — were now unfolding. Now I was sharing their experiences, thinking the same thoughts, seeing what they had observed and feeling what they had felt.

I knew now what Miller meant when he described how his calves became caked in dirt because his boots brushed against them. When Shaffer observed how the rain rolled in, how the mist was dense and muggy in the low spots but shifted and swirled further up, I now saw in front of me. The emotions that Brill had struggled with when saying farewell to his injured friend, Victor, who left the trail, I was also to share.

Even my friends who I had met on the Pacific Crest Trail two years earlier also inspired me. Dinosaur, Pockets, Grey Fox, Texas Walker Ranger, Swiss Miss and more had all shared their AT memories, offering me guidance and painting their own

Balancing on Blue

pictures.

As I passed certain points on the trail, I, too, was to feel what they had. Like the ruined homestead where Pockets had collected water from a well. He had expressed to me his unease with the place, almost a fear that although he was alone there; a bad presence lurked. I was also to feel it.

When Swiss Miss described the freezing rain, that intolerable point just before it turns to snow and soaks through your jacket to the very core, my body had also experienced.

Or the delight that Grey Fox had revelled in when he described how he had crested a hill in Maine and finally seen Katahdin for the very first time.

How Dinosaur told me that I should take the time out to contribute to some trail maintenance, and imparting in detail the planning and physical strength it takes for two people just to move a boulder two feet I would soon be able to relate to.

I held onto moments like those, passed on by my friends and tales from many years ago. They pulled me onwards, the anticipation building the nearer I got, almost to the point that sometimes I screamed for them to arrive so I could finally see, or feel, what others had.

All the history, stories, legends and myths, all the way back to Lief Ericson and up to haunted homesteads were nestled in the back of my mind. The little nooks, crannies and crevices that filed those thoughts away, some place safe where one day I would unlock them were now, piece by piece, being opened.

And what of my memories? I viewed the trail in three perspectives: the past, present and future. The past was gone, from Springer Mountain to a point a fraction of a second behind me where I had taken my last step. The present I observed as I watched my foot fall on the precise part of the trail between those two roots that I had hoped it would. And the future was the next step, visible but unknown, all the way up to Mt Katahdin.

As I walked, my memories were being filed away. Some would be more vivid than others, some I would look back on with happiness, others with sadness. They would remain with me for the rest of my life for me to share with others. As Grey Fox had shared his vision of Katahdin, as Shaffer had observed that fog, I would also reminisce and pass on. I hoped that my passion, shared with others, would spur them to come and walk in these woods and up these mountains.

And what of my words? As you read them, what do you picture? I hope you take them, tuck them away and at some point in your future you place your foot in that same spot between those roots on your journey to Katahdin.

***

I hovered along the trail from Brown Fork Gap Shelter at about 3800 feet, the trail swapping constantly from the chilly west side where the sun had yet to make any inroads and spots of ice mirrored the trail, over to the east where it was noticeably warmer as sunlight found a way through the trees. It had been a cold night and I had slept wearing most of my clothing. My down bag wasn't performing and it wasn't until closer inspection revealed that most of the down had migrated to the bottom of the bag that I spent a good hour, on Daffy's advice, impatiently trying to ease the insulation back to the top. The fact I had run out of coffee hadn't helped until Eastwood jump-started me by brewing and handing me a mug of his.

I topped up with water at Cody Gap, sped up the 800 feet from Cable Gap shelter and let gravity ease me down the 2000 foot descent to bring me out on the NC28 road crossing. My data book advised that this was the place to get the required permit for the Smoky Mountains ahead which I duly did and just over a mile later I pulled into the Fontana Dam shelter, affectionately known to hikers as the Fontana Hilton.

With an impressive capacity of twenty, plus nearby toilets and a shower, the Hilton earned its reputation from the relative luxury and amenities it afforded to us hikers. It was, however, brimming — and unable to decide whether to stay there or not with the crowds, I spent another hour continuing to fluff up my sleeping bag before hunger got the better of me. I caught a ride to the Fontana general store a couple of miles up the road to stock up with food for the Smoky Mountains. The Pit Stop restaurant dished me up a generous portion of nachos before I managed to get another ride back to the Hilton.

Even more hikers had arrived, and beating a hasty retreat, I

Balancing on Blue

took a quick shower before bumping into Phillip who shared similar concerns about the full shelter. He had performed a quick scout of the area and found a small island just opposite the dam which he showed me. It looked perfect for a little stealth camping, as we called it, so suffering from slightly wet shoes crossing the few feet over, we settled down to sleep.

The Smoky Mountains, or Smokies as they are known, are one of the most renowned and revered sections of the AT. So named after the natural fog that hangs over the range which commands views of the Tennessee and North Carolina border, they are also home to the highest point of the entire trail, Clingmans Dome at 6643 feet. Designated a UNESCO World Heritage Site, they are home to 187,000 acres of old growth forest and, somewhat worryingly, the densest black bear population in eastern America. I had been told by several hikers that my chances of seeing a bear were far greater in the Smokies than any other part of the trail.

I left with this firmly on my mind, unable to decide whether it was a positive statistic or not. Eager to get up there and experience it all, I made a good start at 7 a.m., albeit an hour after Phillip who was becoming fond of his early departures.

The trail joined the road over Fontana Dam itself which sits at an elevation of 1864 feet and shortly after, I began to climb into the Smokies. Despite the usual up and downs of the trail in between, the climb carries on pretty much all uphill to Clingmans Dome which means an AT hiker has a 4779 feet ascent stretching out over thirty-three miles. This is the literal difference between the two points, when the dips and dives are taken into account; you can easily throw in a few more thousand feet. Further progress was confirmed as I crossed over into my third State, Tennessee from North Carolina at mile 174.

Despite gaining height and cooling, the Smokies were alive with the new season. Flowers splashed colour everywhere. Sarvis trees had blossomed and were cloaked in tiny, white flowers. When I saw my first one I mistook it for a layering of snow. The ever reliable rhododendron bushes were yet to flower but their buds appeared to be at bursting point, poised to unleash their purple, white or pink blooms in a few weeks' time. Laurel bushes were also eager to please, the buds firm to the touch and seemingly about to explode.

I reached a small break in the trees and peered back at the Fontana Reservoir, already a tiny speck lost in the green furrows and folds of its surroundings. Although this stretch of trail was still covered in trees, they appeared less dense, almost thinned out. Regular gaps appeared offering far reaching views. Seemingly the AT was compensating me for the thick forest I had experienced up to that point.

I was feeling at ease with my world and starting to become accustomed to the AT, its whims, moods and habits. The trail rarely routed around a mountain, or cut along the side, but took a far more direct approach usually straight up and over. A flat, three-mile section would take most hikers an hour to complete. Straining up and down the various peaks often meant it took two hours to do that distance. My natural hiking speed is between three and three and a half miles an hour, but after a few days on the AT it was hovering around two to two and a half. I had been warned not to get complacent by other hikers who had already completed the trail. They advised that just because I had a few thousand miles under my belt, and the PCT, not to consider this trail as easy bagging. I was beginning to understand what they meant.

Statistics for the total amount of elevation gained on the AT are not definitive and vary from source to source but it is considered to be around 464,500 feet. To provide a comparison, Ben Nevis, the highest mountain in Britain and no mean feat to summit, is 4409 feet which means you'd have to summit Nevis just over 105 times to achieve the same elevation gain. If you thought Everest a tough prospect, by the time an AT thru-hiker finished their mission they would have climbed Everest sixteen times. Some sources even claim that the altitude gain on the AT is greater than the Continental Divide Trail.

Many hikers, after the initial romance of the trail has subsided, become frustrated by the AT, especially the pointless ups and downs (known as *puds*). I often joked that when the AT was originally constructed, they chose the hardest route possible. In the vast majority of cases, the trail would always climb up and over an obstacle instead of skirting around it. It annoyed me sometimes, usually at the end of a long day with just a couple of miles to camp when I'd notice the elevation graph showing a 1000 foot climb. In the main it didn't bother me, I had done my research and knew, roughly, what to expect.

The AT is shorter than the PCT by around 462 miles. However, even after just a couple of weeks in arguably one of the less demanding sections, physically at least, I already considered the AT tougher.

***

"Do you snore?" enquired Bridget as she squeezed into the gap between PJ and I in Spence Field shelter. Heavy rain was expected so it was full.

"Sometimes, yes. But only when I sleep on my back. On the occasions I have slept with someone else ..." She interrupted me with a mild glare.

"Sorry, *near* to someone else, then I make sure I sleep on my side."

When I accused her of snoring in the morning, an accusation she firmly denied, I felt rather smug when both PJ and Beacon backed me up.

Phillip had run out of food so was making the best of a tortilla with no filling for breakfast. I had food but had run out of alcohol for my stove. Dreading the thought of starting the day with no coffee, everyone had kindly chipped in with a few dribbles each after seeing my onset of mild panic. Eric informed me his trail name was now Bowser, and no one had seen Daffy for a few days although Phillip informed us that he was a few days behind walking with another group.

"Daffy likes to change those he socialises with sometimes," he explained.

Misjudging a re-supply and running out of food or fuel was common. The great thing about hiking the AT and the amount of hikers on trail meant that it never proved a problem and, in fact, was a wonderful lesson in camaraderie. If someone had run out of oats for breakfast, was short of a main meal, didn't have any sugar or was despondently shaking their gas canister with a concerned look, then someone would always offer to help. Without asking, we could always count on someone to offer an item from their supplies to make up the deficit. In true outdoor spirit, something was usually offered in return, but often declined because we knew that at some point, we would be in the same situation and the karma would return full circle.

***

After a sixteen-mile uphill slog I arrived at Clingmans Dome and sat with PJ, Phillip and Bowser. I didn't really know what to expect from the highest point on the trail except a decent view but I was sadly disappointed. As is common with our infatuation towards high places, some idiot had deemed it necessary to celebrate the location by cutting a swathe through the trees, laying down a road and building what I can honestly say was the ugliest structure I had ever witnessed — not just on a trail, but anywhere, period.

The tower on top of Clingmans Dome, built in 1959, was at the time probably a much-praised example of modern architecture. Unfortunately, as with most of these eyesores, it now resembled something like a concrete, spiral car ramp often found by the side of multi-storey car parks. Half a mile down the road, hordes of tourists on their annual vacation would park their cars, kit themselves out with their Walmart hiking accessories and plod, out of breath, up to this monstrosity to lay claim to standing on top of the highest point in Tennessee.

Kids wailed, adults complained that there wasn't a coke machine or a McDonald's, others posed for photos whilst the rest of the area was littered with out of breath, dehydrated holidaymakers. Some even asked us to take photos of them so I quickly resorted to my habit of picking imaginary items of debris from my beard and eating them whilst Phillip and PJ removed their shoes and socks to act as a deterrent. We sat at the base of the tower resting and at one point a Japanese man walked cautiously over to me as if I were some sort of wild animal who had just emerged from the woods after a few weeks. Actually his observation bore some credit. He hesitantly handed me his camera.

"You take picture please?"

I finished wiping my nose on my left sock and took his

Balancing on Blue

Nikon, whilst he walked to the base of the tower. This I just found puzzling and hilarious, although with a little restraint I remained relatively polite. Instead of climbing up the spiral walkway to the top of the tower where the view was, he merely stood at the bottom and requested I include the tower in the shot.

"Why would you walk up here and not actually go to the top of the tower?" I asked Phillip. "And, why the hell would you want to include that hideous thing in the photo? What the fuck?"

Phillip, PJ and Bowser looked as puzzled as I was and just shrugged their shoulders.

We relaxed for an hour until early evening and the last of the mob had disappeared down to the car park. Phillip proposed that it would be a great idea to actually sleep at the top of the tower which didn't exactly excite anyone's wild camping instincts but as it was a pretty original idea, and something we could potentially get into trouble for, I was all for it. It was under cover after all.

Clingmans afforded a vast view from the top of the tower and we spent a good hour taking it all in. The wind started to whip up just before sunset and the temperature dropped alarmingly. We were high up and exposed so had expected a chilly night, although not as windy. A three feet high wall circled the observation platform which provided a wind break as we hunkered up next to it. I made a brief effort to move more down insulation to the top of my bag but became so cold that, eventually, life preservation instincts got the better of me and I retrieved every item of clothing out of my bag and pulled it on. I abandoned my sleeping bag revival once more but Phillip came up with the obvious, interim solution.

"Fozzie, turn it over!"

***

Newfound Gap, where the AT intersects US-41 is a renowned spot for trail magic. A large parking area provided ample space for vehicles coming up from Gatlinburg, a large town fifteen miles down the road, to park and set up welcome refuelling spots for hikers, as well as rides into town.

To add to my sleeping bag woes, my air mattress had sprung

a leak. At 3.30 a.m. on Clingmans Dome, I was roused by a weak hissing sound somewhere near my right ear and shortly after, my comfortable perch was reduced to an airless strip of plastic. Not only that, the air chambers inside had deteriorated and I was forced to get a ride into Gatlinburg to buy a replacement as well as a food re-supply.

The AT lifts a hiker's expectations of their world. We become used to seeing magnificent views, towering mountains and serene surroundings. When we have to leave the trail for town, our hopes continue as we dream of old, quiet, historical settlements rich in history where we can re-supply and take it all in over a civilized meal.

As if I had written these wishes down, Gatlinburg glanced momentarily at them, smirked rudely and scrunched them into a tight ball. Tossing them onto the ground, and for good measure, it jumped up and down on them and then set them alight.

I didn't know what to expect of the place but as soon as I arrived, I made plans to run my errands as quick as possible and make for a quick escape. It was seething with holidaymakers and Gatlinburg was well set up to cater for them. Tacky shops lined the main street, selling everything from overpriced T-shirts to ice cream. Spotless cars and motorbikes cruised up and down just for show in between long periods of gridlock, whilst I became frustrated trying to weave a route along the crowded sidewalk. The supermarket was way out of town so I had to settle for the meagre supplies offered by Walgreens — which meant no fresh food, a limited display of boxed, undesirable stock such as Pop Tarts and an uninspiring selection of main meals. The only saving grace was the NOC store which was well-stocked and I managed to buy a respectable brand of sleeping mattress. The NOC shuttle even took us back to Newfound Gap where I quickly disembarked and ran for the cover and solitude of the woods.

I passed Bowser quickly and although he tried to stick with me, my momentum, need to escape civilization and a desire to get to Pecks Corner Shelter before sunset meant he gave up after twenty minutes. The fact that I covered the eleven miles to the shelter in less than three hours I put down to the psychological damage that Gatlinburg had inflicted on me. Pecks Corner shelter was busy and as usual I pitched my tent before chatting to Phillip and Fonsworth, who was taking his choice of a trail name very seriously. He explained his intention to think of an extended title which he hoped would result in a somewhat posh sounding air.

"You could put a Horatio in there," I suggested. "Nice ring to it."

"I like it, Fozzie."

"By the way, did you know, back in England, that you can buy a Lordship title?"

"You can?"

"Yeah. Don't quote me on it but I'm sure I read it somewhere. Pay whatever organisation is responsible a few bucks and you can legally start your name with Lord."

The ball was rolling and Fonsworth, subject to further elaborations, was now Lord Horatio Fonsworth.

My main source of food for the next few days consisted of oats, which had been the only edible option available at Walgreens. As I forced down the apricot variety over breakfast, in between re-packing, I opened my pack to see a mouse curled up at the top. He yawned, appeared even to rub his eyes and nonchalantly climbed out to disappear under the shelter.

The trail bobbled along around 5500 feet for a few miles and I pulled into Tri-Corner Knob Shelter for lunch. Bemoaning my lack of dinner supplies, Walking Man and his nephew, Ninja Turtle, handed me a generous bag of homemade dried chicken and vegetable casserole. Along with two packs of Beef Ramen Noodles that someone had left in the shelter, my stomach quit complaining at the prospect of a good feast that evening.

Cosby Knob Shelter was also crowded and despite my chilly night at Clingmans Dome, I hoped the lookout tower on top of Mt Cammerer would provide more sheltered accommodation. Situated half a mile off the AT, it had been built in 1937 by The Civilian Conservation Corps and was manned by a fire ranger up until the 1960s.

I caught up with Phillip and PJ and the tower proved to be a real gem. Not only did it have a far more luxurious wooden floor, even a roof, but it was fully enclosed on all sides and sported several windows. It is amazing how trail life simplifies our expectations of what makes us content. Forget whining that your smartphone is out of date, that your car is too old or the coffee you just bought is too weak, we were over the moon at the simple prospect of having somewhere to sleep with a roof, walls and windows.

Mary Poppins, so named because of his umbrella, sprung through the door shortly after and introduced himself, further helping bulk out my food supplies by handing me half an avocado. I offered a pack of Beef Ramen as an incentive for further bartering but not surprisingly, he declined.

The preference for shelters and other under cover buildings was becoming the norm during this stretch because of constant bad news on the weather front. We had somehow managed to miss the rain that had been forecast during the past few days, save an occasional shower — but on pulling into Standing Bear Hostel it finally caught us up.

The place was busy, understandably, as over the course of the day the sound of rain on the roof became louder until that corner of the Appalachian hills sat under a constant, heavy deluge. We were thankful for the shelter.

I decided a little trail magic of my own was called for at breakfast. The rain was still downing spirits so I figured a good old cooked breakfast would go down well with Phillip, Daffy and PJ. Taking hiker appetites into consideration, I calculated twenty-four eggs would suffice for the four of us plus an alarmingly high stack of bacon. No sooner than it had hit the plates, it was devoured with much lip smacking, finger licking and approving nods.

The rain was still falling mercilessly the following morning. The usual train of thought is to sit out inclement weather because it's obvious that it will never last that long. Phillip and I stared out at our soaked environment from the seclusion of an overhanging roof and discussed one of two options: either go or stay. The problem with waiting is that it could go on for days and those are then days wasted being stationary.

It's not particularly pleasant starting out in the rain but waterproof gear is pretty efficient these days and once you're warmed up it's actually quite a novelty. I looked at Phillip; he looked at me. We shrugged our shoulders, hoisted our packs and

Balancing on Blue

I popped the umbrella up.

The steep climb from Standing Bear Hostel wasn't helped by a slick surface coated with wet leaves, which stuck in several layers to the points of our trekking poles. We brushed past wet bushes and contorted our bodies around poison ivy.

We warmed on the five-mile, 2500-foot climb to pop out of the woods onto the lovely sounding Snowbird Mountain, and then bounced along the top to Max Patch Bald. Up there I felt like I was in my home county of Sussex. It looked just like the downland near where I grew up, played as a kid and still go now. A low hanging cloud added to the similarity and occasionally a weak, yellow sun tried in vain to break through making us squint. The rain stopped but our feet remained wet as they brushed through the wet grass.

Continuing to Roaring Fork shelter, I counted twelve hikers inside and another five brushing away leaves to make space underneath. Phillip had secured a new hammock and was extolling its virtues as I tried in vain, again, to fit my tent onto one of the designated tent areas. I eventually crawled in, pulled down a rain flap at the front for use in bad weather and commenced a gear drying operation. When I tried to exit I discovered I couldn't. The release clip for the beak was by the tent peg, beyond my reach. It was like being locked out the house, except I was stuck in a tent.

I peered under the flap and saw Bridget strolling past through the trees.

"Bridget! Help!"

She stopped and cocked one ear, looking around aimlessly trying to fathom out who was calling her.

"Over here!" I implored.

"Wassup? What are you doing?" she said whilst crouching down and trying to peer under.

"Look, don't take the piss but I can't get out. I'm stuck."

She started giggling and after pausing for what I thought was a few seconds more than necessary, just for a little self-satisfaction, she eventually released the small karabiner and I was a free man.

The rain lashed down all night and constantly smacked on the tent. Unable to sleep I rose and was gone by 6 a.m. Phillip caught me mid-morning as we summited Bluff Mountain and then sped down the 3500 feet to emerge from the woods at Hot Springs. As usual there were a few errands to run in town but none were as important as the Smoky Mountain Diner, conveniently one of the first stops. We ate like bears, tearing at steaks like wild animals between forkfuls of vegetables and gravy, our plates wiped clean with bread rolls.

We secured a cabin at The Hot Springs Resort and Spa, taking one which slept four in anticipation of Daffy and PJ arriving, which they duly did. The bench outside of the laundrette seemed a good place to watch the world go by as my clothes dried.

"Are you Fozzie?"

I looked up to see a guy around my age (but with a far superior beard) and a young girl who I took to be his daughter.

"Yes, that's me?"

"I'm Balls; this is my daughter, Sunshine. I bought your PCT book."

"Ah, so you're the one!" I replied, smiling. "Thank you very much. You two are going for the Triple Crown right?"

"Sure are, it's going well."

Sunshine peered round her Dad and said hi, all freckles, red hair and a huge smile. Even at the end of the day she appeared to have enough energy to walk further. I relayed the conversation to PJ later to which he replied that he had bumped into them the day before and heard her say to her dad: "Come on dad, let's do a twenty-five!"

We spent a day in Hot Springs. I liked the place. It was a compact town with all the amenities lined up along the main street. Red brick buildings flanked the railway line and it was a short walk from our cabin in the woods squeezed between Spring Creek and the imposing French Broad River. The trees had sprung to life down from the mountains in a vibrant chartreuse. The calmer waters by the river bank, sheltered by half-immersed boulders soothed my tired feet as I dipped them and I spent time reading, occasionally swapping boulders for those bathed in the early spring sunshine. Children screamed as they played by the campsite and the occasional waft of meat grilling on barbecues made my mouth water.

I collected my new water filter, poncho and power pack from the post office then ventured into the library to take advantage of the free Wi-Fi and to update my blog. Krista was doing the same and we chatted briefly about our progress.

She was due to travel to Japan for work so only had a few weeks to enjoy the AT. Her mother had since returned home as she was only joining her daughter for a week. Krista was the focus of most of the male hikers' attentions. She was attractive and initially reserved, because of the attention she was receiving I think, but after we had spoken a few times she opened up somewhat. She explained that her new trail name, Pork Chop, had come about because she had recently packed out an impressive supply of meat to the trail. She dealt with the male attention she was receiving nonchalantly, often ignoring it. She smiled as she spoke, slightly embarrassed and she was very endearing. I joked that as she hiked with a blithe disregard for the guys, most of them were left in her wake in varying states of love-struck despair, littering the trail. Frankly, I just thought she was a goddess.

The community centre was packed that evening after news that an AYCE (all you can eat) was up for grabs. Tables lined the room, and dishes of pasta, garlic bread and salads disappeared quicker than the staff could replace them. Chatter was minimal — hikers were occupied with fuelling up and made several visits to satiate their appetites.

I bumped into Bridget who declared she had given herself a trail name and was now to be referred to as 'Lady Forward'.

"How did that come about?" I asked, confused and eager for an explanation.

"Well, it's the name of the statue on top of the capitol building in Madison. The motto of Wisconsin is forward, for whatever reason and as I'm a lady who's planned on moving forward for 2000 miles, it seemed appropriate. And, there is the added bonus of fending off any unsavoury names that could be given to me by, say, a creepy Englishman."

"Ouch. It's nowhere near as good as Pink Bits," I retorted.

PJ was immersed in his guidebook in between shovelling pasta into his mouth.

"We've done 274 miles," he announced with little emotion,

easing an escaped segment of pasta back into his mouth. I couldn't tell if he was impressed or disappointed.

"It's progress, mate," I offered. "Just don't look at the bigger picture too much."

We were often reminded of the bigger picture by a renowned map of the AT, produced by The Appalachian Trail Conservancy. As it follows the trail northward, it is, understandably, not so wide but quite long. I regularly saw it displayed in restaurants, libraries and other establishments but tried not to pay much attention to it because it was daunting. I had checked it at the Smoky Mountain diner with Phillip, who had proudly declared that we had completed just short of the width of a little finger. In other words, after three weeks on trail, we were just 12% done.

I had learnt on the PCT, and other hikes, never to look at the bigger picture because progress was slow and could wear you down psychologically. Despite doing an activity that we love, focusing on the distance covered can make a hiker a little despondent.

I take each week at a time, manageable chunks to concentrate my efforts on and when I complete that section, I give myself a pat on the back and look at the next one. Even those sections are broken down further by looking at each day and then split again into hours. Two to three hours, or six to ten miles, and then I would take a break. Do the same again, have some lunch, look at possible options for a camp and then repeat the process in the afternoon. Slowly, day by day, week by week and month by month, the bigger picture gradually reveals itself.

***

It had started raining and the temperature had also dropped. I worried about how cold it would be up at the higher elevations. Hot Springs sat at just over 1300 feet and as I left with PJ and Pink Bits — sorry, Lady Forward — it became colder as we climbed. By the time we pulled into the Spring Mountain Shelter after eleven miles, thankfully, the rain had stopped. Wet gear hung from every available space as hikers blew into cupped hands, pulled on extra layers and stomped their feet to try and warm up. Everyone had become a little complacent after the great conditions we had been blessed with and the Smokies were living up to expectations. I pitched my tent on a little section of raised ground commanding a good view of the shelter to watch the evening's events.

The Smokies continued to play a guessing game with the weather over the next few days. Dry, wet, hot, cold; we never knew what was around the corner.

Earthling was huddled in the Little Laurel shelter trying to keep warm as we arrived and Pops turned up shortly after. We all remarked on how the weather seemed to be turning for the worse and even stopping to rest was becoming difficult because all our body heat drained quickly.

PJ stopped briefly before we both left to climb the 876 feet to Big Firescald Knob before descending to our destination for the day at the Jerry Cabin shelter. The further we climbed the colder it became. The main problem was the rain which seemed undecided as to whether to remain be, or change to sleet. It soaked us, seeming to leach through our waterproofs and chilling our very cores. I couldn't feel my hands despite my gloves and straining on the incline, I just couldn't warm up.

The shelter appeared in the gloom as a fine mist engulfed us. A wisp of smoke spluttered from the chimney as a blue tarpaulin stretched across the front. I entered and as my eyes struggled to see in the darkness, I made out several hikers wrapped in sleeping bags or sat by the fire rubbing their hands. The place was full. A meagre pile of wet firewood promised little and after spending a few minutes trying to wriggle nearer the heat I retreated back outside to set up my tent in the rain.

My hands, now numb, struggled with the guy lines as I tried to push the tent pegs into a sodden soil. Forsaking anything else I quickly blew up my sleeping mat and climbed inside my sleeping bag where I lay for an hour until, slowly, my body eventually warmed up. Rain continued to hammer on the tent and I cooked a warming meal before darkness forced me to sleep.

Overnight, as the temperatures had dropped further, snow had fallen and I woke to a world of white. I peered out, coloured tents dotted the area, lightly coated with powder. I reached for my shoes which had frozen; my waterproofs were stiff with the cold and a chunk of ice slid down my water bottle as I tried to drink. I had to place my socks into my sleeping bag to defrost them. After three days without washing them, this was none to pleasant an experience.

I jumped over frozen puddles and followed footprints in the snow down the 1000 feet to Devils Fork Gap which shivered under the snow line but was, at least, dry. The sun fought a battle with the rain and every time I looked up through the canopy it was difficult to fathom whether the next few minutes would be wet or dry. I repeatedly changed my layers to keep a constant temperature.

In a matter of a few days, I had gone from the relative warmth of Hot Springs back to what seemed like midwinter. The trail fluctuated so much between different elevations that the weather was a constant puzzle. Up high was cold, down in the gaps it was bearable and anything in between was pure confusion. It started to affect me and play games with my head. Coupled with the dense woods my mood slumped and although there was little I could do about the weather, I longed for a bald where I could have some sense of space as compensation and occasionally the trail obliged.

Once in my sleeping bag at night I warmed for the first time that day. I often left the flaps of the tent open so I had wonderful views stretching to distant mountains.

The Appalachians are essentially one long, wide ridge. Because of the abundance of woods and forest, a hiker rarely actually sees the surrounding landscape, so balds, or gaps at the edge of the woods, made wonderful surprises, an escape from the sometimes claustrophobic environment of the woods. I frequently took breaks there to survey a blanket of trees stretching as far as I could see.

Often, in the fading light of early evening, those distant hills — sometimes one, more often two, three or more, peeking up from behind each other — took on varying tones of blue. Like gentle waves in shades of beryl, azure, cerulean and sapphire fading away to merge into the sky. I used to wonder if someone, somewhere out there, was also sitting down and looking back at me, wondering exactly the same thing.

Balancing on Blue

At times the mountain tops narrowed to a rocky ridge a few feet wide, where I felt as though I were balancing, edging along with my arms outstretched as a counterbalance. Occasionally, I lost touch with my feet as I focused on the trail in front, becoming mesmerised and detached, almost in another world. I forgot the ground under me and floated, gliding without any sensation, just balancing on blue.

Chapter 6

Throwing down the Gauntlet

April 24th to May 8th
Mile 309 to 523

I wear a leather strap around my neck with three silver pendants. The first is a St Christopher, the patron saint of travellers, given to me by my boss at the time in 1994 before I left on a cycling trip to Israel. I'm not a religious person but I do like to think that Christopher looks over me on my travels.

The second is a cedar tree, symbolic of the country of Lebanon. On that same cycling trip, during a harsh winter in early 1995, I stayed overnight with a family in a simple, three-roomed house in Syria. It was basic to say the least as they clearly had little money, but they gave me shelter after seeing me in town one afternoon, trying to warm up in a snowstorm. When I left, the son handed me the pendant. At first I refused because it had some value and they had already shown me enough kindness and generosity. I felt somewhat guilty accepting it but he insisted.

The third is a small Celtic cross, synonymous with Galicia, a province in North West Spain. Monica, a cook working at the Refugio Ave Fénix, in Villafranca del Beirzo, a small town on the Camino de Santiago, gave it to me after I had rested there for a few days.

I like to think of them all as my lucky charms. In twenty

Balancing on Blue

years of travelling since being given the first one, I have stayed out of trouble. I always hike with them and even if I am out for a day's walk, a week's cycle ride, or indeed a few months on trail, I do not feel safe without them.

Sometimes I touch them where they hang, halfway down my chest. I rub them between my fingers and even place them between my teeth. I wear them when I sleep and I keep them on in the shower. They are as much a part of my travels as the associated memories.

They also serve a double purpose, being a great indicator of my walking posture and rhythm. I don't like to mess much with the mechanics of my walking because I believe it is a natural process that we are born with. However, having read a few books on the subject such as *Chi Walking* and *Born to Run* , I have become curious about how we actually walk.

Both authors advocate making changes to various aspects of the body whilst hiking and running to encourage landing on the forefoot, the theory being that a lot of injuries associated with walking and running are caused by striking the ground, incorrectly, on the heel. A forward strike of the foot makes one less susceptible to injury, increases speed and means a hiker can cover more miles in a given amount of time. These advantages are not deliberate, merely an unintentional influence of making these changes

I made two main adaptations to my walking after reading, in particular, *Chi Walking* by Danny Dreyer. These were to shorten my stride and to lean forward. A shorter stride encourages a forward strike of the foot. Leaning forward, not from the waist but from above the heel (imagine a hinge at the back of each ankle), whilst keeping the body straight also promotes a forward strike.

When I first started to change the way I walked two years ago, it took a little getting used to. My body's natural reaction was to revert to how I had walked since I could first stand upright. I had to constantly remind myself to implement both changes — but slowly, with much practice, I have now reached the point where it is just about becoming natural and I don't have to think about it.

As well as watching over me, my neck pendants are a great

indicator that I am walking correctly. As I lean slightly forward, they swing away from my chest; as each trailing leg comes forward to strike the ground, the momentum of my body comes forward and these pendants hit my chest, resulting in each pendant chinking an audible reminder. As the next foot reaches forward, they swing forward and then return again.

Once I'm walking, regardless of how fast or slow, they stay in rhythm as long as my body is hinged forward and each foot strike is accompanied by a clink of silver. If I become lazy and revert to my walking style of old, I lay back somewhat, resulting in a strike nearer to the heel but more importantly, my pendants fall silent. They sound a little like loose change in your pocket when you're running for the bus and it's become a very reassuring sound.

Others carried similar lucky charms or items they felt incomplete without. Kori 'Rocket' Feener from Topsfield, MA, had a propensity to fall. In fact, she fell or rolled her ankles every single day up until the last sixty miles. She put this down to losing focus, getting lost in her head and not concentrating on what was actually on the ground in front of her. "The Trail doesn't like multitasking," she told me.

When she first saw Mt Katahdin, visible from miles away because of its sheer size, she stopped to take in the view. As she geared up to go, she noticed a hawk feather on the ground which wasn't there when she sat down. "It looked beautiful," she said. "Grey with white stripes, it was soft and something about it made me feel like I needed to hold onto it. I ended up tying it in my hair and, for the last sixty miles of the hike, I didn't trip or roll my ankle once. I still have it — it hangs in my apartment and it can be seen in my summit photo, poking out of my pony tail."

***

PJ and I emerged from the woods onto the I-26 somewhat sodden from the trees dripping on us. It was a further five miles to Bald Mountain shelter and as we looked up, moody clouds raced overhead. The Little Creek Café was three miles down the I-26 although we didn't know if it was open and Wolf Creek

Balancing on Blue

Market store was a further half mile.

As we sat by some rubbish bins contemplating our options, and our hunger, Trooper David L Buckner from the North Carolina Highway Patrol pulled up. His window slid down which gave me the opportunity to ask a question I had been dying to know the answer to for thirty minutes.

"Morning, officer," I started with. "You see that sign up there?" I gestured to my right.

"Yes?" he replied with a curious and confused expression.

"Well, what does it mean? Read it, it makes no sense does it?"

His head turned to face the sign which read 'Permitted trucks not allowed'.

I continued. "If a truck is not allowed down that road then how can it be permitted to go there? Conversely, if a truck is permitted to go down that road, how can it not be allowed?"

He scratched his head, smiled and looked at PJ who just shrugged his shoulders and offered, "He's British, I apologise."

"PJ, English mate, please," I corrected.

Trooper Buckner could not offer an explanation but it was a good way to open up a friendly conversation, and in turn, perhaps get a lift. PJ knew this was what I was gearing up for and whispered discreetly "Fozzie! You *can't* ask a cop for a ride!"

I carried on. "You don't, by any chance, know what time the Café shuts do you?"

"I do, yes. You've missed it by a few minutes."

"Damn, I'm starving. How far is the store?"

"It's about three miles. I can take you there; I'm not busy, happy to help out. I can only get one of you in the car though, it's full with gear."

I had a quick debate with PJ and we agreed I should go.

"What do you want to eat mate?" I asked.

"Chicken, Fozzie. Anything with chicken, I need chicken."

Not only did Trooper Buckner take me down to the store, he waited and gave me a lift back as well. We even discussed the relative merits of wild food foraging in the patrol car as he flicked through pages on his laptop showing me different plant species. As I left he handed me a badge with 'North Carolina

Highway Patrol' embroidered on it.

I have always had good encounters with the cops in America. I think the English accent works wonders, especially when partnered with a little ignorance about local laws. Play the dumb tourist and all sorts of avenues open up.

I do, however, have problems with those in positions of so called authority. Where it stems from I don't know. Subsequently, I am generally not too fond of the police because of some past experiences in England where they abused their authority and assumed they were above me. I didn't like being told what to do by my parents, bosses, friends or my teachers and I still struggle with it.

Immigration and customs are my worst nightmare, especially in the States although my passage through Miami airport was, for once, smooth because of a genuinely smashing officer who let me through with two months over my visa allowance when he found out that I was hiking the AT.

In the most part I find immigration run by a rude bunch of individuals who, having seen my backpack, assume I am just bumming around the country for a few months with little money. They are more often than not impatient, intolerant, ask stupid questions, don't wait for an answer and act as if they are better than me because they wear a uniform, which they falsely believe puts them in a position of power.

I do not, and never will, consider anyone to be above or below me. And correspondingly, I do not consider myself above, or below, anyone else.

Trooper Buckner was an absolute gem, wished us well and sped off. As we stood under a bridge where highway US-23 went over us it became clear that bridges made excellent shelters. The I-26 was a small country lane with few cars and the traffic noise on the busy freeway over us was dampened by the actual structure itself.

A hiker called Honey Badger arrived, also a little on the damp side and after a quick check to make sure no one was looking, we scampered up the concrete embankment and found a flat platform completely sheltered from the rain.

The only apparent hazard of bridge life was taking a pee which entailed walking sideways along the steep slope in a crouched position aiding a lower centre of gravity, to avoid slipping. This was not made any easier wearing Crocs and by the time I reached open air and commenced operations, a strong wind blew most of my bodily fluids back up my shirt and into my face. Despite this — and the occasional vehicle hissing past below us on the wet road — we slept well, no doubt relaxed at the thought of a dry night. Bridge life held much potential.

Now out of the Smoky Mountains and, except for some parts where the elevation went up to 6000 feet, we were enjoying warmer conditions down around the 3000 feet mark. I continued to walk with PJ and Phillip. Sometimes we travelled within earshot of each other, but in the main we walked alone and teamed up in the evening to camp or to share a motel room in town.

The familiar faces I had become friends with popped up and crossed my path every once in a while: Bowser, Byline, Fonsworth, Mary Poppins, Pink Bits, sorry, Lady Forward, Pops and Earthling to name a few. Daffy tinkered with his alternative socialising habit, made appearances now and again and a constant stream of new faces entered my world.

***

Despite my inability to spot wild ramps, Phillip became very excited one morning after passing the Clyde Smith shelter. We had both been preoccupied admiring the golden ragwort, whose golden yellow flowers often carpeted sections of the trail, when he stopped dead in his tracks causing me to bump into the back of him.

"Fozzie, are these ramps?"

We sniffed, prodded, stroked, observed and studied the possibilities. Slender, vibrant green leaves thinned into red stems before changing to white just before they disappeared under the soil. We pulled one out and smelt it; undeniably it was an onion. A couple of minutes searching on our phones for images and we both agreed we had found the elusive source of food. The identification was positive which was ideal, because we were bloody hungry.

Pulling out probably more than our fair share, we toiled up the steep, 2000-foot climb to summit Roan High Knob. Finding the spring and addressing the immediate problem of borderline dehydration, we gulped down water as though we hadn't drunk for days.

Peering into the depths of our respective food bags, we took stock of the culinary opportunities. I had several of my usual rice meals and Phillip produced not only a bag of sliced salami but a sachet of olive oil as well.

Before long our pots were brimming with handfuls of wild ramps as the salami sizzled and spat in the hot oil. A wonderful aroma of fried onions acted as a homing beacon for the few day hikers spread around the shelter. We handed them a few of the surplus stock and devoured our new found source of fresh, wild sustenance with gusto, licking our lips.

For a few miles after Roan High Knob the AT opens out briefly and entertains the claustrophobics. The trail twisted, turned and I bowed to its every whim, revelling in the wide, open spaces. I passed the imposing Overmountain shelter, dipped into short sections of thin woodland which opened out into vast, green, boulder speckled moors. I crossed over into Tennessee which at times looked and felt like the Yorkshire moors, Dartmoor, or the South Downs. I felt the sun on my back and ran my hands through bushes, which were now bursting with vivid green leaves, alive and thriving in the warm sunshine.

The contrast of an occasional ivory cloud against a deep, electric sky was highlighted by rounded hills intense with deep greens. It was early May and winter had been defeated, stubborn to the last but now behind us. The mornings and evenings were brighter; hikers could start their days in the light and enjoy extended, warmer evenings. Summer was looming and although every AT hiker was relishing the prospect of hotter days, little did we know at that point just what it had in store for us.

Phillip was a day ahead with PJ as I had decided to take a zero at the Mountain Harbour Hostel. Departing I was soon joined by a hiker called Nito. He had short, curly, black hair and spoke with a Latin accent that made him sound somewhat like a gangster. He made good company and we sped easily along, enjoying the flatter section between Bear Branch Road and the

Kincora Hiking Hostel at Denis Cove Road.

After leaving the Smoky Mountains the talk turned to a man called Bob Peoples. Hugely respected by hikers for the work he has done maintaining a long section of trail around where he lives at the Kincora Hiking Hostel, he is a legend in hiking circles. So much so that quotes often appear scribbled onto shelter walls in the area.

'When Bob Peoples stays in a shelter, the mice bring him *their* food.' Or, 'The bears hang Bob Peoples's food bag for him.'

Since 1988 he has logged several thousand miles of hiking just to maintain the trail and every May around a hundred past and present thru-hikers join him for a two-day intensive trail maintenance event known as 'Hardcore Kincora'. His hostel, set back from Denis Cove road, asks for a mere $5 donation which includes a bed, shower, laundry, use of the kitchen and rides into town.

Unfortunately I never got to meet Bob. I arrived late evening and he was out on a shuttle run. Byline and PJ were sitting down looking ill with upset stomachs claiming a pizza from town was responsible. Phillip was checking on a lasagne in the oven fit for five people but had plans to consume all of it and Fonsworth was cooking the healthy lentil option with Margaret. Cats were everywhere; postcards from previous hikers covered the walls and I sat outside after enjoying a shower, relishing the quiet around Kincora.

Phillip seemed a little despondent that evening. When I enquired why he looked so glum he simply explained he was tired and a little fed up with the rain. He continued.

"They should put Wi-Fi in all the shelters," he began. "And electrical outlets. The path should be cleared five feet wide and there should be an awning over the entire trail."

Well rested I left the following morning as the trail descended sharply from the hostel down to Laurel Falls, which at eighty feet high is so named because of the laurel bushes in the area.

It was hot and very humid, seeming to sap the very strength out of me. I toiled up the 1659 feet towards Pond Flats where Deep, a German hiker, and Fuurther, who pointed out his trail name was spelt with two u's, sat by a fresh spring drinking the cool water. Deep's name had come about literally because he spoke with a deep voice. We had tried to name him Arnie, as in Schwarzenegger, because of the similar tone but he had settled on Deep.

He left before Fuurther and I but returned a few seconds later looking shaken.

"What's up mate?" I enquired, seeing the ashen look on his face.

"There's a big snake on the trail," he replied, stony-faced and deadpan.

Fuurther cautiously walked up the trail as I tucked in behind him, peering over his shoulder. He was a local so snakes were nothing new to him. Just off the trail a large rattlesnake basked in the sun with a bulge halfway down its body, no doubt the remnants of lunch.

"God dang!" exclaimed Fuurther. "Biggest god damn snake I ever saw!"

As we crept closer it let off a warning rattle but seemed docile, possibly full from its meal, so I approached slowly to take a photo. Snakes are the main reason why manufacturers install a zoom function on cameras and after getting closer than I should have, I quickly fired off a couple of shots and retreated hastily.

I passed Iron Mountain shelter and a concrete structure caught my eye. I had been coasting along enjoying the flatter trail which bumbled along around 4000 feet when over to the left, just by a wooden seat, stood a stone pillar with what appeared to be a gravestone embedded into one side. I went for a closer look and read the inscription

Uncle Nick Grindstaff
Born
Dec 26, 1851
Died
July 22, 1923
Lived alone, suffered alone and died alone

The inscription sparked my curiosity and I took a photo but

was unable to find out any details surrounding this man until I returned back home and did some digging around. Nick lived alone on the ridge between Stoney Creek and Doe Valley for forty years. He was orphaned as a child and raised by relatives until he reached adulthood, when he married and inherited part of the family farm.

He made a living farming for a few years but suddenly moved to Missouri for reasons that are unclear. Some stories say his wife died, others say she left him. Further accounts detail him being robbed of everything he owned. He eventually moved back to Iron Mountain where he lived out his remaining years as a hermit with his dog Panter, a horse, and some say a pet rattlesnake.

In July 1923, his friend Baxter McKewen stopped by to check on Nick but found him dead with Panter guarding the body. The dog had to be prised way from its vigil. To his day, no one knows how Nick died.

Relatives constructed the chimney shaped structure we now see on Iron Mountain a couple of years after his death. To add to the sense of mystery, years after the AT was constructed, hikers camping near the spot reported hearing the howls of a dog through the night.

You've got to love a good mystery ...

***

I had only managed sixteen miles in eight hours and was sweating copiously. The air was oppressive and, suddenly, shelters were not the targets that many were aiming for — it was the water sources too. Over the course of a summer, especially a hot one, some creeks dry up and the chances of obtaining water become slimmer. It was still only May but temperatures had shot up and everyone was complaining. Instead of fantasising about food, our attention turned to our favourite cold drinks. PJ told me he had been dreaming about an ice-cold cranberry juice for days and as he walked away from the TN-91 road crossing, I couldn't resist getting a lift to the charmingly named town of Shady Valley, just over three miles away.

A local called Kirby dropped me off at the General Store. A

couple of Harleys were propped up outside, the doorbell tinkled as an occasional customer walked in or out and I looked at the signs above the door offering a deli, fuel, general merchandise, restrooms and 'Home of the Shady Dog', whatever that was.

A can of Coke settled the immediate thirst crisis and I ordered two hamburgers whilst picking up a few items for the food supply, including the coldest carton of cranberry juice I could find.

I was back on trail in an hour after another quick lift back to the trailhead by Joe, a local section hiker. Lord Horatio Fonsworth passed me as I was gearing up by the roadside and commented on the cranberry juice, still ice-cold with condensation bubbles forming on the outside as I wrapped it in my jacket for insulation.

"Man that looks good!" he said, whilst walking off with his head turned back.

"It does dunnit! I'm going to surprise PJ with it," I explained. "He's been hankering after one for days."

It was only four miles to Double Springs shelter and I walked through pleasing, yellow-coloured meadows splattered with buttercups and dandelions whilst catching glimpses of the agricultural landscape back down in the valley. A collection of hikers had congregated to sit out the afternoon heat and take advantage of the cool spring water by the shelter. I figured word may have reached PJ about my purchase and sure enough when he saw me approach, he got up and came swiftly over.

"Fozzie!" he exclaimed with a desperate expression that only the thought of a chilled carton of cranberry juice on a hot afternoon could bring on. "I heard you went to the store and got me cranberry juice!" Saliva was almost dribbling down his chin.

Alas, for poor PJ's salivation at least, satiation salvation was not imminent.

"Yes, PJ, I did."

He looked excited and his eyes opened wider in anticipation, looking like they would pop out.

"The problem is," I added, "I drank it all."

His expression changed in a millisecond to a mix of shock, disappointment, anger and possibly a small smattering of hatred.

"I'm really sorry mate but that last three miles was stinking hot and what with all the salt from the burgers, I just ... well ... I just couldn't resist it. PJ, I'm really sorry, I'll buy you another one."

He stared at me, gormless, and said nothing.

"PJ, Come on! Don't make me feel guilty! I may have drunk it but at least I bought it for you in the first place!"

This explanation, admittedly, didn't offer much consolation.

Lord Horatio Fonsworth chipped in. "Fozzie, I can't believe you drank it."

There was an uncomfortable silence for a few seconds, during which I feared PJ would grab my throat and try and throttle me. I felt I was being cross-examined in a court room after a very weak defence. Eventually he started laughing, along with Lord Horatio Fonsworth plus a few others and a strange feeling that I was now on the end of a wind up surfaced.

"Fozzie, I'm just messing with you! It was nice of you to buy it, even if you did drink it. Don't worry, it's all good!"

I spent the night camped near the Abingdon Gap shelter, waking briefly at 4.30 a.m. when a small group of hikers woke me as they left early. I couldn't get back to sleep, especially after hearing what sounded like a large animal around camp. Too scared to peer under the tent to be confronted by a bear, I pulled my sleeping bag over me and prayed.

The chatter was rife in the morning when several others also recounted hearing similar sounds during the night. One was Margaret who, having pitched near me said:

"I heard it too and spent most of the night with my knife ready, just in case."

"Blimey!" I retorted, "Remind me not to creep into your tent during the night!"

I talked briefly with a new face, Cheddar, so named after his fondness for my native English cheese.

"It's a good cheese with a great reputation," I said. "But, I have to say that my personal favourite is Stilton."

"What's that like?" he enquired.

"Completely different. Softer, creamier, smellier and it has blue veins of mould running through it which some people dislike. As far as English cheeses go, I think it's the champion."

"Really?" His curiosity seemed aroused so I took the

opportunity, instead of trying to give someone a trail name, of improving the one they already had.

"Far superior to Cheddar in my opinion. I think you should consider changing your name to Stilton — I think it will command a lot more respect, enhance your reputation and show off your cheese knowledge."

I left him to ponder the idea and headed off with Phillip who informed me he had given himself the trail name of Lazagne, which he purposely spelt with a z. He had reached the decision after his mammoth portion of said dish at Kincora.

We walked with excitement, and for good reason. Damascus is quite possibly the most famous and revered town on the entire Appalachian Trail, and it lay just a few miles down the trail. It is renowned for an annual event known as 'Trail Days' where thousands of hikers both past and present converge on this small town in Virginia, swelling the population from around 1000 to 20,000. Most camp a short way from the centre of town and enjoy huge campfires, food and drink, foot washes, medical check-ups and a host of other services often laid on free by the local community.

Unfortunately, we were too early by about ten days for the event but the plan was to carry on north and hopefully hitch a lift back for the experience.

It was a small, cute town and I liked it immediately. Old, timber-clad houses lined the main street in subtle, pastel shades. Gardens were well kept and spring flowers danced by picket fences. The local trails were busy with people jogging, cycling or walking the dog and a collection of local shops catered for everyone. Damascus nestled in the green folds of the surrounding hills as cloud shadows passed over creating occasional respites from the heat.

We camped in the grounds of one of the hostels run by the local Methodist Church which was known simply as 'The Place', and took a zero the following day. I shared a room with PJ, Lazagne and an English hiker called Chez 11, spending the day relaxing. Chez 11 was the first English guy I had met so it was good to catch up on some news, especially our respective football teams' performance.

He was 20, and had worked, amongst other places, for the

Balancing on Blue

railways at Leeds train station as well as Debenhams department store. He supported Everton, which I didn't hold against him and spoke animatedly, with great fondness about his brother, who suffered from cerebral palsy. He was always relaxed and spoke slowly, choosing his words carefully.

Our room was positioned directly in front of the stairs which gave us a good view of who was coming up and if we fancied a chat, or they did, we'd call them in. I started to think of our little room as the reception.

Pink Bits, sorry, Lady Forward, was one such example who popped her head around the door after hearing us discuss who would be the first to summit Katahdin. The AT was never a race and most of us really didn't care who would be the first to finish, but egos defend themselves rigorously when provoked. The finishing point, and which one of us would get there first, was always on our minds.

In a good-humoured, brief discussion, she claimed she would be there before all of us.

"Are you throwing the gauntlet down?" I probed.

"Perhaps, but whichever one of us two is behind has to carry it."

"It's a done deal," I confirmed.

She approached, smirking, and handed over an imaginary gauntlet. Obviously, being a heavy, armoured glove, its weight caught me by surprise.

"This thing is heavy!" I exclaimed. "Whoever is behind and has to carry this thing will be at a serious disadvantage."

"I know," she replied. "That's why you have it now because I'm leaving. See you up the trail."

"You can count on it."

I left Damascus with Chez 11 in the afternoon with aims to reach Lost Mountain shelter, fifteen miles away. Nito was loitering outside the store and offered me a shot of bourbon for the trail which I duly accepted. We generally didn't carry alcohol into the woods because of the weight so opportunities to indulge had to be grabbed without hesitation.

"I have too much weight," he said. "I need to lose some. The bourbon is yours if you want to carry it."

It was a fair sized bottle and, as much as a wee tipple in the evening for the next few days appealed, I thanked him but declined.

The rain started again and, feeling stubborn, I delayed stopping to don my waterproofs until it approached the downpour stage. Eventually and reluctantly, I removed my pack, put on my poncho, put up the umbrella and started to walk again. One minute later I rounded a corner to see the shelter right in front of me.

Daffy rolled in to everyone's surprise and dispensed some decent hugs. When PJ realised he was back in the fray Sam was on the receiving end of his frightened bear cub up a tree hug routine.

I saw Nito approaching out of the corner of my eye as I was erecting my tent. A mixture of urgency, impatience and inquisitiveness creased his furrows.

"Fozzie, you got any TP?"

"Any what? What's TP?"

"Toilet paper."

He looked a little embarrassed and spoke softly so no one would hear. He was also grimacing, walking around a little agitated and kept crossing his legs.

"Nito me old mate, do you need the bog?"

"Yes, I'm a little desperate. I can trade you, I've run out."

Now, I was more than prepared to offer a few squares out of kindness; I didn't expect anything in return and knew the trail would return the favour at some point when I needed something. However, Nito was obviously desperate for the toilet and as he had mentioned the 'trade' word, I thought, shamelessly, the opportunity should be taken full advantage of.

"Well, Nito, let me see. I could do with a generous dram of that bourbon for this evening and what's that you have in the bag there? Is that a pack of dehydrated veggies? How many squares do you need?"

I started to rummage round in my bag for the paper.

"Six will do it," he implored.

"Six? Just six squares?" I offered in surprise. "That's impressive, mate. I'd struggle to get by on six squares. I usually double up as well, you know, just in case of tearage? And what about tomorrow? You may need to go then as well."

Balancing on Blue

Nito's expression was now borderline panic.

"Fozzie, that's fine! Bourbon is there, here's the veggies."

I counted out six squares, possibly slower than I should have done, and handed them to him as he raced off to the privy. TP was not an item that thru-hikers buy in stores because of the bulk of two roll packs so usually we procure it in public toilets. I had a few squares of inferior quality which I hadn't used since picking it up at the diner in Hot Springs. The thickness was concerning and its texture reminiscent of baking parchment. I was pleased to get rid of it although did feel a little guilty and fully expected a little bad karma in return for my greed. Especially, even though Nito was unaware, as it was only one-ply as well.

Lazagne sauntered over as I was cooking my dinner.

"Chess, Fozzie?" he enquired.

"Sure, take a pew."

We had both discussed bringing a travel chessboard on the trail but discounted it because of the weight, when he came up with the bright idea of downloading the game onto his phone. Subsequently, the England vs. America competition had been underway for a couple of days. If a game went on too long, perhaps past hiker midnight, then we just picked up from where we had left it the next time.

We were both around the same skill level — that being poor amateurs — so the games were fairly well balanced. After two games we were drawn level at one game each. As I checked my meal cooking, he made a move and handed me the phone. I perused the possible options as he chatted to Daffy or quickly started pitching his hammock. The entire game would usually stretch over the course of an evening or two.

The annoying aspect of the game was that when one person won and checkmate was reached, a deadpan, computer synthesised voice exclaimed *checkmate!* Either Lazagne or I, having just made the killer move would still be holding the phone and simply smiled smugly, holding it aloft near the other's ear to announce our victory. Tonight was his turn and, having finalised his options, he sat back confidently and held his phone aloft. It was 2-1 to the States.

Checkmate!

Lazagne's playful ego, and desire to rub his victory in, continued the following morning as I woke, rubbing my eyes at 6 a.m. As I lay there contemplating the day ahead, I heard footsteps creeping up to my tent. They paused a couple of feet away and as I cocked one ear to try and find out what was happening, the immortal, electronic voice wafted through the woods.

Checkmate!

Promptly followed by Lazagne giggling like a school kid.

"See you up the trail Fozzie!"

***

Once in a while, the AT breaks out from the seclusion of the woods and, for anything from a few minutes to perhaps a day, a thru-hiker suddenly revels in a new found freedom. These open spaces were little treats along our 2178-mile journey and offered rare glimpses of the landscape surrounding us.

It was a new playground and as simple as it might sound, always exciting. Suddenly we could see our surroundings, feel the sun on our backs, and hold our face against the wind. A clear pathway cut over the landscape, sometimes visible from miles away: either a bare dirt track or silvery grass that had been flattened by the boots of others. We could see if the trail was going up or down, if it skirted a mountain or climbed deliberately up and over it. We saw thru-hikers ahead and behind. The sudden, new-found freedom of these open spaces had us giggling and behaving like school children.

One such place was the Grayson Highlands in Virginia. Regarded as a highlight of the trail, it leaves a lasting memory with most thru-hikers. The 4522-acre area passes near Mt Rogers and Whitetop Mountain, Virginia's two highest peaks.

Grayson, as with most areas where I broke out of the woods, caught me by surprise. First of all the sun blinded me, then the heat hit me and I dropped my pack scrabbling around for my sunglasses and cream.

This is fantastic! Look at all this space!

I had lost track of Daffy again, hearing through the hiker grapevine that he was a couple of days back. I had no idea of

Lazagne's location and rumour had it that PJ had slowed down drastically because of some sort of foot ache. It didn't bother me; I enjoyed their company but to be honest, sometimes the nomad kicked in and all I yearned for was space, solitude and quiet. I had all three in abundance.

The light was mesmerising. Early morning sunrays spliced through a low, weak mist like probing searchlights. Dew glistened on wet grass, infinite clusters of sparkling jewels — and clouds drifted lazily across the landscape as the sun lifted higher, their shadows speeding over me. I could see weather patterns miles distant. Brooding clouds tormenting the land, toying with it until the storm unleashed its anger.

Grayson is home to herds of ponies introduced to control the grass and most are used to humans. Stop for a break, rustle a food bag and before long a curious few will wander over hoping for a titbit and some even demand a few strokes.

I reached the Wise Shelter and pitched my tent nearby. After tallying up my mileage for the day, I was pleased to see another hundred miles had been passed, bringing me up to 500 in total. I was just under 25% done.

Rain fell overnight, perhaps seeming heavier because I had no trees for protection and after lying in my tent watching tiny explosions of water erupt as the rain smacked into the ground, I decided it wasn't going to stop and set off. The trail was transformed into dark mud and large pools had formed. Some sections had become creeks in themselves and I squelched through, the dirt muddying my shoes before being washed clean by the torrent further on.

I reached the Scales livestock corral and made a beeline for the only sheltered area, a roof overhanging the privy. Snot Rocket and Anchor joined me as we peeled off waterproofs, steam rising from our bodies in gratification for the release.

I walked with Tripping Yeti in the afternoon and, after the rain had finally stopped, spent time observing how my environment came back to life.

After the noise of the rain gradually subsided, little changes happened around me. Where the tree canopy thinned, the residual drips stopped; and once back in denser woods, water plopped with a satisfying smack onto my head. It became quieter, the sun emerged and started to dry the land out, steam rose making the air humid and wet plant leaves appeared polished. The birds chirped, sounding like an orchestra and slowly, the insects emerged and buzzed around me. Just like us thru-hikers after hiding from a storm, we tentatively peek out from our shelters and gradually venture out once more.

Balancing on Blue

Chapter 7

The Wapiti Shelter Murders

May 9th to May 16th
Mile 523 to 620

Infatuated by the prospect of pizza and lost in thought, I sped along an easy trail towards the Partnership shelter before stopping abruptly in mid-stride, alarmed at the cacophony behind me. For a few seconds I dared not turn around, confused and afraid of whatever was responsible for the deafening roar that was rapidly closing in on me.

Eventually, cautiously, I turned around to see a wall of water speeding towards me through the woods. I was on the very front edge of a rainstorm and it was coming right for me. In panic, I reached for the side pocket where I kept my poncho and umbrella. They both snagged on the pack strapping as I desperately tugged to release them. I looked up — so heavy was the downpour that it appeared like a waterfall, bearing down on me with frightening speed.

Shit! SHIT! Fozzie! Do something and make it quick!

Of the limited options available, I chose to run. I realised as I sped through the woods that the whole idea was just plain ridiculous.

What are you doing?! You can't outrun a storm!

Like a frightened hiker running from a rampaging bear, I continued to flee. Focusing on the immediate trail ahead, I quickly scanned the ground for obstacles, jumping over tree roots, leaping for boulders before springing off into mid-air and landing, the momentum making me slide on the slick ground. I darted from side to side avoiding obstacles whilst occasionally flicking my head around to see if I was making any headway. Unfortunately I wasn't.

Oh crap! Go faster! Run you bloody idiot! Run for fuck's sake!

I started giggling like a child, laughing at the absurdity of it all. The mad turmoil was gaining on me and eventually, after a couple of minutes, I could go no further. Collapsing in a heap of sweat and gasping in air, I watched as the wave raced the final few feet towards me like a surfer might study a breaker and I braced myself.

The dispersed wind hit me first, smashing into me, almost knocking me over. Then the torrent engulfed me and within a minute it had passed. I sat there soaked, drunk and intoxicated by the sheer energy of the elements that I had been fortunate enough to witness. It was unbelievably invigorating.

***

The abundance of time that a thru-hiker is blessed with means thinking becomes a novelty. During our normal lives we believe we do have time to think but, actually, we merely skim the surface. With not much else to do except walk, we become lost in our own thoughts, almost meditating. We can study any topic with a depth of detail that is hard to explain. Instead of spending a few minutes trying to solve a problem before something interrupts us, on the trail I used to spend days pondering various subjects — and not just the usual, boring topics such as finances, or work, but a host of diverse areas as simple, even, as the rain. And boy, when it rained out there, it really rained.

The physical side took care of itself and left the mind free to wander, so once the legs were warmed up the mind started to drift. I pondered what I was doing and how lucky I was to be experiencing it. Would dinner be rice or pasta? Would I camp that night or sleep in a shelter? Or I got the chance to spend time studying everyday things like the weather, or as I liked to call it, precipitation observation studies.

It's not that I got bored, far from it. When life was simplified, the grey matter spent valuable time exploring subjects that we didn't normally bother with because we think of them as mundane and not worthy of focus in our busy lifestyles. However, even areas that we perceive as possibly boring, or unworthy of our attention, can prove fruitful.

Rarely did we get a light shower; more often than not it was a torrential downpour. We had been lucky: the first two weeks were amazing weather, a couple of nights a storm passed over but during the day I had only been rained on, briefly, about five times. Thing is, those times had all been in the last week. Because I was enclosed by the forest most of the time, it was difficult to see the sky for a clue as to what was coming. Occasionally I glimpsed a dark cloud, or just overcast skies through the foliage so I began to employ my other senses for clues. The wind picking up was often a sure sign that there may be a storm blowing in, and if the temperature dropped that backed up the assumption. There was another sense which I couldn't put my finger on — it wasn't a smell or taste, more a sensation that rain was imminent, this I referred to as the 'Alert Stage'.

During the alert stage I looked up, checked on the clouds and if a few tiny droplets brushed past my cheek, this put me on 'Red Alert Stage'. I stopped and listened. Sound was the biggest clue to what nature intended. If I heard the rustling of water as it hit the leaves and undergrowth then a decision had to be made. Did I stop, don my poncho and have umbrella at the ready? Or did I, often foolishly, kid myself into thinking it would stop and I didn't need to bother?

The pattern was similar every time: the droplets became heavier, increased in frequency and then, reluctantly, I stopped to prepare. All hell usually broke loose during the procedure of wrapping up. The thunder roared, fierce winds whipped through my surroundings bending over tree limbs and it was a race to weatherproof myself. During an Appalachian storm the roar of water cascading down through the canopy onto the forest floor was deafening. The path was transformed into a torrent, cascading down the trail as if it owned it. After five minutes or fifteen, maybe an hour, the deluge abated and for another half hour I kept the umbrella up to see off the last of the droplets spilt from the trees. Then, the amazing experience was the birds, signalling that it was all over — quiet one second then an avian orchestra filled the air and told me it had past, everything was safe.

Apart from the initial warnings and using my senses to gauge if it would rain, I also spent time observing the rain itself. First was the temperature of the water, which was often cold during the first month, the tail end of winter — especially at the higher elevations. Exposed skin such as hands, and my lower legs which my poncho didn't cover, became numb in minutes. Also, my arms, protruding from the poncho, became goose pimpled in retaliation and, eventually, my hands ceased to function properly. As the elements warmed, so did the rain but even so, it was often an invigorating experience to be cooled.

Velocity also came into play. Sometimes, at one end of the spectrum, I experienced just a fine spray, almost a mist, that gently stroked over me and caused me to wipe my face, eyes and the droplets that collected in my beard. At the other end were the angry torrents which were sometimes so heavy that it felt as though I were underwater. Appalachian storms were often so intense that it was a battle to stay dry; hikers were beaten into submission and we longed for a shelter to escape the anger.

Then there was the angle of onslaught. In the woods the trees sheltered the winds somewhat so the rain often hit the west side of the Appalachian hills before being subdued and falling vertically. However, in the rare open spaces, such as meadows, it slammed into me from one side. I pulled my umbrella down to my side, bracing it against me from a near-horizontal pounding. Coming from the front, there was little I could do. The umbrella would obscure my field of vision so I had to hold it slightly aloft and study the ground just visible in front of me. Often resigned that the rain had gotten the better of me from a headlong attack, I merely let it slam into me and scrunched my eyes nearly shut, bowing my head down to escape the stinging on my face.

These storms did follow similar patterns. I knew, roughly, what to expect taking in all these factors so I knew how to deal with them. Thankfully, save a few days when it rained for hours, the storms eventually passed over, chased by the wind — and there were long respites to dry myself and keep an eye out for the next one. For the most part I enjoyed the novelty of them. The forest was spring-cleaned, the air became fresher and the experience was invigorating.

***

I reached the Partnership shelter quickly, chatted to Tyvek who was breaking camp and reached the Mt Rogers Visitor Center shortly after. Several despondent hikers including Snot Rocket and Anchor informed me that a pizza delivery was out of the question because no one was answering their phone. I called Dinosaur.

"I'm at the Visitor Center, just got in!"

"OK, I'm on my way!" she replied.

Dinosaur had already walked the AT in 2006 and I had met her on the PCT in 2010 with Swayze, her boyfriend at the time. Our paths had crossed several times on the journey. She had always taken the time to chat and her infectious personality shone through. Her trail name came about after lack of funds for the AT meant she had to use her Dad's forty-year-old Kelty backpack from his days in the Scouts, which managed just over 600 miles and several dental floss repairs before giving up. She called it her Dinosaur and subsequently took the name for herself. A true outdoors lover, not just content to spend time in the outdoors whilst thru-hiking, she carried this passion over to her work as a member of the Konnarock trail crew based out of Sugar Grove. This group did a lot of work in the Grayson Highlands but co-operated with several other trail clubs, the Appalachian Trail Conservancy and the US Forest Service to look after sections of the trail from Rockfish Gap, near Waynesboro, Virginia, all the way back to the start at Springer mountain itself.

I had never done any trail work but Dinosaur had suggested a little food and lodging in exchange for a couple of days' work which I had jumped at. The Konnarock crew hosted several volunteers each week who gave a week or two of their time to maintain the AT and stay at the Sugar Grove premises.

She pulled up in an ageing '93 Toyota Corolla which squeaked when she went round corners, gave me a hug and off we squeaked. Stopping briefly, so I could solve my hunger crisis with a huge sandwich, we arrived at Konnarock where I was introduced to Dave Hebert, AKA Czar, or the Louisiana Bear who ran the show.

The original building of the AT was only part of the story. The trail is subject to constant wear and tear, not just from hikers but more often from the weather. Maintenance involves surface repair in high traffic areas and protection from the elements. Water will always follow the path of least resistance and often it's the trail itself that unintentionally acts as drainage. Water bars, which are designed to direct water off the trail, consist of either wooden or stone barriers built across the trail to divert water off to the side. Steps are often built, especially in areas of high traffic such as trailheads near roads where day trippers also use the trail. Then there is the clearing of undergrowth encroaching onto the trail, removal of fallen trees and a host of other areas to contend with. It's a constant battle to keep the AT open and the hard, physical work is untaken by a dedicated band of maintenance crews working long hours in all sorts of conditions: rain, snow, cold and heat. Their toil is appreciated, but often taken for granted. Not only was I looking forward to the experience but, as with a lot of thru-hikers, giving something back to the trail which has been a big part of their life is something they do gladly.

We worked for two days in the Grayson Highlands on a section of steep trail suffering from erosion. A series of steps had to be constructed mainly from incredibly heavy boulders, utilised from the immediate area. It was hard work; the logistics and sheer physical effort required just to move these beasts were huge. An approximate hole was excavated by eye according to the size of a nearby boulder and then, using a series of straps and several volunteers, it was hauled in short bursts over to the site where it was manoeuvred into place. Adjustments were carried out such as filling in the hole to accommodate the stone so it became stable and didn't rock, and then we moved onto the next one. With around twelve of us on site, I received some small insight into how much work must have been required for the whole of the AT when it took most of us the whole day to install just two of these blocks.

Apart from the exhausting but rewarding work, the other great part of my experience was the food. Dave usually stayed at base camp dealing with the office side of things but also cooked an absolute feast for us every morning and evening.

Appetites were borderline dangerous and as we patiently queued through the kitchen, each edging closer to the pile of food awaiting us, lips were licked, stomachs rumbled and excitement grew. Slowly, each one of us edged closer to various dishes until we were able to pile our plates high, retire to the canteen and placate our hungers. Then we returned for more.

I always voiced my appreciation, as did most thru-hikers, when we walked through a trail maintenance area and after my time at Konnarcok, I had a new found respect for these people that do such a wonderful job of keeping the AT open and usable. My hat is bowed not just to Dinosaur, Dave and the rest of the Konnarock crew but to all the maintenance teams who toil tirelessly.

***

It's not often during my life off trail, when I work my day job that I wake up in the morning with a smile. The prospect of another mundane day rarely excites me so it's with reluctance that I tip myself out of bed and head off to work. On trail, however, once the sun has woken me, smiling is the first thing I do. The prospect of lying in my tent for a few minutes, gearing up to move and planning out the day visually always makes me happy. It's where I'm content in my life at that moment.

More often than not I'm smiling during the day as well and as I reached the Lindamond school, part of an early settlement built in 1894, I ventured inside to view a bygone era and check the visitors book where Lord Horatio Fonsworth, having clearly done some homework on extending his title, had signed off his message as 'Lord Horatio Fonsworth Belvidere Bentley Tiberius III, Esq.' I was smiling for the rest of the day.

The trail left the school through a meadow, one of several that dotted Virginia. A silver, flattened line of grass wove through, snagging my trekking poles. I often caught a tantalising glimpse of these open spaces from the confines of the woods above as I descended. Farms dotted the area and as well as the teasing little views from the hills, there were audible clues too: the distant hum of a tractor or mower, dogs barking, livestock, or perhaps a car engine humming along a narrow country lane.

The plan, loose as always, was to put in five, twenty-mile days to get to Pearisburg. There I hoped to catch a ride back to Damascus to experience Trail Days.

I passed Pops and Apollo sheltering from the fierce sun in the middle of a meadow under a giant oak tree. They invited me to sit with them and as I lay down my pack and took a rest in the grass, Pops handed me a cold beer fresh from a recent resupply. I felt no urge to move; the heat was intense and the beer refreshing. We all stayed there for a couple of hours, relaxing, catching up on the trail gossip, watching birds soar above us and taking in the sounds of a quiet afternoon in the Virginia countryside.

Pops was highly respected on the trail. 53 years old and with long grey hair tied back into a ponytail, his beard reached his chest and he was tanned from a life outdoors. His lean frame suggested he looked after himself, and often he would hold court in a conversation, delivering his own insights, thoughts and views on all manner of subjects wisely and with great insight. Everyone loved Pops.

It wasn't until after I returned from the trail and was watching a film called *Hard Way Home*, made by Kori 'Rocket' Feener who had hiked the AT that same year, did I realise how wise Pops was. Kori filmed him on a few occasions and one of the lines he delivered had me nodding in agreement.

And those great souls that have learnt to let go, out here like us we let go, we put on packs, we hike in mountains. We've let go of the TV, the illusions, the jobs, the insurance and all these other concepts that have been holding us into this man made world, instead of being lifted up into God's creation in this life we have.

So, let go.

Balancing on Blue

***

The overnight weather didn't bode well. I had camped in the woods, miles from anywhere after coming up just short of my twenty-mile target with a nineteen. As my water boiled ready to make coffee, I packed up my stuff, occasionally grabbing a handful of granola. Enjoying the caffeine rush, I sat and watched my world slowly wake up. A stream quietly gurgled to my side as it weaved through rhododendron bushes, the sandy bottom clearly visible through its waters. The woods were silent save the birds heralding another day and a weak mist occasionally floated past only to disappear, letting the sun warm me once more.

I had earmarked Chestnut Knob shelter to escape the rain. Despite its meagre capacity of eight, I figured arriving mid-afternoon would secure me one of the spots. AWOL's guide also promised that the shelter not only boasted four concrete walls but a door as well. Time spent outdoors has a wonderful way of teaching us what we perceive is important and it puts our lives into perspective, reminding us of how little we need to be content — case in point that I was excited to be spending the night with the bonus of four walls and a door. Life couldn't have been much simpler.

There were eighteen miles to Chestnut Knob but also around 4500 feet of climbing to get there. A clear sky and piercing sun suggested the weather forecast may have been wrong as I watched emerald leaves turn silver with light bouncing off them, and chinks of sunlight blinded me as the leaves occasionally lifted in the breeze, providing a clear passage through.

Relishing the meadows, I followed blazes painted on posts driven into the ground, sentinels pointing the way. My shoes and trousers became soaked from the overnight dew which coated the grass and glistened in a low sun. Virginia rolled casually, somewhat easier than the previous states and although it boasted some big mountains, the climbs seemed gentler. I crossed wooden stiles over quiet, potholed country roads as an occasional tractor bumped along. Deer bounded away as I startled them and cows eyed me curiously from a distance. I longed for the shade of the woods when out in the open and, conversely, looked forward to the warmth of the sun when walking through the woods. At the top of each hill, I stopped and looked back at where I had travelled. I was once told that the best views are sometimes behind, and more importantly, it would probably be the last time I ever saw them. Then I turned away, held the image, stored it somewhere safe and carried on towards Maine.

I took a break by some unexpected trail magic just off the small country lane left by Lumberjack and Labrat who were previous thru-hikers. Two coolers excited me as it was another hot day and I longed for a sweet drink; anything else was a bonus. Sure enough, one was brimming and unashamedly I took the last cold Coke, opening the other to see what goodies it contained. Joy of joys! Peanut butter and jelly sandwiches accompanied by a note saying they had been made just that morning. There was even a piece of paper detailing the latest weather forecast, confirming the news I had heard from others that rain was on the way. Thirsty, a thru-hiker who I had met briefly at the Fontana Hilton arrived and lived up to his trail name as he gladly popped open another can. We subsequently spent fifteen minutes belching and laughing at our good fortune.

He left just before me and I spotted him half a mile ahead as we finished off the final four miles. A pond two miles before the shelter signalled our water source and several other hikers were filling up. There was a queue of about six before me on account of the limited space around the shallow stream. I looked back to see more hikers approaching and, concerned that I would miss a place at the shelter, I scrabbled through some undergrowth. Further upstream a small pool emerged and I dipped my mug in the shallow water and poured the contents into my water bag. By the time I had finished I had bypassed the line and nipped out before those coming up the hill.

Chestnut Knob shelter sat in a clearing commanding fine views back down the trail. Not only did it sport four walls and a door, but also a couple of windows as well. I grabbed a bottom bunk closest to the door as slowly, a steady stream of hikers dribbled in and the shelter filled.

With a recommended capacity of eight, after everyone had squeezed in, the number rose to twenty. Far from being cramped, everyone took care with their space and it was surprisingly comfortable. Some sat on their bunks, like me, cooking their evening meals, writing their journals and other tasks, whilst Pops took a place at the small table and made hot chocolate with bourbon for everyone who wanted one. Laughter filled the air, conversation was animated and good cheer echoed around.

As each of us slowly succumbed to tired limbs, Chestnut Knob quietened until the last light went out and Pops blessed us all.

"Good night my friends, be safe and God bless you. I love y'all, you hear? I love y'all."

"Night Pops."

The woods were a murky, damp world when I left Chestnut Knob. A mist hung low and intermittent rain fell for most of the morning. There was no wind, and it was eerily quiet save the gentle plopping of water on the sodden ground around me. I made my way down a slick trail onto a dirt track, just off the VA-623. Thirsty was huddled under some trees with Embassador and Flint, trying unsuccessfully to roll a cigarette and debating taking up an offer of lodgings posted on a tree by the local church. I nodded a greeting and, eager to keep warming up, I carried on into the trees.

I paused momentarily, thinking I had heard a cry from behind me.

"Fozzie!"

I had; it was Thirsty.

"Yeah?" I called back.

"A guy called Bush Goggles is down the trail. We're staying at the church place. Tell him we ain't gonna make camp tonight!"

I caught the gist of what he was shouting but misheard the name.

"Who?" I called.

"Bush Goggles!" he cried.

"I'll tell him!"

I didn't catch him up until some four miles later at the Jenkins shelter. There was no one else about and Bush Goggles sat on the edge of the sleeping platform, swinging his legs and taking a rest from the rain. I sat beside him, keen also to spend a few minutes out of the damp.

"Are you Bush Goggles?" I asked.

"Yup, sure am," he replied.

"I have a message from Thirsty. They're gonna stay at the church place tonight."

"Oh OK, thanks. Where you heading?"

"Dunno. Helveys Mill shelter looks good for the mileage I'm doing."

Dallas 'Bush Goggles' Nustvold was 23 and came from Minneapolis, Minnesota. He grinned a lot, mischievously, as though he had just played a prank on someone and was anticipating the moment they found out. His hair was short but his beard was sprouting proudly; in fact he had more hair on his face than his head. He was so named after casting some admiring glances at a member of the fairer sex one day in Gatlinburg. When she turned around and wasn't as attractive as the rear view had suggested, Trevelyan 'Walkabout' Edwards, an Australian hiker, chastised him.

"Christ mate, you got your bush goggles on!"

Bush goggles is an Australian slang term describing someone's attraction to a — let's say — *homely* person of the opposite sex caused by isolation, such as working in a mine, or in this case, too long spent in the woods.

He was young, in good shape and eager to put in some miles. Walking quickly, perhaps a little above my normal pace, it was like walking behind a pacemaker. I could stay with him but it was a decent workout. His official employment title was an environmental contractor site superintendent. This was far too much of a mouthful so I decided to refer to him as a builder to simplify things.

Chez 11, Deep and a few others were spread about Helveys Mill shelter. Bush Goggles preferred to sleep in a tent, a bright yellow tunnel model which was unusual in that the entrance was on the top; instead of crawling in, it was more a case of stepping in.

Gear hung from every available hook drying out. Seeing the privy a way off in the trees, and eager for a visit, when I opened the door I discovered there was no roof so I went back to retrieve my umbrella. I had several unusual experiences on the AT but sitting on the bog, with my umbrella in the rain was a first.

***

I planned to return to Damascus Trail Days for a weekend so I had put in a couple of twenty-five-mile days to make up for the mileage deficit that Trail Days would incur. I had also passed the 600-mile mark and was into the fourth state of Virginia. Fighting fit, I had not suffered from any blisters. My legs felt strong, my head in order and despite the AT still proving difficult in terms of the ascents and descents, I was hiking well and confidently.

Daffy had dropped back again and although I hadn't seen him, Chez 11 said he had seen a couple of messages in the trail registers from him. PJ had disappeared and I hadn't seen Lazagne for a couple of days. When I checked my email, a message from Lazagne solved everyone's whereabouts, advising they were all in Bland. The bad news was that PJ had suffered a possible stress fracture in his foot. Although I hoped he would be OK to carry on and the diagnosis was wrong, I knew deep down that he had a problem.

Injuries, depending on the severity, can and do end thru-hikes. Most of us are a stubborn bunch, and despite what the doctors or physios tell us (on the rare occasions when we actually bother to see one), we usually ignore it. Some carry on with injuries, and it is possible to do so depending on the type, but the risk is that the repercussions later on can be more serious.

The standard joke on trail about doctors is that whenever a thru-hiker pays a visit, regardless of the problem, the advice is always 'get off trail'. Therefore we usually don't bother making an appointment. A few may rest for a day or two if something hurts and then carry on ignoring the problem, hoping it will go away. If I'm not thru-hiking, the advice I remember from a physio a few years back is to wait for the pain to stop, then rest for a further two weeks without exercise. Invariably, the pain usually takes ten to fourteen days to stop, meaning an injury can mean taking a month out. If I'm hiking and somewhere starts hurting, I may slow down but normally I hope, pray to the god of muscles and injuries, grin, bear it and carry on.

Stress fractures are common to the feet where repetitive stress over long periods of time mean the muscles, unable to cope, transfer the load to the bones which results in hairline fractures. When I read about PJ's problem in Lazagne's email I feared the worst. I had full faith in PJ — he was focused, determined and intent to finish the trail. However, stress fractures aren't something to be ignored, thru-hiking or not. PJ, for the time being at least, appeared to be out of the hunt.

Hikers, runners, cyclists and most sportspeople have experienced injury and it's a huge disappointment. Even with drugs and remedies it is often weeks before they can return to training. Rest is the only sure fire method to cure most problems. Not only do you have to rest, but most of the hard work spent training is then subsequently lost.

I have been fortunate, except for one occasion on El Camino, not to have been injured on a thru-hike. Pushing hard one day in Spain I pulled my right calf. I slowed my pace somewhat but carried on to the end in Santiago. Twelve years later and it still aches if I ask too much of it.

Six weeks before I was due to travel to California to start my Pacific Crest Trail hike, whilst out running, I pulled up quickly with a sharp pain in my right knee. The diagnosis was runner's knee, a common injury with sportspeople, especially, unsurprisingly, runners. The prognosis was not good; my local physio advised it could mean up to eight months of rest. I looked at him in horror, said I had six weeks maximum and asked him to do everything he could to fix it. A week before my departure it still hurt, albeit only a fraction of the original pain. It was a risk, he admitted, but advised that I go and hike. If anything, the actual exercise would strengthen the surrounding area and support the injury. Thankfully, it was fine although as with my ankle, it still twinges from time to time.

On the North Downs Way, a 140-mile trail local to where I live in south east England, I was into day one of the hike when my right extensor digitorum longus, a muscle running down the outside of the lower leg, began to ache. I ignored it but later the same day, I rolled my ankle on a right hand camber which pulled it sharply and a pain shot up my leg. I foolishly carried on and amazingly, given that I rarely roll my ankles, I did exactly the same thing later.

The pain did subside but I was hobbling for a week after

returning home when I had finished. The physio ordered rest, which put me out of hiking for three months. The result is that now, although it never hurts, I can only describe the sensation of a Velcro strip running down the outside of my leg — which, on a bad day, feels as though it is constantly being pulled away and stuck back repeatedly.

The drug of choice for thru-hikers is Ibuprofen. Although now associated with stomach ulcers, it is the preferred pain reliever and also reduces swelling. I always carried it but used it sparingly, usually when I was flagging in the afternoon and the legs started to ache a little. Most took 200 mg — although some thru-hikers became immune to the lower doses with constant use and would take up to 800 mg, sometimes even more.

I also carried caffeine tablets. Due to an unfortunate lack of coffee bars in the middle of the Appalachian woods, I enjoyed the hit. The energy boost was almost immediate and come the middle of the afternoon, along with a couple of Ibuprofen, my body reacted gratefully. For at least two hours, the aches subsided, the energy rocketed and if I had a flattish trail, I could quite happily cover eight miles in less than two hours. The negative side of this was that I increased the chances of injury by pushing too hard so had to reign in my enthusiasm.

Often it was the easier, flatter sections of trail where I got injured because I could push harder. Virginia was a classic example and kinder — the severe ups and downs had subdued somewhat. Bush Goggles and I enjoyed a more relaxed hike, thankfully without aches and pains. We passed Jenny Knob shelter, scampered down the hill to the wonderfully-sounding Lickskillet Hollow, cranked out a further five miles to the Kimberling Suspension Bridge and shortly after, popped out on the VA-606.

Trent's Grocery was a mere half-mile west. I turned to Bush Goggles.

"Hungry? Burger?"

He merely grinned and shortly after, re-fuelled, we sped along the eight miles to the Wapiti shelter, dodging and running scared of thunderstorms. The small shelter sat just off trail, and a faint track wove down to a creek through thin woodland. The rain had stopped and sunlight filtered through the canopy, dancing on the ground. There was no wind and only birdsong broke a still, quiet evening.

Its beguiling atmosphere offered no clues to the bloody events that happened there in May, 1981. Or perhaps the ethereal woods were still in mourning.

Robert Mountford Jr. and his hiking companion Susan Ramsay had pulled into the Wapiti shelter to stay for a night during their thru-hike. They had befriended a local, Randall Smith, who had charmed his way into their trust and also stayed at the shelter. Smith lived nearby in Pearisburg and knew the area well. Having a fondness for the woods he made regular trips there. A welder by trade, he worked occasionally when he needed money.

After they had settled down and were sleeping, Smith shot Mountford Jr. in the head with a .22 calibre handgun. Having woken, Ramsay was then repeatedly and violently stabbed. Post mortem reports revealed her hands had received injuries, suggesting she was awake and had tried to defend herself. When both hikers failed to turn up in Pearisburg, police first searched the Wapiti shelter as it was the nearest one to town. Blood was discovered between the floorboards and a search of the immediate area revealed both Ramsay and Mountford Jr. buried in the sleeping bags.

Smith was arrested a few weeks later, subsequently found guilty and sentenced to thirty years in jail. There are numerous theories about why he carried out the killings, one being that he had made a pass at Ramsay which Mountford Jr. had intervened in. Some say the killings were revenge for Ramsay's rebuke and his dislike for Mountford Jr. Unfortunately Smith, despite his incarceration, didn't change.

He was released on parole in 1996 after serving just fifteen years. He caused no trouble in jail and was in fact described as a model prisoner. Over the subsequent twelve years, he scraped a living from welding and, when out fishing in 2008, had camped in the woods again just a mile and a half from the Wapiti shelter.

He befriended Scott Johnston of Bluefield, VA, out on a fishing trip with his friend Sean Farmer of Tazewell, VA. Smith chatted to Johnston, complaining that he had caught nothing and Johnston, feeling sorry for him, opened his cooler and handed him a bag of his fish. Johnston told him where he was camped with Farmer and invited him to dinner that evening.

Smith spent several hours with the two men that evening after they cooked trout and beans for him, even feeding Smith's dog. He eventually got up, and having walked a few paces, pulled a gun from his pocket, turned and shot Johnston in the neck. He then turned the gun at Farmer and shot him point blank in the chest. Johnston, despite his injury, fled into the woods as Smith let off another volley of bullets after him, and one hit him again in the nape of the neck.

Farmer struggled to his truck a few yards away as Smith caught him and pointed the gun at him once more, but it failed to fire; he had run out of ammunition. Farmer drove off. His headlights picked out his friend staggering into the road and he swung the door open for him. They both escaped.

They received treatment for their wounds and lived to tell the tale. Smith fled the scene in the vehicle that Johnston had abandoned, but subsequently crashed and was picked up quickly by the police, to whom he was well known. He was taken to the police cell where later, an officer knocked on his cell door to bring him food and received no answer. He knocked again to no avail and Smith was discovered dead in his cell. It is believed that he died from his injuries sustained in the crash.

I never found out about the killings until after my return from the AT and realised I had not only slept in the shelter where the murders had taken place, but quite possibly slept in the same spot that either Ramsay or Mountford Jr. had met their demise.

***

Just over six miles from the Wapiti shelter a thru-hiker meets a dirt road at Sugar Run Gap. Half a mile east lays Woods Hole Hostel, a place previous thru-hikers had recommended I stay. Set down this quiet road, amongst the surrounding woods, Woods Hole was opened in 1986 by Roy and Tillie Wood; their granddaughter, Neville, continues to run it with her husband Michael.

I crunched down Sugar Run Road, walked through the gates and sat down admiring the chestnut-coloured, red-roofed house built back in the 1880s. Vegetable plots lined the front of the house with healthy, vibrant plants growing strongly. I took off my shoes and walked down a grassy slope to an outbuilding where a few hikers mingled, relaxing. Ken, Margaret, Flint, Thirsty and Bush Goggles all dribbled in as well as Lazagne, fresh from his two-day stopover in Bland sitting out the rain. Even Lord Horatio Fonsworth Belvidere Bentley Tiberius III, Esq. turned up.

It was a beautiful setting, miles from anywhere and away from any noise intrusion. The atmosphere rubbed off on everyone and we soon relaxed. I showered, did my laundry by hand as there was no machine, read sitting on a log and even managed a game of chess with Lazagne on the hostel's own, real chess board.

We ate like kings and queens that evening, spoilt by a table groaning with home produce. The tradition at Woods Hole dictates that just prior to eating, all thru-hikers gather in a ring around the fire and, holding hands, introduce themselves and say a short piece. I was one of the first and as I watched the introductions filter down the line, I saw it was only a matter of time before Lord Horatio Fonsworth Belvidere Bentley Tiberius III, Esq. had to introduce himself.

I couldn't stop giggling. Before he had even started, just the thought of his eight-worded title was too much. After some tweaking, lengthening, shortening and playing around with, Lord Horatio Fonsworth Belvidere Bentley Tiberius III, Esq. was where he had settled.

I slept in the loft of the outbuilding, next to an open window where the breeze kept me cool and a little moonlight filtered through.

I was excited — Trail Days was imminent.

Chapter 8

Trail Days

May 17th to May 31st
Mile 620 to 800

The Plaza Motel in Pearisburg was quiet but the car rental businesses weren't. I made several calls in vain to try and secure transport for Lazagne and I back down to Damascus, just over 100 miles south. Eventually, tired of trying, we walked through town, placed our packs on the verge beside us and stuck out a thumb. The locals are used to hikers and putting the pack beside me when trying to get a lift is something I always did — it showed that I was not a rampant murderer. Butch Simpkins pulled over a mere five minutes later and took us an hour down the road to Wytheville, as far as he was going. We had barely raised another thumb before Steve and Annie Chambers waved us over from the petrol station and took us all the way to the main street in Damascus. It couldn't have been easier.

The hostel known as the Place, where we had stayed a few days before, was brimming. We were about to pitch in the grounds when Daffy came over and beckoned us to what is known as tent city at the other end of town. A field and the surrounding woods near the creek was packed with hundreds of tents, hammocks, and hikers. The police milled around conspicuously.

Food stalls plied their trade effortlessly as a steady queue of hikers kept them solvent. Equipment manufacturers extolled their latest products and after meeting Ron Bell, owner of Mountain Laurel Designs, he kindly struck me a great deal for one of his Spirit quilts. The advantage of the quilt was that it just lay over me, instead of getting into a sleeping bag which I had always found restricting. I also chatted with the legend that is Tom Hennessy, owner of Hennessy Hammocks and I returned to the woods to sling my new hammock between two suitable trees under the guidance of Lazagne and Daffy. With both the quilt and the hammock, I was relishing the prospect of a good sleep every night.

One of the local churches offered free medical check-ups and after my blood pressure was deemed excellent, they cleaned up a wound on my leg, the result of some overzealous scratching of a mosquito bite in the middle of the night. They washed and massaged my feet and even threw in some cake and a cup of coffee, although I hasten to add not on my feet.

I was delighted to bump into some PCT hikers I had met in 2010 on my thru-hike. Detective Bubbles, Karma and Wiffle Chicken all came over to say hello and Stanimal surprised me in the diner when he walked in the door. Scott 'Squatch' Herriot, who had made a name for himself by producing several films on the PCT, was busy advertising his effort on the AT: 'Flip Flop Flippin', which he had filmed the year before. 'Flip Flop Flippin 2' was a work in progress and he was hiking up and down the AT to film. We parted with a promise to bump into each other at some point on the trail.

I awoke the following morning in the same position as I had gone to sleep; the hammock was that comfortable. At last, I hoped, my lack of sleep in tents was behind me. Walking back through town with Daffy and Lazagne, we dodged an onslaught from the traditional water fight and hiker parade before getting a ride back to Pearisburg with K2 and Tarp Water who had managed to hire a car. They dropped us at the Plaza Motel, I debated staying another night but the need for mileage got the better of me — although I did take up Earthling and Yodler's offer of a quick shower in their room. I left alone and made a quick five miles to camp.

The ensuing days were quiet. Hiker numbers had dwindled,

partly due to some still working their way back from Damascus and also because, approaching the end of the second month on the AT, many had given up. The first month sees many hikers drop out of their thru-hike for various reasons: it was physically and psychologically harder than they had thought, finances weren't holding up, blisters were too much to handle or the experience just didn't suit them.

Daffy and Lazagne had travelled back from Pearisburg to take five days out with relatives so I was on my own for much of the time, albeit with some familiar faces cropping up. I didn't mind the solitude — in fact I bathed in it. I am met with surprised looks from people when I tell them about thru-hiking and even further amazement when they realise I go alone. On any thru-hike, there are many others going solo and I often spend the first couple of weeks socialising briefly with others, chatting and finding out about them. I quickly realise who I could spend more time with and subsequently I do hike with others, but equally relish the prospect of time alone. On the PCT I thrived over one section of the Sierra Nevada, where I saw no-one for five days.

On the AT there are literally thousands attempting a thru-hike each year, less on the PCT and under a hundred on the CDT, although the figures enjoy a steady upward curve. The option is always there for company if needed. Friendships are tested to their limits on thru-hikes, even if you go out with your best friend — suddenly spending twenty-four hours a day in their company stretches even the closets of alliances and it is something I have never done for that reason. I prefer to spend time with those that I meet and connect with but I can honestly say that I could have quite happily hiked the whole of the AT on my own, seeing no one.

I'm an introvert by nature. Shy as a kid, it is only the last ten years that I have come out of my shell and become more confident. During my twenties I suffered from long bouts of depression because of an inability to socialise in groups of more than four people. I hated being the centre of attention, struggled expressing myself and hid away at home, sometimes not venturing out for weeks except to work. I declined invitations to attend social events because I couldn't deal with them.

Introverts have always had a raw deal. Society has pushed the extrovert on us as the successful human being, the one we should all strive to become but I don't buy into that. Their confidence does indeed give them the ability to make a success of careers and their characters handle social situations easily. They thrive and gain energy from being amongst others.

Introverts prefer to stay in the background. We recharge through solitude and easily drain with too much social stimulation. This, you would think, may suggest that the extroverts make more successful people and although around 50 to 65% of the population are extroverts, bear in mind that Bill Gates is an introvert, as were Abraham Lincoln, Albert Einstein and Mahatma Gandhi. The extrovert may be the one at the helm of the board meeting, holding court and controlling the room but it's the quiet person sat at the back who is digesting the events, turning them over and coming up with the great ideas.

Being introverted is a great attribute for which I am grateful. I wouldn't change it. My best ideas come when I am alone and I feel energised through solitude, I live for it and I thrive through it. I will always escape to my local hills when I can, usually in the middle of the week when they are quieter — and within minutes, my escape from the madness of society makes me happy. I am able to think clearly on my own.

My ability to thrive away from people often reaches extremes. During my time on the AT not only did I revel in the occasional bout of solitude, as rare as it was, but often I escaped further. At the end of the day, I'd take a side trail, or even tramp through the undergrowth to get away. I'd spend a solitary evening there, and quite often the following morning as well, immersed in my own company and thoughts. If I heard hikers ahead of me I would take a break to let them move on. Conversely, if I knew people were behind me I'd increase my pace to escape.

At the far end of the solitude spectrum, where I could push the boundaries of this world no more, I dreamt up scenarios to please my isolation further. I fantasied about the apocalypse, the final days of humankind where I never saw another soul — a lone survivor drifting through a world of decaying cities and towns. Surveying a legacy rotting, crumbling and deteriorating, I was free to wander, a dromomaniac indulging their ultimate fantasy. As extreme and intense as it may sound, I know I would be happy there.

Thru-hiking is my escape. It is the only time that I am free to spend several months devoid of regulations and to live my life with minimal constraints. Or, to quote James Thurber:

"Two is company, four is a party, three is a crowd. One is a wanderer."

***

I crossed the VA-630 and walked over a footbridge, neglecting to collect water for the evening camp. The AT climbed 1300 feet to Bruisers Knob and I swallowed harshly as I reached the summit, my mouth dry and starved of moisture. I grabbed my water bottle from the side pocket of my pack and poured out a last, warm, pathetic dribble.

Shit, Fozzie. Why didn't you pick up water?

The trail emerged from the shade of the woods and an afternoon sun blazed. Sweat dripped down my face; my shirt was dark and sodden with perspiration. I sat down, wiped a hand across my forehead and looked at my palm as a mix of dirt, sweat, salt and sunscreen left an oily mess. My hair was oily, matted and smelt, as did I. My fingernails appeared like black crescent moons, dark with ingrained dirt and my legs were caked with a layer of dust and sweat, interspersed with red, swollen mosquito bites.

I checked the guidebook. Sarver Hollow shelter nestled, somewhat annoyingly, half a mile down a steep hill off the trail and the water source was even further down. It was the only water for five miles and my day was coming to an end. I didn't need the walk down — and more importantly back up again — and I didn't want to see anyone at the shelter. I wanted to be alone. Begrudgingly I sat up, hoisted my pack and trudged down. Faces I didn't recognise were setting up for the night in Sarver Hollow, but I nodded a greeting to Tinkerbell whom I had already met and carried on down to collect water. Slowly, in the sapping heat I walked back up to the ridge.

The views either side opened out majestically as I made my

way along the ridge towards Sinking Creek Mountain. Ominous clouds piled up the east side and rain shadows darkened the lowlands. I glanced to the west, felt a strong wind coming straight at me with more threatening clouds getting closer. The heavens opened in a matter of minutes so I ducked into the woods and searched for a suitable camp spot. The ground sloped sharply down the west side of the ridge which didn't bother me because I now had the hammock which could pitch over any uneven ground. I took it out and searched for the two support slings which wrapped around the trees at either end. I couldn't find them.

Wind started to tear through the woods. I looked up as trees creaked overhead and gales tore at the leaves. I was a little exposed but the woods offered some shelter and it wasn't cold; at worst I would get wet. I retrieved the waterproof flysheet and fashioned two, weak anchor points between the trees, low to the ground. I had sent my air pad back because it wasn't used in the hammock and instead, piled up leaves for insulation and a modicum of comfort. For a little more insulation, I lay my groundsheet and pack down. The fly was perfect for the hammock but, not designed for use low to the ground, it was a little narrow and as I cooked my meal, the sides lifted in the gusts and rain worked underneath.

I spent an uncomfortable night with little sleep. Although I stayed relatively dry, stones protruded from the uneven ground and I had to adjust my position constantly. As I lifted my pack to clear away, the two, lost hammock slings peered at me mockingly.

Clouds had congregated in the valley appearing like a vast ocean below me. Distant ridges appeared briefly through the cloud before disappearing like huge serpents. I descended down to Craig Creek road, passing Juggles and Rainbow Eyes collecting water just before the Niday shelter. I had met Juggles briefly and we chatted. He had also heard that PJ's stress fracture was confirmed and he was taking a month off trail to recuperate.

I struggled up Cove Mountain and onto the jagged, fluctuating ups-and-downs of a section appropriately known as the Dragon's Tooth which tired me quickly. I wasn't progressing well, my speed was slow, albeit hampered by a difficult section; but I felt lethargic, as though only firing on three cylinders. I put it down to my lack of sleep the previous night.

It was warm, each week the temperature seemed to be increasing and the humidity was creeping up as well. I don't mind walking in a dry heat; on the PCT it often went over 100 F in the Californian desert but there was no humidity so I coped well. However, as soon as it became muggy I struggled, along with everyone else.

The water sources were, thankfully, still flowing and up in the mountains it ran clear and cold. Very often, where we passed these sources, be it usually a creek or spring, we were near the top of the Appalachian hills where the water drained off the summits so the quality was excellent. I filtered everything I drank, even the spring water. My filter unit required no pumping; I just filled up the bottle and screwed the unit on top, then sucked the water through the filter so water stops were quick. I pulled my bottle from a side pocket, dipped it in a creek, screwed the filter back on and I was off, the whole process often taking as little as fifteen seconds.

But as the summer became hotter, the smaller water sources lower down were drying up or reducing to pathetic dribbles so I couldn't dip my bottle in — they were becoming too shallow. To solve the problem, most hikers would take a leaf, fresh from a nearby bush, and wedge it into the dribble, weighed down with the help of a stone. Often, the water sources would still have these leaves there, thoughtfully left by someone else. The leaf funnelled the water down to its tip where we could hold our bottles underneath.

***

I smiled as I finally reached the top of the hill and saw McAfee Knob. This famous rock outcrop, appearing to protrude like a diving board, is thought to be the most photographed spot on the entire trail. Pick up any AT calendar, or search the internet for Appalachian Trail and sure enough, McAfee Knob will appear somewhere with a hiker sitting on the edge, legs dangling over the precipice.

Unfortunately it was bustling with day trippers when I arrived so I decided to keep going and a good idea it turned out to be. Seven miles further on was the delightfully named Tinker Cliffs, a half-mile section where the trail skirts along the edge of the same precipice, weaving up to and away from the drop. I wondered why this section wasn't more popular. The view was easily on par, if not better and it wasn't centred on one spot, but more of a ten-minute travelling delight. It was also quiet, away from the tourists so only the occasional thru-hiker passed by. Taking full advantage of my loose planning approach, even though it was only 10 a.m., I smiled, dropped my pack and slung up the hammock twenty feet from the edge to indulge in a little randomness.

A cooling breeze lifted up from the valley and swept over me. There I lay, sometimes taking my trekking pole and pushing the ground to sway the hammock. If anyone passed by I occasionally received a greeting which I either ignored, offering a fake snore so I didn't appear rude, or just waved a casual arm in lazy recognition. After days of pushing out miles, it was a wonderful tonic to just stay in one place and experience a small section of the trail for a day instead of a flashing glimpse.

As the sun lowered, a receding light chased it, fighting a losing battle with skies above becoming an inky canvas. Reds joined the celebration brushed with oranges, caressed with yellows and flicked by casual violets. Slowly, my surroundings darkened and I waved my hand, pretending to orchestrate the playing of the stars. They obliged willingly, each one joining in the symphony, visual musical instruments sharing the ensemble.

The moon appeared shyly, peeking over distant mountains and slowly bathed my world in silvers and greys. As it rose, becoming more confident like a child making friends at nursery, its initial coyness fading as it climbed higher to take command of the sky.

I was alone, a solitary hiker, making a small section of the Appalachian Trail my own. This was my home, at least for the night and it welcomed me. There were no noise interruptions save a few leaves rustling. I heard no cars, no planes, nothing except what nature offered me.

Daleville, by stark contrast, was completely the opposite.

Situated just off the US-81, it epitomised everything I loathed about some US towns. The VA-220 carved a straight line straight through the middle of a collection of fast food restaurants, garages and motels. It did have everything a thru-hiker could hope for, just lacked character and presentation. I checked into the Howard Johnson Motel, a short walk from where the trail popped out of the woods. Juggles arrived in the afternoon as we had agreed to share a room.

It had been five days since my last wash, which was about normal. Salt stains streaked my shirt, my shorts were blotched with dust and dirt and I picked out debris from the wool entwines of my socks. A clear line of dirt around my ankles contrasted with the white skin of the sock line and my wrinkled feet sported ingrained dirt around the toes and nails.

The problem with laundry day was that everything needed washing, which in turn meant I had nothing to wear. You can always spot a thru-hiker in the laundry because they will either be sitting there sweating in Gore-Tex, the only item of clothing available, or with a meagre towel wrapped around them as they sit tightly crossed legged. I usually did my laundry first because I hated taking a shower to get into dirty clothes. All I had was my poncho so there I sat, in the Howard Johnson laundry room, with a silver section of cuben fibre wrapped around me, scanning the singles ads in some obscure local magazine.

I watched dark brown trickles of water slide off me in the shower and helped myself to a generous portion of shampoo which failed to lather and eventually, after two washes, the drainage ran clear. A sweat rash circled both ankles caused by my socks and a speckled fungus wove in and around my toes as I dusted them with foot powder.

Being filthy on a thru-hike is hard to accept at first but, once resigned to the fact that there is little that can be done, a thru-hiker becomes used to it. Just a day's walk in summer is enough to make most people smell somewhat undesirable, but after five or more days without washing or laundry the aroma reaches a stage where it's borderline dangerous. We don't notice it, as someone may forget they are wearing perfume, and the nose becomes immune after a while.

However, having reached town, if food is first priority

(which it often is), once in the air-conditioned environment of a restaurant the smell of our bodies suddenly reaches our noses and we grimace. Arms are raised and arm pits smelt, invitations to smell each other are accepted and waiting staff casually point fans in our direction.

"There you go," a waitress may say, coyly standing as close as she dare. "You'll be more comfortable in this cooler air. Or perhaps you'd like a table outside?"

***

Chris 'Juggles' Chiappini was patching up and repairing some war wounds to his gear when I got back to the room. He came from Midland Park on the outskirts of New York City. As his trail name suggested, he was a professional juggler. Having learnt his craft from a young age, and encouraged by his father, he worked for agencies who found him work. Albeit a niche trade, there isn't exactly an abundance of jugglers out there so he found gigs fairly regularly.

He also wanted to be a stand-up comedian which may paint a picture of a guy that runs off a series of jokes every time you see him. Not so, but it wasn't his lack of material that I found funny, it was his delivery. Even during conversation, I would often ask him a question and he would pause, raise his hand with one finger extended, and look somewhat confused with his mouth slightly ajar, suggesting he was going to answer. But he didn't — for a few seconds, he would ponder the question, occasionally make a false start to respond, and eventually he'd answer. Why I found this funny I don't know, but it just made me laugh.

Bush Goggles appeared in the evening, then Thirsty, and we all spent the evening chatting in the room.

I was glad to get out of Daleville; not an unpleasant place, just lacking identity. I disappeared off into the woods and despite a climb up to the Fullhardt shelter, the hiking was easy. With no big elevation changes, the trail floated along between 2000 to 3000 feet in a series of short, non-taxing ups-and-downs. I stopped briefly to chat to Kaleidoscope and Not Worthy at the Wilson Creek shelter before bouncing up and down the trail

Balancing on Blue

further.

Strange insects called from the woods and the mosquitos were out in force. I don't know why I attract mosquitos, or mozzies as I call them. The accepted theory is based on their ability to detect carbon dioxide which all humans emit. Others speculate that increased body temperature and metabolism, blood type and the colour of clothing all have an impact. I don't know what it is I have but if I'm in the vicinity of mozzies, which at that point of my thru-hike was basically everywhere, then I got mauled.

They weren't so prevalent during the hotter daytime temperatures, but came out for feeding when it cooled in the late afternoon and early evening. I prayed for wind, or even a breeze as they couldn't fly well in those conditions and, after a while, I learnt to seek out the ridges at the edge of the tree line where I could count on some airflow. That was the only weapon in my armoury I could rely on.

During the still evenings, as soon as I stopped for camp, I was pounced on. I might have been sitting down eating my dinner when a familiar droning circled around my ear. In between mouthfuls I would swipe the air erratically and slap myself, becoming more frustrated. As their numbers increased, so did my temper. After perhaps thirty minutes of trying to stay calm, I'd eventually just flip out and lose it, much to the amusement of anyone in the vicinity.

"Fuck off will yer?!" I'd yell, jumping around camp smacking the living daylights out of my exposed skin. "Just fuck the fuck off! Seriously! FUCK OFF!"

Deet never worked and I hated using it anyway. The only effective method I'd employed in the past was to don my waterproofs, which they struggled to bite through. Apart from the fact that I'd just sit there with my Gore-Tex slowly filling up with sweat, I hadn't brought them anyway as I used just the poncho. Often I'd retreat into my hammock which, unless one of them stole in before I could zip up the netting, was the only effective method. But, once inside I was restricted to staying there except for mad dash pee breaks.

Thirsty and I had discussed the dilemma and agreed to trial a little known method which we had both read about and agreed made sense. Eating garlic is not the first deterrent that springs to mind for most people but it does, apparently, work. Garlic gets quickly into the blood stream and judging by the smell of most garlic lovers, is also emitted from the pores. Mozzies don't like the smell, or indeed the taste.

Thirsty claimed that it took a week to kick in so I stocked up in town and started throwing two fat cloves into my dinner every evening. Breakfast, however, was proving a problem. Garlic does compliment a lot of food but granola isn't one of them. Believe me, I tried it — it's not good. I love garlic and I really don't care who smells it, on or off trail. However, a raw, fat, garlic clove first thing in the morning on an empty stomach was too much even for my digestive system.

I had managed to chew and swallow some for two mornings but on the third, as I sat there with coffee in hand, staring at a worryingly obese clove, it proved a bad idea. I weighed up the option of either drinking my coffee with a bowl of granola first to line the stomach, or starting with the garlic to get it out of the way and letting the food and drink take the strong taste away. I chose the latter. Garlic is great chopped up into slices and spread around a meal but raw and all at once wasn't a good idea.

I started chewing. The heat hit me first and I started to sweat. Then my sinuses flooded with onion and my eyes watered. Valiant to the last I forced it down, wincing, convinced I was a small way further down the road of insect immunity. My stomach, however, had other plans and immediately ordered an emergency evacuation.

I vomited a mix of brown masticated dinner from the previous night and dark roast Italian coffee. My body immediately felt better but I bemoaned the waste of a decent mug of coffee. After that incident, I stuck to two or three cloves mixed in with my evening meal.

The rhododendrons were now in full bloom and I entered shaded tunnels awash with pink flowers and sweet scent. It was hot and sticky, even up in the mountains, albeit slightly more bearable at higher altitude. The land was green, all the plants were growing quickly and the trees, now sporting a coat of foliage, sheltered me from the sun. I remembered a conversation with Daffy some weeks earlier when I commented on the stark landscape of post winter. "Don't worry Fozzie," he said, "Give it a few weeks and it'll be a God damn jungle out there."

He was right. Whilst the peaks were just changing from browns, the lower elevations were awash with a thousand shades of green. Plants encroached onto the trail, their moisture wetting my clothing and slowly the paths had narrowed as the season wore on. I dodged around poison ivy, ducked under branches and squeezed through overgrown sections.

I loved life in the woods. Many found the confined world amongst the trees too much, some even quitting for that reason, but I was revelling in it. I adored both the open spaces and the trees when I walked anywhere and England offered a varied mix of both. The AT reminded me of home.

I lived in the woods, respected them and in return they looked after me. They shaded me from the fierce sun and shielded me from strong winds. During light showers the canopy above dealt with most of the rain before it even reached me. Streams offered water to drink and at times wild food was found. Occasionally a pool or creek would offer itself up so I could wash and every single night, two stout trees held me aloft as I slept in my hammock. The woods provided firewood for the colder nights and during the warmer nights the smoke chased away some of the mosquitos. I was given logs to sit on or trunks to rest my back against. Sand from the creek beds washed my mug, spoon and even cleaned the grime off my hands.

Take a look at a map of east America and you'll see a broad swathe of green stretching from Georgia all the way up to Maine. The Appalachian Mountains were now my home and the best was still to come. When society collapses, for whatever reason, I will pack my rucksack and run for the woods. I know I can survive there and I know they will help me. I bow to the woods.

***

It was May 28th. I had been on trail for 59 days and covered 745 miles. This was slow progress but expected after my successful anti-blister plan, and it was the first hike I had ever done without suffering from them. My careful start and low-mileage days had worked. The soles of my feet had formed the usual hard covering of skin, the body's method of dealing with constant wear and tear. Two, small ridges ran along the underside of my little toes which always happened on thru-hikes and the pads below my big toes were hard and calloused.

Now on full throttle and fighting fit, I slowly started making inroads into the mileage deficit. My mileage was hovering around twenty-five each day and I'd even thrown in a couple of thirties.

I passed under the guillotine, a gap between two vertical slabs of rock with a round boulder wedged above, and then I plummeted down 3412 feet over fifteen miles to arrive at the James River footbridge, the longest pedestrian-only bridge on the AT, some 650 feet long.

Crossing the VA-130 the 2700-foot climb up to Bluff Mountain wasn't as severe as I had anticipated. I passed Day-Glo, Slim and Sun on the way up and by the time I'd reached the top I was sweating already as the heat of the day intensified. A clear cut provided a great view as power lines stretched over me and I admired the landscape to both sides as the mountain dropped away to the lowlands, dotted with rivers and towns.

I leaned back against a rock and glanced to my right; something had caught my eye. It was a hiker, his small pack suggested he was out for the day.

"Hey, how's it going?" I asked.

He glanced in my direction but said nothing.

"Hey," I repeated, "You doing OK?"

Again there was no response. He was wiping his brow and walking unsteadily. I figured he just didn't hear me so ate a quick snack and thought I would ask again as I passed him. Instead, he came over a couple of minutes later, still looking slightly disorientated.

"Hey," he said. "I'm sorry, I heard you but ..." he trailed off.

"Mate, are you OK? Is everything all right?" I stood up.

"I ... I ... don't know."

I noticed he had grazes to his face, his lip was swollen and he had cuts to his legs.

"I think I fell, I ... I, don't remember. Where am I?"

He looked beaten up. As well as his injuries he was shaking, sweating and his face was pale.

"Mate, sit down. Here." I offered my shaded perch against the rock as he dabbed blood from his lip. "You have any water?" I asked.

"Yes." He took his bottle but fumbled aimlessly with the cap. I took it, unscrewed the lid and handed it back.

"Drink some water," I said. "Rest, take some deep breaths, move into the shade here and just take a few minutes. I ain't going anywhere."

"Thanks."

He gulped down his water and took big, heavy breaths, his chest rising and falling.

"Do you have any electrolytes, sugar maybe? A salty snack, something like that?"

"No."

I handed him a sachet of electrolyte mix and some peanuts. "Take it easy on the nuts but drink that. Do you have more water?"

"Yes. No. I don't think so."

I filled his bottle with some of mine and slowly his pale complexion coloured.

"I fell," he confirmed. "I did fall. I felt terrible, nauseous, weak, shaky. I did fall."

His injuries were minor but his condition worried me. He was slowly coming back to normal but a long way off being capable of hiking. The heat was unbearable and he was eleven miles from the road.

"Do you have any medical issues? Do you take any medication?"

"Just blood pressure pills."

"Look mate, I think you've probably just pushed yourself a little hard. It's hot, and you look dehydrated. The electrolytes will kick in but keep drinking and rest for thirty minutes OK?"

"OK, thanks."

I stayed with him for an hour, still concerned for his condition.

He eventually got up, took a deep breath and smiled.

"I'm OK, I'm good, really."

"You sure?"

"Yup."

"Where you heading?"

"Down to the James River."

"Do you want me to walk down with you?"

"No, I'm fine, really."

"Listen mate, I've just climbed eleven miles to get up here. Believe me, the last thing I want to do is go all the way back down again and then come back up. But, BUT, if you're not up to getting down there, you need to tell me. I will come back down with you."

I looked him in the eye and he returned the gaze, solidly.

"I will come back with you if I don't think you're OK, or you want me to," I added.

"I'm fine, thank you, really, I'm good to go."

"This is my cell number." I wrote it on a scrap of paper. "Please message me when you get down so I know you're OK. There are other hikers behind me — stop them if you need to, they'll help you out."

I gave him the last of my water as I knew there was more a further mile away at the Punchbowl shelter, and another sachet of electrolytes. He shook my hand and set off back down the hill.

I downed a litre of water at the Punchbowl shelter spring and took another litre with me. Rounding a switchback I came face to face with a fawn. We stopped just six feet apart and for a few fleeting seconds just stared at each other. I saw the colour of its eyes and the sun shining through its fur. It was beautiful. It stood motionless looking at me, and its eyes showed no fear. It didn't seem startled — more curious. Suddenly my phone beeped and it darted quickly to one side, bounding through the undergrowth but turned, head over its shoulder and took one last look. Then it was gone.

I checked my phone: 'Got down. I'm all good, thank you so much for your help, Dave.'

I smiled; it was good to know he'd made it.

I was keen to get to Brown Mountain shelter, or at least near it. I was later than usual, partly due to taking time to help Dave and I was also tired.

Deep, Bush Goggles, Turbo Toes, Dayglo and Sun had made

camp by a sweet little flat area bordering the creek. I slung the hammock between two trees that could almost have been put there for me. A small fire illuminated our surroundings as the day came to an end and Brown Mountain Creek slid quietly past.

Talk was of the Shenandoahs. The Shenandoah National Park is held in high esteem by hikers. The terrain is easier and there are numerous places to stop and eat along Skyline Drive which caters to the many motorists enjoying the scenic stretch of road, which the trail crosses several times. Gabriele had arranged to come out for a week with her son Max, and the area seemed like the ideal place for them to experience a little bit of the AT.

However, as always when friends joined me for a portion of a thru-hike, things never went quite as planned.

Chapter 9

Half Way Done

June 1st to June 16th
Mile 800 to 1089

I tended to score the towns I stayed in according to various criteria. Amenities, appearance, compactness, quality of the restaurants, cafés and suchlike. I compared everything else against Hot Springs after my excellent stay there. It had been relaxing — a smattering of old, red brick buildings reminded me somewhat of home, a great café tended to my coffee needs and all the conveniences were close to hand. Damascus was also wonderful and I was to experience more great trail towns as I travelled further north.

On initial inspection, Waynesboro wasn't one of them. Although historic, it wasn't visually stimulating. Most of the buildings were fairly new and uninspiring. It wasn't a huge place but neither was it small, which meant walking about to shop, to do laundry and to eat. It's ironic how a thru-hiker can negotiate several thousand miles without grumbling but ask them to walk around town on a rest day and they'd look at you as if you're insane.

The Comfort Inn provided accommodation and Juggles, Goggles, Thirsty and I shared a room. Walking to the laundrette with Bush Goggles we realised we had no spare clothing to wear, as usual, because we had to wash everything. So we sat

Balancing on Blue

watching the clothes go round whilst wearing a couple of dangerously small discarded towels around our waists, much to the amusement of the locals.

Relaxing over a beer back in the room, I became curious about Juggles. He had written his email address down for me, which was associated with his website, so I took a look.

"Holy Shit!" I cried out.

Bush Goggles looked up from his ice cream, spoon still in his mouth.

"Wasup?!" he spluttered.

"Juggles was a World Champion!" I exclaimed.

"No shit?"

"Straight up, mate. He won the title in 2000! We're walking with a World Champion! I don't know about you, but if you're going to be World Champion at something, juggling has to be right up there for originality!"

Gabriele had travelled up to Waynesboro from Florida with her son Max for their week's taster on the trail. I experience confusing feelings when friends join me for a few days. It's great to see people I know, they invariably bring luxuries like dark chocolate and to have different faces around is wonderful. Conversely, the main problem is one of fitness. Two months into any trail and most hikers are in great shape, approaching the top of their game. The muscles are strong, lungs are working efficiently and the feet are hardened. Suddenly, when eager eyed and keen individuals join the fray, it invariably all goes wrong.

Mileage plummets, breaks are frequent, pace drops off and your opinion, help and knowledge are sought frequently. Despite this, I was keen to see them both and compromise was inevitable.

Gabriele arrived in my life at a time when I was beginning to figure out what I actually wanted out of it. Her farm back in Homestead had advertised for seasonal help in exchange for food and board. I had just returned from walking El Camino de Santiago in Spain. England was cold and damp, and I was eager to seek out warmer climes for a few months at minimal expense, so when she replied positively to my emailed plea, I jumped on the next available plane.

She was a very spiritual person, living healthily and had

transitioned from a vegetarian diet to eating completely raw food. Always viewing the world positively, she had made a success of her farm from difficult beginnings. I had great memories from the three months I spent there and left feeling rejuvenated after a diet change, good hard work and plenty of opportunity to reflect and plan for the future.

Under his mother's guidance and direction, Max was destined to turn out good and he had. He was only twelve when I first met him on the farm and it was hard to believe this twenty-two-year-old man was the same person. He was studying hard and doing well. Softly spoken and with a gentle demeanour, he was easy to get on with.

They were both eager to spend time in the woods and taste this classic trail for a week. I had deliberately chosen a section in Virginia as the terrain was relatively easy and, just into June, the weather warm. After a few chores around town we hit the trail late, managing only seven miles before pulling up at the Calf Mountain Shelter. Gabriele had hiked well, never out of eyesight but Max was already struggling. They had hit the ground running but realised quickly that most of it was uphill.

Calf Mountain Shelter sat on top of a 3000-foot peak, but tucked away in the woods it felt more like a dark hollow. Wise Guy, Socks, Atlas and several others were milling in and around the full shelter. Gabriele and Max needed little guidance, having quickly set up their tent. Food as always was next on the agenda and they sat down to cook, making friends quickly with the others. A few raindrops found a way through the canopy but not enough for anyone to take evasive action as we congregated around the fire, our bodies flickering silhouettes around the woods.

I had faith in both of my new companions' abilities. They had researched their gear well and had even done a reasonable amount of training in preparation for their little outdoor foray. However, a couple of hours into day two and plans were not going well. I had slowed my pace to take their abilities into account and, although Gabriele was progressing well, Max very clearly was having problems. I took regular breaks, feeling obliged to act as their guide and look after them — although I was of course glad to do so. Gabriele always rolled in within a couple of minutes and was still either visible behind me, or walking with me. Max, however, was dropping further and further behind.

A mere three miles into the day, I reached the Turk Mountain Trail junction with Gabriele. We stopped to wait. The weather had turned for the worse, alternating between drizzle and heavy rain. The temperature had also plummeted; it felt more like October, not the start of summer. As we kept peering down a tunnel of trees behind us, eventually a lone, sodden figure emerged through the mist with a pronounced hobble.

"Max, you all right?" I enquired, fully aware he wasn't.

"No. My legs hurt, and I'm tired."

He put on a brave face, forcing down some energy snacks as Gabriele delved into her bag of natural remedies and wonder fixes. I tried to persuade them to push through to the Blackrock Hut, a further ten miles down the trail, making a potential thirteen mile total for the day but after a quick discussion, it was clear Max wasn't up to par. They stood by a road that intersected the AT many times in that section, and attempted to get a lift as I carried on to the Blackrock Hut. The understanding was that a decent meal, some rest, and maybe a shower would revitalise Max. We agreed to meet later that evening at the hut.

Despite seeing Max struggle, and the constant rain and chill, back on my own I felt like an unstoppable powerhouse. My legs in particular had never felt stronger and I began to toy with their limits, dipping in and out of my lactic thresholds. I approached hills and momentarily eyed them up as a boxer would an opponent. At times I ignored the elevation statistics in my data book, purely to revel in ignorance. Without breaking pace or stride, my eyes narrowed as each ascent came into view and I sized them up. Steepness, camber, length, surface, obstacles. My head buzzed in excitement, calculating the optimal form of attack. Hit them hard and quick or go in slower, conserving energy?

In the end I attacked them with no mercy and ascended higher, laughing at my ability to dip in and out of my pain barrier. Planting one foot precisely at the intended point, trusting in the decision that it would hold there whilst scanning the next landing option. On the rock? Land on the tree roots? Maybe not, they look slippery. Risk the wet dirt? Was the camber too much to hold my foot? Making the decisions, trusting them, I stormed on and repeated the process over and over again. Bam! Bam! Bam!

Reaching the limit, legs screaming, I held it there, dealing with the pain, toying with my bounds and discovering what I was truly capable of.

For a few minutes at the top of my game, there was always a sweet moment every day when it all came together. All the judgements, speed, and concentration merged into moments of hiking epiphany. Like a trance, a meditation, the outside world was a memory. My world centred onto a few feet of one of the world's classic hiking trails, in my small bubble where nothing else existed, mattered, or affected me.

I loved cracking along the trail at speed. The focus and judgement was almost euphoric. I demanded complete commitment in my decisions for each step over difficult terrain, focusing on the trail in front ready for each foot placement, the speed of it all, and trusting in my decisions. It was like a meditation. When everything came together and I reached that sweet spot, nothing else mattered because I felt I was in a different world.

I passed three women whom I remembered from earlier in the day. Peeking from under my umbrella I nodded a greeting.

"Didn't you pass us in that downpour earlier?" one of them asked.

"Yes, I did," I replied.

"And you're still smiling?"

I felt no need to reply. I just gave them another smile but it did make me think. I always tried to smile and acknowledge anyone I met on the trail, out of courtesy and because it made me feel good when I was on the receiving end. However, it suddenly made me realise that, despite the rain and cold, I *was* having a great time. Rarely did I feel that content in my everyday life. In fact, one of the few times I did feel happy back home was when I was either out walking for the day, or even better, counting down the days before I left on a thru-hike.

Once out there in the wilds, I always felt as though I belonged, as if it were my home. A friend once collected me from the airport after three months hiking and in the car he asked what my plans were now I was home.

"I'm not home," I replied. "Home is back where the trail is, and I've just left it."

I think my happiness on trail stemmed from the freedom, or being as close to freedom as I could ever hope to be. Although the AT and the terrain it passed through was still part of US society, and its rules and regulations, escaping to the wilds offered me a barrier between what I considered to be two very different worlds. Yes, anyone on trail for a few months is governed by the same restrictions as they were back in the city. But, on the other side of this barrier, out there in the woods, it was easy, thankfully, to forget that they ever existed.

There were virtually no buildings, no one in authority, no signs stating orders, no man-made noise, and there was no need to be in a certain place at a certain time. We were free to escape, to live our lives how we always used to live them, and I believe making this connection with nature reminds our bodies and minds of a time long ago when we were truly free. We all came from the wilds. The history, although long gone and forgotten for all of us, still occupies a small space in the back of our minds. Somewhere, subconsciously, our minds remember the woods where we spent our infancy; and spending time there rekindles those distant times in the past.

It *was* home.

***

The Blackrock Hut nestled in a small clearing a couple of minutes off trail. It slept just six and, being one of the first to arrive, I grabbed one of the bottom bunks in case the rain, which had finally stopped, decided to return.

Gabriele and Max were nowhere to be seen. I checked my phone for a signal but it didn't oblige. I was slightly worried that they may be in trouble, but knew they would be in town as I had last left them trying to get a lift.

I took half an hour to wind down and I stood, smoking, by the side of the shelter. A twig cracked in the woods. As I looked out of instinct, a bear paused perhaps fifty feet away, appearing to berate its mistake. It looked straight at me and carried on. Curious, I followed it, keeping my distance until it sloped off amongst the trees.

A new face had arrived at the shelter when I returned.

"Did you see that bear? Hey, I'm Hotshot!" We shook hands.

"Yes," I confirmed. "I followed it for a short while. I was a little concerned that it was heading in the direction of the trail but I think it's veered off somewhat."

"Ya'll not from around here are you? Where ya'll from? British?"

Oh crikey, not again.

"I'm English, name's Fozzie. Nice to meet you."

Hotshot thankfully didn't pursue the nationality subject but he told me about an incident with another bear earlier that day. He had been on the receiving end of a bluff charge, which is where a bear will run at someone threatening to attack and then, usually, call off the manoeuvre. I generally viewed a bluff charge as a test, for a bear to see if someone would run off and therefore appear weaker. If the hiker stood their ground — which is what we are advised to do — then generally a bear took the argument no further. Hotshot had stood his ground but he described it as one of the scariest moments of his life, comparing it to standing on a railway line when a train is hurtling towards you, hoping it would stop in time.

Frankly, the bear wasn't worrying me. The huge spider that had appeared inside the shelter concerned me more. A hiker called Boots had arrived and was occupying the top bunk, just below what he had identified as a wolf spider. He didn't seem to mind its presence and, in fact, commented that it was looking after him. We don't have big spiders back in the UK, and not being used to such large specimens, I kept a close eye on its location, sleeping fitfully.

***

I didn't listen to music very often on trail, preferring the sounds around me. On this occasion, however, I was keen to carry on reeling in the miles so I selected The Stranglers playlist on my phone. As 'Mercy' wafted through my earphones, my stride

Balancing on Blue

matched the rhythm.

The trail skirted around Blackrock summit, smoothing a path through a crazy mixture of huge boulders and slabs.

"Fozzie!"

I turned to see Juggles approaching from behind.

"Message from Gabriele," he continued. "They're bailing out."

"They are? Where did you see them?"

"At the Black Rock parking area."

I was surprised but part of me had expected it. It was sad to see them go after such a short while, but now I was free to carry on at my own pace.

Bush Goggles also showed and the three of us teamed up, stopping at Loft Mountain Wayside to enjoy a sorely needed burger and fries, nicely washed down with one of their speciality blackberry shakes.

Bush Goggles was complaining about a lack of sleep in the shelters due to what he referred to as the 'snorechestra'. I sympathised; a couple of hikers always kept the others awake with not just any old snoring, but often synchronised playlists reverberating off the wooden walls. I was still following my principle of sleeping in the tent unless there was a particularly bad storm forecast but the snorechestra wasn't my only problem. The shelters weren't exactly renowned for their spacious interiors and often we slept on platforms, raised off the ground. The roofs generally sloped down to meet these platforms and I had hit my head on several occasions, forgetting that there was such a small gap between the two. A bruised head was becoming such a regular occurrence that I had now started referring to the shelters as 'headaches' instead.

Skyline Drive made regular appearances during that section of trail. Running a distance of 105 miles from Front Royal to Rockfish Gap through the Shenandoah National Park. Intersecting the AT many times and being described as one of the most scenic drives in America, it was popular with cyclists and motorists. Subsequently, to our delight, Skyline was dotted with places to eat, known as 'waysides'. We enjoyed regular calorie top ups, and were also able to carry less food. With our packs being lighter, and the terrain in the Shenandoah National

Park being kinder, not only were we crushing good mileage, but stomachs were full and our fatigue subsided.

The Shenandoahs enjoy a great reputation amongst AT hikers. The elevation loss and gain was minimal compared to what we had become used to. It was also stunning to look at. Spoilt with many wide-open meadows commanding fine views over Virginia, it was home to a variety of wildlife such as deer, black bear, bobcat, raccoon, skunk, fox and rabbit.

As we hightailed it up Weaver Mountain, Bush Goggles, Juggles and I bumped into Squatch coming down. We stopped, and he took some video footage for Flip Flop Flippin' 2, whilst Juggles plied his trade in the background, thankfully with no drops.

Spending that night in the Hightop Headache, sorry Shelter, discussion was rife between the three of us that we push ourselves, get an early start and pull in a day with some decent mileage.

We hit the trail at 7 a.m., full of energy. The weather was stunning, the trail smooth and we flew along, albeit aided by some ibuprofen and Five Hour Energy drinks. By 8 p.m. we pulled up to camp having hiked thirty miles and bringing our tally on the AT to 928 miles. After sixty-nine days we were approaching half way and Harpers Ferry was just a few days away.

The mornings, in particular, were proving an exquisite time of day to walk. The cool air and quiet trail before the day trippers appeared was welcome. Early morning moisture dampened the trail to a dark brown, lightening as the day progressed and the sun dried it out. Rhododendron leaves speckled the ground, their red and yellow coats crunching underfoot. There were few sounds; birds chirped, rabbits scampered and rustled through the leaves as an occasional breeze murmured through the tree canopy. Occasional clouds drifted through my world like lost ghosts and my surroundings consisted of three colours: blue sky, green woods and brown ground.

Although I joined Bush Goggles and Juggles for most of the day, we also enjoyed time on our own as well. We had gelled, enjoying each other's company but relishing some solitude as well. With each of us pushing the miles, we had agreed to reach Harpers Ferry on June 11th. This entailed increasing our distances each day and I felt my mileage deficit from the start was gradually being eaten into. Over three days I had covered ninety miles.

I bumped along through the Shenandoahs, cresting regular peaks such as the Pinnacle, Pass Mountain and South Marshall Mountain before falling down from Compton Peak to intersect the US-522.

I was keen to keep up the mileage. Until, that is, I passed the Jim and Molly Denton Headache, sorry Shelter, a few yards off trail. With a large veranda to the front, including tables and chairs, I was tempted to lay up for the night. I managed to resist, just, although I did succumb to a shower and a quick laundry session under the solar-powered shower.

This could catch on. Nip into town, fill your stomach, do a quick resupply, grab a shower and wash your clothes at the same time. Long stops could be history.

A quick energy drink now known as 'rocket fuel', and two ibuprofen to argue it out with a sore shin, I sped off in the direction of the Rod Hollow Shelter, eager to pull in another thirty-mile day. It proved a big mistake.

Leaving at 1.30 p.m., there were eighteen miles to reach my destination. The first four and a half miles took me just an hour. I enjoyed a good rhythm over easy terrain, my trekking poles synchronised with my stride, breathing perfect, focus concentrated. In two hours I had covered nine miles, half the distance. When fully warmed up I felt little need to rest but revelled in my ability to cover distance quickly. I was sweating profusely; I wiped my shirt over my face and dried my trekking pole handles against my shorts. My shin started to ache but I ignored it and the trail continued to flash under my shoes until, finally, the turn off for the shelter signalled day's end. I was buzzing, on a high and soaked in the excitement of the afternoon. I had hiked eighteen miles fully loaded in a little over four hours.

The shelter was quiet; just two other hikers occupied the table outside. I did a double take and recognised one of them.

"Fozzie! Wassup!"

Pausing briefly, I struggled to remember his name.
"Onespeed! Hey! I'm good, how the hell are you?"
"Doing great."
I had last seen him in Irwin where we shared a motel room.
"This is Medic," he added, motioning to the woman sitting next to him.
I introduced myself and we shook hands.
"I'm going to get the hammock set up and I'll be back," I said.

After sitting for just ten minutes, my body had already cooled. I rose to reach for the jacket in my rucksack and pain shot through my shin. Wincing, I ran my hand over it. It was tender and swollen.

"You OK?" enquired Medic.
"Not sure. Does your trail name hold any relevance to your profession by any chance?"
She laughed.
"Yes. Here, let me take a look."
I gingerly raised my leg and rested it on the picnic table seat beside her.
"Any problems with your shin before?" she asked, gently running her hand over the area.
"No, never," I replied.
"How was your day? Have you been taking it easy? Did you fall? Were you pushing yourself?"
"Er, great day, I didn't fall and yes, I was pushing hard."
"This is not my specialised area but being a hiker, and a runner, I know a little about sport injuries. I'm pretty sure this is a shin splint."

I was aware of shin splints although they hadn't affected me in the past. I did know that in the worst cases it meant stopping all exercise and resting. I cursed myself for pushing too hard. Damage to the connective layer of tissue which covers the shin bone, or periosteum, causes inflammation. It can be caused by several factors; a rolling of the feet known as over-pronation during hiking or running is one, but usually it is caused by periods of intense exercise when you ask too much of your body. Even at the peak of physical fitness, we can still push too hard, and pushing too hard was exactly what I had been guilty of.

I faced the prospect of a two-week rest period. Medic saw my disappointment and tried to placate it.

"Don't worry," she said. "It's probably not as bad as you think. Try and be positive. There's an ice-cold spring over there, sit down, hold your shin under the running water for at least ten minutes and take ibuprofen. Both of these will reduce the swelling and help the healing process. Stretch it out when you can and new shoes may help. Yes, you may need rest but I've seen people in exactly this situation and the following morning they've hiked off with no problem at all. Hold it under the water whenever you can. Finally, if it is OK in the morning then carry on. Gently!"

I hobbled off to the spring and sat there for fifteen minutes, letting the water tumble over my shin and swallowed a couple of ibuprofen. The pain subsided somewhat. I ate heartily and slid into my hammock for a decent nights rest.

***

The Roller Coaster is a thirteen-mile section of trail, sixteen miles prior to Harpers Ferry. Its name pretty much describes better than I can what it involves and, whilst the series of ascents and descents aren't particularly high, nor at any great altitude, there are lots of them. Halfway through and I was knackered. The swelling on my shin, amazingly, had gone down and it didn't hurt. Nevertheless, I took the Roller Coaster easy, dropped my pace and continued to hold my shin under water a few times during the day.

Bush Goggles joined me for the afternoon. Whilst we rested, taking in the view from Raven Rocks, a new face going by the name of Dr Attractive sat with us. Bush Goggle's eyes lit up when he saw her and, leaving me to rest, he took off in hot pursuit.

I've explained that 'blue blazing' is the term coined for taking a side trail. Another is 'yellow blazing' whereby a hiker may take the road to cut off a section of trail and this stems from following the yellow lines on a road. Well, Bush Goggles was indulging in what we refer to on the trail as 'pink blazing', when a male deliberately follows a female in the hope of some reciprocal interest. I didn't see him for the rest of the day but eventually caught him just after the Virginia and West Virginia border, perfectly placed exactly on the thousand-mile mark.

Being late evening, the glimmering lights of Torlone's Pizza and Bar winked at us just down the road. With an absence of bars to that point, we promptly went in, ordered a Jack Daniel's and Coke each, and slumped in one corner with instructions to the waitress to keep a watchful eye on our drinks.

"Less than quarter full and feel free to replenish them," I advised, smiling.

We ate, then ate some more and finally, just after dusk, left Torlone's with more than a slight stagger to pitch camp a short way into the woods.

We had a mere five miles left to Harpers Ferry in the morning. The mercury was tickling ninety degrees and humidity was on the increase. The AT cut straight through Harpers Ferry and first stop was the Appalachian Trail Conservancy on Washington Street. Most hikers stopped there to say hello and the staff always insisted on taking everyone's photo out front for a visual, yearly record. It also acted as a great reference to see who was ahead, behind, and at what time they had passed through.

I had high expectations of Harpers Ferry. When I first became aware of the AT some twelve years earlier, the town regularly cropped up during my research. Perhaps the most famous place on the trail, it was considered to be the halfway mark although that actual point was around seventy-two miles further.

My expectations were met. The town nestled beautifully between the confluence of the Potomac and Shenandoah rivers. Crossing the Byron Memorial Footbridge over the Potomac I left West Virginia and entered Maryland, the sixth state of the AT.

Harpers Ferry is bathed in history and named after Robert Harper, who first settled there in 1747. In 1761 he established a ferry service across the Potomac, drawing settlers wishing to head further west into the Shenandoah Valley. Thomas Jefferson visited the town in 1783, referring to it as 'Perhaps one of the most stupendous scenes in nature'.

Thirsty, Juggles, Goggles and I were a little way from the

Balancing on Blue

centre of town, which entailed a lot of walking to reach the amenities but it proved a pleasure. The streets tumbled up and down, bordered by old, rickety wood and red-brick-fronted houses, their front gardens speckled with summer flowers. The restaurants, bars and shops were independent and all around me the surrounding hills kept sentinel. Harpers Ferry surpassed all of my expectations.

We spent our time, as usual, resupplying with food for the next stage as well as filling our stomachs with three good meals. My shoes, having lasted well from the start, now had 1000 miles on them and were finished. I had purchased a new pair back in Waynesboro and mailed them up to the post office. My new shoes were light trail runners — and although I had doubts about their durability, I was looking forward to the comfort they promised.

The guys were in good spirits. Our room quickly became swamped with piles of dirty laundry, opened packages from the post office, beer bottles and food containers. Every available anchor point was utilised to hang damp gear to dry. It smelt fine when we were in there, but after trips to town we returned to hold our noses at the aroma of sweat, week-old socks and damp gear. The cleaners, bless them, never batted an eyelid.

The four of us left late the following morning, clearing up the last of our chores and enjoying a late breakfast at the Town Inn. Most of us sported new shoes and T-shirts and with everything washed, including rucksacks, we could have passed for day hikers, our beards perhaps the only giveaways. We were always excited to arrive in town, especially one as notable as Harpers Ferry, but the feeling never quite lived up to the excitement of returning to the woods.

The trail ran parallel to Shenandoah Street as we passed Jefferson Rock, John Brown's Fort and over the Potomac River by way of the bridge and railway line. A flat, dead-straight path hugged the C&O Canal for two and a half miles and soon the sounds of town faded.

Juggles dropped back but Thirsty, Bush Goggles and I carried on, passing the Ed Garvey, Crampton Gap, Rocky Run and Pine Knob shelters. We enjoyed a delightfully flat trail before pulling over after twenty-five miles to camp near

Annapolis Rocks.

The trail was becoming rockier. The AT through Maryland was just forty miles long before entering the next state of Pennsylvania, famed for its hard-going, rocky trail. I figured the section near Annapolis Rocks was a precursor to this.

The day after a town stop I was constantly hungry. With the amount of food I used to eat when in town, my stomach figured I must have been back in civilisation and therefore expected further gratification. After sixteen miles we reached Pen Mar Park. Noticing some sort of military retirement party, or more importantly, the surrounding tables groaning under copious piles of food, Thirsty made plans.

Looking hungry, he headed off to make some polite conversation. The ultimate aim was to procure some form of sustenance for Bush Goggles and me. He returned a few minutes later looking dejected and empty-handed. If civilisation couldn't help us, the woods certainly did. The summer berries were just starting to ripen and we stopped regularly to feast on blackberries and raspberries. Wild strawberries were also nearly ready and we had little inkling of the feasts that lurked further north, including blueberries. A lack of fruit from that point in the trail was never a problem again.

Having left Maryland that morning, we eventually pulled off trail in Pennsylvania at the Tumbling Run shelters. Curious as to why there were two of them, I presumed it was purely to meet demand until I noticed a sign on each one. One read 'snorers', the other 'non-snorers'. Juggles eventually caught up with us, pitching his home-made tarp and inner mosquito net near to Bush Goggles' tent, whilst Thirsty and I strung up our respective hammocks. Juggles loved his camp setup, it had cost him very little as he had made most of it with the aid of his sewing machine back home.

"That's not my best piece of gear though, Fozzie," he announced. "Take a look at this!"

He delved into this backpack and pulled out his sleeping mat. Thru-hikers often utilised various items of gear for use when trying to get a ride into town at road junctions. 'Hiker to Town' was commonly inked onto anything large enough to be spotted by speeding vehicles and Juggles had used his sleeping mat to good effect.

"There's more," he continued, giggling.

He turned it over. We collapsed laughing after reading what he had written on the other side, for use purely as amusement, and to see the reaction from motorists.

'Psycho Killer!'

We commandeered the picnic table nestled between the two shelters and each of us ate like wolves, desperately trying to placate our respective appetites. We had the place to ourselves and the table quickly disappeared under a pile of food. Stoves were lit and there we stayed for the rest of the evening, occasionally topping up our calorie intake with nibbling and drinking.

When I read the shelter register I saw an entry from a hiker whose name wasn't legible but it said that Nito, who I had last seen near Damascus, had left the trail. He had succumbed to a case of tendonitis, which even after five days rest hadn't healed. There was also a message from Pink Bits — sorry, Lady Forward — dated four days earlier. I was still carrying the gauntlet and eager to return it to her.

Although we had yet to hit any major rocky sections in Pennsylvania, we knew they were coming and, even though the state was relatively flat compared to most, efforts were being made to continue with the high mileage to counteract any possible difficult days. Since Harpers Ferry we had covered eighty-five miles in three days. The trail was indeed easy, lacking any serious climbs and descents and we happily floated along between one and two thousand feet enjoying fine weather.

***

As far as thru-hikes go, Saturday 16th June was always going to be notable. We were all up at 5 a.m. and away by 6 a.m, although I walked with Juggles for the day, losing Bush Goggles and Thirsty during the morning. At mile 1069, both of us downed our packs, shook hands and had a hug before taking a few minutes to rest by a sign that most AT thru-hikers remember.

Appalachian Trail – Maine to Georgia
1069 Springer Mt S
1069 Mt Katahdin N

We were halfway. I felt elated, and surprised. It seemed to have arrived too quickly, and that it was only recently that I had stood on top of Springer Mountain. For a brief moment I felt sad, for I knew that it was only a matter of a few more weeks before, hopefully, I would stand on top of Mt Katahdin and my journey would be finished.

Until that time, I was determined to approach the second half of the AT with the same excitement as I had on the first half.

Chapter 10

Awesomely Nasty

June 17th to June 28th
Mile 1089 to 1300

A small town known as Pine Grove was on the guys' radars. I wasn't too bothered about their reasons why but, just after the halfway point, those few scattered houses were a renowned stop on the AT. The Pine Grove Furnace General Store was famous for a tradition known as the Half Gallon Challenge.

Instead of a hiker's usual preference for beer at reaching halfway, the Half Gallon Challenge of ice cream, or nearly two litres if that's your unit preference, was the accepted method of celebration. But I didn't have a sweet tooth, and besides, the prospect of eating that much ice cream didn't appeal to me. Besides, they didn't stock Mint Choc Chip and Raspberry Ripple just drew blank looks.

Juggles also chose not to participate but Thirsty and Bush Goggles were all over it. They were both successful and Bush Goggles, having had his dessert first and missed out on the first course, resolved that minor dilemma by finishing off a couple of burgers as well.

A few minutes further up trail, Fuller Lake in Pine Grove Furnace State Park also sported a shower block and we all took the chance to clean up. Juggles arrived just as I was leaving, complaining of soreness around his groin, or the 'sac' as the Americans like to call it, and judging by his facial expressions it wasn't too pleasant. I left him with a cotton wool ball and some rubbing alcohol, which I used for pretty much any medical problem. For sore skin, rashes, fungal issues and a decent disinfectant it was very effective. The only downside was it stung like I can't begin to describe, particularly when used for a sore sac. I kid you not when I say I have seen rubbing alcohol reduce a hiker to their knees. Juggles, I think, was also aware of its potency and I left him holding a plastic bottle of alcohol in one hand, cotton wool in the other, pondering whether to start juggling with them or contemplate his fate. Little did I know how those early signs of sore sac syndrome were to affect us.

We settled in a corner of the sports field for the night and I dreamt of being chased by giant cotton wool balls. Not concentrating in the morning, I lost a mile on the approach to the town of Boiling Springs when I inadvertently took a side trail for half a mile, and then had to return when I realised. Thirsty trusted my often dubious navigational skills, and despite an abundance of signs, followed me until I realised my error.

Boiling Springs did not, as you might imagine, refer to any thermal activity. Springs, yes, but the bubbling aspect referred to the pressure at which the water emerged from several artesian wells dotted around the town.

The AT ran straight through the middle and was therefore a popular place to grab some food and use the post office as an easily accessible destination for mail drops, as the trail passed right outside.

Although undeniably pretty, Hot Springs was a little twee for me. Prices were inflated from tourism and the gardeners appeared to have gone a little too far. Verges were neatly trimmed and often bordered with symmetrical rocks, regimental flowers stood guard, the grass was aggressively mown and artificial landscaping was prevalent. I grabbed some lunch at the Caffe 101 with Bush Goggles and Thirsty before they headed off, agreeing to meet me in Duncannon, twenty-six miles up trail. I had a parcel to collect but as usual timed my arrival to perfection on a Sunday, when it was closed, so I had to hang around until Monday morning.

The Allenberry Resort Inn and Playhouse, about half a mile out of town, offered reasonable rates so, unable to hike any further that day, I took care of some chores such as laundry and a small food resupply. I figured my shin, although not causing many problems, would benefit from some rest, just in case.

The weather forecast for the week was excellent and I had considered myself lucky up until that point. The AT's reputation for wet conditions, so far, hadn't come to fruition. The evenings were also cool so mosquitos were rare, and the famous Pennsylvanian rocks had still yet to say hello. It was proving ideal hiking and I wondered if, in the future, 2012 would be regarded as one of the few dry years to hike the AT.

I collected my parcel in the morning and started to make inroads into the twenty six miles to Duncannon where the guys were holing up for the night.

The trail was below 1000 feet for much of the way and gloriously flat, so progress was rapid. The woods thinned, I passed over bridges, crossed through fields and wandered through an agricultural landscape. I admit to actually skipping for a couple of minutes when no one was about.

"Hey! Ya'll hiking the trail huh?"

A man out walking his dog forced me to stop by taking up a stationary position in the middle of the track. His opening question was standard fare and I disguised a groan, knowing he would probably ask a load more. Everyone I met on trail was polite, the locals usually interested despite several thousand hikers passing through each year. However, I did tire of the same questions.

'Ya'll hiking the trail?' was invariably followed by 'where did ya'll start?' 'where ya'll heading?' 'how far do ya'll walk each day?' 'when do ya'll think ya'll finish?' 'how much does ya'll pack weigh?' and so on.

After replying to everything he threw at me, I bode him farewell and spent the rest of the afternoon pondering those questions and inventing scenarios to flip everything around. My favourite was imagining entering a restaurant and cornering an unsuspecting diner. My questions of choice included — "Hey! You're sitting in a restaurant huh? What you eating there? Burger huh? How's it going so far? When did you start? When do you think you'll finish? That's a big burger! What sort of weight we talking? Must be a pound at least!"

A short but steep hill shook me from my daydreams and I rested in the empty Darlington Shelter at the top, taking a quick lunch including some wild strawberries I had collected. Pink Bits, sorry, Lady Forward, had left a progress note in the shelter register and I discovered I had gained ground on her. She was four days ahead and I was looking forward to relinquishing the gauntlet.

"Starting to get rocky!" I said to Easy Rider, a hiker I'd not met before, as he rested on a slab of rock overlooking the approach to Duncannon later that day. The descent to town was one of few rocky sections I had walked through but gave me some idea of what was coming.

"Sure is!" he replied. "Gets worse as well."

Duncannon sported some wonderful architecture. The AT followed the High Street, which, along with the surrounding streets, provided some visual clues to its age. The Doyle Hotel was one of them, being a favourite stop for thru-hikers because of its cheap prices. A balcony ringed the first floor of this red brick building and one rounded front corner looked like a castle turret. Unfortunately the Doyle, and apparently most of Duncannon itself, seemed to be lacking in local funding: faded paint flaked here and there, repairs long overdue. It definitely had charm, perhaps just in need of a little polish to allow it to shine.

I had heard mixed reports about the Doyle on Market Street, ranging from being 'worse than an overflowing privy' to 'an absolute must stop' and even 'awesomely nasty'.

When I swung open the front door my eyes momentarily adjusted to the lower light level. Bush Goggles and Thirsty glanced round and each raised a beer bottle in unison, complete with a suggestive 'come drink' expression. Some unfamiliar faces peered from the corners and baskets of chicken and chips dotted the tables.

Pat and Vicky Kelly, the owners, bought the hotel in 2001. It was originally constructed in the 1770s but burnt down. The current incarnation was built in 1903. The Ritz it wasn't, but with the majority of the clientele sporting beards, rucksacks, appearing in sore need of a shower and muttering 'food', or 'beer', it didn't need to be. The Doyle unashamedly catered for thru-hikers, which was reflected in the $25 room price, even less if shared.

The rumours had made me slightly wary but I immediately loved the place. The bar was the Doyle's focal point, acting as the feeding, drinking, Internet-checking, social and general hanging out point. Tables and chairs made from dark wood skidded and screeched around on a tiled floor. Wood panelling adorned the lower half of the walls, rising to tobacco-stained uppers occasionally interrupted by lighter, rectangular spaces from missing, long-forgotten pictures. A deep polished wood ceiling stared down on hikers catching up with the news.

I stayed for one night but left early with Bush Goggles, eager to return to the trail and preserve my hiking budget after two consecutive nights in a hotel. We followed the High Street as, gradually, Duncannon started showing signs of life. Car exhausts released a slow rise of smoke, drifting to meet a low mist. Front doors slammed, and cries of 'see ya later!' echoed as the locals began their commute.

We crossed the railway line and walked over a short bridge spanning the River Juniata which fell to a narrow strip of land before the Clarks Ferry Bridge, which stretched out and carried us both over the Susquehanna River.

From 400 feet the trail rose sharply to around 1242 feet. Bush Goggles pulled away; having no desire to push my shin, I fell back, spending the rest of the day on my own. It was hot, and as I stopped briefly to chat with Chez 11, he informed me it was 100Â°F with humidity off the scale.

Finally, Pennsylvania had delivered on its rocks — often moist from early morning dew, making them slippery. Several different routes wove through rock sections, around and beside them; clear, worn trails where past hikers had picked out the line of least resistance. Most days there was little wind and mosquitos droned annoyingly as cobwebs constantly wrapped round my face, arms and legs followed by a frantic slapping of my cheeks, praying that the actual spider wasn't also attached. Often, perhaps an hour into the day, hikers would meet coming from opposite directions and relief was palpable from both parties, aware that the other had cleared the trail.

"Oh, thank God!" One sobo exclaimed, wiping her face as we surprised each other. "No more cobwebs!"

There was no getting away from cobwebs. The short-term solution I used was holding one trekking pole in front to clear them; but there was only one, sure-fire winner and that was to walk behind someone else.

Pennsylvania's rock came in all manner of different forms and I soon learnt how to deal with its whims. Often I was confronted by a crazy mess of loose blocks, like a stone wall that had been knocked down and abandoned. A fine balancing act ensued and, as I educated myself to this new obstacle, it became second nature to stick to the high points and 'float' over the surface. Getting bogged down in the indentations, hollows and low points left a hiker plodding through and lifting their legs each time to make any progress. Picking out the pointed, raised rocks, my eyes flicked from one landing point to the next in quick succession. When I became complacent, I had to force myself to lay off the speed a little for fear of making a mistake. Many a thru-hike of the Appalachian Trail has ended unceremoniously in Pennsylvania.

Raised lines of stone, which we referred to as 'shark's fins' or 'ankle breakers', bisected other sections. Hopping from one to the next, I teetered, and flapped my arms ungracefully in a balancing act before regaining my composure. They often came into view only as I climbed higher and scanned the trail ahead for a familiar white blaze. It's not unusual for hikers to inadvertently end up on side trails in Pennsylvania as the need to focus so much on the terrain, with head down, meant they kept missing the white blazes.

I lost time and distance through those sections, but the flat, smooth, dirt trails in between more than made up for it. The relief of hitting soil after an hour negotiating a rock field was almost exciting.

I reached the 501 Shelter, named after the 501 road it stood near. It was a welcome change, boasting four walls, plenty of internal space and a clear, plastic dome on the roof where sunlight poured in. It was June 21st, eighty-three days into my hike and I smiled as I wrote in my diary that evening, having checked the data book, for there were less than 1000 miles to the finish.

I sat outside swatting mosquitos with Bush Goggles, Thirsty and Juggles. The talk turned to the problem of soreness around the groin area. Juggles's condition had deteriorated, whilst the rest of us were rapidly descending also into what most referred to as 'crotch rot'.

The result of walking for hours every day, in high temperatures and humidity, with shorts rubbing was that the area concerned was constantly damp, dirty and chafed, resulting in an incredibly sore and painful rash which became infected. Several days between showers and neglecting our personal hygiene weren't helping matters either. It wasn't as if we had access to a shower every day so little could be done.

"Mate, you could try losing the shorts," I said to Juggles. He had been wearing tight-fitting, Lycra cycling models. "They're black so they heat up and your boys need some air down there. Let them breathe!"

There were mutterings of agreement from the collective but Juggles was very fond of his shorts. However, as he constantly shifted around on his seat, he was clearly not comfortable. Bush Goggles and Thirsty were also suffering from early symptoms. As usual at the shelters in the evening, many minds strived to reach solutions and others also appeared to have fallen foul of crotch rot. With so many casualties, the advice was generous.

Some advocated cleaning the area with a damp cloth, usually a bandana with a little soap, although I hasten to add it was not then used for headwear as well. Before long, wise words and suggestions were aired.

"Drop your shorts and offer your arse to the wind for five minutes every day," floated out from the shelter.

"Cut the lining out of your shorts. Never had a problem, but be careful sitting during rest breaks when talking to the ladies," drifted over from the direction of the privy.

Daily swabs with baby wipes, antiseptic cream, a medicated foot powder known as Gold Bond and rubbing alcohol were also firm favourites. I used a mixture of alcohol and powder and, although sore, it wasn't bothering me as much as some. I dusted twice a day and if things got really sore then out came the rubbing alcohol. 'Rubbing' is not the technique I'd recommend for applying the demon fluid. The upmost respect had to be exercised and, although the actual application took just a few seconds, my personal routine stretched out to at least five minutes as I needed that length of time to summon up enough courage to do it in the first place.

I usually swabbed myself in the evening, retiring to the privy with my cotton wool bud in hand. After a short, but intense period of meditation and deep breathing I looked skyward and prayed to the hiking gods. The sooner the finish, the sooner the stinging subsided — but the initial few seconds, when I hesitantly dabbed and wiped my undercarriage, and subsequent minute's worth of pain brought me to my knees stifling a scream. As I gritted my teeth and rocked back and forth on the toilet, my breathing rate and volume approached that of a woman giving birth during a particularly bad labour. However, in the following days my boys often returned to something approaching normality.

In the morning I rounded a bend in the trail to see Bush Goggles, or 'Goggles' as his trail name had shortened to, standing in the middle of the trail, peering down into the recesses of his shorts and one hand rubbing lotion down there. Seeing me, he looked up smirking with a knowing glint in his eye and just said:

"Pro-active sac day."

***

Several times a day throughout a thru-hike, my head took time to calculate progress. Occasionally in the evenings I would scribble down a few numbers just to keep check on the mileage I had covered, and the distance left. Even checking my diaries now, as I write this, the margins are dotted with scribbles, figures and plans.

I had indulged in this process so many times that embedded in my memory were a series of predictions enabling me to reach certain points at certain times, and every day I repeated the process.

OK, twenty miles each day is 120 miles per week, taking one

Balancing on Blue

day as rest. Up that to twenty-five, Fozzie, and you can cover 150 miles in the coming week. If you make a quick town stop then maybe it's a 170. Let's be cautious and call it twenty-five; this time next month you'll be 600 miles further. You've got another fifty-six to Delaware Water Gap, that's two days — maybe two days and a couple of hours. Get there, get cleaned up quickly and you can avoid an overnight stay. If you can pull in twenty to twenty-five each day, you'll hit Katahdin at the end of August with a sub-five-month trip.

I had worked that out prior to the halfway point. my average daily distance was thirteen miles including days resting, or sixteen miles per day actually walking. The plan to cut into the mileage deficit during the second half was progressing well and I had averaged nineteen miles per day including rest days, or a pleasing twenty-five each day actually walking. During one fourteen-day stretch I had averaged 26.1 miles per day. The guys were covering similar distances. We were all warmed up and in fine fettle, considering twenty-five milers as a minimum goal, and often we pulled in thirties.

Respectable mileage wasn't intended as an ego boost, and we weren't rushing — although thirty-mile days may seem like we were. On my Pacific Crest thru-hike two years earlier, I hadn't paid enough attention to distance targets and took far too many rest days. Most hikers looked to finish the PCT at some point in September, or early October at the very latest, taking on average six months for the entire trail. We never had a choice, really; as with most south to north thru-hikes, the onset of winter and the first snow meant September was the optimal target.

On the PCT I became lax keeping to those targets, and I realised during the latter stages that my hike was in serious jeopardy of failing. I became depressed, and made matters worse by taking even more rest days to swim in my own disappointment because I really didn't think I would make it. I had invested a lot of time and money to complete that dream and, having realised that failure was very possible, I picked myself up, set a demanding target to finish and kept to it. In the middle of November, a good two months over what was generally accepted, I finally reached the end having fought my way through several weeks of snow and cold weather.

I had made mistakes but I never saw mistakes as a bad thing. I always learnt from them and there was no better way to learn on a thru-hike than to nearly fail. I had witnessed others failing, and keeping an eye on my progress was now firmly embedded.

The northern states, especially Vermont, New Hampshire and Maine, were considered the hardest. Steep climbs and descents were the norm, often over rock slabs, slippery and damp from the wetter climes. The weather was sure to be colder and wetter further up.

"Fozzie!" Juggles made me jump as he appeared from behind. "Did you hear the one about the hikers, the soup and a fly?"

I smiled. Juggles harboured dreams of becoming a stand-up comedian and occasionally practiced his repertoire. We had been discussing how little food a thru-hiker wasted the previous day so his gag followed on from that.

"No mate, but go on."

"Well, there's a day hiker, section hiker, and a thru-hiker in a restaurant. They all order the soup. The day hiker notices a fly in the soup, rejects it and asks the waiter for a fresh bowl. The section hiker also has a fly in his, but picks it out, then proceeds to finish the soup."

"Yes, go on," I said.

"The thru-hiker picks up the fly gently, holds it at eye level and says 'Now you spit that back out!'"

I got the impression that Juggles enjoyed his solitude as well as me. Although Goggles, Thirsty and I had now reached the point where we pretty much hiked, camped and shared motels together, Juggles spent a lot of time with us but also drifted in and out. We all did that to a certain extent. Perhaps I wouldn't see Goggles for half a day, Thirsty camped on his own occasionally and sometimes I took a day out in solitude. Juggles regularly disappeared, re-appeared, took breaks on his own or with us but we all considered him to be part of our group.

I had formed a strong bond with Thirsty, Goggles and Juggles. I hoped Lazagne and Daffy somehow caught us up because I had a good feeling they would fit in well. I had heard from PJ that he had got back on trail on June 26th. He was well behind us now, at least a month, so it was highly unlikely that

Balancing on Blue

we would see him again. I sent him a good luck message, knowing he would pull through.

We were aware of each other's behaviour, preferences, speed and habits. Juggles, as I have said, drifted in and out but we all found his sense of humour, juggling antics and overall light-hearted outlook on life amusing. Thirsty was dependable; if he said he would be at a certain campsite at a particular time then I could count on it. He dipped in and out of his limits, sometimes flying along and covering distance at unbelievable rates, but more often than not his hiking style was solid although relaxed and he appeared in no hurry. Goggles was a physical firework. He was young, enjoyed the challenge of pushing miles at high speed, and constantly had his eye on breaking a forty-mile day (or even further). Somehow, we all worked.

Since shortening Bush Goggles to just Goggles, I kept getting his name confused with Juggles — so much so that, on occasion, I referred to one as Guggles, and the other as Joggles. I couldn't get my tongue around it and many times one of them had to correct me, despite my pleas of ignorance.

Goggles was following me after we had taken a break at the Eckville Shelter, and there was a short climb to a hill known as Dan's Pulpit. He was right on my tail; I could hear his footfall just a few feet behind and I sensed he was enjoying the pace I was setting, without feeling the need to overtake me. I was capable of keeping up with him, but being around twenty years younger than me he had the advantages of youth and stamina. Often, begrudgingly, I had to let him go.

On that climb, I thought I'd dip into my reserves and show him that, despite the age difference, I could, hopefully, still show most hikers a clean pair of heels. Gradually, as we made inroads into the climb, I warmed and started to push harder. Every half a minute I increased the pace slightly and took tight lines through the switchbacks to gain a couple of feet. Reaching forward with my trekking poles, I hauled myself up, jumping from one boulder to the next, planted a foot on damp soil and forcing my weight on it to gain purchase.

I glanced back occasionally when I thought he wasn't looking. One aspect of Goggles we all knew well was that when he pushed hard he sweated, particularly his face. His forehead glistened with shiny beads and his T-shirt was damp, as was mine. His expression was one of concentration, tinged with a little hurt. I upped the pace further, trying not to giggle at the game we were involved in.

We were both gulping in lungfuls of air, and my legs started to scream, so for a couple of seconds I backed off slightly to bring them back, then pushed hard once more. I pulled over at a gap in the trees revealing a sun-bathed rock slab with a fine view.

We were exhausted, covered in sweat, our legs burning and capable of nothing more.

"Man! I was digging deep just to stay with you!" he cried, sparing a few seconds of oxygen intake to laugh.

Supported by our trekking poles, we bent over and fought to control our breathing before eventually collapsing on the warm rock. I just smiled at him. It was reassuring to know that I was still capable of pushing others to their limits.

I can't remember whether I lost Goggles in the afternoon, or, more probably, he lost me. The interestingly named Bake Oven Knob Shelter was my planned overnight point, although I now rarely stayed in the shelters, preferring the relative comfort and seclusion of my hammock.

Pennsylvania was still offering flatter terrain and I made quick progress over Blue Mountain, the Knife Edge and Bear Rocks before huge slabs of sloping rock rose up and hindered my way. A recent white blaze confirmed I was on the right track but I took some convincing before realising that the slabs needed to be negotiated. Protruding from the ridge, they commanded fine views north and south to the lowlands but I had little chance to admire them. It took all my concentration and a fine balancing act to manoeuvre through.

I tried to pick the best route and teetered, arms flapping, trying to regain composure. Summoning up courage, I leapt from one rock to the next and inched cautiously down whilst praying my shoes would grip the surface and not whip out from beneath me. Then I moved slowly up the next section, my hands scrabbling for any protrusions to grab. The rocks straddled the ridge itself about thirty feet below so a slip would be high enough to cause injury, but wouldn't result in a 1000-foot fall

Balancing on Blue

down the mountainside to the Lehigh Valley below.

At the tail end I came up behind more hikers, each tentatively finishing off the last rock slab before returning to a dirt trail, and the turn off for the Bake Oven Knob Shelter. Its capacity of six was already accounted for but I had already seen a flat area where one other hiker had set up camp. On closer inspection my companion for the night turned out to be the Kindle Ninja, whom I hadn't seen since the Blue Mountain Shelter back at the start. It was some coincidence that we had just passed over another peak called Blue Mountain. It was great to see he had taken to the trail name I had given him. I strung up the hammock and we chatted the hours away idly. Juggles and Goggles were a no show but Thirsty announced his presence with an ominous thud just after sunset, which reverberated around most of northern Pennsylvania.

"Shit. Fozzie, I fell out of my hammock!"

Eight miles from Bake Oven Knob the following day, Thirsty and I caught up with Juggles and Goggles as we crossed a bridge over the Lehigh River and met the PA-248. We needed a ride to Palmerton, situated a mile and a half down the road. The traffic was moving quickly downhill and there was no verge for them to pull over so we moved uphill a short way to take advantage of motorists waiting by the traffic lights.

We waited for thirty minutes, doing our upmost to make eye contact with the vehicle occupants to make them feel guilty for not offering us a lift. Goggles only put in any effort when the drivers were good-looking members of the opposite sex, but eventually Tom waved us over and we sped off towards town. He subsequently missed the turn off and drove for ages before stopping, taking us pretty much back to square one. It was a first for me; I'd never managed to catch a ride to town and then been left farther away from where I had originally started.

The first aspect that struck me about Palmerton was the open space. The roads were laid out parallel to each other in grid fashion. Avenues and streets were wide and generous, trees dotted the pavements and the locals milled around the park in the centre walking their dogs. No one seemed in a hurry, cars glided past slowly and I wondered whether it was some sort of public holiday.

Goggles and I sorted out a laundry run for everyone and, as I caught up with news on my phone, he snoozed precariously in a chair whilst leaning against a pillar. Somehow, even during sleep, the guy still had a smirk on his face as if he knew something that no one else did. The Jail House Hostel, conveniently situated across the road from the launderette, provided accommodation for the night.

***

Lehigh Gap was a climb that I had seen in countless photos during my AT research. Most of them were taken looking down on hikers ascending, with the road and the Lehigh River just tiny strips some 1000 feet below. We reeled in thousand-footers easily now but the further north we ventured many were becoming far steeper, particularly after Pennsylvania. Lehigh was no exception; the 1000-foot climb was just under a mile in length. Under a mile for a 1000 feet ascent was usually our guide. From one mile to a mile and a half we expected to be hard going but anything under this distance was regarded as steep. It did prove exactly that, but another obstacle on our path to Katahdin was conquered.

Once Lehigh had levelled out onto the flat ridge of yet another Blue Mountain, we were greeted with extensive views north down to Palmerton and the valley it nestled in, before hills rose back up on the distant horizon.

We gorged on blueberries, blackberries and raspberries, our progress impeded by the regular stops but we were thankful that our vitamin C levels had been topped up. An occasional quiet road intersected our path. Passing the Leroy A. Smith Shelter, we ventured further to eventually break camp at Hahns Overlook.

I didn't sleep well, and neither did Thirsty. The temperature had cooled overnight and our first problem with the hammocks had become apparent. If conditions were too cold, we felt the effects under our shelters. With only a thin area of nylon to lie on, we had no insulation below us. Warm on top under our sleeping bags, and being the height of summer, it was an area we had both neglected. The usual solution is to suspend what is known as an insulating quilt below, keeping the warm air of our bodies from escaping beneath. We hoped the overnight temperature would increase until we managed to get hold of some insulation.

There were no plans to stop in Delaware Water Gap, just sixteen miles on from Hahns Overlook. However, both Thirsty and I had to wait for the Post Office to open. Coupled with our usual thinking of grabbing hot food when it was available, before long it was late afternoon. Goggles joined us to share a room in the Pocono Inn which was cheap, especially as the three of us shared, but well past its sell-by date. Juggles left town to link up with a side trail and hike the ninety miles to pop out of the woods not far from where he lived. He wanted to chill at home and we gladly agreed to call him when we reached the Arden Valley Road, where he had agreed to pick us up, share some down time with him and a possible trip for breakfast to The Big Apple. I was humming *Breakfast in America* by Supertramp for most of the evening.

We left weighed down after agreeing to a cook up in camp that evening. Walmart, the American chain supermarket, exchanged our dollars for a kilo of minced pork, several potatoes, peppers, onions and spices. We crossed the Delaware River Bridge and left Pennsylvania, entering the eighth state of New Jersey. I had enjoyed my time in Pennsylvania but, hopefully, our rocky excursion was now over.

The traffic noise slowly faded as we climbed back up into the hills. After five miles enjoying a gentle ascent we crested to the idyllic sight of Sunfish Pond, a glacial lake. Its crystal-clear, calm waters glinted in the mid-day sun as the surrounding low-lying hills circled us, cloaked in the vivid greens of summer. Glorious ivory clouds drifted across our delightful sanctuary, and submerged rocks basked in the sunshine before plunging further down to the depths. No words were needed. We put down our packs by the northern edge and spent a relaxing afternoon in the sun, swimming and listening to music.

We barely spoke for three hours. Goggles caught up with his sleep, Thirsty took regular dips in the cold water in between sitting on the warm rocks, and I split my time doing all three.

I felt a tickling on my arm and slowly opened my eyes to see a dragonfly. A black thorax merged into its abdomen where fine white hairs caught the light. Four transparent wings were divided into small sections by a web of crazed lines and there it rested for two minutes, where I studied it happily. Occasionally, a weak wind passed. Caught by the change, my little friend lowered its body parallel to my arm and I felt the tiny, delicate claws on the end of each leg subtly digging into my skin to ride out the unexpected breeze. Its body pulsated like a heartbeat and, once in a while, eyes flicked up to meet my gaze, as if reciprocating my studies.

We met Hal Evans that evening, a ridge runner who informed us that swimming was prohibited in Sunfish Pond. Ridge runners worked with the public, trail community and officials along the length of the AT, keeping log books and offering assistance if required. When I enquired why no swimming was allowed, he explained that it encouraged erosion.

I have mixed views on erosion. I understand it is a problem for many outdoor areas with high traffic but it seemed just a little ironic that all trails, including the AT, are in fact erosion in their own right because of building them in the first place.

On the Pacific Crest Trail, a parking lot sits at the trailhead of the Cotton Wood Trail not far from Mt Whitney in the High Sierra. A blazing scar of bitumen carved into the side of the hills stretches several miles down to link up with the road system. In the parking lot, signs state not to pick up wood for fires, based on the 'leave no trace' theory. I still find it hypocritical that the authorities erected such signs, and implemented these regulations, after destroying several miles of pristine wilderness by scraping a road up there in the first place.

That memory lurked as I digested Hal's words. Although trails are, in fact, erosion, I don't see them as that. They are a means to provide access to the great outdoors, necessary erosion if you like, but I still struggle to understand how we can then be told not to take part in an activity because it causes damage.

We pulled in at the uninvitingly named Rattlesnake Campground and made camp quickly, excited at the prospect of a huge feast. A camp fire was built and, after letting it settle down to a mesmerising flickering of reds and oranges, the mound of pork began spitting whilst onions, peppers and potatoes sizzled. With a generous dash of spices there was ample food for the three of us. I spent the rest of the evening digesting, and keeping a keen eye out for snakes.

***

Thirsty was rubbing a plant on his leg as the sun rose. I glanced over whilst breaking camp and eventually, out of curiosity, went over and enquired what he was doing.

"It's a plant called Jewel Weed, Fozzie. Apparently it's good for mosquito bites."

Further research on our phones confirmed just that. After rain, water beaded up on the velvety leaves, creating little sparkles of moisture which is how the name came about. It was another weapon in our armoury against bites — and although the mozzies weren't as prevalent as I had feared, they were due to get much worse. The garlic plan was still in force and I always had a few cloves tucked away somewhere to supplement my evening meal. I was also resisting the urge to scratch bites and discovered that if I kept to this plan, the irritation was minor. Jewel Weed, however, became a much-needed alleviant.

New Jersey was spoiling us. Although the AT weaved a meagre seventy-two miles through the state, it took those miles and made the most of them. For much of the day we surfed along a ridge, dipping down into the woods and then returning to the rocky heights, like swimming underwater and occasionally, gladly, coming up for air. Blueberry bushes encroached onto the trail edges and, although we tried to avoid treading on them, the occasional crunch acted like rumble strips at the edge of a motorway, nudging us back to the middle of the trail. Views from the summits revealed a valley either side of us, each cradling a long, narrow lake.

It was windy. Gusts ripped randomly around us bringing our surroundings to life as the woods rustled in reply. The trees were alive, lifting as the torrents struck, then bowing back down when it subsided.

We saw few others that day; New Jersey appeared deserted. Unable to hold a conversation in the wind, we were lost in our thoughts. Occasionally, whoever was out front glanced back to check on the others and a knowing smile confirmed what we all felt — the woods were truly alive and it was an atmospheric day to experience it.

After meeting Hal again we all took some lunch by Stony Brook, enjoying the sunshine. He shared his knowledge of the trail and told us about the White Mountains, where he had hiked regularly. The Whites were a difficult stretch in New Hampshire, and dotted through the park were mountain huts. Not used very often by thru-hikers due to the costs, some did offer work in exchange for stay — if, indeed, there were any places available. Hal explained he had stayed at one once.

"I spent an hour turning over waste from the privy," he explained. "And my wife's job was to empty the fridge of out-of-date food and then clean it."

"Bearing in mind the raging hunger of most thru-hikers," I said, "I don't think asking them to clean out a fridge would be conducive to any business."

Thirsty and Goggles munched and nodded their heads in agreement.

The Whites, still 440 miles up trail, gave us some indication that the second half of the AT may be harder than the first. We were looking forward to the Whites and everything else the trail had in store. We were strong and determined that nothing would impede progress, and success was starting to seem possible even though failure never crossed our minds.

What we hadn't bargained for, however, was what the weather had in store for us.

Chapter 11

Seeking Solitude by the Rivers

June 29th to July 17th
Mile 1300 to 1643

The state lines of New Jersey and New York teased us several times. The trail dipped over into one, then fell back to the other, undecided, so we never knew if we'd left New Jersey or not. Finally, at mile 1360, we began hiking the eighty-eight miles of state number nine: New York.

It was June 29th, day ninety-one of my hike. Although I was happy that the Appalachian rains had generally held off up to that point, a new problem presented itself that was far worse. New York State was sweltering. Temperatures were hovering around or above 100°F and the humidity never fell below 100%. It sapped my energy; I was soaked in sweat all day and most of the night, and prayed for a respite. I wrapped a bandana around my neck, dipping it into water as I passed a creek or stream, and constantly wiped my face. Within minutes it had dried. Suddenly, food was taking second place to a new resource; everyone was chasing water.

We drank constantly, keeping an eye on upcoming water sources, of which New York had numerous. Occasionally we'd pass a hosepipe by the side of a farm or building and took it in turns to hose each other down. The relief was exhilarating and our soaked clothes kept us cool for an hour or so.

Following one hiker, I laughed as instead of taking the bridge over a river, he swerved right and approached the bank, dropped his pack and flinging off his shoes, and continued without breaking stride straight into the water.

I strove for starts around 6 a.m. to pull in some decent mileage before the furnace fired up. Even the nights were hot; I often pulled my quilt to one side and there it stayed.

Goggles and Thirsty were also suffering, but faring slightly better than I, they were usually ahead by a couple of miles. That said, when Thirsty dropped back behind, I knew he was approaching, as his footfall reverberated through the ground like a runaway bear. Most times, when I was aware he was just a few feet behind, I merely stepped off trail for a second and let him steam past as though his brakes had failed.

"Thanks Fozzie!" And off he sped.

The trail tumbled along, rarely flat but without any major hills. It twisted, turned, emerged into sunlight and then plunged back into the woods. Board walks suspended us over swamps and marsh where the mosquitos droned annoyingly. The trail was easy but the heat was taking its toll on all of us. Embittered, I breathed deep, drank and resisted the urge to scratch my insect bites.

Keep going, Fozzie — you must keep going.

We stopped for food at a store in Unionville. The sheltered porch and flickering lights advertising 'deli' and 'breakfast' were too tempting to resist. I devoured a roll stuffed with bacon and two eggs before deciding I was still hungry, then ordered another — all washed down with two pints of chocolate milk, now our preferred choice of protein. I promptly ordered another roll to go.

New York is one of the most densely populated states on the AT but hikers never really notice. Although quiet road crossings were common, and stores, cafés and other amenities cropped up regularly, we were still in the most part oblivious to it as the trail shied away, hidden in the woods.

Bush Goggles was suffering badly from sexual frustration. So obsessed with the fairer sex had he become that when describing anything great, or even just good, it was referred to as 'titties'.

Balancing on Blue

"How was your food?" I asked him outside Heaven Hill Farm, where we had stopped one afternoon.

"Oh yeah," he replied, "Titties."

***

Arden Valley Road, where Juggles had agreed to collect us, was approaching but not before a section known as 'Agonies Grind'. We made short work of the higher areas. The Eastern Pinnacles, Monbasha High Point and Buchanan Mountain all passed as the AT clung to broad, rocky ridges, bordered with forest. The small community of Greenwood Lake was visible below us.

Agonies Grind wasn't marked in our guide so it caught us by surprise. Reminiscent of the Roller Coaster just before Harpers Ferry, it was a section of sharp climbs and descents that, while not particularly taxing, finished us off in a constant, searing heat. We emerged from the woods battered, bruised, and dripping a trail of sweat behind us.

Juggles, true to his word, arrived and took us back to the house he shared with his father James in Midland Park, New Jersey, where we eventually took three days out. Rest was required, I needed new shoes as Pennsylvania had finished my last pair prematurely, and we all had chores to take care of.

Juggles had taken advantage of a few days' work. The TV show *America's Got Talent* had contacted his agent, as they were in need of a juggler to perform, with others, to Will I Am's latest single. He needed a week to prepare under the choreographer and was constantly darting about to and from the city.

Lazagne had emailed stating his intention to come up and join us. He was back on trail but his two weeks out had put him a way behind. When he expressed a wish to walk with us, the guys had no problems with it so I invited him up. His intention was to return to the section he missed after reaching Katahdin and polish off that last little bit. Daffy was also back on trail but content to carry on from where he left off.

We spent a day in the big city. The Tick Tock Diner, on the corner of 34th Street and 8th Avenue, served us breakfast in typical, frantic, New York style. The streets were busy, traffic was noisy; I felt claustrophobic and couldn't breathe. Thank God for Central Park at least, an oasis in the big smoke, where we spent most of the afternoon.

"Wait, listen to this," Juggles said on the way back to the car in the evening. He approached a complete stranger coming towards us and motioned him to stop.

"What do you think of the Appalachian Trail?" he asked the bemused guy.

"I think I like it," he replied.

"How long did it take you?" Juggles questioned, trying not to giggle.

"Two hours."

With this, Juggles turned to me with a look of complete anguish on his face as he tried to suppress a laugh. He pushed one last question.

"What was your favourite part?"

"The top!"

***

Lazagne had arrived the following day and dropping us all back at the Arden Valley Road, Juggles explained he had around a week committed to the TV show but would be back on trail and, hopefully, would catch us up. Our new four-man team was rested and looking forward to the final 800-mile section.

West Mountain Shelter lay thirteen miles up the trail. We stopped there as its position commanded fine views of the New York suburbs and, being Independence Day, with the promise of fireworks, our perch offered the best outlook of the pyrotechnics.

The four of us camped in the woods and took our stoves to settle in front of the shelter. As our dinners cooked, we picked on snacks, and chatted to some locals who had also hiked up to watch the display. What we hadn't anticipated was the added spectacle of a lightning storm. As the fireworks exploded below us, a huge bank of cloud blew in from the west. Passing to the side of our overlook, the black mass bubbled, grew, and lightning bursts illuminated the cloud's interior. Forks of lightning cracked down, ominous rumbles reverberated around us and more firework displays joined the performance. It was better than any movie, even *The Great Escape*.

***

The lowest point on the AT was situated in a zoo, of all places. The Trailside Museum and Zoo to be precise. At just 124 feet above sea level, the trail passed directly through the zoo and didn't charge hikers an entrance fee. A nice gesture, but I wouldn't have paid it anyway. I hate zoos — in fact I loathe them. As it turned out, the zoo was shut and the gates locked. Unbeknown to us, there was a side trail for hikers to use when this was the case. Instead, we shimmied over the gate.

I know zoos educate us to the reasoning that their animals are kept because they were found injured, or orphaned and unable to survive by themselves, so they need to be looked after. I accept this in the cases where it may be true, but my dislike for these prisons stems from the other animals incarcerated there purely for show.

This was brought painfully home as I walked through the Trailside Zoo. I passed at an enclosure and abruptly stopped, saddened by what I saw. A lone fox, in a pen no bigger than most people's lounges, sat motionless and stared at me. I stopped as the guys went on, calling out that I'd catch them up.

I dropped my pack and sat down, watching my new friend. He didn't move, just returned my gaze; and despite the lack of communication, it wasn't needed. I quickly realised how unhappy this creature was. He lowered his head slightly as if ashamed, kept eye contact for long periods but then gazed off aimlessly, lost. Then I swore he was trying to tell me something, although I don't know how. An overwhelming sense of sadness hit me, as if this innocent fox was pleading with me to set him free. At one point he whimpered — a pathetic, lost cry of surrender. Resigned that he would never get out, be free to run through the woods, sleep in the grass, drink from a creek and start a family.

It wasn't right that I was free, and he was imprisoned. Surely it should be the other way around? At times my standard life felt like imprisonment and I longed for the outdoors. Here, the roles had been switched. I was wild and he was locked up, desperate to return.

He looked again, pleading with me almost to the point that I could hear him.

Open the gate. Please, open the gate and let me escape.

I looked around; no one was about and the zoo was still locked. It was quiet. I wished Thirsty was with me. He had a knack of seeing when something wasn't fair and acted on impulse. I knew he would have helped me.

Please. Please, let me free.

Compassion replaced logic, and overwhelmed by what I was seeing, emotions conquered resolve and I started to cry. Looking just inside the outer fence I saw an iron bar lying on the ground. I glanced at his pen; there was just one, feeble padlock on the gate. I reached for the latch.

Grab the bar, Fozzie. Break the padlock and set him free.

I got up and reached for the gate.

"Hey, morning! You know there's a side trail around the zoo when we're closed? You're a thru-hiker right? Are you OK?" she asked, seeing my damp eyes.

I grabbed my pack and ran, eventually stopping at the Bear Mountain Bridge, which passed over the Hudson River. I stopped, caught my breath and composure and walked quickly towards the sanctuary of the trees. If anywhere could heal the hurt, it was the woods.

To this day I still see that fox. I still remember his forlorn expression, I still sense his pleading, I still hear him and I still feel as though I let him down. I would gladly have spent a few days locked up in exchange for his freedom.

And to this day, I still believe — animals shouldn't be locked in cages.

Rising away from the Hudson, trees moved in and huddled all around me as I crunched over gravel roads that intersected the trail. I climbed over Canopus Hill and descended. Lost in my thoughts I missed the turn off for Canopus Lake, eventually pulling up by the Shenandoah Camping Area for the night after thirty-one miles, to camp with the guys.

The heat and humidity continued to tire us the following day. Since Duncannon there had been no let-up. Dust from the trail clouded up around our legs and stuck to the sweat, resulting in a sticky brown residue.

Lazagne had already gelled well with the group. I knew he would; he was easy going, pulled in the miles and got on with the mission in hand without complaining, although he had commented on his sore knees. Goggles and Thirsty were suffering badly from sore sac syndrome, which had now spread between their buttocks. My legs were tired for some reason, and I was also sore in the same places. We had enough creams, powders and sprays to start a small pharmacy and each of us stopped regularly during the day to apply something, somewhere. Water seemed to help. If nothing else it did clean the area and the cold relief was welcome, as well as pleasantly numbing.

However, I couldn't figure out what was wrong with my legs. The point at which the lactic acid became too much, and my legs started to hurt after exertion, seemed to be kicking in earlier. Ascents seemed harder. I couldn't move as quickly and became frustrated. When setting off first thing it was usually my calves that ached, particularly going uphill but my quadriceps were also complaining. Thinking it may be some electrolyte problem, I increased my intake of a powder that replaced lost minerals, salts and electrolytes and hoped for the best.

We were all tired and our bodies were showing signs of wear. We had passed 1,450 miles, with around 734 left. As fit as we were, experience had taught me that the body starts complaining around that mark on any trail. The break in New York had been a good idea — we had refuelled, rested and returned full of enthusiasm. We got up each day, hoisted our packs and carried on walking north. It was now habit, ingrained and accepted. No one spoke of quitting. Katahdin was our focus and Katahdin would be reached.

We kept to around 1000 feet through most of New York State but the trail was starting to ripple. Short, steep hills meant summits arrived just as we started to breathe hard, and we caught up on oxygen going down, just in time for it to start over again.

Old, moss-covered stone walls in the woods marked long-forgotten boundaries. Sometimes I caught glimpses of a solitary building, or what was left of it, the last corner standing defiant amidst a pile of rubble.

I ascended down the 700 feet of Ten Mile Hill to the Ten Mile River, crossed over the Ned Anderson Memorial Bridge as sunlight bounced off the river, blinding me. Passing into Connecticut, the tenth state, I still had four more to negotiate: Massachusetts, Vermont, New Hampshire and Maine. I climbed again to Indian Rocks. Gaps in the trees teased with glimpses of the countryside below.

***

Lazagne and I finished off a long downhill to reach the CT-341 at Schaghticoke Road. Thirsty and Goggles were ahead of us and discovering the best places to renew fat levels in the town of Kent, just under a mile east. Tired and hot, neither of us could fathom which way east was. Having downloaded the data book onto our phones, we both peered helplessly at the screen, trying to see the directions as sunlight blinded us. Eventually we just went with the direction that seemed right and met up with the guys shortly after. Thirsty's uncle, John Lundeen, had agreed to put us up for the night. He collected us and drove us to his house in Darien where we were able to clean up and feast. We even managed to stumble on *America's Got Talent* that evening whilst watching TV and cheered as Juggles plied his trade effortlessly in the background, even managing a cheeky grin for the camera as he sped past on a unicycle. Again, glad of the rest, we left the following morning and were back on trail quickly.

A soft, sandy path hugged the Housatonic River as it kept us company for most of the day. Its wide, shallow and clear waters weaved around submerged boulders. Thinly spaced trees lined the banks. Thirsty and Lazagne floated down river whilst Goggles, unsurprisingly, napped on a warm rock, as did I.

The rivers on the AT were wonderful, particularly from Connecticut north. As the woods were often so dense, we had no idea what was coming up, except for checks made in the data book. Gradually, as I approached, the sound of water filtered over and met me, and the sunlight intensified, creating beams that spliced through lingering mists and silhouetted the trees.

Then I broke out from the forest into the light. After the dark woods it was a revelation to be free. Often I'd pick a route over the rocks until I reached the middle and just stood there. Facing downstream I could do little more than remain motionless, amazed, watching that huge ribbon of water gradually shrink and narrow, lines of perspective decreasing as I lost sight completely.

Although there were plenty of rivers intersecting the AT, I always became excited when I stumbled across one. Sometimes they seemed out of place, strange and unexpected. A long, silver slither parting the trees, a warm and bright oasis that demanded I stop and rest.

In fact I knew when I'd indulged in a little too much river therapy because the guys were always a way ahead. These warm, light strips where the trees parted and the rivers flowed became an addiction. The Housatonic either crossed my path or glided alongside me several times in Connecticut, and one morning was no exception.

It was cooler than usual, goose bumps speckled my arms and I spent several minutes contemplating whether to put on a jacket. A solitary silver birch stood sentry. Then, slowly, the trail descended, its soft sandy surface easing my feet into the day and the woods parted like a theatrical curtain. Mist spectres glided effortlessly across the water, a solitary crow called and I hopped out to a lonely rock. It was quiet. A gentle breeze tickled the tree tops and they replied with a genial rustle. I tilted my head skyward and, grateful for the early morning sun, just sat there.

The Housatonic slid past and, save the occasional gurgle, was silent. My rock was warm and I spent an hour revelling in the solitude, letting the wilds of Connecticut soothe me. I adored the rivers.

I caught the guys in the afternoon and we managed a quick lift into Salisbury to top up the fat levels and buy some food. Riga Roast Coffee solved my immediate caffeine crisis before we holed up in the Country Bistro, eagerly eying the menu. The waitress suggested we move nearer the back door, as 'there was more space on the table'. Returning, she took our orders, placed an industrial-strength fan pointing straight at us, and flicked it onto hurricane mode. Most of the napkins blew off the table and I guessed our aroma wasn't improving.

I was becoming hooked, for some unknown reason, on ginger cookies. The two supermarkets in Salisbury failed to deliver and I left despondent, hands in pockets, kicking the dirt. When I reached the end of a quiet road before disappearing back into the woods, a car pulled alongside me and stopped. The woman beckoned me over.

"Hiking the AT?" she said.

"Yes, I am."

"Well here, take these. I have two and figured you might like one of them."

With that I accepted the pack she held out and, before I could even thank her, she had driven off as if she knew something that I didn't. I looked down to be met by the sight of a pack of ginger cookies nestling in my hand. Go figure.

Stocked with good food we left town and made inroads into the ascent up Bear Mountain. I had concentrated on buying food with not only fat, but healthy sources of it — such as a small bottle of olive oil slipped into the outside of my pack. A tub of fresh pesto was finished quickly, dipping a fresh tear of Kaiser Bread into the green paste. I supplemented my stocks with cheese, olives, various nuts and even carefully wrapped up an avocado in a pair of socks to protect it.

I increased my intake of electrolyte powder and also started to drink a protein shake in the morning. Good, nutritious food wasn't the lightest or easiest to carry but it always revived me.

Passing the Riga and Brassle Brook Shelters, we climbed from 720 feet to 2316 feet strongly and smoothly to summit Bear Mountain. A hiker called Easy Mile was resting at the top, and we exchanged a few pleasantries. I was to bump into her several times that afternoon. We descended to Sages Ravine, crossed the Connecticut–Massachusetts state line and then our path forced us up harshly to the summit of Mt Everett. The afternoon levelled somewhat and we relaxed.

I was happy, content with my world. The 102 days now behind me were already imparting lifelong memories, filtering out the least important and leaving me with vibrant recollections. I was fit. Several weeks of nature's nurturing had calmed my mind and I felt healthy. My breathing seemed easier, problems that played with my consciousness had either been resolved or had vanished, and my body slowly responded to the nutrients I had eaten.

All these factors made me smile but, occasionally, I also felt sad. Sad because I was on the home stretch. Instead of walking away from the beginning, I now felt as if I were walking towards the finish. There were perhaps six weeks left to reach Katahdin, at which point the inevitable feeling of helplessness would come back to haunt me.

Most of the reputable thru-hikes in the northern hemisphere require finishing near the onset of the winter. After months of freedom, escaping the constraints of my normal life and becoming recharged, there was little to look forward to. I would invariably return home to England with nothing more than a bleak winter to battle through. Sounds despondent I know but post-thru-hike depression is common.

It takes time for us to readjust to society. After plentiful time in the wilds the shock of leaving is hard for many to comprehend. I tend to cope reasonably well; I'm not one for wallowing in self-pity, although it may take me a week or two to merge back.

Houses seem confining, the air dry, there are too many distractions and unwanted noise, and I hate dealing with the boring, mundane activities that civilisation demands. It feels like an alien environment and many times I entertain the idea of a walk with no set direction, a walk with no end. An adventure to escape to, forever.

A walk with no end is just that. To spend the rest of my life drifting through the world, with what I need strapped to my back. Perhaps I'd have a dog for company, but one thing is for sure — my route would not be planned. The walk with no end doesn't stick to one, marked trail; it meanders on many, undoubtedly through Europe, probably starting in England. I always dreamt of starting with no ideas other than to walk on an approximate southeasterly bearing.

I didn't want a schedule mapped out of where I was heading. I wanted to be free to go wherever I wished. There would be no daily mileage targets and no overall distant goal. After catching a ferry over the English Channel I'd listen to my senses, be open to suggestion and flow along able to accept opportunities as they appeared.

The only plan I'd entertain would be the approximate direction. I could see myself progressing through northern France in the direction of Switzerland. As the Alps rose up I'd probably veer east and explore the foothills, occasionally rising up higher to the summits. Liechtenstein and Austria seem obvious choices but my options, always open, meant that if the Mediterranean called, I could work over the Alps and hike down through the Dolomites, reaching Italy's Po Valley.

The Adriatic Sea would beckon and, passing Venice, perhaps I'd pay a visit to Trieste before crossing into Slovenia. From there Croatia has always been on the wish list along with the lesser-visited countries of Hungary, Serbia, Romania and Bulgaria before the vast Black Sea came to view. Or perhaps I'd travel further north, taking advantage of the summer through such delights as Slovakia, Hungary, Poland and Belarus.

Live their cultures, taste their cuisine, marvel at the history, and lose myself in the forests and mountains. Perhaps spend a day in town once in a while, drink coffee and read the newspaper then move on, feed the nomad.

And all the while I'd be free, indulging the dromomaniac, satiating its appetite, bowing to its whims. Left? Right? Straight? I wouldn't care, pick the path that seemed right, follow my instincts.

Sweet serendipity. One day ...

***

Bush Goggles was like a whippet in an espresso bar, constantly needing to pull in miles. He had agreed to meet his mum at the finish and travel back home with her. His relationship with her was obviously great, and he beamed as he spoke of his plans. However, his plan was affecting me, and I didn't like it.

To that point, Goggles, Thirsty, Lazagne and I spent most of the day either hiking with each other, or in the same approximate vicinity. Sometimes we'd walk alone but we always pulled in a similar mileage, and at some point in the afternoon we would break and discuss the options of where and when to camp.

Goggles had set himself a tough target to reach Katahdin,

and although he was more than capable of sticking to it, the constant demands to meet his quota were impacting on me.

If anything, I wanted to slow down. I was still on course for a sub-five-month finish and I didn't need to rush, nor pull in huge miles to achieve it. I was also painfully aware that I didn't want the Appalachian Trail to finish.

Thirsty and Lazagne seemed fine with the pace and distance but I was tiring of it. I was more than capable of pulling in the miles that Goggles had set himself; and as we all enjoyed his company, and didn't want to split the group, we met his targets. I didn't want to see him go but I knew that at some point I would talk to everyone and raise my concerns. At that point Lazagne and Thirsty would either keep with Goggles, keep with me, or we'd disband and figure it all out for ourselves.

The town of Dalton shimmered in a heat haze. We made our way down Depot Street after filling up with stove alcohol at the L.P Adams store. The Mill Town Tavern, profitably placed right on the AT, seemed a good choice to grab a beer. I entered and my choice seemed confirmed as Thirsty greeted me with an ale in hand.

Dalton had places to stay but, for some reason, they were all expensive. We agreed to grab a shower at the Sports Hall, which kindly offered its washrooms free to thru-hikers. Laundry was also dealt with in the shower and, after just a couple of hours, we left to start our sixth day on trail without a zero and make dents into the ascent of Mt Greylock, seventeen miles and 2000 feet away. The shores of Gore Pond offered a great camp spot for the night and amongst some crazy mosquitos, I drifted off to the cries of Loons calling and frogs splashing.

Six a.m. was unreasonably dark. Dense evergreens blocked out whatever light managed to escape from cloudy skies and a dog's cry down in the valley was the only sound. I alternated between packing up camp, sipping on coffee and grabbing a handful of granola to fuel the system.

The guys left as I was finishing off. Working my way down outcrops of marble known as the Cobbles, I paused to take in the view of the Hoosic River and the town of Cheshire below, with Mt Greylock rising up behind.

Cheshire was quiet. The AT joined Church Street before

turning right onto School Street. Unable to find the store and grinning at the prospect of being in town at breakfast time, I was soon disappointed to find everywhere shut at 7.30 in the morning. I spotted Lazagne and Goggles coming down a side street and they directed me towards the only open store in town. A bottle of chocolate milk followed by a protein bar worked wonders on my muscles, and I tucked another bottle of protein away in my pack for later that day.

We rested on Mt Greylock, the highest point in Massachusetts, admiring the ninety-three-foot-high Massachusetts Veterans War Memorial Tower, before a cry caught my attention.

"Hey!"

I turned around out of instinct but realised the call probably hadn't been directed at me anyway.

"Hey! Fozzie!"

I turned again to see Pink Bits, sorry, Lady Forward coming towards me. I even got a hug on arrival.

"Pink Bi ... sorry, Lady Forward. How are you?"

"Great!"

She was happy, going strongly and focused on finishing.

"Here," I offered. "This is for you. I've been lugging this thing with me since I last saw you. It's your turn, at least until you pass me."

I handed her the gauntlet and she took it.

"You'll have it on Katahdin, you know," she jested.

"We'll see about that."

Another familiar face appeared later. The Congdon Shelter was quiet and seemed empty as I passed.

"Fozzie!"

I turned to see Chez 11 grinning and poking his head out from the interior.

"Chez 11! How the hell are you, mate?"

"Not too bad. Feet have been in bad shape since Duncannon though. You?"

"Yeah, I'm all good."

A few blisters spotted his feet and he agreed that his new shoes were partly to blame, as he was still wearing them in.

"I'll deal with it," he added. "Too close to quit now.

Balancing on Blue

***

Shortly before the Seth Warner Shelter I left Massachusetts and entered Vermont. Along with the two remaining states of New Hampshire and Maine, this area of northeast America was famed for its autumnal colours. Unfortunately we were early, and being the middle of July, the dynamic greens around me showed few signs of surrender. With our progress to date, we would have finished and left Maine before the majestic shades of yellow, red and orange celebrated the end of the summer.

Even so, Vermont was stunning. Wood and forest still occupied vast swathes of the land, which the AT faithfully followed. But we were blessed with wide-open spaces where sunlight streamed down. The air was clean, the skies deep blue and farm buildings we passed retained a sense of age, their colourful wooden exteriors blending with the area.

The terrain was becoming tougher. It seemed that since Pennsylvania, the further we ventured north, the more demanding the hiking became. Elevations dipped to as little as 400 feet, reaching as high as 4000. Any mountaineer or hiker will tell you that a 4000-foot elevation is relatively minor but it was still the constant ups and downs in between where our energy was expended. Mountains rarely entail a straightforward ascent straight up; there are usually sections going down as well.

With the elevation and occasional winds the temperature had dropped; and although still hot, it was slowly becoming more bearable. Clouds cast shadows and cooled our surroundings further still.

The AT was becoming wilder and more remote. The last three states were prone to harsh winters and less populated; regularly we stopped at vantage points and marvelled at the arena surrounding us. A vast sea of green stretched away in all directions, occasionally broken by rocky mountain summits. Lonely, elongated lakes dotted the valleys and shimmered. The huge expanses of open water caught the sunlight and winds whipped across the surface creating alluring patterns.

We tried to camp high, still escaping the mosquitos, where the breeze chased them away. We were humbled by stunning sunsets of reds and oranges bouncing off the waters and casting infinite shadows. Canada was near and Maine, our last state, jutted sneakily northwards into the next country as if claiming a small portion for itself.

Lazagne, Goggles, Thirsty and I reached Stratton Mountain where the lookout tower and caretaker's cabin kept tabs on the weather. We sat snacking under the tower as one of the caretakers strolled over.

"Bad storm coming!" She said, smiling as if it were meant to be great news. "Get into camp early if you can and hunker down! 'Bout eight o'clock I think."

We looked at each other as Lazagne peered into his phone to corroborate the news but ended up just shrugging his shoulders.

"She knows something we don't," he said.

Veering on the side of caution, and remembering the fickle mountain weather patterns, we agreed to camp at Prospect Rock. I left first, keeping a watchful eye out for the William B. Douglas Shelter, which was situated just under a mile before the turn off for the Prospect Rock camp area.

Daydreaming and concentrating on speed to be sure of getting to camp before the storm rolled in, I missed the sign for the shelter, and for Prospect Rock itself. Luckily Spruce Peak Shelter was close at hand. As I pulled in, nodding to Chez 11 who was setting up in the shelter, the wind started to increase. I looked up through the trees and saw the ominous black clouds stream over.

I strung up my hammock first, just in case I got caught out and retired to the table outside the shelter where the others had congregated, as usual, for some socialising.

Catching up with Chez 11 after our brief encounter earlier that day, he introduced me to three, new faces; Danish, Metric and Don Quixote.

Food stock levels varied between the three of us. I was well stocked after a resupply in Bennington. Danish's head disappeared into his food bag, looking disappointed when he emerged. We supplemented his rations and he reciprocated with a few titbits to liven up our dinners.

Dinner time on trail was an interesting time to study the eating habits of others. Because of our raging hungers, most hikers ate quickly, shovelling ramen, pasta or rice dishes down as quickly as possible. Others savoured their food and dined slowly, taking the time to appreciate the contents of their pot.

Conversations were animated; news on how we were all doing, where everyone else was, the weather, mosquitos, and other relevant topics were discussed.

We each cleaned our pots as we finished. I'm sometimes asked how I do my washing up on thru-hikes. How much washing up liquid did I carry? Did I bother with a cloth, and perhaps a small towel to dry my utensils? I don't think I've ever met a thru-hiker who bothered with any of them. The preferred method of cleaning up utilised just water and a finger.

My pot was a perfect depth to accept my middle finger, which just reached the bottom. A small trickle of water was poured in, and then I swept my finger around the sides of the pot, scraping away any detritus clinging to the sides, sucking my finger after each sweep. Then, I'd swish the water around, discard it, and repeat the finger process again. Finally, a quick tickle on the bottom of the pan, and a final rinse was job done.

The interesting point was watching others do the same, as it was the method most used. As we were usually so hungry, with smaller than ideal rations, every scrap of food was eaten. Pots were cleaned to within an inch of being sterile. Fingers precisely wiped pans, sucked carefully after each pass and savoured as though it were a last meal. Concentration was focused, precise checks and observations picking up any stray morsels. Mugs were tipped skyward as we searched for the last dribble that may, or may not, drop out to an expectant tongue; and again a small splosh of water swilled around with care to retrieve that last dribble of coffee. Cutlery was sucked and inspected for any clingers, which were removed with a fingernail or wiped along a suitable piece of clothing, then sucked again, tongues scanning the surface for any irregularities.

Food was gold and, along with water, a valued commodity. We never had enough of it. Portions were never big enough and variety never up to par. However, such was our hunger that it was never wasted and, despite the limitations, always enjoyed and savoured. Such a change to everyday life where obscene amounts of food are sometimes wasted. We never left a scrap and relished our food.

A few fat raindrops splattered our little haven in the woods. We ran for our shelters. The woods hissed and roared as the deluge gained strength and a fierce wind ripped through that little corner of Vermont. I ran for my hammock, suspended my rucksack under the tarp and sat underneath, observing the torrent as, gradually, the light faded. Occasional gusts lifted my tarp, pulling at the anchor points. Eventually, too tired to sit any longer, I slid into my sleeping bag and watched, enthralled, as the woods lit up with lightning bursts, silhouetting the trees above me.

I fell asleep thinking of mountains. The Whites were coming.

Chapter 12

The Whites

July 18th to July 30th
Mile 1643 to 1841

The storm had stopped during the early hours but nature was still clearing up. The trail, overgrown in sections, was littered with deadfall; plants were dripping wet, dampening my clothes as I brushed past. The woods were silent save an occasional plop of water plummeting from the trees above and hitting small pools nestled amongst tree roots. Swathes of mist glided effortlessly through the canopy, chilling my exposed skin as I entered the murk. I stepped up my pace and put on a warm jacket, occasionally holding my trekking poles under my arm to rub my hands together, but the friction did little to alleviate their numbness. Cobwebs constantly covered my face as I frantically brushed them away.

The guys were somewhere behind. I had made an early start from the Spruce Peak Shelter but, eager for them to catch up, I took regular breaks and enjoyed a leisurely pace.

I paused at the VT-11 and VT-30 to contemplate hitching into Manchester Center for breakfast, just over five miles west, but continued progress won the day over bacon and eggs. I sped up the climb culminating at the summit of Bromley Mountain, descended down to Mad Tom Notch and then rose once more to bag Styles Peak and Peru Peak. As I was resting on a footbridge a few minutes later, Thirsty, Goggles and Lazagne finally rolled in.

The pursuit of the hyper light still seemed to be affecting Lazagne. Having extolled the benefits of the hammock to me, which subsequently influenced my purchase shortly after, he had now ditched the system. A solitary tarp weighing barely a couple of hundred grams now acted as his shelter with a small section of plastic forming a barrier between him and the ground. A sliver of foam provided ground insulation, with a lightweight quilt to sleep under. A new rain jacket barely registered on the scales at ninety grams and he had also, remarkably, ditched his stove, fuel, and associated equipment, surviving on cold food and drink.

His new radical approach was inadvertently having an impact on me and the others, and was fuel for constant, light-hearted jibes in his direction. As he constantly made amendments to his equipment, his tweaks had left him short of gear that others would deem necessary. His knife had been a victim of cutbacks, as well as his camp shoes. Camp shoes were just that — usually a pair of light, comfortable and vented offerings to wear in the evening for a little comfort, and for our feet to air and escape the confines of our smelly, damp hiking shoes.

Lazagne's gear refinements had resulted in the occasional plea to borrow an item. A knife was the most common request but his lack of footwear took the situation a little too far. One evening at camp he strolled over and asked to borrow my Crocs. A knife? No problem, but appeals for personal items such as clothing, and indeed, shoes, were taking things a little far. I mean, I even struggled to put my footwear on — camp shoes or hiking shoes — because of the stench and rapidly increasing communities of microbes calling both of them home.

"Fozzie, can I borrow your Crocs real quick?" he asked, sheepishly.

"Where's yours?" I questioned.

"I sent them home, didn't need them anymore."

"Well, obviously you do need them. Don't you think that your pursuit of the mega-light is pushing the boundaries a little too far, Phillip?"

He stuffed his hands in his pockets and shuffled his feet

guiltily.

"Yeah. Ditching the shoes may have been hasty."

"You can borrow my shoes but just the once because I don't think it's fair. So, you can keep that 'borrow' in the bag for a later time, or feel free to use them now. Either way, it's only the once, sorry."

On the plus side, the Anglo-American chess championship was back and competitive as ever. Picking up from where we had left off weeks prior, the score had now reached three to one in his favour.

The English had mounted a comeback and after game five that evening at Little Rock Pond I had pulled one back to bring the score to three-two.

Checkmate!

***

Wild swimming was the new activity and inadvertently meant we needed to spend less time in town. We were able to wash ourselves and our clothes, which meant motel rooms and laundrette stops weren't needed so much.

A classic example was the Mill River. As we rounded a corner the impressive, if somewhat wobbly, Clarendon Gorge suspension bridge hung precariously over a rocky drop to the river cascading through the narrow rock walls below. A small path picked its way down to the popular swimming hole and we cooled off and discreetly bathed for an hour. Regular washing seemed to be resolving our sore sac issues as well, and in the main there seemed to be some improvements.

The water in Vermont, and further north as we were to discover, was beautiful. The lakes in particular provided calm waters and cool temperatures. Often, rocks poked out a short distance from shore and we swam to them, then hauled ourselves out to dry off and bask in the sun. The activity also cooled off tired muscles.

Most of us were suffering physically so relief was welcome. I was carrying five injuries: an old battle wound to my right calf throbbed constantly, my right ankle hurt on the back and left-hand side, my left knee ached, and my left elbow was swollen for some unknown reason.

Lazagne's knees were still causing him grief, but Thirsty seemed to be either faring well — or he was also suffering but not complaining about it. Goggles seemed fine in the muscle department but had been grumbling about a bad stomach and feeling lethargic. 1700 miles in and with around 484 left, our adventure was taking its toll.

Mentally, however, we had never been stronger. That first month, where most hikers drop out, was now one of many memories we nurtured. Although our surroundings changed by the minute, our routine and mental resolve remained solid.

Each of us approached the day in our own individual styles but we had formed a unique pattern to get us through it. We rose with the sun, which was now well past the summer solstice so each morning it peeked over the horizon a little later. Lazagne was usually the first to rise. Being quick to pack up, he was usually ten minutes up the trail before the rest of us broke camp. I brewed coffee, snatched a little to eat and Thirsty and Goggles usually left just before me.

We still hiked together, occasionally splitting up as the day progressed but joined each other if someone was resting. We shared the views, conquered mountains, forded rivers — and, each day, got just a little closer to Katahdin.

In the evenings our respective routines came into their own once more. I always slung up my hammock first. Then, I'd stretch out my leg muscles with a series of exercises which took perhaps ten minutes. Although often ignored, I had made efforts to stick with this routine on the advice of my physiotherapist back home.

Then I'd hang my sleeping bag over the hammock so the down expanded whilst some water boiled for a hot drink. Slipping into my camp shoes and donning a warm jacket as my body cooled, I'd take some time to update my journal for the day.

Then food, the highlight of every evening and a much-treasured activity. Each of us would usually commandeer the table if we had camped near a shelter; but, more often than not, we now stayed away from them. Congregating at a suitable spot, perhaps by some trees to act as a backrest, we watched our dinners cook and reviewed the day.

It was not just a time to eat, but to catch up. We chatted together, although sometimes one of us, seeking a little solitude, would remain absent and the rest would respect their privacy. Thirsty and I often shared this trait and would remain either in or near our hammocks. He also liked to make camp near the lake shorelines, enjoying the relative calm and therapy of gently lapping water. Close to the lakes there was a lack of trees so hammock spots were rare. Thirsty regularly bagged the prime spots and spent a few minutes standing sentry like a guard dog; get too close to his patch and he'd look disapprovingly in our direction, narrow his eyes in warning and occasionally he'd even growl.

Goggles was easy. He'd employ a quick scout round of the available spots, scratch his head and make himself comfortable in whatever area he'd chosen. He could have pitched on a slope, with umpteen tree roots and a small puddle but still he'd merely grin and utter his catch line: 'Oh yeah, titties.'

Lazagne was happy pretty much anywhere. He'd scout around for a few minutes and, after a little head-scratching, make it home for the night.

Once fed and rested, we'd often retire to the camp fire after sunset to stay warm, catching brief glimpses of each other in the meagre light as the flames rose and fell. Often we were quiet. The fluctuating patterns of the blaze became addictive as we stared into their world. Cracking and spitting, glowing embers escaped and rose up before slowly fading.

And slowly, one by one, we bade each other a good night, crept into our shelters, spent a few minutes still as our sleeping bags warmed to our body heat, and slept soundly.

***

As we spilled out onto the VT-103, we were pleased to see a sign for the Whistle Stop Restaurant, just a half-mile down the road. We sat outside on the grassy area while the owners popped out regularly to top up our coffee levels before bringing an afternoon breakfast over — a delicious feast worthy of any thru-hiker's appetite.

A steep climb up a rocky outcrop followed before the trail dipped down to the Clarendon Shelter and rose once more to Beacon Hill. A ten-mile, 2500-foot climb beckoned to the Cooper Lodge Shelter; but, having become tired, we pulled in early near Robinson Brook to camp.

I slept poorly as the bottom of my hammock was still cold. During the early hours I got up and slung my old quilt underneath for insulation, which worked perfectly, the sleeping bag keeping me warm once back inside.

When I did eventually rise, I was surprised to see Pink Bits's, sorry, Lady Forward's tent lurking in the trees a short way off. I hadn't noticed it during the night. Realising she must have arrived late the previous evening, I snuck over.

"Morning, Pink Bits," I said softly.

"I don't answer to that name anymore," came the groggy reply.

"I'm off shortly," I continued. "Just wanted to bring the gauntlet over for you. Have a great day."

***

While relaxing at camp after a strong afternoon with good miles, Lazagne shuffled over looking a little sheepish.

"You OK?" I ventured.

"Fozzie, I have a bit of a problem," he explained. "I think I might have a tick."

"Well it's not so bad," I said. "They're pretty easy to identify and remove."

"It's not so much the tick, it's the location of it."

I paused from eating my Mexican savoury rice and looked at him.

"Where exactly is it?" I ventured, still chewing.

He paused and scratched his head.

"Between, well, it's between my nuts and my arse."

Laughing was probably not the most sympathetic of responses but I couldn't help it.

"Oh shit."

"Yeah, shit," he confirmed.

He looked at me silently and expectantly until I finally

caught his angle.

"Oh, hold on! Wait a second! No! Absolutely not! I consider you a fine friend and there are many things I'd do for you, including pulling you from a river if you were in trouble, right up to looking after you if you fell. However, there is no way I'm surveying the hidden crevices of your anatomy for either a positive verification, or any form of removal. Sorry mate."

"OK, that's cool."

"You could try taking a photo of it for identification?" I added.

As I returned to my dinner, occasional flashes from the direction of Lazagne's camp silhouetted the outline of his legs as he took several exposures with his phone stuffed down his shorts.

"It's OK, Fozzie!" came the cry a few minutes later. "It's just a bit of dirt!"

Vermont had started to roll. Hills of a constant gradient were rare on any part of the AT, which more often involved short, sharp ascents and descents in between bigger peaks. However, Vermont was noticeably tougher. It was slowing us down although our mileage remained pleasing, between twenty to thirty miles most days — but it was taking longer to pull in the same distances.

This got me thinking how I could better manage my day and I started a list of time-saving methods, more often out of humour to keep me amused as opposed to actually putting them into practice.

Taking the time to roll a cigarette whilst peeing had the potential to save a couple of valuable minutes. With both hands not necessarily required for pee breaks, it seemed obvious to put them to some other use and I did try this method, but discounted it because of the lack of aim and subsequent splash back.

Another potential skill — although not linked with time saving — was the ability to pee in the middle of the night without getting out of my hammock. This proved difficult in a tent but Thirsty and I had already mastered the art of hammock peeing and, often, at some point in the early hours, the sound of splashing on the ground could be heard as one of us relieved ourselves.

I had managed to master the enviable art of either removing or donning my jacket without breaking my stride or completely removing my backpack. This, again, wasn't so much of a time saver, more a personal challenge that I'd seen others employ.

I had perfected the art of weatherproofing when it started to rain. My poncho lived in an outside pack pocket and a quick grope to one side retrieved it whilst I threw it over me and my pack. The umbrella quickly followed as it also lived in the same pocket. I could do all of this without stopping.

Finally, snacking, applying sunscreen, drinking and checking the data book without breaking stride had all been mastered back in the Smokies.

Perhaps I was paying too much attention to time-saving experiments? It was usual to think whilst hiking, and regularly becoming lost in thought; but it had affected my concentration on occasion. Hearing a loud rustle up in the trees, I naturally looked to try and see what was causing it — before walking straight into a tree trunk. Although cursing the mental distraction and a very sore face, shortly after I admit to passing a very attractive female hiker coming from the opposite direction. Turning around to take in the rear view, as is natural for both sexes on trail (she did the same), I promptly walked straight into another tree. Saving any further loss of face, literally, I laughed it off and tried to look more professional.

We skirted the town of Killington, passed Kent Pond and took a side road into town. Food was calling and I also needed batteries, so I entered the Base Camp Outfitters. Whether the woman that served me had seen me lurking around various sections studying equipment and had deemed me prime for a potential sale, or she had excess stock I don't know, but her sales pitch did little to lure me to the object in question.

"Have you seen this, it's brilliant!" she opened with, handing me a silver-coloured piece of cloth about the size of a large handkerchief.

"What is it?" I enquired.

"It's made by NASA," she proclaimed, as if this fact alone would secure a sale. "The technology is amazing. Just soak it in cold water and it stays cool."

I usually turned off when I discovered that anything was

Balancing on Blue

made by NASA — or, as the Americans pronounced it, *Narsore*. Responsible as they may have been for making inroads into the space race, and the subsequent technology associated with it, I noticed that most people in the States take everything they produce, or endorse, as sufficient reason to buy it without question. Well, it's produced by *Narsore* — it must be great!

"How much is it?" I asked the assistant.

"It's forty dollars," she answered, her expression similar to a double glazing salesman trying his luck with a high price.

"Forty dollars is a hell of a lot to ask for a piece of cloth," I said. "I use this," holding up my bandana. "Cost me two dollars fifty and does exactly the same job."

I paid for the batteries and left her staring into several redundant boxes containing NASA Cool Cloths, no doubt wondering whether she had been a little hasty.

I found the others at the Killington Deli. Several empty bottles of chocolate milk and sandwich wrappers dotted the table and the guys looked suitably full.

"How was the food?" I asked.

"Titties," Goggles replied and then changed the subject. "Have you seen the elevation graph?"

I peered at my phone to study the data book, which provided a schematic of ascents and descents. By way of comparison, back in Pennsylvania, this line coasted along with barely a ripple. Now it looked more like a cardiograph screen hooked up to a patient with a serious heart condition.

"Crikey!" I exclaimed.

"That's nothing," chipped in Thirsty. "Check out New Hampshire."

I scrolled forward a few pages.

"Flippin' 'eck!"

New Hampshire, home to one of the toughest sections of the AT through the White Mountains, or *Whites* as they are known, looked positively horrific. Mt Washington itself peaked at 6288 feet, and there were numerous other stiff climbs. The elevation graph bounced up and down, steep ascents and descents appeared everywhere and a new term, *notch* , made its debut. Notches, as we were to find out, were pretty common in New Hampshire and Maine. The name pretty much gives them away, but imagine a V-shaped indentation in the terrain, steep on both sides with a river at the bottom. We English would refer to them as gorges. The Whites were a mere fifty miles away, and Vermont, it appeared, was doing its upmost to get us into gear for them.

Our confidence was high and we knew there was nothing that could stop us, but still, I always doubted my own ability. Despite having around six thousand miles of hiking experience, I still looked at difficult terrain, particularly climbs, and didn't know if I could make it. I always relied on my trail mantra of *never, ever, ever, give up* to see me through. Nothing was ever that difficult, was it?

Every evening and several times during the day I vigilantly made checks in the data book. I often preferred to hike in ignorance; whatever the trail had in store for me wasn't going to change, whether I knew about it or not. However, planning each day was necessary. It was no use planning to pull in a thirty when I didn't know that there were 8000 feet of climbs and descents to take into account.

Most hikers will groan when they know any climbing is imminent, me included. Knowing that an hour is all it takes to knock off three miles, perhaps four or even more, and then suddenly faced with a speed drop to less than one mile an hour was a motivation killer.

Despite my grumbles and lack of confidence, when in full flow I loved hills. Covering ground over flat terrain is undemanding, and dare I say sometimes it can be monotonous. There's little energy expended, minimum effort required, and concentration is limited to avoiding detritus on the trail. Crossing mountain ranges where steep climbs were common always appeared daunting but I relished the challenge.

Climbing was all about keeping near to the limit I had set myself. I knew, roughly, how long a 1000-foot ascent took, and could subsequently adjust my pace, and effort, to see me up to the top without exhausting myself. There were other factors such as the distance those 1000 feet were spread over, what time of day it was, how I was feeling; even the weather played a part. But, after quick mental observations of how those influences could affect me, I then figured out how I needed to react to get up there.

When the hill hit, I went in at the pace I thought best. Sometimes I felt confident and pushed hard, playing around with pain limits and holding it just below them. At other times I completely misjudged them, or was just having a bad day physically, and all the planning went out of the window. But there are few greater pleasures than being at the peak of physical fitness, staring down a mountain and then reaching the top. You just feel superhuman, and nothing in the world is unachievable.

To take it to the next level, after a thru-hike is completed, and all the miles, weeks, physical exertion and metal stamina are behind us, we emerge as stronger individuals. Returning home, we suddenly realise what we have actually achieved and it makes a positive impact on everyday life. To walk 2000 miles and more through the heat, the wet, and the cold tests anyone's resolve — but it imparts strength. Suddenly, anything is achievable. We learnt the power of perseverance, to push through regardless of the odds, to always keep going. Obstacles in everyday life were not viewed negatively, but positively.

I've just walked 2000 miles! I can do anything I want to do!

***

Vermont ended at the Ledyard Bridge spanning the Connecticut River, and heralded our arrival into not only the penultimate state, New Hampshire, but to the town of Hanover as well. We had 161 miles to negotiate through New Hampshire and a further 282 through Maine, the last state — a total of some 443 miles. It was July 22nd, day 114 of my thru-hike.

Hanover was a beautiful town. Dartmouth College sat in an island of grass, occupying a proud position near the centre, its colonial buildings dating back to 1769. With wonderful architecture and old stone buildings, neatly trimmed gardens, parks and clean streets, it was a pleasure to thread a route through town.

We were eager for a motel so we could clean up. Thirsty, Goggles, Lazagne and I loitered outside Dunkin' Donuts as I got stuck into one of their glazed chocolate varieties. The Sunset Motor Inn, situated a couple of miles out of town, seemed to be the only viable option in an expensive area. The logbook stated they were happy to offer rides from town, which a phone call soon confirmed. It was the first time in my thru-hiking adventures that I had ever walked into a town looking for a motel, only to get a ride out again. Normally, I'd be standing by a road trying to get in, not the other way round.

Using a bed rotational system, normally disputed when at a motel, Thirsty and Goggles claimed the two beds whilst Lazagne and I slept on our mats on the floor. A shuttle bus made regular stops outside the motel and, the following morning, I caught an early one into Hanover for breakfast and some gear replacements. My head torch had died, and I needed a new pack towel to replace the one I had lost, not to mention new shorts as well.

The Hopkins Center for the Arts at Dartmouth College was celebrating its 50th anniversary with an unusual but wonderful project called *Hands on Pianos*. The college had dotted brightly painted pianos around Hanover and the surrounding area. The object was simple and invitations open; if you were a half-decent piano player, or indeed couldn't play at all, the idea was simply to sit down and have a go.

Strange as it was to see pianos perched on street corners, they drew regular crowds as participants shared their favourite tunes. I listened to everything from Mozart to Mick Jagger.

We reluctantly prised ourselves away from Hanover and its eclectic music choices at mid-day, managing twelve miles before setting up camp on Holts Ledge. After converging on a rock slab with impressive views down to the lowlands, we sat around watching the sun sink lower whilst slapping mosquitos, leaving bloody streaks on our exposed flesh. I missed the pianos and fell asleep humming songs by the Rolling Stones.

The data book's interpretation of New Hampshire turned out to be accurate, as we would have expected. Plummeting from Holts Ledge at 1937 feet, we bottomed out at the Lyme Dorchester road some 800 feet further down, only to climb again. Passing Lamberts Ridge we carried on to Smarts Mountain at 3237 feet. We climbed the fire tower to get a visual on the terrain surrounding us and bemoaned what seemed like a wasted climb; the trail promptly fell 1787 feet back down to

South Jacobs Brook.

Our maps appeared to suggest that the White Mountain section started shortly before the Beaver Brook shelter, at mile 1793. Mt Cube, about twenty miles before, offered a sweet perch for camp and to take in the outlook. The further we ventured north, the wilder America was becoming. Far-reaching views surrounded us as we sat on the flat summit, the rock warm from the sunshine, eating our dinners. A green ocean of trees rose up to the peaks surrounding us as distant, blue hills faded off to the horizon. Quintessential summer clouds appeared motionless, hanging in a contrasting sky, their reflections mirrored far below us in the lakes.

It seemed an inspiring enough location to discuss our plans for the Whites. There was no doubt that our mileage was due to suffer so damage limitation was the name of the game. Everyone was happy with progress and the estimated finish date wasn't of concern. Approximate plans put us on for a finish before the end of August, making a sub-five-month thru-hike. This wasn't breaking any records, nor was it a bad time either — more a typical thru-hike average for the AT.

However, everyone agreed that the Whites looked difficult. A never-ending series of peaks had to be climbed — but what we didn't realise was that it wasn't the climbs that were going to prove difficult, but rather the descents. Also, having psyched ourselves up for the ninety-odd miles through the Whites, we had become dangerously complacent. Such was the reputation of this section of the AT, we were focusing too much on its difficulty when we should have been looking beyond it. The Whites, as difficult as they looked, were just an entrée for everything afterwards.

Up until Pinkham Notch, near the town of Gorham at mile 1865, the trail just went silly. I had a headache from looking at the elevation profile, which switched from ascents to descents at alarming intervals. Thirsty's eyes peered over his guidebook. His eyebrows rose and fell in quick succession, almost like the mountains themselves.

Notches appeared regularly, and the climbs were long and steep, as were the descents. The surface of the actual trail was getting tougher also. Rock slabs rudely protruded over the trail, and tree roots, searching desperately for soft soil, wove crazy patterns everywhere.

Agreed that our daily distances were due to plunge, damage limitation involved nothing simpler than earlier starts and perhaps later finishes as well. One thing was certain: we were about to get our arses kicked. Not just by the Whites, but most of the rest of the AT itself.

Mt Mousilauke was the first peak to fire an opening shot across our bows with a 3746-foot climb. With Thirsty just a couple of yards in front of me, but his feet still level with my head, I realised it was going to be steep, and not easy. We had to fuel up just a few minutes in as my energy suddenly plummeted. The guys took the opportunity to do the same. I chewed on a packet of dried mango slices and, slowly, a sugar rush navigated a route down to my grateful legs.

The trees thinned shortly before the top and rain began to fall as we picked our way along a clear trail cutting over a stony summit. A howling wind whipped us from the west and, scurrying along, we began to curve downwards to the relative shelter of the trees.

Once out of the wind we took a quick break. Goggles and Thirsty dropped their shorts to carry out some treatment for their sore areas. It struck me at that point that I had two arseholes either side of me.

Switchbacks are not favoured by many thru-hikers, but their absence on the descent from Mousilauke wasn't making the going any easier. Sections of slick, wet rock slabs asked a lot of our fading shoe tread. Pinned to alarming angles, we teetered, eyeing up any promising lines. Trusting the grip on our shoes with arms flapping for balance, we cautiously inched our way down, sticking to the sides of the trail where trees offered hand holds, their roots edging onto the rock for sketchy foot placements. Even a series of steps hewn into the rock were difficult. As Beaver Brook joined us for company, we eventually landed at Kinsman Notch after a descent of 2932 feet in just four miles. Our first day venturing into the Whites had nevertheless reeled in an impressive twenty-three miles.

Sobos were a reliable source of information and Mike, fresh out of the Whites, stopped as we gleaned some advice from him.

Balancing on Blue

"You've got this far," he began. "You'll get through but just keep an eye on the weather, it changes quickly."

The town of Lincoln was just six miles east on route 112. We were all suffering — not just with sore sac syndrome, but with burning rashes where the straps from our packs had been rubbing in the humid atmosphere. Our shoulders, hips and backs were raw and demanded attention. A quick ride dropped us at the Econo Lodge and we each took turns for a shower.

Thirsty emerged cringing a few minutes later.

"That was one of the most painful experiences of my life," he announced, tentatively sitting on the edge of the bed and trying to decide which ointment would be the least painful.

Cries of pain floated out from the bathroom shortly after Goggles went in. Lazagne followed in silence but his facial expressions as he came out did little to placate my concerns.

As I cautiously entered the shower, looking at my beaten and raw flesh, I didn't know which way to turn, literally. My shoulders burned as the water hit them from behind; turning to lower the temperature, my hips fared little better.

I dabbed the towel hesitantly. Unable to face the prospect of actually rubbing in the antiseptic cream, instead I gently smeared a generous squirt over everything that looked like it needed treatment and left it. We spent most of the evening lying horizontal in front of the TV as, gradually, our bodies succumbed to the treatment and the pain slowly faded.

However, it hadn't faded enough for us to contemplate carrying on the next day. Lazagne had made the best progress and left with Chez 11, also in town, to knock off the section over Mt Wolf, South Kinsman Mountain and North Kinsman Mountain. Thirsty, Goggles and I rested in between eating, overdosing on ointment applications and striving to perfect some form of painless walking style.

The rest, several showers and cream applications appeared to work well and, the following day, we got a taxi back to Kinsman Notch. Once again, the rain started just shy of South Kinsman Mountain's summit, complete with lightning and thunder claps although, thankfully, not in the immediate vicinity.

A familiar pattern was already emerging. The AT constantly rose and fell through the Whites, and the name of the game was to bag a high peak or two, usually around the 3000 to 6000-foot mark. Once summited, it was then a steep descent back down to a notch — at which point, the whole process started over again. It made sense to use the areas around the notches as overnight camps. They were situated in sheltered positions and down from the higher altitudes where rain and lower temperatures were common. As sheltered as they were, they didn't benefit from much sunlight.

We didn't consider this a problem; in fact it made complete sense to camp at the notches. However, my problem with the section through the Whites centred on the rules and regulations. The area was popular with hikers — not just AT thru-hikers but day hikers also — and foot traffic presented problems with erosion.

The Appalachian Mountain Club (AMC) maintained a 122-mile section from Kinsman Notch in New Hampshire to Grafton Notch in Maine. They offered hikers overnight stays in eight mountain huts and several shelters. The huts, as wonderful as they were, were basic; most didn't have showers or heating, and the fees to stay there started around $80 each. A couple of positions were usually available on a work-for-stay basis for thru-hikers in exchange for sleeping on the floor, and leftover food.

The Randolph Mountain Club (RMC) maintained the section from Edmands Col to the Madison Hut and maintained four normal shelters in the Northern Presidentials Range, also charging for overnight stays there.

Charging high fees, and charging for shelters period, instead of encouraging us to stay there, did nothing more than to tempt us out to camp off the trail. Stealth campsites, as they were known, were common and information made available on the web by previous thru-hikers was easily obtainable.

Areas within a quarter of a mile from AMC and RMC facilities, and everything above tree-line were part of the Forest Protection Area (FPA). Camping was prohibited in these areas, and within 200 feet of water and trails anywhere. Trail boundaries were often marked with small, rock scree walls, off trail was out of bounds to protect plant life.

Suddenly, after weeks of living free with few restrictions, it wasn't just the amazing environment in the Whites under threat from erosion — it was our freedom.

Thru-hikers take on the challenge of a long-distance trail, and escape to the wilds, for various individual reasons. A yearning for a sense of living free is high on that list. To suddenly be told that camping in most areas was illegal, and to then feel forced to pay over the odds for accommodation, to keep to marked trails and to adhere to restrictions did little more than encourage us to rebel. It felt as though the Mountain Clubs had used erosion prevention to impose an accommodation monopoly with ridiculous prices.

I understand that areas of high traffic in wilderness areas need to be protected. I respect plant life, know to camp away from water sources and follow all the recommendations we were made aware of. However, we seem to forget that carving the Appalachian Trail in the first place — and the building of the AMC and RMC huts, the shelters, and the clearing of the ground surrounding them — is, by definition, erosion from the word go. For all this to happen and to then be told not to camp was hypocritical, especially as the vast majority of thru-hikers were always respectful, and practiced a leave no trace policy.

The net result was that Goggles, Thirsty, Lazagne and I stealth camped for most of the Whites. We were extremely careful: we didn't camp near water, resisted the urge to light a fire, took everything away with us and did our upmost to make no impact. The hammocks were ideal for this, keeping us off the ground and opening up sites on sloping terrain that a tent wouldn't be able to utilise. Although Goggles still had his tent, he often managed to squeeze into a flat space with us.

I never met a thru-hiker who had stayed at one of the shelters or the huts, and the usual reason they offered was that the cost was prohibitive. So stealth camping was how most of them got through.

***

Franconia Notch had proved a good place to stay. Getting ready for our second day in the Whites, I jumped out of my hammock and looked skywards. The sun was up but not yet high, the steep walls of the notch reaching up and covering us in shadows. I pulled on a jacket, started to jump around for warmth and made a coffee. We had a steep climb up to Franconia Ridge, taking in Little Haystack Mountain and Mt Lincoln before culminating at Mt Lafayette, 3831 feet above us. Franconia Ridge was a highlight of the AT, mainly because it was above tree-line for two miles and offered amazing views of the alpine scenery around us. Getting above tree-line was a rare treat in New Hampshire, as well as Maine, and the views offered insights into the wilderness we were travelling through.

"Here, I believe this is yours." I turned to see Pink Bits, sorry, Lady Forward, with an outstretched arm offering me the gauntlet.

"Just finishing my lunch," I replied. "I'll be off before you so you best keep hold of it."

Stuffing my snacks back into my food bag I discovered a rock at the bottom. Goggles started grinning, suggesting he was the culprit.

"How long as it been in there?" I asked.

"What in where?" he replied. "Don't know anything about a rock."

"I never said it was a rock?"

Thirsty also grinned, feigning surprise. I merely smiled and planned revenge.

Our route, for two miles at least, was clearly visible ahead along Franconia Ridge. Hikers speckled its length, clinging to the rocky top. It was so different to what we had become used to, spending days in the woods with few glimpses of what lay around us. Suddenly to be out in the open with views all around was incredible. We were all smiling.

After summiting Mt Garfield, we descended 1000 feet to get away from the exposed peak and tucked into the woods, just off trail, for the night. We had managed just ten miles.

South Twin Mountain faced us the following day but, once summited, it was 3625 feet downhill to Crawford Notch, fourteen miles away. South Twin was steep but we warmed quickly. With muscles loose, we made short work of the descent, pulling in at a small car park next to the US-302 at Crawford Notch.

Crawford Notch was essentially the start of the ascent of Mt Washington, 5000 feet above us and sitting pretty at 6288 feet. The summit was thirteen miles distant and renowned for its highly unpredictable and often violent weather patterns, even in the middle of summer. Despite having hiked just over twenty miles to Crawford Notch, it was a long and steep climb up to Washington. We needed to get up, over, and descend the other side out of any potential bad weather. The trail descended from Washington to the Peabody River, twenty-two miles away — so, keen to get up and over the mountain, we left late afternoon to climb the 2000-foot, two-mile section to Webster Cliffs. This, we hoped, would place us perfectly for the next section over Washington.

The 1000 feet per mile rule, signifying anything steep, was on our minds as we left Crawford and climbed. Progress, as expected, was slow. Tree roots wrapped over the trail to provide natural steps as we climbed, weaving around huge rocks encroaching on the trail edge. Ten minutes in we realised we had no water for camp. Goggles and Thirsty were good enough to track back down to the bottom and collect some water — not just for themselves, but for Lazagne and I too as we sat and waited.

When we reached Webster Cliffs, a large area of flat rock opened up before us with far-reaching views away to the valley below. Some of our gear was damp from the recent rain, so we pulled out our sleeping bags and hung them from the trees, setting up camp in a small clearing behind. The sky over the hilltops at the other side of the valley was streaked with oranges and reds, gradually rising up to blues and higher still to a darkening border as night fell.

The rocks were warm. We sat, cooking our dinners and discussing the big day ahead of us. The Whites were hard and we weren't though them yet. Stunning as they were, the immediate focus was to get through New Hampshire and into Maine, some sixty-one miles distant. After that we figured we could breathe easier on kinder terrain, and push some higher miles in our last state.

How wrong we were.

Chapter 13

Cambers, Sinkers, Bouncers, Sliders, Rockers, Rottens and Floaters

July 31st to August 8th
Mile 1841 to 1953

I was up at 3.30 a.m, unable to sleep. I didn't know if the anticipation of summiting Mt Washington and hiking the Presidential Range was responsible, but for over two hours I sat on Webster Cliffs. The Milky Way blazed its own trail over me and, slowly, the horizon started to glow red. With enough light to have breakfast and pack, I was away before the guys. The forest thinned the higher I ventured. I found regular opportunities to rest on rocky perches with views ahead and behind. As I watched the guys closing on me a little further down, I shouted regular taunts that they were either going too slow, were too far behind, or that their hiking was rubbish. They stopped, looked up at me a couple of hundred feet above, laughed, threw a few insults and started to speed up. At this point I flew off, increased my speed to gain further ground and subsequently re-appeared at another vantage point for further bantering.

With Goggles leading the hunt, they eventually caught me as we rolled over Mt Jackson. The terrain unfolded before us, occasionally broken by solitary, rocky peaks floating on a sea of green. The trail was invisible beneath millions of trees, but our route was clear. Numerous pinnacles, each a little higher than its predecessor, stepped up to the clear outline of Mt Washington itself, standing proud over everything it surveyed. Perched on its majestic throne, we, its subjects, bowed in acknowledgement, humbled.

The Presidential Range, within the White Mountains, contained thirteen mountains named after American presidents and other prominent figures from the eighteenth and nineteenth centuries — Mt Washington, Mt Eisenhower, and Mt Franklin to name just three. The area was a tempting lure for many hikers and mountaineers.

I had read so many accounts of this section that I was convinced we were going to be in for a very wet and windy ride. Washington is a melting pot of weather patterns. Fierce winds regularly rip over the summit and it once laid claim to the fastest wind speed recorded anywhere in the world, of 231 miles per hour. This record, set on April 12th 1934, remained solid until 1996, when a tropical cyclone called Olivia registered 253 miles per hour at Barrow Island, Australia. Mt Washington had lost its claim to fame but still holds the record for wind speed outside a tropical cyclone.

Washington's reputation as the most dangerous small mountain in the world is well founded. Even calm days with clear blue skies can, in a short space of time, descend rapidly into fierce winds, with temperatures plummeting to below freezing. Inexperienced and experienced hikers alike regularly get blown off course. Resisting the urge to battle the gales, they succumb to them and end up disorientated and lost, miles from anywhere. Often on day hikes with no equipment, they die from exposure and hypothermia. It is not a mountain to be taken lightly.

Unofficial fatality lists for the area date back to the 1800s. Figures vary, but around 147 people have reputedly lost their lives there.

It immediately reminded me of a quote by Edward Whymper, an English mountaineer, illustrator and author who was born in 1840.

There have been joys too great to be described in words, and there have been griefs upon which I have not dared to dwell;

and with these in mind I say: Climb if you will, but remember that courage and strength are nought without prudence, and that a momentary negligence may destroy the happiness of a lifetime. Do nothing in haste; look well to each step; and from the beginning think what may be the end.

Always wary that the weather could change, I looked up amazed at how lucky I was. We couldn't have wished for a better day. In fact, a day hiker I met coming south stopped to chat to me.

"How's the view up there?" I opened with.

"Wonderful," he replied, grinning. "I've walked up to Washington many times, and the Presidentials. I can honestly say this is the best weather I've seen up here. Enjoy!"

When we reached the Mizpah Spring Hut and nearby campsite, the caretaker called Bearsweat called us over and brewed hot drinks for us. He had also hiked the AT and shared his experience, confirming we were lucky with the weather.

"The descent from Mt Madison down to Pinkham Notch is long and steep but you're well on course to get down there today. Have a great hike!"

Our next target was the Lakes of the Clouds Hut, five miles further up and itself a mere one and a half miles before the summit of Mt Washington. The trail climbed steeply from the Mizpah Hut over awkward sections of tree roots before emerging above tree-line. With the summit buildings of Mt Washington now clearly visible, we passed the Lakes of the Clouds Hut and the prospect of a hot meal in the summit café was enough to haul us up the final 1200 feet.

Scrambling over the final section of rocks we arrived in a different world. Tourists spilled out of the train, after ascending 3588 feet on the three-mile cog railway built in 1868. Many seemed out of their element, surveying the view in T-shirts and shorts before retreating to the warmth of the café. Warm from the climb, we felt no need to put on another layer, instead queuing for a few minutes for the obligatory summit photo.

We weren't keen on staying, partly due to the crowds and the need to get down to Pinkham Notch. Hot food, however, was on blatant display; and, following our unwritten rule of never passing sustenance by, we retreated inside for a quick bowl of chilli before leaving for the decent.

One of several trail customs on the AT entails baring one's bottom, or mooning, in the direction of the tourist train. So popular was this custom that apparently the authorities had taken a dim view of the practice. Police were known to ride the train and arrest perpetrators on occasion. I was under strict instructions from Pockets, a friend with whom I had hiked a fair chunk of the PCT.

"Don't forget to moon the train," he ordered. "If the police are on board, run!"

Intrigued by the possibility of being arrested, Goggles and I, the first to descend, stopped as the train chugged and strained up the final few hundred feet to the summit. The passengers peered out curiously at two strange-looking, bearded beasts. Goggles turned to me.

"Ready?" he said, smirking.

"Yup."

Not wanting to push our luck further than necessary, a quick drop of the shorts with raised arms was sufficient and we glanced back to applause and shouts. With no police in pursuit, we nevertheless upped the pace a little and sped off north.

At first the descent was relatively easy, over open ground with good visibility. We reached Edmands Col and then the Madison Spring Hut, refuelling once more with snacks. Rising steeply to Mt Madison, the final climb was over and we began the 3100-foot descent to the Peabody River three and a half miles down. Picking our way over rough rock slabs slowed my pace and Goggles, Lazagne and Thirsty pulled away. I fell below the tree-line and negotiated the trail steeply, watching my step, weaving over and around rocks with tree roots reaching out and gripping the surface like giant hands.

Finally I bottomed out at the Peabody River where the guys had set up camp with a new thru-hiker, Grok. We hadn't managed to reach Pinkham Notch, but having pulled in an impressive twenty miles over difficult terrain, no one was complaining.

I was sore, though. A minor stumble had blooded my thigh and my knees were tight from such a long and steep descent. At the end of each day it felt as though I had gone several rounds in a boxing ring. Having won each bout thus far, I seemed to be facing far heavier, tougher opponents every time I ventured out for another round.

"It roughed us up but we won the fight," Goggles commented, wisely, as we chatted with raised voices over the roar of the Peabody River. Grok, also sporting some grazes, complained that he needed several beers for medicinal purposes.

***

After a short, and welcome, four miles from an early morning start we emerged at Pinkham Notch. The visitor centre offered a decent but expensive breakfast, which we declined in favour of getting a ride into Goreham, eleven miles west. Apart from bacon and eggs, we all needed to resupply with food, get cleaned up and wash our clothes. My shoes, also, were on their last legs and pair number four was beckoning.

We had heard of a trail angel called Miriam in Goreham who welcomed hikers at her small house three miles from town. Our ride dropped us in the centre of town at the Moonbeam Café. Timing couldn't have been more perfect; as we emerged with full stomachs she pulled up and took us back.

"I have to go to work," she said. "But feel free to use the washer, make yourself at home and I'll see you later."

I took the opportunity to call Pockets, who had hiked the AT some years prior, and asked him for advice to get through the last state, Maine, just a few miles ahead.

"No problems really," he explained. "Just watch the biting flies."

"Biting flies?" I ventured.

"Yup, come out latish summer, nasty little bastards."

With breakfast already a fading memory, and our clothes drying outside, we walked back to town for more food and also for me to try and get a new pair of shoes. There was just one outfitter in Goreham, and that would have better been described as a hardware store. My first pair at the start, a brand called Inov-8, had lasted an impressive 1000 miles. Pennsylvania fought a running battle with their replacement, a pair of Brooks, which gave up after just 250 miles and some New Balance had

Balancing on Blue

fared well until Goreham, but they too were finished.

Lazagne came to the rescue with a suggestion that, at first, I dismissed. He had ordered a pair of Brooks Cascadia 7's, which had been delivered to the post office in Goreham. They were too small for him but curiosity got the better of me when he offered them to me for the original purchase price. The only problem was the size, which was two full US sizes up from what I normally wore.

Unwittingly, it solved the problem of my wider feet up front. Although clearly too big and with a gap at the ankle I could slide a thumb into, I walked up the road for half a mile and returned. Apart from sliding around at the back, as I might have expected from being too large, they remained firmly secure; and with my feet pushed towards the back, the toes also moved back and away from the narrowest part of the shoe. It was a revelation. Not only were my feet away from the edges up front, they were unbelievably comfortable. I have hiked in Cascadias ever since with no problems. I didn't see them as shoes; they were so comfortable I referred to them as my slippers.

We left Goreham on Thursday, August 2nd. 1865 miles into our adventure, and with 319 miles left to Katahdin. Confidence was high. We had finished the Whites, one of the toughest sections. We climbed the 2000 feet from Pinkham Notch up to Wildcat Mountain, having left most of our gear at Miriam's, taking just lunch and clothing. The trail intersected the US-2 twenty-one miles further up, but taking into account the twists and turns, it spilled out just a few road miles back into Goreham so we could walk back. The chance of hiking with little weight over rough terrain made the decision for us. More wet, slick, green rock hindered our climb. Huge rock sections at alarming angles were becoming more common. It was a big leap of faith to plant a shoe down, taking all my weight, and then hoping it held as the other foot searched for grip. Coming downhill, the horrible feeling that at any second my feet would be whipped out from under me constantly teased. We crawled, slid, shimmied, and grasped anything at the side of the trail that would accept a hand. If the trees and their roots hadn't been there to help, I don't know how we would have got down, or up.

Instead of the AT becoming easier, if anything, it felt much harder. The notches were killing us; always steep on both sides, the only saving grace was that some of them crossed roads at their base and offered the chance of trail magic, or a quick ride to town. We were reduced to a plodding pace, our legs not so much stepping ahead, more lifting up. Breathing hard with legs screaming we eventually reached the open summit of Wildcat.

"I thought this was supposed to be getting easier?" I said. "The further we venture north, the harder it seems to be getting."

Thirsty, bent over double trying to regain his breath, agreed.

"That's not all," Goggles chipped in. "The Mahoosuc Notch is only twenty-four miles away. We'll probably be there tomorrow."

The Mahoosuc Notch took notches up another notch. We had heard stories about this mile-long section of trail, and indeed its reputation preceded itself. Fallen boulders, some the size of houses, littered the passage through. It wasn't so much hiking as crawling.

Goggles and Thirsty moved ahead of Lazagne and me. My lower back was sore after a night on Miriam's unforgiving sofa, and Lazagne's pace had also suffered because he had little grip left on his shoes. He was treading cautiously, especially through the rock sections.

It was exhausting. After recovering from Wildcat Mountain we promptly plunged back down 900 feet, bottomed out near the Carter Notch Hut, and then faced a 1500-foot climb back up to Carter Dome.

As we reached the higher sections, the trees gradually thinned and became more stunted. Light flooded the trail and the wind increased until we met rocky summits with astonishing views. It became a familiar pattern: descend to the dark depths of a notch, sunlight diminishing as the trees grew thicker further down, the walls of each notch closing in like a dungeon. Then, we picked our way back up, through a dank, murky underworld where the environment was quiet, sometimes eerie. The climbs always caused me to overheat. Peeling off a jacket, I remained undecided — too hot or too cold, I never got it right.

After North Carter Mountain and Mt Moriah, we gently eased our way down 3200 feet to the road. The gentle decline was a welcome reward for our hard work — so welcome, in fact, that Lazagne and Thirsty started to jog two miles from the road, free from their pack weight. I followed and before long our legs were scrambling to stay with the momentum. With fading light we leaped over obstacles, not seeing them till the last moment.

"Log!" Lazagne screamed from the murk a few feet ahead. "Stream! Rock, shit! ROCK!"

Swerving, running hard, focusing on the trail, jumping and cutting corners we reached the road crying with laughter from the adrenaline rush, drenched in sweat and giggling uncontrollably.

Goggles, resting and confused as to why we were totally out breath, hoisted his pack and we road-walked back to Miriam's. After hiking twenty-one miles and following every curve of the trail, it was strange to be back, just a short distance from Goreham.

The run had inflamed my shin splint, which had given me no problem for weeks. Obviously my free-spirited jog had caused it to retaliate and I made a mental note to keep my speed down. I debated resting it the following morning but any delay meant the guys would be ahead and I might not catch them.

We were two weeks away from the final 160 miles of the AT. Occasionally I'd flick a few pages ahead in the data book, as did the others; during that final section, the gradients eased, the hills diminished, and the going appeared flat. Of course, there was the small matter of summiting and descending from Katahdin. The mountain entailed a climb of over 4000 feet spread over five miles, the first half of which was renowned for its hard going, and then we had to get back down again.

The weather had also turned and we longed for the heat wave that had plagued us through New York State. Temperatures had dropped, especially at night, but we still wore T-shirts and shorts throughout the day. Angry clouds swept over us and, each minute, threatened to open.

The Mahoosuc Range is a notorious section of trail starting at Mt Hayes and is renowned for many steep climbs on difficult terrain. It hit me for six.

I picked my way over rock slabs, following a weak line of cairns to the top of Mt Hayes after a storm. I was alone. Various injuries screaming at me to slow down had won over my resolve.

I dropped my pack and sat on the summit, enjoying the warm rock. A strong sun somehow discovered chinks in the clouds, casting searchlights all around me and flooding the valleys with light, broken up by racing cloud shadows. Steam rose from the rocky summit as it dried and I surveyed my world. Mt Hayes dropped away, its speckled, grey slopes surrendering to the treeline and merging into green. I could see no trace of man's intervention. No roads or buildings spoilt my panorama; the wilds were just as they had been for thousands of years.

Rivers, like silver ribbons, threaded routes through infinity, sparkling as the sun bounced off them. They emptied into vast lakes, mirrors nestling in the lowlands. Then the land rose majestically once more, cloaked in evergreens before succumbing to the rocky peaks. A weak wind offered the only noise, the trees gently reciprocating, bowing over in surrender and gently rustling. I could have stayed there forever.

In retrospect, Mt Hayes somehow seemed to talk to me. I stayed up there for two hours, just thinking and questioning. This is something I often did at home when I needed space. Escaping to the outdoors often not only forced me to accept problems, but gave me the space and time to resolve them.

I was exhausted — there was no escaping that problem. My shin throbbed, the injured calf complained constantly, my ankles ached; and as I looked at my bloodied legs the solution became obvious. I had to slow down. I was lethargic, sluggish, not just in body but also in mind. My pace was slow and so was my decision making. Everything seemed like hard work, something was wrong.

I needed to make a decision. Bush Goggles was pushing hard, both the miles and the pace. He had agreed to meet his mum at Katahdin where she would drive him home. The target he had set himself had rubbed off on us. We didn't want to lose him; we were a team, and a damn good one, but I was at risk of bailing out if I continued to push myself like this. Confident of reaching Katahdin, and well ahead of schedule, if anything, I wanted to slow down and take more time, not speed up.

My body needed rest. When I hauled myself down from Mt Hayes I was too tired to go on. After covering just four miles for the entire day, I pitched the hammock and made a decision. I would talk to the guys — even let Goggles go, if that's what he needed to do, as much as I didn't want to see him leave. Whether Lazagne and Thirsty would go with him or we would stay as a three-member team I didn't know.

By the morning I had deteriorated. Making decisions was exhausting and hiking was slow. Something was wrong; physical tiredness was a problem I could usually sort out, but with judgements to be made and navigation choices to follow, my mind just didn't seem up to par. At times I just couldn't be bothered with any of it and entertained thoughts of quitting the trail for good.

I caught them mid-morning. We shook hands on passing into Maine and somehow I managed to make it to camp on the west peak of Goose Eye Mountain. Stiff, tight, low vegetation hindered camping and there were no trees to sling our hammocks. As the sun set we sat on the flat, rocky summit and watched the sunset, staying there for hours as the night sky came out to play. Away from the city lights, the stars were intense and the Milky Way arced, soaring above us. Mesmerised, we said little. I woke several times during the night to take it all in again.

Realising the others would be ahead of me straight away, I voiced my concerns over breakfast.

"I'm tired, guys," I ventured. "I'm nowhere near a hundred percent and I need to slow down, if not rest for a day. Something isn't right. Goggles, I know you have to meet your mum but I can't keep with your distances. I'd love to finish with you but I don't think I can."

No one spoke as I turned to Thirsty and Lazagne.

"I don't know what will happen with the group, and we all know there is no commitment to walk together. I *have* to slow down. Chances are I'll rest at the next opportunity and, then, I plan on fifteen-mile days until Katahdin."

We discussed the situation sensibly. Although we came to no decision, we all knew that Goggles would be out front, I would be bringing up the rear, and Lazagne and Thirsty would take time somewhere in the middle to figure out their next move.

Suddenly, everything seemed to be going wrong.

Four miles later, somehow, I had managed to stick with them and a good job it turned out to be. Suddenly, we stared down at the jumbled, rocky calamity otherwise known as the Mahoosuc Notch. Awol had described the notch in his guidebook as '*The most difficult, or fun mile of the AT*'. I guess it depended on your perspective.

Tiredness and group dynamics were pushed to one side as each of us realised that prudence, and a team approach, were advisable to get through. We surveyed the terrain ahead of us. Planning went out of the window. It became clear that the only approach was to descend and take each obstacle as it appeared.

The walls of the notch narrowed towards the base where countless massive boulders had become lodged, blocking the route. Faded white blazes indicated the optimal route but we lost them many times. Balancing on rock ledges, we peered down into dark crevices, seeing the faint gush of water below us as streams also battled a way through. Sometimes we picked a way through the base, crawling, sliding and squeezing. Occasionally we were forced higher up the notch, inching along narrow ledges, all the time scanning ahead for the right line.

Two hours later we emerged, having averaged a dismal half a mile an hour. We smiled, looked at each other's dirt streaked clothes and laughed.

I lost them in the afternoon. After the adrenalin of the notch, my fatigue kicked in once more. I dropped my pack on the shore of Speck Pond, sat down and eased off my filthy socks and shoes, pulled off my T-shirt and waded out into the water. My muscles slowly eased, grateful for the therapy. For an hour I alternated between swimming and sitting on a rock a few yards from shore. The sun warmed me as gentle waves lapped over my feet.

I dried myself off and checked my injuries for any swelling but found nothing. Ten minutes into the next climb, I was stopped by a couple of day hikers who questioned why I had started so late for a south bounder.

"I'm heading north to Katahdin?" I questioned. "I'm north bounding?"

"Well, currently you're headed back towards the Mahoosuc Notch," one replied. "Are you OK? You look done in."

"I'm fine, thanks," I said, offering a weak smile. I turned around and headed back the way I had just come.

It was obvious that I wasn't fine. Somehow I managed to climb 600 feet, passing the turn off for Old Speck Trail. Two more day hikers, Eric and Samantha, enthralled when they discovered I had walked from Georgia, forced me to stop and chat. I couldn't focus on the conversation and felt light-headed, but did my best to appear friendly.

"You sound like, British or something?" Eric said.

Oh crap, not now please.

"I'm from the UK, yes; I'm English."

"You *walked* here all the way from Georgia? That's amazing!" Samantha chipped in.

They wished me good luck and some minutes later I arrived back at Speck Pond. I had walked the wrong way again, all the way back down the hill I had just climbed.

That's it, Fozzie. Get the fuck off trail and rest. Sort this out, you need to take time out.

Again, I plodded back up to the Old Speck trail, sat down and checked the data book. There was a 2500-foot descent to Grafton Notch just over three miles away where the ME-26, a quiet road, offered the chance to get a ride out.

Staggering down, somehow I managed to catch up with Eric and Samantha. I must have looked terrible because, again, they asked me if I felt OK.

"I don't feel great, no," I answered. "I don't know what's wrong with me but I need to get off trail and rest for a couple of days."

Before I knew it, my pack was in the back of their car and they had dropped me at the Pine Ellis Lodge in Andover. David, the owner, checked me in for two nights and provided a brief tour of the hostel.

Pine Ellis was quiet save for a few hikers. Most of them were in bed despite it being mid-day. Being as quiet as possible, I inadvertently woke Rachael, a section hiker sharing my room.

"Sorry," I said. "Didn't mean to wake you."

"That's OK," she mumbled, rubbing her eyes. "Surprised you're not ill."

"Really, why?"

"You haven't heard? Most of the hikers within a ten-mile radius are sick," she explained.

"No, I hadn't heard?"

I walked to the Andover General Store, which also served food from its deli. Two hikers I had not met, Willie and Indiana, along with Bad Dinner and Metric, peered up from their fries and shuffled over to let me in. Everyone looked pale, unimpressed as they poked their food.

"How's the food?" I opened with.

"It's good," Bad Dinner replied, somewhat contrary to his trail name. "Are you not sick?"

"I feel incredibly tired, something is definitely not right but I'm holding on to my bodily fluids. Do you have any idea what's going on?"

"Norovirus," he explained. "Apparently the CDC was in the area recently trying to locate the source but didn't find anything. Everyone is sick. I'd say at least eighty percent of hikers are down with it."

I'd never heard of norovirus but it is very common. With a twenty-four to forty-eight-hour incubation period, the symptoms include vomiting, diarrhoea and tiredness. There is no cure. The usual advice is merely to rest, drink plenty of water and let it run its course. I hadn't been sick, and my bowels seemed fine although I was tired. Either I was in the early stages or I had something completely different.

Lazagne arrived at Pine Ellis the following morning.

"I thought you were ahead?" I asked.

"I was. I got off at Dunn Notch. I'm sick, feel like shit. Thirsty too. He was too weak to even get up."

"Where's Goggles?"

"I think he's at the next notch, South Arm Road."

Dunn Notch was ten miles ahead of where I had bailed out, and South Arm Road was a further ten more.

Despite sleeping for ten hours straight overnight, I was still tired and dozed off again for another four hours. I walked slowly downstairs, sat outside on the porch, drank a Coke and watched a car pull up outside. Goggles got out. Before he could even shoulder his pack, another car arrived and Thirsty emerged, looking very much the worse for wear.

Goggles appeared fine and confirmed he felt OK. Thirsty was far worse, saying he couldn't even muster the energy to get out of his hammock to be sick, so he just poked his head out to vomit.

Rest was on the cards. In between drinking plenty of water, the chess championship picked up from where it had left off. England was making a determined comeback; beating Lazagne twice, I pulled the score to four against five. One more win for me would secure a draw.

Thirsty slept but Goggles only rested briefly, ate some food and set off with David for a ride back to the trailhead. Knowing that we probably wouldn't see each other again — at least not on that trip — we shared a hug before he left. I'd hiked with plenty of companions but was going to miss Goggles for sure. With Thirsty, Lazagne and I all sick, and with his schedule to meet, we all understood that he had to leave.

Andover was quiet, the streets narrow, and we occasionally passed timber-clad houses dotted around the town. Although we were desperate for some vitamins and nutrients, the general store, amazingly, had no fresh fruit. I walked over to the Little Red Hen Diner. The door creaked open to reveal Pink Bits — sorry, Lady Forward — Chez 11 and a new face called Warlie.

"Are you ill?" Lady Forward asked.

"I'm not a hundred percent. Tired but holding on to the fluids. You?"

"We've all been ill, everyone's been ill."

"I think we're out the other side mate," Chez 11 chipped in, his Scouse accent pronounced.

The Little Red Hen, a wonderful little country diner, saved the day with fresh orange juice and a salad. I rested and continued to drink water with rehydration powder. Slowly, my lethargy faded; and, although still not completely up to par, I made plans to leave the following day.

Rising early, I left Lazagne and Thirsty at Pine Ellis. Both had ten miles on me anyway so they weren't in any rush. David drove me back to Grafton Notch.

Johannes, a German thru-hiker, was gearing up to leave as David dropped me off. He had started ten days before me back in Georgia and was struggling through the Mahoosucs. Either he was ill or I was recovering; climbing 2167 feet from the notch up to Baldpate West Peak I left him quickly. There were ten miles to Dunn Notch, where Lazagne and Thirsty had bailed out and I knew they were planning a ride there with David, probably getting there before I did. We knew our plans and agreed that we'd either meet later, or certainly the following day. The beauty of the AT, and other trails, was that firm plans weren't needed. We hiked on a strip of trail perhaps a couple of feet wide. You would always pass others and could never really lose anyone.

I felt almost back to normal. My legs coped without complaints but, more importantly, my head was clear. Decisions came easily and with little effort.

Taking a quick break, I looked around. Broadleaf trees were in the minority in Maine, replaced with evergreen pine and firs. They grew right up to the trailside, their thick growth transforming my surroundings into a dense, eerie darkness. Although the way was clear, stray off trail and it was easy to see how anyone could get lost and never be seen again. Many hikers have gone missing in Maine when they never showed at expected points, despite searches. Not only was it sad but this last state on the AT definitely had a sense of mystery about it.

One thing was for sure — Maine was wild, very wild. Surveying that barren corner of America from many vantage points, there was usually little to remind a hiker that they lived in the twenty-first century. It was rare to see a building or road. Even planes passing overhead seemed scarce.

But wilderness was precisely the reason many people came. The lack of intrusion, and wanting to keep that beautiful countryside unspoilt, drew many outdoor enthusiasts. In fact, the state slogan said it all: *Maine – The Way Life Should Be.*

The winters were harsh. Low temperatures and high snowfall made much of the area out of bounds except for a dedicated few, experienced at winter hiking and other such activities.

Climbing higher, the trees gradually became more stunted. Unable to cope well with the harsher climate at altitude, their height diminished to just a few feet. This feature of subarctic and subalpine trees is known as krumholtz, from the German *krumm,* meaning crooked or bent, and *holz,* meaning wood. The exposed upper sections of the trees were often devoid of foliage. Growth concentrated around the base where it was more sheltered. At

Balancing on Blue

lower elevations, the growth became more normal, away from the upper climes.

The predominant rock in Maine, granite, often covered the mountain tops. Vast sections also stretched down from the summits. Bathed in sun, they were wonderfully warm and great places to sit. Even lower down, the surface alternated between soft, dark soil and this grey, sometimes bluish rock. My shoes stuck to the gritty texture. It was like walking on sandpaper. After a while getting used to its whims, it proved a trustworthy platform to hike on. I could always count on it to hold me securely while ascending steep sections. Striding purposefully uphill, leaping from boulder to boulder, Maine granite held me securely.

However, away from the exposed sections, where the sun made few inroads, this rock was often damp and covered in a slimy texture that demanded caution. Many descents were spread over vast sections of rock, appearing like a flight of steps, each one several feet high. With the weight of my pack bearing down, slips were common; I continued to utilise the edges of the trail where trees steadied me and their roots offered foot holds.

My hiking style had to adapt to these sections. It was common to clamber, slide on my bottom, teeter precariously and generally look completely inexperienced.

The soil, a rich, chocolaty dense brown colour, was wonderful to walk on. The soft texture gave just a little underfoot to cushion each footfall. Even then, at the beginning of August, sections were still wet. Vast amounts of snow melt over the course of the summer, coupled with the rainfall, meant much of the ground never dried out. Puddles speckled the way and boggy sections were common.

To prevent erosion and make the trail negotiable, the authorities had installed many sections of boardwalks. The majority of these were welcome, preventing soaked and muddy feet. The upper sections of these walkways were constructed using two parallel lengths of wood, with shorter planks fixed widthways, similar to what you might expect on a pier.

The dodgy versions consisted of two planks of wood side by side, sometimes logs sawn in half so the underside was semi-circular but the top flat. At the ends, a block or two of wood lay on the ground at right angles for the planks to anchor onto — foundations if you like. To negotiate these boardwalk versions required an awkward stance with legs slightly apart, with one foot on each plank.

Boardwalks became a pet hate for me, so much so that I studied the various types. I divided them into various categories, in order of difficulty starting with the easiest.

There were right or left cambers, sinkers, bouncers, sliders, rockers, rottens and floaters. Most exhibited just one trait but some shared two or even more.

Cambers were the easiest, mainly because they gave themselves away visually. On approach, it was easy to spot the angle, the surface sloping either to the left or right. A slight posture adjustment was enough to counteract most of the cambers.

Sinkers were hard to detect because it wasn't until I had set foot on one that its character revealed itself. They thrived on ground that was either saturated or muddy. Once my weight bore down, one section or more would sink alarmingly into the ground, catching me unawares.

Bouncers were closely related to sinkers. Instead of remaining in the downward position, they mustered enough energy to counter my weight and bounce back up — just at the point when one foot lifted for the next step and the pressure released somewhat.

Sliders were, frankly, lethal. Wood has many positive properties but grip can never claim to be one of them, especially when wet. With the damp conditions and regular traffic, most boardwalk surfaces were slippery. It was the one aspect that was common with all of them. Feet merely skidded when any pressure was applied. Some lured me in with a couple of sections of dry wood; I became complacent and sped up, only to enter *the slider zone* . Once the leading foot was planted it suddenly slid forward, resulting either in a very ungraceful parting of the legs, or the splits, which had me clutching my groin in pain. Sometimes one leg flung up wildly skyward, shortly followed by the other, as in the classic cartoon sketches where someone steps on a banana. During this split second of airborne travel came the realisation that no part of my body was in contact with the ground and I was, in fact, horizontal. My pack, thankfully, cushioned many a hard fall.

Rockers gave an entirely new perspective on fulcrums. Loose ground on the end sections left the base points without any anchor points. I often stepped on the first section only for it to sink and the opposing end to lift up, just like a seesaw. Or, reaching the far end, suddenly the section behind me did the same.

Rottens were easy to spot, but difficult to judge. The older sections, those in need of some maintenance or replacement, gave themselves away with deep surface ridges, chips, breakaways and holes. Tentative steps were crucial to establish just how bad they might be if any progress was to be achieved. Trust in placing all my weight had to come into play at some point. The usual warning was a loud splitting sound when the wood finally decided that life in Maine was not as ideal as it might have hoped for. One foot, sometimes both for double points, fell a few inches to the ground where mud invariably engulfed my new Cascadias and an unpleasant feeling of moisture greeted my socks.

At the far end of the difficulty scale, floaters were extreme. Actually, they were fairly easy to spot because one end was over water. The trick was judging whether they were securely anchored below the surface, or were prime floaters. Applying foot pressure over the suspected area was usually enough to ascertain whether they had a firm base; they either didn't move, sunk a little or, in a worst-case scenario, plunged down into the murky depths. Once more, although testing was obligatory, complacency regularly overruled. With an overwhelming feeling of impending wetness, the universe seemed to pause as my platform sank in anticipation of meeting anything solid. Some merely sank a few inches but the worst culprits, the crème de la crème of floaters, sank into oblivion and called their cousins, the sliders and rockers, into action. Either a quick retreat or a forward jump saved the day; but if I was caught out in the middle sections, the only escape was to jump sideways into the water.

Over time, I became quite adept at judging the boardwalks but one particular specimen, despite appearances, hid a far deeper, evil character. It looked innocent on my approach. A right camber was obvious but not severe, and the ground seemed boggy which made me suspicious of anything in the sinker, bouncer or rocker categories. The surface seemed dry so a slider didn't really cross my mind but the opposing end was hovering over water.

The initial left foot placement held and I felt confident. My right foot swept past, but instead of making firm contact, merely glanced across the camber and was promptly whipped from under me. It collided with my left foot which decided to join its partner in flight. Both feet hurtled out to the left, momentarily leaving me in midair before I fell off the other side.

After dusting myself off and glancing quickly behind for any possible witnesses, I stepped on board once more and progressed to the apparent safety of the middle haven. The centre sank alarmingly and proceeded to bounce, reverberating, as I clung there like a tightrope walker pausing to regain composure.

With half the stage complete, I inched bravely towards the obvious floater but it remained solid. Already bruised and muddy, I figured things couldn't get any worse; and, despite the solid anchor point, little did I know that a small sliver of wood was holding on for dear life on the edge of a submerged rock.

Feeling proud and all-conquering, I reached the end and raised my arms in triumph. Despite an ungainly start, I congratulated myself on a successful finale — until, that is, the aforementioned sliver finally slipped off and my world sank by two feet. I fell backwards, missing the wood behind me which angled off to the right, and clipping the edge I rolled over in mid-flight for an unceremonious finish, head first into a foot of mud.

It wasn't the ideal end to the day but I saw the funny side. A sense of humour through Maine was a welcome attribute but I didn't realise how much I would come to rely on it.

Chapter 14

Why didn't Anyone Tell Me about Maine?

August 9th to August 27th
Mile 1953 to 2184

Old Blue wasn't some ageing old hillbilly — the somewhat friendly sounding name had also been claimed by a mountain. My approach from the south descended gently from Moody Mountain to a wide col and then curved up to the 3600-foot summit. I scampered quickly down to the col, making the most of my momentum to get stuck in to the uphill. My shoes clung to smooth granite, fuelling confidence to plough upwards with firm steps, hopping and jumping through the traverse. Occasionally I had to call my arms into play to hoist myself up natural steps and ledges.

I dropped my pack at the top for a quick rest. I preferred the summits for breaks because I could pick up again straight into a downhill. Krumholtz surrounded me as I rested my back against a weather-beaten post, topped with a sign for Old Blue itself. The limited growth of the trees meant I was taller, allowing for a decent 360-degree view. A clear line of erosion was visible back down in the col where thousands of hikers had etched a faint passage over the rock.

It was incredibly quiet. I heard nothing except the occasional bird call. Quintessential late summer clouds appeared motionless, barely mustering a glide against the blue canvas behind. The sun was hazy, its light bouncing and ricocheting around, making me squint. A storm raged far to the south, angry clouds crowning a distant mountain.

I briefly calculated where I thought Lazagne and Thirsty might be. They had ten miles on me, but taking into account my earlier start by perhaps an hour, I figured they were no more than two hours ahead. Knowing how both of them approached the trail, and their mileage, I estimated they would probably end up at the Sabbath Day Pond Lean-to, meaning I had a twenty-mile day.

I found them sunbathing on a beach at Moxie Pond, half a mile before the lean-to.

"How are we all doing?" I asked.

"OK," Thirsty replied. "Not a hundred percent but a shit load better than yesterday."

I thought Old Blue had been peaceful but the lake was pure nirvana. A thin strip of beach lined the shore before meeting the forest edge. Sand gently sloped away to meet the flat, calm waters that stretched away to the far end where two hills either side shelved diagonally down to frame the view. Despite a lack of wind and our proximity to the water, the mosquitos seemed to have taken a welcome vacation for once. We sat on the warm sand, took an occasional dip and relaxed.

"Heard from Goggles?" I asked.

"No but he'll be at least ten ahead," said Lazagne. "He'll need twenty-five to thirties to meet his mum. I don't think we'll see him."

"Presumably, then, you two aren't hot on his heels and have decided to take it easy?"

"Yup," Thirsty answered.

This was great news. Although I missed Goggles, there was no way I was going to catch him. My plan to drop the mileage down, and take the last 230 miles at an easier pace, seemed to have rubbed off on Lazagne and Thirsty. We hadn't spoken about our conversation to let Goggles go, and I felt no need to bring it up again; but having lost one member, our team appeared to be solid once more.

Lazagne, making further inroads into his pursuit of the pack that weighed nothing, had now ditched his tarp, trekking poles

Balancing on Blue

and one of his quilts. His philosophy for the final section was to sleep in the shelters. This made sense but he was counting on the shelters having space which, although wasn't impossible, might catch him out.

It rained overnight. Packing away at camp, water drops fell and splashed on my back, making me shiver in the colder, early morning hours. I passed a new face, Catwoman, at the Sabbath Day Pond Lean-to. I was warming up as I walked so I didn't stop, but we both nodded an acknowledgement to each other.

We dodged rain showers for most of the day and hiked cautiously over wet ground and slick rock. When we met the ME-4, the town of Rangeley lay nine miles west. We were lucky to get a quick ride down to the supermarket for a food resupply and back again.

Maine liked to refer to its shelters as 'lean-tos' and our destination for the day was the Piazza Rock Lean-to. Thirsty didn't stop; but with rain clouds threatening, Lazagne and I grabbed a spot inside. We were pleased to see Chez 11 and Groc who were setting up their beds along with Catwoman.

The privy had a sign on the outside which read *Your Move* . Curious, I ventured inside to see not one but two seats for doing one's business. In between the two was a cribbage board. Quite why anyone would want to have a crap next to someone else, or even indulge in a game of cribbage at the same time, defeated me. Apart from the strange setup, it did at least have a roof to stop me getting wet. Believe me, taking a toilet stop in the rain presented all sorts of logistical problems.

The rain didn't let up all night. As Lazagne and I watched a few sobos head off, the warmth of our beds did little to persuade us to get up and hike. The forecast was dire: rain all day and the temperature wasn't encouraging either. There was only one solution, a trail zero.

Trail zeros are just that — instead of taking a day out in town, you do it on the trail. I had only ever entertained one, back on the PCT in the Sierra Nevada, where the scenery alone was enough to make me want to experience it for a whole day. At Piazza Rock, the weather had made the decision for us. Our gear was still damp from the day before so it made sense to dry it out, start a fire to keep us warm, and of course have a game of chess.

We played two games. I won the first to bring the scores level at five apiece. Sensing the possibility that I could pull away from America, I focused intently on the game that culminated in a masterly pincer movement utilising my Queen and Knight to finish off Lazagne. I punched the air, grabbed his phone and held it aloft with pride as those immortal words floated around the lean-to:

Checkmate!

The only downside of my victory was that I had forgotten my shoes were drying by the fire.

"These yours, Fozzie?" Groc asked, holding up my right shoe and quickly tossing it between his two hands, the heat too much for him to hold. He blew on the sole as a faint wisp of smoke curled upwards.

"Shit!" I cried. "Shit! Are they OK?"

A small section of the side sole had bubbled slightly but, thankfully, they seemed intact.

We tended the fire all day but Groc took the mission to heart and cared for it like a treasured possession. Constantly glancing over towards the flames, he adjusted the fuel to provide more air, occasionally blew on the embers and placed piles of wet wood on the stone surround to dry out. In between rain bursts, we all raced over to breathe life back into our heating system, sitting at the fire edge and chatting. We tended it well into the evening. Its flickering light danced around the inside of the lean-to and picked out trees before fading into the darkness of the Maine wilderness beyond.

Everyone's mood seemed happy, but I also sensed a little sombreness. I, too, was feeling somewhat sad. The thought of finishing was becoming a real prospect. Mixed feelings played havoc with my moods at the end of thru-hikes. Ecstatic that I would soon be successful, thoughts turned away from the usual day-to-day planning and life after the trail entered the fray.

It wasn't unusual for my feelings to run riot on the final stretch, and it was confusing to know how to deal with them. The high of completion is unmatched by any other feeling of accomplishment I've ever experienced. I become emotional, thoughts turn to family and friends, those people that I love, and the burden of returning to civilisation weighs heavy. My dromomania becomes dormant, satiated by time in the woods; but I knew that even after a couple of weeks back home, my attention would turn to the next adventure. My wandering thoughts would call and there was little sympathy to be found in the upcoming cold and dark winter months back in England.

I sensed it in others as well. Camp fire conversations inevitably turned to home, and my hiking friends began to touch the surface of life after the trail. I think the elation of success, coupled with the inevitable prospect of finishing what many would eventually regard as the best few months of their lives, created confusion. Most thru-hikers become extremely emotional near the end.

It wasn't unusual to see people cry, some openly, some more reserved. I was often tearful; and even though I was aware of why, it still caught me off-guard. In full hiking flow one minute and then bam! Suddenly, I was sobbing.

Often, I paused and battled the urge but many times I shed a few tears openly, albeit when I was on my own. A failed relationship just prior to leaving for the trail weighed heavy. I dwelt on what could have been. Contrary to how this sounds, all these mixed emotions were actually calming and I often tempered them even further by planning the next trip. I think it pleased my wandering side.

I woke at 3 a.m. with an overwhelming feeling that something wasn't quite right. After rubbing my eyes and taking a moment to get centred, I realised that, firstly, I felt terrible; and secondly, I needed to get to the toilet as quickly as possible.

A game of cribbage was the last thing on my mind as I pulled on my camp shoes and raced with clenched buttocks to the faint silhouette of the privy, stumbling on the uneven ground. With not a second to spare, I lifted the lid, sat down and relaxed my muscles with an overwhelming feeling of relief.

As my bowels emptied it became quickly apparent that the consistency wasn't optimal. In fact, the splashing sound from the inner depths of the privy pit confirmed that my stomach was not in a good way.

I stumbled weakly back to the shelter, feeling slightly nauseous, and crawled back under my quilt. By 10 a.m. I felt I had spent more time in the privy than in the shelter, making a further five emergency visits. Groc and Lazagne had left for the climb up to Saddleback Mountain.

I was confused, thinking my lay up in Andover had been due to norovirus and that it had left my system. Perhaps I had just caught a mild case of the illness. I figured I had a stronger immune system than others, and had escaped the diarrhoea and vomiting that others hadn't.

I was also tired again, felt mildly nauseous but hadn't been sick. One thing was for sure — I wasn't going anywhere for a second day and settled down to another trail zero.

"Fozzie!"

I looked up to see an old friend. The sight cheered me.

"Juggles! Where the fuck have you been!"

"Where the fuck have *you* been?! Where is everyone? Lazagne? Thirsty? Bush Goggles? Why are you here?" He paused, tentatively, on his approach. "Are you sick?"

"That's a lot of questions, Mr World Champion. Er, answers in order. They're walking, obviously — Lazagne left this morning, Thirsty two nights back. Goggles has pulled away to get to Katahdin and meet his mum on time. I'm here because I got that bloody norovirus thing which answers your last question; yes I am sick."

He stopped, eyed me cautiously and, throwing caution to the wind, gave me a hug.

"Don't get too close," I said. "Have you had the bug yet? Everyone's had it, mate, or it seems that way."

"No, I've been lucky," he said.

It was mid-day so Juggles had no reason to stop. I said to get the message up trail that I'd be back hiking the following day.

With no more visitors either in the afternoon or the evening, I had the place to myself. I continued to drink water and also some rehydration sachets, along with the occasional mouthful of sugar and a little salt. As my toilet breaks stopped, my nausea faded and my energy levels began to increase. With my hunger returning quickly, I cooked dinner and picked on almonds through the evening.

Despite my almond supplies, a squirrel was taking a dislike to my presence in camp. He screamed loudly at me for most of the afternoon, occasionally jumping up and down on a tree branch as if unable to get his own way.

"He's a local," the shelter caretaker explained when he came over to check on my progress. "Thinks he owns the area, doesn't like visitors and just stomps about airing his feelings."

By 9 p.m. I felt as though I was on the mend. I made the decision to leave early the next morning to catch up with the guys, hoping that Juggles would replace our absent team member, making us four once more.

With no privy visits during the night, I made a strong coffee, wolfed down a bowl of porridge, and was away by 6.30 a.m. I felt strong, amazed at the speed of my recovery. Saddleback towered 2000 feet above me; but, surrounded by trees, I couldn't see it. After a mile I passed Ethel Pond where a low-slung mist hung motionless over the water. The only sound was the occasional plop of a fish.

I thrived on the expectation of views. Since Georgia I hadn't been disappointed and Maine had saved the best until last. I expected magnificence on every mountain and every summit delivered, still managing to throw in a surprise.

Saddleback was no exception and, in retrospect, became one of my favourites. Looking down, endless hills rolled away to the horizon. Bands of cloud stretched across the sky, their ivory tops blending to darker bellies. Rain seemed imminent but never came. A rocky path swept down, curving away around the north side of Saddleback and disappeared into the trees. The trail was still unbelievably quiet. I took an hour at the top to snack, surveying my world.

My illness defeated, I was back. The wind raged and I stood firm, leaning into it, arms and legs outstretched and screamed "I'm back! I'M FREE!" I punched the air and celebrated.

"YES!"

We English are generally a little reserved. At most, if we're having a great day, we don't usually voice our thoughts — certainly not shout them — but linger in the feeling, perhaps the only signal a satisfied smile. The Americans, more unabashed, often feel free to express themselves verbally. On sunny days, or during lively conversations around a camp fire, perhaps breaking for lunch in a jovial mood, they often aired their joy by simply saying "Good times!"

It seemed strange when I first heard it, thinking it somehow wrong that verbal confirmation of happiness should be shared. Realisation of enjoying a moment might seem obvious but we often let it pass by without indulging a little in that feeling. Admitting happiness at a precise moment, and taking a moment to wallow in it, records it for posterity — verbalising it even more so and often resulted in fond recollections after those moments, often months or years later.

***

I was eager to catch up with the guys and concentrated on pulling in a decent day. After bagging Lone Mountain, Mt Abraham, Spaulding Mountain and Sugarloaf Mountain, I eventually reached days end, after twenty-two miles, at the south branch of the Carrabassett River.

The woods parted like a curtain to reveal this gently moving, boulder-strewn ribbon of water. A few tent sites on the opposing bank indicated the perfect spot to spend the night and attack both South and North Crocker Mountains the following day. The ME-27 intersected the AT some eight miles further where the town of Stratton lay five miles west. Lazagne mentioned he was planning to stay there overnight and gear up for the next section.

Small clearings in the wood, just a few feet from the Carrabassett, proved an ideal spot to string up the hammock. A couple of day hikers were my only company. I retreated to the river and took a quick swim, washing a few items of clothing in the process.

I had heard that bears were often spotted at the campsite so nodded off cautiously, keeping one ear cocked for movement. Sure enough, around 2.30 a.m., a paw fall snapped a few twigs as I listened to what could only have been a bear move slowly closer.

"Hey, bear! Sod off!"

Immediately a loud crashing sound reverberated around the woods as the culprit sped off. The annoying aspect of marauding bears is that I could never be content when they left. Experience showed that, more often than not, they usually returned. Sleep never came naturally after the initial visit. By 3.30 a.m. I was resigned to the fact that I wouldn't fall back to sleep, even though a return visit didn't seem likely. I got out of my hammock.

I took my stove to the river and splashed some water on my face, then filled my pot and lit the fuel to brew a coffee. I looked up at the river. Its lines of perspective narrowed as the moon reflected and glinted in the water, throwing around just enough light to see.

My head torch picked out the path on the steep climb up to South Crocker Mountain, dipping momentarily and climbing further to the north peak. Stopping briefly to fill up my water bottle from the spring, I reached the road shortly before 7 a.m. and stuck out my thumb.

Brian pulled up, on his way to work. "Where you heading? Stratton for breakfast?"

"You read my mind," I replied.

He dropped me outside. When I swung open the door of the Stratton Diner, Lazagne, Thirsty and Juggles looked up smiling.

"You OK, Fozzie?" Lazagne asked.

"Fighting fit and back into the fray! How's the breakfast?"

"Awesome," Thirsty mumbled with a mouth full of eggs.

The Stratton Motel and Hostel was just over the road. The owner kindly allowed me to use the laundry facilities. Whilst waiting for my clothes to dry, a sheet of paper pinned to the wall caught my attention.

It concerned Paul 'Parkside' Bernhardt, who had set out on his AT thru-hike well before me on February 17th. Registering as the eleventh thru-hiker to start, he was at the front of pack. Making camp near Pierce Pond on June 15th, thirty-three miles up trail from the Stratton, he went to the pond to take a swim, not thinking it necessary to tell anyone of his intentions.

Shortly after, those at the shelter heard cries from the pond and raced down to see Paul go under the water. He never surfaced again. Despite brave attempts by Achilles and Carpenter, they couldn't find him. His body was discovered later that evening by rescue workers.

The likely cause of death is unknown but thought to have been cramp. Parkside had covered twenty miles that day — not an unusually high amount at that stage of the trail but still a hard day's hike, taking the terrain into account. Low potassium levels may have played a part as well as the notoriously cold water.

Achilles, Dropout, Germanator, Swivel, Spiral and Catwoman took time out from the trail to attend Paul's funeral in Queens, New York. Two weeks later, on June 29th, they carried Paul's ashes to the summit of Mt Katahdin.

With such an uncommon trail name, I assumed the Catwoman I had met the previous day was the same hiker who was with Paul and had returned two months later to hike some more. I never saw her again to ask.

It's a sad and sobering thought to know that some hikers never come back. Worse, always at the back of my mind was the fear that I, one day, could be one of them.

Maine seemed to be the state where most hikers go missing, and many were never found. With such hazardous terrain, one slip or fall could mean a hiker ended up in inaccessible areas at the base of cliffs or gorges. It's a sobering thought, and one that many try not to dwell on. Besides, if we all took notice of the warnings associated with some outdoor activities, we probably wouldn't get involved in them.

The clothes drier beeped, shaking me from deep thought. Rain had started to fall once more and we paused, contemplating staying at the hostel but eventually caught a ride back to the trailhead and hiked the five miles up to Horns Pond Lean-to.

The caretaker turned up late evening and took time with us, expressing his sadness surrounding the events at Pierce Pond. He also confirmed that Avery Peak, three and a half miles further on, was the last major peak of the AT except for Katahdin itself. It was downhill to East Flagstaff Lake. The final, flatter section we had studied in our data books was close.

We had just 183 miles left to call ourselves AT thru-hikers.

***

Light rain fell as we broke camp in the morning. We glanced up to see the cloud level tickling the mountain tops. Climbing strongly and warming quickly, we reached South Horn first, with views of the west peak of Bigelow Mountain ahead. Above treeline our direction was clear. Despite heavier rain and a ferocious wind we eventually summited Avery Peak and hunkered down behind some rocks to take in the view and eat some snacks.

We were smiling. Nothing could stop us now, not even Katahdin. That icon was the last in a long stretch of mountains starting 2000 miles and 138 days behind us.

Dropping from Avery, we met the East Flagstaff Road and suddenly remembered our mileage total had exceeded 2000. For the second time in my life I had passed this point. We marked the moment by taking a soft rock and writing '2000' on the road.

We called it a day after just thirteen miles, and had good reason to stop. East Flagstaff Lake glinted through the trees to our left as a beach shelved gently into the waters. With more rain due it seemed a good excuse to stop, but I think, secretly, we knew that the end was close. The fewer miles we hiked each day, the more time we had to stretch out our remaining time on trail.

Lazagne, being without a shelter, carried on to the West Carry Pond Lean-to whilst Juggles, Thirsty and I set up camp on the beach, alternating between swimming and resting before the rain came.

The pattering on my tarp didn't abate all night. The following day, soot-black clouds offered little to suggest any let-up so there we stayed, indulging in our decision to slow down and make the most of our last days.

The temperature dropped that night. I woke cold and pulled on a jacket. Despite the chill, I knew the reason for the sudden cold was that the clouds had cleared and that the morning, hopefully, should dawn bright.

I wasn't disappointed. I woke to calling loons, a gentle breeze lifting the tarp, and a perfect morning.

***

River crossings were common in Maine, as were wet feet. The Kennebec River, thankfully, was the only exception. With its fast-flowing water and wide berth, the Kennebec had a ferry service in operation.

Dave Corrigan of the Kennebec River AT Ferry Service was on the opposite bank. As soon as he saw us waving, he was in his canoe quicker than an otter taking a dip. There was no fee and Dave gave us a quick briefing on what to expect. There wasn't room for all of us so I went first with Thirsty, figuring if anyone could paddle with power it would be him, whilst Juggles and Lazagne waited for the return voyage.

Dave had been ferrying hikers and other outdoor enthusiasts for the previous six years and told me that already he had carried around 1500 hikers over the waters that year. It was just starting to get busy as the nobos were in full flow and closing in on their goal. We thanked him and left.

Despite the kinder terrain away from the mountains, there was one final test of our resolve in addition to river crossings as we reached the last town on the AT. The ME-15 heralded the start of a section of trail known as the Hundred-Mile Wilderness. It ended at Abol Bridge, itself just fifteen miles from the finish. Northbound hikers often caught a ride to Monson, four miles east, to resupply before the section.

The Hundred-Mile Wilderness was just that: no towns, no road crossings, nothing except the occasional desolate logging track. We had figured on five twenty-mile days to get through. We could have done it in four, perhaps even three; but with the end of our adventure closing, we wanted to make the most of it.

We secured a quick ride into Monson. Shaw's Lodging provided a bed for two nights, taking a final zero to get cleaned up and resupplied for the final assault.

I was walking back from lunch at the Lakeshore Pub. I turned around to see Snot Rocket, Anchor and Chef getting out of a car. I hadn't seen them for weeks and welcome hugs were freely dispensed. It reminded me that even though I had lost contact with those I had met, they occasionally turned up when I least expected it.

The Lakeshore Pub, being the only place to serve draught beer, tempted me back in the evening where I sat with Lazagne, Thirsty and Juggles.

"Goggles made it! He reached Katahdin today!" Juggles screamed, passing me his phone. There he was, Goggles, astride the summit sign proudly holding a flag with 'Wisconsin' emblazoned across it.

"He's on his way back home now," I said. "What are you

going to do when you get back, Juggles?"

"A different kind of survival," he answered wisely as Thirsty and Lazagne smiled and nodded in silent approval.

We left Monson the following morning, still in no hurry, keen to eke out every last minute.

A campsite caught our eye late afternoon, but getting there meant fording Little Wilson Stream. Lazagne crossed last; when the rest of us had made it over safely, we turned to check on his progress.

Reaching half way, he decided a better approach would be to throw his pack to the bank, leaving him unencumbered for the last few feet. Unfortunately, before we could grab it, the pack slid slowly down to the water's edge and slipped gently into the stream before floating in the direction of Little Wilson Falls. 'Little' was not the first adjective that sprung to mind for the cascading torrent disappearing alarmingly over an abyss to our left.

"Fuck!" Lazagne screamed as he increased his wading speed. He reached a small rock and leapt for another to cut off his pack's own little adventure. He promptly fell sideways into the water but re-surfaced just in time to grab his pack before it disappeared over the edge.

I negotiated Little Wilson carefully the following morning and was away before the others had broken camp. Maine continued to amaze me with its dense forest, regular river crossings and quiet hiking. True to form, we continued to hike together but often drifted off on our own, occupied with thoughts of finishing and what we would do after trail life.

All 3650 feet of White Cap Mountain rose up before me. I appeared to have missed that while checking the last 'flat' section of trail in my logbook. I filled up with water from a stream near the Carl A. Newhall Lean-to, where Meat, whom I had just met, joined me to do the same.

"Meat, I still look at mountains after all this time and doubt my own ability to get up them," I offered as we sat on a rock drinking.

"I know exactly what you mean, I do the same," he agreed. "Always doubt if I can make it up."

"See you up the top then?" I said.

"Hell yeah!"

White Cap wasn't just famed for being the last major peak apart from Katahdin on the AT. A side trail along the north summit, through a short section of trees, offered the first view of what most AT thru-hikers had spent several months dreaming about.

I crested White Cap, turned north through the woods and, after a minute, emerged from the other side. The land swept down, rippled along the lowlands dotted with a few lakes, then rose majestically. My eyes slowly eased upward to settle on a sight I sometimes thought I'd never see. I cried as emotions caught me out.

There, seventy-three trail miles north, Mount Katahdin soared skywards to command absolute dominance over all it surveyed. The upper plateau, known as the Tableland, was clearly visible. Forest ascended its lower flanks, finally surrendering to the harsher conditions further up. A few wispy clouds tickled the summit; I hoped the fine weather held, for I, hopefully, would be standing on the summit in days.

With White Cap behind me, the trail settled down to the level section I had hoped for. A smooth trail wove through the forest. My feet were gently cushioned by soft soil and a sprinkling of pine needles. It was easy hiking all the way to a waterside camp at Nahmakanta Lake, where the guys arrived later.

Discussing logistics that evening, it was agreed that a 3.45 a.m. alarm call followed by a start time of 4.30 a.m. would be prudent. We wanted to see Katahdin at first light around 5.30 a.m. and our logbooks advised that Nesuntabunt Mountain was a great vantage point.

I struggle with early morning calls on trail. It's invariably chilly and the complete darkness doesn't lend itself to getting out of a sleeping bag. Usually I waited until someone else stirred before moving myself.

The next morning, we took a short side trail on Nesuntabunt to reach a cliff where the trees cleared. Sitting down near the edge, our finishing point was clearly visible. An orange glow brushed the eastern skies, softened by blankets of mist caught in the valleys.

Katahdin's silhouette beckoned.

Balancing on Blue

***

On the afternoon of the 25th of August, I emerged from the Hundred-Mile Wilderness onto Golden Road, frantically grabbing my sunglasses as the sun caught me off-guard. A small café and store were pretty much the only buildings there. With a hunger that was borderline dangerous, and an unhealthy yearning for fat, I ordered two large burgers, two packets of crisps, ice cream, three coffees, a chocolate milk and an orange juice. My choices wouldn't have made the front cover of any healthy diet magazine. Lying outside on the ground after the indulgence, my stomach certainly regretted it. I wobbled over to the Abol Pines campsite where Lazagne, Thirsty, Juggles and I warmed with a camp fire and watched the Penobscot River glide sweetly past.

We woke to find Juggles missing. He had mentioned that he needed to get a ride to Millinocket, nineteen miles east, to collect some juggling batons that he had mailed to the post office. His plan was to juggle with fire on the summit. We sent him a text explaining our intentions of taking advantage of a decent weather window on the Monday, two days away, so he could join us for the finish.

He also had a suspected broken toe but didn't intend to visit the doctor for fear of a confirmed prognosis. Talking to Meat about walking with broken bones that morning, he relayed some unfortunate news about Danish. I had met him a couple of days before and we had shared a brief conversation. He explained that it was his second attempt on the AT; the previous year, his visa had run out before he could finish the trail.

"What happened?" I asked Meat.

"Got one foot caught in a tree root or something. Momentum carried him forward and now he's got a broken tibia and fibula," he replied, cringing somewhat.

"Oh shit! So, he's off for the second year?"

"Knowing Danish," Meat said, "He'll be back next year again."

It was a welcome short day to the Birches Lean-to and campsite. At least fifteen thru-hikers had congregated for the final approach and our last day's hike to Katahdin in the morning. Our base camp was bustling. Juggles had shown and, along with my regular companions Thirsty and Lazagne, we also had Pedestrian, Houdini, Great Dane, Banjo, Meat, Skunkape, Roadhouse, Chesty, Stingray, Poncho, and Jonathan the caretaker for company.

We built a roaring fire in the evening and Houdini invited everyone over for a smudging ceremony. Common amongst the Native Americans, smudging or purifying the air by burning herbs creates a positive atmosphere. Sage is a common choice for this; but Houdini, unable to find any, had settled for the noble alternative of a cedar bundle.

We sat in a circle around the fire. Having lit the cedar, Houdini blew it out and wafted the smoke over each of us with the aid of a feather. He explained that every person was then invited to speak about their experience, adding that each of us should hold the feather in turn. The rest of the group should be silent as the person with the feather spoke. When finished, they handed it to the next person.

It was a wonderful ceremony, of particular poignancy because everyone respected the feather and the person that held it as they spoke. There were no interruptions. I thought what a pleasant change it made for each of us to offer our story without disruptions.

Stories of a serious nature were openly told, as well as humorous tales and everything in between. We laughed, joked, pondered, reflected and left for our beds feeling positive.

My thoughts centred on the rumour that Katahdin was the first landmass in America to receive light from the rising sun. Anyone standing on the summit would be the first in America to witness sunrise, but in fact this is not true. According to the time of year and the equinoxes, Cadillac Hill, Mars Hill, and West Quoddy Head share the claim.

However, Katahdin was right up there. I peered in annoyance at my alarm which broke my slumber at 2 a.m. I packed, and hung around for a few minutes waiting for Lazagne, who had agreed to join me. No one stirred. At 2.26 a.m., I left and began my final day of the Appalachian Trail.

I was still hauling the gantlet. Pink Bits, sorry — Lady

Balancing on Blue

Forward — had beaten me to the post a few days before.

I glimpsed clear skies studded with stars through breaks in the trees. It was warm and the climb soon had me shedding clothing and walking in just shorts and a T-shirt. The hiss of Katahdin Stream Falls filtered through the trees as I passed, and then faded. My head torch easily picked out trees with white blazes. A stream glistened and frogs hopped out of my way as I picked my way up the trail. Not even the drone of a mosquito spoilt a definitive silence and occasionally I stopped, turned off my light and looked skyward to swaying pines framing a magical night sky.

I caught Skunkape, who had started a few minutes before me, fumbling with his failing head torch. I offered to share my light. As the going steepened, I took the lead, crawling and scrambling over rock slabs, occasionally turning around to shine my light for him.

After just over three miles, at 4538 feet, the ascent suddenly eased onto the Tableland. Meagre light spread from a glowing horizon and picked out our passage through a rocky environment. An occasional lonely white blaze was caught in the dawn fire. I turned back to see two head torches behind, sweeping around the landscape like lost astronauts on a distant planet.

And suddenly, there it was ahead of me. Backlit with orange, as if rightly commanding a solitary presence on stage, the silhouetted, iconic summit sign that I had seen so many times in photos straddled the summit.

At 5.15 a.m., just under three hours after leaving, I placed my palm on its cold and damp surface, and slowly ran my hands over the carved letters.

KATAHDIN
Baxter Peak – Elevation – 5267 FT
NORTHERN TERMINUS OF THE
APPALACHIAN TRAIL
A mountain footpath extending over
2000 miles to Springer Mtn. Georgia

A fierce wind ripped over the Tableland. I pulled on my

jacket and sheltered behind a rock with Skunkape, soon joined by Banjo and Meat whose lights we had seen behind us. We faced east and watched, mesmerised but impatient for our sunrise. At 5.51 a.m. a hazy, ruby circle tentatively poked over distant hills, battling for supremacy with lingering cloud. The Knife Edge Ridge to our right gradually illuminated, dropping and arcing away to the north. The light met our faces, inching down our chests as Katahdin gradually brightened.

We stayed there for three hours, observing the light change, watching the shadows appear and the temperature rise. Finally, after weeks of carrying my imaginary gauntlet, I launched it over the side of Katahdin and watched it plunge down before smashing into the rocks to disintegrate into a thousand pieces.

I heard footsteps behind.

"YEAH! FUCK YEAH!"

I peered over rocks behind me to see Thirsty beyond excitement, punching the air and yelling. Lazagne arrived shortly after. Juggles, somewhat emotional, greeted me with a wobbly bottom lip and watery eyes. Others gradually filtered in. From a quiet, reflective and silent atmosphere, the mood turned to celebration.

Juggles had indeed carried up his juggling batons. He held a lighter under each one, and the flames caught, licking skyward. He balanced on top of the sign, plying his trade for several minutes with no drops and to rapturous applause.

After a group photo I shook some hands and left, descending back over the Tableland and occasionally turning back. The group slowly faded. Unable to control a barrage of emotions but trying to resist the urge to cry, I suddenly let everything go and burst into tears.

Months of planning and hiking, time spent thinking about my life, reflecting on my past and pondering my future, and the uncertainty about my next step all surfaced — but they weren't sad tears, they were joyful. I had made it. I was a Double Crowner, an Appalachian Trail thru-hiker, and a member of a rare breed of individual successful in completing the most iconic hiking trail on Earth.

Before dipping away from the Tableland I turned for one last, lingering look at Katahdin. Visually it was exceptionally beautiful, but also a decisive and poignant landmark offering confirmation that I had been successful. It stirred massive emotions, so powerful I couldn't ignore them even if I wanted to.

It had made people cry, sing, and dance. They basked in their own glory and that of those around them. It held them in the moment and, suddenly, realisation dawned that they had achieved possibly the biggest challenge they would ever face, that they are capable of far more than they ever thought possible. Katahdin offered encouragement to pursue dreams and a life away from the ordinary. It wasn't so much a realisation that the adventure was over, but that new ones were just beginning.

My dromomania was silent, still and satiated; but it stirred as I descended, eager for sustenance. Hungry for the next adventure, the nomad already demanded feeding.

Chapter 15

Epilogue — The Separating

Peter 'PJ' Semo

Resting my injury was a hard and frustrating decision to make. For a few short weeks I had been given a wilderness present and then, abruptly, it was taken away before I could properly unwrap it. But rest was what I had to do — an obvious choice to make when the only other option was to quit. Returning to continue my hike after a month's break, I reached Katahdin on October the 5th. I'm immensely proud of what I achieved.

I don't often bring my adventure up in conversation but I do find it holds a common bond, being an easy story to make small talk with. Most of the time people's eyes light up when they realise what I have achieved. It helps people understand where I have come from in life and what type of person I am. It imbues a certain wonder and curiosity, and that's all I could hope for — to inspire others to experience nature and possibly go and hike the AT for themselves.

Post-hike I went to Dalton, Massachusetts, to work at a hostel and then I decided to return to my original home near Latrobe in Pennsylvania. Readjusting to society was very difficult, and post-hike depression, which I had heard about, was disturbing. It was a sense of tremendous loss like a family member had died. A part of me had disappeared and the memories became foggier and foggier. The winter was tough. I wasn't sure where I wanted my life to go and, frankly, at times, I couldn't really care either.

My mood improved during the spring of 2013. I started to work at an adventure park, making some fantastic friends. In the summer I was promoted to rides supervisor and now I'm very happy.

The trail imparted a certain understanding of life and helped me on the journey, like finding a meaningful book in the library with answers to a specific topic. Having hiked I now understand life more. With increased confidence in myself, I know where I want to go; and more importantly, I have the confidence to get there. My big goal is to hike the Pacific Crest Trail and the Continental Divide Trail to earn my Triple Crown.

Socialising and communicating are easier now and I'm able to discover areas that excite people. I can inspire them to do something that is really meaningful in their lives. Everyone is full of possibilities, capable of wonderful things and I hope they view me in the same way.

I value my friends much more and my family is really important. Not a day goes by in which I don't think about my dad. I miss him dearly. But he would be proud of the journey I undertook and the mental effort I put into sorting everything out, both the tangible and intangible. Whilst I have regrets about the events between us, I have made peace with myself. I'm blessed to have my family back in my life and I love coming home from work where I can talk to my brother and mum, or my sister when she visits. I'm grateful I have learnt the importance of friendships.

I feel loved and I couldn't be happier. The trail has been a philosopher's stone for my life and I wouldn't be where I am today without it.

Phillip 'Lazagne' Colelli

The train was a wise choice of transport to return home on. I had nine hours to ponder my adventure but never really figured much out. My dad was waiting to collect me and I was overjoyed to see him. Realising how important family was to me, we had grown even closer.

I had little idea of what my next move should be but I knew I had to work. Returning to my old job was the easiest option; despite my original yearning to escape from grilling burgers, at least I had money coming in, breathing space to calculate my next move. That was a big mistake.

I was still peaking from the AT, on a high from what I had achieved and no one else's negative energy could affect me. However, after a couple of months I realised that I was back where I had been before I began my hike, and I didn't like it. I missed the trail, the amazing people I had met and the simple existence I had thrived on.

I started to plan more adventures. If getting away made me happy, then I thought planning another trip would take my mind off work. I researched North Carolina's Mountains to Sea Trail and cycling across America. The anticipation of this planning woke me up to the mistake I had made of returning to a job I hated.

"Shannon, I'm done, I'm leaving now," I said to the general manager after my last shift, right before the Friday night dinner rush.

"You realise you won't be rehire-able if you don't work your two weeks' notice, right?" she replied.

"I don't care."

In retrospect, subconsciously, I think I left them in the lurch so I wouldn't be rehire-able. I didn't want to go back.

Working with my dad in construction gave me more time to think. He knew I was viewing it as a stopgap until I figured out my next move. Then Sam called. He was contemplating a move to Denver, Colorado, to rent a house there and asked me if I would be interested. I said no, on the basis that I wasn't 100% sure — but called him a week later and said I had changed my mind.

Packing most of what I owned into my tired old car made me realise what the trail had taught me about materialism. It had 200,000 miles on the clock and was only worth about $500 but I loved it. I had no desire to own anything other than the crappiest car in existence. It also acted as a people-filter. I had little time for anyone who judged me on the basis of my car, and you would be surprised how few people that left.

I had high hopes for Denver but it was tough at first. A few dead-end jobs came and went until one day I saw an advert for a vacancy at a marijuana-growing facility, shortly after the plant became legal in Colorado. I had no experience but figured it would be a complete change of scene. The interview went well, I got the position and I've now been there for a few months. The people are great and the managers treat me with respect, which was always more important to me than money.

A co-worker called Adam mentioned that his lease was running out, and as mine was also coming to an end we looked for somewhere together. This proved difficult as he had a dog — albeit a service dog — and landlords were reluctant to take it on. After a few weeks of wasting our time I suggested the mad idea that we go and live in the woods. I had the gear, there was no rent to pay, it was quiet with no neighbours and it just seemed like a brilliant (if somewhat crazy) idea. Adam jumped at the chance, so for the summer that's exactly what we did.

It was something I had always wanted to do. We packed up and found a nice spot in Pike National Forest, although we abide by the forestry regulations and move camp every two weeks. I still get a shower every day, decent meals and I'm warm at night.

I suppose I have been unsettled since I completed the trail but that is possibly something that the trail has done to me. I realise that I have to work to earn money for the everyday expenses that we all have, but I'm unsettled because for a few, short months, I had complete freedom. Indeed, I now realise that long-distance hiking, or whatever adventure I choose, is the best method for being as truly free as I can ever hope to be.

I live my life day by day and I have no idea what may come along next. Tomorrow I could be living on the other side of the country, but to taste true freedom — or as close as I could wish for — at some point I'll pick up my pack and head off for another long-distance hike to rekindle how I really love to live.

Sam 'Daffy' Ridge

I swore I'd never do it again. Don't get me wrong, it was fun, but directly after finishing, believe me, the last thing on my mind was doing it again. As much as I loved my journey, there's only so much rain, so much hunger, tiredness and time in your own head that a man can take. I felt beaten up. It hurt physically and mentally I was exhausted as well, but elated that I finished.

The negativity wore off quickly. After a week or so I started planning the next one, which is going to be the Pacific Crest Trail in 2015. Day hikes just don't do it for me anymore. Why escape for a day when you can immerse yourself for months? It's different out there if you commit the time. Generous periods in the outdoors are rewarded by leaving them with an entirely different perspective and appreciation.

I did the AT to get away from people, otherwise known as the world. I hated both at the time; but, over the course of those summer months in 2012, my opinions of both changed dramatically. I'm now sure that I couldn't have done it without the people.

I made new friends, some of whom I now share a place with. I met my girlfriend on the trail too. I moved to Colorado to be nearer the outdoors and because the weed's legal here now.

I smoked marijuana almost every day on the trail and concluded that it wasn't as limiting or bad as the masses perceived. I now work legally at a weed growers for a living. I just received manager of the quarter and I'm in charge of more than fifty people.

I'm still on my trail, or *the* trail, in many ways. I still read poems that I wrote on the AT and look at the pictures. I do feel like I was stronger, more at peace, or more Zen on the trail.

John 'Thirsty' Beshara

I returned to Juggles' place in New York and stayed with him, Fozzie and Lazagne. Of all the things we could have done, we decided to return to the woods and spent a few days by Lake Placid. It was by mutual agreement, mainly to experience just one, small, isolated place amongst the trees without moving on. Perhaps we just didn't want to leave.

Before my flight home, I was milling around near the ticket

counter as the flight crew walked in. The pilot noticed my pack and we starting talking about hiking. It turned out he was a section hiker who had done much of the southern half of the AT. We talked about the Smokies for a minute before he went off to prepare for the flight. It was a short trip back to Minneapolis; I don't think they were even offering a snack. So you can understand my surprise when the stewardess came over to my seat.

"You're the hiker, right?"

I considered the question for a moment, wondering if there had been a complaint about the odour coming from seat 34A, before eventually responding.

"Yes," I replied, tentatively.

"What would you like? The pilot wants to buy you a beer."

It was one final, uplifting gesture of trail magic before I returned to locations where that concept wouldn't have any meaning.

I stayed in Minneapolis for about a month. The beard and hair were big hits with my friends, but eventually I shaved and trimmed in favour of a less conspicuous look.

I didn't have much trouble re-integrating. People are different when you're in the city. You have to get used to the idea that you can't just walk up to someone and expect them to be friendly as they were in the mountains. Most were very interested to hear about the trail, but their interest would wane the longer I rambled on. They wanted to hear about the animals, the weather and the food. I ended up with a couple of anecdotes about bears and snow that served me well whenever someone asked about the trail.

I left Minneapolis in October with a one-way ticket to Saigon. My plan since graduation had been to go abroad and teach English. I gained a contact through my sister who was teaching in Vietnam and I got in touch with him. He sold the lifestyle well, so I packed my stuff and took off. After completing the trail I was confident in my abilities to make it on my own in a place very different from anything I had known — to be able to adapt to new people and surroundings, to sleep anywhere, and eat just about anything. The first week or so in Vietnam was difficult. I kept getting lost, I couldn't understand anything that was said to me, and it was sweltering hot. But it got easier, if not less hot, as time went by.

My experience in Vietnam lasted for a little over a year. Taking advantage of the opportunity, I also travelled around much of Asia. The highlights were Koh Rong Island off the coast of Cambodia, where I met my beautiful Argentinian girlfriend; and a one-month motorbike tour down the coastline of Vietnam. I'm currently in Barcelona, Spain, and I'll be heading to Buenos Aires soon.

Spending time outdoors is still a big part of my life. I haven't done anything longer than a few days since the AT, but I still get out fairly often. I just finished four days in the Catalonian Pyrenees, and the GR-11 trail is now on my long-distance list. The PCT will likely be my next attempt, though. I hope to be on the border of Mexico in May 2016. When I get there I'll be adopting the trail name 'Moses', which Fozzie unofficially gave me on the AT due to my apparent likeness to the biblical character.

Hiking the AT didn't breed any wanderlust in me that wasn't already present. It did give me the foundation of skills and confidence that allowed me to pursue the life of adventure that I've always dreamt of.

Advice on the AT? None really. Just pack your shit and go!

Dallas 'Bush Goggles' Nustvold

I finished my thru-hike on August 20th. I missed the guys and it was a hard decision to leave them but sometimes life is about making tough decisions. I was incredibly proud to have made it, and sitting on top of Katahdin I felt very optimistic about my future. All those weeks of hiking provided plenty of time to think about what was ahead of me.

Optimistic, that is, until I returned home. I fell back into the old routine and returned to my old job. I moved in with my parents to give me some time to find a place of my own. Whilst interesting at times, I never really liked my job. Then I stumbled into a post-hike depression. All I wanted to do was lie around, relax and eat. Even though I stopped hiking, my appetite remained. By Christmas I had gained forty pounds. It's worrying how easily we can change from being a thru-hiker at the peak of our game to lying around doing nothing.

I knew there and then that if I didn't make some radical changes to my life I would be unhappy so I hit the gym. It felt good and the fat just burned off. With my body back in shape, my mind quickly followed. I focused, realised I missed the hiker lifestyle and decided to take on the Ice Age trail in Wisconsin.

I left on March 15th 2013. Winter hadn't subsided and it was too early for hiking season. The trail was deserted. It was a different kind of hike — obviously it was colder, but I also missed my hiking family, especially in the evenings.

I faced a lot of challenges. It was bitterly cold but I still had a blast. I finished 700 miles of the 1050 before the weather finally defeated me and my deadline to return back to work arrived. I even managed to hike fifty-four miles in one day.

I spent the following summer training to run a marathon, which I completed. I finished another one in the fall. In just over a year I hiked 3000 miles and ran two marathons.

Not a day passes in which I don't think about the AT. I daydream about those morning climbs, fresh spring water and beautiful sunsets. I think I will be a slave to my wandering ways forever. Something deep and strong inside just urges me to go and explore. I know that another thru-hike, somewhere, will happen at some point.

I have learned to slow down and live in the moment. I allow my anxieties to take hold sometimes and I start rushing for some reason. I'm not in a race to my death, so I have to remind myself to relax, just like I did on the AT.

I just wish every day could be like that Appalachian Trail hike in the summer of 2012.

Chris 'Juggles' Chiappini

I guess perseverance pays off eventually. If you want something badly enough, I think you need to put in the effort and never admit defeat. This was true for the trail; and, having hiked it, I carried away that philosophy to my everyday life. We are capable of truly wondrous things, but it's not until a challenge is undertaken and completed — whether it be the AT or anything else — that we fully comprehend them.

I returned home to New York to pick up my life where I had left it. In March 2013 Lazagne came to stay and we hiked the New Jersey section of the AT. That August I took a trip to Colorado to climb some 14,000-foot peaks.

In September 2013, the chance of my dream job came out of the blue. A juggler I knew was leaving his position and they needed someone to replace him. He put my name forward as the ideal replacement and even said he wouldn't train anyone else. Eventually, after a nerve-wracking wait, I received a call from their HQ in Vancouver asking me to come for an interview.

More waiting followed before I knew if I had been successful but finally the news came. I couldn't believe I had landed it. After a lot of training, I'm now proud to say I juggle for Cirque du Soleil all over the world.

Although I get a few weeks off between shows, it's not enough time to go back and do another long-distance hike. I take trips out between shows, in whatever country I'm lucky enough to be in. So far I've seen New Zealand and Australia. I'm incredibly happy and very lucky to be doing what I love.

I nurture fond memories from the AT, and made many friends whom I still keep in contact with. Such a beautiful and eye-opening way to spend a few months. I miss the mountains and often reflect on my adventure there. I will do another long-distance hike someday.

I was very taken by Maine — so much so that I would like to return to live there. I have a dream of buying some land, building a log cabin and letting some close friends have separate parcels of land to do the same. It's wild up there, quiet, beautiful, and I can't think of a better place to put down some roots.

Keith 'Fozzie' Foskett

From Georgia, I had traversed north on a slim ribbon of trail over the Appalachian mountain chain for 150 days. Through

Balancing on Blue

snow, ice, rain, storms, humidity and unbearable heat I inched a little closer to Katahdin every day.

I witnessed stark, bare trees come alive as my world turn green. Riding a series of rocky waves I smiled, emerging above tree-line to survey America's wild lands from a lofty perch. I had battled fatigue, illness, stress and emotional storms, clung stubbornly to my resolve and refused to give up.

Some mornings I woke and doubted if I could go any further. I stood in valleys, mesmerised by the hulk of mountains towering before me. I willed myself up to summits that I never thought I could conquer. Despite all my fears of failure, I stood strong and arrived at camp knowing that, for another day, I had won.

The continual search to placate my dromomania, to satisfy the nomad, and to appease my travelling addiction continues. But I've written another chapter of a never-ending adventure to be as close to freedom as can ever be truly possible.

From a teenager that initially viewed my wanderlust as a curse, I learned over time that it was, in fact, a valuable and cherished attribute. I accepted my feelings, nurtured them, learned from them and acknowledged how I was supposed to be, instead of trying to pick a more conventional life that I know would have made me unhappy.

I know I'd be just as fulfilled cycling around the world, taking a long road trip or bumming around Europe for the summer. The ultimate goal has, and always will be, to be as free as is ultimately possible in this world.

As I write this, in January 2015, a piece of paper nestles on the corner of my desk. There are a few scribbles haphazardly inked in one corner, a list of actions, plans needing to be implemented in order to fulfil my next adventure. The culmination of years of planning, months spent in the wilderness — training, if you like, for the big one.

That scrap of paper is titled 'The Continental Divide Trail'. The last of the big three American hikes. 3000 miles from the Mexican border to the Canadian border along the length of the continental divide. From the lowest point, Waterton Lake in Glacier National Park at 4200 feet, soaring to 14,270 feet on Grays Peak in Colorado, this is the next instalment of my life adventure.

My dromomaniac ways still beckon. I doubt they will ever be truly satisfied. In the unlikely event that the nomad shrinks into obscurity and declares, *OK, I've had enough, I'm full up*, that will be a sad day.

My wanderings keep me alive, urge me ever forward, constantly searching for the next adventure, a new escape. The call to freedom, the cries of the wilderness, the desire to roam is all I dream of.

Can I recommend you walk the AT? Of course! However, if hiking isn't your cup of tea, perhaps take whatever pastime you prefer and make a plan to do it for a few months.

If you're stubborn enough to make it happen, when you get there, open your eyes. Observe and admire everything as much as possible. Take mental photos, study them for a few seconds, remember them, hold on to them, and tuck them into an imaginary file. Place that file in the back of your mind and label it:

The Best Few Months of my Life.

No, wait.

I don't mean in some weak font, in lower case, and printed when your black ink level is low.

I mean use a striking font, in capital letters, bold, and with a fresh ink cartridge:

THE BEST FEW MONTHS OF MY LIFE.

Acknowledgements

First and most importantly, thank *you* for buying this book. Following an unconventional dream of hiking and writing is a long road, full of setbacks which require a strength and stubborn determination to follow. It is people like you, who buy my books that allow me to continue to live it.

The proof readers who took time out to help me: Caroline Morse, Chris Partridge, Dan McCormack, Tom Moose, Cliff Martin, Derek Vreeland, Charley Seger, Frank Patriot, Sarah Van Vliet, Nina Smirnoff, Michelle Markel, Patti Kulesz and exceeding the call of duty honourably — Kate Bryant.

Alex Roddie of Pinnacle Editorial for pointing out my dangling participles, and for his top notch editing.

Jeremy 'Obs da Blobs' Rowley and Samantha 'Mumfa' Rowley for the continued dedication to the formatting cause.

For those who provided quotes — Daniel Neilson, Alastair Humphreys, Jennifer Pharr Davis, David Lintern, Andrew Skurka, Rosie Fuller and Chris Townsend.

The Appalachian Trail Conservancy, whose help with trail and history facts was much appreciated.

Those that helped me prior to starting the trail and their hospitality; Gariele Marewski, Keith 'Hiker X' Baitsell, Sarah 'Sami' Van Vliet, Lauren 'Swiss Miss' Moran and Kathryn 'Dinosaur' Herndon.

The group that I hiked most of the trail with comprised of Peter 'PJ' Semo, Sam 'Daffy' Ridge, Chris 'Juggles' Chiappini, John 'Thirsty' Beshara, Dallas 'Bush Goggles' Nustvold and Phillip 'Lazagne' Colelli. My thanks to them for keeping such a great group together and also for their individual work on the first and last chapters.

All the hikers I met on trail, friendships made, and missed; PJ, Lady Forward, Chatterbox, Bowser, Byline, Pork Chop, Lazagne, Daffy, Bill, Kindle Ninja, Juggles, Bush Goggles, Thirsty, Desperado, Ninja, Jack, Shakespeare, Eastwood, Susan, Poco 'n Poco, Beacon, Mousy, Cheryl, Patrick, Cassie, Daniel, Tom and his dog Dakota, Tyler, Dirt Farmer, Central Booking, Jonathan, Grady, Turtle, Funny Bones, Slayer, Wildflower, Ken, Hoot, Lord Horatio Fonsworth Belvidere Bentley Tiberius III Esq, Tree Hugger, Mary Poppins, Honey Badger, Road Runner, Walking Man, Ninja Turtle, Jonah and his dog Dingleberry, Onespeed, W, Balls, Sunshine, Pops, Earthling, Carrie, Willy, One Speed, Honey Badger, Margaret, Roadrunner, Spam, Mattress Pad, Chez 11, Nito, Bonk, Saint, Cheddar, Hill Walker, Snot Rocket, Anchor, Tripping Yeti, Embassador, Flint, Tyvek, Wiffle Chicken, Apollo, Ken, Yodler, K9, Tarp Water, Tinkerbell, Rainbow Eyes, Plant Man, Socks, White Wolf, Kaleidoscope, Not Worthy, Chef, Turtle, Day-Glo, Sun, Slims, Turbo Toes, Wise Guy, Socks, Atlas, Hotshot, Hippity Hop, Medic, Easy Rider, Dog Whisperer, Easy Mile, Danish, Don Quixote, Two, Bad Dinner, Grok, Metric, Willie, Indiana, Warlie, Johaness, Cat Woman, Meat, Connect 4, Stingray, Resource, Whoop, Danish, Houdini, Pedestrian, Great Dane, Banjo, Skunkape, Roadhouse, Chesty, Stingray and Poncho.

The immense artistic talent of Derek Smith, whose sketches illustrate this book. David Taylor and Faye Fillingham's advice and tweaks to the front cover.

Thanks to David 'Awol' Miller, whose excellent book — The AT Guide, I used both on trail and in writing this book. It was invaluable for both.

The equipment manufacturers, and suppliers who helped me with gear for the trip; Rand Lindsly of Trail designs, Jake Bennett at Numa Sport Optics, Dan Thompson at Rab, Chris McMaster at ULA Equipment, Niels Overgaard Blok of Backpacking Light Denmark, Richard Codgbrook from Smartwool, Ron Bell at Mountain Laurel Designs, Tom Hennessy at Hennessy Hammocks and Joe Valesko at ZPacks.

Balancing on Blue

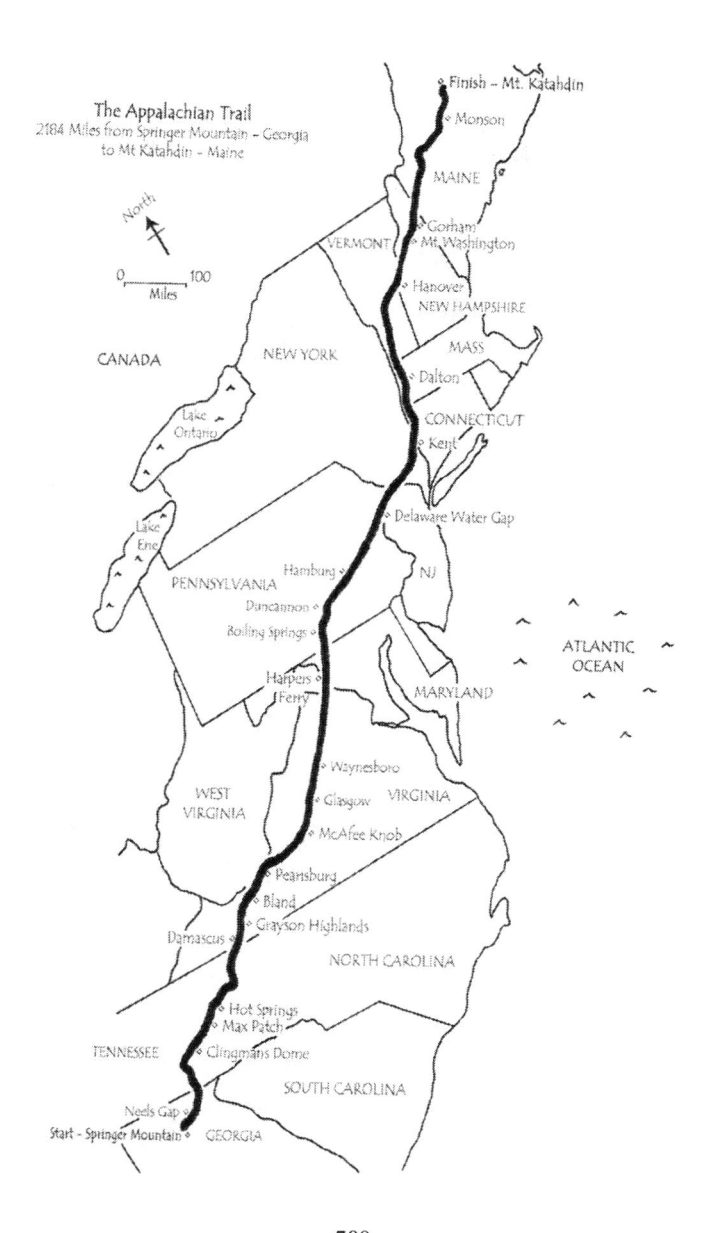

Keith Foskett

Printed in Great Britain
by Amazon